CHRISTOPHER MARLOWE

A contemporary of William Shakespeare and Ben Jonson, Christopher Marlowe was one of the most influential early modern dramatists, whose life and mysterious death have long been the subject of critical and popular speculation. This collection sets Marlowe's plays and poems in their historical context, exploring his world and his wider cultural influence. Chapters by leading international scholars discuss both his major and lesser-known works. Divided into three sections, 'Marlowe's works', 'Marlowe's world', and 'Reception', the book ranges from Marlowe's relationship with his own audience through to adaptations of his plays for modern cinema. Other contexts for Marlowe include history and politics, religion, and science. Discussions of Marlowe's critics and Marlowe's appeal today, in performance, literature, and biography, show how and why his works continue to resonate; and a comprehensive further reading list provides helpful suggestions for those who want to find out more.

EMILY C. BARTELS is Professor of English at Rutgers University and Director of the Bread Loaf School of English, Middlebury College. She is author of *Spectacles of Strangeness: Imperialism, Alienation, and Marlowe* (1993), which won the Roma Gill Prize for Best Work on Christopher Marlowe, 1993–94, and *Speaking of the Moor: From Alcazar to Othello* (2008). She has edited *Critical Essays on Christopher Marlowe* (1997) and published essays on early modern drama, race, gender, and survivorship. Her newest project centres on Shakespearean intertextuality.

EMMA SMITH teaches at Hertford College, University of Oxford, and is the author of a range of works on Shakespeare and early modern drama, including *The Cambridge Introduction to Shakespeare* (2007) and *The Cambridge Shakespeare Guide* (2012). She has contributed numerous articles to publications including *Shakespeare Studies* and *Shakespeare Survey*, and her iTunesU lectures on Shakespeare and on other early modern plays have been downloaded more than 300,000 times.

CHRISTOPHER MARLOWE IN CONTEXT

EDITED BY
EMILY C. BARTELS
and
EMMA SMITH

CAMBRIDGE
UNIVERSITY PRESS

University Printing House, Cambridge CB2 8BS, United Kingdom

Cambridge University Press is part of the University of Cambridge.

It furthers the University's mission by disseminating knowledge in the pursuit of education, learning and research at the highest international levels of excellence.

www.cambridge.org
Information on this title: www.cambridge.org/9781107559363

© Cambridge University Press 2013

This publication is in copyright. Subject to statutory exception and to the provisions of relevant collective licensing agreements, no reproduction of any part may take place without the written permission of Cambridge University Press.

First published 2013
Reprinted 2014
First paperback edition 2015

A catalogue record for this publication is available from the British Library

Library of Congress Cataloguing in Publication data
Christopher Marlowe in Context / edited by Emily C. Bartels and Emma Smith.
pages cm
Includes bibliographical references and index.
ISBN 978-1-107-01625-5 (hardback)
1. Marlowe, Christopher, 1564–1593–Criticism and interpretation. I. Bartels, Emily Carroll, editor of compilation. II. Smith, Emma (Emma Josephine) editor of compilation.
PR2674.C58 2013
822'.3–dc23
2012051607

ISBN 978-1-107-01625-5 Hardback
ISBN 978-1-107-55936-3 Paperback

Cambridge University Press has no responsibility for the persistence or accuracy of URLs for external or third-party internet websites referred to in this publication, and does not guarantee that any content on such websites is, or will remain, accurate or appropriate.

Contents

List of illustrations	*page* viii
Notes on contributors	ix
A chronology of Marlowe's life and works	xv
Catherine Clifford and Martin Wiggins	
List of abbreviations	xxviii
Introduction	1
Emily C. Bartels and Emma Smith	

PART I MARLOWE'S WORKS   5

1. Marlowe's chronology and canon   7
   Martin Wiggins

2. Marlowe's magic books: the material text   15
   Leah S. Marcus

3. Marlowe and the limits of rhetoric   27
   Catherine Nicholson

4. Marlowe and character   39
   Laurie Maguire and Aleksandra Thostrup

5. Marlowe's dramatic form   49
   Sarah Dewar-Watson

6. Marlowe's poetic form   57
   Danielle Clarke

7. Marlowe and the Elizabethan theatre audience   68
   Brian Walsh

8	Marlowe and classical literature *Syrithe Pugh*	80
9	Marlowe's medievalism *Chris Chism*	90
10	Marlowe's libraries: a history of reading *Elizabeth Spiller*	101
11	Marlowe's translations *Jenny C. Mann*	110

PART II   MARLOWE'S WORLD — 123

12	Geography and Marlowe *Jacques Lezra*	125
13	Marlowe, history, and politics *Paulina Kewes*	138
14	Marlowe and social distinction *James R. Siemon*	155
15	Marlowe, death-worlds, and warfare *Patricia Cahill*	169
16	Education, the university, and Marlowe *Elizabeth Hanson*	181
17	Marlowe and the question of will *Kathryn Schwarz*	192
18	Marlowe and the self *Lars Engle*	202
19	Race, nation, and Marlowe *Emily C. Bartels*	212
20	Marlowe and religion *Gillian Woods*	222
21	Marlowe and queer theory *David Clark*	232
22	Marlowe and women *Alison Findlay*	242

23	Marlowe and the new science *Mary Thomas Crane*	252
24	The professional theatre and Marlowe *Tom Rutter*	262

PART III RECEPTION 273

25	Marlowe in his moment *Holger Schott Syme*	275
26	Marlowe and Shakespeare revisited *Thomas Cartelli*	285
27	Marlowe in Caroline theatre *Lucy Munro*	296
28	Marlowe's literary influence *Lisa Hopkins*	306
29	Marlowe in the movies *Pascale Aebischer*	316
30	Editing Marlowe's texts *Andrew Duxfield*	325
31	Marlowe's biography *Thomas Healy*	334
32	Marlowe and the critics *Adam Hansen*	346
33	Marlowe now *Paul Menzer*	357

Further reading 366
Index 378

Illustrations

1. Portrait of Tamburlaine, from the 1590 edition. Reproduced by permission of the Huntington Library, San Marino, California. *page* 19
2. Portrait of Zenocrate, from the 1597 edition of *Tamburlaine*. Reproduced by permission of the Huntington Library, San Marino, California. 20
3. Marlowe's *Doctor Faustus* (1616), title page. © The British Library Board. 22
4. Thirteenth-century T-O map. Copyright The Bodleian Libraries, The University of Oxford. 128
5. Paul Ive, *The Practise of Fortification* (1589). Copyright The Bodleian Libraries, The University of Oxford. 174
6. Marlowe's *Tamburlaine* (1590), title page. Reproduced by permission of the Huntington Library, San Marino, California. 264

Contributors

PASCALE AEBISCHER is Senior Lecturer at the University of Exeter and the General Editor of *Shakespeare Bulletin*. She is the author of *Shakespeare's Violated Bodies: Stage and Screen Performance* (2004), *Jacobean Drama* (2010), and *Screening Early Modern Drama: Beyond Shakespeare* (2013). She is the editor of 'Early Modern Drama on Screen: A Jarman Anniversary Issue' (*Shakespeare Bulletin* (2011)) and, with Kathryn Prince, of *Performing Early Modern Drama Today* (2012).

PATRICIA CAHILL is Associate Professor in the Department of English at Emory University and author of *Unto the Breach: Martial Formations, Historical Trauma, and the Early Modern Stage* (2008). Her current book project explores how skin surfaces and the sense of touch signify in early modern drama and culture.

THOMAS CARTELLI is Professor of English and Film Studies at Muhlenberg College in Allentown, Pennsylvania. He is the author of *Marlowe, Shakespeare, and the Economy of Theatrical Experience* (1991) and *Repositioning Shakespeare: National Formations, Postcolonial Appropriations* (1999), co-author (with Katherine Rowe) of *New Wave Shakespeare on Screen* (2007), and editor of the Norton Critical Edition of *Richard III* (2009).

CHRIS CHISM is Associate Professor at the University of California, Los Angeles, and author of *Alliterative Revivals* (2002). Her projects range from medieval friendship to medieval Arabic travel writing. She regularly teaches medieval and early modern drama, juxtaposing performance theory with late medieval theatrical practices, texts, and contemporary reconstructions.

DAVID CLARK is a senior lecturer at the University of Leicester. His publications include *Gender, Violence, and the Past in Edda and Saga* (2012), and *Between Medieval Men: Male Friendship and Desire in Early*

Medieval Literature (2009). He has edited a number of volumes and translated *The Saga of Bishop Thorlak* (2012). He is currently working on friendship in medieval European literature and medievalism in contemporary children's literature.

DANIELLE CLARKE is Professor of English Renaissance Language and Literature at University College Dublin. She has published widely on a range of topics, including gender, sexuality, paratexts, textuality, and rhetoric. Her most recent book is *Teaching the Early Modern*, edited with Derval Conroy (2011).

CATHERINE CLIFFORD is an adjunct instructor at the University of North Texas. Her research interests are in sixteenth- and seventeenth-century English drama and, in particular, dramatic performance in English royal palaces.

MARY THOMAS CRANE is the Thomas F. Rattigan Professor in the English Department at Boston College. She is the author of *Framing Authority: Sayings, Self, and Society in Sixteenth-Century England* (1993) and *Shakespeare's Brain: Reading with Cognitive Theory* (2000).

SARAH DEWAR-WATSON has published widely on early modern genre and classical literature, including in *Shakespeare Quarterly* and the *International Journal of the Classical Tradition*. Her monograph *Shakespeare's Poetics: Aristotle and Anglo-Italian Renaissance Genres* will be published in 2013. She is the author of *Tragedy* in the Readers' Guides to Essential Criticism series (2013). Her current research engages with contemporary as well as Renaissance translation.

ANDREW DUXFIELD is an associate lecturer at Sheffield Hallam University. He is the winner of the 2009 Hoffman Prize for distinguished publication on Christopher Marlowe, and his published essays include 'Doctor Faustus and Renaissance Hermeticism' in the Continuum Guide to *Doctor Faustus*, 'Doctor Faustus and the Failure to Unify' in *Early Modern Literary Studies*, and 'Modern Problems of Editing: The Two Texts of Marlowe's *Doctor Faustus*' in *Literature Compass*.

LARS ENGLE, James G. Watson Professor of English and Department Chair at the University of Tulsa, is the author of *Shakespearean Pragmatism* and a co-editor of *English Renaissance Drama: A Norton Anthology*. He has published many articles and book chapters and has served as a Trustee of the Shakespeare Association of America, as the Lloyd David Professor of Shakespeare Studies at Queensland, and as Frank and Eleanor Griffiths Professor at the Bread Loaf School of English.

ALISON FINDLAY is Professor of Renaissance Drama and Director of the Shakespeare Programme at Lancaster University. She is the author of *Illegitimate Power* (1994), *A Feminist Perspective on Renaissance Drama* (1998), *Women in Shakespeare* (2010), and, most recently, *Much Ado about Nothing: A Guide to the Text and the Play in Performance* (2011). Alison has also published on women's drama, including *Women and Dramatic Production 1550–1700* (2000) and *Playing Spaces in Early Women's Drama* (2006). She is currently a general editor of the Revels Plays series.

ADAM HANSEN is Senior Lecturer in English at Northumbria University. He has published *Shakespeare and Popular Music* (2010), as well as articles and chapters on many aspects of early modern literary culture. He is currently working on a project titled *Shakespeare's Cities*.

ELIZABETH HANSON is Professor in the Department of English, Queen's University, Canada. She is the author of *Discovering the Subject in Renaissance England* (1998, 2008) and of a range of articles on early modern drama, poetry, and women's writing. Her current project is a book on the so-called 'education revolution': *Education and Social Distinction in Early Modern England*.

THOMAS HEALY is Professor of Renaissance Studies and Head of the School of English at the University of Sussex. He is the author of studies on Crashaw, Marvell, and Marlowe (Writers and Their Works, 1994) as well as *New Latitudes: Theory and English Renaissance Literature* (1992). He co-edited *Literature and the Civil War* (1987), *The Arnold Anthology of British and Irish Literature in English* (1997), and, most recently, *Renaissance Transformation: The Making of English Writing 1500–1650* (2009).

LISA HOPKINS is Professor of English at Sheffield Hallam University and co-editor of *Shakespeare*, the journal of the British Shakespeare Association. Her publications include *Christopher Marlowe, Dramatist* (2008), *A Christopher Marlowe Chronology* (2005), and *Christopher Marlowe: A Literary Life* (2000).

PAULINA KEWES is Fellow and Tutor in English Literature at Jesus College, Oxford, and a Fellow of the Royal Historical Society. Her books include *Authorship and Appropriation: Writing for the Stage in England, 1660–1710*

(1998), *This Great Matter of Succession: Politics, History, and Elizabethan Drama* (forthcoming), and, as editor or co-editor, *Plagiarism in Early Modern England* (2003), *The Uses of History in Early Modern England* (2006), *The Oxford Handbook of Holinshed's Chronicles* (2013), and *Doubtful and Dangerous: The Question of Succession in Late Elizabethan England* (forthcoming). She is writing a study of the transmission and application of Roman history in the reign of Elizabeth.

JACQUES LEZRA is Professor of Spanish, English, and Comparative Literature at New York University. His most recent book is *Wild Materialism: The Ethic of Terror and the Modern Republic* (2010).

LAURIE MAGUIRE is Professor of English at the University of Oxford, a tutorial fellow at Magdalen College, and the author or editor of eight books, including *Shakespeare's Names* (2007) and *Helen of Troy: From Homer to Hollywood* (2009).

JENNY C. MANN is an assistant professor of English at Cornell University and the author of *Outlaw Rhetoric: Figuring Vernacular Eloquence in Shakespeare's England* (2012). She is currently working on a project that investigates how early modern writers think about the power of fiction and its relationship to other knowledge practices.

LEAH S. MARCUS is Edwin Mims Professor of English at Vanderbilt University. She is the author of *Childhood and Cultural Despair* (1978), *The Politics of Mirth* (1986), *Puzzling Shakespeare* (1988), and *Unediting the Renaissance* (1996). Over the past decade and a half she has done a lot of editing, including two Norton Critical Editions (*The Merchant of Venice* and *As You Like It*), two volumes of the *Works of Queen Elizabeth I* (co-edited with Janel Mueller and Mary Beth Rose), and an Arden edition of Webster's *Duchess of Malfi*. She has now returned to writing books and is currently at work on two: *How Shakespeare Became Colonial* and *Reading Elizabeth I Writing*.

PAUL MENZER is an associate professor at Mary Baldwin College, where he directs the Shakespeare and Performance graduate programme. He is the author of *The Hamlets: Cues, Q's, and Remembered Texts*, editor of *Inside Shakespeare: Essays on the Blackfriars Stage*, and President of the Marlowe Society of America.

LUCY MUNRO is a senior lecturer at Keele University. She is the author of *Children of the Queen's Revels: A Jacobean Theatre Repertory* (2005) and the editor of plays by John Fletcher, Richard Brome, and Edward

Sharpham. She is currently working on editions of Thomas Dekker, John Ford, and William Rowley's *The Witch of Edmonton* and James Shirley's *The Gentleman of Venice* and is completing a study of the functions of outmoded style in early modern drama and poetry, provisionally entitled *The English Archaic: Outmoded Style in Early Modern Literature, 1590–1660*.

CATHERINE NICHOLSON is Assistant Professor of English at Yale. Her current research focuses on the emergence of self-consciously strange theories and practices of vernacularity in sixteenth-century England, and she has recently published on *Othello* (in *English Literary Renaissance*) and on Spenser (in *Spenser Studies*).

SYRITHE PUGH is a lecturer in English Literature at the University of Aberdeen. Her research focuses on imitation of and allusion to classical literature in English literature of the sixteenth and seventeenth centuries, particularly in relation to politics. She has published two monographs, *Spenser and Ovid* (2005) and *Herrick, Fanshawe, and the Politics of Intertextuality: Classical Literature and Seventeenth-Century Royalism* (2010), as well as numerous articles.

TOM RUTTER is Lecturer in Shakespeare and Renaissance Drama at the University of Sheffield. He is the author of *Work and Play on the Shakespearean Stage* (2008) and *The Cambridge Introduction to Christopher Marlowe* (2012), and he co-edits the journal *Shakespeare*. He is currently working on the repertory of the Admiral's Men playing company.

KATHRYN SCHWARZ is Professor of English at Vanderbilt University and the author of *Tough Love: Amazon Encounters in the English Renaissance* (2000) and *What You Will: Gender, Contract, and Shakespearean Social Space* (2011). She is currently at work on a study of intent, subjectivity, and the body, entitled *Disposable Bodies, Provisional Lives*.

JAMES R. SIEMON is Professor of English at Boston University. He is the author of *Shakespearean Iconoclasm* (1986) and *Word against Word: Shakespearean Utterance* (2002), and the editor of Christopher Marlowe's *The Jew of Malta* (1994, 2009) and William Shakespeare's *King Richard III* (2009) and *Julius Caesar* (forthcoming).

ELIZABETH SPILLER is Associate Dean, College of Arts and Sciences, Florida State University. She is the author of *Reading and the History of Race in the Renaissance* (2011) and of *Science, Reading, and Renaissance*

Literature (2004, 2007). She is the editor of *Seventeenth-Century English Recipe Books* (2008) and is currently working on a new book on matter theory and poetic practice in the Renaissance.

HOLGER SCHOTT SYME is Associate Professor of English at the University of Toronto. His essays have appeared in *English Literary Renaissance*, *Shakespeare Quarterly*, *Shakespeare Survey*, and elsewhere. He is the author of *Theatre and Testimony in Shakespeare's England: A Culture of Mediation* (2012) and has co-edited *Locating the Queen's Men, 1583–1603: Material Practices and Conditions of Playing* (2009). For the third edition of the *Norton Shakespeare* he is writing a new introduction to the theatre of Shakespeare's time, and he is editing *Edward III* and *The Book of Sir Thomas More*.

ALEKSANDRA THOSTRUP is a Marlowe scholar who lives and works in Oxford.

BRIAN WALSH is Assistant Professor in the English Department at Yale. He is the author of *Shakespeare, the Queen's Men, and the Elizabethan Performance of History* (2009) as well as several articles on the early modern history play, Shakespearean commemoration, and other topics.

MARTIN WIGGINS is the author of *British Drama, 1533–1642: A Catalogue* (2012–). He co-edited *Edward II* for New Mermaids, and he was awarded the Hoffman Prize for his work on the dating of *Dido, Queen of Carthage*.

GILLIAN WOODS is Lecturer in Renaissance Theatre and Drama at Birkbeck College, University of London. She is the author of *Shakespeare's Unreformed Fictions* (2013) and has published articles on a range of Renaissance drama, including work by Shakespeare, John Ford, and Anthony Munday. Her current research focuses on visual arts in early modern theatre.

A chronology of Marlowe's life and works

Catherine Clifford and Martin Wiggins

	LIFE
1564	Born in Canterbury, second child and first son of shoemaker John Marlowe and his wife Katherine; baptised 26 February. His siblings were Mary (1562–8), Margaret (1565–?1641), Jane (1569–?83), Anne (1571–1652), Dorothy (b. 1573), and Thomas (b. 1576).
1579	Elected to a scholarship at the King's School, Canterbury.
1580	Elected to a Matthew Parker scholarship at Corpus Christi College, Cambridge; arrived in December, matriculated on 17 March 1581.
1584	Graduated B.A. in February.
c. 1585–7	Apparently engaged in clandestine government work entailing some prolonged absences from Cambridge.
1587	Cambridge authorities attempted to prevent him from graduating M.A. on grounds of his absence and suspected intention to take up residency at the Anglo-Catholic seminary in Rheims; on 29 June, the Privy Council wrote to the authorities in his support. Wrote *Tamburlaine* Parts I and II.
1588	Wrote *Doctor Faustus* and *Dido, Queen of Carthage*, both in collaboration, the former possibly and the latter certainly with Thomas Nashe.
1589	Wrote *The Jew of Malta*. Imprisoned in Newgate on 18 September along with Thomas Watson, after becoming embroiled in a street fight during which William Bradley was killed; released on bail on 1 October and discharged on 3 December.
1590	On 9 May, bound over to keep the peace after a scuffle with two constables in Hackney; sued for assault in September after a violent altercation with a Canterbury tailor.
1591	Sharing a writing chamber with Thomas Kyd.

1592	Arrested in Flushing (Vlissingen) in January, suspected of counterfeiting foreign coins; wrote *Edward II*, the Latin dedication of Thomas Watson's *Amintae gaudia* (published posthumously) to Mary Herbert, Countess of Pembroke, and a Latin epitaph on Sir Roger Manwood (who died on 14 December).
1593	Wrote *The Massacre at Paris* and (probably) *Hero and Leander*. Living at Sir Thomas Walsingham's house in Scadbury. Named by Thomas Kyd, under interrogation at Bridewell on 12 May, as the owner of heretical papers found in his room. Summoned on 18 May to appear before the Privy Council on a charge of atheism; answered the summons on 20 May and was required to be in attendance daily. Murdered by Ingram Frizer on 30 May after a fight in a Deptford eating-house. Buried on 1 June at St Nicholas' Church, Deptford. Richard Baines sent the Privy Council a report about Marlowe's 'damnable opinions'. Frizer was tried in the Court of Chancery on 15 June and pardoned on 28 June.

THE POEMS

mid 1580s?	Translated Ovid's *Amores*, perhaps while still at Cambridge.
before 1589	'The Passionate Shepherd to His Love' written.
1592	Manwood epitaph written; never printed.
1593	*Hero and Leander* probably written.
1598	*Hero and Leander* first published; the book had been in the printer's hands since September 1593. Later in the year, the second edition was printed, with additional sestiads by George Chapman. There were eight subsequent early editions (1600–37).
c. 1599	*Epigrams and Elegies* by Sir John Davies and Marlowe printed, containing a selection from the translation of Ovid's *Amores*; a second edition followed soon after. In June 1599, the Archbishop of Canterbury ordered all copies of 'Davies's Epigrams, with Marlowe's Elegies' to be seized and burnt.
1599	Abbreviated version of 'The Passionate Shepherd' printed in *The Passionate Pilgrim*, and followed by a single-stanza 'Love's Answer'.

A chronology of Marlowe's life and works xvii

1600	Complete text of 'The Passionate Shepherd' printed in *England's Helicon*, ascribed to Marlowe and followed by 'The Nymph's Reply to the Shepherd'. First publication of the translation of Lucan, the only early edition; the text had been in the printer's hands since September 1593.
after 1602	*All Ovid's Elegies* printed, undated and with a false imprint (Middleburg for London); there were three subsequent early editions (to *c.* 1640), all with the same false imprint.
17th century	Manwood epitaph transcribed into the MS commonplace book of the Kentish poet Henry Oxinden (1609–70).

THE *TAMBURLAINE* PLAYS

1336–1405	Life of Timur Khan, known as Timur the Lame, and later as Tamburlaine.
1444	Battle of Varna, the basis for the Sigismond episode in *2 Tamburlaine*.
1543	Publication of Antoninus Bonfinius' *Rerum Ungaricum*, source of the second play's Sigismond episode.
1553	Publication of Pietro Perondino's *Magni Tamerlanis Scythiarum Imperatoris vita*, source of the first play's account of Bajazeth, and of elements of the second play.
1570	Publication of Abraham Ortelius' *Theatrum orbis terrarum*, the source of the plays' geography.
1586	Publication of George Whetstone's *The English Mirror*, main source of the first play.
1587	Both plays written, and performed in London; according to its prologue, the second was a commercially inspired sequel rather than a part of the original design.
1590	First publication of both plays; the printer claimed to have excised comic scenes. As in the three subsequent early editions (1592–1605), no author's name is given: the plays are presented as anonymous works.
1594–5	Performed at the Rose by the Admiral's Men. Cast included Edward Alleyn (Tamburlaine).
1630s (?)	Performed at the Red Bull.
1919	A conflated and abridged version performed by the Yale Dramatic Association.

1951	A conflated and abridged version performed at the Old Vic, London, directed by Tyrone Guthrie. Cast included: Donald Wolfit (Tamburlaine); Leo McKern (Bajazeth); Jill Balcon (Zenocrate); Richard Pasco (Agydas); Kenneth Griffith (Mycetes); David Waller (Cosroe); Lee Montague (Usumcasane); Alun Owen (Arabia); Wolfe Morris (Governor); Colin Jeavons (Calyphas); John Abineri (Celebinus). In 1956, the production was later revived at the Shakespeare Stratford Festival (Ontario) and on Broadway, with a cast including: Anthony Quayle (Tamburlaine); Barbara Chilcott (Zenocrate); Douglas Rain (Bajazeth); Coral Browne (Zabina); and William Shatner (Usumcasane).
1964	BBC radio production directed by Charles Lefeaux. Cast included: Stephen Murray (Tamburlaine); Joss Ackland (Theridamas).
1972	A conflated and abridged version performed by the Glasgow Citizens' Theatre Company at the Edinburgh Festival, directed by Keith Hack. The role of Tamburlaine was split between three actors: Rupert Frazer, Jeffery Kissoon, and Mike Gwilym.
1976	A conflated and abridged version performed by the National Theatre Company at the Olivier Theatre, London, directed by Peter Hall. Cast included: Albert Finney (Tamburlaine); Susan Fleetwood (Zenocrate); Denis Quilley (Bajazeth/Callapine); Barbara Jefford (Zabina); Brian Cox (Theridamas); Oliver Cotton (Techelles); Philip Locke (Mycetes); Robert Eddison (Orcanes).
1992–3	A conflated and abridged version performed by the Royal Shakespeare Company at the Swan, Stratford-upon-Avon; and at the Pit, London, directed by Barry Kyle. Cast included: Antony Sher (Tamburlaine); Malcolm Storry (Bajazeth); Claire Benedict (Zenocrate); Jasper Britton (Meander/Calyphas); Toby Stephens (Prologue/Argier/Celebinus); Trevor Martin (Sultan); Emily Watson (Perdica); Sophie Okonedo (Anippe); Tracy-Ann Oberman (Ebea).
1997	Part I performed at the American Theatre of Actors, New York City, directed by Jeff Dailey.

1999	Part I performed at the Cochrane Theatre, London, directed by Sam Shammas.
2003	Part II performed at the American Theatre of Actors, New York City, directed by Jeff Dailey.
2005	A conflated and abridged version performed at the Barbican Arts Centre, London, directed by David Farr. Cast included: Greg Hicks (Tamburlaine); Rachael Stirling (Zenocrate).
2007	A conflated and abridged version performed by the Shakespeare Theatre Company at Sidney Harmon Hall, Washington, DC, directed by Michael Kahn. Cast included Avery Brooks (Tamburlaine); David McCann (Bajazeth); Mia Tagano (Zenocrate).
2011	Part I performed at the Blackfriars Playhouse, the American Shakespeare Center, Staunton, Virginia, directed by Jim Warren.

DOCTOR FAUSTUS

1519–56	Reign of the Emperor Charles V, the play's loose historical setting.
1588	Publication of *The History of the Damnable Life and Deserved Death of Doctor John Faustus*, a translation by P. F. (Paul Fairfax?) of the German 'Faustbuch'. (The first extant edition dates from 1592.) Marlowe and a collaborator (Nashe?) wrote the play, and it was probably performed at the Bel Savage (though probably without the guest appearance by the devil himself that was alleged by William Prynne in 1633).
1594–7	Intermittent performances at the Rose by the Admiral's Men. Cast included Edward Alleyn (Faustus).
1597–1626	Intermittent performances in Europe as part of the repertory of the Anglo-German company led successively by Thomas Sackville and John Green; known performances took place in Strasbourg (1597), Graz (1608), and Dresden (1626).
1602	Revived at the Fortune by the Admiral's Men, in a new version (designated the B-text) prepared by William Bird and Samuel Rowley.

1604	First publication of the A-text. The play had been in the hands of the printer since 1601. There were two subsequent early editions (1609 and 1611).
1616	First publication of the B-text. There were five subsequent early editions (1619–31).
c. 1620	Revived at the Fortune by the Palsgrave's Men.
c. 1640	Revived at the Fortune by Prince Charles's Men.
c. 1660–3	Revived in a new version (designated the C-text); a performance at the Red Bull in 1662 was attended by Samuel Pepys.
1663	First publication of the C-text.
1675	Intermittent performances by the Duke's Company, attended by Nell Gwyn.
1688 or earlier	'Farce' adaptation by William Mountfort performed at the Queen's Theatre, Dorset Garden, and later at the theatre in Lincoln's Inn Fields. Cast included: Anthony Leigh (Faustus); Thomas Jevon (Mephistopheles).
1697	Mountfort's version published.
1885	Performed in an adaptation by W. G. Wills at the Lyceum Theatre, London. Cast included Henry Irving (Mephistopheles).
1897	Performed by the Elizabethan Stage Society at St George's Hall, London, directed by William Poel. Revived in 1904 at the Court Theatre, London, with a cast including: Hubert Carter (Faustus); George Ingleton (Mephistopheles).
1910	Performed at the Garden Theatre, New York City, produced by Ben Greet.
1925	Performed by the Phoenix Society at the New Oxford Theatre, London, directed by Allan Wade. Cast included: Ion Swinley (Faustus); Ernest Thesiger (Mephistopheles); Elsa Lanchester (Envy); John Gielgud (Good Angel); Stephen Jack (Scholar).
1937	Performed at Maxine Elliott's Theatre, New York, directed by Orson Welles, who also played Faustus. Cast also included: Jack Carter (Mephistopheles); Joseph Cotten. The production was revived in Paris in 1950, with music by Duke Ellington and a cast including Eartha Kitt (Helen).

1946	Performed at the Shakespeare Memorial Theatre, Stratford-upon-Avon, directed by Walter Hudd. Cast included: Robert Harris (Faustus); Hugh Griffith (Mephistopheles).
1948	Performed at the Old Vic, London, directed by John Burrell. Cast included: Cedric Hardwicke (Faustus); Robert Eddison (Mephistopheles); Harry Andrews (Lucifer); Mark Dignam (Beelzebub/Emperor); Donald Sinden (Envy); Faith Brook (Helen); Timothy Bateson (Ralph).
1959	BBC television production directed by Ronald Eyre. Cast included: William Squire (Faustus); James Maxwell (Mephistopheles); Alex Scott (Lucifer); Felicity Young (Helen).
1961	Serialised television production directed by Ronald Eyre. Cast included: Alan Dobie (Faustus); James Maxwell (Mephistopheles); Patrick Godfrey (Wagner); James Grout (Cornelius); Terence Lodge (Valdes); John Ringham (Chorus).
	Performed at the Old Vic, London, directed by Michael Benthall. Cast included: Paul Daneman (Faustus); Michael Goodliffe (Mephistopheles).
1963	'Montage' adaptation by Jerzy Grotowski performed at the Theatre Laboratory, Opole, Poland.
1967	Film version directed by Richard Burton and Nevill Coghill, developed from Coghill's Oxford University Dramatic Society production of 1966. Cast included: Richard Burton (Faustus); Andreas Teuber (Mephistopheles); Ian Marter (Emperor); Maria Aitken (Sloth); Elizabeth Taylor (Helen).
1968	Performed by the Royal Shakespeare Company at the Royal Shakespeare Theatre, Stratford-upon-Avon, directed by Clifford Williams. Cast included: Eric Porter (Faustus); Terrence Hardiman (Mephistopheles); Maggie Wright (Helen).
1970	Performed by the Royal Shakespeare Company at the Abbey Theatre, Dublin, directed by Gareth Morgan. Cast included: David Waller (Faustus); Alan Howard (Mephistopheles).

1974	Performed by the Royal Shakespeare Company at the Aldwych Theatre, London; and the Royal Shakespeare Theatre, Stratford-upon-Avon, directed by John Barton. Cast included: Ian McKellen (Faustus); Emrys Jones (Mephistopheles).
1981	Performed at the Royal Exchange Theatre, Manchester, directed by Adrian Noble. Cast included: Ben Kingsley (Faustus); James Maxwell (Mephistopheles).
1989	Performed by the Royal Shakespeare Company at the Swan Theatre, Stratford-upon-Avon; and at the Pit, London, directed by Barry Kyle. Cast included: Gerard Murphy (Faustus); David Bradley (Mephistopheles).
1997	Performed by the Royal Shakespeare Company at The Other Place, Stratford-upon-Avon, directed by Jonathan Best. Cast included Darryl da Silva (Faustus).
2002	Performed by Natural Nylon Theatre Company at the Young Vic, London, directed by David Lan. Cast included: Jude Law (Faustus); Richard McCabe (Mephistopheles).
2011	Performed by Creation Theatre Company in Blackwell's Bookshop, Oxford, directed by Charlotte Conquest. Cast included: Gus Gallagher (Faustus); Gwynfor Jones (Mephistopheles).

DIDO, QUEEN OF CARTHAGE

29–19 BC	The play's source, Virgil's *Aeneid*, written.
1588	Marlowe and Nashe wrote the play, and it was performed by the Children of the Chapel Royal at an unknown theatre.
1594	First publication: the only early edition.
1792	Operatic adaptation, composed by Stephen Storace, premiered at the King's Theatre, London.
1993	Performed by the Stage One Theatre Company at the Steiner Theatre, London, directed by Michael Walling and Richard Allen Cave.
1995	Performed by the Moving Theatre Company at the Bird's Nest Theatre, London.
2001	Performed at the Target Margin Theatre, New York City, directed by David Herskovits. Cast included: Nicole Halmos (Dido); Adrian LaTourell (Aeneas).

2003	Performed at Shakespeare's Globe, London, directed by Tim Carroll. Cast included: Raike Ayola (Dido); Will Keen (Aeneas).
2005	Performed at the American Repertory Theatre, Cambridge, Massachusetts, directed by Neil Bartlett. Cast included: Diane D'Aquila (Dido); Colin Lane (Aeneas).
2006	Performed by Angels in the Architecture at the House of St Barnabas, Soho, directed by Rebecca McCutcheon. Cast included: Sarah Thom (Dido); Jake Maskall (Aeneas). The production was later revived in Kensington Palace, London.
2009	Performed at the Royal National Theatre, London, directed by James McDonald. Cast included: Anastasia Hille (Dido); Mark Bonnar (Aeneas); Siobhan Redmond (Venus); Susan Engel (Juno); Alan David (Ilioneus).

THE JEW OF MALTA

1565	Siege of Malta, the play's loose historical setting.
1589	Marlowe wrote the play, probably for performance at the Rose. (The play seems to have been the property of the theatre owner, Philip Henslowe.)
1592–3	Performed by Lord Strange's Men at the Rose. Cast included Edward Alleyn (Barabas).
1594	Performed at the Rose by Sussex's Men and the Queen's Men.
1594–1601	Intermittent runs at the Rose and also at Newington Butts (in 1594) and the Fortune (in 1601), performed by the Admiral's Men (in 1594, in collaboration with the Lord Chamberlain's Men).
1597–1646	Intermittent performances in Europe as part of the repertory of the Anglo-German company led successively by Thomas Sackville and John Green; known performances took place in Strasbourg (1597), Passau (1607), Graz (1608), and Dresden (1626, 1646).
1630–3	Performed at the Phoenix by Queen Henrietta's Men, with a new prologue and epilogue by Thomas Heywood; also a court performance at the Cockpit-in-Court. Cast included Richard Perkins (Barabas).
1633	First publication, with Heywood's prologue and epilogue: the only early edition.

1645	Dutch version by Gysbert de Sille, entitled *Joodt van Malta, ofte Wraeck door Moordt* (*The Jew of Malta; or, Revenge through Murder*), printed at Leiden.
1818	Adaptation by Samson Penley performed at the Drury Lane Theatre, London, with Edmund Kean (Barabas).
1923	Performed by the Phoenix Society at Daly's Theatre, London, directed by Allan Wade. Cast included: Baliol Holloway (Barabas); Ernest Thesiger (Ithamore); Isabel Jeans (Abigail).
1964	Performed at the Victoria Theatre, Stoke-on-Trent, directed by Peter Cheeseman. Cast included: Bernard Gallagher (Barabas); Alan Ayckbourn (Machiavel). Performed by the Royal Shakespeare Company at the Aldwych Theatre, London, directed by Clifford Williams. Cast included: Clive Revill (Barabas); Tony Church (Ferneze); Ian Richardson (Ithamore); Michele Dotrice (Abigail); Glenda Jackson (Bellamira); Michael Bryant (Calymath); Derek Godfrey (Machiavel). In 1965, the production transferred to the Royal Shakespeare Theatre, Stratford-upon-Avon, with a mainly new cast including: Eric Porter (Barabas); Tony Church (Machiavel); Donald Burton (Calymath).
1987	Performed by the Royal Shakespeare Company at the Swan Theatre, Stratford-upon-Avon; and at the Pit, London, directed by Barry Kyle. Cast included: Alun Armstrong (Barabas); John Carlisle (Machiavel/Ferneze); Phil Daniels (Ithamore); Stella Gonet (Bellamira); Gregory Doran (Mathias).
1999	Performed at the Almeida Theatre, London, directed by Michael Grandage. Cast included: Ian McDiarmid (Barabas); Adam Levy (Ithamore); David Yelland (Ferneze).
1999	Performed by the Marlowe Project at the Musical Works Theatre, New York, directed by Jeff Dailey, featuring Bart Shattuck (Barabas).
2007	Performed at the Theatre for a New Audience, New York City, directed by David Herskovits. Cast included: F. Murray Abraham (Barabas); Arnie Burton (Ithamore).

EDWARD II

1307–27	Reign of King Edward II.

A chronology of Marlowe's life and works

1587	Publication of the second edition of Raphael Holinshed's *Chronicles of England, Scotland, and Ireland*, the play's main source.
1592	Marlowe wrote the play, and it was performed by Pembroke's Men in London, probably at the Theatre.
1594	First publication. The play had been in the printer's hands since July the previous year. There were three subsequent early editions (1598–1622).
1610s(?)	Performed at the Red Bull by Queen Anne's Men.
1903	Performed by the Elizabethan Club, directed by William Poel. The cast included Harley Granville Barker (Edward).
1905	Performed at the Shakespeare Memorial Theatre, directed by Frank Benson, who also played Edward.
1923	Performed by the Phoenix Society at the Regent Theatre, London, directed by Allan Wade. Cast included: Duncan Yarrow (Edward); Ernest Thesiger (Gaveston); Gwen Ffrangcon-Davies (Isabella).
1924	Adaptation by Bertolt Brecht and Lion Feuchtwanger, performed in Munich.
1947	BBC television production by Stephen Harrison. Cast included: David Markham (Edward); Nigel Stock (Kent); Patrick Troughton (Baldock).
1956	Performed by Theatre Workshop, Stratford East, directed by Joan Littlewood, featuring Peter Smallwood (Edward).
1958	Performed by the Marlowe Society, Cambridge, featuring Derek Jacobi (Edward) and John Barton (Mortimer).
1969	Performed by Prospect Theatre Company, directed by Toby Robertson. Cast included: Ian McKellen (Edward); James Laurenson (Gaveston); Timothy West (Mortimer); Diane Fletcher (Isabella); David Calder (Spencer Junior); Robert Eddison (Lightborne). The production was televised by the BBC in 1970.
1975	Produced at the Harkness Theatre, New York, directed by Ellis Rabb. Cast included: Norman Snow (Edward); Sam Tsoutsouvas (Mortimer); Peter Dvorsky (Gaveston); Mary-Joan Negro (Isabella); Kevin Kline (Lightborne).
1982	Television production of Françoise Rey's French translation, directed by Bernard Sobel. Cast included: Philippe Clévenot (Edward); Bertrand Bonvoisin (Mortimer); Hélène Vincent (Isabella); Daniel Briquet (Gaveston).

1986	Performed at the Manchester Royal Exchange, directed by Nicholas Hytner. Cast included: Ian McDiarmid (Edward); Michael Grandage (Gaveston).
1990–1	Performed by the Royal Shakespeare Company at the Swan, Stratford-upon-Avon; and at the Pit, London, directed by Gerard Murphy. Cast included: Simon Russell Beale (Edward); Grant Thatcher (Gaveston); Ciarán Hinds (Mortimer).
1991	Film adaptation by Derek Jarman. Cast included: Steven Waddington (Edward); Andrew Tiernan (Gaveston); Tilda Swinton (Isabella); Nigel Terry (Mortimer); Jerome Flynn (Kent); Dudley Sutton (Winchester).
1995	Ballet adaptation by David Bintley, premiered at Stuttgart.
2000	Adaptation by Paul Wagar performed by the ARK Theatre Company, Los Angeles, directed by Don Stewart, featuring Donald Robert Stewart (Edward); Ryan Gesell (Gaveston).
2001	Performed at the Crucible, Sheffield, directed by Michael Grandage, featuring Joseph Fiennes (Edward).
2003	Performed at Shakespeare's Globe, London, directed by Timothy Walker. All-male cast included: Liam Brennan (Edward); Gerald Kyd (Gaveston); Chu Omombala (Isabella).
2007	Performed by the Shakespeare Theatre Company at Sidney Harman Hall, Washington, DC, directed by Gale Edwards. Cast included: Wallace Acton (Edward); Vayu O'Donnell (Gaveston); Andrew Long (Mortimer).
2011	Performed at the Manchester Royal Exchange, directed by Toby Frow. Cast included: Chris New (Edward); Samuel Collings (Gaveston); Emma Cunniffe (Isabella); Jolyon Coy (Mortimer); David Collings (Mortimer Senior).

THE MASSACRE AT PARIS

1572	Massacre of the Parisian Huguenots on 24 August (St Bartholomew's Day).
1573	Publication of François Hotman's *The Furious Outrages of France*, a source for the early scenes.
1576	Publication of Jean de Serres' *The Life of … Jasper Coligny Chatillon*, in a translation by Arthur Golding: another source for the play's early scenes.

A chronology of Marlowe's life and works xxvii

1588	Assassination of Henry, Duke of Guise on 23 December.
1589	Assassination of King Henry III of France on 2 August.
1593	Marlowe wrote the play, and it was performed once in January by Lord Strange's Men at the Rose, under the title *The Tragedy of the Guise*. (Further performances were forestalled by the closure of the London playhouses because of plague.)
1594	Performed at the Rose by the Admiral's Men; after the first performance it was retitled *The Massacre*.
1590s(?)	First publication, in a garbled, abridged text: the only early edition (though there is a fuller manuscript version of one passage)
1601–2	Revived by the Admiral's Men at the Fortune.
1981	Performed by the Citizens' Company at the Citizens' Theatre, Glasgow, directed by Phillip Prowse. Cast included: Robert Gwilym (Guise/Admiral); Jill Spurrier (Catherine); John Breck (Anjou).
1985	Performed by the Royal Shakespeare Company at The Other Place, Stratford-upon-Avon, directed by Paul Marcus, featuring Hilton McRae (Guise).
1999	Performed by the Marlowe Project at the Producers Club, New York, directed by Jeff Dailey.
2001	Performed by the Royal Shakespeare Company at The Other Place, Stratford-upon-Avon, directed by Lucy Pitman-Wallace.
2003	Performed by Blood and Thunder Theatre Company at the Marlowe Society Conference, Cambridge, directed by Kelley Costigan. Cast included: Gregory de Polnay (Guise); Sally Mortemore (Catherine); Sebastian Bates (Henry); Martin Carroll (Cardinal); Jonathan Milton (Navarre); Patrick Marlowe (Chatillon); Martin Wiggins (English Agent).

Abbreviations

DQC	*Dido, Queen of Carthage*
DrF	*Doctor Faustus*
EII	*Edward II*
Ep.	Epilogue
HL	*Hero and Leander*
JM	*The Jew of Malta*
MP	*The Massacre at Paris*
OE	*Ovid's Elegies*
Pro.	Prologue
Tamb.	*Tamburlaine*

Introduction

Emily C. Bartels and Emma Smith

The paradox of Christopher Marlowe is that he is both too familiar and rather evasive. The frequent abbreviation 'Kit' suggests an intimacy that the works themselves both solicit and repel; more appropriate, perhaps, is the slippery range of his name in official records: Marlow, Marloe, Marley, Marlin, Malyn, Morley, Merlin, Mar. Atheist, intelligencer, heretic, spy, overreacher, tobacco-loving sodomite, intellectual queen, radical tragedian, who held monstrous opinions, wrote the plays attributed to Shakespeare, did not die in Deptford in 1593 or did, and was murdered by the Queen: these are some of the rumors that have been attached to Christopher Marlowe. His characters too have correspondingly outrageous reputations – Tamburlaine for 'working words' that conquer kingdoms and dare gods out of heaven, Faustus for a demonic 'form of fortunes' that do or don't produce his damnation (who can tell?), Edward II for queerness, and so on. Marlowe's lyric 'The Passionate Shepherd to His Love' reverberated across the poetic and musical culture of the period, like the pop hit that is the soundtrack for a generation, and, like all the best pop stars, he died violently and young. Marlowe's literary canon is all essentially juvenilia.

In part Marlowe's mythic reputation is an inevitable supplement to the biography of Shakespeare. His life is political where Shakespeare's seems studiedly neutral; his light burns bright and brief, while Shakespeare looks back on a long career in the theatre; Marlowe's own personality seems to shape his writing, while Shakespeare slips behind the mask of his characters; his work is transgressive where Shakespeare's is bourgeois. As Al Pacino found in his vox pop in *Looking for Richard* (1996), Shakespeare now circulates largely as textual fragments: 'what's in a name?'; 'alas, poor Yorick'; 'to be or not to be'; 'neither a borrower nor a lender be'; 'now is the winter of our discontent'; 'all the world's a stage'. In the case of Marlowe, however, our first step is more often one or more oversized myths. Just as contemporaries constructed Marlowe's life in the light of his violent death, so too have Marlowe aficionados afterwards built his reputation via retrospection. To encounter Christopher Marlowe is almost inevitably to read from the end to the beginning, from the outside in, and from his life and world to the works themselves. It is not surprising that Marlowe's most prominent place in modern culture is as a proto-Romantic hero, a Caravaggio or Byron, played in the Oscar-winning film *Shakespeare in Love* by Rupert Everett, nor that even as biographical approaches to literature have waned, the most pressing critical context for Marlowe's works has tended to be Marlowe's life.

It seems all the more important, then, that we look closely at multiple contexts and recover, explore, augment, and critique the literary and historical narratives that frame the study and appreciation of Marlowe. We are used to an idea of Marlowe as socially, dramatically, poetically, and sexually subversive, but this, too, is a construct in need of fresh assessment. This collection attempts to anchor Marlowe and 'Marlowe', to consider the multiple textual and theatrical practices that bear on Marlowe's work and reputation; the social and political issues that arise with Marlowe, during his moment, as before and after; the shifting circumstances and conceptions that may prove Marlowe to be at least as ordinary as he is extraordinary as a poet, playwright, translator.

The chapters that follow do not pretend to provide the key to all Marlovian mythologies, once and for all. All of our contributors engage the norms, assumptions, and protocols of twenty-first-century academic scholarship, whose outlines it is too early either to codify or to decode. Instead of completeness, our aim as editors and authors is to model heterogeneity, offering diverse ways of defining what actually counts as context and deciphering how it counts, when, and for whom. If we're lucky, the differences between the approaches and conclusions in the chapters here together will underscore, at once, both the contingency that comes with any reading or frame for reading history, literature, life and, at the same time, the pointedness of any connections that we, as critics, readers, and spectators make between text and context. Accordingly, we have encouraged the contributors to use their own preferred editions of Marlowe, recognising that as readers we choose the text, as well as the context, in which to encounter his works. And in the same vein, we have not sought to resolve differences in the dating of the plays and early performances.

The British plantsman David Austin has recently bred a new variety of rose, called 'Christopher Marlowe'. The description is a suggestive one. The rose is 'of a colour not usually associated with English roses', 'the growth is short but very vigorous', and, best of all, 'Christopher Marlowe should be useful whenever a bright splash of red is required.'[1] We hope this volume will be read in that spirit.

Notes

[1] www.davidaustinroses.com/english/showrose.asp?showr=4080.

PART I
Marlowe's works

CHAPTER ONE

Marlowe's chronology and canon

Martin Wiggins

We know what plays and poems Marlowe wrote, but when did he write them and how do they fit together as a coherent literary career? The dating and chronology of literary works is only straightforward when there is an unbroken sequence leading from composition to first publication, generally in fairly short order. Printed books are usually empirically datable: most bear a year of publication in their imprint (at the foot of the title page) or colophon (at the back of the book). A publisher might occasionally have reason to suppress or falsify this information – Marlowe's sexually explicit translation of Ovid appeared in a series of undated editions that misleadingly claimed to have been printed in the Netherlands – but for the most part the date of a book's publication is a secure fact. But relatively few of the significant Elizabethan authors wrote for the print market in the first instance: between composition and print there was a gap, of indeterminate duration, defined in part by the original purpose for which the work was produced. It might have been written solely for the author's personal amusement and that of his friends, and passed around in manuscript. It might have been presented to a patron in a handwritten copy, which was deemed in the sixteenth century to have more social cachet than a vulgar printed book which anyone could buy. A playwright would sell his work to an acting company, which would only release it for printing, if ever, when it was commercially advantageous to do so, usually when the play was nearing or past the end of its box-office potential. All this meant that it might be many years before a play or poem reached the hands of a printer; Marlowe had been dead for four decades when *The Jew of Malta* was first published in 1633.

This means that dating an Elizabethan play is an analytical procedure, rather than one that entails the mere location and collation of information that already exists, and the resultant chronology – which might be the basis for a history of changing theatrical fashions, or of the development of a genre, or of an author's career – is either solid or porous depending on the quality and quantity of the available evidence. In Marlowe's case, the starting-point is a broad correlation of biographical with professional circumstances. Play-writing was fundamentally a commercial activity that required the author to have easy access to his market, the mostly London-based acting companies. Marlowe's plays were therefore most likely to have been written during the six years after his leaving Cambridge in the spring of 1587, when he too was mainly based in London. The poems could have been written earlier, as private exercises during the Cambridge period of 1581–7, though it is usually, and reasonably, assumed that the unfinished *Hero and Leander* belongs to the other end of his career, its writing interrupted by his murder at the end of May 1593. It was also often argued that *Dido, Queen of Carthage* was written at university, and that in consequence it was Marlowe's first play. In the 1580s, however, all college drama at Cambridge was written in Latin: asked to arrange a performance in the English language for a prospective royal visit in 1592, the university authorities were forced to admit that they had no English plays to offer.[1] Moreover, *Dido*'s cast includes two roles, Ganymede and Ascanius, written to be played by little boys who can be dandled on the laps of adult-sized characters. Such diminutive performers were less likely to be found among Cambridge undergraduates than in the personnel of a London choirboy acting company like the Children of the Chapel Royal, to whom the play is ascribed on the title page of its first edition of 1594. So *Dido* also seems to belong in the London period, and specifically in its first half, before the city's boy companies collapsed in 1590.

Marlowe's output is easiest to pin down at the beginning and end of his play-writing career. Late in the autumn of 1587, a performance by the Admiral's Men came to a premature end when a child and a pregnant woman were accidentally shot dead by one of the actors, and another member of the audience was wounded in the head. The incident, reported as news in a letter written on 16 November, occurred during a scene where a character was tied to one of the stage posts and shot; the borrowed firearm turned out to be loaded, and the gunman's aim was off.[2] It is a good match for the scene towards the end of *The Second Part of Tamburlaine*, which belonged to the same company's repertory, in which the Governor of Babylon is hung up in chains and shot at by Tamburlaine's men; no similar scene occurs in any other known play of the time. It is true that the letter-writer, who was not an eye-witness, did not explicitly identify the play, and in theory this might open the way to speculate that it was an otherwise wholly unknown work; but the company would hardly have wanted to repeat the business in 2 *Tamburlaine* if it had already gone so spectacularly wrong in a different play, and so there are no good grounds to doubt the identification. In short, 2 *Tamburlaine* opened in London in or before November 1587. The prologue tells us it was written to capitalise on the commercial success of its predecessor, which must therefore have been written and staged earlier the same year, and must have been Marlowe's first play for the commercial theatre.

It is even more straightforward to date his last play, *The Massacre at Paris*. It appears, under its original title, *The Tragedy of the Guise*, in the theatre financier Philip Henslowe's note of his receipts at the Rose playhouse on 30 January 1593, when the take was £3 14s. Henslowe compiled his records in arrears, rather than adding a new entry each day, and he sometimes got muddled: the true date of the performance was 26 January, four days earlier. (The actual 30 January play, listed at the top of the next page of the account-book, was *Friar Bacon*.) In the misdated entry, he marked the play as 'ne', his spelling of the word 'new'.[3] Marlowe would have been writing the tragedy during the second half of 1592, when the plague was virulent and the London theatres were closed as a public health measure. It was the second new play in the Rose repertory since its reopening at the end of December, and the resident company, Lord Strange's Men, probably began preparing the production soon after the first, *The Jealous Comedy* (a lost play by an unknown author), premiered on 5 January.

The Massacre was the only play Marlowe is known to have written for one of Henslowe's companies during the period covered by the surviving accounts (which start in February 1592), and there are no comparable records that would enable the same degree of exactitude in placing the others. Even so, we can be fairly sure that, immediately before writing *The Massacre*, he devoted some of the first half of 1592 to *Edward II*. The title page of the 1594 edition establishes that it was performed by the Earl of Pembroke's Men, a company created in mid 1591 and resident at James Burbage's playhouse, the Theatre. Two factors suggest that Marlowe probably did not write the play for them in the first months of their existence. In the process of composition he followed the typical Elizabethan practice of occasionally borrowing verbal figures from his fellow dramatists; and some of these debts are to plays written in late 1591. For example, London audiences had recently heard a queen carp at a well-dressed social inferior who 'bears a duke's revenue on her back', just as Gaveston wears a lord's revenue on his, and remark that an enemy 'commands the narrow seas', as is also said of the Danes in *Edward II*; Marlowe was drawing on the original two-part version of *Henry VI*, which Shakespeare probably wrote for the same company, Pembroke's Men.[4] Likewise, when Spencer Senior wishes that Edward will reign 'in peace triumphant, fortunate in wars', he is repeating, word for word, the hope expressed of Queen Elizabeth in the 1591 Lord Mayor's inaugural pageant, scripted by George Peele and performed in the streets of London on 29 October.[5] This evidence pushes *Edward II* towards at least the end of 1591, where we collide with Marlowe's other, murkier career. He was overseas during the winter of 1591–2, apparently engaged in an espionage operation that ended with his arrest, towards the end of January, as an accomplice in a criminal counterfeiting racket in Flushing; after interrogation by the town's English Governor, Sir Robert Sidney, Marlowe was shipped back to England. What he did next was, in all likelihood, write *Edward II*.

Aside from this kind of substantive chronological evidence and analysis, it also helps if, subjectively, a dating 'feels' right. *Edward II* and *The Massacre at Paris* seem to belong together. Both tragedies deal with the conflict between royal authority and ancient baronial rights, centred on the role and influence of the King's parvenu minions. Both eschew exotic settings in favour of political realism, figuring power in terms of competing interests within a monarchy, rather than as an offshoot of some outside force such as war, magic, or mercantile wealth. Both are written – as far as it is possible to judge *The Massacre* from the boiled-down, pirated text that survives – in a 'greyer', less florid style than Marlowe's other plays, localising his distinctively lush, allusive, metaphorical writing into arias by characters indulging their imagination with either sexuality or sadism. But the trouble with subjective impressions based on literary assessments of the plays is that they can come unstuck if the criteria for assessment change. For instance, there was once a consensus that *Doctor Faustus* was written in 1592, because it was considered Marlowe's greatest achievement and must therefore belong to a 'mature' phase of his work; whereas today we accept that judgements of maturity or otherwise, which can seem natural when applied to the two decades and nearly forty plays of Shakespeare's professional career, are somewhat less meaningful in the littler confines of Marlowe's six years. But is this shift essentially any different from the way a case becomes vulnerable when there is a change in the profile of the factual evidence on which it is founded? A late dating of *Doctor Faustus* used to seem inevitable because its likely narrative source, P. F.'s *The History of the Damnable Life and Deserved Death of Doctor John Faustus*, appeared to have been published in 1592; it was later shown that the earliest extant edition was a reprint of a work that first appeared in *c.* 1588.[6]

With that instance in mind, if we apply to *Doctor Faustus* the same approach that indicated the likely proximity of *Edward II* and *The Massacre*, it becomes apparent that, imaginatively, *Faustus* starts more or less where *2 Tamburlaine* left off. Tamburlaine dies with a powerful sense of a life's work unfinished, dreaming of future achievements that he can never have, thanks to the physical limitations and frailties of his mortal human body: 'And shall I die, and this unconquerèd?'[7] Faustus, in contrast, has peaked too soon: he begins his play 'glutted … with learning's golden gifts', facing the terrible prospect of living on with nothing left to accomplish, and so crosses the last academic frontier into the forbidden art of magic.[8] Its appeal, as expressed in his early speeches, lies partly in the same sensuous engagement with the thought of far-off lands that was previously articulated by Tamburlaine; but whereas Tamburlaine travels to those lands and takes possession of them, Faustus talks of sending spirits out to bring the best bits back home to him while he will never have to leave Wittenberg. And where Tamburlaine finds a sense of pity in the death of a beloved woman, Zenocrate, Faustus repeatedly uses his magic to defy mortality and seemingly bring the dead back to life, ultimately conjuring himself a paramour in the shape of Helen of Troy.

Just as the two plays have some cognate preoccupations, so they seem to have had a comparable impact on their audiences and fellow dramatists. *Tamburlaine* sparked off a fashion for similar 'conqueror plays', usually set in the Islamic countries or beyond, starting with Robert Greene's *Alphonsus, King of Aragon*, a cash-in written in 1587 probably even before the premiere of *2 Tamburlaine*; Tamburlaine's chariot drawn by vanquished human beings was also quickly imitated in Thomas Lodge's Roman tragedy, *The Wounds of Civil War* (1588). (Since this play also belonged to the Admiral's Men, it would have been literally the same chariot.) Likewise, the years after 1588 saw an upsurge of interest in magicians, with Greene again an early adopter in *Friar Bacon and Friar Bungay* (1589; probably not the same play as was performed at the Rose in 1593); and in their biblical history play, *A Looking-Glass for London and England* (1589), Greene and Lodge burlesqued *Faustus* in a comic scene where a prankster comes disguised as the devil to claim another character's soul, only to a get a beating when he is found to be less supernatural than he seemed.

From *Doctor Faustus*, the thematic trail leads on to *Dido, Queen of Carthage*, and not only because both casts feature survivors of the Trojan War, Helen and Aeneas. Aeneas' dilemma, drawn from Marlowe's source in Virgil's *Aeneid*, is the incompatibility between his desire as a man, to stay in Carthage with Dido, and his duty to the gods, who have ordained that he must sail away to Italy and establish the dynasty that will found Rome.

Faustus' circumstances are wholly different, but the conflict is fundamentally the same. It is true that the two plays' theatrical contexts could not be more different, one written for adult performers in an open-air amphitheatre, the other for boys in an indoor, candle-lit hall; but this would not be the only example, then or now, of a striking new talent being head-hunted to work in a more elite branch of his profession. In one respect, however, the two tragedies show a significant continuity of play-writing practice. Marlowe's younger contemporary Thomas Nashe left Cambridge and came to London in 1588, and became involved in controversial pamphleteering the following year. He is named as the co-author of *Dido* on the 1594 title page. Marlowe's only other collaborative play was *Doctor Faustus*: the comic scenes in which Wagner shadows Faustus' career of legerdemain were written by another author with different linguistic habits. Circumstantially, this *should* have been Nashe, whose early connection with the play is evinced by a quotation from the opening scene that he copied into the margin of a printed book in *c*. 1589.[9] To date, however, only unsystematic efforts have been made to trace his hand in the play, and the results have not been promising. But even if Marlowe worked with different men on the two tragedies, the very fact of collaboration tends to reinforce the other signs associating those plays with one another.

This leaves us with *The Jew of Malta*. The play was not 'ne' when it first appears in Henslowe's records, on 26 February 1592, and Shakespeare drew on its language in *3 Henry VI* in the latter part of 1591. The only firm internal evidence of its date is an allusion in the prologue, spoken by the ghost of Machiavel, who says he has come to England 'now the Guise is dead'.[10] The Duke of Guise was assassinated on 23 December 1588, an event that Marlowe later dramatised in *The Massacre at Paris*. The chronological significance of the allusion will depend on precisely how topical we take it to have been. It evidently wasn't so ephemeral that it had become meaningless by the time the play was printed in 1633 (albeit in a text apparently based on Marlowe's original manuscript rather than on some interim adaptation), but the notion that Machiavellianism had now left French politics would have rung more and more hollow as the months and years rolled on. An early date in the spring or summer of 1589, before Marlowe went to prison in September, would make the allusion consistent, in a much smaller way, with his speedy exploitation in *Doctor Faustus* of the dramatic potential of a recently published book. Moreover, a revival at the Rose just under three years later would also be consistent with the repertory practice of the time; *A Looking-Glass for London and England* also had a Rose revival in 1592 after a similar interval.

The shape of Marlowe's career as it emerges from this analysis raises an enormous question about the Marlowe canon. There is a gap of more than two years separating *Edward II* and *The Massacre* from the five earlier plays, which makes good sense in terms of those plays' tonal differences from their predecessors, but which includes a period when we have definite testimony that Marlowe was actively working as a writer. Under interrogation in 1593 after a heretical text was found in his possession, Thomas Kyd explained the document away as Marlowe's property, which must have got mixed up with his papers when they were 'writing in one chamber two years since' – that is, in mid 1591.[11] So what was Marlowe writing then, and during the rest of the unoccupied years? There are three possibilities. He might have written some of his extant non-dramatic poems, such as his hard-to-date translation of Lucan. He might have written works that are extant, but that have not been securely identified as his. Or he might have written plays or poems that are lost and that we may or may not know about through other surviving evidence. And that is where we begin to lose our grip on empirical knowledge and slip from certainties to likelihoods to sheer, unverifiable speculation.

Marlowe did not write *Lust's Dominion*, which was published as his in 1657, but written for Henslowe by Thomas Dekker, William Haughton, and John Day in February 1600. He did not write the mid-1590s jig of rustic courtship sometimes called *The Wooing of Nan*, whose surviving manuscript is endorsed 'Kit Marlowe' in a later hand. He is very unlikely to have written *The Maiden's Holiday*, a lost comedy entered for publication in 1654 and ascribed in the register to him and Day, whose ignominious expulsion from Cambridge took place less than four weeks before Marlowe was murdered in Deptford. He *ought* to be the author of *Arden of Faversham*, who was evidently a man with a classical education and an intimate knowledge of north Kent; but the tragedy's considerable dramatic power is coupled with such rank ignorance of theatrical practicalities that it can hardly be the work of an experienced playwright.[12] But there is a list of lost plays from this period, none of them ever before associated with Marlowe's name, to which he might plausibly have contributed an item or two.

Kyd told the authorities in 1593 that, when they first met, Marlowe was writing for the players patronised by Kyd's master, usually identified as Lord Strange. We don't know how early the encounter took place, nor what Marlowe was writing for Lord Strange's Men at the time (the only possible candidate among his extant plays is *The Jew of Malta*); but if they were his clients during the 1591 room-sharing period, there is a good chance that in that year he sold them one or more of the lost plays that continued in their repertory the following year when Henslowe's records begin. There are fourteen candidates – too many to list them all here – and there is simply no way of knowing which of them, if any, might have been his. Perhaps we could be tempted by *Pope Joan* and *Machiavel*, the titles that offer the most obvious bridge from the concerns of *The Jew of Malta* to those of *Edward II*; but that is probably a hypothesis too far. All we can ultimately say is that there is a large hole in our knowledge of Marlowe's literary career; that, in all likelihood, not every piece of his writing made it through the haphazard, contingent processes that led to their survival in print; and that, short of an improbably lucky find, there is nothing whatever that we can do to get those lost works back.

Notes

1 Alan Nelson, ed., *Cambridge*, Records of Early English Drama (University of Toronto Press, 1989), Vol. I, 347.
2 *Letters of Philip Gawdy*, ed. Isaac Herbert Jeayes (London: J. B. Nichols, 1906), 23.
3 R. A. Foakes and R. T. Rickert, eds., *Henslowe's Diary*, 2nd edn (Cambridge University Press, 2002), 20.
4 William Shakespeare, *2 Henry VI*, I.iii.83, and *3 Henry VI*, I.i.240, in William Shakespeare, *The Complete Works*, ed. Stanley Wells and Gary Taylor (Oxford University Press, 1986); compare *Edward II*, ed. Martin Wiggins and Robert Lindsey, New Mermaids (London: A. & C. Black, 1997), iv.408 and vi.165. For further debts to the *Henry VI* plays, see the Revels edition of *Edward II*, ed. Charles R. Forker (Manchester University Press, 1994), 24.
5 *Edward II*, x.33; George Peele, *Descensus Astraeae*, line 39, in *The Life and Works of George Peele*, ed. Charles Tyler Prouty (New Haven and London: Yale University Press, 1952–70), Vol. I, 214–19.
6 R. J. Fehrenbach, 'A Pre-1592 English Faust Book and the Date of Marlowe's *Doctor Faustus*', *The Library* 7th ser., 2 (2001), 327–35.
7 Christopher Marlowe, *Tamburlaine the Great*, ed. J. S. Cunningham, Revels Plays (Manchester University Press, 1981), Part II: V.iii.150, 158.
8 Christopher Marlowe, *Doctor Faustus*, ed. David Bevington and Eric Rasmussen, Revels Plays (Manchester University Press, 1993), A-Text, Pro., 24.
9 Peter Beal, *Index of English Literary Manuscripts*, Vol. I: *1450–1625* (London: Mansell, 1980), MrC 20.
10 Christopher Marlowe, *The Jew of Malta*, ed. N. W. Bawcutt, Revels Plays (Manchester University Press, 1978), Pro., 3.
11 Park Honan, *Christopher Marlowe: Poet and Spy* (Oxford University Press, 2005), 378.
12 Martin Wiggins, ed., *A Woman Killed with Kindness and Other Plays*, Oxford English Drama (Oxford University Press, 2008), 284–7.

CHAPTER TWO

Marlowe's magic books: the material text

Leah S. Marcus

The first English printer was William Caxton, who learnt the fledgling art of creating books through movable type on the Continent and set up a printing press in Westminster in 1476. More than 100 years later, Christopher Marlowe's writings began to appear in print, the first of these an edition of the two parts of *Tamburlaine* in 1590. We cannot be sure that this printing was, in fact, Marlowe's earliest: editions of individual plays were typically issued in cheap, unbound paper format and were sometimes read to death as they were passed from one consumer to another, so that copies failed to survive into the present. But we can be sure that the printed *Tamburlaine* was popular: it was reprinted in 1592, 1597, 1605–6, and after.

During the late sixteenth century, printed playbooks were usually issued only after a play had been successful on stage; they were designed to extend the play's afterlife to an audience of readers who could peruse the printed version and recapture some of the élan of watching it in the theatre. However, printing plays that had recently been acted was a new enough practice that many would-be readers found it disconcerting. Contemporaries complained that the playbooks were drab and still, lacking the 'soule of lively action' that animated plays in performance.[1] One of the things that made Marlowe popular on stage was his ability to ravish and amaze audiences by dramatising fascinatingly horrific spectacles like mass murder or the conjuring of demons, spectacles that 'balanced on the nervous razor edge between transcendent heroism and dangerous blasphemy', creating what I have elsewhere termed the 'Marlowe effect'.[2] This chapter will contend that early printers of Marlowe sought devices beyond the mere reproduction of the language of the plays to keep the 'Marlowe effect' alive in their editions, specifically in the early printed editions of *Tamburlaine* and *Doctor Faustus*.

Printing on paper is to us now an increasingly outmoded and vanishing technology. But when it was new in the late fifteenth century it aroused strong emotions of fear and wonder: how was it possible, in an age before mass production, for a mechanical process to produce duplicates so quickly, when manuscript copying had always been very slow and only capable of creating single, unique copies? Printing in the West was invented by Johannes Gutenberg and its most famous exemplar was the Gutenberg Bible. When Gutenberg's associate Johann Fust, sometimes called Johann Faust and associated with the legendary necromancer Doctor Faustus, took early examples of the Gutenberg Bible to the French court, he was accused of being in league with Satan because the copies were all uncannily identical.[3] Similar rumours dogged Albertus Manutius, the founder of the famous Aldine Press in Venice. Printing as a process of reproduction initially appeared either godlike or demonic because it replicated divine creation, producing a dizzying number of quick simulacra where only a single entity had existed before. As Elizabeth Eisenstein has argued, it also helped disseminate demonic practices by printing both the magic spells and the criteria used to recognise them, as in the comprehensive guide to witchcraft, *Malleus maleficarum* (1486).[4]

By Marlowe's time, much of the anxiety surrounding the process of printing had abated through familiarity, though the term 'printer's devil', used for apprentices in the printshop, may register its continuing presence (the first *OED* citation of the phrase is from the late seventeenth century). But Marlowe on stage was another matter. *Doctor Faustus* in particular, which included several scenes of conjuring on stage, was dogged by sensational episodes of demonic interference in performance. In Exeter, an extra devil appeared on stage, causing panic among actors and spectators; in London, the playhouse cracked loudly during one performance, frightening the audience; at another performance, a 'visible apparition' of the devil appeared on stage, to the amazement of all present.[5] Was it possible that a performance of conjuring could actually summon a devil, or that a stage utterance of blasphemy could call down divine judgement upon the actors? Puritans who wrote tracts against the theatre contended that the answer to both questions was yes: many contemporaries feared theatrical performance because of its potential to contaminate the world beyond the stage, and in 1606 an 'Act to Restrain Abuses of Players' prohibited spoken profanity in any dramatic production. But what was bad for public morals was often good for business. Marlowe's printers, I shall argue, devised mechanisms designed to revive some of the frisson that had accompanied early printing by associating Marlowe's printed texts with the transgressive world of plays in performance and with their divine – or demonic – capacity for performative speech.

'Performative speech' as understood by speech-act theorists is language that brings into being the thing being referenced, as in the biblical story of creation: 'God said, Let there be light: and there was light.'[6] Or a commonly cited human example might be the marriage vow, 'I do' (in the USA) or 'I will' (in the UK), which states the bride or groom's acquiescence to being married but also performs the marriage. Marlowe's plays display enormous fascination with the theatrical potential of performative speech. In *Tamburlaine*, as is frequently noted, the hero's 'working words' frequently appear to conjure into being what they ask for. On stage, Tamburlaine's invocation of an image through the power of his speech is often followed by its material appearance as stage business, so that his declamatory language carries an aura of magical efficacy. After many incantatory repetitions of the word *crown*, actual crowns appear on stage, and the same thing happens to other words – thrones; swords; and the colours white, red, and black. A particularly arresting case is the idea of fire, which, in the language of Jill Levenson, 'becomes apparent verbally' in Act II of Part I but 'threads its way through the drama' until it emerges visually on stage when Tamburlaine burns the town where Zenocrate dies in Act III of Part II.[7] At another point, Tamburlaine predicts that the defeated kings will draw his chariot and, behold! they do so. According to the stage directions in the 1590 octavo, Tamburlaine is 'drawn in his chariot by Trebison and Soria, with bits in their mouths, reins in his left hand, in his right hand a whip with which he scourgeth them'.[8] This arresting moment closely resembles the familiar iconic image of the Gallic Hercules on his cart drawn by auditors chained to his tongue, an emblem of the great power of rhetoric to mobilise and control its audience.[9] Through the figure of Tamburlaine, a master rhetorician who enacts swift conquests via language, Marlowe dramatises the power of performative speech. We can speculate that Tamburlaine's magical ability to conjure up 'reality' through his 'working words' was a major element of his fascination for the playgoing public. He was an alien, a Scythian, at least at some points a Muslim and a heretic, but he simultaneously ventriloquised early modern rhetorical culture's belief in the material power of language.

In Act V of *Tamburlaine*, Part II, shortly before his own death, Tamburlaine calls for a huge pile of Korans and other 'superstitious books' to be burnt, daring Mahomet to save his holy writings through a 'furious whirlwind' or some other deus ex machina. The conqueror does not survive for long after the conflagration of the books, but he comes alive again for readers in the printed version of *Tamburlaine*, Parts I and II. Speech-act theorists contend that a written document can carry the efficacy of the 'performative speech' it commemorates: a marriage licence, for example, records the effects of the spoken language that cemented the marriage. Similarly, the book of *Tamburlaine* preserves some of the transgressive power of the plays on stage. All of the early editions of the play were printed in octavo – a very small format that was relatively unusual for the printing of plays: with one exception, for example, all of Shakespeare's plays that appeared in print before the First Folio in 1623 were published in quarto, and so were other plays by Marlowe.[10] Octavo books could vary in size but were designed to be easily portable 'pocket books' narrower and smaller than quartos. The Aldine Press had published a series of octavo editions of literary classics; in England, the small format was frequently used for prayer books, books of hours, and the like. As Ramie Targoff has argued, George Herbert's volume of devotional poems *The Temple* (1633) was issued in small format to echo the shape and size of a prayer book.[11] Readers of an early octavo edition of *Tamburlaine* may have noticed the correlation in format between the playbook and books of devotion, but the 'devotion' in this case was parodic and transgressive, giving the book, perhaps, an aura of delicious danger. Its typeface, likewise, echoed prayer books and other devotional materials. It was printed in blackletter (Gothic type), which was still common in the 1590s for many kinds of popular literature but was used most consistently for devotional manuals and law books. In addition, the 1590 *Tamburlaine* included a portrait of the play's great hero at the beginning of Part II (sig. F2v). Such portraits in play texts are unusual at this period; this one helps bind the text to its earlier performances by depicting a late-middle-aged, very English-looking warrior in armour, much as the ageing hero of Part II may have appeared on stage (Figure 1).[12] Subsequent early editions continue the same format except that by the 1597 edition the visual effect is amplified by the addition of a portrait of Zenocrate (Figure 2) at the end of Part I (sig. F5r). The 1590 printer's preface 'To the Gentlemen Readers and others that take pleasure in reading Histories' expresses the hope that his readers will delight as much in the book as they have earlier in seeing the play 'shewed in London vpon stages' (sig. A2r); but the printer also throws himself upon their 'protection' (sig. A2v) – perhaps a mere gesture of courteous humility, or perhaps an acknowledgement that the book's publication could be interpreted as flirting with blasphemy. What would we know of Marlowe's *Tamburlaine* were it not for its early printings? The book of *Tamburlaine* gives a kind of permanence to its otherwise evanescent stage hero, his monumental exploits, and his gloriously dangerous power of performative speech.

Figure 1   Portrait of Tamburlaine, from the 1590 edition

Unlike *Tamburlaine*, Marlowe's *Doctor Faustus* was not published until the early seventeenth century. The earliest extant text is a quarto dated 1604, but that edition exists in only a single copy, and there may have been earlier printings that have not survived. It was reissued in 1609 and

the Scythian Shepheard.
Thy first betrothed Loue Arabia,
Shall we with honor(as beseemes)entombe
With this great Turke,and his faire Emperesse,
Then after all these solemne Exequies,
We will our celebrated rites of mariage solemnize.

Finis Actus quinti & vltimi huius primi partis.

Figure 2   Portrait of Zenocrate, from the 1597 edition of *Tamburlaine*

1611. A much amplified text was printed in 1616: most notably from our perspective here of the history of the book, the 1616 quarto's title page includes an image of Faustus holding one of his magic books, standing within a circle of mysterious signs and confronting a black demon whom he has evidently just conjured up (see Figure 3). If Tamburlaine excelled in producing seemingly spontaneous 'working words', Marlowe's Doctor Faustus is an actual magician who has learnt the art of performative speech by following the formulae offered in his tomes. Mephistopheles does at one point tell Faustus that he comes to the magus not because of the power of Faustus' spells but because of the prospect of tempting a Christian soul into perdition.[13] But why would the Father of Lies necessarily speak truth? As we have already seen, the play's conjuring scenes were often seriously unnerving for early audiences in the theatre: on those occasions when an extra being magically appeared on stage, or so the actors thought, they were either conjuring successfully or (to take the perspective of enemies of the theatre) they were provoking a demonic visitation through their blasphemy. As Andrew Sofer has cogently argued, *Doctor Faustus* gets much of its energy on stage from its conflation of magic and theatrical power: is performance mere empty gesture or is it efficacious, and if the latter, how and in what degree? *Faustus* unleashes the energies of conjuring by blurring the boundary between representing magic and performing it.[14]

All of the early printings of *Doctor Faustus* use blackletter type, which was becoming increasingly uncommon for playbooks by the seventeenth century and may therefore have helped give the text a distinctive and faintly theological air. Editors have disagreed about the respective quality and authority of the two early texts of the play. The 1604 quarto (commonly known as the A-text) is shorter and lacks many of the rather frivolous stunts that mark Faustus' progressive decline in the 1616 quarto (the B-text), which may well reflect the 'new additions' belatedly advertised in the titles of subsequent quartos of 1619 and 1624. It is beyond the scope of this chapter to discuss the textual differences in detail. However, it is worth noting that older editors preferred the B-text because it was fuller and more crowded with stage actions, while more recent editors have preferred the comparative sparseness and tautness of A.[15]

As might be expected given its date of 1616, the B-text of *Doctor Faustus* shows intermittent signs of stage censorship introduced by the 1606 'Act to Restrain Abuses of Players'. At several points where the A-text reads 'God', B substitutes 'heaven'; two A-text references to 'Christ' are deleted

Figure 3 Marlowe's *Doctor Faustus* (1616), title page

in B and the oath "Swounds', meaning 'God's wounds', disappears at points in B.[16] However, the necromancy in A remains intact in B, and B draws emphatic attention to the such matters through the woodcut on its title page. This image of Faustus is not particularly well carved and may not have attracted 'Gentlemen Readers' to the volume. But it was surely successful as advertising: it reminds would-be purchasers of the thrilling moments of Faustus' conjuring on stage, moments that they can now recapture by buying the book. As the clown Robin within *Doctor Faustus* steals one of the magus' books so that he can raise demons on his own, perhaps naïve would-be readers even hoped to use the playbook as a manual for casting their own spells – or for protecting against them. As Georgia E. Brown has recently argued, *Doctor Faustus* is 'obsessed with the relationship between writing, print and performance', with the ways that 'textuality and corporeality might overlap', and with the 'opportunities and dangers of writing'.[17] The fear of Johann Fust (or Faust) and of printing as demonic that had been common a century before hovers in the background of the play. Even handwriting is associated with danger. Not only does Faustus sign his demonic contract in his own blood, but words of warning – '*Homo, fuge!*' (II.i.77) – appear mysteriously written on his arm. In the B-text of *Doctor Faustus*, the magician's scholars enter at the end of the play, anxious to confirm Faustus' safety after a night of terrifying shrieks and cries. They discover his mangled body on stage, his limbs 'All torn asunder by the hand of death' (V.iii.7). According to Christian moralists of the period, blasphemy was a particularly dangerous form of performative speech in that it tore apart the body of Christ, thereby sacrificing him anew. Faustus' bodily dismemberment in the B-text is therefore a fitting punishment for a blasphemer, performing on his own flesh what he had done to Christ through language. The material playbook is, among many other things, an extension of Faustus' body, written over with cryptic spells and warnings yet restored to material intactness.

Although the A- and B-texts of *Doctor Faustus* are profoundly different in terms of content, they have a curious motif in common. At the end of the text in all early printings of the play, after Faustus has exited accompanied by devils and the chorus have uttered their final words of admonition, we encounter the following inscription: '*Terminat hora diem. Terminat Author opus.*' Since this line, with its curious lacuna in the middle, is followed by a printer's device (a decorative emblem) in the 1604 edition, most critics have assumed that it is non-Marlovian and have given it little attention. But the line is, I would contend, key to the functioning of the printed book, especially for early readers, in that it suggests connections among three seemingly discrete events. 'The hour [that] ends the day' is midnight, the hour of Faustus' exit with demons on the stroke of twelve. At the same hour, readers are allowed to infer, 'The Author ends his work' – Marlowe finishes writing or, possibly, the supreme 'Author', God, consummates the damnation of Faustus. The gnomic suggestiveness of the line allows a conflation of natural process (the end of the day), Marlowe's shaping of the play, and the power of the divine to create and destroy. The tag line gives a mysterious aura to the text, drawing a potentially blasphemous connection between human authorship and divine creation and thereby heightening the play's emphasis on – or status as – performative speech. With succeeding printings, the tag line became absorbed into the text. The 1604 and 1609 texts end with the tag line and after it a printer's device, but in 1611 the printer's device below the tag line is replaced by 'FINIS' and subsequent printings keep this pattern. From 1611 onwards the tag line is therefore part of the play and reads as the author's final send-off to the reading public. Small wonder that *Doctor Faustus* was frequently reprinted: it too, like *Tamburlaine*, enticed readers to flirt with theological danger, to imagine human plastic powers as verging on the divine. Modern readers who consult early printed versions of dramatic works are often unimpressed with the printers' artistry and degree of editorial accuracy. But early printers of Marlowe's plays exploited the resources of the material book in subtle, ingenious ways in order to replicate, or at least gesture towards, the thrilling, transgressive 'Marlowe effect' that had captivated audiences in the theatre.

Notes

I would like to thank my graduate students Jane Wanninger and Erin Pellarin, whose work on demonic contracts and performative speech stimulated my interest in the topic of this chapter.

1. John Marston, *The Malcontent* (London: for William Aspley, 1604), sig. A2r.
2. Cited from Leah S. Marcus, *Unediting the Renaissance: Shakespeare, Marlowe, Milton* (London and New York: Routledge, 1996), 42.
3. See Philip B. Meggs, *A History of Graphic Design* (New York: Van Nostrand Reinhold, 1983), 80–4; and Eric Frederick Jensen, 'Liszt, Nerval, and *Faust*', *Nineteenth-Century Music* 6 (1982): 151–8.
4. Elizabeth Eisenstein, *The Printing Press as an Agent of Change: Communications and Cultural Transformations in Early-Modern Europe*, 2 vols. (London and New York: Cambridge University Press, 1979), Vol. I, 433–9.

5 See John Russell Brown, 'Marlowe and the Actors', *Tulane Drama Review* 8:4 (1964): 155–73; E. K. Chambers, *The Elizabethan Stage,* 4 vols. (Oxford: Clarendon Press, 1923), Vol. III, 423–4; and Michael Goldman, 'Marlowe and the Histrionics of Ravishment', in *Two Renaissance Mythmakers: Christopher Marlowe and Ben Jonson,* ed. Alvin Kernan, Selected Papers from the English Institute, 1975–6 (Baltimore: Johns Hopkins University Press, 1977), 22–40.
6 Genesis 1.3. On speech-act theory, see J. L. Austin, *How to Do Things with Words* (Cambridge, MA: Harvard University Press, 1962); and for recent revisionist theory of performative speech in the theatre, W. B. Worthen, 'Drama, Performativity, and Performance', *PMLA* 113 (1998): 1093–107; and the articles cited in n. 14 below.
7 Jill L. Levenson, '"Working Words": The Verbal Dynamic of *Tamburlaine*', in *'A Poet and a Filthy Play-Maker': New Essays on Christopher Marlowe,* ed. Kenneth Friedenreich, Roma Gill, and Constance Brown Kuriyama (New York: AMS Press, 1988), 99–115 (112).
8 Christopher Marlowe, *Tamburlaine Parts One and Two,* ed. Anthony B. Dawson, 2nd edn (New York: W. W. Norton, 1997), II.iv.4.
9 See Neil Rhodes, *The Power of Eloquence and English Renaissance Literature* (New York: St Martin's Press, 1992), 86–7; and more generally, Wayne A. Rebhorn, *The Emperor of Men's Minds: Literature and the Renaissance Discourse of Rhetoric* (Ithaca, NY: Cornell University Press, 1995), 66–79.
10 The 1594 edition of Marlowe's *Edward II* was published in 'quarto-form octavo', which means that it was based on octavo-sized sheets but printed like a quarto.
11 Ramie Targoff, *Common Prayer: The Language of Public Devotion in Early Modern England* (University of Chicago Press, 2001), 111–17.
12 Tamburlaine's portrait in relation to those of eastern potentates is discussed in Leah S. Marcus, 'Marlowe *in tempore belli*', the 'Epilogue' to *War and Words: Horror and Heroism in the Literature of Warfare,* ed. Sara Munson Deats, LaGretta Tallent Lenker, and Merry G. Perry (Lanham and New York: Lexington Books, 2004), 295–316. See also Jonathan Burton, *Traffic and Turning: Islam and English Drama, 1579–1624* (Newark: University of Delaware Press, 2005), 68–91.
13 Christopher Marlowe, *Doctor Faustus, A- and B-Texts (1604, 1616),* ed. David Bevington and Eric Rasmussen (Manchester University Press, 1993), A-text 1.45–52, 128–9.
14 Andrew Sofer, 'How to Do Things with Demons: Conjuring Performatives in *Doctor Faustus*', *Theatre Journal* 61 (2009): 1–22. See also Eric Byville, 'How to Do Witchcraft Tragedy with Speech Acts', *Comparative Drama* 45 (2011): 1–33.
15 For representative views, see Christopher Marlowe, *Marlowe's* Doctor Faustus, *1604–1616: Parallel Texts,* ed. W. W. Greg (Oxford: Clarendon Press, 1950); Christopher Marlowe, *The Complete Works of Christopher Marlowe,* 2 vols., ed. Fredson Bowers, 2nd edn (Cambridge University Press, 1973, 1981), Vol. II,

123–59; Marlowe, *Doctor Faustus*, ed. Bevington and Rasmussen; Christopher Marlowe, *Christopher Marlowe's* Doctor Faustus*: A 1604-Version Edition*, ed. Michael Keefer (Peterborough, ON and Lewiston, NY: Broadview Press, 1991); and Marcus, *Unediting*, 38–67.
16 See Marlowe, *Doctor Faustus*, ed. Bevington and Rasmussen, 76.
17 Georgia E. Brown, 'The Other Black Arts: *Doctor Faustus* and the Inky Worlds of Printing and Writing', in *Doctor Faustus: A Critical Guide*, ed. Sara Munson Deats (London and New York: Continuum, 2010), 140–58 (142).

CHAPTER THREE

Marlowe and the limits of rhetoric
Catherine Nicholson

Eloquence, says Erasmus in the opening chapter of *De copia*, Christopher Marlowe's grammar-school guide to the art of rhetoric, is a 'godlike power of speech'.[1] Marlowe seems to have attended carefully: his plays animate the fantasies of linguistic mastery on which sixteenth-century rhetoricians founded their art. The well-trained orator, writes Henry Peacham, 'leade[s] his hearers which way he liste, and drawe[s] them to what affection he wille';[2] he may 'winne Cities and whole Countries ... without bloodshed', according to Thomas Wilson;[3] the pursuit of eloquence, claims George Puttenham, makes men 'apt to receave visions, both waking and sleeping' and 'utter prophecies, and foretell things to come'.[4] And so it proves on Marlowe's stage. Aeneas, 'eloquent in all his speech', masters Dido's affections with the 'more than Delian music' of his voice: '[B]e thou King of Libya, by my gift', she exclaims.[5] Tamburlaine 'play[s] the orator' before a thousand Persian horsemen and wins their captain to his side with the 'strong enchantments' of his speech (*1 Tamb.*, I.ii.129, 224): 'Not Hermes, prolocutor to the gods, / Could use persuasions more pathetical', the captain responds, 'I yield my self, my men, and horse to thee' (210–11, 229). Tasked with explaining his defection to the Persian king, he says simply, 'You see, my lord, what working words he hath' (II.iii.25). Faustus overgoes even that feat, his utterances summoning visions from hell: 'I see there's virtue in my heavenly words', he marvels (*DrF*, iii.28).

It is tempting to conclude, as many Marlowe critics have, that this faith in the incantatory power of eloquence is the poet's own sole orthodoxy. 'What the common reader finds in Marlowe', according to Harold Bloom, 'is ... above all else a sheer exaltation of the possibilities of rhetoric, of the persuasive force of heroic poetry'.[6] Harry Levin famously reads Marlowe himself as an embodied figure of speech, Puttenham's overreacher, whose hyperbolic rhetoric makes poetry into power, 'taking metaphors literally' and 'convert[ing] symbols into properties',[7] while A. Bartlett Giamatti claims him as exemplary of the Renaissance belief that man 'had the power to transform himself because he had the power of language'.[8] And Stephen Greenblatt attributes to Marlowe a 'Gorgian conception of rhetoric … borne out in [his] heroes'; 'each of his plays constitutes reality', Greenblatt writes, by 'embracing a fiction rendered desirable by the intoxication of language'.[9] But there have always been those in whose ears Marlowe's 'high astounding terms' (*1 Tamb.*, Pro., 5) have rung somewhat hollow, and this chapter classes the poet himself first among them. For Marlowe is less persuaded by his own potent rhetoric – and less persuaded by the potency of rhetoric – than most modern accounts suggest. Neil Rhodes' caution that Marlowe's 'pioneering demonstrations of the power of eloquence must be placed in the context of his intellectual skepticism' is well taken, for Marlowe proves no more pious about eloquence than he is about anything else.[10] Indeed, the suspicion of dissenters like T. S. Eliot, who dismissed Marlovian rhetoric as 'a pretty simple huffe-snuffe bombast', is endemic to Marlowe's own writing, which conceals behind its grandiloquent displays a counter-narrative, both embittered and amused, about the limits of linguistic power.[11] Marlowe may excel in bringing to life humanist fantasies of eloquence, but he is equally adept at exposing the half-truths and wishful thinking on which those fantasies depend.

It's worth recalling that the one actual rhetorician who appears on his stage – the French humanist Peter Ramus, a minor character in *The Massacre at Paris* – is murdered in a scene that parodies his theory of persuasion: 'To contradict which', jibes the Duke of Guise, 'I say: Ramus shall die. / How answer you that?' (ix.35–6). Here, emphatically, words are not swords, and the Gorgian conception of rhetoric has no force: 'Your *nego argumentum* / Cannot serve', the Guise continues, 'sirrah. Kill him' (ix.36–7).[12] A suspicion of this brutal disregard for language – the antithesis of the humanists' celebratory rhetoric about rhetoric – shadows even those scenes in which eloquence seems most powerfully to serve the purposes of Marlowe's characters. His Dido, after all, merely believes herself to be in thrall to Aeneas' voice; in truth, it is Cupid's arrow that has mastered her.[13] Her misplaced faith in eloquence is her downfall, as her own plaints are dismissed by Aeneas as 'female drudgery' (*Dido*, IV.iii.55): 'In vain, my love, thou spend'st thy fainting breath', he declares, 'If words might move me, I were overcome' (V.i.153–4). *If* words might move me: for all their rhetorical opulence, Marlowe's plays treat this premise as all too conditional. The Persian king and his army may be won without bloodshed by Tamburlaine's verbal 'enchantments', but his kidnapped bride responds more cynically to his elaborate professions of love; noting the threats of enslavement to which they are explicitly coupled, she pronounces herself 'pleased perforce, wretched Zenocrate!' (*1 Tamb.*, I.ii.259). As for Faustus, his delight in the power of his own words is fatally misplaced: 'Did not my conjuring speeches raise thee?', he demands of Mephistopheles, and the devil answers,

> That was the cause, but yet *per accidens*.
> For when we hear one rack the name of God,
> Abjure the Scriptures and his Saviour Christ,
> We fly in hope to get his glorious soul.
> (*DrF*, iii.46–50)

Faustus may believe 'there's virtue in [his] heavenly words', but Mephistopheles suggests the reverse: the artfulness of his incantations is purely superfluous – any casual curse would do.[14]

The opening scene of *Edward II* urges a similar conclusion, returning Marlowe's audience to a primal scene of his boyhood training in rhetoric the reception of a letter from a beloved friend – only to strip eloquence of virtue in either sense of the word. 'Ah, words that make me surfeit with delight!', exclaims Gaveston upon reading a letter from the newly crowned Edward (i.3). His response – twenty floridly figured lines likening himself to a swooning Leander, London to Elysium, and Edward to the arctic sun – parodies the famous thirty-third chapter of the *De copia*, in which Erasmus offers his first 'practical demonstration' of the godlike power of rhetorical amplification: nearly 150 variations on the sentence *Tuae litterae me magnopere delectarunt*, from the plainspoken ('Your letter mightily pleased me') to the comically extravagant ('The lotus tastes not sweet to any mortal man as your letters do to me'; 'When your letter was delivered, you might have seen us tipsy with excess of delight').[15] Erasmus offers this prodigious display as a two-fold testimony to the generative magic of *copia*, a tribute both to his own inventive powers – strengthened by the exercises prescribed in his treatise – and to the suasive effect of a well-crafted epistle. Gaveston's effusions might likewise be taken as sincere testimony to the power of Edward's 'amorous lines' (i.6), were it not for the fact that he begins the play by reading aloud the letter itself, a two-line missive whose style is most charitably described as to-the-point: 'My father is deceased; come, Gaveston, / And share the kingdom with thy dearest friend' (i.1–2). In Erasmus' imagined scene, *copia* begets *copia*; his eloquence is devoted to and stimulated by the eloquence of his friend. But paired with Edward's bluntness, Gaveston's ornate expressions of delight seem less copious than compensatory, rhetorical filigree designed to obscure the naked fact of ambition. In fact, as the remainder of the scene suggests, Gaveston regards susceptibility to eloquence as mere folly.

His ecstasies over the letter are interrupted by the pleas of three beggars, whose plaints he first mocks and then forestalls with false assurances, noting in an aside that 'it is no pain to speak men fair' (i.41). Poetry and wit, he observes, are Edward's 'delight' – means to 'draw the pliant king which way I please' – but 'words … move me as much / As if a goose should play the porcupine / And dart her plumes, thinking to pierce my breast' (i.52–3, 38–40).

According to Gaveston, it isn't simply that eloquence can be turned to bad ends – the usual complaint of rhetoric's enemies, from Plato's Socrates on – but that it holds a vastly inflated view of its own efficacy: silly goose. This latter charge is the more subversive of the two, as it turns the serious enterprise of humanist rhetorical training into the stuff of comedy. A similar transformation marks Marlowe's *Hero and Leander*, which mounts a witty take-down of rhetoric's self-mythology by way of a poem that epitomises that mythology, identified by its humanist readers with the very purest strain of antique eloquence. For according to an erroneous but widespread scholarly tradition, the author of the Greek text on which Marlowe based his poem was the same poet hailed by Virgil as 'Musaeum ante omnis', pupil and companion of Orpheus himself, one of the aboriginal company of poets Puttenham classes as 'from the beginning the best perswaders and their eloquence the first Rhethoricke of the world'.[16] The text of Musaeus' poem made its way into the Renaissance as a veritable emblem of the process of cultural and linguistic *translatio*, chosen by the Venetian printer Aldus Manutius for his first parallel-text edition of an ancient Greek work in the original language and in Latin translation.[17] Aldus' edition promotes the poem as the source for Ovid's *Heroides* XVIII and XIX and the most antique trace of classical poetry's Orphic inheritance. Renaissance writers hastened to graft their own poetry to this rarefied stock, translating the narrative into various European vernaculars and confirming its status as the privileged node linking modern literary ambition to antique inspiration.[18]

Late in the sixteenth century Isaac Casaubon conducted a stylistic analysis of the poem that exposed all these claims as hogwash, proving that the Greek 'original' was the production of a late antique schoolmaster living on the margins of the Roman Empire, a fifth-century Byzantine known as Musaeus the Grammarian. Far from anchoring modern vernacular verse in a pristine point of origin, the poem turned out to be distinctly and recognisably belated, an embroidered hybrid of earlier texts; its character 'went from radical innocence to over-sophistication in the course of a few decades'.[19] But word of the reattribution spread slowly and, in England at least, failed to undo *Hero and Leander*'s association with an essential and fundamental version of eloquence. The poem was by then deeply embedded in the primitive stages of rhetorical education, serving as a popular introductory text in the English grammar-school curriculum in the language arts. Even if it had lost its stature as the so-called 'first poem', it was still one of the first poems English schoolboys learnt to read. The poem was ideally suited for this purpose: itself the product of its author's schoolmasterly desire to synthesise the full range of classical rhetorical techniques, the Greek text of *Hero and Leander* became a template for acquiring the 'rudiments of eloquence' – the basic strategies of amplification, description, and declamation outlined in Erasmus' *De copia* and other Renaissance arts of rhetoric.[20] Moreover, its erotic plot provided a compelling fable of language's sensuous power, its ability to turn resistance to consent and indifference to passion. Leander's first speech to Hero prompts her to compare him to the mythical orator Amphion: 'Stranger, likely with your words you might rouse even a stone', she replies, 'Who was it taught you the paths of devious utterance?'[21] The answer, for a generation of English schoolboys, was Musaeus himself.

What Marlowe inherits, then, is a poem saturated from within and without by the romance of rhetoric, imbued with the promise that learning to speak or write well means gaining access to a world of pleasure and power. What he produces in response to that poem is a far more equivocal text, one that indulges in richly ornamented displays of rhetorical skill while contriving to represent eloquence itself as inessential, ineffectual, or downright counterproductive. Georgia Brown's claim that *Hero and Leander* 'sets up a mutually constitutive relationship between artistic mastery and erotic success', whereby '[t]he more accomplished their rhetoric, the more successful the characters are in getting what they want',[22] offers a perfectly accurate account of what Marlowe's readers would have expected to find in a poem founded on the *Ur*-text of the classical tradition, but a rather misleading representation of what is actually there. For the poem's notoriously unstable tonal register has much to do with the fact that its style teeters on the precipice of self-parody, remaining paradoxically invested in linguistic commodities that it simultaneously and systematically devalues.[23]

Consider for instance Leander's pivotal address to Hero in the temple of Venus, which Warren Boutcher identifies as '*the* most important occasion according to a conventional rhetorical reading of the story'.[24] The narrator presents Leander to us as the quintessential earnest schoolboy: 'At last, like to a bold sharp sophister, / With cheerful hope thus he accosted her' (197–8).[25]

His theme, the relative advantages of marriage over virginity, is a favourite topos of humanist debate: Erasmus' well-known disquisition on the subject in *De conscribendis epistolis* serves as a pedagogical model of how to amass commonplaces in service of an argument and is Englished by Thomas Wilson in his *Arte of Rhetorique* as an exemplum of persuasive force.[26] But Marlowe's hyperinflated version – Leander speaks, virtually uninterrupted, for 120 lines – manages to suggest that *copia* is itself an obstacle to Hero's assent: she simply can't get more than a word or two in edgewise. The profusion of end-stopped rhyming couplets emphasises the static quality of his commonplaces, which achieve the rhetorical equivalent of hopping up and down in one place: 'A stately builded ship, well-rigged and tall, / The ocean maketh more majestical' (225–6); 'Like unturned golden strings all women are, / Which long time lie untouched, will harshly jar' (229–30); 'Rich robes themselves and others do adorn, / Neither themselves nor others, if not worn' (237–8); 'One is no number; maids are nothing then, / Without the sweet society of men' (255–6).[27] The narrator himself seeks refuge, at last, in summary: 'These arguments he used, and many more, / Wherewith she yielded, that was won before' (329–30).

The preposterous redundancy of Leander's speech – oratory deaf to its audience's need for persuasion – is highlighted by the lovers' instantaneous *silent* intimacy: they 'parled by the touch of hands … while dumb signs their yielding hearts entangled' (185–7). Here and elsewhere Marlowe synaesthetically reassigns the stock imagery of rhetorical suasion – of minds enthralled and transported – to the realm of physical contact and visual appeal: Leander's 'speaking eye' shines so that 'the barbarous Thracian soldier, moved with naught / was moved with him' (85, 81), while Hero's 'beauty' calls to viewers like the Sirens' 'inveigling harmony' (105–6). Leander's superfluous speech is delivered, moreover, on ground – the painted pavement of Venus' temple – that mocks his verbosity with images of desire satisfied with much less ado: 'gods in sundry shapes, / Committing heady riots, incest, rapes' (143–4). The closest that erotic tableau comes to ascribing power to language is in the image of Jove 'for his love Europa bellowing loud' (149), and Marlowe's poem implies that such inarticulacy is in fact the natural and most effective lexicon of desire. For seductive language, when it finally occurs, sounds a lot like stammering: 'Come thither', Hero says, and '[a]s she spake this, her tongue tripped, / for unawares "Come thither" from her slipped' (357–8).

Hero's tripping tongue prompts a lengthy interlude that crystallises the poem's ironic attitude towards its own rhetorical polish. On its surface, the story of Mercury – god of eloquence – and the shepherdess who succumbs to his advances so as 'to hear his tale' (418) frames a conventional moral about the potency of rhetoric: 'Maids are not won by brutish force and might, / But speeches full of pleasure and delight' (419–20). But the etiological digression in which this moral is embedded is spurred not by eloquence but by a cascade of rhetorical misfires. First, of course, there are Hero's repentant vows and prayers, which 'Cupid beats down … with his wings' (369). Then, penitent himself, he pleads with the Destinies to reverse her tragic fate; they refuse to 'vouchsafe so much / As one poor word, their hate to him was such' (383–4). That hatred is explained through the story of Mercury, whose courtship of the country maid relies rather more heavily on brutish force and might than its sententious tag allows: he 'did charm her nimble feet and made her stay' (399), and when she disdains his wooing, tackles her and pins her to the ground. Her silence – she 'yet was mute, / And neither would deny, nor grant his suit' (423–4) – proves far more powerful than his 'smooth speech' (402), making him 'ready to accomplish what she willed' (433). The fable's true lesson makes eloquence emphatically the loser, with poets and scholars displaced by 'servile clown[s]' (481): the Destinies punish Hermes by 'conclud[ing] / That Midas' brood shall sit in Honour's chair, / To which the Muses' sons are only heir' (474–6).

Hero and Leander can seem to enact a similarly punitive displacement upon its source text, allowing scenes of clownishly unsuccessful seduction – Leander's of Hero, Hero's of Leander, Neptune's of Leander – to unseat a narrative that once promised modern poets access to a truly Orphic inheritance. But Marlowe doesn't wholly disallow the possibility that language might make things happen; instead, he concentrates its power paradoxically, in tropes of evasion, understatement, and incompletion. As Judith Haber has argued, the poem derives much of its own seductive appeal from dilation and delay.[28] Most famously, there is the narrator's tantalisingly unfinished description of Leander's body, which begins at his face and neck and makes its way teasingly on down:

> I could tell ye
> How smooth his breast was, and how white his belly,
> And whose immortal fingers did imprint
> That heavenly path with many a curious dint
> That runs along his back, but my rude pen
> Can hardly blazon forth the loves of men,
> Much less of powerful gods: let it suffice
> That my slack muse sings of Leander's eyes.
>
>   (65–72)

This stagy *occupatio* – the sudden fit of poetic impotence at the very precipice of readerly satisfaction – becomes the signature technique of the poem. Paired with wilful understatement – *meiosis*, the figure Puttenham named 'the Disabler' – evasion is a strategy Marlowe employs to obscure not simply the most delectable bits of his characters' bodies but also the choicest expressions of their eloquence. At lines 498–9, for instance, just after Hero's dropped fan has utterly failed to convey its intended message to Leander, the pair achieve a breakthrough in communication, exchanging letters that express their mutual yearning to meet. It is an episode invented by Marlowe and seemingly tailor-made for rhetorical dilation, an excursus in the style of Ovid's *Heroides*, but the narrator retreats instead into a calculated vagueness, telling us simply that the letters are written 'in such sort' (499) as to fill their recipients with hope. So too at the lovers' first tryst, when we are told of a rapturous reunion but prevented from overhearing it:

> O who can tell the greeting
> These greedy lovers had at their first meeting?
> He asked, she gave, and nothing was denied.
> (507–9)

Such dodges have the odd effect of suggesting that rhetoric is precisely what is excluded – either as unnecessary or as insufficient – from moments at which people finally get what they want. Here, contrary to what Erasmus and his English counterparts teach, the satisfaction of desire is not the fruit of persuasion but its antithesis. 'He asked, she gave, and nothing was denied' is an ideal outcome, romantically, but it leaves no room for the *sic et non* rituals of rhetorical invention, no room for *copia*.

Ultimately, in Marlowe's poem, such outcomes are possible only when the rituals of argument are set aside. Once he has gained access to Hero's tower Leander is at a loss, fondling her 'as a brother with his sister' and 'supposing nothing else was to be done, / Now he her favour and good will had won' (536–8). William Weaver reads this moment as an allegory of rhetorical incompetence – Leander fails to interpret the text of Hero's body[29] – but Leander's formation in the rhetorical arts seems rather to be the very thing that stymies his erotic ambitions: rhetorically speaking, after all, nothing else *is* to be done. So long as Leander persists in treating lovemaking like an Erasmian exercise – 'as in plain terms (yet cunningly) he craved it; / Love always makes them eloquent that have it' (555–6) – his eloquence can get him only *most* of the way there: 'She, with a kind of granting, put him by it, / And ever as he thought himself most nigh it, /

Like to the tree of Tantalus she fled' (557–9). His second visit to Hero's tower seems doomed to a similarly frustrating outcome: 'she lets him whisper in her ear, / Flatter, entreat, promise, protest, and swear' (751–2), but all that talk makes her no less willing to surrender her virginity – and the litany of synonyms turns verbal *copia* into a self-satirising device: so many ways of saying *blah blah blah*.

Finally, however, Leander does manage to say something that – as Renaissance rhetorical manuals promised it should – overwhelms Hero's defences and secures her willing surrender. What? Well, *something*:

> Leander on her quivering breast,
> Breathless spoke something, and sighed out the rest;
> Which so prevailed, as he with small ado
> Enclosed her in his arms.
>
> (762–5)

This unspecified utterance, less oration than exhalation, accomplishes what all Leander's schoolboy rhetoric cannot; it gains for him an experience that the narrator, predictably, declares himself incompetent to narrate. An elegant metaphorical shift transplants Hero's body from Tantalus' hell to 'the orchard of th' Hesperides', where Leander, like 'Theban Hercules', plucks and eats – but the fruit turns to ashes in the narrator's mouth, for 'none rightly can describe [it] but he / That pulls or shakes it from the golden tree' (781–4). Sexual bliss escapes from rhetoric into the realm of first-hand experience; it is the subject of an eloquence proper to those whose mouths are otherwise – and better – occupied.

This wilful narratorial inarticulacy at the moment of erotic satisfaction inverts and answers Leander's earlier suspicion that, in the midst of his garrulity, something remained undone – 'some amorous rites or other were neglected'. It isn't simply that rhetoric proves irrelevant to the achievement of Leander's desire; the consummation of that desire also exposes the simultaneous inadequacy and superfluity of poetic expressivity. This melancholy insight finds a meta-textual echo in the Latin inscription with which Edward Blunt's 1598 edition of the (purposefully?) unfinished poem concludes: 'Desunt nonnulla'; something is missing.[30] Humanist rhetoricians – like some Marlowe critics – insisted that nothing remains outside the boundaries of eloquence; *Hero and Leander* suggests that an unspoken something always does. It does so, of course, by means of its own artfully chosen tropes, its conspicuously learned similes and metaphor, its copious Erasmian ingenuity. *Hero and Leander* isn't merely a critique of the Renaissance art of rhetoric; it is also a compelling demonstration of all that one schooled in that art – yet suspicious of its totalising pretensions – might achieve. As the poem that puts a period to Marlowe's dazzlingly brief career, it also opens a set of questions by which we might interrogate the necessarily partial working of words in his famously eloquent plays.

Notes

1 Desiderius Erasmus, *De duplici copia verborum ac rerum comentarii duo* (1512), trans. Betty I. Knott, in *Collected Works of Erasmus*, 56 vols., Vol. XXIV, ed. Craig R. Thompson (University of Toronto Press, 1978), 295. On Marlowe's grammar-school curriculum, see Constance Brown Kuriyama, *Christopher Marlowe: A Renaissance Life* (Ithaca, NY: Cornell University Press, 2011), 22–8.
2 Henry Peacham, *The Garden of Eloquence* (London: H. Jackson, 1577), sig. Aiiir.
3 Thomas Wilson, *The Arte of Rhetorique* (London: Richard Grafton, 1560), sig. Aiiv.
4 George Puttenham, *The Arte of English Poesie* (London: Richard Field, 1589), sig. Ciiv.
5 Christopher Marlowe, *Dido, Queen of Carthage*, III.i.64; III.iv.51, 63; in *The Complete Plays*, ed. Frank Romany and Robert Lindsey (London: Penguin, 2003). All citations from Marlowe's plays refer to *The Complete Plays*, ed. Frank Romany and Robert Lindsey (London: Penguin, 2003).
6 Harold Bloom, 'Introduction', in *Christopher Marlowe: Modern Critical Views*, ed. Harold Bloom (New York: Chelsea House Publishers, 1986), 1.
7 Harry Levin, *The Overreacher: A Study of Christopher Marlowe* (Cambridge, MA: Harvard University Press, 1952), 23–4.
8 A. Bartlett Giamatti, *Exile and Change in Renaissance Literature* (New Haven: Yale University Press, 1984), 103.
9 Stephen Greenblatt, *Renaissance Self-Fashioning: From More to Shakespeare* (University of Chicago Press, 1980).
10 Neil Rhodes, *The Power of Eloquence in English Renaissance Literature* (New York: St Martin's Press, 1992), 117.
11 T. S. Eliot, 'Some Notes on the Blank Verse of Christopher Marlowe', in *The Waste Land and Other Writings* (New York: Random House, 2002), 130. Eliot's jibe follows in a critical tradition inaugurated in the sixteenth century by rival poets like Thomas Nashe, who disparaged the 'spacious volubility' of Marlowe's 'drumming decasillabon' ('To the Gentlemen Students of Both Universities', in Robert Greene, *Menaphon* (London: Thomas Orwin, 1589), sig. **), and Robert Greene, who expressed mock-regret that his own verses did not 'iet vpon the stage in tragicall buskins, euerie worde filling the mouth like the fubarden of Bo-bell, daring God out of heaven with that Atheist Tamburlan': Greene, *Perimedes the Blacksmith* (1588), in *Marlowe: The Critical Heritage*, ed. Millar Maclure (London: Routledge and Kegan Paul, 1979), 27.

12 See R. W. Serjeantson's analysis of this scene as a particular spoof of Ramist theories of effective disputation in 'Testimony: The Artless Proof', in *Renaissance Figures of Speech*, ed. Sylvia Adamson, Gavin Alexander, and Katrin Ettenhuber (Cambridge University Press, 2007), 134–5.
13 Marlowe emphasises this reality by reversing the order of events in Virgil's poem, so that Cupid wounds the queen only *after* she listens to Aeneas' narration of the fall of Troy. Before she receives her wound, the telling of his story – to which she retrospectively attributes her passion – inspires only pity, and perhaps a hint of impatience: 'O end, Aeneas! I can hear no more', she interrupts, and bids him, 'Aeneas, leave!' 'Trojan, thy ruthful tale hath made me sad', she concedes at its end, but adds, 'Come, let us think upon some pleasing sport, / To rid me from these melancholy thoughts' (Marlowe, *Dido, Queen of Carthage*, II.i.243, 289, 301–3).
14 'Faustus' deepest illusion at this point', writes Rhodes, 'is that his words have virtue in the sense of power … If Faustus' words have any power it is the self-enthralling power of his own rhetoric which allows him to be deceived by the devil' (Rhodes, *The Power of Eloquence*, 110–11).
15 Desiderius Erasmus, *De copia*, 348–54.
16 Virgil, *Aeneid*, VI.667; Puttenham, *The Arte of English Poesie*, sig Ciiiv; on the poem's reputation in the sixteenth and seventeenth centuries, see Stephen Orgel, 'Musaeus in English', *George Herbert Journal* 29:1–2 (2005–6): 67–75.
17 Warren Boutcher, '"Who taught thee Rhetoricke to deceive a maid?": Christopher Marlowe's *Hero and Leander*, Juan Boscán's *Leandro*, and Renaissance Vernacular Humanism', *Comparative Literature* 52:1 (2000): 11–52. Boutcher's marvellous essay situates Marlowe's poem in relation to Aldus' edition and the Continental versions of *Hero and Leander* that precede it – a context that further emphasises its irreverence towards its source.
18 Bernardo Tasso's *Favola di Leandro et d'Hero* appeared in 1537, Clément Marot's *Museus ancient poete grec, des amours de Leander & Hero, traduict en rithme francoise* in 1541, and Juan Boscán's *Leandro* in 1543. See Boutcher, 'Who taught thee Rhetoricke', 20–4.
19 Orgel, 'Musaeus in English', 67.
20 William P. Weaver, 'Marlowe's Fable: *Hero and Leander* and the Rudiments of Eloquence', *Studies in Philology* 105:3 (2008): 388–408.
21 Musaeus, *Hero and Leander*, lines 174–5, trans. Cedric Whitman, in *Callimachus: Aetia, Iambi, Lyric Poems, Hecale, Minor Epic and Elegiac Poems, and Other Fragments and Musaeus: Hero and Leander*, ed. Thomas Gelzer (Cambridge, MA: Harvard University Press, 1975), 367–9. On the relationship between Musaeus' Greek and Marlowe's English style, see Gordon Braden, *The Classics and English Renaissance Poetry: Three Case Studies* (New Haven: Yale University Press, 1978).
22 Georgia E. Brown, 'Marlowe's Poems and Classicism', in *The Cambridge Companion to Christopher Marlowe*, ed. Patrick Cheney (Cambridge University Press, 2004), 117.

38   Catherine Nicholson

23 Elizabeth Bieman, 'Comic Rhyme in Marlowe's *Hero and Leander*', *English Literary Renaissance* 9 (1979): 69–77, summarises the long critical debate over whether Marlowe wrote an unfinished tragedy or a deliberate comedy.
24 Boutcher, 'Who taught thee Rhetoricke', 40.
25 All citations from Christopher Marlowe, *Hero and Leander*, are to *The Collected Poems of Christopher Marlowe*, ed. Patrick Cheney and Brian J. Striar (Oxford University Press, 2006).
26 See Desiderius Erasmus, *De conscribendis epistolis*, trans. Charles Fantazzi, in *Collected Works of Erasmus*, Vol. XXV, ed. Craig R. Thompson (University of Toronto Press, 1975), 129–45; and Wilson, *The Arte of Rhetorique,* sigs. Fiv–Iiiv. Erasmus' epistle also, of course, yields material for the first seventeen of Shakespeare's *Sonnets*.
27 For example, Stephen Booth precisely anatomises the poem's odd dissociation of rhetorical energy from actual consequences in speeches like this: the 'eventfulness' of the poem, he writes, lies not in its slow-progressing plot but in its 'substantively irrelevant, altogether extra' displays of stylistic finesse; Stephen Booth, 'On the Eventfulness of *Hero and Leander*', in *Christopher Marlowe the Craftsman: Lives, Stage and Page*, ed. Sarah K. Scott and M. L. Stapleton (Burlington, VT: Ashgate, 2010), 125–36 (129).
28 Judith Haber, *Desire and Dramatic Form in Early Modern England* (Cambridge University Press, 2009), xxx.
29 Weaver, 'Marlowe's Fable', 404.
30 Christopher Marlowe, *Hero and Leander* (London: Edward Blunt, 1598), sig. Eiiiv. Blunt's is one of two editions of the poem produced in 1598; the other, published by Paul Linley, includes George Chapman's continuation of the poem.

CHAPTER FOUR

Marlowe and character

Laurie Maguire and Aleksandra Thostrup

Like their author, Marlowe's dramatic characters were quickly pigeon-holed in attitude, language, and ontology. Within a year of *Tamburlaine*'s first performance, Robert Greene wrote of 'that atheist Tamburlaine', 'daring God out of heaven'.[1] As late as the Caroline period, Ford's antic courtier, Mauruccio, in *Love's Sacrifice* (Q 1633) practises a 'stalking … gait' and plans '[t]o ride in triumph through Persepolis' (II.i.72–3, 119).[2] In Munday's *John a Kent and John a Cumber* (1590 or 1596) and Jonson's *The Devil Is an Ass* (1616) characters allude to the transformative power of the devil in (probably) *Doctor Faustus* ('able to make a man a Munkey in lesse then halfe a minute of an houre') and Faustus' misuse of infernal assistance.[3] In 1593, overreaching character and larger-than-life author were conflated to serve as a gesture of dangerous dissent when Tamburlaine's 'signature' stood in for Marlowe's iconoclasm on the inflammatory notice pinned to the door of the Dutch Church. Even Marlowe's characters view their Marlovian predecessors stereotypically: in *The Massacre at Paris* the Guise wants to be Tamburlaine ('Give me a look that when I bend the brows / Pale death may walk in furrows of my face; / A hand that with a grasp may gripe the world').[4] These shorthand epitomes are understandable. We 'know' that Tamburlaine was the 'scourge' of God (*1 Tamb.*, III.iii.44), that Faustus' 'waxen wings did mount above his reach' (Pro., 21), and that Barabas is a disciple of Machiavelli because the plays tell us so. But the same prologues and epilogues that provide interpretive summaries also unmoor us hermeneutically. We are instructed to applaud Tamburlaine and his achievements 'as you please' (*1 Tamb.*, Pro., 8); Machiavelli invites us to grace Barabas 'as he deserves' (*JM*, Pro., 33); Faustus, like his fortunes, is antithetically 'good or bad' (*DrF*, Pro., 8). But how do we know how to interpret – actions, morality, character – on Marlowe's stage? This chapter focuses on the last of these terms but all three are linked.

When Faustus speaks of 'characters' he is talking of the kind that make up words, whilst the 'characters' Tamburlaine perceives 'graven in [Theridamas'] brows' (*1 Tamb.*, I.ii.169) invoke the kind of brand one might find a 'bloody and insatiate' tyrant (II.vii.11) transferring from a bond-slave to an enemy figure's forehead; but both uses imply the etymological origin of the term 'character' (from Latin *charactēr*, and Greek χαρακτήρ: instrument for marking or graving, impress, stamp, distinctive mark, distinctive nature).[5] In the drama preceding Marlowe, character is as legible and immutable as the graphic mark from which the term derives. The ruffians and roisterers of the late moralities *The Conflict of Conscience* and *All for Money* are functions of a pre-scribed narrative and a prescriptive dramatic ideology. Actions, even those of the seemingly subversive Vice figure to which Marlowe's plays consistently gesture, are determined by the logic of exemplarity and endorse some essential 'truth' about the collective, morally decrepit world; their role is to play to audience expectation and through performance dictate the terms of interpretation. In contrast, as we will show, Marlowe's sceptical dramatic treatment of 'distinctive natures', of emblematic and exemplary experience, turns static sign towards a marker of human complexity. *Doctor Faustus*, for example, transfuses morality drama into tragedy where fixity of character (linguistic and dramatic) becomes fluid, equivocal, indeterminate – what Ruth Lunney calls 'debateable'.[6]

Ironically, the trend in Marlowe criticism of the sixteenth and seventeenth centuries is to undo this amorphous and illegible concept of character and make fluid shapes fixed. This trend is clear in the contemporary stereotypes cited above (just as 'character', which derives from writing, comes to mean something reproducible, so 'stereotype', which derives from printing, comes to mean something repeated without change); but we see it also in the revisions and revivals of Marlowe's work. When a prologue to *The Jew of Malta* is added for a later performance 'at court', it promises the audience simplistic characterisation and interpretive ease: 'you shall find him still, / In all his projects, a sound Machevill; / And that's his character' (7–9). Here, 'character' signifies the written, the distinctive mark of a stock type; yet throughout the play Barabas proves adept in manipulating the anti-Semitic bugbears of folklore. Inscribed 'character' (the Jew, the Merchant, Job) is invoked only to be overturned; what had earlier been understood as given nature becomes something to be 'cunningly perform'd' (II.iii.368) by an adroit player who accumulates and enacts character(s). He thus intimates that something – his true 'character' – is kept in reserve.[7] Similarly, the B-text of *Doctor Faustus* ruthlessly silences the inner voices A-text Faustus hears 'buzz[ing] in mine ears' (II.iii.14). Although both texts contain this line, following it with a speech beginning 'My heart's so hardened [B: 'is hardened'] I cannot repent. / Scarce can I name salvation, faith, or heaven', only the A-text continues with 'But fearful echoes thunder in mine ears / "Faustus, thou art damned!"' (II.iii.18–21). This B-text revision functions as a virtual denial of any inward recesses of character. The voices A-text Faustus hears come from within, prompted by his own vocabulary, echoes of thoughts he himself has articulated. The B-text cuts the expanding and complex Renaissance mind down to size, returning character to a medieval dramatic aesthetic of a passive humanity swayed by external force – what *The Jew of Malta* calls a 'senseless lump of clay' stamped in the same mould as 'common men' (I.ii.217, 220). Thus B-Faustus becomes what A-Faustus abhorred (and his author eschewed): undifferentiated and reproducible character, 'man' as an exemplum. Marlowe is made medieval and moral, character made singular and legible.

Character and self-presentation

It is worth looking at the dramaturgical techniques by which Marlowe presents this kind of fluid character. We may begin with that most theatrical of figures, Barabas, who, as a self-conscious performer, occupies the ontological hinterland of the 'aside'. Poised between the world of the stage and the world of an audience, between inner and outer spaces of character, he performs an interiority through outward caricature; his 'character' is disturbingly plural and deliberatively 'put on', plotted and enacted until he seems an embodied *mise-en-abîme* of performances, of stereotyped 'Jews' and potential selves. 'Who … knows not Barabas?', he says (I.i.67). Everybody, it would seem, knows *of* Barabas but not even the audience, complicit in his secret machinations by being privy to soliloquies and asides, can be said to know Barabas.

Although 'character' refers to 'handwriting', the character of Marlowe's Jew is not autograph but indelibly scripted by someone else: 'What tell you me of Job? I wot his wealth / Was written thus …' (I.ii.183–4). Barabas succinctly dismisses the ontological taxonomy that underlies the condemnatory rhetoric directed at him throughout the play. 'Tut, Jew, we know thou art no soldier: / Thou art a merchant and a money'd man' (I.ii.52–3), says the First Knight, and patronisingly shunts Barabas into type.[8] Yet, paradoxically, the character of the Jew, so clearly visible behind his bags of gold and prosthetic nose, grows protean and elusive as he plays up to the typology that should render him simple and easily recognisable. The semiotics of the anti-Semitic grow confused. The 'Barabas' everybody 'knows' is largely the 'Jew' made and moulded by Christian policy, as fake as the subhuman entity conjured up by Ithamore later in the play (IV.iv.65–71). *The Jew of Malta* turns characters from expository persons into contingent and expedient postures. Consequently (or is it causally?), the play unfolds an amoral world of such scope it cannot be contained by the ostensible moralistic frame. The play thereby renders dubious the very notion of definitive 'character': 'No, Barabas is born to better chance, / And fram'd of finer mould than common men / That measure naught but by the present time' (I.ii.219–21). Mocking the reproducible character, Barabas claims a composite being of outer and inner – both a 'frame' and a 'mould'.

Barabas may be an extreme case but in locating himself in the liminal, in the space between caricature and aside, he is not unrepresentative of Marlovian dramaturgy. Marlowe depicts character by ironising distance – between the character and his theatrical predecessors, between the character and his role, between (as we shall see) two terms in a simile. Faustus even ironises the theatrical equivalent of sumptuary laws when he instructs Mephostopheles to dress as a friar, since that holy shape 'becomes a devil best' (I.iii.27): he is simultaneously making and mocking stage-devils and the semiotics that render the staged body and its character assimilable to a specific way of seeing and interpreting dramatic action. Throughout *Doctor Faustus* the very shape and meaning of the devilish become a source of crisis, growing ever more disturbing to inherited modes of theatrical experience. As Mephostopheles answers honestly and Lucifer, in a single scene of theatrical 'show', stands impotently by, it is Faustus who assumes the role of tempter and seducer, of the word-juggler who cites Scripture to his purpose. Not the devil but Faustus' words mould his thought. In presenting Faustus as his own tempting devil, Marlowe collapses the distance between the externally and the internally diabolic.

Character and language

And so we come to language, a crucial component of Marlowe's indecipherable characterisation. Tamburlaine, the 'scourge of God', collapses all conceptual structures of analogy. The problem he poses is explicitly a problem of how to understand character: thus Ortygius muses on 'What god, or fiend, or spirit of the earth / Or monster turned to a manly shape, / Or of what mould or mettle he be made' (*1 Tamb.*, II.vi.15–17).

Linguistic and cognitive attempts to ascertain the 'mould and mettle' that compose 'this monstrous slave', 'this devilish shepherd' who aspires with 'such a giantly presumption' to 'dare the force of angry Jupiter' (*1 Tamb.*, II.vi.1ff.), are consistently frustrated, turning rigid 'character' into something amorphous and unreadable – to both onstage and offstage spectator.

Myth might help us here. 'What better precedent than mighty Jove?' (*1 Tamb.*, II.vii.17), ponders Tamburlaine, offering us a straightforward parallel for his character and his actions. But 'precedents' and analogues pose deceptive hermeneutic structures. Tamburlaine does not invoke myth so much as remake it (he turns Icarus from an image of pride into one of military daring; *1 Tamb*, IV.ii.49–52).[9] Other, less imaginative, rulers cannot do this – Mycetes asks Theridamas to come home triumphantly 'as did Sir Paris with the Grecian dame' (*1 Tamb.*, I.i.66), hardly an auspicious analogue. In *The Jew of Malta* Barabas explains that he has 'one sole daughter, whom I hold as dear / As Agamemnon did his Iphigen' (I.i.135–6) but we know (as Barabas may or may not) that the mythical king was notoriously willing to sacrifice his daughter for his own gain. Character becomes a hieroglyph of layered meaning as parallels in myth, in fact, function as ironic counterpoise. The linguistic relationship is not one of correspondence but of collision or divergence, of collapsing into another story or, as Faustus with his succubus-Helen, being cruelly, irrevocably severed from it.

As he remaps the world, Tamburlaine also redraws lines of comparison between dramatised character and mythological precursor as a marker of absolute difference. He is not 'like' anything that has gone before. Linguistically, he outdoes the 'prolocutor to the gods'; materially, he is celestially and infernally mixed (*1 Tamb.*, II.vi.9–10). The eponymous figure of Marlowe's first staged play is theatre in defiance of theatrical practice. Character is part of this defiance. Mythical analogues function to imply the limitation of analogical understanding, to invoke and revoke a topography of character. As the *Jew*'s Ithamore says, 'the meaning has a meaning' (IV.iv.84) but Marlowe does not spell it out. His dramatic characters are as multiple as Faustus' written ones, as capable of being 'forward and backward anagrammatised' (I.ii.9).

They are also, all of them, enamoured of words. Dramatic character is a multiple thing, composed of words, actions, costumes, actors, but in Marlowe the linguistic dimension frequently operates in tension with these other aspects of person-making. Tamburlaine effects a self-metamorphosis from shepherd to conqueror through 'high astounding terms'(*1 Tamb.*,

Pro., 5); Faustus flourishes 'necromantic books' (I.i.52) and inscribes magic circles on the floor but emerges less like the figure of the *Faust-Book*'s 'damnable life and deserved death' and more like the self-seducing, self-deluding subject of a 'tragical history'. Words (as Faustus warns the scholars at V.i.25) are dangerous. In *The Massacre at Paris* the Guise condemns Ramus for his 'epitomes' and 'axioms', for reductive interpretations that 'did ... never sound anything to the depths' (ix.30, 33, 26). This is a slanted summary of Ramus' position but Guise's accusation that Ramus is a 'flat dichotomist' is apt (ix.29). A dichotomist is the ultimate in anti-Aristotelianism, someone who questions the unity of the sign, who turns unity into dichotomy, who (in our terminology) prises apart signifier and signified. Marlowe's characters die not by the sword but by the word. Marlowe was a 'Poet' first and a 'filthy Play-maker' second,[10] and his plays show hypnotic fascination with the power of language to make worlds and break characters' minds. *Doctor Faustus* begins with the doctor's desire to be resolved 'of all ambiguities' (I.i.82) – an impossible desire because it implies living without language (which is complex, ambiguous, polysemous). In fact, the pact with the devil works in the other direction: it resolves nothing but *dis*solves everything (language, self, 'reality'/'show') into ambiguities.

The scholars of the A-text, sympathetic to Faustus' human predicament, are revised in the B-text to become explicators of a didactic theatre: 'The devils whom Faustus served have torn him thus' (B-text, V.iii.8). The B-text amasses devils, thrusting them onto the stage prior to Faustus' conjuring and thus divesting the play of its ambiguous treatment of agency. Faustus becomes a pawn to ulterior, non-human forces, rather than a puppet strung along by the lines of his own verse. The grammatical delirium that sends Faustus reeling from first- to second- to third-person pronoun and into the self-alienation of the proper name (in both texts) encapsulates this shifting play at the level of language:

> Sweet *Analytics*, 'tis thou hast ravished <u>me</u>! ...
> Is to dispute well logic's chiefest end?
> Affords this art no greater miracle?
> Then read no more; <u>thou</u> hast attained the [B: that] end.
> A greater subject fitteth <u>Faustus</u>' wit.
> (I.i.6–11, underlining added)

Marlowe deprives audience and Faustus alike of a stable interpretive frame for experience; words slip and slide; and the mind (and character) made up in words will not stay still.

Consequently, Marlowe's central figures are remarkably lonely ones and thus have more ontological verisimilitude than they are generally seen to have. Barabas converts social marginality into dramatic centrality; but the centre of the stage, like the apex of political power or the empty space bounded by a conjuror's circle, is a lonely place to be in Marlovian drama. Beneath the emotionally anaesthetised stereotype of 'the Jew' stirs a very human need for companionship and sympathy – the very things from which Barabas's designated 'character' excludes him. (But he is human: if you drop him in a cauldron, does he not boil?) Attempting to mitigate loneliness has grim repercussions for monarch and scholar alike. Faustus fantasises about filling up a world that seems sinisterly empty, depleted of humanity even before he begins to conjure (an attitude that some have linked to the disillusion of the late Elizabethan graduate). At the most pragmatic level, Faustus seems to want either an equal with whom to have intellectual argument ('I think hell's a fable' could be a debating motion as much as a denial; II.i.130) or a wife (his instructions to Mephistopheles to be pliable, obedient, and appear whenever summoned sound like an early modern male's vision of marriage). Barabas is a 'Jew', Edward II a 'king', and Faustus a 'scholar', but all are strangers in the company that their 'character' prescribes them to keep. 'Yet art thou still but Faustus and a man' says Marlowe's scholar (I.i.23), finding constraint in names and categories imposed upon him from without, in those character-building forces of religious, political, and theatrical ideologies that Marlowe's characters consistently rebel against. As a result, Marlowe's characters simultaneously encompass their play and exceed it.

Staging Marlowe's characters

Contemporary actors have difficulty with Marlowe's characters. Stevie Simkin explains that Marlowe's plays 'are fairly intractable material for anyone determined to approach the text with a "naturalistic" or "realistic" methodology'.[11] We want to conclude with a modern production that dealt successfully with a 'realistic' approach to the isolated Marlovian character.

Michael Grandage's production of *The Jew of Malta* for the Almeida Theatre in London (1999) offered an extended reading of emotional loneliness and loss. By cutting a mere thirty-five lines – the prologue, spoken by Machiavelli – the play was removed from its sixteenth-century context and its many references to 'policy' were left freefloating. Characterised instead by indeterminate and timeless visual images (sun-drenched Maltese walls, Abigail's white cotton sundress), the production's surprisingly specific concluding tableau was all the more shocking: Barabas (Ian McDiarmid) fell into his cauldron not as a medieval Vice-figure descending into a hell mouth, nor as an outwitted overreacher comically plunging to a 'Microcook' barbecue (as in Peter Benedict's production at the Donmar Warehouse in 1984), but as a Jewish father heroically resisting a Nazi death-oven. The verbal specificity of Machiavelli at the start of the play was thus replaced by the visual specificity of the holocaust at the end.

The image was doubly disturbing for it replayed, in a different register, an image that concluded the first half. The interval came at the end of III.iv, where Barabas stirs poison into the porridge with which he plans to poison the nuns. McDiarmid stirred no domestic porridge pot but a large witches' cauldron, delivering lines 97–106 ('As fatal be it to her as the draught / Of which great Alexander drunk and died …') in incantatory fashion, accompanied by offstage diabolic sound effects that would not have been out of place in *Macbeth*. The egregious revenge perpetrated by Barabas foreshadowed the egregious revenge later meted out to him, and neither seemed just.

But people in pain do strange and excessive things, and this Barabas was a man in pain. Not at the loss of his fortune – he was blasé in his acknowledgement of the value of what he had lost, and matter-of-fact about the ease with which he had regained and surpassed the original sum. Barabas' pain stemmed from the emotional loss of Abigail. This was a father who lived for his daughter: his tone changed to great tenderness whenever he talked of her, and the exaggerated Yiddish accent and the plotter/performer's relish, vanished. 'All I have is hers' revealed a merchant genuinely concerned to provide for his only child (I.i.137); the description of Abigail as 'the loadstar of my life' was rapturous (II.i.42); and the diabolic spells with which he accompanied the stirring of the convent's poisoned porridge broke down into heart-wrenching human gasps on the last line: 'envenom her / That like a fiend … *hath left her father thus*' (McDiarmid's emphasis).

Barabas' aphoristic advice in I.ii about bearing wrongs gently was itself full of gentleness, intended to comfort his outraged daughter, for in this scene Abigail was more angry and upset than her father. But Abigail was feisty throughout and less in need of comfort than her father might want or think. Her independent will and action in choosing an Aryan suitor wounded her father deeply. 'Are there not Jews enow in Malta?', Barabas shouted in anger and hurt (II.iii.359), clearly feeling not just religious but personal betrayal. The father–daughter relationship was severed irrevocably in III.iv when Barabas entered reading a letter from Abigail (as the quarto instructs) in which she explains her conversion to Christianity. Line 2 – 'false and unkind' – was delivered not as Barabas' judgement on the apostate Abigail but as a direct quotation from the letter in which Abigail clearly chastised Barabas for his treatment of Don Mathias. With Abigail's conversion, Barabas lost his daughter (as he had in her choice of suitor) to religious difference and – more significantly – to adult independence. This time the loss was final. Abigail's subsequent poisoning was a technicality; to Barabas she was already dead.

And so the relationship with Ithamore took emotional centre-stage. Grief is defined as love with nowhere to go, and McDiarmid's Barabas, like King Lear, transferred his love for his daughter onto his servant/slave. Ithamore's later betrayal was simply too much for Barabas to bear. The stage position of Ithamore's dead body paralleled that of the poisoned Abigail and called attention to Barabas' double loss.

It is no coincidence that Grandage's interpretation came in the year that Roberto Benigni's *Life is Beautiful* won an Oscar for best foreign language film. This holocaust comedy was a contradiction in terms (we don't make comedies about the holocaust), and the unsettling feelings and generic perplexity it occasioned in viewers were similar to those responses to *The Jew of Malta* by viewers and readers from T. S. Eliot on. Cued by Benigni, Grandage's combination of farce and atrocity, of comic gags and father–child poignancy led to a Marlovian tragicomedy that was centred plausibly, psychologically in family life.

But Marlowe's play needed this filmic referent to make the transition to realism. Like the critical reactions with which we began, it is an approach that, however successful on its own terms, reduces the plural and inscrutable Marlovian character to the singular and legible. Fully fledged psychological realism is Shakespeare's domain, not Marlowe's. Marlowe's characters, we have argued in this chapter, do not hold the mirror up to nature so much as put her out of office: they flutter between the fixity of type and a tantalising, unfathomable depth.

The consequent inscrutability invokes an analogous affective response in audiences (then and now): like the protagonists, we desire, want to know and to possess more than the immediate script provides. From Tamburlaine with his maps to Faustus with his books and Barabas with his bags of gold, characters are motivated by 'wants' (*2 Tamb.*, v.iii.125), by the itching of 'aspiring minds' that, 'still climbing after knowledge infinite', by various strategies seek to redraw 'the wondrous architecture of the world' (*1 Tamb.*, II.vii.24, 22). It is a reshaping that begins in character.

Notes

1. Robert Greene, *Perimedes the Blacksmith* (1588, 'To the Gentlemen Readers').
2. John Ford, *Love's Sacrifice*, ed. A. T. Moore, Revels Edition (Manchester University Press, 2002). 'Stalking' is associated with Tamburlaine (and/or Edward Alleyn) in Joseph Hall's *Virgideriarum* (1597), Thomas Middleton's *The Black Book* (1604), Thomas Dekker's *The Wonderful Year* (?1603), and Everard Guilpin's *Skialethia* (1598).
3. Anthony Munday, *John a Kent and John a Cumber* (Oxford: Malone Society, 1923), lines 1037–8; Ben Jonson, *The Devil Is an Ass and Other Plays,* ed. M. J. Kidnie (Oxford University Press, 2000), I.ii.35–9.
4. Christopher Marlowe, *The Massacre at Paris*, ii.101–3. All Marlowe quotations come from *Christopher Marlowe*, ed. E. D. Pendry and J. C. Maxwell (London: J. M. Dent, 1976) with the exception of *Doctor Faustus*, which is quoted from Christopher Marlowe, *Doctor Faustus, A- and B-Texts*, ed. David Bevington and Eric Rasmussen (Manchester University Press, 1993). We cite the A-text unless otherwise indicated.
5. See Jacques Bos, 'Individuality and Inwardness in the Literary Character Sketches of the Seventeenth century', *Journal of the Warburg and Cortauld Institutes* 61 (1998): 142–57; Peter Holland, '"A kind of character in thy life": Shakespeare and the Character of History', Sam Wanamaker Lecture, Shakespeare's Globe, 2010.
6. Ruth Lunney, *Marlowe and the Popular Tradition: Innovation in the English Drama before 1595* (Manchester University Press, 2002), 126.
7. On Barabas as performer, see Sara Munson Deats and Lisa S. Starks, '"So neatly plotted, and so well perform'd": Villain as Playwright in Marlowe's *The Jew of Malta*', *Theatre Journal* 44 (1992): 375–89.
8. Emily C. Bartels explores this tactic in relation to the words 'stranger' and 'profession' in the play and shows how their shifting meanings expose the tactics of colonialism. See 'Malta, the Jew, and the Fictions of Difference: Colonialist Discourse in Marlowe's *The Jew of Malta*', *ELR* 20 (1990): 1–16, esp. 10–11.
9. See Richard A. Martin, 'Marlowe's *Tamburlaine* and the Language of Romance', *PMLA* 93 (1978): 248–64.
10. The accusation comes from Edmund Rudierd in 1618; quoted in *'A Poet and a Filthy Play-Maker': New Essays on Christopher Marlowe*, ed. Kenneth Friedenreich, Roma Gill, and Constance Brown Kuriyama (New York: AMS Press, 1988), ix.
11. Stevie Simkin, *Marlowe: The Plays* (Basingstoke: Palgrave, 2001), 66–7.

CHAPTER FIVE

Marlowe's dramatic form

Sarah Dewar-Watson

> Only this, gentlemen: we must perform
> The form of Faustus' fortunes, good or bad.
> To patient judgements we appeal our plaud.[1]

For a tragedy that ends as starkly as *Doctor Faustus* – not only with the protagonist's death, but with the prospect of eternal damnation to boot – the Chorus is oddly equivocal about the form of the play that is about to be presented. The coordinating conjunction 'or' (8) refuses to prioritise between good fortune or bad, pleasure or suffering – briefly, perhaps, even between tragedy and comedy. Up to line 20, the prologue steadily focuses on Faustus' achievements and his prosperity: 'The fruitful plot of scholarism graced, / That shortly he was graced with doctor's name' (16–17). The word 'graced', ostensibly refers to proceeding to an academic degree. But emphatically repeated as it is here, the reference to 'grace' absorbs some of the theological context in which it is situated and audaciously conjoins – rather than rigorously separates – the ideas of Faustus and grace. The preposition 'Till' ('Till, swoll'n with cunning of a self- conceit…'; 20) therefore becomes heavily weighted because it suggests a specific point in time at which Faustus' fortunes change for the worse and vice begins to have its consequences.

The prologue, therefore, subtly complicates Calvinist determinist readings of the play, which see Faustus as predestinately damned rather than condemned to hell by his own choices and actions.[2] The prologue is not straightforwardly expository and does not provide a simple slipstream into the main action. Later in the chapter, we will be looking further at this dynamic relationship between Marlowe's surviving prologues and the plays that they introduce. But first, when *Doctor Faustus* was originally performed in 1588, what did Marlowe and his audience take dramatic – and in particular tragic – form to be?

The first purpose-built playhouse, the Red Lion, had opened in London in 1567, just two decades before Marlowe was writing for the stage. The 1560s had witnessed another important landmark: Sackville and Norton's *Gorboduc* (performed 1561, published 1565), the first English tragedy to be written in blank verse, a form of versification that was to become a vital resource for Marlowe and his contemporaries. At the time *Gorboduc* was written, rhyming fourteeners were commonly used. As an example, we can look at the protagonist's death speech in Thomas Preston's *Cambises* (published 1570): 'I feele myself a-dying now, of life bereft am I, / And Death hath caught me with his dart, for want of blood, I spy.'[3] As we can see from this couplet, the verse form does not easily lend itself to conveying pathos. But with the emergence of blank verse as the dominant metrical form for the tragedies of the 1580s, Martin Wiggins notes, 'the sound of drama had changed forever'.[4]

During the sixteenth century, one definition of tragedy, inherited from classical antiquity, was shaping contemporary ideas about tragic form. According to the fourth-century grammarians Donatus-Evanthius:

> inter tragoediam autem et comoediam cum multa tum inprimis hoc distat, quod in comoedia mediocres fortunae hominum, parui impetus periculorum laetique sunt exitus actionum, at in tragoedia omnia contra, ingentes personae, magni timores, exitus funesti habentur, et illic prima turbulenta, tranquilla ultima, in tragoedia contrario ordine res aguntur.[5]

> But many things distinguish comedy from tragedy, especially the fact that comedy is concerned with the average fortunes of people, the onset of moderate risks, and actions with happy endings. But in tragedy, everything is the opposite: great people, immense terrors, and deathly endings. Furthermore, in comedy what is stormy at first becomes smooth at the end; in tragedy the action has the opposite pattern.[6]

This definition of tragedy was frequently printed in editions of the popular Roman comic playwright, Terence, and is cited by Thomas Heywood in his *Apology for Actors* (1612): 'Tragedies and Comedies ... differ thus: In Comedies, turbulenta prima, tranquilla ultima; In Tragedyes, tranquilla prima, turbulenta ultima: Comedies begin in trouble and end in peace; Tragedies begin in calmes and end in tempest.'[7]

This tradition assumes a perfect antithesis between tragedy and comedy. Paradoxically, given how widely circulated this account was, it was a vision of dramatic form that very few English dramatists, including Marlowe, shared.[8] In his well-known assault on Elizabethan dramatists Philip Sidney complains that 'their plays be neither right tragedies, nor right comedies, mingling kings and clowns'.⁹ Here Sidney might well have had in mind Preston's *Cambises* itself, a play in which the king of Persia rubs shoulders with comic, native characters called Ruf, Huf, and Snuf. While Marlowe scorned the rhyming fourteeners in which much of *Cambises* is written, he seems to have sympathised with its comic vein. Among Marlowe's plays, *Doctor Faustus* is distinctive in the way that it alternates, like Preston's play, between comic and tragic scenes; indeed the comic elements of *Doctor Faustus* are expanded in the 1616 version, testimony to their popularity with audiences.¹⁰

Thus *Doctor Faustus* richly exemplifies some of the tensions that existed between Elizabethan dramatic theory and practice. Indeed, Marlowe was working with a form that was not fixed but that exhibited remarkable heterogeneity. It is now fairly commonplace to characterise Marlowe as an ideological radical, particularly in reference to sexual politics or the ethical and theological framework of his plays.¹¹ But it is in no way to diminish our sense of his radicalism to say that in terms of dramatic form, Marlowe was not, in any straightforward sense, writing against the grain. To claim this is not to try to reconstruct Marlowe as a conservative: rather, it is to recognise that the form itself, as he encountered it, was still – and indeed continued to be – diverse and pliable.

Some of Marlowe's thinking about tragedy is distilled in the highly programmatic prologue of *1 Tamburlaine* (first performed 1587, published 1590):

> From jigging veins of rhyming mother-wits
> And such conceits as clownage keeps in pay
> We'll lead you to the stately tent of War,
> Where you shall hear the Scythian Tamburlaine
> Threat'ning the world with high astounding terms,
> And scourging kingdoms with his conquering sword.
> View but his picture in this tragic glass,
> And then applaud his fortunes as you please.
>   (Pro., 1–8)

Marlowe's explicit rejection of rhymed fourteeners ('jigging veins of rhyming mother-wits'; 1) reminds us that blank verse is still a relative novelty on the English stage. Yet taken as a whole, the prologue asserts not a driving sense of innovation, but a sense of tragic decorum that many in the 1580s would recognise and approve: in terms of subject matter (war and conquest), the rejection of comic elements in tragedy ('clownage'; 2), and the affirmation of the play's commitment to the pleasures of elevated – even bombastic – diction ('high astounding terms'; 5). If Marlowe is ever capable of conservatism, this surely is it.

Then comes the imperative: 'View but his picture in this tragic glass' (7). By the end of the prologue, Marlowe has built up a semantic context in which the implications of the word 'tragic' seem very reliable. So how else to take this statement, other than as an indication that the protagonist will die? If we recall Donatus-Evanthius, 'in tragoedia ... exitus funesti habentur' ('tragedies ... end in death'). And those in the audience who had not read Donatus-Evanthius would only have to call on their experience of watching any other tragedy to know that the protagonist must surely die. By explicitly declaring the play's conformity to a variety of tragic conventions concerning subject matter, diction, and so on, Marlowe paves the way to breach a more fundamental expectation: *1 Tamburlaine* ends not with a death but with a marriage, and with Tamburlaine still on an upward trajectory. Indeed when Tamburlaine does die at the end of Part II, Marlowe still withholds a sense of climax. Tamburlaine dies not in battle; rather, it is an unremarkable illness that finally halts his conquest of the world. As he observes, 'Shall sickness prove me now to be a man / That have been termed the terror of the world?' (v.iii.44–5). Thus, far from clarifying the form of the play, the prologue's self-reflexive reference to the 'tragic glass' complicates and teases the audience's initial sense of how the play will unfold.

Marlowe is not the only dramatist in the period to experiment with tensions between the prologue and the main body of the play. In Q2 *Romeo and Juliet* (published 1599, but written in the early 1590s), the Prologue-Chorus' focus on the prospect of the lovers' death is strikingly juxtaposed with the comic movement of Acts I and II.[12] The effect is to heighten the pathos of these early comic scenes: against the background of the prologue, we know that the lovers' attempts to evade parental opposition are doomed. In *Romeo and Juliet*, the play's ending enacts and confirms what the prologue foretold: however, in *1 Tamburlaine*, the ending of the play more radically contradicts the prologue through the survival of the protagonist.

In *Doctor Faustus*, the prologue is spoken by a chorus that reappears at several points. Marlowe's treatment of the Chorus shows him experimenting with its composition and function. In the 1604 quarto (the A-text), the Chorus appears at the beginning of Act IV and delivers the epilogue. Interestingly, at the end of the play, the Chorus once again entertains the view that Faustus' fortunes were not divinely ordained, but might have turned out otherwise ('Cut is the branch that might have grown full straight', Ep., 1). Thus the Chorus frames the play with a sense of alternative possibilities that Faustus himself frequently and determinedly discounts (for example, 'I am resolved Faustus shall ne'er repent', II.iii.32). In the 1616 quarto (the B-text), the Chorus introduces Act III and, as in the A-text, also speaks the epilogue. In their edition of the A-text, Bevington and Rasmussen identify Wagner's speech at the beginning of Act III as 'Chorus', though it is not identified as such in the 1604 quarto. The fact that modern editors see the role of Wagner and Chorus as to some extent interchangeable is significant: in Greek tragedy, the main characters and the chorus are sharply differentiated, and indeed would have occupied separate parts of the stage. Thus the editorial question that hangs over the designation of Wagner's speech could never arise in a classical tragedy.

The early modern chorus is therefore a dynamic rather than a fixed entity. We see echoes of this dynamic aspect in *The Spanish Tragedy*, written c. 1587–90 by Thomas Kyd, a friend of Marlowe, who shared lodgings with him in the early 1590s. At the end of Don Andrea's expository prologue, Revenge says: 'Here sit we down to see the mystery / And serve for Chorus in this tragedy.'[13] Here Revenge expresses a radically new idea that a character can become assimilated into the chorus. Unlike Wagner, a minor character who temporarily takes on a choric role, dramatic convention suggests that a nobleman like Don Andrea would have been a protagonist in the play, had he lived. Instead, killed by Balthazar, he is socially demoted to the ranks of the chorus and spatially relegated to the side of the stage.

However one assigns the beginning of *Doctor Faustus*, Act III, it is clear that the part of the Chorus in the play refers to just one figure and not a group of people (or even a pair, as in *The Spanish Tragedy*). The single-figure chorus that Marlowe uses here appears recurrently in Shakespeare. As well as in *Romeo and Juliet*, Shakespeare uses a single chorus-presenter in *Henry V* (1599) and introduces 'Time, as Chorus' in *The Winter's Tale* (1611) at the beginning of Act IV. In its classical origins, both Greek and Senecan, the plural nature of the chorus is essential to its identity.[14] In the sixteenth century, this aspect of choric identity becomes all but lost. A key moment of transition is, once again, *Gorboduc*, which uses a chorus of just four persons. In their *Jocasta* (performed 1566 and first published 1573), Gascoigne and Kinwelmersh were quick to imitate their Inns of Court contemporaries and also opt for a chorus of four. It is, perhaps, somewhat surprising that Inns of Court dramatists should choose to reduce the chorus in this way, since they have at their disposal a large cast of players. But both *Gorboduc* and *Jocasta* also include sequences of dumbshow, and the dramatists divert much of their resources, in terms of players and spectacle, in that direction.[15]

In the public playhouses, the imperatives to reduce the chorus would have been largely financial: it would be difficult to justify a group of players speaking in unison when one actor could suffice. In spite of this impetus towards reducing the chorus in scale, dramatists like Marlowe and Shakespeare clearly recognised the utility of the chorus as a theatrical device. Whereas in Greek and Senecan drama the chorus never introduces the play, this becomes a relatively commonplace function of the early modern chorus: so commonplace, in fact, that during the performance of *The Mousetrap* Hamlet is acclaimed by Ophelia for being 'as good as a chorus, my lord' (*Hamlet*, III.ii.229), simply for identifying the characters. This is a long way from the model of the classical chorus that characteristically contributes layers of mythological or philosophical complexity to the play. In classical drama, the social and regional identity of the chorus is crucially important to its function in the play. Even in *Gorboduc*, which seemingly authorises a reduction in the role of the chorus, the age, gender, and regional identity of the chorus are explicitly identified ('Four ancient and Sage men of Britain'). In *Doctor Faustus*, the Chorus is not localised in this way. Indeed if any identity is attributed to the Chorus, it is as the acting troupe performing the play: 'Not marching in the field of Trasimene … Intends our muse to vaunt his heavenly verse' (1–7).

As we have seen, contemporary definitions of tragedy placed considerable emphasis on a play's ending as a crucial determinant of its genre. *Doctor Faustus* is a play much concerned with endings, and it is a nice irony that the play is most concerned with endings in its opening scene: "*Bene disserere est finis logices*. / Is to dispute well logic's chiefest end?" (I.i.7–8); 'The end of physic is our body's health. / Why Faustus, hast not attained that end?' (I.i.16–17). In Act II, Faustus avows 'Now will I make an end immediately' (II.i.72), a declaration freighted with irony: the 'end' to which he refers is the completion of the contract, and in the act of writing he seems momentarily distracted from the mortal ending that it signifies. As the play draws to an end, conversely our sense of an ending seems only to recede from view:

> Impose some end to my incessant pain.
> Let Faustus live in hell a thousand years,
> A hundred thousand, and at last be saved.
> O, no end is limited to damnèd souls.
> (v.ii.93–6)

Kyd's *The Spanish Tragedy* similarly concludes with the promised continuation of suffering after death: Revenge vows to pursue Balthazar and others in the Underworld and 'there begin their endless tragedy' (IV.v.48). There is a playful irony in ending a tragedy with the words 'endless tragedy'. More sobering, perhaps, is the shared emphasis in this play and in *Doctor Faustus* not on death itself but on the spiritual torments that may follow. While Greek tragedy maintains a strict unilateral focus on death as an event in the temporal world, early modern English tragedy takes on new eschatological dimensions. Thus *Doctor Faustus* reflects an interest not just in death itself as the climax of a play (as it is characterised in the Donatus-Evanthius tradition), but in heightened anxieties about what – and where – death leads to.[16] 'Terminat hora diem, terminat author opus' ('The hours ends the day, the author ends the work'). So end both texts of *Doctor Faustus* with a motto that may or may not be authorial. Either way, it is an emphatic flourish: an attempt, perhaps, to enforce a sense of closure on a play that trains our thoughts beyond the ending of the protagonist's life and towards eternity.

Notes

1 Christopher Marlowe, *Doctor Faustus*, i.7–9. All references are taken from Christopher Marlowe, *Doctor Faustus and Other Plays,* ed. David Bevington and Eric Rasmussen (Oxford University Press, 1995). All references to *Doctor Faustus* refer to the A-text unless otherwise indicated.
2 On the play's involvement with Calvinist thought and the doctrine of predestination, see Pauline Honderich, 'John Calvin and Doctor Faustus', *Modern Language Review* 68 (1973): 1–13.
3 Thomas Preston, *Cambises*, in *Minor Elizabethan Tragedies*, ed. T. W. Craik (London: J. M. Dent & Sons, 1974), 1162–3.
4 Martin Wiggins, *Shakespeare and the Drama of His Time* (Oxford University Press, 2000), 34.
5 Evanthius, 'De fabula: Excerpta de comoedia', IV.ii.9–17, in *Aeli Donati commentum Terenti*, ed. P. Wessner, 3 vols. (Stuttgart: Teubner, 1966), Vol. I, 21. The passage is sometimes ascribed, as in Wessner's edition, to Evanthius, but because of textual difficulties it is more usual to refer to the source(s) of this critical tradition in the hyphenated form, 'Donatus-Evanthius'. For further discussion of Donatus-Evanthius, see Henry Ansgar Kelly, *Ideas and Forms of Tragedy from Aristotle to the Middle Ages* (Cambridge University Press, 1993).
6 Translation mine.
7 Thomas Heywood, *Apology for Actors*, ed. Richard H. Perkinson (New York: Scholars' Facsimiles and Reprints, 1941), sig. F1v. On the widespread circulation of the essay in editions of Terence, see Howard B. Norland, *Drama in Early Tudor Britain, 1485–1558* (Lincoln: University of Nebraska Press, 1995), 65–83.

8 Ben Jonson maintains a strict separation between comedy and tragedy, though notably neither of his tragedies, *Sejanus* (performed 1603) and *Catiline* (1611), enjoyed popular success.
9 Philip Sidney, 'A Defence of Poetry', in *English Renaissance Literary Criticism*, ed. Brian Vickers (Oxford: Clarendon Press, 1999), 383. The *Defence* was written *c.* 1580 and first published in 1595.
10 For twentieth-century defences of Marlowe's mixing of tragic and comic elements in *Doctor Faustus*, see Robert Ornstein, 'The Comic Synthesis in *Doctor Faustus*', *English Literary History* 22 (1955): 165–72 (165); and Cleanth Brooks, 'The Unity of Marlowe's *Doctor Faustus*', in *To Nevill Coghill from Friends*, ed. J. Lawlor and W. H. Auden (London: Faber, 1966), 109–24.
11 On Marlowe's radicalism, see for example Jonathan Dollimore, *Radical Tragedy: Religion, Ideology and Power in the Drama of Shakespeare and His Contemporaries*, 3rd edn (Durham, NC: Duke University Press, 2004), 109–19.
12 See Ruth Nevo, 'Tragic Form in *Romeo and Juliet*', *Studies in English Literature, 1500–1900* 9 (1969): 241–58.
13 Thomas Kyd, *The Spanish Tragedy*, ed. Philip Edwards (Manchester University Press, 1977), I.i.90–1.
14 On the communal nature of both choral and audience experience, see John Gould, 'Tragedy and Collective Experience', in *Tragedy and the Tragic: Greek Theatre and Beyond*, ed. Michael Silk (Oxford: Clarendon Press, 1996), 217–43.
15 For the interplay between chorus and dumbshow in these two plays, see Sarah Dewar-Watson, '*Jocasta*: "A Tragedie Written in Greeke"', *International Journal of the Classical Tradition* 17 (2010), 22–32.
16 The seminal studies of the Reformation as a cultural stimulus for early modern tragedy are Robert Watson, *The Rest Is Silence: Death as Annihilation in the English Renaissance* (Berkeley: University of California Press, 1994); and Michael Neill, *Issues of Death: Mortality and Identity in English Renaissance Tragedy* (Oxford: Clarendon Press, 1997).

CHAPTER SIX

Marlowe's poetic form

Danielle Clarke

Marlowe's impact on English Renaissance poetics is wholly disproportionate to his output and, additionally, rests on only a selection of his extant poetic writings. As Millar Maclure notes: 'It is not, in perspective, an impressive corpus: a fragment of narrative verse, a song, two translations in two modes, and two occasional pieces of Latin composition.'[1]

Moreover, as numerous critics have pointed out, this unexpected impact is ultimately marked by a high degree of exceptionalism, as Marlowe carves out a trajectory with quite different assumptions, priorities, and sources from that of most of his contemporaries.[2] Marlowe chooses to work in poetic genres that lack clear outlines or that come without an established or available discourse in the English tradition, and to rework, rewrite, and hybridise them from within. His extant poetry (*Hero and Leander*; *Ovid's Elegies*; his translation of Lucan; and 'The Passionate Shepherd') represents both resistance to established conventions and a concern to work playfully within classical models, with a scholarly interest in the return *ad fontes* combined with a desire to subvert the very idea of origins and originals. *Hero and Leander* plays multiple back-and-forth textual games with the very idea of literary tradition and authority, by subverting the very texts that he purports to reverence. Marlowe's poetry tends to reject the dominant Petrarchan mode (with its implied abjection of the disempowered masculine self) – formally as well as stylistically – and to look to Latinate models for the articulation of desire. This apparent undermining of the humanist inheritance is all the more pointed owing to the heavy indebtedness of Marlowe's output to methods and techniques perfected within the highly programmatic education system of early modern England: the use of *ekphrasis* (vivid description, often using extensive visual detail), the deployment of *ethopoiea* (putting oneself into the position and voice of another), and the sustained interest in copious variation of every kind – almost to the point of problematic narrative inertia, together with the knowing appropriation and hybridisation of multiple genres.[3] Yet, for all this dependence on literary heritages of various kinds, Marlowe's verse continues to strike the reader with its freshness, vitality, and sheer mercurial brio.

Marlowe embraces two poetic forms at the very inception of their life in English – namely the epyllion (variously labelled the minor epic, erotic complaint) and the elegy in its Ovidian formulation (as distinct from the poem of consolation, a distinct, but linked tradition).[4] Both forms are tricky to define, and they modulate repeatedly and with each subsequent use whilst being anchored loosely to particular source materials, modes, and tonal qualities. It is fair to say that Marlowe's *Hero and Leander* (printed 1598, but entered in the Stationers' Register in 1593) is by far the more influential of the two texts ('The Passionate Shepherd' notwithstanding). Not least, *Hero and Leander* can lay claim to the inauguration of a genre – a genre that has a peculiarly strong hold on the Elizabethan imagination – as well as to a specific way of reworking and alluding to the classical legacy. Both elegy and epyllion, it is fair to say, break down distinctions and boundaries, yet in ways that nonetheless place literary convention ludically at the very heart of literary production and reception. Marlowe's powerful invigoration of the flexible muscularity of dramatic blank verse is undisputed, but his formal innovations in printed verse are perhaps less obvious, particularly in relation to *Ovid's Elegies* which, as Patrick Cheney notes, have been sidelined within the Ovidian canon and within the Marlovian one.[5] The *Elegies* are rarely anthologised and not often cited or read – perhaps a symptom of the low esteem in which modern culture holds translations. The framework within which the *Elegies* might signify is difficult to reconstruct, and their direct purpose is oblique. This marginality to the centre might – in one way or another – be said to characterise much of Marlowe's poetic output, as he works mischievously, but extensively, with a body of inherited material, yet places it under certain kinds of pressures. For Marlowe the act of rewriting and reworking the classical heritage is a kind of making new, a literal textual rebirth. Russ McDonald has rightly noted that much of Marlowe's energy derives from 'his unmediated acquaintance with rediscovered classical texts'; yet perhaps this assessment downplays the degree to which Marlowe's poetic diction renders classical topoi and tropes in an English style that is supple, subtle, and 'natural'.[6]

Whilst Marlowe's translation of Ovid's *Elegies* is fascinating in its own right, this chapter largely focuses on the experiments with form that Marlowe undertakes in *Hero and Leander* – partly because of the influence of the poem in its own time, and partly because of the text's open-endedness (formal, generic, and stylistic), which allows Marlowe to stitch together multifarious materials in innovative ways.[7] A couple of brief examples from *Hero and Leander* will illustrate the way that Marlowe troubles any clear distinction between form and meaning and thus questions some of the key assumptions that structure Renaissance thought (although not practice) on language and culture – for example, the notion that the world may be divided into words (*verba*) and things (*res*).

In the second sestiad, Leander's father intuits that his son has fallen in love (a passage that has no analogue in Marlowe's known sources):

> His secret flame apparently was seen,
> Leander's father knew where he had been,
> And for the same mildly rebuk'd his son,
> Thinking to quench the sparkles new begun.
> (II.135–8)

A reader familiar with the Petrarchan tradition would expect the monosyllabic 'sparks' here (picking up on the common metaphor of love as consuming fire),[8] but Marlowe – observing the ten-syllable line – picks the arresting plural noun 'sparkles' instead. Despite being a noun, the word carries with it the force and energy of the related verb, so that Marlowe's vocabulary choice enshrines the idea of the power and unpredictability of desire. 'Sparkle' as a noun dates from the late medieval period and traverses a range of literal and figurative meanings:[9] 'a small spark' (1a); 'with allusion to the kindling of a fire or conflagration' (d. fig.); but also 'a slight beginning, trace, indication, or manifestation *of* something' (2). Further historically relevant available meanings include 'a vital or animating principle' (3); 'a glittering or flashing point of light' (5a. fig.); 'lively brightness' (6a); and 'brightness or liveliness of spirit' (6b); all of which might be mobilised as a way of glossing the advent of a potentially ruinous desire in Leander.[10] Like his contemporaries, Marlowe gleefully exploits the polysemy offered by an as yet unfixed language, whilst simultaneously demonstrating its copious potential for eloquence. This is an indicative example of Marlowe's subversion of expectation at the level of lexical choice, with an additional inference of the burning fires of religious sacrifice and to a set of metaphors throughout that allude to desire in terms of fire: 'Stone still he stood, and evermore he gazed, / Till with the fire that from his count'nance blazed / Relenting Hero's gentle heart was strook' (I.163–5).

Continuing the repeated set of variations on the common topos of love/desire as fire, a passage in the second sestiad reveals the way in which Marlowe manipulates the poetic line (echoing the techniques of

Latin prosody), by self-consciously reordering words to achieve patterns of sound and meaning, rather than allowing them to be dictated by purely grammatical imperatives. Leander's fumbling attempts at consummation are described:

> She, fearing on the rushes to be flung,
> Striv'd with redoubled strength; the more she strived,
> The more a gentle pleasing heat revived,
> Which taught him all that elder lovers know.
> And now the same 'gan so to scorch and glow,
> As in plain terms (yet cunningly) he crav'd it;
> Love always makes those eloquent that have it.
> She, with a kind of granting, put him by it,
> And ever as he thought himself most nigh it,
> Like to the tree of Tantalus she fled,
> And, seeming lavish, sav'd her maidenhead.
>
> (II.66–76)

This passage encapsulates much that typifies Marlowe's poetry – including its reflexive cultural misogyny – the tension between rejection and desire, the expression of complex emotional ideas by recourse to classical reference, and the repeated use of apparent contradictions. Marlowe stretches out the dependent clauses to such an extent that the reader almost forgets that the subject is 'heat', rather than Hero herself. The use of antistrophe (the repetition of a word at the end of successive lines or clauses) in lines 71–4 serves to underline the instability of the referent of 'it', a pronoun that is marked by its instability (subject/object) and substitutes for an unspoken noun (or nouns).[11] 'It' euphemistically implies a range of meanings, where 'it' might denote desire, sexual intercourse itself, and by association the 'it' of Hero's virginity, concretised into the objectified 'it' of Hero's genitalia. Like other passages of Marlowe's poetry, this unstable 'it' registers grammatically the exploration of the complexities of gender, desire, and identity, together with the complexities of interpreting consent ('She, with a kind of granting, put him by it'). 'It' here is the subject that is everywhere, but precisely the thing (sex) that cannot be spoken. It is at the level of precise lexical choice and stylistic arrangement that Marlowe's texts register his complex understanding of cultural norms and ideologies; the naming/non-naming dynamic traversed here by 'it' suggests the vagaries and instabilities of the language of courtship and the ways in which discourses often float dangerously free of the acts that they suggest, or substitute for.

Throughout *Hero and Leander* questions of speech, as in Ovid's *Heroides* (and rather differently in the *Metamorphoses*)[12] are inextricably tied up with the erotic rather than with the inscription of virtue – rhetorical thought is largely preoccupied with the relationship between good or eloquent style and moral status rather than with desire. In the passage quoted above, two lines amount to a puzzlingly complex statement about the relationship of language to desire: 'As in plain terms (yet cunningly) he crav'd it; / Love always makes those eloquent that have it' (II.71–2). The poem consistently opposes theory and practice; what it says about style and eloquence is not at all the same as what it does. But even as the poem attempts to equate 'love' and 'eloquence', poetic description is repeatedly elided with the sexual. In the first sestiad, where Marlowe famously blazons Leander's body, the passage is introduced by the poet's assertion that

> my rude pen
> Can hardly blazon forth the loves of men,
> Much less of powerful gods: let it suffice
> That my slack muse sings of Leander's eyes,
> Those orient cheeks and lips.
> (I.69–73)

Like so much else in *Hero and Leander* words point in unusual directions; all is not as it seems. When Marlowe states that 'my rude pen / Can hardly blazon forth the loves of men' (and again, the idea completes the line, until the reader realises that it is but one term of a comparison), we assume that we are reading a standard humility topos (a standard convention, conceit, or idea), the effect of which is to aggrandise the poet's claims to skill.[13] Yet the blazon that follows, together with the Neptune passage in the second sestiad, prompts us to read these lines with a different set of referents in mind; not only are they a statement about the status of English poetry, but they are also covertly glancing at the (im)possibility of scripting homosexual desire. 'Rude' is a code word for the alleged shortcomings of English verse, but here, as elsewhere in the poem, also signals an inequality of social status; 'hardly' means 'scarcely', but also implies that the subject ('the loves of men') might lie outside the traditional scope of poetry, whilst also suggesting the traditional division between mortals and gods. It thus becomes a claim to a different kind of poetic innovation, one that links Marlowe directly with his classical forebears, by writing *in* the homoeroticism of (particularly) Greece and not writing it *out*, as key humanist pedagogues such as Erasmus often advocated. 'Hardly' additionally contrasts with the undoubtedly sexualised (and cross-gendered) image of the 'slack muse'. Here the traditionally female muse is imagined to be an emasculated male. The plural 'loves of men' again moves counter to expectation, suggesting not simply mortal as opposed to divine entanglements, but also the multiplicity of such encounters, an inference that is redoubled by the resolutely corporeal focus of the previous lines – a rare instance in English Renaissance verse of the aestheticisation of the male body:

> Even as delicious meat is to the taste,
> So was his neck in touching, and surpass'd
> The white of Pelops' shoulder. I could tell ye
> How smooth his breast was, and how white his belly,
> And whose immortal fingers did imprint
> That heavenly path with many a curious dint,
> That runs along his back
>
> (1.63–9)

The phrase 'I could tell ye' is a form of *aposiopesis* (an unfinished thought, a broken-off speech or utterance), at least when followed by the 'but' that continues line 69 ('That runs along his back, but my rude pen / Can hardly blazon forth the loves of men'; 69–70), a turning away from the subject that nonetheless establishes the absent description in the reader's mind. In other words, Marlowe repeatedly uses established rhetorical techniques and devices, designed to persuade an audience to a particular point of view, to gesture at an absent subject, to suggest an idea or subject that is, at one level, literally unspeakable.

The connection between eloquence and sex, between description and eroticism, is pursued repeatedly in *Hero and Leander*. For all of Leander's avowed baseness (1.219–22), the beauty of his person proves the most powerful eloquence. By contrast, Hero's speech suggests that she does not own her own body and that it escapes discursive control; what she *says* is opposed or undermined by what her body *does*. The extent to which Marlowe relies on stock ideologies regarding the nature of women – at the same time as he carefully dissects the problematics of male desire in relation to them – has often gone unremarked, or in the case of the *Elegies*, attributed to the source rather than to Marlowe. *Hero and Leander* has frequent recourse to the early modern default position in relation to femininity. Woman, as exemplified by Hero, is the object of male scopic desire ('for men to gaze upon', 1.8; 'So ran the people forth to gaze upon her', 1.117; 'stone still he stood, and evermore he gazed', 1.163), largely passive, and initially impervious to his attempts at wooing her away from chaste virginity (paradoxically denoted by her devotion to Venus).[14] Leander's arguments have frequent recourse to standard assertions: that use confers value (1.232–6); that the failure to couple leads to death ('Lone women like to empty houses perish', 1.242); and that women are mere ciphers without connection to a male term:

> One is no number; maids are nothing then,
> Without the sweet society of men.
> Wilt thou live single still? one shalt thou be,
> Though never-singling Hymen couple thee.
> (1.255–8)

Hero represents a familiar disjunction between speech and intention, as her body betrays a socially proscribed desire: 'Hero's looks yielded, but her words made war; / Woman are won when they begin to jar' (1.331–2).

Hero's externality to rhetorical culture is stressed (and thus her status as object rather than as subject), as she focuses on the speaker rather than on the argument (1.338–40) and as her discourse unconsciously betrays her 'true' desire:

> 'Come thither.' As she spake this, her tongue tripp'd,
> For unawares 'Come thither' from her slipp'd,
> And suddenly her former colour chang'd,
> And here and there her eyes through anger rang'd.
> (1.357–60)

The term 'tripp'd' compounds the ambiguity of where agency is to be located – are the words 'Come hither' that trip from Hero's tongue something willingly spoken (see Ia in the *OED*: to 'tread, step lightly, walk, skip etc.'; and II.6: to 'stumble or fall'); or are they an error, a betrayal (see 9: 'fall into an error; make a mistake or false step', and 8b: 'to stumble in articulation, to falter in speaking')?[15] All of these meanings are potentially in complex interplay. This passage provides another example of implied *aposiopesis*, as the thought or idea is left unfinished (conforming to Lanham's definition as 'sometimes from genuine passion') once Hero realises what she has said.[16] The moment can be allied with a prevalent idea in early modern discourses that women's language does not signify unproblematically, particularly where questions of sexual consent are concerned, namely the standard conceit whereby 'no' means 'yes'.[17] Resistance provokes an increase in pleasure:

> She trembling strove; this strife of hers (like that
> Which made the world) another world begat
> Of unknown joy.
> (II.291–3)

In this context, the Mercury 'digression' that follows can be seen as providing a parallel example of passion between unequals, but where the maid ('Her mind pure, and her tongue untaught to glose' (1.392)), *resists* Mercury's forceful advances and tricks him both by refusing to speak and by demanding a gift that she knows will ensure Mercury's punishment: 'yet was mute, / And neither would deny, nor grant his suit' (1.423–4).[18] The example is presented as a way of underlining the power of the language of courtship and of confirming Leander's rhetorical power: 'Maids are not won by brutish force and might, / But speeches full of pleasure and delight' (1.419–20).

As with the preceding discussion, there has been a tendency to stress the originality of *Hero and Leander* rather than to note the extent to which many of its key assumptions about sex, desire, and gender are articulated in terms that are familiar to an early modern readership. The description of Hero in the first sestiad involves a famously distended *ekphrasis* (yet another of the rhetorical set-pieces that convey liveliness, vividness – as per Sidney's famous praise of this form of description in the *Apology*),[19] which is followed by a reference to a personified, abstracted Nature:

> So lovely fair was Hero, Venus' nun,
> As Nature wept, thinking she was undone,
> Because she took more from her than she left,
> And of such wondrous beauty her bereft.
> (1.45–8)

The topos of a beautiful man or woman outdoing nature is widespread in Renaissance writing, notably in Shakespeare's *Sonnets* (1609), especially 1–17, and in demonstrably contemporary texts such as Shakespeare's *Venus and Adonis* (1593). Similarly, ideas such as 'Beauty alone is lost, too warily kept' (1.328), or the use of agricultural, legal, and financial metaphors to explore the nature of love are familiar from a range of Renaissance texts and have the status of commonplaces. The representation of Leander as polymorphous in his appeal to both men and women, mortals, and gods, is hardly unique either ('Some swore he was a maid in man's attire, / For in his looks were all that men desire' (1.83–4))[20] – again Shakespeare's *Sonnets* provide an analogue, as does the 1590 ending of Book III of *The Faerie Queene* where the figure of the hermaphrodite, combining male and female within a single body, provides an ideal figuration of love.[21]

Paradoxically, the dependence on traditions in regard to the representation of gender affords Marlowe the licence to pen explicitly homoerotic passages by taking a conventionally bisexual image for the depiction of love as an ideal and resituating that image in the context of same-sex passion:

> He clapp'd his plump cheeks, with his tresses play'd,
> And smiling wantonly, his love bewray'd.
> He watch'd his arms, and as they open'd wide
> At every stroke, betwixt them would he slide
> And steal a kiss, and then run out and dance,
> And as he turn'd, cast many a lustful glance,
> And threw him gaudy toys to please his eye,
> And dive into the water, and there pry
> Upon his breast, his thighs, and every limb
> And up again, and close beside him swim,
> And talk of love.
>
> (II.181–91)

Marlowe self-consciously, or even perversely, eschews those poetic forms and genres that we most associate with the Elizabethan period: no courtly sonneteer he. Equally, critical consensus allies him very strongly with the Ovidian strain in English poetry, a line that runs parallel to Petrarchan influence, yet one that arguably is more productively transformed into the English idiom. Not that Marlowe is immune from the Petrarchan mode, as his experiments with the form of the blazon and the received vocabulary of the Petrarchan tradition suggest. In *Hero and Leander* his direct source is not Ovid in any straightforward way; nonetheless, Ovidian themes and texts are reflexively deployed throughout. Cleland argues that Marlowe's rejection of the sonnet form (he is one of the few major late Elizabethan writers not to have used the sonnet form) 'signifies his resistance to the inactive, and thus effeminate, subject position of the Petrarchan lover' (218); yet the poems collectively reveal a sustained interest in the culturally anomalous figure of the disempowered male (tellingly, to be a male without power is to signify as female).[22]

As Georgia Brown notes, '[t]hrough his shameless reinterpretations of the classics, Marlowe made his independence from inherited values the basis of his authority'.[23] *Hero and Leander* is a consummate example of the ways in which Marlowe manipulates questions of form (conceptually and pragmatically understood) in order to piece together the fragmented pieces of the classical inheritance in new and surprising ways. Even though Marlowe's reception of conventional Renaissance traditions diverges from the norm, his particular mode of innovation is nonetheless grounded in the very practices, texts, and histories that he reinvents.

Notes

1. Christopher Marlowe, *The Poems*, ed. Millar Maclure (Manchester University Press, 1968), xxxix. All subsequent references are to this edition.
2. Just as much of the interpellation of Petrarch in the English poetic tradition is at several removes from the work of Petrarch himself, having resolved into a series of topoi and ideas – the sources of, for example, *Hero and Leander* may conjure the *Heroides* – its actual sources are many and various and range across the classical tradition, including Musaeus, a poet widely referenced by key Latin poets and associated strongly with the figure of Orpheus: a connection that Marlowe implicitly and playfully exploits. See Gordon Braden, *The Classics and English Renaissance Poetry: Three Case Studies* (New Haven: Yale University Press, 1978); and Stephen Orgel, 'Musaeus in English', *George Herbert Journal* 29:1–2 (2005–6): 67–75. George Chapman, who 'completed' Marlowe's potentially intentional fragment, also translated Musaeus. Although my chapter will focus on the first printing of 1598 (the first two sestiads, by Marlowe, which conclude '*desunt nonnulla*'), most early modern readers would have encountered this popular text as a collaboratively authored text.
3. See Georgia Brown, 'Marlowe's Poems and Classicism', in *The Cambridge Companion to Ovid*, ed. Patrick Cheney (Cambridge University Press, 2004), 106–26. For definitions of key rhetorical terms, see Richard A. Lanham, *A Handlist of Rhetorical Terms*, 2nd edn (Berkeley: University of California Press, 1991); *Silva rhetoricae*, http://rhetoric.byu.edu/ also provides useful definitions.
4. See Clark Hulse, *Metamorphic Verse: The Elizabethan Minor Epic* (Princeton University Press, 1981); and William P. Weaver, 'Marlowe's Fable: *Hero and Leander* and the Rudiments of Eloquence', *Studies in Philology* 105:3 (2008): 388–408.
5. Patrick Cheney, *Marlowe's Counterfeit Profession: Ovid, Spenser, Counter-Nationhood* (University of Toronto Press, 1997), 49–67.
6. Russ McDonald, 'Marlowe and Style', in Cheney, *The Cambridge Companion to Ovid*, 55–69 (57).
7. The poem was printed twice in 1598 (the second being George Chapman's continuation), and then in 1600, 1606, 1609, 1613, 1629, and 1637.
8. Marlowe uses 'sparks' in the conventional way at 1.187–8: 'Thus while dumb signs their yielding hearts entangled, / The air with sparks of living fire was spangled.'
9. See Judith Haber, '"True-loves blood": Narrative and Desire in *Hero and Leander*', *English Literary Renaissance* 28 (1998): 372–86.
10. *OED Online*, www.oed.com, accessed 23 February 2012.
11. Haber discusses these inversions in detail.
12. See Heather James ('one thinks of its dazzling array of mythological characters who seek out the resources of speech and writing – in say, prophecy, lament, and weaving – to contend with hostile opposition to their will or their views'): 'The Poet's Toys: Christopher Marlowe and the Liberties of Erotic Elegy', *Modern Language Quarterly* 67:1 (March 2006): 103–27 (108).

13 See, for example, William Shakespeare, Sonnet 103.
14 This gives a particular edge to the identification of Hero with Diana through the framework of the Actaeon myth (II.259–62).
15 *OED Online*, accessed 2 March 2012.
16 Lanham, *Handlist*, 20.
17 See Sir Philip Sidney, *Astrophil to Stella*, 63.11–14: 'But Grammar's force with sweet success confirm, / For Grammar says (O this dear Stella weigh,) / For Grammar says (to Grammar who says nay) / That in one speech two Negatives affirm.' In *Sir Philip Sidney: The Major Works*, ed. Katherine Duncan-Jones (Oxford: World's Classics, 2008), 177–8.
18 See also I.311–14.
19 Like other structurally distinct elements of Marlowe's poem, this too was one of the exercises prescribed in the progymnasmata, mostly likely encountered through Erasmus' *De copia*. See Peter Mack, *Elizabethan Rhetoric: Theory and Practice* (Cambridge University Press, 2002), 31–2, 149–52.
20 This passage, however, is subject to the same potential (mis)construction as that discussed above.
21 For this argument in relation to Shakespeare's Sonnet 20, see Margaret Healy, *Shakespeare, Alchemy and the Creative Imagination: The Sonnets and A Lover's Complaint* (Cambridge University Press, 2011).
22 See Bruce Smith, 'Rape, Rap, Rupture, Rapture: R-Rated Futures on the Global Market', *Textual Practice* 9 (1995): 421–44; and Ian Frederick Moulton, '"Printed Abroad and Uncastrated": Marlowe's *Elegies* with Davies' *Epigrams*', in *Marlowe, History, and Sexuality: New Critical Essays on Christopher Marlowe*, ed. Paul Whitfield White (New York: AMS Press, 1998), 77–90.
23 Georgia E. Brown, 'Breaking the Canon: Marlowe's Challenge to the Literary Status Quo in *Hero and Leander*', in Whitfield White, *Marlowe, History, and Sexuality*, 59–75 (71).

CHAPTER SEVEN

Marlowe and the Elizabethan theatre audience

Brian Walsh

Marlowe's audience, like most aspects of the Elizabethan theatre for the modern scholar, is elusive. We know, of course, that when Edward Alleyn donned a false nose to play Barabas in *The Jew of Malta*, or when a fellow company member served as his stool in *Tamburlaine*, there were people there to look on.[1] And, given how widely these and other plays by Marlowe were imitated by fellow dramatists and playing companies hoping to attract paying customers, we can reasonably surmise that most of those present were entertained or otherwise gained pleasure from the experiences.[2] But many key questions remain beyond our ken. When Barabas poisons and kills a host of nuns, including his own converted daughter, did those assembled for the play laugh at the outrageous trick or recoil in horror? Did some admire the audacity and cunning but at the same time condemn the villainy? Similar questions can be asked about Tamburlaine and the humiliation of Bajazeth. Was there widespread satisfaction or amusement in seeing Tamburlaine's foe, caged, fed, and watered like a dog? Was such a response heightened when, after an agonised speech expressing his abjection and misery, the defeated Turkish Emperor 'brains himself against the cage'?[3] Or was this a moment when audiences felt regret or sorrow over the man's miserable end? There are even more basic, general questions that precede these and encompass more than Marlowe's audience. Who were playgoers in the first place? What types of people attended theatres? How did they behave while there? What made them choose one playhouse over another on any given day? How did plays intersect with the spectators' experiences and with whatever level of education the spectators may have had? How did plays affect the audience's sense of themselves or of their world? That is, however they responded to individual plays or moments within plays, were audience members ever fundamentally *changed* by the experience of seeing and hearing stage enactments?

Proposed answers to both sets of questions are scarce and often highly qualified. Historical-sociological research has yielded some credible hypotheses about types of playgoers, but there is no current consensus on the demographics of the playgoing public.[4] Likewise, while there are eye-witness testimonials that attest to various individuals' reactions to plays, these are largely isolated and, as far as we know, sufficiently idiosyncratic to prevent us from building too broad a set of conclusions upon them.[5] We remain, then, far from possessing a full portrait of Elizabethan theatre patrons, either as individuals or as variously conceived heterogeneous or homogeneous groups, and the goal of ever knowing precisely or on a wide scale how they reacted to or used their experiences in the playhouses is largely unattainable. Recognising such difficulties is nothing new. But those interested in understanding Elizabethan plays in their historical context must continually confront the sceptical, and in some ways unassailable, view that such difficulties mean that to hypothesise about audiences or audience response in any meaningful way is pointless.

We can begin to confront that outlook by returning to the basic notion that institutional theatre such as that which provided the framework for Marlowe's plays cannot properly exist without an audience. As one common-sense definition puts it, theatre as a form 'occurs when one or more human beings, isolated in time and/or space, present themselves to another or others'.[6] The 'another' or 'others' who attended plays in the 1590s, however difficult to pin down, were constitutive elements of the achievements of Marlowe, Shakespeare, and their peers. As such these attendees are part of the ontology of the theatre, and any attempt to analyse what was produced on the Elizabethan stage that does not attempt to account for them by some means will always be limited. We must engage them through the scanty evidence, internal and external to the plays, that we have, and something more. Jeremy Lopez offers a useful assessment of what that 'more' ultimately involves: 'Given the state of the documentary evidence in the field [of early modern drama], there is a point at which imagination must take over where evidence leaves off.'[7] Between a refusal to speculate beyond the confines of the evidence and a willingness to assume *carte blanche* power to mould Elizabethan audiences to resemble our own contemporary desires, we must find a space for responsible conjecture about how the fact of the audience affected the composition and production of plays, and about how the experience of being part of an audience inflected the reception of the drama.

Such work is rooted in historical research as well as in performance-sensitive close reading of the plays' language, staging directions, and implied cues. Charles Whitney, a pioneer in recent studies of Renaissance audience response, offers an intriguing local instance of such work, in his article about the playgoing habits of 'journeymen, apprentices, and servants', collectively labelled for his purposes as 'subalterns'. Whitney offers a granular survey of various guild records that reference or attempt to regulate playgoing by its younger members. Given that such people were sometimes discouraged from attending plays at all, Whitney suggests that 'subalterns made to feel that their playgoing was transgressive might be predisposed to respond more positively to staged transgression than they otherwise would have. Here, a play such as *1 Tamburlaine the Great* would have supplied a lot of material.'[8] Such scholarship – combining as it does detailed historical research with cultural analysis of the implications of the performance of a particular play – is inspiring to those who remain committed to exploring ways of revitalising and expanding the possibilities of audience study. In Whitney, as in Lopez, imagination is not a flight of fancy, but rather a key intellectual faculty that is central to scholarship in all fields, especially scholarship that deals with the past.

A recent, relevant essay collection proclaims this insight as central to its project in its very title: *Imagining the Audience in Early Modern Drama*. The editors of that collection, Jennifer A. Low and Nova Myhill, propose that we do the work of imagining the early modern audience by keeping in mind the fact that, from the playwright's side of things, 'imagined audiences shape dramas at the inception of the composition process' and that the 'playwright and actor ultimately had little control over' audience response.[9] Low and Myhill further ask scholars to consider both audience and audiences. They define the distinction thus: 'The first term implies a collective entity – one that the dramatists might know and appeal to (and even create) as a group; the second emphasizes the variety of experiences and viewing practices that individuals brought to the early modern theater.'[10]

In the remainder of this chapter, I will draw attention to moments from Marlowe's oeuvre where we can track the dialectic of performance between the play and the playgoers in these terms. My method will involve the imaginative, more than the strictly historical, mode of audience analysis. I will pay attention to the ways that the playwright invites both the audience and audiences to experience his work. Marlowe recognised that being successful in the popular theatres meant pleasing audiences in conventional ways. But his work does far more than please with standard lines, characters, or plots. The audience that Marlowe imagined and that shaped his work at the composition stage was evidently one that wanted to be challenged with novel, often difficult and uncomfortable, situations. For this audience he offered moment after moment that could nonplus, elicit an array of conflicting feelings, cause self-reflection among, or awe playgoers. I will consider here three different ways that Marlowe's plays delivered a heightened and unusually engaging experience for the audience. The moments I focus on are not ones that merely present complicated or conflicting views. Rather, they are moments that seem calculated to disturb and elicit the imaginative participation of playgoers in the questions, problems, and sensations being enacted. First, I will consider Marlowe's penchant for provoking variegated, mutually exclusive feelings in audience members about situations and characters; second, I will consider an instance where Marlowe makes the fact of the gathered group aspect of any audience a means to force playgoers to think of their potential to act, or, more importantly, not act, as a violent mob; and third, I will consider a Marlowe play that deploys sound effects at a strategic moment in order to unify audiences, if not intellectually then emotionally, producing a powerful, theatre-specific sensation of fearful wonder before the drama that is unfolding.

The examples from *The Jew of Malta* and *Tamburlaine* with which I began are instances where Marlowe forces playgoers to orient themselves along a spectrum of possible – often mutually exclusive – responses to his plays.[11] Such provocation is conventional in his works and examples are plentiful, although each has its own particular inflections. Another scene from *The Jew of Malta* provides an opportunity to think about this dynamic of provoking conflicting responses within an audience or within audiences in Low and Myhill's senses more fully. In this play, Barabas' slave Ithamore has fallen in love with the prostitute, Bellamira, and finds a moment to 'lie in [her] lap' (IV.ii.85) while she uses him to extort Barabas. Ithamore by now has already revealed himself to be thoroughly craven, stating in his interview with Barabas: 'One time I was an ostler in an inn, / And in the night-time secretly would I steal / To travellers' chambers and there cut their throats' (II.iii.208–10). This is just one item on his résumé of villainy, much of which is reported, but some of which he enacts directly for audiences to see. His desire for Bellamira and her apparent interest in him produce a wholly unanticipated poetic reverie. When she offers to marry him, Ithamore declares:

> Content, but we will leave this paltry land,
> And sail from hence to Greece, to lovely Greece,
> I'll be thy Jason, thou my golden fleece;
> Where painted carpets o'er the meads are hurled,
> And Bacchus' vineyards overspread the world,
> Where woods and forests go in goodly green,
> I'll be Adonis, thou shalt be Love's queen.
> The meads, the orchards, and the primrose lanes,
> Instead of sedge and reed, bear sugar-canes.
> Thou in those groves, by Dis above,
> Shalt live with me and be my love.
>
> (IV.ii.91–101)

The content of the poem is at times directly incompetent ('by Dis above' incorrectly places Dis, or the classical god of the underworld, in the sky), and the allusions to a classical love story like that of Venus and Adonis that ends in tragedy is awkward, given the situation of the poem's utterance. Richard Wilson points out that Ithamore here is 'travestying Marlowe's most quoted lyric', 'The Passionate Shepherd to His Love':

> Come live with me and be my Love,
> And we will all the pleasures prove.
> That valleys, groves, hills and fields,
> Woods, or steepy mountain yields.[12]

But how total is the travesty? The poem is, after all, formally pleasing and is replete with compelling images of comfort and plenty: 'The meads, the orchards, and the primrose lanes', and 'Bacchus' vineyards overspread the world'.

The poem's images and its romantic intent contrast with the dark edge of the invoked Jason and Adonis stories as well as with the foolish nod to a celestial Dis. Its effect in the theatre may be complexly discordant as well. It is easy to imagine the moment as pure, low comedy. Ithamore is overdetermined in his otherness. His precise ethnicity is ambiguous, but he certainly would read on stage as a Turkish subject and a Muslim, and he is debased in social standing through his status as a slave.[13] By convention there is something inherently ridiculous about such a figure, and so he presents as distasteful even before audiences witness him serve as an assistant in horrible acts of cruelty, such as the poisoning of the nuns who have taken in Barabas' daughter against her father's wishes or the murder of Friar Barnardine who had sought to blackmail Barabas. The incongruity of this man articulating tender feelings of love with rapturous delight is itself comical, and the irony of his emotional sensitivity is compounded by the fact that he does so to a whore who is conspiring with one of her clients to manipulate him for gain. The sordid situation of the poem's emergence possibly frames it as entirely risible.

And yet, for all the oddities of its content and the context, the lyric nonetheless offers evidence of an expansive poetic imagination at work. Ithamore brings forth exotic locales and evokes the pastoral world's longed-for otium, which is often expressed in this period by aristocratic poets of refined sensibility. Ithamore envisions a release from his mundane existence in 'this paltry land', but his aspiration is not necessary egotistical, as is the case with other Marlovian antiheroes like Tamburlaine or Faustus. Rather, it is a fantasy of *sharing* ease, abundance, and beauty with a beloved. It is a fantasy of escape that likely aligns with the desires of some playgoers – perhaps among them some of Whitney's 'subalterns' – who may themselves long to ditch their bosses and flee to a land of plenty to enjoy natural riches and sexual fulfilment.

I'm not proposing here that we overlook how the lurid situation in which the poem emerges contaminates its reception in the playhouse, or that we be blind to the ways Ithamore's words demonstrate his laughable limits as a reader of the classics. Travesty is in the air and perhaps overwhelms everything else. But the moment the words are spoken could easily be a tantalisingly brief, aesthetically and affectively powerful interruption of the squalid scene around it. No audience member would consciously identify with Ithamore here; beyond the fact of his otherness he is, after all, being (somewhat obviously) gulled. And yet the poem expresses longing for a sublime, sensual experience of intimacy that is doomed to fail and so offers playgoers a surprising entry point to sympathise with a character who speaks to more poignant effect than one might have expected.

While each playgoer's mind is his or her own, theatre is ultimately a group experience. In considering Marlowe in the playhouse, we must consider also how the fact of being part of a group may have framed the experience of particular plays for those in attendance. One of Marlowe's least-known works today is *The Massacre at Paris*, although it was very popular in the 1590s.[14] It provides an extended uneasy experience for the audience in part because it is about one possible outcome of a crowd gathering: mob violence. The play represents the infamous St Bartholomew's Day Massacre of 1572, in which French Catholic forces, under the leadership of the Duke of Guise, slaughtered a group of prominent French Protestants, or Huguenots, and thus incited wider mob rage against Protestants throughout Paris and elsewhere in France.

Julia Briggs has offered a compelling argument that the play, despite being in some regards an over the top anti-Catholic diatribe, could actually have created some uneasiness in its Protestant audience, an argument that Sara Munson Deats extends when she calls *The Massacre at Paris* an 'interrogative drama' that encourages 'audience ambivalence'.[15] It makes sense to assume that English audiences would watch the killing of Protestants by bloodthirsty Catholics with horror. But, as Briggs and others have noted, complications arise both when we consider the charisma of the killing scenes, achieved by Marlowe's deft use of dark humour throughout, and when we consider that Elizabethan English Protestants attending the play were in their country in the powerful majority rather than in an oppressed minority. While the play could frighten audiences by showing them the possibility of being violently persecuted for their religion, it might be just as frightening for suggesting how easily a majority group within a society where different faiths exist can themselves become the frenzied perpetrators of violence. Mainstream Protestant playgoers were challenged to consider the shift in responsibility majority status affords them when it comes to confessional divides.

At one point after the Massacre, the Guise articulates his expansive plans for more confessional cleansing, stating that, 'being animated by religious zeal', he will do all he can to 'overthrow those sectious Puritans' (xix.42, 43). What is brought up for scrutiny here is not so much the Guise's Catholicism as the concept of 'religious zeal' itself when it is used to muster legions of hateful killers. The choice of the word 'Puritan' is intriguing for an English audience. Puritan was a term of abuse used by mainstream Protestants to denigrate those who agitated for further reform.[16] Marlowe transvalues it by putting it in the Guise's mouth at this moment. While ostensibly referring to the French, the label cannot but be heard by an English audience with a local resonance, and this marginalised group may suddenly appear sympathetic as the targets of the Guise's hate. The non-Puritan majority at the playhouse is forced to see itself reflected in the Guise's murderous fantasies and thus to feel the potential for social tensions over religious divides to spill into acts of group violence.

The play suggests a way to mediate within a society rather than use group force to compel conformity. Early in the play, Charles IX, the Catholic king of France, resists his vicious mother's desire to initiate a massacre against the Protestants. Aside from the infamy it would bring on France, he claims that

> my heart relents that noble men,
> Only corrupted in religion,
> Ladies of honour, knights, gentlemen,
> Should for their conscience taste such ruthless ends.
>   (iv.9–12)

Although steeped in the language of a transcendent notion of aristocratic solidarity as much as anything else, the words do articulate a vision of religious tolerance, and perhaps even make a case for the desirability – and indeed, the *possibility* – of a religiously pluralistic society. Such a sentiment prompts English playgoers to reflect on the problem of religious difference in their own time and place and on the impulse among majorities to coerce uniformity through terror and violence. Later in the play, another French king, Henri III, has his Catholic co-religionist the Duke of Guise murdered. He says of the Guise 'This is the traitor that hath spent my gold / In making foreign wars and civil broils' (xxi.98–9). The distaste for the Massacre expressed here is framed in practical terms: 'civil broils' are costly and disruptive, and they weaken the nation. Whether a matter of 'conscience' or of order, the play in these moments articulates a rationale for religious toleration amid its louder and more sensational representations of the internal and international threat Catholics pose to Protestants everywhere, and especially to the English queen and her people (e.g. xxiv.55–68).

Finally, we can consider a moment when Marlowe has sought to unite his audience, at least around a shared sensation, by capitalising on the live moment of performance through use of a theatrical effect. Elizabethan audience members could, we know, be inattentive to the play at hand if they preferred to chat, mingle, flirt, proposition, rob, or otherwise interact with fellow playgoers instead of minding the dramatic action.[17] Playwrights and players could never count on having the total attention of the audience. Sound effects could be a way to startle the inattentive into engaging with the performance, and there are many indicated instances of jarring noises in Marlowe's work: loud fireworks in *Doctor Faustus*, alarums during battle scenes in *Edward II*, or the bells tolling to signal the Massacre in *The Massacre at Paris*. Such theatrical effects, strategically deployed, can, at least for an instant, shock playgoers into a moment of collective attentiveness. In many cases, this probably passes as quickly as it came about. Alarums may start to seem routine after the first two or three times they are deployed, and audience members inclined to follow other happenings within the playhouse could easily turn away again. One instance where we discern Marlowe working extra hard to gain and hold attention through a sound effect, and so to bind his audience together in shared tension and anticipation, comes at the climax of *Doctor Faustus*. At stake in the play's end is the fate of a human soul, and, through a skilful blend of stage technology and subsequent urgent language, Marlowe creates the conditions for collective contemplation of a universal anxiety over damnation. Early on, Faustus proposes 'four-and-twenty years' as his term to enjoy power and live in 'voluptuousness' (iv.93–4), and this temporal expanse creates a loose notion of time passing. Time up until the end of the play has moved uncertainly through the initial, dreamlike scenes of incantation and interviews with Mephistopheles through the episodic middle vignettes. When the scholars exit and leave Faustus alone at the end, the twenty-four years now expire, and the movement of time becomes, for an instance, terrifyingly precise. The text indicates a sound effect: 'The clock strikes eleven.' Faustus articulates the implications: 'Ah, Faustus, / Now hast thou but one bare hour to live, / And then thou must be damned perpetually' (xiv.61, stage direction; 62–4).[18] From here time begins to move rapidly again, this time within the tight framework of the putative final hour that transpires over the course of a few lines, the inevitable temporal movement towards the midnight of Faustus' final moments when 'the clock striketh twelve' (xiv.112, stage direction), another moment when audiences must wait through the dramatic tolling.

Insofar as it is possible to herd an audience into a collective feeling, a sound effect like the clock striking – especially in an era when this was the primary way that most urban dwellers could know the time, and so a phenomenon to which most people would be habitually attentive – is a most efficient means of controlling an audience's perceptions and focusing, perhaps even fusing, their attention on the chronological sequence of tolls. The striking clock in *Doctor Faustus* transmits information to be decoded, and it does so over a sequence of chimes, the end-point of which is uncertain in the first instance of establishing eleven o'clock, and then in the second instance armed with a sense of what the final number of tolls will be, anticipating each beat as the clock moves towards twelve. It thus elicits, if not impels, auditors to participate en masse in the act of listening through the tolls to count up the chimes and learn the time the play wishes to establish. The aural sensation of gleaning temporal movement amounts to a phenomenological awareness of progress towards doom for the play's protagonist. The playwright here manipulates theatrical time through the repeated references to it and through the device of the toll to focus and heighten audience awareness of its passing into ultimate, eternal grief for Faustus. The uniting of audience attention does not mean that every person will think about the play in the same way. Some playgoers may have sympathy for Faustus; others may not. Some may find the play Calvinist, while some may see hints of Pelagianism, and condemn or praise it on those lines according to their confessional preferences. But collectively what the audience, rapt with attention as the second clock-tolls progress, probably feels most strongly is a sense of relief that this is a fate they are watching, not experiencing themselves. Marlowe here turns the heterogeneous Elizabethan audience into Lucretian spectators, comforted that they are on shore while Faustus' boat splits on the rocks.[19]

Marlowe does not make it easy for audiences to take any one message with them from the playhouse. It might sound as though I am giving total power to the dramatist to vex or otherwise easily manipulate audiences, but I hope it is clear from these examples that the kind of engagement his difficult plays allow is both respectful of and empowering to playgoers. The audience that Marlowe *imagined* when he wrote his emotionally and intellectually complex plays was filled by people who evidently wanted, and were prepared to grasp and negotiate, distinct tones and registers. The audience he *inspired* through the experience of his immensely popular works was one that came to expect from theatre formal artistry and amusement as well as provocations to thought and feeling. We remain limited in our capacity to say how directly these encounters changed audiences in their day-to-day lives. But it is easy to imagine that as Marlowe's plays asked playgoers to assess critically the values and ideas on display, as well as to experience viscerally the feelings the plays conveyed, the habits of heart and mind exercised in the theatre became mobile and found application and expression outside the confines of the playhouses.

Notes

1 This assertion can be made based on entries in Henslowe's *Diary* for the plays' gate receipts on various days. See Philip Henslowe, *Henslowe's Diary*, ed. R. A. Foakes, 2nd edn (Cambridge University Press, 2002), 6–17 (*The Jew of Malta*), 23–4 (*Tamburlaine*). William Rowley refers to the 'artificiall Jewe of Maltae's nose' in his 1609 *A Search for Money* (London: C. Richards, 1840), 19.
2 Lisa Hopkins, 'Marlowe's Reception and Influence', in *The Cambridge Companion to Christopher Marlowe*, ed. Patrick Cheney (Cambridge University Press, 2004), 282–96 (282–3).
3 Christopher Marlowe, *Tamburlaine the Great, Part One* (V.i.304, stage direction). All quotations from Marlowe are taken from *Christopher Marlowe: The Complete Plays*, ed. Frank Romany and Robert Lindsay (London: Penguin, 2003).

4 The landmark studies are: Alfred Harbage, *Shakespeare's Audience* (New York: Columbia University Press, 1941); Ann Jennalie Cook, *The Privileged Playgoers of Shakespeare's London* (Princeton University Press, 1981); and Andrew Gurr, *Playgoing in Shakespeare's London*, 3rd edn (Cambridge University Press, 2004). See also Charles Whitney's article '"Ussually in the Werking Daies": Playgoing Journeymen, Apprentices, and Other Servants in Guild Records, 1582–92', *Shakespeare Quarterly* 50 (1999): 433–58.

5 For instances of individual responses, see Charles Whitney, *Early Responses to Renaissance Drama* (Cambridge University Press, 2006). Tanya Pollard's survey of audience reception in the period gathers evidence to warrant some generalisations, e.g. 'audiences actively sought out the experience of being powerfully moved, and enjoyed it'; 'Audience Reception', in *The Oxford Handbook of Shakespeare*, ed. Arthur Kinney (Oxford University Press, 2012), 469.

6 Bernard Beckerman, *Dynamics of Drama: Theory and Method of Analysis* (New York: Drama Book Specialists, 1979), 10.

7 Jeremy Lopez, 'Imagining the Actor's Body on the Early Modern Stage', *Medieval & Renaissance Drama in England* 20 (2007), 187–203 (188–9).

8 Whitney 'Ussually in the Werking Daies', 448. Alan Dessen gives us another model for audience-oriented readings by attempting to recover Elizabethan stage conventions: *Elizabethan Stage Conventions and Modern Interpreters* (Cambridge University Press, 1984).

9 Jennifer A. Low and Nova Myhill, 'Audience and Audiences', in *Imagining the Audience in Early Modern Drama, 1558–1642*, ed. Jennifer A. Low and Nova Myhill (New York: Palgrave, 2011), 1–18 (1).

10 Ibid., 2.

11 On *Edward II*, see Meg F. Pearson, 'Audience as Witness in *Edward II*', in Myhill and Low, *Imagining the Audience*, 93–111.

12 Richard Wilson, 'Tragedy, Patronage, and Power', in Cheney, *The Cambridge Companion to Christopher Marlowe*, 207–30 (218). Poem quoted from *The Norton Anthology of English Literature*, ed. Stephen Greenblatt, M. H. Abrams, Jack Stillinger, and Deidre Shauna Lynch, 8th edn (New York: Norton, 2006), 1022.

13 On Ithamore's origins, see Mark Hutchings, '"In Thrace; Brought Up in Arabia": *The Jew of Malta* II.iii.131', *Notes and Queries* 47 (2000): 428–30.

14 On the play's popularity, see Kristen Poole, 'Garbled Martyrdom in Christopher Marlowe's *The Massacre at Paris*', *Comparative Drama* 32 (1998): 1–25 (4).

15 See Julia Briggs, 'Marlowe's *Massacre at Paris*: A Reconsideration', *RES* 34 (1983): 257–78, esp. 277–8; Sara Munson Deats, '*Dido, Queen of Carthage* and *The Massacre at Paris*', in Cheney, *The Cambridge Companion to Christopher Marlowe*, 193–206 (200, 202). Poole, 'Garbled Martyrdom', esp. 18–19, disputes the claim that the play could inspire any real ambiguity.

16 See Patrick Collinson, 'Ben Jonson's *Bartholomew Fair*: The Theatre Constructs Puritans', in *The Theatrical City: Culture, Theatre and Politics in*

London, 1576–1649, ed. David L. Smith, Richard Strier, and David Bevington (Cambridge University Press, 1995), 157–81.
17 On the varieties of the 'theatrical event', see Charles Hirrell, 'Duration of Performances and Lengths of Plays: How Shall We Beguile the Lazy Time?', *Shakespeare Quarterly* 61 (2010): 159–82.
18 These lines are taken from the A-text.
19 See Lucretius' famous lines 1–4 in Book II of *The Nature of Things*.

CHAPTER EIGHT

Marlowe and classical literature

Syrithe Pugh

Jonson's *The Poetaster; or, His Arraignment* opens with the Augustan poet Ovid, alone on stage, reading lines he has just written: 'Then, when this body falls in funeral fire, / My name shall live, and my best part aspire. / It shall go so.'[1] This is the end of Ovid's *Amores*, I.xv, read in full later in the scene; the translation is Jonson's emendation of Marlowe's, reprinted in Marlowe's *All Ovid's Elegies*. Marlowe's translation of Ovid's *Amores*, the first into any vernacular, was publicly burnt in 1599. Marlowe himself had been killed in 1593. The lines quoted here must have gathered poignancy from the fate of Marlowe and his book, as well as from that of Ovid, sent into exile later in the play.[2] Ovid and Marlowe both furnish examples of the dangers besetting poets and of the immortality of their verse. By quoting at once Ovid and Marlowe here, Jonson defiantly shows that their verse survives them. This figure on stage even has a body, reintroducing the uncanny physicality with which Marlowe imbued the lines.

It is tempting to say that the play opens with Ovid declaiming Marlowe, but this would not be quite true. Ovid is perfecting his elegy, and the lines we hear first are very different from Marlowe's, which read 'Then though death racks my bones in funerall fire, Ile live, and as he puls me downe mount higher.'[3]

Marlowe's distinctive focus on the body here is not in Ovid, who makes no mention of his 'bones' and who claims only that a 'great part' of him – his poetry – will survive. But Jonson presents the moment of decision after drafting: 'Ovid' could have deleted Marlowe's lines moments before. This correcting process is of course what Jonson has done with Marlowe's version. While Jonson pays tribute to a dead contemporary, resuscitating him on stage and identifying him with one of the greatest classical poets, he simultaneously boasts that his own poetry is more perfect.

The play identifies Horace, its main character, with Jonson himself, and Marston and Dekker, its satirical targets, with Crispinus and Demetrius. Might 'Ovid' be Marlowe?[4] Later in the play Ovid and his companions, dressed up as gods, hold a riotous drinking party. The glasses are filled by a 'catamite' playing Ganymede, and Ovid as Jupiter threatens to cudgel a jealous Juno, played by Augustus' daughter Julia. Stumbling on the irreverent scene, Augustus banishes Ovid. It is reminiscent of the opening of Marlowe's *Tragedie of Dido*, which also features an attractive Ganymede and a quarrel between Juno and Jupiter. If 'Ovid' represents Marlowe, Jonson identifies a strain of counter-classical irreverence expressed in Marlowe's Ovidian poems, but also in his Lucan translation and adaptation of Virgil. Rewriting classical literature entails an often antagonistic engagement with ideas and values central to Augustan and to Elizabethan society.

Ovid

Ovid's *Amores* wittily narrates an adulterous affair in a recognisably everyday contemporary Rome. The speaker, a promiscuous and apparently adulterous lover, presents himself as the author, but is clearly a persona, emerging as comically boastful, deceitful, and shameless. Stephen Orgel calls Marlowe's translation 'in a sense ... Marlowe's sonnet sequence',[5] a label that is telling not just because, like a Petrarchan sonnet sequence, Ovid's collection hovers between lyric poetry and a narrative of desire, uttered in the first person by a changeable male lover as interested in his own art as in his mistress, but also because sonnets are this period's 'norm' for love poetry, from which Marlowe's translation deviates. The translation appears at the height of the Petrarchan vogue in England, when Petrarchism had become a conventional way of seeking patronage. At the top of the patronage system was the Virgin Queen, and Elizabethan sonnets often have a political flavour. The languishing pose of Petrarchan amorous courtship had become a convention of life at court. By ventriloquising Ovid's defiant eroticism, Marlowe launches an assault on this whole system – on its prime value, the chastity of the unyielding Petrarchan mistress, and on the stance considered appropriate to the young man seeking advancement.

But Marlowe's *Elegies* are so rough as to be scarcely recognisable as his. Marlowe's use of the 'heroic' couplet to translate Ovid's elegiacs was pioneering, and would become the norm for Ovid translation. But he handles metre and matter clumsily. There are mistakes of translation – though sometimes merely because Marlowe was misled by contemporary commentaries.[6] But the translation also lacks musicality. Ovid's *Amores* are stylistically as polished as any English sonnet, though much funnier, but

Marlowe is often crabbed and clumsy. To fit unpromising rhyme-words he strains syntax: 'Thy service for nights scapes is knowne commodious / And to give signes dull wit to thee is odious' (I.xi.3–4). Sometimes the iambic pentameter breaks down under pressure of literal fidelity to the (densely inflected) Latin, as in: 'Let Marchants seeke wealth with perjured lips; / And being wrackt carowse the sea tir'd with their shippes' (II.x.32–3). The lines can with difficulty be made to fit the metre, but the effect is unnatural. This work dates from early in Marlowe's career, however, and perhaps at this stage Marlowe planned to make his name through drama rather than through poetry. It has been argued that the translation announces an Ovidian career combining both forms: Ovid wrote a tragedy, *Medea*, sadly lost, and refers to his intention to write tragedy several times in the *Amores* (e.g. II.xviii, III.i).[7]

Be this as it may, Marlowe's translation marks a watershed in Ovid's reception. Medieval commentators, favouring the more easily allegorised *Metamorphoses*, saw Ovid as shrouding philosophical truths under pleasant fables. The Ovid of the *Amores*, however, is witty, urbane, and mundane, eager to obtain sex, and explicitly using poetry to that end. The translation was originally published, attributed only to 'C. M.', together with John Davies' *Epigrammes* in 1599, and burnt by order of the Bishops' Ban.[8] Davies' satires were probably the target, but they sit very comfortably with their urbane partner-piece. Reading these satires alongside Marlowe's translation encourages an ironical reading of Ovid's persona, who fits Davies' description of a 'gull' in many ways, being boastful, lecherous, and a dandy. This is the most striking thing about the volume: Renaissance authors were slow to read Ovid as speaking through a persona, while modern criticism emphasises this trait.

As well as displaying irreverent immorality and evasive irony, however, Ovid in the *Amores* is also concerned with immortality as a poet, a concern that sits oddly with Marlowe's clumsy translation. Again, it is helpful to think of the companion-piece in Marlowe's volume, which expresses an attitude to poetic immortality pointedly different from Ovid's. Davies is evidently proud of his skill – he targets fellow-poets 'put down since my light muse arose'.[9] Yet his final poem, 'Peace, idle Muse, have done, for it is time' (XLVIII.i), though evoking the final elegy of the *Amores*, claims that his chosen genre, epigram, is merely fashionable and as brief-lived as the feathers sported by vain 'gulls'. Perhaps Marlowe intends the vaunts of Ovid's persona to be read with irony as symptoms of boastfulness, and, like Davies, he would be indifferent to the immortality of this early work, concerned more with its immediate satirical effect. His later work in translation, poetry, and drama, however, shows a skill matching Ovid's and worthy of the enduring fame it has won.

Marlowe's Ovidianism flowers fully in *Hero and Leander*, the most celebrated poem of the brief Renaissance vogue for what was later dubbed the Ovidian epyllion. 'Epyllion' means little epic, and all the English Renaissance examples take their erotic subject matter and light tone from Ovid. Marlowe's chief source is a Greek poem by the late classical Musaeus, but Marlowe expands his original greatly, taking every opportunity to slip in allusions to other myths dealt with by Ovid, amplifying the themes of the dangers of sexual desire and divine violence. The couplet of the *Amores* translation is here perfected, becoming flexible and capable of wit and beauty. The poem is infused with charged eroticism, Ovidian humour (especially ironising Leander's naïveté), and allusion to myth, recalling the *Metamorphoses*. The heavy use of *ekphrasis*, describing Hero's garments or the decor of Venus' temple, is also very Ovidian. Marlowe inserts a long digression on Mercury's seduction of a shepherdess, an original story whose etiological purpose (it explains why scholars are poor) also recalls the *Metamorphoses*.

But Marlowe tells only half the story – Leander's falling in love with Hero and successful swimming of the Hellespont to spend a night with her – omitting his subsequent drowning and Hero's grief-stricken suicide. He defers the consummation of Hero and Leander's love, swiftly accomplished in Musaeus. Leander returns to Abydos after the fatal meeting, and, when he finally finds himself in bed with her, works out only gradually what to do. The poem ends with Hero's shame at her lost virginity. In the first edition the editor appended 'Desunt Nonnulla' to signal that Marlowe breaks off before the final tragedy, and two contemporaries composed 'continuations'. But Marlowe's poem should be allowed to stand alone. By finishing the tale where he does (despite occasional glances forwards to the familiar ending), Marlowe converts the tale almost into a comedy of fulfilled love. The expansion of the consummation scene is funny, in keeping with the treatment of the naïve Leander throughout, but also allows the development of a psychological realism still fresh today. But it is not optimistic – the lovers face a changed reality now that Hero has lost that 'inestimable gem', her virginity, its significance paradoxically emphasised by Leander's lengthy disquisition on its ultimate worthlessness at their first meeting. Quite apart from our knowledge of Neptune's and Venus' hostility and the lovers' destiny, we feel that their relationship is on a different footing now that desire has been fulfilled, and we sympathise with Hero's discomfiture on the threshold of this new world.

Virgil

When Marlowe turns his attention as translator to Virgil in *The Tragedie of Dido Queene of Carthage*, a similarly Ovidian approach engenders a more antagonistic treatment of the original. With our retrospective knowledge of the great dramatist Marlowe would become, his turn to the stage for this translation and adaptation may seem merely natural, but in fact even the choice of genre here is part of a counter-Virgilian strategy.

The play excerpts the liaison of Dido and Aeneas from Books I to IV of the *Aeneid*. This was the most widely read section of Virgil's epic, but it marks the one major digression in Aeneas' epic quest. In his quest to lead his band of Trojan survivors to their promised homeland in Italy, Aeneas obeys the gods' behests throughout the poem, placing his duty to his race's public destiny above private desires, which might cause him to curtail the voyage. His encounter with Dido is the greatest challenge to that forward trajectory: forgetful of his task, Aeneas wallows in effeminate ease at Carthage until reprimanded by the gods. Virgil alerts us almost to a change of genre on Aeneas' arrival: as Aeneas approaches, the Carthaginian harbour is described in theatrical terms, the wood above forming a *scaena* (*Aeneid*, I.164). His treatment of Dido is heavily indebted to tragedy.[10] The poem strays with its hero away from its epic directedness. In the wake of his departure, Dido curses Aeneas' descendants in a glimpse of the future Punic Wars and kills herself, a sacrificial victim to the poem's *telos*. This moment, when the poem flirts with a genre and values inimical to epic, has appealed to generations of readers, poets, and commentators keen to detect or exploit alternative possibilities in Virgil's monumental work. Ovid, for instance, exploiting the echoes of Roman love-elegy with which Virgil also infuses the episode, composed a letter supposedly written by Dido to Aeneas as he departs in his *Heroides*, isolating her sympathetic voice from Virgil's controlling narrative and encouraging identification with this prime Virgilian victim.[11]

Marlowe's adaptation is similarly counter-Virgilian. He transforms Virgil's episode fully into tragedy, the genre with which it self-consciously aligned itself, removing like Ovid the epic framework justifying Aeneas' desertion. Where Ovid's Dido doubts Aeneas' report that the gods commanded him to leave, however, Marlowe's treatment of Virgil's supernatural justification is different, though no less undermining. Marlowe's tragedy is interspersed with scenes populated wholly by gods, diminishing Aeneas' responsibility just as Virgil had done; yet they are stripped of their Virgilian dignity. The play was written for pre-pubescent boy actors, surely exacerbating the effect of Marlowe's irreverent portrayal: one remembers Shakespeare's Cleopatra (in a play influenced by this one) choosing suicide rather than 'see / Some squeaking Cleopatra boy my greatness / I' the posture of a whore' (*Antony and Cleopatra*, V.ii.218–20). Marlowe's play opens to 'discover' (a diminutive) Jupiter '*dandling* GANIMED *upon his knee*' – the boy whom, in a story that delighted Marlowe and Ovid, an enamoured Jupiter ravished to heaven in the shape of an eagle. Jupiter's jealous wife Juno has struck Ganymede, and Jupiter pleads with him to return his favours, promising to humiliate all the gods 'to make thee laughing sport' (I.i.32). He also promises rich gifts, decking Ganimede in jewels that were Jupiter's wedding gift to Juno. Their exchange ends with the calculating Ganimede begging more jewels, 'And then Ile hugge with you an hundred times', to which Jupiter replies 'And shall have *Ganymed*, if thou wilt be my love' (I.i.48–9), the whole exchange echoing Marlowe's lyric 'The Passionate Shepherd to His Love', which itself draws on the comically blustering serenade of Ovid's Polyphemus to the uninterested nymph Galatea in the *Metamorphoses*. The scene anticipates the drama, as Dido dandling Cupid disguised as Ascanius on her lap recalls our opening vision of Jove. Marlowe Ovidianises Virgil's gods, presenting them as foolish and driven by their desires, as they appear in Ovid's *Metamorphoses*. Aeneas too is diminished. For instance, where Virgil has Aeneas present gifts to Dido (I.647–55), Marlowe reverses the direction of the gift (II.i.80), encapsulating his emphasis on shipwrecked Aeneas' beggarly status and dependence on the munificent queen. He also expands Virgil's minor characters, Dido's disappointed suitor Iarbus and her sister Anna (in love with Iarbus in Marlowe): their suicides cap Dido's at the end of the play. Though incorporating much direct translation, Marlowe inverts the significance of Virgil's episode, amplifying Dido's tragedy and undermining the values to which she is sacrificed in the *Aeneid*.

Lucan

Hostility to Virgil's imperial project is also a fundamental trait in the classical work that elicited Marlowe's most brilliant translation, Book I of Lucan's *Pharsalia*. Here, Marlowe allows himself the freedom of what Dryden would call 'metaphrasis', often paraphrasing the original to achieve an exhilaratingly vigorous translation, very different from the tame literalism of his *Amores*. In doing so, Marlowe ends up paradoxically closer to his original, conveying much of Lucan's mood: the passion, irony, and rhetorical brilliance of the two poets were evidently akin. What Jonson would call 'Marlowe's mighty line' operates here at full force.

Lucan's poem is fiercely anti-Caesarian. In many ways, it subverts the imperialist agenda identified with epic since Virgil's *Aeneid*. Whatever nuances have been found by critics, the *Aeneid* presents history as teleologically driven by divine providence towards the foundation of Rome and ultimately Augustus' rule – a glorious end justifying sacrifices made en route. The overarching unity of this design is matched both by the singularity of rule prophesied under Augustus and by the singular Aeneas, the poem's hero and saviour of his escaped Trojans. Lucan omits Virgil's vision of divine providence: no gods are present or intervene in the unremitting slaughter and human tragedy that form his subject. Instead of looking forwards, Lucan's poem looks back to a lost republican past, the present offering only hopeless suffering, confusion, and fragmentation. Virgil's one hero is replaced by at least two antiheroes. Though Caesar's ambition and cruelty make him evidently a dangerous villain to be resisted, the forces ranked against him are far from unambiguous: the aged Pompey is a mere shadow of his great name, having exchanged military might for idle popularity, and his Stoic supporter Cato, who takes over as leader when Pompey is murdered after Pharsalia, is not only unattractively *durus* (rigid or hard; II.380), but opposes Caesar largely because he fears that Pompey too, if left to his own devices, would become a tyrant.

The pessimism that presides over Lucan's poem has made some modern commentators see it as an epic without a cause. Yet, though the overweening ambition of Caesar evidently exerts a fascination over the poet, Lucan frequently condemns him as a villain. Central to Lucan's poem, moreover, is the notion that the republican cause transcends hero-worship. After Pompey's flight, the Battle of Pharsalus continues, purified now from any taint of mere personal loyalty to Pompey: the struggle is now between Liberty and Caesar (VII.696).

Both the fascination and the villainy of Lucan's Caesar obviously made a deep impression on Marlowe, several of whose stage-villains and ambiguous heroes are indebted to him. In his ruthless rise to world-domination, Tamburlaine sweeps the principle of hereditary monarchy aside as carelessly as Caesar did Roman republicanism. Tamburlaine explicitly compares his triumph over Bajazeth to Caesar's at Pharsalia (*1 Tamburlaine*, III.iii.152–5); Machiavel and the Guise also compare themselves to Lucan's antihero.[12]

A passage often cited by those who contest the *Pharsalia*'s republicanism is the encomium to Nero near the beginning of Book I, the authorial voice here directly addressing the poem's dedicatee:

> Yet *Room* is much bound to these civil armes,
> Which made thee Emperor, thee (seeing thou being old
> Must shine a star) shal heaven (whom thou lovest,)
> Receive with shouts: where thou wilt raigne as King,
> Or mount the sunnes flame bearing charriot,
> And with bright restles fire compasse the earth.
>
> (44–9, in Marlowe's translation)

Taken 'straight' and out of context, this passage would argue fidelity to the emperor. But, though making it difficult for Nero to punish the author for his outspokenly republican poem, this fulsome praise, as Renaissance commentators realised, 'is meere Ironicall flattery'.[13] Lucan began by cataloguing the horrors of the civil war, but then he proclaims that Rome must be grateful for them, because they led to Nero's reign! The note of lament at tragic suffering is constant throughout the poem; through this dedication Lucan lays it all at Nero's door, also twisting the conventional apotheosis of the ruler into an absurd reference to Nero's weight-problem: the passage continues by asking the bulky emperor to station himself in the middle of the heavens rather than off-centre, lest the whole cosmos collapse. Marlowe's use of parentheses arguably highlights the tongue-in-cheek tone of this passage, isolating subordinate clauses as though they were 'asides', implying a dramatic irony separating the addressee gulled by the encomium from the reader who recognises its ironical intent.

Marlowe dilutes Lucan's republicanism, however. Near the end of *Lucan's First Book*, Figulus' prophecy climaxes

> What boots it then the *Gods* to pray,
> This misery to turne away?
> For peace againe we shall not haue,
> Till all become a Tyrants slaue.[14]

This is the translation of Arthur Gorges, the first to put the entire *Pharsalia* into English: his octosyllabic couplets may sound inappropriately sing-song beside Marlowe's resounding pentameters, but in these lines, as often, he is much closer to the Latin sense. Marlowe, by contrast, produces here the paradoxical 'Many a yeare these furious broiles let last, / Why should we wish the gods should ever end them? / War only gives us peace' (667–9 in Marlowe's translation). Omitting all reference to a tyrant, he seems motivated only by some sense of Rome's innate militarism, as if

Romans will somehow enjoy the civil war. With less said for republicanism as a positive good, Marlowe's poem seems more nihilistic than Lucan's.

But if Marlowe dilutes the politics, he introduces his own rhetorical effects to further Lucan's more general ends. For instance, Lucan's theme of fragmentation is pointed up in Marlowe's recurrent use of the words 'share' and 'shiver'. Lucan's simple apostrophe at lines 85–6 to Rome *facta tribus dominis communis* ('When thou wert first made slave to three', in Gorges' translation), Marlowe translates compellingly as 'Thy selfe thus shivered out to three mens shares' (85), the idea of fragmentation implicit in the English 'share' – a cognate of *shear* – emphasised by alliteration with 'shivered'. A few lines later, Lucan asks what availed the triumvirate before the war to unite their strength and hold the world in common, but Marlowe translates with an ominous echo of the earlier line, 'Why joine you force to share the world betwixt you?' (88) The initial combination of strength to which Lucan refers here merges into the opposition that ensued, the submerged meaning of 'share' importing the image of their cutting up the world. This idea is certainly present in Lucan's *dividitur ferro regnum* at line 109. Marlowe's translation gains force by echoing his earlier lines in the emphatic 'Swords *share* our kingdom' (109), where the previously submerged meaning 'cut' is now foremost. Marlowe finally assigns responsibility when he translates the end of Lucan's great lightning simile describing Caesar, 'Falls, and returnes, and *shivers* where it lights'.

Sadly, Marlowe translates only Book I of Lucan's (unfinished) ten-book epic: the task of translating the whole poem was left to Gorges. Yet what we have feels complete. Book I ends with a prophecy of the terrible events to follow, foreshadowing the rest of the poem. Lucan was particularly relevant to England when Marlowe was writing. It must have felt as though the peace of the Tudor dynasty, threatened by the great Catholic powers of Europe, could be almost over, and England might be plunged again into the horrors of civil war that preceded it. Marlowe's single book warns England of a possible but still uncertain outcome. The closing prophecy ends 'o *Phoebus* shew me *Neptunes* shore / And other regions, I have seene *Philippi*' (692–3). (Roman poets habitually talked of the Battle of Pharsalus in 48 BC, where Pompey's troops were defeated, and the Battle of Philippi in 42 BC, where Octavius and Antony defeated Julius Caesar's assassins, as fought on the same ground.) The despairing sense of impending cyclicity speaks directly to later readers on the brink of war.

Classical translation and adaptation were no dry scholarly exercise in Marlowe's hands. Displaying a demystifying and irreverent counter-classical urge throughout his work, Marlowe's Ovidian eroticism and Lucanian violence hit out at contemporary culture with topical and iconoclastic force.

Notes

1. Ben Jonson, *Poetaster*, ed. Tom Cain (Manchester University Press, 1995), I.i.1–3.
2. Ian Donaldson, *Jonson's Magic Houses* (Oxford University Press, 1997), 206.
3. Christopher Marlowe, translation of Ovid, *Amores*, I.xv.41–2. Quotations are from Christopher Marlowe, *The Complete Works of Christopher Marlowe*, 5 vols., Vol. I, ed. Roma Gill (Oxford: Clarendon Press, 1987).
4. Jonson, *Poetaster*, 23; Philip Hardie, *Ovid's Poetics of Illusion* (Cambridge University Press, 2002), 105.
5. Christopher Marlowe, *Christopher Marlowe: The Complete Poems and Translations*, ed. Stephen Orgel (Harmondsworth: Penguin, 1971), 233.
6. Christopher Marlowe, *The Collected Poems of Christopher Marlowe*, ed. Patrick Cheney and Brian J. Striar (Oxford University Press, 2006), 27.
7. Patrick Cheney, *Marlowe's Counterfeit Profession: Ovid, Spenser, Counter-Nationhood* (University of Toronto Press, 1997).
8. Richard McCabe, 'Elizabethan Censorship and the Bishops' Ban of 1599', *The Yearbook of English Studies* 11 (1981): 188–93.
9. Epigrammes and Elegies by *I.D.* and *C.M.* (Middleborough, 1599), C2v.
10. Elaine Fantham, 'Virgil's Dido and Seneca's Tragic Heroines', *Greece & Rome* 22 (1975): 1–10.
11. On Renaissance treatments, see Craig Kallendorf, *The Other Virgil: 'Pessimistic' Readings of the* Aeneid *in Early Modern Culture* (Oxford University Press, 2007); and John Watkins, *The Specter of Dido: Spenser and Virgilian Epic* (New Haven: Yale University Press, 1995).
12. Christopher Marlowe, *The Jew of Malta* (Pro., 18–22); *The Massacre at Paris* (ii.95–6). See William Blissett, 'Lucan's Caesar and the Elizabethan Villain', *Studies in Philology* 53 (1956): 553–75.
13. Arthur Gorges, *Lucans Pharsalia* (1614), 4.
14. *Ibid.*, 40.

CHAPTER NINE

Marlowe's medievalism

Chris Chism

This chapter explores the following question, which has a double answer. What would you call a dramatic protagonist, who is struggling in a world of hostile sovereign powers and banal profiteers, who knows with absolute and enabling certainty that he is actually a god and in that knowledge throws himself against his world until it destroys him? Answer A: Tamburlaine, Faustus, Guise, Barabas, and various other overreaching protagonists from Marlowe's plays. Answer B: The many Christs of the medieval civic cycle passion sequences.

There is a sizable gap between the registers in which scholars have been taught to think of the characters in propositions A and B and the dramatic genres those characters represent. Marlowe's plays, inaugurating the 'mature' period of Tudor drama, have capped many genealogies from university classicism, Catholic theology, the medieval morality plays and their Tudor descendants,[1] and Italian drama and other Continental plays. David Bevington's groundbreaking study, *From 'Mankind' to Marlowe*, traces a practical genealogy of staging practices, troupe composition, and dramatic structure, between the fifteenth-century so-called morality plays, through sixteenth-century Tudor drama to the late-sixteenth-century advent of the professional theatre. In so doing, Bevington usefully undermines the mythical rift separating (and creating) the 'Monkish Darkness' of pre-Reform cultural production and the apparent cultural regenerations of the sixteenth and seventeenth centuries.[2] Marlowe's plays (and later Shakespeare's) have become instrumental in the construction of the Renaissance. What happens, however, when we view Marlowe's plays as Janus-faced, invested in recollecting and redirecting specifically dramatic medievalisms in order to capitalise on new modes of dramatic production? What happens if we resist false dichotomies between sacred and secular histories and temporalities that place the 'medieval' imagination overwhelmingly in the sacred realm and the 'renaissance' imagination at the fountainhead of a secular culture, oversimplifying both in the process?[3]

One aspect of Marlowe's medievalism has been understudied, an emotional and affective one that hinges on the dramatic power of transecting the human and the divine – a power that both the cycle dramas and Marlowe's plays exploit. Marlowe adapts the cycle dramas' ethical juxtaposition of divine and fallibly human forms of sovereignty when he creates characters who imagine themselves as gods, only to punish them through tragic falls. However, he also diverges from the cycle dramas' dramaturgies of audience involvement, by mobilising a more distant, spectacularised relationship to audiences and a more poetic form of writing – strategies capitalising upon the sixteenth-century development of permanent and professional theatres and the post-reform censorship of biblical drama, which impelled dramatists to draw from literary and historiographical sources and fed the growth of literary and secular theatre.

Constellating Marlowe to the public, historical civic cycle dramas rather than to the moralities casts light on Marlowe's power as national playwright, consciously addressing the fragile and venturesome network of English imperial outreach and the larger, stranger worlds within which such claims were staked.[4] The civic cycle plays have a similarly dizzying scope and reach, extending over the span of biblical history and human ethical agency and addressing a range of social structures and institutions, from the family, to Church, to monarchy, to the geographical mapping of regional politics. And, like Marlowe's plays, the civic cycle plays traffic in the familiar and the strange, whether anachronistically transplanting explicitly English regional divisions into the pastures of the Holy Land (the Wakefield Second Shepherds' pageant) or playing the ecclesiastical/legal/monarchical rivalries of occupied Judea in an implicitly late medieval key (the York Trial and Passion pageants). The civic cycle dramas involved audiences in dramaturgies that remained so ethically and affectively involving that the plays endured for two centuries and well into reform, despite their enormous cost, the continually shifting rosters of participating cities and guilds, and their connection with a censored Catholic past.

Marlowe need not have personally seen civic cycle plays in order to reconfigure the passional spectacle at their heart, the story of the incarnation, trial, execution, and resurrection of a human god, which after 200 years of sustained performances had sunk deeply into English cultural memory – though it is difficult to miss one of the wilder staging effects of a Last Judgement play echoing in Faustus' cry: 'See see where Christs bloud streames in the firmament!'[5] Moreover, the cycle dramas were current event as well as cultural memory; Marlowe's lifetime coincides with the controversies of their surveillance, suppression, and Protestant cooptation in the last third of the sixteenth century. Their demise was not the surrender of an obsolescent form; cities and parish guilds fought it bitterly.[6] They were suppressed at York after 1569, at Wakefield in 1576, and at Chester in 1575, where Protestant and Catholic citizens contested over their production. Farther south at Coventry, about sixty miles from Oxford, the plays were cancelled for the year 1575 and then reinstated, only to be suppressed altogether in 1580 and then replayed once in 1584.[7] As late as 1591, the Commons of the city were pleading for their reinstatement.[8] Thus, well into Marlowe's lifetime cycle dramas were a divisive regional civic issue, an opportunity for both Protestant and Catholic empire-building.[9] Marlowe would have known of them, and he was nothing if not attentive to the kinds of controversies they sparked.

The civic cycles were dangerous to Tudor censors not only because the plays were associated with a Catholic past but also because they juxtaposed human and divine forms of power to implicate sovereign institutions in the societies that those institutions served. In both the civic cycle dramas and in Marlowe's plays sovereignty is a locus for inciting desire and fear in pleasurably aestheticised forms. However, dramatic sovereigns interpellate and involve audiences differently across the complex cascade of effects consequent upon Reform, the nationalisation of the English Church, and the professionalisation of theatres.[10] Overall, the cycle dramas exploit second-person confrontational modes of address, while Marlowe's plays capitalise on third-person spectacle. For instance, the first part of the East Anglian cycle called the N-Town Passion Play opens with an address by Lucifer himself, who comes out in the guise of a court gallant to address his subjects, the audience, as his own people:

> I am your lord Lucifer, that out of helle cam,
> Prince of this wer[l]d and gret Duke of Helle –
> …
> Gyff me youre love! Grawnt me myn affeccyon,
> And I wyl unclose the tresour of lovys alyawns [love's alliance]!
> And giff yow youre desirys, afftere your intencion.[11]

This opening address gives us a seductive Lucifer who approaches the audience as a recognisable social figure, a court schemer, and as a consummate and self-aware actor letting us in on his game: he instructs the audience to admire 'the divercité of [his] disgisyd variauns' (65). Spotlighting his double theatricality as an actor playing an actor, he follows with a twenty-two-line blazon on his exquisitely fashionable costume from his 'long pekyd schon' (69) to his 'hey small bonet' (87). He then capitalises on the contagious erosion of ethics that his duplicity can precipitate, transforming the Seven Deadly Sins into social virtues by giving them new linguistic costumes: Pride becomes Honesty, Lechery becomes Natural Begetting, Covetousness Husbandry, Wrath Manhood, and so on.[12] As both courtier and actor Lucifer thus implicates not only the hypocrisy by which the rich and the courtly at once exploit and disdain the poor, but also the ethical legerdemain by which we transform our socially and morally corrosive faults into social and moral strengths. In this speech, Lucifer conjures the audience as demonic familiars in at least three senses of the word: we are related; we are of Lucifer's intimate council; we are possessed. His last words to the audience before exiting insinuate an allegory-shattering intimacy: 'I am with yow at all times whan ye to councel me call, / But for a short time myself I devoide' (123–4). He leaves the stage but he does not leave the audience, because we, now and constantly, are invoking *him*. There is no disentangling moral dilemma from social behaviour in this intimate performativity.

Audiences are implicated very differently by the seduction and threat of sovereignty in Marlowe's plays. Marlowe takes medieval spectacles of intimate power and distances them in order to grip audiences through the power of spectacle itself. *1 Tamburlaine* was Marlowe's first London play and so had to be doubly arresting to win over an indifferent audience. From its flagrant poetry to its passionate staging of the beauties of power, *Tamburlaine* foregrounds its own aesthetic capacity to overpower and seduce audiences. The minute the short prologue begins, the play's own *superbia* is apparent:

> From jygging vaines of riming mother wits,
> And such conceits as clownage keepes in pay,
> Weele leade you to the stately tent of War:
> Where you shall heare the Scythian Tamburlaine,
> Threatning the world with high astounding tearms
> And scourging kingdoms with his conquering sword.
> View but his picture in this tragicke glasse,
> And then applaud his fortunes as you please.[13]
> (Pro., 1–8)

This prologue takes a familiar figure – the fierce sovereign who 'threat[ens] the world with high astounding terms': the blustering Herod, Pilate, and Caesar – and places it in a very different relationship to the audience. The world is on stage, not for the first time, but here it is a world from which the audience is separated.[14] The stage becomes a 'tragicke glasse' into which the audience gazes to see the threatening sovereign in the display of his power, but rather than being positioned either as seduced familiar or threatened victim, the audience becomes a wilful consumer, leisured and pleasured by the now-distanced spectacle of the play. But that interpellation of distracted appraisal is a dare. It is the ground for the seduction of the audience, not by a particular character but by the play itself. The very freedom the audience is given to appraise the play energises the play as an agent provocateur that must spectacularly incite and seize across the gap it has created. This flair creates not only the play but the idea of its writer as author and animates the composite creature called Marlowe that has been situated as its source. Having conjured its author, *Tamburlaine* then proceeds to create a world in which the audience can trace the very processes of force and theatrical seduction that its prologue had invoked, poetically alluring the audience by showing the enticement of characters. It is no accident that after an opening scene excoriating the ineffective lordship of King Mycetes, Tamburlaine himself strides onto the stage and immediately begins to attract followers. His first seduction – of Zenocrate, his future queen – is perfunctory and unconvincing; its political motives remain transparent, and it is no wonder that Zenocrate resists. However, a much more effective seduction follows, that of Mycetes' captain, Theridamas, beguiled to Tamburlaine's side by a gorgeous speech that joins power with poetry, culminating in the appeal: 'May we become immortall like the Gods' (1.ii.201). This scene makes sovereign outrageousness into a form of masculine social bonding, an alliance that is not only political but amorous – and gambles on drawing in not only Theridamas, who is enchanted, but also the audience.

However, when Marlowe distances *Tamburlaine* into the past and recreates it as a 'tragicke glasse' for the audience, he both gains and loses a source of dramatic power. Tamburlaine's spectacle can become imaginatively larger in scope because now it can opportunistically forget or recall its locality and contiguity to the present world of its audience. It can capitalise on its distance from them to create the diegetic world as a historical panorama. Diegetic timespan and geographical distance can be at once logically ordered and fiercely compressed. And because the play must now threaten and seduce its audience by proxy, using diegetic characters like Theridamas, rather than using direct address in a shared present, it has to hone its techniques – dramaturgical, affective, narrative, and stylistic, to arresting new levels of virtuosity. At the same, time, however, the play becomes past rather than present to its audience and it loses the capacity to provoke audiences through the proximity of a shared temporality.

By contrast, the civic cycle dramas had operated very differently, using techniques of dramatic expansion and temporal intimacy. They took spectators from Creation to Judgement Day over several days and across numerous civic playing spaces. They broke the Bible into dramatic segments, allowed many actors to play Christ or Mary simultaneously or consecutively, and redressed the inevitability of the audience missing crucial sequences by yearly repetition. The N-Town Passion Play's two parts were so elaborate that they were probably played in alternate years; Christ would be condemned one year but crucified in the next. The parts could also be abstracted from the cycle to become a single enormous Passion play, as could the Mary Play whose pageants nest around the Passion sequence like a romance emboîtement. Thus the civic cycle plays were adaptably enmeshed in larger rhythms of diurnal, seasonal, and liturgical civic commemorations, working simultaneously to stabilise and allow innovation in the city's image of itself.[15] They became part of the ongoing chronotope that cities created for themselves: to bring honour to the city by showcasing and individuating its guilds of merchants and artisans who produced the plays. The plays also became opportunities for challenges to orderly configurations, for seizing upon the tensions between the capitalising merchants and the producing artisans, among the citizens of the city, its disenfranchised, and the visitors who were both necessary and threatening to its ongoing prosperity.[16]

Civic cycle plays routinely disdain historic distance in order to position the audience as partner in a shared temporality that uses anachronism for ethical provocation. For instance, the N-Town Passion II begins with Herod threatening the external audience to shut up and allow the play to proceed, but then he transitions seamlessly into a diatribe against Christ's followers within the diegesis:

> Not o word, I charge you that ben here present;
> Noon so hardy to presume, in my hey presence,
> To onlose hese lippys ageyn myn intent!
> I am Herowde, of Jewys kyng most reverent,
> The lawys of Mahownde my powere shal fortefye ...
> To kylle a thowsand Chrysten, I gyf not an hawe
> To se hem hangyn or brent. To me is very plesauns
> To dryven hem into doongenys, dragonys to knawe,
> And to rend here flesche and bonys, onto here sustenauns!
> (N-Town Passion II, 21–5, 33–6)

The anachronism and threat here hinge upon the word 'Chrysten' – whereby the Christian audience of the play can imaginatively join hands with the pre-ecclesiastical followers of Christ within the play, under the pressure of Herod's verbal violence. This anachronism does necessary work. It implicates the Christian audience at this moment as followers of a criminal 'Chrystyns' in the face of a threatening sovereignty. Over the course of the cycle, this sovereign threat will proliferate, implicating social institutions of the monarchy (Herod), the nobility (Lucifer), the Church (Caiaphas and Annas), and the law (Pilate). By aligning the audience as criminal 'Christyns' the play invites them to occupy a series of alienated standpoints from which they can criticise the sovereign institutions whose actions of threat and seduction, limitation and pressure, right of death and power over life configure the everyday social experience of the audience. By staying in the now of the audience the play performatively recreates a Christian community that can think itself as a resistance movement. The performance of civic cycle dramas, other civic pageants, and associated feast days such as Corpus Christi are sporadically associated with riots and regional uprisings throughout the period.[17]

In order to underscore this shared temporality and inscribe the plays within the common time shared by players and audience across the performance, the N-Town plays revolve around the paradox of the Incarnation, a divine being who embodies himself in a human body in order to recuperate the human. This corporealising and making present of God doubles and can be exploited by the theatrical paradoxes involved in playing itself: the representing of something brought into being by and across the performance in the now of the audience. Thus the civic cycle dramas capitalise on the perplexed mimesis of a double incarnation, God to human Christ, human actor to divine role, whose doubleness places the spectacle of Christ in a theatrically uncanny and present relationship to its audience rather than in an institutionally privileged and past one.[18]

This double and temporally intimate role provides a launch-pad both for ethical inquiry and aesthetic power. The ethical provocation of the audience becomes most severe during the Passion sequences at the heart of the cycles. Across multiple plays we see many human Christs deliberately cut off from their own divine power and at the mercy of the sovereign powers – monarchical, imperial, legal, and ecclesiastical – of the contemporary, and anachronistic, social world. The multiple trial and judgement plays radically objectify their many Christs as passive material to be arraigned and abjected by all-too familiar regimes, while simultaneously intimating that Christ is the most important being in Creation. The torture, scourging, and crucifixion plays situate the audience as the crowd that gathers to consume the spectacle of punishment, using the passivity enforced by the role of audience itself to raise the ethical stakes of ignoring, enjoying, and justifying the ill treatment of peasants, criminals, sorcerers, and heretics: the positions Christ occupies in the plays. This guilty implication of the audience is brilliantly clear in the York Crucifixion Play, which renders the death of Christ uncomfortably familiar to its audience by making that death a routine construction project. The play reduces a pivotal moment in Christian history to the casual brutality of working men, struggling with recalcitrant materials – wood, nails, wedges, a body, a god – to get a job done. The civic cycle dramas' segmentation of the story of a state execution into multiple plays intensifies the intimacy of this history by serialising it into a continuous present, all closure provisional. The necessary interpolation of the everyday time of the city between pageant segments, as audiences move to or wait for the next pageant, also intensifies the vulnerability of these multiple human Christs by separating them from the diegetic vindications of resurrection, harrowing, and ascension. These plays invest their Christs with a sense of enormous bated power by dramatising the martyr as a singular stillness at the centre of a vortex of hostile, inventive, increasingly frantic sovereign enemies. Across the plays, each of Christ's judges and executioners provokes Christ to break his silence, to express himself, to implicate himself – and he doesn't. That refusal of expression not only displays the Christ character's power of resistance, but it also invites the audience to project their own emotions into a space opened for general consumption by that very withdrawal of expression. The Christ of a Passion play doesn't feel *at* his audience – rather he adjures them to feel *for* him.[19]

Where the civic cycle dramas are riveted by the affective spectacle of absolute divinity diminished to mortality, many of Marlowe's plays find an equal fascination in the spectacle of a humanity that dares to seize upon the divine, leaping at a freedom beyond social and institutional boundaries – and failing. The spectacle of a divinely exalted human who falls remembers and inverts that of a humbled god who rises. Faustus' blitzkrieg through the human sciences telescopes all merely mortal intellectual labour into ant-hill insignificance in order to grasp at magical sublimations that retransect Eucharistic, alchemical, and humanist relationships between flesh and spirit. He spurns 'divinitie' as a human science for a reincarnation as a semi-divine being: 'that Faustus may be a spirit in forme and substance' (II.i. 485). This reverse transubstantiation of body into spirit divides Faustus' body from his intent, inducing his very blood to rebel against his will and eventuating in the comic and tragic scenes of dismemberment and disintegration in which both A- and B-texts culminate. In *The Jew of Malta* Barabas excommunicates his oppressors as though he were God (I.ii.166) and dedicates himself to their ruin in the unbreakable certainty that he 'is borne to better chance, / And fram'd of finer mold then common men, / That measure nought but by the present time' (I.ii.218–20); his sense of privilege spurs him not towards apotheosis but rather towards a self-delighting diabolism. In *The Massacre at Paris* Guise makes peril his road to happiness in an explosion of ambition so extraordinary that it can only claim divinely incarnational origins: 'For this, hath heaven engendred me of earth' (ii.113).[20] In the speech seducing Theridamas, Tamburlaine stages an apotheosis by conquest that uses Roman paradigms rather than biblical ones, but it bears remembering that Jove was not the only divine being who started life among shepherds to ascend to heaven – a favourite trope in nativity plays. Very particularly Marlowe is not simply referencing paradigms of Catholic theology, but also drawing upon powerful theatrical tropes that had incited two centuries of performed soteriology – the study of salvation – in the civic cycle plays.

The extraordinary energy yielded from Marlowe's plays' seizure of past forms comes from the satisfaction of twisting at their central tensions. Like the civic cycle passion sequences, which make Christ an outsider and victim in the face of violent regimes, Marlowe highlights outsiders, the strangers whose daring and ambition are outrageous enough to attempt to transcend the scholastic, imperial, and social boundaries of their day. Yet instead of the uncanny passivity of the Christs in the cycle dramas, we get a new but equally heart-wrenching crux of the divine and the human – a figure who fights back against the powerful of his world.

In each of Marlowe's plays, this struggle ultimately becomes more gripping than all the flashpoints of divine bravura – because it is doomed to fail. In this way, Marlowe's plays at once remember the helpless Christ of the cycle dramas and move him beyond recuperation and resurrection, towards tragedy. *Edward II* in particular centralises human vulnerability; the play appeals to audiences through the dynamisms of unfolding characters whose devolutions they can witness, as in a 'tragicke mirror', in a range of eloquent and aesthetically gripping self-expressions. Its hero operates as a kind of martyr to a world of courtly and baronial politics that refuses to accommodate his love. Marlowe foregrounds Edward's anger and resistance, his fierce dedication to his own desires, and his sorrow for the loss of his lovers. At the same time, however, Edward's tragedy, unlike the constantly re-*present*ed and immanent suffering of the Christs in the cycle dramas, operates most powerfully across a distance – through the hindsight of his miserable death. Ultimately Marlowe's medievalism operates most effectively by recreating the medieval – Edward II, Tamburlaine, Faustus, these fourteenth- and fifteenth-century kings, conquerors, and scholars – as most urgent when lost. Thus even as Marlowe innovates new forms of dramatic virtuosity and audience address, he conducts a form of *amour de loin* for the mortality of the medieval itself.

Because of this urgency in mortality, the falls of Marlowe's heroes ultimately extend similar ethical provocations to those implicit in the Passion plays. The civic cycle dramas are absolutely clear that Christ has to die: soteriology dictates it. But what they actually perform is a drama of human mercy that invites cynicism about institutional sovereignties and adjures sympathy for the outcast, the alien, and the criminal. By humanising and aestheticising power in its most aspirational campaigns and desperate devolutions, Marlowe captures a sense of possibility and social agency that undercuts tragic inevitability. He looks both forwards and backwards, building a theatre of Renaissance possibility by remembering and redirecting medieval dramaturgies of social critique and transformation.

Notes

1 David Bevington, *From 'Mankind' to Marlowe: Growth of Structure in the Popular Drama of Tudor England* (Cambridge, MA: Harvard University Press, 1962).
2 *Ibid.*, 2. See also Ruth Lunney, *Marlowe and the Popular Tradition: Innovation in the English Drama before 1595* (Manchester University Press, 2002), 186.
3 For a survey of medieval popular drama based on secular romance, historical, and classical themes, see Lynette R. Muir, *Love and Conflict in Medieval Drama: The Plays and Their Legacy* (Cambridge University Press, 2007), 79–201.
4 Emily Bartels, *Spectacles of Strangeness: Imperialism, Alienation, and Marlowe* (Philadelphia: University of Pennsylvania Press, 1993).
5 Christopher Marlowe, *Doctor Faustus* (A-text), V.ii.1939. Quotations from Marlowe are from *The Complete Works of Christopher Marlowe*, 2 vols., ed. Fredson Bowers, 2nd edn (Cambridge University Press, 1973, 1981) unless otherwise noted.
6 Sarah Beckwith, *Signifying God: Social Relation and Symbolic Act in the York Corpus Christi Cycle* (University of Chicago Press, 2001), 121–66.
7 Alexandra F. Johnston, 'Tudor Drama, Theater and Society', in *A Companion to Tudor Britain*, ed. Robert Tittler and Norman Jones (Oxford: Blackwell, 2009), 430–47.
8 Paul Whitfield White, 'Reforming Mysteries' End: A New Look at Protestant Intervention in English Provincial Drama', *The Journal of Medieval and Early Modern Studies* 29:1 (1999): 121–47 (139).

9 *Ibid.*; Beckwith, *Signifying God*, 121–60.
10 Sarah Beckwith, *Shakespeare and the Grammar of Forgiveness* (Ithaca, NY and London: Cornell University Press, 2011), 15–34.
11 *N-Town Passion II*, 1–2, 61–3. All quotations from the N-Town plays are from Douglas Sugano, ed., *The N-Town Plays*, TEAMS Middle English Texts Series (Kalamazoo: Medieval Institute Publications, 2008).
12 John Alford, '"My Name is Worship": Masquerading Vice in Medwall's *Nature*', in *From Page to Performance: Essays in Early English Drama*, ed. John A. Alford (East Lansing: Michigan University Press, 1995), 151–77.
13 See Lunney, *Marlowe*, 1–13.
14 Martin Stevens, 'From Mappa mundi to Theatrum mundi: The World as Stage in Early English Drama', in Alford, *From Page to Performance*, 25–49.
15 Beckwith, *Signifying God*, 42–55.
16 Mervyn James, 'Ritual, Drama, and the Social Body in the Late Medieval English Town', *Past and Present* 83 (1983): 3–29; Charles Phythian-Adams, *Desolation of a City: Coventry and the Urban Crisis of the Late Middle Ages* (Cambridge University Press, 1979).
17 James, 'Ritual', 28–9. Beckwith, *Signifying God*, 42–58.
18 Beckwith, *Signifying God*, 59–71.
19 *Crucifixio Christi*, line 256, in *The York Corpus Christi Plays*, ed. Clifford Davidson, TEAMS Middle English Texts Series (Kalamazoo: Medieval Institute Publications, 2011).
20 Christopher Marlowe, *The Complete Works of Christopher Marlowe*, ed. Roma Gill (Oxford: Clarendon Press; New York: Oxford University Press, 1987).

CHAPTER TEN

Marlowe's libraries: a history of reading

Elizabeth Spiller

In the early modern period, numbers and availability of printed books increased exponentially, and reading became a newly important activity. Indeed, the greatest 'invention' of the Renaissance was arguably not so much the printing press itself but the multiple and competing forms of reading that developed around it. In the *sola scriptura* tradition, reading was often a pathway to salvation, but in ways that differed from the contemplative medieval model of *lectio divina*. For humanists, reading was at the heart of the imitation and creation of virtue, while Galenic medicine made it clear that reading stimulated the passions and could not be separated from the humoral balance of a healthy body. Yet, there were others who wondered at the risks that such power implied. Were books not an instrument of the devil? Was reading not the way to hell?

These are questions one might well ask of Christopher Marlowe's *Doctor Faustus*. *Doctor Faustus* is a play about books. The 1592 edition of the English *Faust-Book* that forms the key source text for Marlowe's play introduces its readers to a character who 'applied not his studies, but toke himself to other exercise'.[1] Marlowe's play instead gives us a man who loses his way because he has read too many books, not too few: the opening Chorus's 'this the man that in his study sits' provides our first and defining introduction to Faustus.[2] Much of the action of the play takes place in Faustus' study, and books often become the props that move forward the dramatic action. In the opening scene, Faustus' turn away from the traditional areas of scholastic education (rhetoric, physic, jurisprudence, and theology) is figured in the physical act of taking up and discarding volumes of the works of Aristotle, Galen, Justinian, and Jerome, before turning to a fifth book, this one filled with the 'lines, circles, signs, letters, and characters' of a more devilish book, an illicit book of necromancy (1.i.53).

From this scene forward, books are everywhere. As Paul Budra notes, '*Doctor Faustus* is as much about books – the physical objects – as knowledge and its use. More than any other English drama of the sixteenth century, *Doctor Faustus* revolves around the text, the reader's manipulation of it, and its manipulation of the reader.'[3] Valdes and Cornelius promise Faustus that 'these books' will enable him to acquire the power he seeks (I.i.121). They initially enjoin him to bring various books – works by the medieval natural magicians and philosophers Roger Bacon and Petrus Albanus, the Hebrew Psalter, the New Testament, and 'whatsoever else is requisite' (I.i.158) – to begin his conjurations. Both Mephistopheles and Lucifer give Faustus strange and powerful books to add to his library, while the comic subplot turns on the illiterate Robin's theft of one of Faustus' conjuring books. Books are a source of desire and temptation: Faustus dreams not just of having books that might allow him to know everything, but indeed of having spirits who might 'read me strange philosophy / And tell the secrets of all foreign kings' (I.i.88–9). In *Faustus*, the sin of *invidia* is a bookish one: as the Envy that Faustus sees makes clear, she 'cannot read, and therefore wish all books were burnt' (II.iii.128). Faustus begins as a reader of books. By the end, Faustus comes to wish that he had 'never read book' (V.ii.19) and, vainly, hopes to make one final deal with the devil, offering to burn his books if only he might avoid the hell he sees coming (V.ii.115).

In *Doctor Faustus*, books often seem to be instruments of the devil, and libraries perhaps hard to distinguish from hell itself. Indeed, it is probably not a coincidence that Mephistopheles is in Faustus' study when he insists that 'this is hell, nor am I out of it' (I.iii.77). Such conclusions might not have surprised many sixteenth- and seventeenth-century readers and audiences because, as Sarah Wall-Randell succinctly puts it, the early modern narrative of printing history 'begins with a man called Faust'.[4] Through one of those curious, but perhaps fated, misconstruals, the identity of Johann Fust, or Faust, who had been the partner of Johannes Gutenberg and a key figure in the invention of the printing press (who died *c*. 1466), became confused in the popular imagination with that of the necromancer Johann Georg Faustus (who was not born until about 1484). In stories that grew ever more detailed over time, the printing press became an instrument and invention of the devil. As Daniel Defoe notes in his history of great inventions and discoveries, early readers imagined that printed books were 'done by Magic and Witchcraft … [and that] poor Faustus (who was indeed nothing but a meer Printer) dealt with the Devil'.[5]

If the figure of Faustus was at the heart of what Elizabeth L. Eisenstein has characterised as one of the 'foundation myths' surrounding the invention of printing,[6] Marlowe's *Doctor Faustus* and its unusually detailed attention to books provides an opportunity to consider early modern reading practices and the consequences that they were understood to have on the minds, bodies, and souls of those who used them. It is certainly compelling to think about the books that Marlowe, or any other great writer, may have read and how those encounters may have shaped his dramatic imagination. Was there a now lost edition of the *Damnable Life* available as early as 1588? Did Marlowe read the copy of Holinshed's *Chronicles* in the Matthew Parker Library while he was at Corpus Christi? If Marlowe did indeed write *Tamburlaine* with a copy of Abraham Ortelius' 1570 *Theatrum orbis terrarum* open in front of him, where did he get this very expensive book? These are important questions, but here I am more concerned with taking *Doctor Faustus* as an occasion for thinking not so much about what Marlowe himself may have read but rather about what, for Marlowe and for *Faustus*, reading might mean and how it was understood to work. What does Faustus do with his books? And what do his books do to him?

In the opening scene, Faustus signals his intellectual malaise by ranging through the volumes in his library. He takes up, reads brief passages from, comments on, and then sets aside Aristotelian rhetoric textbooks, Galenic works on physic, the law books of Justinian, and the Bible itself. Faustus reads his Galen in the Greek, and, while he is sometimes accused of wilfully misreading and misconstruing the meanings of the texts he cites, he seems to know both the traditional scholastic interpretations of Aristotle and the new anti-Aristotelian rhetoric of Peter Ramus. The kinds of books and the range of interests represented in Faustus' study would not have been out of place in many early modern libraries. From December of 1578 until the time he matriculated at Corpus Christi College in 1580, Marlowe attended the King's School in Canterbury. The then headmaster, John Gresshop, had an extensive library – more than 350 volumes – which included many of the kinds of books that Marlowe imagines in Faustus' hands.[7]

Gresshop's upper study included copies of 'Aristoteles de arte rhetorica graece' and 'Aristoteles de mundo' as well as the pseudo-Aristotelian 'Problemata Arist'.[8] Gresshop's collection likewise encompassed key works on physic, including 'Galeni de compositione pharmacerum' (valued at eight pence) as well as an expensive compendium of 'Galenus de temperamentis cum aliis' (housed in the collection of folios in the lower study and valued at two shillings).[9] The Gresshop library did not have significant holdings in jurisprudence, but it included the Vulgate, the Geneva Bible, and an extensive collection of polemical theological works by Martin

Luther, Philip Melanchthon, Theodore Beza, Martin Bucer, and John Fisher, among others.

A library is more than a record of how one uses, values, and categorises information, or even knowledge. Rather, a library stands as a record of shared reading, both achieved and hoped for. Equally importantly, a library is also at least in part a material expression of a theory and practice of reading that is implied by the books on its shelves. Taken as an example of an early modern school library, the Gresshop library at the King's School embodies a commitment to several of the central reading practices that came to define the experiences of many sixteenth-century English readers.

The first of these was humanism. Renaissance humanism was committed to what Pico della Mirandola in 1486 saw as that which made man singular: his indifferent and indeterminate nature. The rest of God's creation was fixed in its essential being, but, 'with no limit and no bound … neither heavenly nor earthly, neither mortal nor immortal', man was responsible for making himself who and what he would be.[10] In sixteenth-century England, this humanist commitment expressed itself as an educational philosophy, an attitude towards texts, and several key practices of reading. Roger Ascham's *The Scholemaster* (1570) and the other works on humanistic pedagogy that Gresshop owned were expressions of commitment to a model of *imitatio* as a way of shaping the 'matter' of students. (Gresshop's octavo copy of Thomas More's *Utopia* expressed a similar impulse in fictional form.) Students began with basic grammar books and then moved on to the translation of carefully selected texts, and finally to composition itself.[11] Such imitative practices were designed not just to teach students to copy appropriate textual models but also to embody them. In this educational model, the purpose of reading a book like Xenophon's *Cyropaedia* was not so much to learn about Cyrus the Great but, through the imitative practice of reading an account of the *paedia*, or education, of Cyrus, to become him. As Philip Sidney puts it, such books serve 'not only to make a Cyrus, which had been but a particular excellency as nature might have done, but to bestow a Cyrus upon the world to make many Cyruses' of its would-be readers.[12]

Humanism encouraged reading practices that aligned with this educational philosophy. In searching for appropriate models of virtue, readers were expected to assemble books of commonplaces as they read.[13] Organised with headings such as 'prudence', 'temptation', or 'vanity', such texts stood as a kind of textual imagining of the kind of person a reader might hope to become or, equally, hope to avoid becoming. By dismantling and reassembling disparate texts, commonplace books encouraged readers to construct a life out of texts. In doing so, humanists developed active reading practices, often adding detailed *adversia* in the margins of the texts that they rewrote as they read. As William Sherman notes, humanist reading strategies were deeply engaged, and marginal *adversia* stand physically '"opposite" the text and sometimes in opposition to it'.[14] We cannot open Faustus' books or read his annotations, but we see a staging of the failure of those forms of reading in I.i. When Faustus picks up the Bible, begins reading and paraphrasing '"*Stipendium peccati mors est*." Ha! / "*Stipendium*", etc.', and concludes 'That's hard' (I.i.39–40, 41), Marlowe dramatises Faustus' 'adverse' relationship to the books of the Bible from which Faustus is culling and his utter failure to bring the appropriate lessons of these texts into conversation with one another in his life.

Faustus does not embody the reader that Renaissance humanism hoped to create. The book of Galen that Faustus tosses aside may give us one reason why. Galen's account of how the four elements were digested by the body into sustenance was the core of Renaissance medicine. Connecting the by-products of digestion to humoral imbalance and human passion, Galenism functioned as a powerful materialist psychology. Galenic medicine was also the basis for understanding how reading worked. Galen had assumed that the humoral balance of the body could be altered through a variety of external forces, the non-naturals, and Renaissance philosophers clearly regarded reading as one of those forces. In neo-Galenic accounts of how the 'faculties' of the brain worked, visual images entered the *sensus communis*, the warm and moist first ventricle of the brain. These images were then transferred to the central ventricle, the site of reason and imagination, and then from there to the third ventricle, cool and dry, to be stored for later use.[15] Sometimes, though, 'fancy' and 'fantasy' would overcome 'wit' (I.i.105, I.i.121). In these cases, the 'estimative faculty' of the second ventricle came to focus unduly on a particular image or text, drawing heat and moisture from the other parts of the brain and body.[16] It is this kind of condition that Faustus seems to suffer from as reader. He has been reading books of necromancy, and they have not been good for his brain. He thus complains that 'mine own fantasy, / That will receive no object, for my head / But ruminates on necromantic skill' (I.i.105–7). Having read the wrong books and for too long, Faustus is now unable to accept any new 'object' – any new sense impression – into his brain. He is arguably no longer able to bring his 'wit' to inform his reading and is in precisely the kind of physiological state that might cause him to imagine 'Lapland giants, trotting by our sides' and 'huge argosies' filled with gold

(I.i.128, 132). Whatever his earlier skills as a scholar, Faustus can no longer read properly.

Faustus sets aside his books, ready to turn to some new form of knowledge, in much the same way that bibliophiles ransacked the monastic libraries to create the great 'new' libraries of Renaissance England. One of the greatest of these was certainly the library that Archbishop Matthew Parker donated to Corpus Christi College in 1575, five years before Christopher Marlowe matriculated there.[17] Comprising nearly 600 books and manuscripts, the volumes in this remarkable library were largely collected by Parker and his agents during the dissolution of the monasteries. Since Parker and other Reformation book 'collectors' destroyed or discarded perhaps a thousand medieval books or manuscripts for every one they kept, the great English library collections built by men like Archbishop Parker, Sir Thomas Bodley, and Sir Robert Cotton were the realisation of carefully articulated principles of discrimination, a separating of the bibliographic wheat from the chaff. This same practice also became, as Jennifer Summit notes, the basis for a 'distinctive technology of reading', which made it possible to 'ransack' old books, separating dangerous theology from good history.[18]

As a reader, Faustus does not succeed in separating the good from the bad, the textual wheat from the chaff, in the way that Reformation bibliophiles suggested, any more than he embodies the imitative self-realisation of the Renaissance humanists. Even as the good angel implores Faustus to 'lay that damnèd book aside' (I.i.73), Faustus is wishing for spirits who might 'ransack' the globe to bring him gold, pearls, and yet new books of 'strange philosophy' (I.i.84, 88).

Faustus' great wish as a reader is not to acquire wisdom, virtue, or knowledge. What he 'most desires' from his books and studies is the 'world of profit and delight, / Of power, of honour, of omnipotence' that is 'promised to the studious artisan!' (I.i.55–6, 57). As he makes clear, the 'art' of reading is about the acquisition of power. The phrase 'studious artisan' is the key one here, for it provides us with the means to comprehend the two remarkable books that Mephistopheles and Lucifer give Faustus in the play's key temptation scenes.

In II.i, when Faustus asks for a wife, Mephistopheles diverts that desire by instead offering him a new book: 'Hold, take this book. Peruse it thoroughly' (II.i.157). In the comic give and take that follows, Faustus' desires for a whole library of new books are frustrated by Mephistopheles' repeated insistence that this one volume contains all he would want. Even as he asks for yet more books, Mephistopheles insists 'Here they be' (II.i.175).

Mephistopheles promises that this book will make it possible to control the elements, call up spirits, and comprehend the motions of the heavens and the plants of the earth (II.i.160–74). With this book, Faustus would thus become the 'studious artisan' he had imagined.

Mephistopheles' book is a dramatic expression of one of the great fantasies that came off the Renaissance printing press: the Book of Secrets. Descendants of the medieval pseudo-Aristotelian *Secretum secretorum*, Books of Secrets included such works as the German *Kunstbüchlein* (1530s), Alexis of Piedmont's *Secreti* (Venice, 1555), and Giambattista della Porta's *Magiae naturalis* (1588). Integrating a range of mechanical and artisanal practices (printing, dyeing, mining, alchemy, physic, cosmetics, and distilling, among others), the Books of Secrets were among the most popular and profitable products of sixteenth-century printing houses. They also made almost Satanic promises to their readers that through 'Art' one could control nature and, in so doing, acquire human power.[19]

'Artisanal' in nature, such books were inherently a rejection of both traditional scholastic learning and the new humanism. Perhaps equally tellingly, in terms of returning us to the devilry of printing, the Books of Secrets were intimately connected with the art of printing in both their form and their content. Yet, even here, Mephistopheles' Book of Secrets is not one we ever see Faustus reading, and it does not seem to be one that works. As most audiences and readers realise more quickly than Faustus himself does, Faustus is able to simulate 'lively' resemblances but cannot conjure 'true substantial bodies' (IV.1.44–8). With his book, Faustus does not gain the power to change nature in the ways that the *Secretum secretorum* had promised; he can only alter appearances.

In the original *Faust-Book*, Faustus is depicted as an epicurean whose temptation by the things of the flesh figures his theologically mistaken belief that there is no soul that survives the body. Marlowe eliminates both this component of the story and the theological arguments that go with it. Faustus, the epicure, becomes Faustus, the bibliophile, an ever covetous reader who believes the devil's promise of a book with which 'thou shalt turn thyself into what shape thou wilt' (II.iii.162–3). In doing so, Marlowe's *Doctor Faustus* rehearses a range of contemporary attitudes towards books and reading that give us some sense of the experiences of reading that were tempting early modern England. Was Faustus bad before he read, or did he become bad because he read? To some extent, Faustus is simply a bad reader, one who fails to understand and properly practise the right forms of reading. Through Faustus we can see both the appeal and the dangers to the reading practices advocated by humanist *imitatio*, the 'ransacking' of old books and libraries of the Reformation bibliophiles, and even the medical complications that Galenic medicine warned would-be readers against. Marlowe, himself very well read, certainly invokes the major claims that associated reading with the creation of virtue. Yet, in depicting Faustus as a bibliophile more strongly than his sources did, Marlowe also sets bibliophilia alongside gluttony, lust, and envy, making it the newest sin of the age of print. Finally, Marlowe refuses these questions in much the same way that he refuses any easy answer to the question of whether Faustus is reprobate, his name written to be read in *A Table of praedestination*, or whether he damns himself.

Notes

1 P[aul] F[airfax], trans., *The historie of the damnable life, and deserved death of Dr. John Faustus* (London, 1592), A2r. On the possibility of an earlier edition of the Fairfax translation, see R. J. Fehrenbach, 'A Pre-1592 English Faust Book and the Date of Marlowe's *Dr Faustus*', *The Library* 2:4 (2001): 327–35.
2 Christopher Marlowe, *Doctor Faustus and Other Plays*, ed. David Bevington and Eric Rasmussen (Oxford University Press, 1995) Pro. i. 29. I have followed the A-text.
3 Paul Budra, '*Doctor Faustus*: Death of a Bibliophile', *Connotations* 1:1 (1991): 1–11 (2).
4 Sarah Wall-Randell, '*Doctor Faustus* and the Printer's Devil', *SEL* 48:2 (2008): 259–81 (261).
5 [Daniel Defoe], *History of the Principal Discoveries and Improvements in the Several Arts and Sciences* (London, 1727), 223–4; cited in Elizabeth L. Eisenstein, *Divine Art, Infernal Machine: The Reception of Printing in the West from First Impressions to the Sense of an Ending* (Philadelphia: University of Pennsylvania Press, 2011), 1–2. On the conflation of the printer Johann Fust with the necromancer Johann Faustus and related confusions in the early history of printing, see also Adrian Johns, *The Nature of the Book: Print and Knowledge in the Making* (University of Chicago Press, 1998), 343–79; and Wall-Randell, '*Doctor Faustus*', 259–62.
6 Eisenstein, *Divine Art, Infernal Machine*, 1.
7 See William Urry, *Christopher Marlowe and Canterbury*, ed. and intro. Andrew Butcher (London: Faber and Faber, 1988), 47–8, 108–22; and Constance Brown Kuriyama, *Christopher Marlowe: A Renaissance Life* (Ithaca, NY: Cornell University Press, 2002), 178–86. For early library collections more generally, see the magisterial *Private Libraries in Renaissance England*, 9 vols., ed. Robert J. Fehrenbach, Elisabeth Leedham-Green, and Joseph Laurence Black (Binghamton, NY and Tempe, AZ: Medieval and Renaissance Texts and Studies, 1992–2009). The library that would have most closely emulated what Marlowe imagines for Faustus is John Dee's *Bibliotheca mortlacensis*.

See William H. Sherman, *John Dee: The Politics of Reading and Writing in the English Renaissance* (Amherst: University of Massachusetts Press, 1995), 29–52.
8 Urry, *Christopher Marlowe*, 116–18.
9 *Ibid.*, 117, 119.
10 Pico della Mirandola, *On the Dignity of Man*, trans. Charles Glenn Wallis (Indianapolis: Hackett, 1998), 4–5.
11 Foster Watson, *The English Grammar Schools to 1660* (Cambridge University Press, 1908). On the pedagogy of *imitatio* and mimetic literary practices, see Jeff Dolven, *Scenes of Instruction in Renaissance Romance* (Oxford University Press, 2007), 15–38; and Andrew Wallace, *Virgil's Schoolboys: The Poetics of Pedagogy in Renaissance England* (Oxford University Press, 2011).
12 Philip Sidney, *The Defence of Poesy* in *Sir Philip Sidney*, ed. Katherine Duncan-Jones (Oxford University Press, 1989), 217.
13 Mary Thomas Crane, *Framing Authority: Sayings, Self, and Society in Sixteenth-Century England* (Princeton University Press, 1993), 4.
14 Sherman, *John Dee*, 66. See also Antony Grafton, 'The Humanist as Reader', in *A History of Reading in the West*, ed. Guglielmo Cavallo, Roger Chartier, and Lydia G. Cochrane (Amherst: University of Massachusetts Press, 1999), 179–212; Antony Grafton and Lisa Jardine, '"Studied for Action": How Gabriel Harvey Read His Livy', *Past and Present* 129 (1990): 30–78; and Daniel Wakelin, *Humanism, Reading, and English Literature, 1430–1530* (Oxford University Press, 2007).
15 Walter Pagel, 'Medieval and Renaissance Contributions to Knowledge of the Brain and Its Functions', in *History and Philosophy of Knowledge of the Brain*, ed. F. N. L. Poynter (Oxford: Basil Blackwell, 1958), 95–114.
16 Elizabeth Spiller, *Reading and the History of Race in the Renaissance* (Cambridge University Press, 2011), 30–5.
17 See http://parkerweb.stanford.edu/parker/actions/page.do?forward=home. On Marlowe's possible access to these texts, see R. I. Page, 'Christopher Marlowe and the Library of Matthew Parker', *Notes and Queries* 24 (1977): 510–14.
18 Jennifer Summit, *Memory's Library: Medieval Books in Early Modern England* (University of Chicago Press, 2008), 109–10, 113, 116–21.
19 William Eamon, *Science and the Secrets of Nature: Books of Secrets in Medieval and Early Modern Culture* (Princeton University Press, 1994), 45–50, 93–167.

CHAPTER ELEVEN

Marlowe's translations

Jenny C. Mann

> The translation of Ovid's 'Amores' was burnt on account of its indecency in 1599, and it would have been no loss to the world if all the copies had perished. The interest of these translations is mainly historical. They testify to the passion for classical poetry, and in particular to that special fondness for Ovid of which the literature of the time affords many other proofs.
>
> A. C. Bradley

A. C. Bradley's dismissal neatly summarises the standard view of Marlowe's translations.[1] Though Marlowe's translation of Ovid's love elegies was salacious enough to earn a Bishops' Ban in the sixteenth century, one reads it now mainly for its 'historical interest', a dry sort of phrase that conjures hard work in a dusty library rather than the variety of assignations enjoyed by the poet and his lover. (The *Elegies* narrate the poet's adulterous relationship with an unhappily married woman, and the most notorious elegy features an extensive description of male impotence.) Although Marlowe and his works have rebounded from centuries of neglect, until fairly recently his translations were still rarely read, studied primarily by scholars hoping to catch a fleeting glimpse of the verse forms and themes that animate his greater works.[2] In this chapter I will follow Bradley's advice and allow Marlowe's translations to 'testify to the passion for classical poetry' in the Renaissance; however, I will ignore the claims of 'decency' and preserve the sexual connotations of this passionate testimony. For it is essential to the story: Ovid sexualises verbal skill ('Toys and light elegies, my darts, I took, / Quickly soft words hard doors wide open strook'), and this alignment of poetic technique and sexual performance places English poets such as Marlowe in a difficult predicament.[3] Since vernacular verse is doomed to fall short of its classical models, what does that failure suggest about the virility of the English poet?

Two of Marlowe's translations were printed in the early modern period: the three books of Ovid's *Amores* and the first book of Lucan's epic poem

De bello civili, commonly known as the *Pharsalia*.[4] As Bradley rightly observes, Marlowe's translations attest to an interest in classical literature widely shared by sixteenth-century writers; however, the pairing of these particular texts is idiosyncratic enough that it encourages speculation about the personality that selected them for translation. Ovid and Lucan are two of Rome's most prominent counter-imperial poets, and so these translations may indicate that Marlowe was at odds with the avowed priorities of Elizabethan culture, at least as expressed by the aspiring laureates of his generation, who preferred to follow the *cursus Virgili*.[5] Yet although Ovid's and Lucan's poems are alike in that both are, perhaps meaningfully, not-by-Virgil, these texts otherwise make for a strange pair. As Harry Levin memorably puts it, they derive from two very different classical exemplars: 'Lucan, the clangorous laureate of civil war, and Ovid, the mellifluous singer of the loves of the gods'.[6] As the adjectives 'clangorous' and 'mellifluous' suggest, the poems embody alternate modes of classicism available for translation by the English writer: the heroic vigour of epic poetry and what Ovid calls the 'tender measures [*teneris ... modis*]' of 'unwarlike [*inbelles*]' elegy.[7] The opposition of these two poetic modes, one characterised by *virtus* (manliness, excellence, bravery) and the other by *otium* (leisure, ease, repose), enables the expression of a series of interconnected cultural norms in Roman culture and of Renaissance imitations of that culture. As Brian Vickers explains, for moralising Roman writers, *virtus* yokes masculinity with civic and military action, while *otium* signifies activity with no practical outcome and is pursued by men who are over-talkative, soft, and lazy.[8] The distinction between *virtus* and *otium* thus helps to identify proper masculinity and appropriate poetic pursuits with one another, and favours epic poetry over elegy.

This chapter focuses on the troubling association of classical elegy with inactivity and effeminacy. The association weirdly prefigures the disdain many modern readers have for Marlowe's translation of Ovid's *Elegies*, which are generally regarded as inept. Yet despite the air of disappointment that often characterises critical responses to these texts, *All Ovid's Elegies* (c. 1599) and *Lucan's First Book* (1600) are watershed sixteenth-century translations in a technical sense: the former is the first translation of Ovid's *Amores* into any modern European vernacular, while the latter is the first sustained heroic poem composed in English blank verse since the Earl of Surrey's partial translation of the *Aeneid* in the 1540s.[9] The heroic couplets Marlowe uses to translate *All Ovid's Elegies* eventually became the standard verse form for non-lyrical love poems written in the vernacular; moreover, the translation provides an unexpected view of how the passion for classical literature shapes Marlowe's English poetry.[10]

Given post-Romantic investments in the originality of poetic composition, the practice of translation can seem to the modern reader more a technical than a creative activity, but in the sixteenth century translation was perhaps the paradigmatic form of literary invention.[11] Renaissance culture revered the texts of the ancient world as idealised models of thought and expression, and Marlowe, a Matthew Parker scholar at the famous King's School in Canterbury, was the glittering product of an educational system designed to reachieve the accomplishments of the classical world. The founders of the early English grammar schools agreed that good civic and moral character would emerge from a deep acquaintance with classical writing, and so pedagogical methods revolved around the practice of translation: turning Latin texts into English and back again into Latin.[12] In the school environment, whatever the reality of such drudgery, translation was conceived of as a powerful site of creative energy and cultural transformation. Given this method of education, literary production in this period was almost inescapably bicultural, and Marlowe in particular seemed imaginatively to inhabit what Dympna Callaghan calls 'the uncannily parallel universe of Augustan Rome'.[13]

In addition to orienting aspiring English poets towards the texts and culture of the classical world, this programme of education generated a number of noteworthy socio-cultural effects.[14] Humanist schools provided a means of social advancement for men outside the ranks of the nobility, endowing the class of governing elites with a distinctive language and range of cultural reference points and thus providing them with the equipment of a gentleman.[15] Because it was a means of social distinction, knowledge of classical Latin was of more than academic significance. The learning of Latin constituted what Walter Ong influentially termed a 'Renaissance puberty rite', marking the moment when boys left the domestic realm and entered the space of public culture, the province of adult men.[16] Latin, or the 'father tongue', was the gateway to intellectual life in Renaissance Europe, and the distinction between Latin and English, or the 'mother tongue', was often expressed in gendered terms as a split between the cultural and the material worlds.[17] To use this education to return to the language of one's infancy was thus a fraught endeavour, in that it might compromise a writer's hard-won masculinity.

Apart from the derogatory associations of the vernacular, there were also serious practical difficulties inhibiting the translation of classical poetry into English. The rules of Latin versification, a focus of instruction in English schools, do not apply to English poetry.[18] Ancient poetic feet consist of time durations (as in long or short syllables) rather than the heavy and light stresses that comprise metrical feet in vernacular poetry; thus it was well-nigh impossible to translate the 'numbers' or 'quantity' of classical measure into English (though many writers of Marlowe's generation expended a great deal of energy in the attempt).[19] In addition, because English is an uninflected language in which grammatical sense depends on word order, the control of syntactical rhythms wielded by the great Roman poets cannot be easily replicated in vernacular verse. Attempts to translate classical poetic measures such as the alternating dactylic hexameters and pentameters of elegiac verse thus highlight the seemingly insurmountable inadequacies of the vernacular language. As a result, to quote Ann Moss, a 'fear of impotence' necessarily 'haunted those whose natural talents were nurtured under the shadow of superior models'.[20] This 'fear of impotence' redoubles the core fear of Renaissance humanists, who were anxious about the virility of their cultural enterprise and worried about their potential effeminisation as men of words rather than of action.[21]

The 'impotence' of English poets in comparison to Roman exemplars seems to be borne out by Marlowe's translations, and scholars have been fairly harsh in their assessment of his *Elegies*.[22] In fact, it may be fitting to think of the *Elegies* as a site of Marlowe's poetic failure, given that Ovid's sequence features a poet who aims to write epic poetry but finds his energies diverted into love elegy, which, as Ian Frederick Moulton argues, produces effeminacy and subjection rather than military or political achievement.[23] As Georgia Brown observes, Marlowe's translation indicates that he may share Ovid's sceptical engagement with the usual themes of epic poetry, particularly the heroism, militarism, and masculinity embodied in the Roman concept of *virtus*.[24] Impotence, that is to say, may be the point of the entire sequence.

Ovid's *Amores*, like Marlowe's translation of them, are the productions of a youthful poet. Yet the hallmark concerns of Ovid's later work are already apparent in this collection of forty-nine poems: like the *Metamorphoses*, the *Amores* link rhetorical power to transgressive sexuality, while the *Elegies* also wrestle with their own status as verbal productions and material objects.[25] In addition to detailing the relationship of the poet with his lover, the poems also meditate on the distinctions between love elegy and other poetic genres, particularly epic and tragedy. Ovid's poems thus tweak the conventional topoi of love elegy, expanding upon its erotic discourse in order to include a self-conscious commentary on elegiac poetry and its poetic alternatives.[26] For example, at various moments in the sequence, Ovid appropriates the values associated with the Roman *vita activa* on behalf of his besotted speaker, suggesting that service in love stirs one to activity as much as does service to the state ('Sooth, lovers watch till sleep the husband charms, / Who slumb'ring, they rise up in swelling arms' (I.ix.25–6)). At other times he celebrates the paralysis and lassitude associated with being in love ('In summer's heat, and mid-time of the day, / To rest my limbs upon a bed I lay' (I.v.1–2)). Most significantly, the poems figure reading and writing as erotic exchanges ('What need she tire her hand to hold the quill? / Let this word, "Come", alone the tables fill' (I.xi.23–4)). (Each of these translations derives from Marlowe's *Elegies*.) The poems thus ally poetic and sexual activity in a witty resistance to the conventional values of Roman *virtus*.[27]

The *Amores* famously begin with 'Arma', the first word of Virgil's *Aeneid*, thus creating the expectation of epic poetry and military achievement. But then, in the fourth line of the first poem, Cupid appears and steals one metric foot from the line, transforming epic hexameters into elegiac couplets. In a prose translation, these lines read, 'Arms, and the violent deeds of war, I was making ready to sound forth – in weighty numbers, with matter [*materia*] suited to the measure [*modis*]. The second verse was equal to the first – but Cupid, they say, with a laugh stole away one foot' (I.i.1–4).[28] Thus the metre of the first poem conveys the conflict of a speaker who aims to write epic poetry but is sidetracked by erotic concerns. In this way the poem draws attention to the close intertwining of content and form, or matter and measure, in classical poetry. As O. B. Hardison explains, classical metre creates a complementary relationship between phonetic-rhythmic materials and the sensations associated with them; thus metre is as important as subject matter in constituting generic form in classical poetics.[29] Interestingly, in *Amores* I.i the change in metre comes *before* the speaker has discovered his passion for his mistress; thus form rather than content drives the transformation of his poetry. Before he has accepted his subjection to love, the speaker complains that 'I have no matter [*materia*] suited to lighter numbers [*numeris levioribus*] – neither a boy, nor a maiden with long and well-kept locks' (19–20). Elegiac form comes before the matter of desire, and Ovid's first elegy thus suggests that poetry rather than sex constitutes the chief interest of the sequence.

This elegy poses an immediate problem for the English translator, since vernacular poetry has no measure like the Latin elegiac couplet. Indeed, the very concept of 'measure', a term for the rhythm of classical poetry as defined by syllabic quantity, was a vexed topic in sixteenth-century literary theory. Here is how Marlowe copes with this predicament:

> With Muse prepared I meant to sing of arms,
> Choosing a subject fit for fierce alarms.
> Both verses were alike till Love (men say)
> Began to smile and took one foot away.
> Rash boy, who gave thee power to change a line?
> (1.i.1–5)

Marlowe's translation preserves the *content* of the verses even though its metre cannot enact Cupid's thievery. Instead, despite the allusion to Cupid's stolen foot, the entire sequence unfolds in rhymed heroic couplets (pairs of iambic pentameter lines). Because rhyme drives the organisation of Marlowe's lines, 'arms' comes at the end of the first line. Thus Marlowe, like Cupid, also 'changes' Ovid's line, introducing in the fifth line a new term that evokes the famous *Metamorphoses* but that is nowhere in the original poem, which reads instead, 'Who gave thee, cruel boy, this right over poesy [*carmina iuris*]?' (1.i.5).[30] This 'changed' verse replaces 'poesy' or 'song', *carmina*, with 'line', a term that came to be particularly associated with Marlowe's dramatic poetry – what Jonson calls Marlowe's 'mighty line'.

Yet unlike the notorious swagger of Marlowe's dramatic writing, the 'lines' of his *Elegies* describe themselves not as 'mighty', but rather as 'soft' and 'loose'. Marlowe continues to emphasise the transformation of Ovid's *Amores* into his own changed 'lines' in the first elegy of Book II, when he speaks in the voice of Ovid:

> I, Ovid, poet of my wantonness,
> Born at Peligny, to write more address.
> So Cupid wills; far hence be the severe:
> You are unapt my looser lines to hear.
> (II.i.1–4)

Ovid's 'tender measures [*teneris ... modis*]' become Marlowe's 'looser lines', and this translation suggests that the elegiac metre of the original will be replicated in a looser form of English verse. The upended word order of this line, in which the infinitive is delayed to the end of the line – 'You are unapt my looser lines *to hear*' – is awkward, perhaps intended to evoke a Latinate word order while also making up the necessary rhyme. Although Marlowe's line describes itself as 'loose', the demands of English word order render it a much more inflexible language than Latin, constraining the syntax of vernacular poets. Thus when Marlowe employs a convoluted word order, as is frequently the case in the *Elegies*, his 'lines' don't read as 'loose' so much as nonsensical, resulting in a series of what Roma Gill memorably dismisses as 'schoolboy howlers'.[31]

Although Marlowe cannot replicate the effects of Cupid's thievery in the measures of his poetic line, later in the first poem he introduces a new way of accounting for the shift from epic to elegiac poetry in English verse: he makes it a moment of detumescence. His speaker explains: 'When in this work's first verse I trod aloft, / Love slacked my muse, and made my numbers soft' (I.i.21–2). Using rhyming couplets to pair 'aloft' and 'soft', Marlowe depicts the shift from the arms of epic to the idleness of love as a slackening and softening of his verse. Ovid's text reads instead: 'My new page of song rose well with first verse on lofty strain, when that next one – of thy making – changes to slightness the vigour of my work [*cum bene surrexit versu nova pagina primo, / attenuat nervos proximus ille meos*].' The lines pun on male detumescence (*nervos* means both 'vigour' and 'penis'), implying that the poet is effeminised by what Marlowe calls the 'change' from talk of 'arms' to 'Love', which is the work of an 'idle bosom' (I.i.30). The interplay of rising and softening mimics an image from the end of the original poem, which reads, 'In six numbers let my work rise [*surgat*], and sink again in five [*residat*]. Ye iron wars, with your measures, fair ye well!' (I.i.27–8). Thus Ovid figures the alternation of six- and five-foot verses in elegiac measure as a rising and sinking, and while Marlowe cannot mimic this metre, he transforms the movement of expansion and contraction into a trope for the shift from epic to elegy, as well as for the waxing and waning of desire.

This association of poetic composition with bodily impotence returns later in the sequence, in Elegy III.6 (III.7 in Ovid's *Amores*), which connects poetic composition with a failed sexual performance. I read this poem as a kind of allegory for the difficulties of translating Ovid's 'tender measures' into English lines. However, although the poem narrates the experience of sexual failure, it also forges an unexpected link between the subjection of impotence and the activity of poetic creation. After going on at length about his lover's failed efforts to arouse him, the speaker wonders if 'my sinews be enchanted …? [*quid vetat et nervos magicas torpere per artes?*]' (II.vi.35). The word 'sinews' translates Ovid's *nervos*, which, as Patricia Parker has argued, is a hinge word between the subjects of sex and of writing style from antiquity to the Renaissance. The term recurs in the works of Seneca, Longinus, Quintilian, and Montaigne as a means of distinguishing a 'manly' writing style from a soft or effeminate eloquence.[32] *Nervus*, as Parker explains, also means 'penis', as well as 'vigor, force, strength'. The use of the word 'sinew' in this context thus connects masculinity and sexual activity with poetic expression. However, in a departure from the usual association of masculine vigour and appropriate writing style, the allusion to 'sinews' occurs in a poem featuring impotence rather than sexual activity. The term appears at the moment the poet's 'vigour' or 'force' 'grow[s] faint' (III.vi.36). This line also evokes the first elegy in the *Amores*, which declares that Cupid lightens the 'vigour' (*nervos*) of the speaker's verses, an alteration that Marlowe translates as a slackening and a softening. From the very first elegy we are told that the composition of the entire sequence is predicated on the sudden impotence of the aspiring poet. By suggesting that the experience of subjection results in a subsequent act of writing, the sequence demands that we resist the enabling tropes of epic poetry and instead align softening with poetic creation.

With classical Latin as the exemplar, English verse looked like a poor vehicle for poetic expression in the 1580s. Nevertheless, writers of Marlowe's generation began to use the discursive mastery provided by their educations to expand the capabilities of the vernacular. Looking backwards, it is easy to regard these decades as marking the 'triumph' of the English language, but at the time it was by no means certain that English had the capacity to achieve the artistry of classical Latin.[33] Marlowe's *Elegies*, engaging though they often are, certainly do not make the most persuasive case on behalf of vernacular poetry. In addition, Marlowe's translation of Ovid's *Amores* contradicts the central conviction of Renaissance humanism: namely, that the reading of classical literature readies young men for service to the state. Rather, quite the opposite: *All Ovid's Elegies* suggests that the reading of classical literature slackens male bodies, rendering them impotent. At times Marlowe seems to feel this poetic impotence keenly, as when the technologies of early modern printing become figures for the speaker's flaccid member:

> Like a dull cipher or rude block I lay,
> Or shade or body was I, who can say?
> What will my age do, age I cannot shun,
> When in my prime my force is spent and done?
> I blush, that being youthful, hot and lusty,
> I prove neither youth nor man, but old and rusty.
> (III.vi.15–20)

At other, rarer moments, we see the promise of a poetic arousal that will follow hard upon this slackening:

> Let base-conceited wits admire vile things,
> Fair Phoebus lead me to the Muses' springs.
> About my head by quivering myrtle wound,
> And in sad lovers' heads let me be found.
> The living, not the dead, can envy bite,
> For after death all men receive their right.
> Then though death rakes my bones in funeral fire,
> I'll live, and as he pulls me down mount higher.
> (I.xv.35–42)

The poet's promise to throw off downward-pulling forces and 'mount higher' sounds like the Marlowe whose poetic achievements have prompted the current volume. Indeed, it sounds like Faustus, who quotes Ovid's *Amores* in his final hour of life: 'O lente, lente, currite noctis equi!' (*DrF*, V.ii.143, *Amores*, I.xiii.40). Marlowe's *Elegies* may not convey the artistry of vernacular poetry, but they do suggest how English poets might move beyond translations of the classics towards new poetic uses of the vernacular language. When viewed in the context of his subsequent career, Marlowe's attempts to accommodate Ovid's tender measures in English verse indicate how Renaissance writers must allow themselves to be softened and slackened by classical poetry before they can rise up and move others with verse of their own.

Notes

1 A. C. Bradley, *The English Poets: Selections* (1880), quoted in *Marlowe: The Critical Heritage 1588–1896*, ed. Millar Maclure (London: Routledge and Kegan Paul, 1979), 129.
2 If one assumes, as most scholars do, that Marlowe composed his translations early in his career, the heroic couplets of his elegies foreshadow the metre of *Hero and Leander*, which in turn influenced the cadence of eighteenth-century Augustan measures. Of even greater interest has been the blank verse of the *Pharsalia*, which precedes Marlowe's transformation of that measure into the standard form of English popular drama. Important recent studies of Marlowe's translation of Ovid's *Amores* include Georgia E. Brown, 'Marlowe's Poems and Classicism', in *The Cambridge Companion to Christopher Marlowe*, ed. Patrick Cheney (Cambridge University Press, 2004); Patrick Cheney, *Marlowe's Counterfeit Profession: Ovid, Spenser, and Counter-Nationhood* (University of Toronto Press, 1997); Heather James, 'The Poet's Toys: Christopher Marlowe and the Liberties of Erotic Elegy', *Modern Language Quarterly* 67:1 (March 2006): 103–27; Ian Frederick Moulton, '"Printed Abroad and Uncastrated":

Marlowe's *Elegies* with Davies' *Epigrams*', in *Marlowe, History, and Sexuality: New Critical Essays on Christopher Marlowe*, ed. Paul Whitfield White (New York: AMS Press, 1988); and M. L. Stapleton, 'Marlowe's First Ovid: "Certaine of Ovids Elegies"', in *Christopher Marlowe the Craftsman: Lives, Stage, and Page*, ed. Sarah K. Scott and M. L. Stapleton (Farnham: Ashgate, 2010).
3. Christopher Marlowe, *All Ovid's Elegies*, in *The Complete Poems and Translations*, ed. Stephen Orgel (New York: Penguin, 2007), II.i.21–2.
4. We might also consider Marlowe's play *Dido, Queen of Carthage* as a translation, or adaptation, of Virgil's *Aeneid*.
5. Patrick Cheney points to these translations in arguing that Marlowe was consciously pursuing a counter-Virgilian, Ovidian *cursus* rather than following what Richard Helgerson terms the 'laureate' model of a poetic career followed by writers such as Spenser and Milton. Cheney, *Marlowe's Counterfeit Profession*; Richard Helgerson, *Self-Crowned Laureates: Spenser, Jonson, Milton, and the Literary System* (Berkeley: University of California Press, 1983).
6. Harry Levin, *The Overreacher: A Study of Christopher Marlowe* (Cambridge, MA: Harvard University Press, 1952), 10.
7. Ovid, *Heroides and Amores*, trans. Grant Showerman, rev. trans. G. P. Goold (Cambridge, MA: Harvard University Press, 1977), II.i.4, III.xv.20.
8. Brian Vickers, 'Leisure and Idleness in the Renaissance: The Ambivalence of *Otium*', *Renaissance Studies* 4:1 (1990): 1–37 (7).
9. Patrick Cheney, '"Defend his freedom 'gainst a monarchy": Marlowe's Republican Authorship', in *Textual Conversations in the Renaissance: Ethics, Authors, Technologies*, ed. Zachary Lesser and Benedict Robinson (Aldershot: Ashgate, 2006), 27–44 (33). Both translations were first published well after Marlowe's death, likely by booksellers hoping to capitalise on his personal notoriety as well as the popularity of his stage works. There are two undated surreptitious printings of the *Elegies* in the Elizabethan period. The first is a collection of just ten of Marlowe's translations bound together with Sir John Davies' *Epigrammes* and titled *Certaine of Ovids Elegies*. This was entered in the Stationers' Register in 1599 and was the text that received the Bishops' Ban. The second edition, titled *All Ovids Elegies*, contains Marlowe's complete translation and is also undated. For more details on the publication history of these texts, see Stapleton, 'Marlowe's First Ovid', 141–2. Despite the mystery surrounding the dates of composition and publication, scholars generally agree that the translations are probably the work of Marlowe's Cambridge years and were thus likely completed between 1580 and 1587, before Marlowe began writing for the professional stage. See Cheney, *Marlowe's Counterfeit Profession*, 5.
10. Moreover, the blank verse of *Lucan's First Book* not only became the primary means of translating epic hexameters into the vernacular, but through Marlowe's theatrical writing it also became the standard verse form of English popular drama. Christopher Marlowe, *The Complete Works of Christopher Marlowe*, 5 vols., Vol. I, ed. Roma Gill (Oxford: Clarendon Press, 1987), 4.

11 Moreover, the practice of biblical translation was at the centre of the political and religious convulsions of the Protestant Reformation in Europe. For example, Martin Luther's translation of Romans 3.28 – *per fidem* – in his 1522 version of the New Testament as 'by faith alone' is perhaps one of the most consequential translations in European history. See Valerie Worth-Stylianou, '*Translatio* and Translation in the Renaissance: From Italy to France', in *The Cambridge History of Literary Criticism*, 9 vols., Vol. III: *The Renaissance*, ed. Glyn P. Norton (Cambridge University Press, 1999), 127–35 (128).

12 For a comprehensive description of grammar-school and university education in the period, see Peter Mack, *Elizabethan Rhetoric: Theory and Practice* (Cambridge University Press, 2002); and Quentin Skinner, *Reason and Rhetoric in the Philosophy of Hobbes* (Cambridge University Press, 1996).

13 Dympna Callaghan, 'Marlowe's Last Poem: Elegiac Aesthetics and the Epitaph on Sir Roger Manwood', in Scott and Stapleton, *Christopher Marlowe the Craftsman*, 159–76 (160). See also Mary Thomas Crane, *Framing Authority: Sayings, Self, and Society in Sixteenth-Century England* (Princeton University Press, 1993).

14 For a detailed accounting of these effects, see Lynn Enterline, *Shakespeare's Schoolroom: Rhetoric, Discipline, Emotion* (Philadelphia: University of Pennsylvania Press, 2011).

15 Ann Moss, 'Humanist Education', in Norton, *The Cambridge History of Literary Criticism*, Vol. III, 145–54 (154).

16 Walter Ong, 'Latin Language Study as a Renaissance Puberty Rite', *Studies in Philology* 56 (1959): 103–24.

17 The pre-eminence of classical Latin in Renaissance culture created what Richard Waswo calls a form of 'psychosexual schizophrenia' for English writers; Richard Waswo, 'The Rise of the Vernaculars', in Norton, *The Cambridge History of Literary Criticism*, Vol. III, 409–16 (410).

18 For a discussion of the translation of Ovid's verse as taught in the schools, in exercises that asked that students translate prose excerpts of classical poets back into Latin verse, see Jonathan Bate, *Shakespeare and Ovid* (Oxford: Clarendon Press, 1993). For the social and psychological implications of such an educational system, see Richard Halpern, *The Poetics of Primitive Accumulation: English Renaissance Culture and the Genealogy of Capital* (Ithaca, NY: Cornell University Press, 1991); and Lynn Enterline, *The Rhetoric of the Body from Ovid to Shakespeare* (Cambridge University Press, 2000).

19 For an analysis of sixteenth-century attempts to translate quantitative verse into English, see Derek Attridge, *Well-Weighed Syllables: Elizabethan Verse in Classical Metres* (Cambridge University Press, 1974); and O. B. Hardison, Jr, *Prosody and Purpose in the English Renaissance* (Baltimore: Johns Hopkins University Press, 1989).

20 Ann Moss, 'Literary Imitation in the Sixteenth Century: Writers and Readers, Latin and French', in Norton, *The Cambridge History of Literary Criticism*, Vol. III, 107–18 (115).

21 Ong, 'Latin Language Study', 116; Patricia Parker, 'Gender Ideology, Gender Change: The Case of Marie Germain', *Critical Inquiry* 19:2 (1993): 337–64 (364).
22 As M. L. Stapleton notes, Roma Gill, one of Marlowe's most important modern editors, devotes not one but two long essays to Marlowe's incompetence as a translator. See Stapleton, 'Marlowe's First Ovid', 139; Roma Gill, 'Snakes Leape by Verse', in *Christopher Marlowe*, ed. Brian Morris (New York: Hill and Wang, 1968), 133–50; and Roma Gill, 'Marlowe and the Art of Translation', in *'A Poet and a Filthy Play-Maker': New Essays on Christopher Marlowe*, ed. Kenneth Friedenreich, Roma Gill, and Constance Brown Kuriyama (New York: AMS Press, 1988), 327–42.
23 Moulton, 'Printed Abroad and Uncastrated', 81.
24 Brown, 'Marlowe's Poems and Classicism', 121.
25 Colin Burrow, 'Re-embodying Ovid: Renaissance Afterlives', in *The Cambridge Companion to Ovid*, ed. Philip Hardie (Cambridge University Press, 2002), 301–19 (302).
26 Stephen Harrison, 'Ovid and Genre: Evolutions of an Elegist', in Hardie, *The Cambridge Companion to Ovid*, 79–94 (80–1).
27 This is characteristic of the writers of Latin elegiacs, who flaunted their idleness as a defining characteristic of being in love. See Vickers, 'Leisure and Idleness in the Renaissance', 19.
28 The first four lines in Ovid read: 'Arma gravi numero violentaque bella parabam / edere, materia conveniente modis. / par erat inferior versus – risisse Cupido / dicitur atque unum surripuisse pedem.'
29 Hardison, *Prosody and Purpose*, 29.
30 See Cheney, *Marlowe's Counterfeit Profession*, 53.
31 Gill, 'Snakes Leape by Verse', 137.
32 Patricia Parker cites a passage from Montaigne's essay 'On Some Verses of Virgil', which adopts this framework in praising ancient poetry: 'This is not a soft and merely inoffensive eloquence; it is sinewy and solid [*nerveuse et solide*], and does not so much please as fill and ravish; and it ravishes the strongest minds most.' See Parker, 'Gender Ideology, Gender Change', 352–3.
33 For a history of attitudes towards the vernacular that emphasises English's victory over competing forms of expression, see R. F. Jones, *The Triumph of the English Language: A Survey of Opinions Concerning the Vernacular from the Introduction of Printing to the Restoration* (Stanford University Press, 1953).

PART II
Marlowe's world

CHAPTER TWELVE

Geography and Marlowe

Jacques Lezra

> Geography laye hidden many hundred yeeres in darknesse and oblivion, without regarde and price. of late who taketh not upon him to discourse of the whole worlde, and eche province thereof particularly, even by hearesay, although in the first principles of that arte, he bee altogether ignorant and unskylfull? This tyme is now.[1]

We have known for almost a century that Christopher Marlowe had before him Abraham Ortelius' great atlas, *Theatrum orbis terrarum* of 1570, when he traced out the regions covered in the two *Tamburlaine* plays: we understand him to be, in words of the critic Emrys Jones, 'the first dramatist to incorporate cartographical passages in a play'.[2] Recent scholarship has taught us to distinguish between an 'old cartography' and a 'new' one, the former (still residually at work in the late sixteenth century) imprecise and mythopoetic, the latter based upon systematic geometric projections largely indebted to the Flemish mathematician and cartographer Gerardus Mercator, whose 1569 world map was the first to provide parallel lines of longitude and latitude.[3] Both cartographies, in tension at times, often not, are at work in Marlowe's plays and poems, which combine residual and emergent notions of mapping, 'world', place, projection. Just what these 'cartographical passages' might amount to – what they might have meant when brought before the plays' audiences or the poems' readers, what their cultural function would have been in Marlowe's time, what social and aesthetic work they might have done – these are questions we are only beginning to ask.

When we do ask these questions we are caught in a peculiar bind. The fascination with maps and mapping that we have learnt to register across early modern societies has found companion critical fascinations today.[4] In place of primarily interpretive, 'imprecise … mythopoetic' forms of criticism (characterological, formalist, biographical, psychoanalytic), we cherish 'new' approaches, notionally more scientific in hewing more closely to the archive: histories of the book, material culture, new textualism, and so on. The supersession of the 'old' by the 'new', of the mythic by the rational: the shift in geographical paradigms lived in Marlowe's time is the story of triumphant modernisation. No wonder the topic excites current scholars. Studying the emergence of the 'new' geography from the mists of the 'old' means confirming the value of the twenty-first-century critic's own approach to the map of the past. A very old narcissism is staked on the analogy: the geography of Marlowe's time is the distant map of our critical successes.

Marlowe's geography, however, is neither new nor old in the senses intended, and it is not amenable to the corresponding contemporary critical practices. We will not get very far with the works if we hold fast to a distinction between interpretive approaches and archival or materialist ones, between mythopoesis and science, old and new – in part because the distinctions were not drawn as firmly or in the same spots in Marlowe's lifetime as they are today, and in part because Marlowe consistently shifts the borders between types of geography and sorts of criticism in ways great as well as small. Take as an example Tamburlaine's famous lines:

> I will confute those blind geographers
> That make a triple region of the world,
> Excluding regions which I mean to trace
> And with this pen reduce them to a map,
> Calling the provinces, cities, and towns
> After my name and thine, Zenocrate.
> Here at Damascus will I make the point
> That shall begin the perpendicular.
> (*1 Tamb.*, IV.iv.73–80)[5]

'I will confute those blind geographers'; yes – but it isn't clear in what the geographers' blindness consists (or, indeed, whether these blind geographers are of the *old* or the *new* variety, or both). Are Tamburlaine's 'geographers' blind because their maps exclude 'regions' they should include – regions that *will be* included when Tamburlaine conquers them and retraces the maps, or that are *already included* in more up-to-date maps that take account of recent discoveries in the East and West Indies? Thomas Blundeville's almost exactly contemporaneous pamphlet *A briefe description of universal mappes and cardes* of 1589, which proposes to 'instruct those that have not studied Geographie … without the knowledge whereof me thinkes that the necessarie reading of Histories is halfe lame, and is neither so pleasant, nor so profitable as otherwise it would be', closes with a prayer that might seem, oddly, and with considerable allowances made, to announce the coming of Tamburlaine:

For though *Ptolemy, Appian, Gemma Frizius, Gastaldus, Orontius, Munsterus, Ortellius* and others have set downe certaine names, both auncient and moderne together with their longitudes and latitudes, yet they are but very fewe in comparison of all the names that are wanting ... Wherefore I pray God with all my heart, that some good man that is a skillful Cosmographer may shortlie traveile hearein to the profit of all Students of Geographie.[6]

Are Tamburlaine's geographers blind because they set the foot of their compass on the wrong originating spot and draw their maps' centre at Jerusalem rather than in Damascus, where Tamburlaine proposes to drop his 'perpendicular'? Tamburlaine is thinking of the old, pre-Mercator maps called T-O maps or projections (see Figure 4) because they set a sort of 'T' within the round world – the 'O' – and usually place Jerusalem at the crossing of the 'T''s two strokes, the horizontal and what Tamburlaine refers to as the 'perpendicular'. Are they blind because they misdivide the earth into a mere 'triple region'? This is Blundeville again: '[T]he auncient Cosmographers, not knowing then the West *Indies*, nor manie other places situated both Northward and Southward ... devided the whole Earth onely into three partes, that is, *Europe, Aphrike* and *Asia*.'[7]

Manifestly, Tamburlaine's geographers are blind in *all* these ways: the maps are incomplete and misdivided as well as centred upon the wrong point. Tamburlaine's purpose, however, is not to replace blind cartography with another, a mythopoetic interpretation of the world with a scientific or mathematical projection, but to refigure the contents of the blind geographers' map – with himself at its centre and its contours in his hands. He stands at the centre of the map, but also circumscribes all the regions of the earth: he is centre as well as circumference – and also the radius, the line that defines the relation between the two, force-vector, arm, sword, sceptre. Tamburlaine is not only a figure for the imperial hyperbole of the traveller and the conqueror who extend the great 'O' of the world; he also provides a tense compromise between 'blind' and more accurate geographies and geographers. And since the sword that marks the new perpendicular of Tamburlaine's map is an old stand-in for the playwright's pen, the hyperbolic conqueror also sets before the audience Marlowe's reflection about the functions of geography on stage, about what it means to plot or to occupy a position *in the theatre, for an audience*.

Even in this early play, then, the practice and the theory of geography involve for Marlowe more than tracing likenesses of lands after 'imagining ... wheresoever you are, a point or pricke directly over your head, which is called Zenith', as a contemporaneous pamphlet put it.[8] The circuit his works describe is richly circular. On one hand, the appropriation,

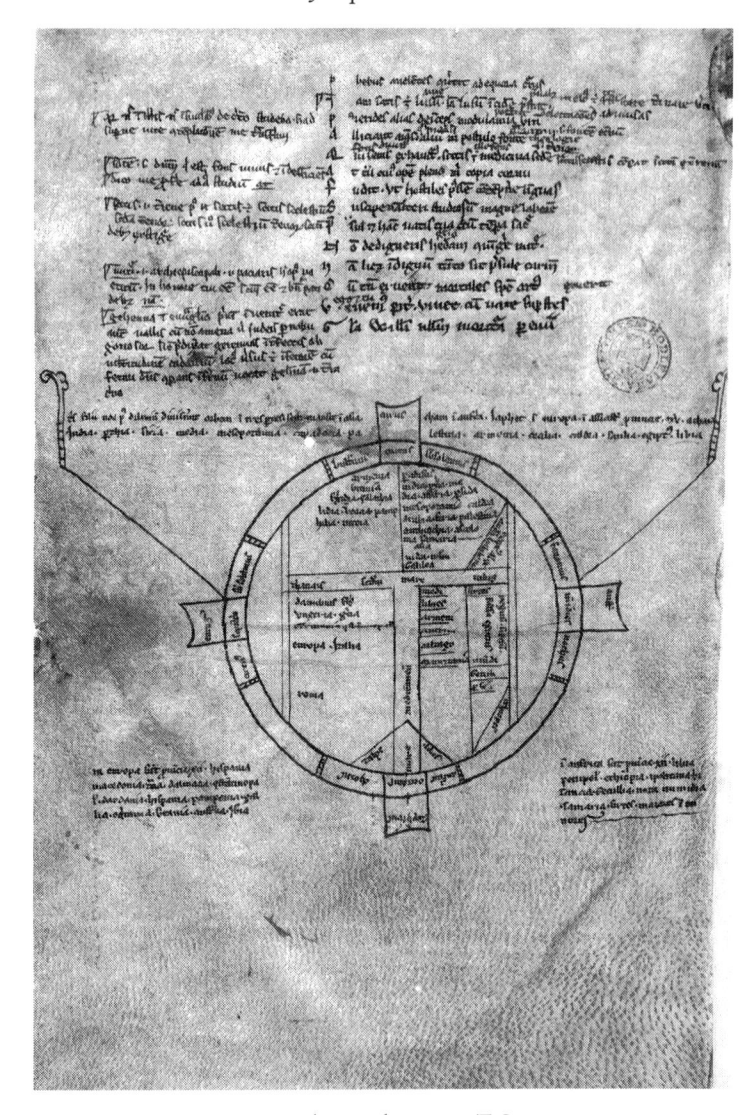

Figure 4 Thirteenth-century T-O map

or indeed the seeming 'confutation', of the geographers' practice, theory, and lexicon in the plays is an aspect of Marlowe's broader reflection on the staging of human action – a very visible, commercially useful (because culturally recognisable) trope conveying a rather recent, breathless sense of horizons at once expanding (the Americas, trade with the eastern Mediterranean) and, suddenly, accessible (print and pamphlet culture making it possible, as Richard Willes had put it in 1577, 'to discourse of the whole worlde, and eche province thereof particularly, even by hearsay'). On the other hand, the theatre and its own lexicon, economics, and conventions are the means and figures for Marlowe's hyperbolic effort to span 'the whole worlde' of his time: the theatre is a figure for geography, extensively understood. When its characters draw attention to their hyperbolic improbability, to their theatricality, the stage makes visible for audiences in the imagined globe of this or that theatrical space the 'blindness' of customary maps of 'the whole worlde'. The theatre is a figure for the world; the world a figure for the theatre.

This rich and constant circulation we find in Marlowe's work between theatre and world, metatheatrical figures and figures for geography, reflects and contributes to a cluster of ambiguities at work in the conceptualisation of geography in Marlowe's time. (There are parallel ambiguities in Elizabethan reflections on the theatre at the time, of course: think 'All the world's a stage'.) Say that we set about plotting just where 'geography' sits in the conceptual map of mapping practices in early modernity. We find it at the hinge between 'Cosmographie' on one side, a 'description of the world: as well his Aethereall part, as Elementall', and on the other 'Topographie called also Corographie ... the describing of any particular place without relation to the whole, not leaving out the smallest contents thereof': thus John Blagrave in 1585. He continues: geography 'is a certaine form and imitation of the picture of the earth, and of his chiefest and knowen parts'.[9] Blagrave's definition – despite an oddity to which I will return in a moment – is generally consistent with others of the period. Philonicus, one of two speakers in the opening dialogue of William Cunningham's *The Cosmographical glasse* of 1559, tells his interlocutor Spondaeus that 'Geographie doe deliniat, and set out the vniuersal earth, no respect had vnto the forna[m]ed circles of the heaue[n]s: but by Hylles, Mou[n]tayns, Seas, fluddes, and such other notable thinges, as are in it co[n]teined.'[10] More sparely, William Bourne's *A booke called the treasure for traueilers* of 1578 calls geography 'the description of Countries, or Kingdomes'; Bourne is borrowing from and summarising John Dee's preface to the English translation of Euclid's *Elements*, which provides a much more extended and nuanced definition:

> Geography teacheth wayes, by which, in sundry formes, (as *Spherike*, *Plaine* or other) the Situation of Cities, Townes, Villages, Fortes, Castells,

Mountaines, Woods, Havens, Rivers, Crekes, & such other things, upon the outface of the earthly Globe (either in the whole or in some principall member and portion thereof contained) may be described and designed, in commensurations Analogicall to Nature and veritie: and most aptly to our vew, may be represented.[11]

Geography in Marlowe's time – whether we call it 'old' or 'new' – sits upon a middle ground between the grand arcs of astronomical observation and the particulars of local description, between the 'circles of the heavens' and earth's 'known parts'. The earth's surface, 'face', 'picture', 'outface' – these are geography's province: they are what geography describes, *geos* to its *graphein*. On this side, geography is akin to mathematics and explicitly to geometry; it deals in what is calculable about the surface of the earth, what is measurable about its 'outface'; it traffics in the 'commensurable', as Dee puts it. *This* geography expresses itself in atlases, map-books, corographic manuals, treatises on the mathematics and technologies of topography, even on the sciences of warfare (the measurement of battlements, layout of battlefields, and so on).

At the same time, however, geography in Marlowe's period (again, whether of the 'new' or 'old' sort) takes shape where 'the world' abuts upon 'any particular place *without relation to the whole*' (my emphasis). Settling geography *between* 'the world' and 'any particular place *without relation to the whole*' means at least that geography no longer serves as a scalar step between a 'particular' and the whole to which it belongs, as though one were moving up or down a gradient according to 'commensurable' units. Geography marks a boundary between *in*commensurables; it is where we 'discourse', as Richard Willes puts its, about 'the whole worlde, and eche province thereof particularly', while acknowledging that some or all of these particular provinces have 'no relation' to the 'whole' of which they are 'parts', including the relation of part to whole. The 'discourse' of geography results in impossible topologies and in strange, heterogeneous works like Willes' *History of Travayle*, which feed the 'late' fashion for discoursing on 'the whole world' with composite collections of travelogues and 'merchants' adventures' to the particular provinces of the known world. Descriptions of that 'discourse' abound in near-paradoxes or in symptomatic, even compensatory overstatements: thus Blagrave's 'Geographie is a certaine form and imitation of the *picture* of the earth' – the term 'picture' here straddling the early senses of image, representation, portrait; a three-dimensional rendering, a tableau in a play; and, provocatively, a counterfeit. But why the 'imitation of a picture'? Does this not amount to the *imitation of an imitation* or the *picture of a picture*? Why both a 'form' and an 'imitation'? Even the words of a much more careful scholar, John Dee, go awry: 'Geography', he writes, 'teacheth wayes, by which … the Situation of Cities … upon the outface of the earthly Globe … may be described and designed, in commensurations Analogicall to Nature and veritie: and most aptly to our vew, may be represented.' What does he mean, we ask, by qualifying 'commensurations' with a term drawn, not from the domain of mathematics, but from the domain of rhetoric, 'Analogical'? Why must he double the object of these 'analogical commensurations': 'Nature and veritie'? Does his 'and' stand in for the particle *or* (as *id est*: commensurations 'analogical' to nature, that is, to the truth)? Is 'and' contrastive? Enumerative? ('Lions and tigers and bears' and 'Apples and oranges'.) The tense Marlovian compromise between geographies figured in characters like Tamburlaine will be unsustainable; geography's middle ground will be anything but solid or single.

What sorts of works, then, *are* Marlowe's plays and poems? Do they trade in the 'commensurable' or in *in*-commensurables? If in both, how are we to measure the *relation* between what the works present as measurable and what they present as immeasurable? This sort of question puts us on an even more treacherous map than the one on which John Gillies beautifully places Shakespeare, in the groundbreaking *Shakespeare and the Geography of Difference*. Marlowe's time – Shakespeare's, too – saw battles about geography in every domain: battles about how areas could be imagined, how they could be brought under the dominion of different powers, how their resources could most conveniently and efficiently be secured for colonial regimes. 'I will confute those blind geographers', we hear Tamburlaine exclaim, 'That make a triple region in the world, / Excluding regions which I mean to trace.' The line is itself 'confuting' at every level. The projects of mapping and of domination, long akin, are here brought together, confoundingly. Tamburlaine's term 'region', used twice in these famous lines, condenses the sense of a spatial extension with the sense (etymologically related to the post-classical Latin *regere*, meaning to rule or direct) of a kingdom, a domain over which a *regent* might *reign*. Tamburlaine will 'trace' these regions or kingdoms by conquering them – and here too manifold senses of the word are brought together, braided: the old meaning of 'trace' understood as the verb 'to write or inscribe'; the verb 'to pass through or across; to traverse'; and the less common sense of 'to trace' as 'to tie up, to braid, to put in traces or in a sort of harness' (*OED*).

For Tamburlaine, and for many of Marlowe's characters, the map of the world is the occasion for consolidating, conquering, confuting. For Marlowe, however, the figure of geography is more complicated. His plays are closely attentive to different landscapes and lexicons and meditate on the special problems that are entailed when one brings geography, a discipline concerned to all appearances with designating and measuring the relations between really existing things, into the domain of fiction, and especially into the domain of theatrical fiction. (Is Jerusalem at the world's centre, or Damascus? Can a really existing location be 'confuted' by a trace or a fiction, the stroke of a sword or a pen, as Tamburlaine seeks to do?) Marlowe's plays are also, however, concerned with understanding and with exploiting the commercial value attached to names and to the naming of exotic lands – and, more remarkably still, with exploring ways in which the lexical surplus-value attaching to place-names can then 'confute' the bounds of the mere atlas and spread to other terms that are *not* place names. '[A]ll the names that are wanting' from the 'old', 'blind' geographers' lists of 'certaine names, both aunciant and moderne together with their longitudes and latitudes' are also words like 'region' or 'trace', or even the pronoun 'I', that function metadiscursively, designating just *how* geography works on stage and on the page: indexical words with a surplus-value, or surplus function, of pointing to the ways or to the subjects in which theatrical and geographical lexicons determine and overdetermine each other, each taking value from the other, a specular loop on which the plays mount and display a new sense of their commercial value-form, though not only that. We can call this specular loop 'theatre-geography'.

Marlowe's 'theatre-geography' puts into relation alternative models of the self as well as of wealth, value, and rhetoric. Take the opening of *The Jew of Malta*. Here – as in Shakespeare's *The Merchant of Venice* – geography serves as a bridge between mercantilism of all sorts and conquest of all sorts. The regions Barabas imagines, the distances on display in his soliloquy, provide Marlowe's audience with indices for gauging the value of the products Barabas describes in his opening lines:

> So that of thus much that return was made,
> And, of the third part of the Persian ships,
> There was the venture summed and satisfied.
> As for those Samnites and the men of Uz,
> That bought my Spanish oils and wines of Greece,
> Here have I pursed their paltry silverlings.
> Fie, what a trouble 'tis to count this trash!
>
> (1.i.1–7)

From here – from the 'paltry silverlings' of Samnites and 'men of Uz'; mere chump's change; 'trash' occupying too much space to count and in this sense being an entirely uneconomic, inefficient means of representing value – Barabas famously moves, through commodities of increasing value and exchange-tokens of corresponding worth, to describe how

> Should men of judgment frame
> Their means of traffic from the vulgar trade,
> And as their wealth increaseth, so enclose
> Infinite riches in a little room.
>
> (1.i.34–7)

The rhetoric of compression, whose affective equivalent is miserliness, is a counter-hyperbole – the opposing fantasy to Tamburlaine's, for whom the conquest of 'regions' involves expanding the map and attributing to himself the colossal capacity to stand with one foot at its centre, like a great compass, and with the other to trace out the new confines of the enlarged world. For Barabas, the misery of wealth consists, for the man of good 'judgment', in the hyperbolic condensation of space into an atom, an indivisible 'point or pricke'.

For Marlowe, then, theatre-geography is the privileged trope assembling the registers of selfhood, wealth, value, and rhetoric, the device for 'tracing' them together, in the complex sense the word assumes in *Tamburlaine*: theatre-geography furnishes the map in which subjects, forms of valuing wealth, and sorts of rhetoric co-exist with antagonists who are at the same time 'commensurate' and incommensurable. Theatre geography works, one might say, by hyperbolically compressing expansive subjectivity while simultaneously capitalising upon that compression-hyperbole. This capitalisation is achieved when theatre-geography designates expansive subjectivity alongside and within every other act of designation on stage (place-names, personal names, pronouns, shifters). This is the peculiar circuit on display in Marlowe's plays, most obviously at the moments when the character who says 'I' is indicating at once himself as actor, as part, and as allegorical figure: he compresses 'in a little room' different spaces and value-forms; he imports semantic merchandise from distant markets; and he traces space, value-form, and (semantic) merchandise (he assembles, maps, draws them into one harness: 'I') in himself.[12]

Marlowe's tactic holds distinct dangers for the phenomenology of the theatrical experience, however. If theatre-geography depends upon tracing the space of the stage in every utterance, it runs the twinned risks of inflation and of paradox – of increasing the number of things designated, while at the same time reducing the sense and the value of each of them, and of finally designating a name or a space, a position, improperly. Every place on stage, every place-name beyond the stage, even those outside the ken of 'blind' geographers' 'certaine names, both auncient and moderne together with their longitudes and latitudes' – all these are indeed indicated, brought into the imperial circumference of the theatrical globe, of the map of the world the play can now, directly or indirectly, indicate. The play is the point from which the circumference of the world is traced, all things plotted to its 'perpendicular'. But this must also mean that all things, all the names in the register of the world, are commensurable – that they occupy the same flat, commercial space or can be brought into it. And yet at least one thing both does and does not occupy that space – the theatre itself, the point on which the foot of the discursive-commercial compass stands: it is a point in the space of theatre-geography and also a point outside it. Like Jerusalem, like Damascus, the theatre is an earthly, walled city as well as a symbolic operator that produces the *relation* between what can and cannot be measured. When the play draws attention to the indexical prolixity on which theatre-geography stands, it risks destroying the fantasy that governs that prolixity. Here, at this point, Marlowe's work ceases to be either a projection or a mythopoetic fantasy alone and draws its perpendicular in a space that is simultaneously both and neither.

Marlowe is not unaware of the risks he is taking. Indeed, in *The Jew of Malta* he opens addressing this sort of risk and showing how a playwright-geographer such as Barabas goes about capitalising upon that risk itself: a speculative trade, in which the risk to the phenomenology of theatre-geography becomes a source of value – thus the rather irritating surplus of deictical or pointing terms in Barabas' soliloquy (demonstrative and personal pronouns; markers of aspect, quantity, time, and place): 'So *that* of *thus much* that return was made, /... *There* was the venture summed and satisfied. / As for *those* Samnites and the men of Uz / *Here* have *I* pursed *their* paltry silverlings. / Fie, what a trouble 'tis to count *this* trash!'[13] It is not only a characterological feature being described – the self-centred Jew, the hoarding merchant whose index of value is himself alone. Marlowe sets on stage a model for surplus-valuation, for the expansion of the region that the 'I' controls – and also for the assertion that these riches, mapped across the actors' bodies, are attached at last to the moment of enunciation, the 'little room' of the indivisible circumstance of expression. It is this simultaneous expansion and contraction that keeps theatre-geographies incommensurable with (unamenable to) the critical insight that in Marlowe's period a residual, mythopoetic conception of the tracing of the world and its subjects subsists, however tensely, alongside an emergent scientific geography. In the register of theatre-geography, place-names, proper names, metadramatic indices, and pronouns work in, and take their value from, two registers simultaneously: they work in the sort of index that Blundeville calls for, lined up alongside their latitudes and longitudes, their value assessed according to their distance from the point the audience occupies; *and* they carry the surplus value of exoticism that comes precisely from being singular, the 'point or pricke' about which the world's axis turns or on which we stand. The *audience* at Marlowe's plays finds itself at every moment, wrenchingly, in two different spaces: it is called upon to assess what it is watching and to establish *from where* it is watching, according to incommensurable criteria; and it is called upon to trace these incompatible spatialities and systems of valuation within the span of one confuted subjectivity – a paradoxically *divided* atom. Theatre-geography in Marlowe's plays and poems designates the register Marlowe explores most savagely in *Edward II*: the cloacal sublime, the abjected body of the 'tenderly' brought-up sovereign who 'sees [his] tragedy written' on his murderer's brow (*EII*, v.v.74). Marlowe's theatre-geography gathers into a 'little room' two incommensurable points: the 'point / That shall begin the perpendicular' of the hyperbolical, imperial map and the 'unpointed' letter that spells out the sovereign's death. ('Gurney, it was left unpointed for the nonce' (*EII*, v.v.16)).

Notes

1 Richard Willes, 'To the right noble and excellent Lady, the Lady Brigit', in *The History of Travayle in the West and East Indies* (London, 1577).
2 We owe the insight to Ethel Seaton's groundbreaking article, 'Marlowe's Map', *Essays and Studies by Members of the English Association* 10 (1924): 13–35; see, however, John Gillies' critique of Seaton, in his *Shakespeare and the Geography of Difference* (Cambridge University Press, 1994), 52–3. The characterisation of Marlowe's use of 'cartographical passages' is drawn from Emrys Jones' astute and illuminating discussion of the uses of such passages in non-dramatic works prior to Marlowe (and which may have influenced Marlowe), in his '"A World of Ground": Terrestrial Space in Marlowe's *Tamburlaine* Plays', *The Yearbook of English Studies* 38:1–2, Tudor Literature (2008): 168–82 (169).
3 The characterisation of the 'old' geography as 'imprecise and religious or mythopoetic' is Garrett Sullivan's, in his 'Geography and Identity in Marlowe', in *The Cambridge Companion to Christopher Marlowe*, ed. Patrick Cheney (Cambridge University Press, 2004), 231–44 (232).

4 A review of recent scholarship on maps and mapping confirms as much. See Henry Turner, 'Literature and Mapping in Early Modern England, 1520–1688', in *The History of Cartography*, 6 vols., ed. J. B. Harley and David Woodward, Vol. III (University of Chicago Press, 2007), 412–26.
5 Christopher Marlowe, *Tamburlaine the Great, Part I*, in *Tamburlaine, Parts I and II; Doctor Faustus, A- and B-Texts; The Jew of Malta; Edward II*, ed. David Bevington and Eric Rasmussen (Oxford: Clarendon Press, 1995). All references are to this edition. For a defining account of the cultural functions of mapping in the period, see Gillies' important *Shakespeare and the Geography of Difference*. Gillies' monograph takes Shakespeare as its exemplar, but the characterisation of the insistence of 'poetic geography' (a term Gillies draws from Vico) works well for Marlowe too. Gillies' remarks about these lines from *Tamburlaine* are characteristically subtle (52–7). They conclude:

> The irony of the passage arises from Marlowe's awareness of the profound incongruity, the incommensurability, of the medieval and the Renaissance constructions of space. My point is to suggest why cartography is not to be taken as a transparent or merely 'given' aspect of geography and why geographic contexts are not to be constructed as the inert 'ground' of the poetic text. (57)

In *Maps and the Writing of Space in Early Modern England and Ireland* (Basingstoke: Palgrave, 2001), Bernhard Klein follows Gillies, but proposes a further interpretation of '*Tamburlaine*'s violent cartography'. The scene, he suggests, 'stages the explosion of the spatial paradigm that encoded space as an inherently social category: space is no longer represented, nor experienced, in terms of human corporeality ... the scene is thus evidence of two opposing conceptions of space – one social, one geometric – overlaying the medieval/renaissance divide of its cartographic referents' (19).
6 Thomas Blundeville, *A briefe description of universal mappes and cardes, and of their vse* (London: printed by Roger Ward, for Thomas Cadman, 1589), A2v, E4r–v.
7 *Ibid.*, B3v.
8 D. P., *Certaine brief and necessarie rules seruing for the vnderstanding of chartes and mappes* (London: by Henry Binneman, 1573), A4r.
9 John Blagrave, *The mathematical ievvel* (London: by Walter Veng, 1585), 6.
10 William Cunningham, *The Cosmographical glasse* (London: Ioan. Daij, 1559), 5–6.
11 William Bourne, *A booke called the treasure for traueilers* (London: by Thomas Dawson, 1578). He is citing from John Dee's introduction to Euclid, *The elements of geometrie of the most auncient philosopher Euclide of Megara, with a very fruitfull praeface made by M. I. Dee*, trans. H. Billingsley (London: by Iohn Daye, 1570).
12 For a different interpretation of deixis, see Russell West, *Spatial Representations and the Jacobean Stage: From Shakespeare to Webster* (Basingstoke and New York: Palgrave, 2002), especially his chapters 2 and 3, which, though focused on a later period and a slightly different sort of performance from the ones

Marlowe is putting together (West is interested in masques particularly), offer a nuanced account of dramatic self-staging.

13 An intriguing account of the function of soliloquy in *The Jew of Malta* may be found in Ruth Lunney's 'Speaking to the Audience: Direct Address in the Plays of Marlowe and His Contemporaries', in *Christopher Marlowe the Craftsman: Lives, Stage, and Page*, ed. Sarah K. Scott and M. L. Stapleton (Farnham: Ashgate, 2010), 109–22 (111–12): 'The early audiences at Marlowe's *The Jew of Malta* expected to be spoken to … In the rhetoric of performance, to interrupt the dialogue or appear alone on stage signaled, in simple terms, "look at me" … Direct address thus functioned as "deictic" rhetoric, as "pointing to" specific contexts or locations or relationships between speakers.'

CHAPTER THIRTEEN

Marlowe, history, and politics

Paulina Kewes

> And in the chronicle enrol his name
> For purging of the realm of such a plague.[1]

Marlowe touches on historical themes in his earlier plays, whether of late medieval Turkey and Persia in *Tamburlaine, Parts One and Two* (1587), Continental Reformation in *Doctor Faustus* (c. 1588), the founding myth of Rome in *Dido, Queen of Carthage* (c. 1589), or a noted Mediterranean siege in *The Jew of Malta* (c. 1589). But nowhere do history and politics commingle more effectively than in his last two works for the stage, *Edward II* (1592), a depressing and oddly anachronistic vision of England's medieval past, and *The Massacre at Paris* (1593), a blood-soaked chronicle of near-contemporary France.

Why this turn to history in 1592–3? In what follows, I shall consider the likely purposes of Marlowe's recasting of his sources – Holinshed's and others' chronicles in *Edward II*, recent French pamphleteering in *The Massacre*. I shall compare, too, the distinctive topical slant Marlowe gives to the materials with that found in works by his contemporaries, both Protestant and Catholic. While Marlowe's imaginative writings always transcend their immediate moment, these two historical tragedies make no bones about bending the past to tackle some of the most pressing issues of the day: the stature of monarchy and proprieties of resistance; the consequences of religious conflict; the vagaries of royal succession. So the challenge is to figure out how and why the two plays do so, and what audiences may have made of them.

The matter of England

The troublesome raigne and lamentable death of Edward the second, King of England: with the tragicall fall of proud Mortimer, based, like most late Elizabethan history plays, on the second edition of Holinshed's *Chronicles* with a few bits gleaned from Fabian and Stow,[2] retails the story of the medieval king's obsessive predilection for unsuitable favourites, which provoked stiff baronial opposition, civil war, deposition, and regicide. Modern critics have often read Marlowe's sensational piece in quasi-allegorical terms. For some, *Edward II* is a parable of Elizabeth's relations with her courtiers and advisers. Others have discerned in Marlowe's king a thinly disguised portrait of James VI of Scotland (1566–1625), who, by the early 1590s, had made no secret of his pretensions to succeed her on the English throne; and still others, of Henri III of France (1551–89), assassinated by a fanatical Catholic cleric barely three years before Marlowe's tragedy reached the stage. These competing identifications are neither mutually exclusive nor consistent. As an examination of the evidence that could be adduced in favour of each will demonstrate, Marlowe does not allegorise history in *Edward II*. Rather, he deploys topical allusion to make broader political points.

The putative association of Edward II with Elizabeth rests on two sets of arguments: first, that Marlowe deliberately echoes charges levelled at the queen's most powerful counsellors in a series of searing Catholic libels, and second, that he forges other connections with the present, for instance by describing the court revels designed for Edward by Gaveston in terms that recall the entertainments mounted for Elizabeth at Whitehall or at her courtiers' country estates (for example, Kenilworth, Cowdray, and Elvetham). With respect to the latter claim, an immediate caveat is necessary, for only current entertainments could give vivid and relevant substance to Gaveston's imaginings, whether or not these were topically loaded. What, though, of the former?

With England's confessional politics becoming increasingly polarised in the late 1560s and beyond, Catholics had vehemently attacked the godly pillars of the Elizabethan regime, Nicholas Bacon (1510–79), William Cecil (later Baron Burghley, 1520/1–98), and Robert Dudley (later Earl of Leicester, 1532/3–1588), in due course also targeting newer royal favourites such as Sir Walter Ralegh (1554–1618). From the manifesto issued at the time of the Northern Rebellion in 1569 and the anonymous libel *Treatise of Treasons* in 1572, to the still more toxic salvo *Leicester's Commonwealth* in 1584 and the slanderous pamphlets by Robert Persons and Richard Verstegan in the early 1590s, Bacon, Burghley, and Leicester were routinely vilified as atheist timeservers and ambitious Machiavellian upstarts whose advancement had come at the expense of the (Catholic) nobility, Elizabeth's natural counsellors.[3] Although the queen was ostensibly exempt from criticism and portrayed as the unwitting dupe and victim of her ministers' nefarious schemes, the venom with which those were lambasted could not but redound to her dispraise.

Marlowe's departures from his chronicle sources in *Edward II* pointedly allude to such allegations. For the play presents Edward's beloved favourites, Gaveston and then Spencer, as lowly social upstarts even though their historical prototypes were in fact well born. (Almost exactly at the time Marlowe was preparing the piece, Verstegan, Persons, and Thomas Stapleton dwelled with relish on the base origins of Burghley and his son Robert Cecil, likening the Cecils *père et fils* to evil counsellors in the mould of Gaveston and the Despensers.)[4] It also associates the haughty medieval peers and their seditious courses with current Catholic resistance theory – that is, belief in the temporal power of the pope to remove a recalcitrant monarch seen as the enemy of the Church. Meanwhile, the no less anachronistic portrayal of the king serves as a typological image of the Protestant Reformation, which had spelt England's break with Rome and rejection of papal authority in both Church and state, and which was reaffirmed by the 1559 Parliament in what came to be known as the Elizabethan Settlement. Marlowe's Edward is made to sound at times like a proto-reformer akin to the eponymous protagonist of *The troublesome raigne of John King of England* (1589–90), a jingoistic and militantly Protestant history play probably by George Peele, another University Wit.[5] *Inter alia*, Edward's exasperated exclamation 'Why should a king be subject to a priest?' would have struck an immediate chord with the mostly Protestant audience, followed in its turn by his threat of bloody destruction of 'proud' Rome's 'superstitious taper lights', 'antichristian churches', and 'priests' (iv.96–102).

In Holinshed, when the Bishop of Coventry is deprived of his see, the king and barons share in the spoils; Marlowe, in a scene of farcical priest-baiting reminiscent of Peele, which sees the cleric brutally divested of his gaudy popish vestments ('Throw off his golden mitre, rend his stole'; i.186), humiliated, and packed off to prison, has Edward bestow them all on Gaveston. Holinshed's king also tries to gain papal support against his wife Isabella and the revolted peers. By contrast, Marlowe's prelates and peers join forces to threaten the wayward monarch with excommunication and deposition unless he agrees to banish Gaveston:

> CANTERBURY: You know that I am legate to the Pope.
> On your allegiance to the See of Rome,
> Subscribe as we have done to his exile.

MORTIMER [*to* CANTERBURY]: Curse him if he refuse, and then may we
    Depose him and elect another king.

(iv.51–5)

These lines plainly advert to the excommunication of Elizabeth by Pope Pius V in 1570, which gained renewed topicality later in the reign after its alleged endorsement in 1588, the year of the Spanish Armada, by Pius' successor, Sixtus V.[6] Freeing her subjects from allegiance, the Bull of Excommunication, as Holinshed damningly noted, served as the pretext for papist efforts to topple the queen and promote a Catholic ruler in her stead.

Marlowe's transplanting of Catholic subversion into the early fourteenth century, like Peele's overtly topical redaction of England's thirteenth-century past, must have supplied an instant thrill of recognition. But the historical parallels Marlowe intimates are neither stable nor consistently sustained. For Edward's passionate homoerotic entanglement with Gaveston could not be further removed from Elizabeth's relations with the sombre and bureaucratic Cecils who, following the deaths of Bacon and Leicester, had emerged as the main power brokers at the English court and, by default, as the most hated objects of Catholic vilification. (They were also attracting the growing resentment of Leicester's political heir, Robert Devereux, second Earl of Essex.) Besides, the play appears to conjure up similarities between the stylish and suave Gaveston, whom the king elevates, *inter alia*, to the earldom of Cornwall (i.155), and Sir Walter Ralegh, Elizabeth's dashing and flamboyant lord lieutenant of Cornwall.[7]

The evocation of such suggestive if fleeting and contradictory associations between the favourites of, respectively, Edward and Elizabeth is emblematic of Marlowe's larger method in the play. Scarcely a straightforward allegory of the Elizabethan court along the lines proposed by Curtis E. Breight,[8] *Edward II* sprinkles liberal hints insinuating, and then thwarting, the application of the story not only to domestic affairs, a predominant concern, but also to late-sixteenth-century French and Scottish courts. Marlowe's aim, we shall see, is to draw out the challenges facing princes and nobles alike in an age of religious conflict.

Henri III of France, whose career and death Marlowe would dramatise in *The Massacre at Paris*, had been widely reviled by his ultra-Catholic subjects for his lukewarm embrace of the cause of the faith manifest in his readiness to grant toleration to the Protestants (called Huguenots in France); pusillanimity in his failure to oppose the danger of a Protestant succession (by 1584, the next in line to the French throne was the Huguenot Henri Bourbon, King of Navarre (1553–1610), whose claim Henri III endorsed); and *entente* with that arch-Jezebel, the queen of England. The opposition to Henri III was coordinated by the Catholic League, a pan-national alliance led by the Guises, France's premier aristocratic family, with the assistance of Spain and the papacy. The League's propaganda machine churned out a profusion of printed attacks lambasting Henri for, among other things, his obsession with male favourites, chiefly the dukes of Joyeuse and Epernon, unworthy of the titles, gifts, and influence conferred on them. In one exceptionally scandalous missive of 1588, with which Marlowe must have been familiar, a Leaguer publicist Jean Boucher drew a close analogy between Henri's passion for the detested Epernon (Joyeuse had died in 1587) and the English Edward's infatuation with Gaveston: the title page advertised the squib as a tragical and memorable history.[9]

Marlowe's tragedy exploits the topicality of Boucher's libel and the overall thrust of the League's polemical output. The prominence of the homoerotic bond between Edward and his young male followers, which, we have seen, militates against the application of the story to Elizabeth, conversely underscores the affinity between the stage King Edward and the historical Henri III. So does the ubiquity in the play of the word 'minion', derived from the French *mignon*, widely used on both sides of the Channel with reference to Henri's companions. And while Elizabeth was famously hostile to her favourites' matrimonial plans – Leicester had suffered a temporary disgrace and Ralegh a more lasting one following the revelation of their respective secret nuptials – Henri, like Marlowe's Edward, who promotes a match between Gaveston and his niece, the daughter of the Earl of Gloucester, had been instrumental in orchestrating his favourite Joyeuse's marriage to the queen's sister in 1581, and footed the bill for the magnificent wedding at court to boot.[10] Marlowe may also be glancing at French politics when he has Gaveston counsel Edward to have his arch-opponent, Mortimer Junior, 'privily made away' (vi.235) – exactly how Henri had disposed, in late December 1588, of his nemesis, the Duke of Guise, an episode Marlowe would represent in *The Massacre*.[11]

As with the English and French frames, so with the Scottish one. Marlowe goes out of his way to suggest a possible connection between Gaveston and Esmé Stuart, first Duke of Lennox (*c.* 1542–83), the French cousin and erstwhile favourite of James VI of Scotland, only to frustrate any attempt to infer a coherent reading of their relationship.[12] The stage favourite's status as a foreigner (the real Gaveston was a Gascon, and in the play he is repeatedly denounced as a Frenchman) and his inordinate sway over and intimacy with his king support the identification; so does the aristocratic insurgency against Edward that tallies with the Protestant nobles' capture and imprisonment of James in late August 1582, the so-called Ruthven Raid, which, as Holinshed relates, led to Lennox's downfall and death in exile the following year. (Tellingly, in 1583 Elizabeth's envoy to Scotland, Sir Francis Walsingham, had admonished the young king to mend his ways or else risk suffering the fate of England's Edward II.)[13] What undercuts the identification, however, is the fictive Gaveston's low birth (Lennox's lineage was illustrious) and vocal anticlericalism: 'What should a priest do with so fair a house? / A prison may beseem his holiness' (i.205–6). Lennox, it was feared, had tried to seduce James to popery, and his own conversion to Protestantism was widely dismissed as a sham. Besides, by 1592 Lennox had long been dead; reviving his memory would have been pointless, unless to glance at the Scottish king's new Catholic favourite, George Gordon, sixth Earl of Huntly (1561/2–1636), and perhaps foretell another ultra-Protestant coup. (One would in fact be attempted in 1596.) The Scottish and French subtexts of the play momentarily merge in the scene of Gaveston and the Lady's reunion at Edward's court (Scene vi), since, like Henri for Joyeuse, James had procured a lavish court wedding for Huntly who, in 1588, married Lennox's eldest daughter; two years later, James also arranged an advantageous match for another of his favourites, Alexander Lindsay, first Lord Spynie (*c.* 1563–1607).[14] In *Edward II*, though, Gaveston's wedding is foiled by the outbreak of civil war, and all that the favourite and his intended manage to accomplish before their final separation is jointly prefer to the king Spencer and Baldock, who will become his new followers.

Hitting too close to home by reinforcing the likeness between Elizabeth and Edward would have been inadvisable, but Marlowe could easily have forged a stronger link with either Scottish or French affairs. Other writers did so. Robert Greene took a barely concealed swipe at James VI in his romantic tragicomedy *The Scottish Historie of James the fourth* (*c.* 1590), and Peele drew a transparent parallel between King John and Henri III in his *Troublesome raigne*, a piece Marlowe seems to have had in mind when composing both *Edward II* and *The Massacre*. In Peele, the baronial rebellion fomented by the papal legate in early-thirteenth-century England, a staple of Protestant agitprop against Rome, is made to look like the civil war incited in late 1580s France by the Catholic League; the French invasion brings to mind the Spanish Armada; and John's poisoning by a monk recalls Henri's murder in 1589 by a Jacobin friar. The upshot is a stark warning against Catholic conspiracy at home and abroad epitomised by the papists' attempts to assassinate Elizabeth and conquer her country.[15] Marlowe, though he courts topicality, avoids peddling so simple a message.

The three topical frames that *Edward II* evokes would have been variously recognised and interpreted depending on the spectators' education, cultural competence, and degree of being in-the-know. If Marlowe adjusts the chronicle material to set up intermittent correspondences between his king and, in turn, Elizabeth, Henri, and James, there is another possible application that stems not from the playwright's tampering with the historical record but rather from his very choice of subject matter. Anyone au fait with England's medieval past would have known that the downfall of Edward II, constrained to give up the crown to his young heir, the future Edward III, and formally demoted by Parliament in 1327, furnished a compelling precedent for the enforced abdication of Mary, Queen of Scots in favour of her infant son James, and for her consequent deposition by Parliament in 1567. Although nothing in the play directs the audience to guess at the analogy, it would have been available to any politically savvy viewer (or reader) and obvious to those familiar with Holinshed's account of the two debacles, complete with verbatim transcriptions of the relevant legal instruments of deposition, in his English and Scottish chronicles respectively.[16] In this, admittedly far-fetched, scenario, the ascent of the reluctant Edward III, whose first action is to avenge his father's death (Scene xxvi), might well be taken as both a retrospective on James' coming of age and a presentiment of a Jacobean future.

Ultimately, Marlowe's goal in tweaking medieval history is not to put forward a tendentious appraisal of the politics of England, France, or Scotland, but rather to draw attention to the common condition of monarchy in these states. In all three, the burning question, which the prince's relationship with his or her counsellors or favourites crystallises, is the extent of the royal prerogative and the proprieties of resistance. Unlike his contemporaries, however, who typically inflect the spin they give to the past in line with their confessional preference, or else avoid mixing religion and politics altogether, Marlowe complicates the resonance of his story by inviting the audience to consider the contingent religious colouring of the conflict between the crown and the nobility. Unlike in England and France where the rebels are Catholic, in Scotland, he tacitly reminds us, the ultra-Protestants are the ones who resort to violence to bring their king to book.

Marlowe's target, I think, is the widespread use of religion to justify political heterodoxy. A case in point is how godly Protestants manipulated Edward's story. The account of his reign in John Foxe's *Acts and Monuments* (1563 and later editions), a massive ecclesiastical history popularly known as the 'Book of Martyrs' – familiar to both Marlowe and many in his audience, not least given its official sponsorship by the regime – could not be more different from the play. Unlike Marlowe who, for all his unsparing analysis of Edward's misgovernment, in the final scenes excites profound sympathy for the king, Foxe is relentlessly hostile towards Edward, whom he denounces as a cruel tyrant, and is uniformly supportive of the barons' actions.[17] Foxe's bishops and barons emerge as proto-reformers – they will not stomach papal interference in England's affairs, while Edward, dangerously susceptible to evil counsel and favouritism, and so depraved that he wants his wife and first-born son murdered, appears to be in cahoots with the pope. It is no less instructive to compare Marlowe's and Foxe's handling of the murder of Gaveston. In the play, the barons are divided about whether to yield to the king's request and grant him one last interview with his minion. They finally acquiesce, only for Warwick to break the code of arms by seizing Gaveston from his ally Pembroke's men and murdering him, a deed that casts a dark shadow over the integrity of the baronial cause (Scenes ix–x). Conversely, Foxe, downplaying the gravity of the abduction, has a conveniently unnamed sage persuade the barons to take advantage of having the hated favourite in their hands and to put him to death for the good of the country; they heed his wise counsel and unanimously resolve to kill Gaveston – which they proceed to do.[18] There is no dissent among the barons, and Foxe makes clear his approval for their resolute stand.

If, like Foxe, Marlowe's sources, Holinshed and Stow, are united in their negative assessment of Edward's reign, they seem more equivocal about the barons' actions. Consider, for example, the shocked interjection added to the second edition of Holinshed by its general editor, Abraham Fleming: 'Ah lamentable ruine from roialtie to miserable calamitie, procured by them cheefelie that should haue beene the pillers of the kings estate, and not the hooked engins to pull him downe from his throne!'[19] Unlike the playwright and the martyrologist, moreover, the chroniclers largely avoid importing current confessional divisions between Protestant and Catholic into England's medieval past except in the case of polemically sensitive reigns such as, for example, that of King John. Foxe subordinates his treatment of Edward to the overall ideological programme of the *Acts and*

Monuments: bad kings are those who rule wilfully and persecute the true believers, Edward was one of them, ergo he was justly – and providentially – defeated and deposed, and his proto-Protestant opponents deserve praise for standing up to the wicked despot allied with Rome. According to Foxe, 'where the church of Christ either through the negligence of Princes, or thorough their setting on, the poore members of Christ be persecuted and deuoured: shortly after ensueth some iust recompence of the Lord vpon those Princes, that eyther their liues do not long continue, or else they finde not that quiet in the common wealth, which they looke for'.[20] Like Foxe, Marlowe gives the story a contemporary spin. Unlike Foxe, he taints the barons, not the king, with popery.

In sharp contrast to Foxe's godly and public-spirited nobility, the readiness of Marlowe's peers to countenance the pope's deposing power is born of political expediency, not faith or concern for the common good, whatever claims they make to the contrary. And, as we have seen, their obsessive insistence that the king expel baseborn favourites recalls Catholic denunciations of those favoured and elevated by both Elizabeth and Henri III, something Marlowe's demotion of Gaveston works to reinforce.[21] In the play, the baronial cause is discredited. A far cry from Foxe's nobles, whose defection stems from patriotism and piety, Marlowe's become increasingly arbitrary, corrupt, and factious, a process culminating in Mortimer Junior's transformation from self-righteous rebel and the people's darling to a hubristic Machiavellian tyrant grimmer than Edward has ever been: 'I seal, I cancel, I do what I will. / Feared am I more then loved. Let me be feared, / And when I frown, make all the court look pale' (xxiv.50–2). We could be forgiven for deducing that Marlowe does no more than tap into the pervasive rhetoric of antipopery.

And yet, the play's fusion of political subversion and Catholicism is not watertight. Not only do the Abbot and monks offer shelter to the defeated king and, unlike their regicidal counterparts in Peele's *Troublesome raigne*, voice outrage at his rough usage by the captors in what could be construed as a telltale image of Catholic loyalism under Elizabeth (Scene xx), but the antipapist jibes spouted by Edward sound every bit as opportunistic and hollow as his adversaries' appeals to Rome. Besides, Mortimer's revealing simile in his despot's manifesto – this one-time champion of papistry now compares the hypocrisy with which he cloaks his overweening ambition to that of 'a bashful Puritan' (xxiv.58) – alerts the viewer to the easy reversibility of the confessionalised tools of political persuasion.

Marlowe's seemingly flippant, though in reality deadly serious, engagement with the religious politics of resistance underpins the insertion of further topical touches. Those turn our attention to the international ramifications of domestic conflict in its confessional aspect. For instance, the French king is unhistorically said to have landed in Normandy (vi.9) – the site of England's military intervention on behalf of the French Huguenots led as recently as 1591 by the Earl of Essex. Think also of Marlowe's depiction of Sir John of Hainault whose forces aid and abet Isabella and the rebel Catholic peers' invasion of England. In a neat reversal of the armed assistance currently being extended by Elizabeth to Dutch (and French) Protestants, Marlowe's Hainault, suggestively referred to as both 'Flanders' and 'Belgia' in the text (xvi.32; xvii.3), doubles up as Spain, widely feared in the early 1590s to be hatching another Armada.

Edward II's elusive and multilayered handling of royal despotism and aristocratic opposition to it furnished a structural model and inspiration for Shakespeare's *Richard II* (c 1596), a history play about the fall of a medieval monarch, whose politics are in many ways yet trickier to pin down. Here too the rights and wrongs of each side are finely balanced, and the overall movement proceeds from condemnation of the king to compassion for his plight. But Shakespeare relegated the evil favourites to the background and eschewed overt linkage of religion and political subversion. Above all, in raising the thorny question of the legitimacy of resistance, he refrained from assailing the audience with a barrage of topical allusions such as those *Edward II* continuously invites them to scrutinise, interpret, and apply.

The matter of France

If less subtle than its predecessor, *The Massacre at Paris* is a good deal more sophisticated than modern commentators have allowed. In a series of short, rapidly changing scenes, this earliest extant French history play covers seventeen turbulent years, from the cross-confessional match between the Huguenot Henri of Navarre and the Catholic Marguerite de Valois, sister of the French King Charles IX, and ensuing slaughter of the Huguenots on St Bartholomew's Day in 1572 to the assassination of Charles' successor, Henri III in 1589.[22] Critics used to write off *The Massacre*, which survives only in an abbreviated and mangled text, as a lurid recycling of Huguenot propaganda designed to whip up anti-Catholic and anti-Spanish sentiment.[23] We know now, thanks to Julia Briggs' luminous article, that for the second half of the play Marlowe also consulted League pamphlets, as well as relying on insider information.²⁴ Briggs has rightly challenged the view of *The Massacre* as 'crude Protestant propaganda' – the play is indeed more than that, but in offering a valuable corrective to previous readings, she may have overemphasised the near-symmetry of emotional response generated by the scenes of the Parisian Massacre and the violence against the Guises carried out on the orders of Henri III, respectively. For however revolting the latter, the fact remains that papists of one kind or another are behind both, as also behind the climactic act of regicide. Divided among themselves and ruthless as well as cunning and duplicitous, they must be encountered with prudence and forethought, and that may in turn require a certain slackening of the ethical basis of political action. How, though, can a leader aspiring to political effectiveness in a 'good' cause guard against compromising his or her morals in the manner of a Machiavellian villain? In addressing this question, Marlowe engages with the newly fashionable doctrine of reason of state, a body of thought advanced in the late 1580s by the Flemish thinker Justus Lipsius and the Italian Giovanni Botero, which controversially underwrote resort to extreme and often dubious measures in meeting the political needs of the moment – and the public good.²⁵

Marlowe's tactics and techniques in *The Massacre* diverge considerably from those he pursued in *Edward II*. In that play, he updated the story of a medieval English king to probe the dilemmas and hazards of modern kingship without, however, proposing any viable solutions. Now, bringing living or newly dead French royalty onto the stage, he tackles raw contemporary events with immediate and sweeping repercussions for his audience. Aside from eliciting revulsion for popish brutality and dissimulation in the at once grotesquely droll and deeply disturbing massacre scenes, and in the only marginally less violent sequence centring on the contest between Henri III and the Duke of Guise, the French lens serves to search England's foreign policy and confessional divisions.

With Parliament due to assemble on 19 February 1593, less than three weeks after the premiere of *The Massacre* on or around 30 January, it was no secret that heading the agenda would be the fraught situation in France, where the Huguenot champion Henri of Navarre (now also Henri IV of France) battled the Catholic League for control of the country. Accordingly, William Cecil, Lord Burghley – Elizabeth's Treasurer and Marlowe's government paymaster who only the previous year had extricated the playwright from an imbroglio on the Continent – and other members of the regime pushed for a large subsidy in support of Henri's offensive against the League; they urged, too, a grant of further privileges to stranger merchants, mostly French and Dutch Protestants, resident in London. Yet the festering religious tensions at home also came to the fore, as MPs clashed over the campaign, spearheaded by John Whitgift, Archbishop of Canterbury, against the reformers voicing dissatisfaction with the current shape of the English Church. The Puritan godly, to whom Burghley was sympathetic, were on the defensive, as Whitgift and his episcopal allies, with the backing of the queen, redoubled efforts to clamp down on all Protestant dissent, from Puritans to the more radical sectarian movements. The conservatives eventually succeeded in converting a bill aimed at popish recusants into a double-edged sword that would apply with equal force to Protestant dissenters.[26]

Marlowe was no government hack. But the confessional and political tenor of *The Massacre* does bear a close resemblance to Burghley's views. Powerfully anti-Catholic and anti-League, Burghley was also far more tolerant of Protestant dissent at home than Whitgift, whom the Presbyterians had mocked during the late Marprelate Controversy as 'the Pope of Lambehith'.[27] Marlowe's piece highlights the various Catholic atrocities, subtly downplays Navarre's espousal of resistance theory, and concludes with the dying Henri III's hearty encomium of Elizabeth, followed – in flagrant violation of fact – by the king's rousing call to arms against the Romish Antichrist, loudly seconded by Navarre. Like the ever proliferating translations of Huguenot writings, published with Burghley's connivance, *The Massacre* would have supplied effective agitprop in favour of further military and financial aid for Henri IV.[28] In addition to being dubbed 'Huguenots' and 'Protestants', the French reformers (who followed Calvin's teaching) are reviled by *The Massacre*'s papist villains as 'Lutherans' and 'Puritans', which evinces a sort of reformed brotherhood *sans frontières*.[29] European Protestants of all stripes, the play seems to imply, must unite against the popish Holy League and, if necessary, even collaborate with the Catholic politiques. On the domestic front, moreover, *The Massacre* works to bring the Puritans into the fold of the Church of England and set them apart from other sectarians.

To urge, as I believe Marlowe does in *The Massacre*, that English and Continental reformers must overlook doctrinal differences between them and make common cause against popery was to counter the subversive pamphleteering by Hispanophile Catholic exiles such as the anonymous author of *The Treatise of Treasons*, Cardinal William Allen, Persons, and Verstegan, with which, as we have seen, Marlowe had already engaged in *Edward II*. Those argued, first, that by adopting the Elizabethan Settlement in 1559, England had set herself apart from other reformed churches, risking isolation on the international scene, and, secondly, that the country was riven by confessional tensions, with conflict between Protestants and Catholics severely compounded by acute dissension within the Protestant community. Middle-of-the-road members of the Church of England, said the Catholic publicists, were now in open conflict with the Puritans (covertly patronised by Burghley) and more radical sects such as the Brownists. These charges cut close to the bone. Only in 1589, Richard Bancroft, Whitgift's right-hand man, had preached a sermon at that most public of London's pulpits, Paul's Cross, lamenting intra-Protestant feuds and impugning the left-of-centre critics of the Elizabethan Church as more pernicious than its popish adversaries: 'When brethren fall out, they growe to great extremities. The Papists did never deale with more egernes against us than these men do now.'[30]

What made Marlowe's call for confessional unity among reformers all the more timely was the increasingly fraught issue of religious refugees in the capital. In 1590s London, xenophobia often flared up despite common faith.[31] Protestant exiles from France and the Low Countries, perceived as commercial competitors being given unfair advantage by the regime, were objects of rising resentment and jealousy. The anti-alien (and, implicitly, antigovernment) feeling might be usefully counteracted by the spectacle of fellow-Protestants being butchered by vicious and treacherous papists. This spectacle had the further benefit of reaffirming Huguenot martyrdom in the St Bartholomew Massacre (since 1583 also part and parcel of Foxe's *Acts and Monuments*) at a time when the papist exiles were garnering political capital from publicising the anti-Catholic atrocities supposedly perpetrated by heretics in France, the Low Countries, and England. Verstegan's Latin counter-martyrology, *Theatrum crudelitatum haereticorum nostri temporis* (1587; French translation 1588), complete with shocking engravings to rival those in Foxe, attacked the Elizabethan state for its Machiavellian tactics in pretending to punish Catholics for treason and not religion. The prime target of Verstegan's book was none other than Burghley, the architect of the regime's anti-Catholic policy. A later pamphlet by Persons, *Newes from Spayne and Holland* (1593), retailed the slanderous report that Burghley, aware his policy of repression and persecution was but steeling the resolve of the English Catholics, would soon resort to 'massacring and murthing' them 'uppon the sudden'.[32]

A stunning commercial success, Marlowe's *Massacre*, it seems, signally failed in promoting popular solidarity with Continental Protestants. The 1593 Parliament, in session until April, toughened laws against non-conformity (much to Burghley's chagrin, for now both Catholic and Protestant outliers were subject to equally severe penalties). It also voted a hefty subsidy to back Henri IV's fight against the League. One of the measure's Commons sponsors passionately urged 'the preservacion of that brave and worthie kinge of our religion and therin most zealous ... His cause is ours; his enimyes ours ... His countrie is nowe the stage of Christendome wherin all nacions our enimyes seke to play their tragicall partes.'[33] However persuasive such rhetoric may have been at Westminster, elsewhere anti-alien and antiwar sentiments were on the rise, not least because foreign merchants had just received still further privileges. The collective paranoia climaxed with the appearance on 5 May of the so-called Dutch Church Libel, probably by Thomas Deloney, a silk-weaver and popular ballad-maker, which charged the Dutch and French immigrant communities with greed, hypocrisy, and Machiavellian corruption. In doing so, the piece, signed 'Tamburlaine', cleverly seized on the rhetoric reserved in official propaganda for the country's Catholic enemies – the pope, Spain, and expatriate papists. While poor Englishmen 'dy like dogges as sacrifice for you', the apparent victims, 'counterfeitinge religion for your flight', benefit at once from government patronage and from Spanish gold. In threatening violent retribution, the libel ominously alluded to Marlowe's French play. 'Weele cutte your throtes', it warned, 'in your temples praying / Not paris massacre so much blood did spill / As we will doe iust vengeance on you all.'[34] But whereas Marlowe's Huguenots fall victims to the fury of their Catholic compatriots, here the aliens will be slaughtered by their exasperated English co-religionists. One can imagine how high tempers must have run when, in July, the much-vaunted star of the international Protestant cause, Henri IV, converted to Catholicism in order to secure the French crown. Were not Deloney's charges of religious hypocrisy amply borne out? By the time of its 1594 revival, *The Massacre* had acquired fresh, and profoundly unwelcome, currency. Spoken by the apostate's alter ego, the closing lines – 'Rome and all those popish prelates there / Shall curse the time that e'er Navarre was king' (xxiv.110–11) – would have rung hollow indeed.

Both resolutely topical, Marlowe's English and French history plays are quite disparate in their effects. *Edward II* tempts the audience to apply the nation's medieval past to current concerns while scattering insufficient or misleading clues to do so with any confidence. Even the play's antipopery is only skin-deep, as Marlowe exposes religious bias of whatever sort as but an expedient political tool. By contrast, *The Massacre*'s take on contemporary events directly affecting the spectators' lives seems both far more clear-cut and more orthodox, though of course this simpler picture may relate to the state of its text and the conditions of its transmission. Unfairly disparaged as mere agitprop, the piece offers a probing exploration of political behaviour and the rhetoric used to justify it. *Au courant* with the latest trends in political thought, which it sceptically reviews, *The Massacre* advocates support for Henri IV not only because he is a Protestant – after all, even Henri III can mouth antipapal platitudes – but because supporting Henri is in England's interest.

In *Edward II* and *The Massacre*, the most 'historical' of Marlowe's history plays, the interaction between the past and the present operates in very different ways and to rather different ends. The former aims at a multiplicity of topical targets to raise a general question about the position of monarchy in a confessionally polarised world which, however, it refuses to resolve; the latter advances a fairly coherent interpretation of foreign and domestic affairs in a bid to under-prop a particular, politically expedient course of action. Playwrights wanting to stage a topical piece needed to get the right balance between sensational audience appeal and less overt political significances: Marlowe's last two plays, however divergent in other respects, both did.

Notes

I wish to thank Sue Doran, Richard Dutton, Tom Freeman, Simon May, Glyn Parry, Richard Proudfoot, Arthur Williamson, and Blair Worden for conversation and advice, and the Huntington Library staff for being as ever wonderfully helpful and efficient.

1 *Edward II*, in Christopher Marlowe, *The Complete Plays*, ed. Frank Romany and Robert Lindsey (London: Penguin, 2003), iv.269–70. Further references to Marlowe's works will be to this edition.
2 Vivien Thomas and William Tydeman, eds., *Christopher Marlowe: The Plays and Their Sources* (London and New York: Routledge, 1994), 341–50; Paulina Kewes, Ian W. Archer, and Felicity Heal, eds., *The Oxford Handbook of Holinshed's* Chronicles (Oxford University Press, 2013). To compare the texts of the two editions of Holinshed, see www.cems.ox.ac.uk/holinshed/.
3 Simon Adams, 'Favourites and Factions at the Elizabethan Court', in *Leicester and the Court: Essays on Elizabethan Politics* (Manchester University Press, 2002), 46–67; Michael C. Questier, 'Elizabeth and the Catholics', in *Catholics and the 'Protestant Nation': Religious Politics and Identity in Early Modern England*, ed. Ethan H. Shagan (Manchester University Press, 2005), 69–94.
4 Curtis E. Breight, *Surveillance, Militarism and Drama in the Elizabethan Era* (Basingstoke: Macmillan, 1996), 134ff.; Victor Houliston, *Catholic Resistance in Elizabethan England: Robert Persons's Jesuit Polemic, 1580–1610* (Aldershot: Ashgate, 2007), 51ff.

5 For the attribution to Peele, see Brian Vickers, '*The Troublesome Reign*, George Peele, and the Date of *King John*', in *Words that Count: Essays on Early Modern Authorship in Honor of MacDonald P. Jackson*, ed. Brian Boyd (Newark: University of Delaware Press, 2004), 78–116; and 'Introduction' to *The Troublesome Reign of John, King of England by George Peele*, ed. Charles R. Forker (Manchester University Press, 2011), 6–30.
6 Ronald Knowles, 'The Political Contexts of Deposition and Election in *Edward II*', *Medieval and Renaissance Drama in England* 14 (2001): 105–21 (115); Paulina Kewes, 'History Plays and the Royal Succession', in Kewes et al., *Holinshed's* Chronicles, 497–513 (506), and *This Great Matter of Succession: Drama, History, and Elizabethan Politics* (Oxford University Press, forthcoming 2014).
7 Susan Doran, 'Elizabeth I and her Favourites: The Case of Sir Walter Ralegh', in *Elizabeth I and the 'Sovereign Arts': Essays in Literature, History, and Culture*, ed. Donald Stump, Linda Shenk, and Carole Levin (Tucson: University of Arizona Press, 2011), 157–74.
8 Breight, *Surveillance, Militarism*, 134ff.
9 Jean Boucher, *Histoire tragique et memorable de Pierre de Gaverston* (1588).
10 Stuart Carroll, *Martyrs and Murderers: The Guise Family and the Making of Europe* (Oxford University Press, 2009), 238.
11 *Ibid.*, 289–92. Marlowe's barons, for their part, discuss having Gaveston assassinated.
12 John M. Berdan, 'Marlowe's *Edward II*', *Philological Quarterly* 3 (1924), 197–207; and, more recently, Lawrence Normand, '"What passions call you these?": *Edward II* and James VI', in *Christopher Marlowe and English Renaissance Culture*, ed. Darryll Grantley and Peter Roberts (Aldershot: Scolar Press, 1996), 172–97.
13 Conyers Read, *Mr Secretary Walsingham and the Policy of Queen Elizabeth*, 3 vols. (Oxford: Clarendon Press, 1925), Vol. II, 218.
14 J. R. M. Sizer, *ODNB* article on Huntly.
15 Kewes, 'Royal Succession', 502–6.
16 Kewes, *This Great Matter*.
17 John Foxe, *Acts and Monuments*, 4th edn (London, 1583), 389ff., at www.johnfoxe.org.
18 *Ibid.*, 391–2.
19 In Raphael Holinshed, *Holinshed's Chronicles of England, Scotland, and Ireland*, 3 vols. (London, 1587), Vol. III, 341.
20 Foxe, *Acts and Monuments*, 800.
21 Blair Worden, 'Favourites on the English Stage', in *The World of the Favourite*, ed. J. H. Elliott and L. W. B. Brockliss (New Haven and London: Yale University Press, 1999), 159–83; Curtis Perry, *Literature and Favouritism in Early Modern England* (Cambridge University Press, 2006), 193.
22 On plays dealing with current events, see Paulina Kewes, 'Contemporary Europe in Elizabethan and Early Stuart Drama', in *Shakespeare and Renaissance*

Europe, ed. Andrew Hadfield and Paul Hammond (London: Nelson, 2004), 150–92.
23 Paul H. Kocher, 'Contemporary Pamphlet Background for Marlowe's *The Massacre at Paris*', *Modern Language Quarterly* 8 (1947): 151–73, 309–18.
24 Julia Briggs, 'Marlowe's *Massacre at Paris*: A Reconsideration', *RES* 34 (1983): 257–78.
25 I owe this point to Mr Simon May's 'Marlowe and Monarchy' (D.Phil. thesis, University of Oxford, in progress).
26 Patrick Collinson, *The Elizabethan Puritan Movement* (London: Jonathan Cape, 1967), Part VIII, esp. 431.
27 Martin Marprelate, *Theses Martinianae* (1589), sig. D3v.
28 Lisa Ferraro Parmelee, *Good Newes from Fraunce: French Anti-League Propaganda in Late Elizabethan England* (University of Rochester Press, 1996).
29 Christopher Marlowe, *The Massacre at Paris*; 'Lutherans': vi.11, 39; 'Puritans': xiv.55, xix.45.
30 Richard Bancroft, *A Sermon Preached at Paules Crosse the 9. of Februarie, being the first Sunday in the Parleament* (London, 1588 [1589]), 52.
31 Laura Yungblut, *Strangers Settled Here amongst Us: Policies, Perceptions, and the Presence of Aliens in Elizabethan England* (London: Routledge, 1996), 41–2; Lien Bich Luu, '"Taking the bread out of our mouths": Xenophobia in Early Modern London', *Immigrants and Minorities* 19 (2000): 1–22.
32 Robert Persons, *Newes from Spayne and Holland* ([Antwerp], 1593), fo. 21r.
33 *Proceedings in the Parliaments of Elizabeth I*, ed. T. E. Hartley, 3 vols. (Leicester University Press, 1981–95), Vol. III, 56. Amid growing unrest, a bill aimed at immigrants was passed by the Commons but thrown out by the Lords.
34 Arthur Freeman, 'Marlowe, Kyd, and the Dutch Church Libel', *English Literary Renaissance* 3 (1973): 44–52 (50–1). For the attribution to Deloney, see Matthew Dimmock, 'Tamburlaine's Curse: An Answer to a Great Marlowe Mystery', *Times Literary Supplement* (19 November 2010): 16–17.

CHAPTER FOURTEEN

Marlowe and social distinction

James R. Siemon

While critics overwhelmingly agree that Marlowe's works launch 'provocative attacks on traditional ideas of place, belief and status', the plays and poems also articulate positive notions of social distinction in non-traditional terms. Forms of distinction appear repeatedly imagined, achieved, measured – or lost – by means of such qualities or capacities as wit or emotional and aesthetic sensibility.[1] Taken together, these attitudes, tastes, styles of expression, and modes of behaviour and perception suggest a Marlovian *habitus*, a disposition derived from Marlowe's own history and responding to the social and economic challenges confronting him as an articulate, ambitious, and highly educated commoner of lowly, provincial origins and few economic resources.[2]

Marlowe's *Hero and Leander* and *Ovid's Elegies* invoke terms that are highly relevant to social distinction and do so in striking ways.[3] For example, *Hero and Leander* employs the most widely recognised, vaguely defined, and frequently contested early modern social category – the 'gentle' – and, completely ignoring period accounts that based gentility on birth, wealth, and public reputation, affirms distinction based on affect:

> In gentle breasts
> Relenting thoughts, remorse and pity rests.
> And who have hard hearts and obdurate minds,
> But vicious, harebrained, and illit'rate hinds?
> (*HL*, II.215–18)[4]

The claim here that only 'hinds' – rustics (cf. *OE*, I.xiii.15) – have hard hearts is particularly odd, since Marlowe frequently represents the well-born, the well-reputed, the publicly recognised as especially pitiless. In *The Massacre at Paris*, for example, the Guise boasts aristocratic birth, rejects demands that 'gentle minds should pity others' pains', and taunts Ramus, the 'scholar' he murders, by calling him 'peasant' (*MP*, I.iv.13; I.vii.54). In *Tamburlaine*, Damascus' rulers show their 'obdurate breasts' in

155

repulsing the town's pleading Virgins (*1 Tamb.*, V.i.28).⁵ Ferneze, Governor of Malta, displays his 'unrelenting ... stony [breast]' in twice refusing to 'relent' and pity Barabas (*JM*, I.ii.143–4; V.v.71–2); Ferneze's 'gentle' son angrily calls his rival a 'base-born peasant' before killing him (*JM*, II.iii.280). But the phrase 'illit'rate hinds' introduces another factor into the definition of gentility in characterising its opposite social condition.

While many Elizabethans conceded that learning was a good thing even for wealthy aristocrats and that a university education could confer the nominal status of 'gentleman' even on one who, like Marlowe, was born to non-wealthy, tradesman parents and studied on scholarship, Marlowe's works repeatedly associate learning with landless poverty, an economic condition that many contemporaries saw as practically contradicting, if not quite barring, gentility.⁶ As Marlowe's Ithamore asks rhetorically, 'what gentry can be in a poor Turk of ten pence?' (*JM*, IV.ii.36–7). In Thomas Deloney's *The Gentle Craft* (1597), the aspiring tradesman Simon Eyre argues that truly to become a 'Gentleman forever' requires not birth, title, or office, which confer gentility 'only ... in name', but landed wealth sufficient to join 'that sort' – i.e. that class-like group of people – 'whose lands are answerable to their vertues, and whose rents can maintain the greatnesse of their minde'.⁷ If education might earn some modicum of respect or title, Marlowe makes learning the virtual antithesis of wealth: 'I am a scholar!' Ramus protests, 'How should I have gold?' (*MP*, I.vii.17). Scholars like Baldock in *Edward II* may assert their 'gentry' fetched 'from Oxford, not from heraldry' (*EII*, vi[II.ii].240–1), but Marlowe reduces the historical figure of Baldock, who was a doctor of Oxford and a cleric, into a poor 'servant' who tutors for a living (*EII* v[II.i].30).⁸ *Hero and Leander* represents poverty as an unavoidable curse which 'always' renders 'every scholar' poor 'to this day', while 'gross gold from them runs headlong to the boor'. Furthermore, the poem continues:

> Midas' brood shall sit in Honour's chair,
> To which the Muses' sons are only heir :
> And fruitful wits that [in aspiring] are
> Shall discontent run into regions far.
> And few great lords in virtuous deeds shall joy,
> But be surprised with every garish toy,
> And still enrich the lofty servile clown,
> Who with encroaching guile keeps learning down.
> (*HL*, l.471–82)⁹

This passage suggests standards that cut across traditional social categories. Despite enormous differences, the rustic 'boor', the public officer holding civic 'honour's chair', and the courtier (the 'lofty servile clown') appear lumped together as competitors with the learned for scarce economic resources. Marlowe labels their tactics against 'fruitful wits' with the heavily charged term 'encroaching', a word frequently used to characterise the actions of exploitive landlords in expropriating land from the weak. Great lords, indifferent to the 'virtuous deeds' they should recognise, reward instead those who '[surprise]' them with 'every garish toy', leaving truly 'aspiring' wits to flee to 'regions far'. Such wandering refugee intellectuals included Marlowe's close associates, Thomas Watson and Thomas Nashe, writers who, like Marlowe himself, were university educated. Whether the journeys of such scholars were compelled by religious or economic necessities, the imaginary portrayal of wandering 'Scholars' as 'rare-witted gentlemen ... learned and liberal' (*JM*, III.i.7–8), rich enough to patronise the Maltese prostitute Bellamira in *The Jew of Malta*, sounds like a compensatory fantasy.

But not even all 'wits' are the right sort. Marlowe translates Ovid's famous self-justification of refined poetic pursuits despite the crowd's bad taste, 'Vilia miretur vulgus' ('Let common people admire common things'), with a sneer at 'base-conceited wits' who admire 'vile' things (*OE*, I.xv.35). Thus, in Marlowe's imagination, one form of 'wit' opposes another: the intrinsic, if socially unrecognised, value of the poet's 'fruitful wit' opposes the vile tastelessness of 'base-conceited wits', no matter their birth, wealth, or standing. Furthermore, although this elegy proclaims the superior values of 'immortal ... verse' over the authority of 'kings ... and kingly shows' and of the Castalian spring over the 'gold-bearing' Tagus, elsewhere in Marlowe 'wit' appears in a close but by no means simple relationship to discursive powers of language – to 'poetry' of course – and also to learning.

Ovid's elegy I.xv rebuts the claims of competing scales of social standing with considerable Elizabethan importance. Marlowe's Ovid resists the limited temporal and geographical 'scope' of those who dismiss his poems as 'fruits of an idle quill'; instead, he claims a universal context in which 'all the world may ever chant my name', while opposing distinction based on military achievement, legal profession, or political office: 'War's dusty honours', 'brawling laws', or putting one's 'voice to sale in every cause'.

Understood in their Roman dialogical contexts, the 'light love' and the 'idle quill' affirmed by Ovid's *Elegies* thus express 'dissent from the heroic and patriotic line of thinking' that had in Ovid's day become institutionalised.[10] If the poet-speaker admits that 'when Caesar should be writ, / Alone Corinna moves my wanton wit' (III.xi.15–16), such phrases do not mean that politics or social distinction go unimplicated in the Ovidian bedroom. Sometimes Ovid is brutally specific: the speaker's impotence prompts an attempt to arouse him by grotesquely exaggerated social deference, as his girl 'soothed me up, and called me "Sir"' (III.vi.11). Other times, his erotic humiliation by the 'rich churls', the 'judge and knight' who compete for his lover's attentions, compels Ovid's speaker to demand, 'What man will now take liberal arts in hand, / Or think soft verse in any stead to stand? / Wit was sometimes more precious than gold, / Now poverty great barbarism we hold' (III.vii.1–4). These sexual disappointments even provoke atheistic outbursts: 'God is a name, no substance, feared in vain' (III.iii.23). In such passages, Marlowe's Ovid suggests proximity to Marlowe's other works, a resemblance also registered by the translation of Ovid's self-confessed sexual promiscuity, his 'ambitiosus amor', into an affirmation of mental distinction as 'my ambitious ranging mind' (II.iv.48), a phrase that closely echoes the 'aspiring mind ... still climbing' of Tamburlaine (*1 Tamb.*, II.vii.20–3).

However, Ovid's rejection of officially recognised social distinctions sometimes gets complicated. The final elegy grants criticism of his 'weak elegies' as 'wanton toys' but also reasserts the poet's aristocratic standing: he is 'not only by war's rage made gentleman' but also 'heir of an ancient house' (III.xiv). Thus, the Ovidian poet-speaker displays multiple minds: his art might promise 'all the world' will 'ever chant my name', but he keeps open other lines of credit, social and economic. Marlowe lacked these options. His M.A. degree gave him officially certified 'learning', and he had obvious discursive gifts that might attract patrons. Conceivably, he could compete with the 'lofty servile clown' to provide 'garish toys' to 'surprise' great lords for 'gross gold' as Gaveston enlists 'wanton poets, pleasant wits' to titillate King Edward and enrich Gaveston himself, 'Midas-like' (*EII*, i[1.i].50–2; iv[1.iv].409).

But consider Tamburlaine's own negative relation to 'gross gold' and his surprising affirmation of scholarly endeavour. Tamburlaine's forces prove indifferent to the gold spread about the field by the Persian martial nobility who intend to entrap their 'base-born' and thus presumably 'greedy-minded' natures (*1 Tamb.*, II.ii.65–7). In fact, Tamburlaine's own terms for his complex economic attitudes derive from Elizabethan discussions of gentle distinction: he calls the 'prizes' he takes 'friends' to establish his 'state' and 'maintain [his] life exempt from servitude' (*1 Tamb.*, I.II.28–31). While 'prizes' derives from the language of contemporary privateering, Tamburlaine's other terms echo familiar discourse about social distinction: a gentleman's 'state' or standing demanded countenance by 'friends' and economic 'maintenance' sufficient to avoid 'servitude' – i.e.

actual labour or dependency.[11] Tamburlaine's euphemistic appropriation of the language of English gentility to turn economic booty into socially acceptable terms is striking but hardly compares to the daring and complex transformation of values in Tamburlaine's praise of 'aspiring minds':

> The thirst of reign and sweetness of a crown,
> That caused the eldest son of heavenly Ops
> To thrust his doting father from his chair
> And place himself in the empyreal heaven,
> Moved me to manage arms against thy state.
> What better precedent than mighty Jove?
> Nature, that framed us of four elements
> Warring within our breasts for regiment,
> Doth teach us all to have aspiring minds:
> Our souls, whose faculties can comprehend
> The wondrous architecture of the world
> And measure every wand'ring planet's course,
> Still climbing after knowledge infinite
> And always moving as the restless spheres,
> Wills us to wear ourselves and never rest
> Until we reach the ripest fruit of all.
> That perfect bliss and sole felicity,
> The sweet fruition of an earthly crown.
> (*1 Tamb.*, II.vii.12–29)

Whatever the revolutionary implications of this speech in affirming ambitious struggle over the peaceful stability and established lineal order praised virtually everywhere else in Elizabethan discourse, its dialogical origins and its onstage response both deserve emphasis.

For those who had ears – educated ears – to register its classical cosmology and its parody of Calvinist learning, Tamburlaine's credo suggests an author with considerable intellectual capital and a disposition to deploy it with bold irreverence.[12] Furthermore, the definition of human nature as inherently driven to pursue 'knowledge infinite', though far more relevant to scholarly Faustus than 'warlike' Tamburlaine, surely resonated with Marlowe's highly educated, demographically disadvantaged peers who might dream of attaining marketable recognition for the value of their 'knowledge'.

On stage, Theridamas, a Persian warrior-gentleman, 'reknowned', 'noble and mild' (*1 Tamb.*, I.ii.239, 162), is so inspired by Tamburlaine as to renounce his own impeccable social qualifications and translate Tamburlaine's intellectual questing into terms derived from the early modern language of distinction:

> And that made me to join with Tamburlaine,
> For he is gross and like the massy earth
> That moves not upwards nor by princely deeds
> Doth mean to soar above the highest sort.
> (*1 Tamb.*, II.vii.30–3)

Although most Elizabethan commentators allowed that social strata divided into vaguely defined but relational 'sorts' of people should be theoretically open to 'rise' in status by one's 'deeds', Theridamas here affirms an openly *competitive* desire by *anyone* to get 'above the highest sort'. Pursued drives replace recognised limits; one is defined by how one strives to get 'above' others; deeds, not birth, are 'princely'. Indifferently as regards birth or wealth, one is 'gross' only in failing to 'mean' to soar above other 'sorts'. This redefinition of distinction and grossness according to performance directly counters royal Dido's ontological sense of 'the people' as so base by nature that 'their gross eye-beams' will 'taint' gentle Aeneas (*DQC*, III.i.72–4). It also clarifies the surprising insults hurled by 'base and obscure' Gaveston at the English nobles for being 'base' and 'leaden', since, rather than striving to greatness by princely deeds, they passively 'glory in [their] birth' and rest content to 'eat [their] tenants' beef' (*EII*, vi[II.ii].74–5).

But Marlovian notions of distinction depend on more than desire to rise over others; it is crucial how one deports oneself to achieve and display superiority. Thus, Tamburlaine, the 'base usurping vagabond' and 'peasant ignorant / Of lawful arms or martial discipline' (*1 Tamb.*, IV.iii.21, IV.i.64–5), overturns the insulting assessments of his noble and professional opponents by conceiving and observing his own unconventional rules of conduct and combat. Rather than stooping to mere calculation and 'labour', he conceives his military campaign as a 'pretty jest' when he launches a daring headlong charge against 'twenty thousand men' (II.v.90–6).[13] And the play seldom lets us forget about the potential distinguishing value of poetic sensibility, even in the context of military strategy.

A chance allusion to a learned interpretation of classical myth by the royal counsellor Meander in discussing military strategy with the 'witless' hereditary monarch, Mycetes, prompts the king's own meagre reflections on the status of poets and on the usefulness of learning:

> And 'tis a pretty toy to be a poet.
> Well, well, Meander thou art deeply read
> And, having thee, I have a jewel sure.
> Go on, my lord, and give your charge I say.
> Thy wit will make us conquerors today.
> (II.ii.54–8)

Here a king trivialises the 'poet' per se, but still dimly recognises 'wit' in a 'deeply read' interpreter of poetry and credits such wit as a capacity for military command.

This exchange offers a fantasy resolution to the problem that faced educated Elizabethans with too few opportunities to employ their humanist learning in the weighty positions for which they presumed it qualified them. It is hard to grasp that this desirable outcome was ever more than fantasy; yet the case of Gabriel Harvey, a product of a distinguished education who resembles Marlowe in forgoing the obvious value of that education in the Church, provides a comparison. Whether studying at Cambridge or later toiling in London's Court of Arches, Harvey read voraciously, wrote everything from popular pamphlets to literary theory, and imagined himself among world historical figures: 'What woold Caesar do, or suffer in this case?' Harvey's marginalia ask; or 'What woold … Machiauel aduise in this Case? … What course of proceding, or conueiance, woold ye cunningest, & deepest witt in ye world, take?'[14] Harvey's classical education and capacity to engage imaginatively with his reading were taken seriously in military and political deliberations by Sir Thomas Smith when Smith was planning his Irish colonial enterprise in the 1570s. Sir Thomas, his son, Sir Humphrey Gilbert, and Walter Haddon debated the cases presented by Livy's historical figures of Marcellus and Fabius to determine military strategy. These notables and 'others of gentle birth' credited the son of a ropemaker for his strategic advice, while Harvey, for his part, imagined himself a Roman, proclaiming 'There are times when I would rather be Marcellus, times when Fabius.'[15]

Harvey's situation here might suggest Faustus, born to 'parents base of stock' but patronised by Emperor Charles V for his ability to conjure up imaginary classical figures like Alexander the Great (*DrF*, Scene x), but Harvey's advice had military and political consequences. When it came to a career, however, things went wrong. The literary intellectual who presumed to evaluate the great Romans and Greeks as 'all uery quick of witt, and passingly eloquent in speach… There noble audacity, inuincible corage, jndustrious actiuity, and speedy dexterity: with many witty pollicies, & sum wily suttletles' failed to secure a position.[16] Like Marlowe, Harvey could attract notice from a high patron, but Harvey's failure to retain the post of secretary to the Earl of Leicester, being told that he was 'fitter for the Universitie then for the Court', according to Thomas Nashe, prompted Harvey's sweeping complaint:

Common Lerning, & ye name of A good schollar, was neuer so much contemn'd, & abiectid of princes, Pragmaticals, & common Gallants, as nowadayes; jnsomuch that it necessarily concernith, & importith ye lernid ether praesently to hate yr books; or actually to insinuate, & enforce themselues, by uery special, & singular propertyes of emploiable, & necessary vse, in all affaires, as well priuate, as publique, amounting to any commodity, ether oeconomical, or politique.[17]

Harvey laments the prevailing demand for specialisation, for the 'good' scholar's being required to reduce his 'Common' – i.e. general – learning to market demands for applied skills, for any 'singular' and marketable use. Suffering the contempt of nobles, professionals, and courtiers, Harvey's lament for learning recalls Marlowe's complaint about great lords, office holders, and 'lofty servile clown[s]'. Harvey had in fact been warned, early and clearly enough, that if he desired 'to live as a free man' he should 'devote [himself] to some lucrative profession as soon as possible', but he wanted more.[18] Marlowe's Faustus comes to mind, with the fantasy of polymath scholarship capable of dismissing all professions political, academic, and religious in pursuing a power-knowledge beyond all disciplinary and occupational definitional boundaries. Yet Thomas Nashe, a university product so taken with Faustus' grand dismissal of any mere career as to record Faustus' 'Che sara sara deuinynitie adieu' twice in his own marginalia, mocked Harvey not as Faustus but as a disappointed Tamburlaine.[19] In a hilarious lampoon, Nashe imagines Harvey striding onto the stage – 'Heere enters Argumentum a *testimonio humano*, like *Tamberlaine* drawne in a Chariot by foure Kings' – only to launch an oration about what a world-famous, though modest, schoolboy he had been: 'I THAT IN MY YOVTH FLATTERD NOT MY SELFE WITH THE EXCEEDING COMMENDATION OF THE GREATEST SCHOLLER IN THE WORLD, &c.'[20] Nashe's would-be Tamburlaine need only speak a slightly misquoted version of Harvey's own words to expose the ridiculousness of a faux-humble pedant's delusionary self-aggrandisement. So much for Harvey's dreams of embodying 'noble audacity' and 'wily suttelties'.

In the terms that measure Harvey's ponderous, pontificating, predictable failure, Marlowe's *Tamburlaine* comes again into relevance. If there had ever been anything more surprising on the Elizabethan stage than Marlowe's refusal to stage Tamburlaine's expected downfall after five acts of outrageous overweening, then surely it is Tamburlaine's witty, nobly audacious, subtly self-reflexive, and strangely pathetic soliloquy while his soldiers massacre the Virgins of Damascus. Other Marlowe plays conclude with remarkable surprises – Faustus' bizarre romantic gallantry, inquiring 'Was this the face that launched a thousand ships', despite knowing full well the 'Helen' he kisses before being carted off to hell to be a soul-sucking demon of his own conjuration (*DrF*, Scene xii); Barabas' self-deluded peace-making with his Christian enemies, despite recognising their proclivity for hypocritical 'policy' (*JM*, V.ii.110–23), just before dropping to his death in the boiling cauldron. In both cases, the attribute each character claims as the chief basis for his self-distinction – Faustus' unbounded learning, Barabas' politic 'wit' – fails him utterly. By contrast, Tamburlaine's Damascus soliloquy surprises not with a failure but with a sublime, if paradoxical, fulfilment.

If, as Sir Philip Sidney urged, martial greatness and poetry could and should go together, it is hard to believe he would have embraced their conjunction in Tamburlaine's speech. Sidney's claim that a poet's 'fore-conceit', the image conveyed by the work of art, could reproduce itself in the world, with one imagined Cyrus potentially producing real Cyruses to live out the virtues of the original idea, appears turned inside out and backwards in Tamburlaine's musing on violence, poetry, conceit, beauty, and virtue.[21] Here too, gentility shows up along with wit and oddly relevant affects.

Surprisingly, the martial besieger is really the one whose soul is under 'siege': the sorrows of victimised Zenocrate at the destruction of her birthplace, her every tear appearing as a 'resolved pearl' to Tamburlaine, become his own 'sufferings'. This famous passage answers the demand of *Hero and Leander* that the truly 'gentle' breast experience 'relenting thoughts' and 'pity', but answers it bizarrely. The violator of female victims turns his pitying glance upon himself for the pains that arise from his own exquisitely 'effeminate' capacity for pitying those he physically violates, lamenting that Zenocrate's 'sorrows lay more siege unto my soul / Than all my army to Damascus' walls' and trouble 'my senses with conceit of foil' (v.ii.92–5).

This overwrought state prompts Tamburlaine's academic disquisition – 'What is beauty saith my sufferings then?' – which rapidly becomes an affirmation of the supreme value of poetry and poetic vocation:

> If all the pens that ever poets held
> Had fed the feeling of their masters' thoughts,
> And every sweetness that inspired their hearts,
> Their minds, and muses on admired themes,
> If all the heavenly quintessence they still
> From their immortal flowers of poesy,
> Wherein as in a mirror we perceive
> The highest reaches of a human wit,

> If these had made one poem's period
> And all combined in beauty's worthiness,
> Yet should there hover in their restless heads
> One thought, one grace, one wonder at the least,
> Which into words no virtue can digest.
> (*1 Tamb.*, V.ii.98–110)

Here creative energy is imagined channelling backwards from pen to brain, while 'virtue' and 'conceit' are recast. If Sidney maintained that the poet's artistic conceit realised in the work of art could go on to incite virtue in the world, Tamburlaine renders 'virtue' as a power in the poet himself struggling to digest 'conceit' into words. The metaphor of feeding that begins with 'pens' that feed their 'masters' thoughts' concludes in 'thoughts' that no poet's virtue can 'digest'.

The act of writing itself creates inevitable discursive failure, but it is just at the point of the poet's inevitable defeat that there arises the largest significance of the poetic as pointing to something beyond the 'highest reaches of a human wit'. Though poesy is all we have to suggest the 'highest reaches' of wit and Tamburlaine envisions a poesy with power to condense 'all' poetry, and a poet's 'virtue' strong enough to capture it, yet even this super-poet and his super-poesy remain insufficient to name an always undigested, uncapturable supplement. Not learning or knowledge but the poetic process, unfulfilled by definition, points beyond the 'highest reaches of a human wit' to suggest what it might mean to soar above all sorts and powers of sorting.

Tamburlaine applies this imaginary poet's dilemma to 'warriors' and all 'men', taking up elements of social distinction in language that enlists familiar standbys of humanist debate about the relation of 'virtue', 'chivalry', and 'birth' to 'true nobility'.[22] Bizarrely, Tamburlaine discounts his own 'birth' and chivalry – as if he had claims to either – to enforce an alternative description of distinction as rightly gained through the double greatness of a 'wit' that possesses the capacities for sublime conceptions and the capacity to endure the power of those conceptions to destabilise all forms of identity by the, literally endless, desire they provoke:

> But how unseemly is it for my sex,
> My discipline of arms and chivalry,
> My nature and the terror of my name,
> To harbour thoughts effeminate and faint!
> Save only that in beauty's just applause,
> With whose instinct the soul of man is touched –
> And every warrior that is rapt with love

>   Of fame, of valour, and of victory,
>   Must needs have beauty beat on his conceits –
>   I thus conceiving and subduing both
>   That which hath stooped the topmost of the gods,
>   Even from the fiery-spangled veil of heaven,
>   To feel the lovely warmth of shepherds' flames
>   And march in cottages of strewèd weeds,
>   Shall give the world to note, for all my birth,
>   That virtue solely is the sum of glory
>   And fashions men with true nobility.
>   (*1 Tamb.*, V.ii.111–27)[23]

Ultimately, not possessions – not what the poet writes, the scholar knows, or the warrior does, much less what the wealthy have or gentlemen inherit – but a capacity for experiences in the internal battleground of conceit constitutes the distinguishing capital of 'true nobility'. Then abruptly, this ringing conclusion is shattered by the surprising, brutal query, 'Hath Bajazeth been fed today?'[24]

This strange credo, with its stark transformation of physical suffering and material feeding into delicate poetic conceits, its logical turns, and its sudden violent surprise, fits uneasily with the possibility that Marlowe's works advertise his employability. They may display detailed knowledge of military tactics, Roman and English history, courtly factionalism, Mediterranean trade, Asian travel, and French religious politics, but this passage suggests a wit eagerly pursuing thoughts and feelings that violate recognised categories and then risks their articulation.[25] If Harvey could honestly claim competence in many fields, Marlowe's plays construct an author pretending autonomy unconstrained by any field or its expectations.

Pretences of autonomy came easier to aristocrats. Ovid reminds readers of his house and pedigree when he indulges his wanton toy. Sidney surely mocked Harvey when he recommended that Harvey read Sacrobosco and Valerius 'with diligent studie, but sportingly, as he termed it'.[26] Such oxymoronic combinations of labour and sport might be tough for the academic commoner to embody, but traces of such a *habitus* pervade Marlowe's complex art. *Sprezzatura* is suggested by Tamburlaine's dismissal of earnest calculation in favour of the 'pretty jest' of a sudden charge against overwhelming forces (*1 Tamb.*, II.v.90), or by Lightborn's refusal to reveal his special 'tricks' before horrifically violating King Edward (*EII*, xxiii[V.iv].38), or by Barabas' 'secret purpose' (*JM*, V.ii.120–4). The stylistic appeal of such attributes to frustrated university scholars appears when Spencer Junior admonishes Baldock to 'cast the scholar off' and 'court it like a gentleman', by acting 'proud, bold, pleasant, resolute' but also 'now and then, stab[bing], as occasion serves' (*EII*, v[II.iv].43). Thomas Kyd's allegation that Marlowe would 'sodenlie … slyp out' blasphemous 'iest[s]' and do others 'soden pryvie iniuries' suggests this *habitus*, taken literally.[27] Thomas Nashe's mockery of schoolboy Harvey as 'a desperate stabber with pen-kniues' jokes about its misappropriation by scholars.[28]

After Marlowe's death the *Parnassus* plays portray university scholars desperately confronting an occupational market for which they had little to offer besides pedantry, pious hypocrisy, and poetic sensibility. Among those revolted at the prospect of joining 'ragged vicars and forlorne schoole-maisters', Luxurio proclaims himself having 'alwaies more than naturallie affected [the] poeticall vocation'; and, fearing the death of his 'witt' if he spends more time in 'base premeditation' upon grammar and punctuation, he affirms a parodic version of Tamburlainean social-aesthetics: 'I'le have my pen run like a spigot, and my invention answer it as quick as a drawer. Melancholick art, put downe thy hose; here is a suddaine wit that will lashe thee in the time to come!'[29] One wonders what Marlowe would have made of this jesting invocation of his own affirmed values: superiority of wit, poetic sensibility, and sudden violent surprise.

Notes

1 Andrew Hadfield, *Shakespeare and Republicanism* (Cambridge University Press, 2005), 59.
2 *Habitus* is a socially acquired, internalised 'disposition that generates meaningful practices and meaning-giving perceptions'; Pierre Bourdieu, *Distinction*, trans. Richard Nice (Cambridge, MA: Harvard University Press, 1984), 170.
3 Marlowe's poetry is quoted from *The Collected Poems of Christopher Marlowe*, ed. Patrick Cheney and Brian J. Striar (Oxford University Press, 2006).
4 For the values of birth, wealth, and public office defining gentility in early modern England, see Penelope J. Corfield, 'Landed and Other Gentlemen', in *Land and Society in Britain, 1700–1914*, ed. N. B. Harte and R. Quinault (Manchester University Press, 1996), 1–33.
5 *The Massacre at Paris* and *Dido, Queen of Carthage* are cited from *Christopher Marlowe: The Complete Plays*, ed. J. B. Steane (Harmondsworth: Penguin, 1969); *Tamburlaine*, *Doctor Faustus*, *Edward II*, and *The Jew of Malta* are cited throughout from *Christopher Marlowe: Four Plays*, ed. Brian Gibbons (London: Methuen, 2011).
6 For Marlowe as 'generoso' ('gentleman'), see William Urry, *Christopher Marlowe and Canterbury* (London: Faber and Faber, 1988), 131. His bachelor's degree rendered Marlowe 'Dominus' ('Sir') in university records; Constance Brown Kuriyama, *Christopher Marlowe: A Renaissance Life* (Ithaca, NY: Cornell University Press, 2010 [2002]), 51.

7 Thomas Deloney, *The Works of Thomas Deloney*, ed. F. O. Mann (Oxford: Clarendon Press, 1912), 112. For 'sort' as a standard term for social and economic categorisation, see Keith Wrightson, 'Estates, Degrees and Sorts: Changing Perceptions of Society in Tudor and Stuart England', in *Language, History and Class*, ed. Penelope J. Corfield (Oxford University Press, 1991), 30–52.
8 On Baldock's transformation, see Christopher Marlowe, *Edward the Second*, ed. Charles Forker (Manchester University Press, 1994), II.i.30n.
9 The 1598 edition (*STC* 17414) reads 'in aspiring' rather than 'inaspiring'. Cf. *Lucan's First Book*, 166–7: 'Poverty (who hatched / Rome's greatest wits) was loathed, and all the world / Ransacked for gold, which breeds the world decay.'
10 Heather James, 'The Poet's Toys: Christopher Marlowe and the Liberties of Erotic Elegy', *Modern Language Quarterly* 67:1 (March 2006): 103–27 (114).
11 See Laura Caroline Stevenson, *Praise and Paradox: Merchants and Craftsmen in Elizabethan Popular Literature* (Cambridge University Press, 1984), esp. 82–5.
12 Cf. Anthony Brian Taylor, 'Tamburlaine's Doctrine of Strife and John Calvin', *ELN* 27 (1989), 30–1; David Riggs, 'Marlowe's Quarrel with God', in *Critical Essays on Christopher Marlowe*, ed. Emily C. Bartels (New York: G. K. Hall, 1997), 39–60 (51).
13 This affirmation of battlefield *sprezzatura* – or recklessness – is remarkable given Elizabethan citing of Tamburlaine's bad example in condemning 'wanto[n] behauiour' displaying 'courage, but not the gouernment' of an ideal soldier; George Whetstone, *The Honorable Reputation of a Souldier* (London: 1585, *STC* 25339, DIV).
14 Gabriel Harvey, *Gabriel Harvey's Marginalia*, ed. G. C. Moore Smith (Stratford-upon-Avon: Shakespeare Head Press, 1913), 148; citations are from this edition.
15 Lisa Jardine, 'Encountering Ireland: Gabriel Harvey, Edmund Spenser, and English Colonial Ventures', in *Representing Ireland*, ed. Brendan Bradshaw, Andrew Hadfield, and Willy Maley (Cambridge University Press, 1993), 63.
16 Harvey, *Marginalia*, 142.
17 *Ibid.*, 151.
18 Virginia F. Stern, *Gabriel Harvey: His Life, Marginalia, and Library* (Oxford: Clarendon Press, 1979), 11.
19 See Paul H. Kocher, 'Some Nashe Marginalia Concerning Marlowe', *MLN* 57 (1942): 45–9.
20 Thomas Nashe, *The Works of Thomas Nashe*, 5 vols, ed. R. B. McKerrow (London: A. H. Bullen, 1904–10), Vol. I, 293.
21 Philip Sidney, *An Apology for Poetry; or, The Defence of Poesy*, ed. Geoffrey Shepherd and Robert W. Maslen, 3rd edn (Manchester University Press, 2002), esp. 85. For a nuanced socio-analysis of Sidney, see Robert A. Matz, *Defending Literature in Early Modern England* (Cambridge University Press, 2000), 56–87.

22 Cf. Stephen Shapin, *A Social History of Truth* (University of Chicago Press, 1994), 42–64.
23 Early editions have 'tempest' for 'topmost' in V.ii.121.
24 For sublimity in this speech, see Kimberly Benston, '"Beauty's Just Applause": Dramatic Form and the Marlovian Sublime', in Harold Bloom, ed., *Christopher Marlowe* (New York: Chelsea House, 1986), 207–27. Among useful accounts of its ironies, see Judith M. Weil, *Christopher Marlowe: Merlin's Prophet* (Cambridge University Press, 1977), esp. 130–3. For conjunctions of 'conceit' with feeding or wounding, cf. *1 Tamb.*, III.ii.9–17; V.ii.352; *DrF*, i.78.
25 Cf. David Riggs, *The World of Christopher Marlowe* (New York: Henry Holt, 2004), 203; Riggs suggests that Tamburlaine's soliloquy might have intended rhetorical effect rather than strict intelligibility (212).
26 Stern, *Gabriel Harvey*, 79.
27 Millar Maclure, ed., *Marlowe: The Critical Heritage 1588–1896* (London: Routledge and Kegan Paul, 1979), 35–6.
28 Nashe, *Collected Works*, Vol. III, 60.
29 *The Pilgrimage to Parnassus with the Two Parts of The Return from Parnassus*, ed. William Dunn Macray (Oxford: Clarendon Press, 1886), 19, 38–9.

CHAPTER FIFTEEN

Marlowe, death-worlds, and warfare

Patricia Cahill

While it is widely acknowledged that *Tamburlaine* displays what a critic once described as Marlowe's 'singular affection for wholesale slaughter', scholarly accounts of the play have focused far less on its martial preoccupations than on its staging of the allure of otherness.[1] In *Renaissance Self-Fashioning* (1980), for example, Stephen Greenblatt influentially linked the play's exoticism with 'the acquisitive energies of English merchants, entrepreneurs, and adventurers', and, subsequently, scholars have often characterised *Tamburlaine* as a narrative about rapacious desire.[2] The play has thus served as a touchstone for Renaissance drama's concern with such matters as Anglo-Ottoman trade and cross-cultural encounters, Elizabethan colonial and imperial pursuits, and the beginnings of global capitalism. While such scholarship rarely overlooks the staging of war, it frequently represents martial violence as merely instrumental, assuming, for example, that war serves an underlying longing to possess the world imaginatively or to stake a claim for rule or riches.

But is warfare so straightforwardly instrumental in *Tamburlaine*? Certainly, the play evokes siege tactics like those ruthlessly used by the Spanish and the Dutch in the Low Countries. Many English soldiers saw such tactics first-hand, and others read about them in early modern English works on warfare.[3] But, as I argue in what follows, *Tamburlaine* also engages with nascent forms of 'necropower', a term coined by Achille Mbembe to analyse regimes in the colonial and post-colonial era.[4] For Mbembe, necropower and necropolitics signal 'the various ways in which, in our contemporary world, weapons are deployed in the interest of maximum destruction of persons and the creation of *death-worlds*, new and unique forms of social existence in which vast populations are subjected to conditions of life conferring upon them the status of living dead'.[5] That *Tamburlaine* represents a yearning not simply for violence but for the 'maximum destruction of persons' seems clear, especially when one considers Tamburlaine's extravagant threats in Part II, where, for example, he declares, 'I will with engines never exercised / Conquer, sack, and utterly consume / Your cities and your golden palaces'.[6] But that each part represents mass death as the goal of warfare rather than as an incidental outcome, and that each renders destruction a (paradoxically) creative act – at times, even, an act of ingenuity – have not yet been adequately explored. By examining these performances of military violence – especially the siege of Damascus in Part I and that of Babylon in Part II – I aim to demonstrate why conventional understandings of this work in terms of English 'acquisitive energies' need revision. If *Tamburlaine* represents a simple desire to claim the wealth of – or even trade with – global others, why then does it focus so steadily upon devastation?

The broad outlines of *Tamburlaine*'s necropolitical imaginary are suggested by the play's structure; for each part charts a martial trajectory culminating in scenes of siege and slaughter. Part I moves from the 'champion plains' of Scythia, where the army of the hapless Persian king meets Tamburlaine and his troops, to the walls of Damascus, where a death-world comes into view as Tamburlaine lays siege to the city (II.ii.40). Part II moves from Larissa Plains, where Tamburlaine gathers soldiers for battle with the Turkish armies, to the walls of Babylon, where another death-world comes into view through another siege. *Tamburlaine*'s engagement with necropower thus has to do with how each part finds its *telos* not in a pitched battle between soldiers (à la Shakespeare's famous scenes at Shrewsbury or Bosworth field) but rather in the enactment of his threats of mass murder, threats that often encompass the desire to destroy an entire world, as in Tamburlaine's boast in Part I: 'Were in that city all the world contained, / Not one should 'scape, but perish by our swords' (IV.ii.121–2). Significantly, Marlowe reserves his most spectacular pageantry precisely for such murderous violence: Tamburlaine's 'martial observations' (V.ii.59) thus entail that on Day One, he dresses in white, pitches white tents, and offers to show mercy to the besieged; on Day Two, he turns to scarlet and threatens bloodshed; and on Day Three, he embraces black and orders massacre. As each part enacts this colour-coded system – Part I shows all three days; Part II starts with Day Three, but glances back at Days One and Two – the play works to contain killing within the rationality of law. Accordingly, as each part moves from battle to siege, it also performs warfare as finding its end – both its literal conclusion as well as its aim – not in riches or rule, but rather in the codified administration of death.

These narrative vectors towards massacre may recall Michael Neill's claim that Tamburlaine is modelled on King Death, the allegorical figure familiar from Italian Renaissance artwork showing the Triumph of

Death. For Neill, the topos of the Triumph is omnipresent in both parts of *Tamburlaine*: 'This self-proclaimed Scourge of God sweeps through the world, meting out destruction like some catastrophic pestilence, his chariot-wheels rolling, like those of Death's car, over heaps of carcasses.'[7] But however much Marlowe evokes the pageantry of the Triumph, the progress of his Scythian shepherd hardly seems analogous to the silent transmission of 'pestilence' or the passive 'rolling' of chariot-wheels. Rather, as the siege scenes abundantly illustrate, Tamburlaine characteristically proceeds by ferocious and noisy military assault. Indeed, rather than evoke Death's car, the chariot, which appears as part of a martial scene in Part II, suggests, in debased form, the vehicle that transported Homeric heroes to battle.[8] More broadly, the play's allegorical narrative about the invincible power of Death repeatedly collides head-on with the brute materiality of sixteenth-century siege warfare – and above all with the vast armies, conflagrations, and gunpowder weaponry that are central to Marlowe's necropolitical imaginary.

While the siege scenes of Parts I and II culminate in offstage slaughter by sword and drowning, both parts foreground the period's 'maximalist' martial technologies. In Part I, Tamburlaine's claim to outnumber the immense army of an ancient Persian king summons up early modern gunpowder weaponry: alongside 'quivering lances shaking in the air' are 'bullets [i.e. cannonballs] like Jove's dreadful thunderbolts, / Enrolled in flames and fiery smouldering mists' (II.iii.18–20). Focusing on the loud sound and incendiary fury of artillery – the way gunpowder produces, as a now-obsolete definition of 'smouldering' indicates, a 'Smothering, suffocating, stifling' atmosphere[9] – Marlowe recalls the fiery topics discussed by Peter Whitehorne in the treatise published with his 1560 translation of Machiavelli's *Arte della guerra*, among them 'Howe to Make Saltpeter, Gunpoulder, and Diuers Sortes of Fireworkes or Wilde Fyr'.[10] In fact, Marlowe evokes the force of gunpowder even in the play's most rhetorically overblown moments – as, for example, in Part I, when Bajazeth, the Turkish emperor, evokes not only Senecan furies and the 'black Cocytus lake' but also the innovations of 'pike and shot' warfare in which armed soldiers move in uniform, geometrical formations (V.ii.155, 157–8); and in Part II, when Tamburlaine orders his soldiers to 'raise cavalieros higher than the clouds / And with the cannon break the frame of heaven, / Batter the shining palace of the sun / And shiver all the starry firmament' (II.iv.103–6).[11] As is suggested by the messenger who in Part I breathlessly reports on the vast size of Tamburlaine's forces and then declares that 'their warlike engines and munition / Exceed the forces of their martial men'

(IV.i.28–9), in *Tamburlaine* gunpowder technology is synonymous with an excess beyond excess.

In the Rose Theatre, where *Tamburlaine* likely had its first performances, martial stage properties and special effects undoubtedly helped to realise its necropolitical imaginary. Part II explicitly calls for guns when Tamburlaine's henchmen transport 'minions, falc'nets, and sakers' as they lay siege to Balsera (III.iii.6), and the depiction in Act V of the onstage death by shooting of the Governor of Babylon is notorious for its use of firearms. Indeed many scholars believe that during a 1587 performance of this scene real bullets were mistakenly used, leading to the death of two playgoers and the injury of a third.[12] Both parts probably followed the playhouse custom of employing gunpowder to create dazzling explosions, so that, for example, in Part II, fireworks may have created the smoke and flames accompanying Tamburlaine's gleeful pronouncement: 'So, burn the turrets of this cursèd town, / Flame to the highest region of the air / And kindle heaps of exhalations' (III.ii.1–3). And both parts probably called on the small cannon known as chambers, which were loaded with blank charges to signal offstage battles and onstage sieges. As black tents and streamers visually signalled massacre, then, gunpowder presumably evoked the loud sounds, stifling atmosphere, and sulphuric stench of warfare.[13] Indeed as is emphasised by Part I's comparison of Egyptians to 'crocodiles that unaffrighted rest / While thund'ring cannons rattle on their skins', the reverberating sounds of gunpowder-fuelled explosions were probably felt as well as heard (IV.i.10–11). In short, *Tamburlaine*'s death-centred martial scenes likely engaged the entire sensorium.

Quivering on their city walls

One measure of *Tamburlaine*'s necropolitical investments is the frequency with which Marlowe invites playgoers to understand military violence as a matter of city walls rather than of battlefields. In Part I the siege begins with the sound of the destruction of the walls of Damascus. Commanding his soldiers to 'hear the basilisks / That, roaring, shake Damascus' turrets down!' (IV.i.2–3), the Soldan conjures the impact of cannon that might weigh as much as 9,000 lb and discharge a 60 lb iron or stone ball. Soon after, Tamburlaine, though clad in white, nevertheless anticipates Damascus' 'lofty towers' and 'city walls' subject to his 'battering shot' (IV.ii.102, 106–7). In subsequent scenes, the Soldan sends his soldiers 'to Damascus' walls' (IV.iii.62); Zenocrate begs Tamburlaine to 'raise [his] siege from fair Damascus' walls' (IV.iv.70); the Governor laments that

Tamburlaine continually 'batter[s] our walls and beat[s] our turrets down' (v.i.2); and the First Virgin decries the 'danger beat[ing] upon our walls' (v.i.30). Military architecture was, of course, deeply important to many Elizabethans, including Elizabeth, who, following the example of her father, spent enormous sums of money strengthening the fortifications at Berwick and elsewhere. It was also, of course, of interest to Marlowe, who in Part II famously paraphrases military engineer Paul Ive's 1589 treatise *The Practise of Fortification*, the first English book on the subject, as he depicts Tamburlaine instructing his sons how the best fort locations are chosen, why certain shapes are best suited for particular sites, and how angled designs can take advantage of different terrains (see Figure 5).[14] As Ive's book indicates, many in England were enthralled by the work of Italian military engineers who built low-lying and angled *trace italienne* fortifications; walls constructed according to such geometrical principles, unlike the high walls and turrets of the medieval era, could be counted on to withstand the force of gunpowder assaults. In making walls so central to his staging of war, Marlowe clearly engages with a palpable fear of gunpowder technologies, one that is writ large in militarist Peter Whitehorne's 1560 admonition that 'the violence of the artillerie is such, that ther is no wall, how great so ever it be, which in ten dayes it battereth not doun'.[15]

If the battered walls of Part I materialise a violence that cannot be defended against, they also evoke the play's construction of something new: a zone of living death. Day Two of the siege thus opens with Tamburlaine's description of figures aloft on the walls:

> Now hang our bloody colours by Damascus,
> Reflexing hues of blood upon their heads
> While they walk quivering on their city walls,
> Half dead for fear before they feel my wrath.
> (IV.iv.1–4)

Marlowe's 'quivering' walkers on the city walls suggest the 'quivering lances' of Tamburlaine's army, thereby proleptically linking the two in a tremulous and fatal identity. Indeed, the phrase also connects the walkers to an earlier description of injured bodies – namely, the Persian king's description of 'how those ... hit by pelting cannon shot / Stand staggering like a quivering aspen leaf / Fearing the force of Boreas' boisterous blasts' (II.iv.3–5). Moreover, the vague pronouns identifying both the walkers and the figures on whom the overhanging reflects its 'bloody colours' ensure that Marlowe's evocation of the soldiers *on* the walls shades into an emblematic image of the citizens *behind* the walls. Those who stand on

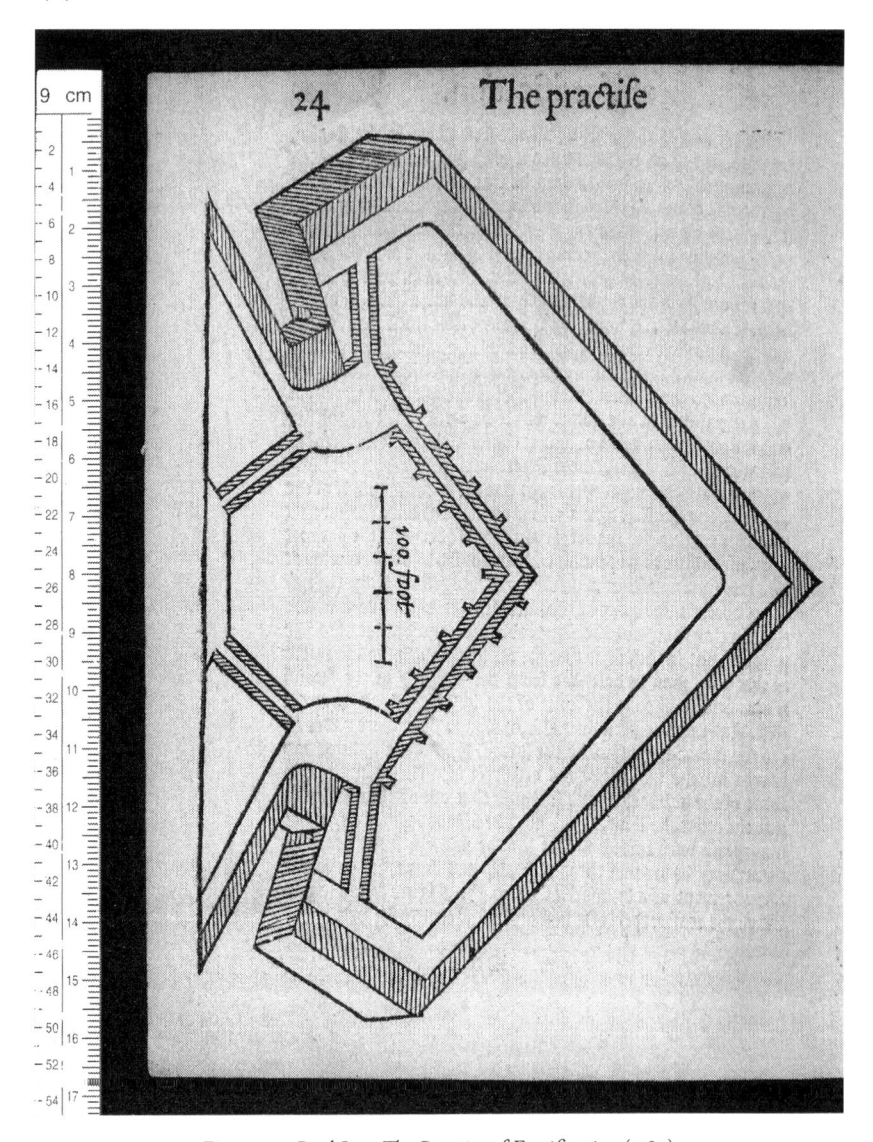

Figure 5   Paul Ive, *The Practise of Fortification* (1589)

its walls thus stand in for the vulnerable populace beneath its blood-red streamers.

But Part I does not simply conjure a terrorised realm on the other side of the walls. Rather, it shockingly brings that death-world onto the stage in the subsequent scene in which the Damascus virgins plead for mercy. Dressed in white, the virgins encounter the black-clad Tamburlaine, who describes them as 'turtle[doves] frayed out of their nests' (v.ii.1), yet responds to them only by berating their city leaders:

> They know my custom. Could they not as well
> Have sent ye out when first my milk-white flags
> Through which sweet mercy threw her gentle beams,
> Reflexing them on your disdainful eyes,
> As now, when fury and incensèd hate
> Flings slaughtering terror from my coal-black tents
> And tells for truth submissions comes too late?
> (v.ii,4–10)

By personifying 'fury' and 'hate' and linking these affects with Tamburlaine's practice or 'custom' rather than with his person, Marlowe figures 'slaughtering terror' as 'administered' violence and as necessity rather than desire. Moreover, even as Tamburlaine proceeds to draw his sword, Marlowe identifies the blade with a separate juridical realm, one presided over by Death, who 'Keep[s] his circuit by the slicing edge' (v.ii.49). As Tamburlaine announces that Death, as if of its own accord, has taken up new residence on his 'horsemen's spears' (v.ii.51), Marlowe frames the death sentence Tamburlaine delivers as something to be carried out rather than something that has been authored: Tamburlaine thus declares that on the 'points' of these spears '[Death's] fleshless body feeds' (v.ii.52) and orders Techelles to instruct his horsemen to 'charge a few of them / To charge these dames, and show my servant Death / Sitting in scarlet on their armèd spears' (v.ii.53–5). Insofar as this luridly cannibalistic image of skeletons feeding on spear points emerges before Tamburlaine issues his order, Death would seem to be independent of Tamburlaine. And yet, even as Marlowe thereby pluralises the command to kill, his repetition of the word 'charge', which equates Tamburlaine's verbal order with the bloody piercing of the virgins' bodies, emphasises Tamburlaine's intimacy with this slaughter. In short, this scene identifies the unavoidably plural and virtually anonymous action of 'charging' as at the heart of Part I's necropolitical vision.

As Part 1 ends, Marlowe devotes remarkably little stage time to the massacre of the inhabitants of Damascus. In a brief encounter with his soldiers, Tamburlaine learns that they have 'hoisted up [the] slaughtered carcasses' of the virgins on the city walls, and he responds to this news by laconically ordering his men to 'put the rest to the sword' (v.ii.71). But while the brevity of this command may seem to represent the play's departure from necropolitics, it actually signals something else: massacre need not be staged because Part I, through its account of the disposition of the virgins' bodies, has already fully realised its death-world. Indeed, the revelation of the fate of these 'slaughtered carcasses' explicitly recalls the image Bajazeth summoned in response to Tamburlaine's threats: 'Let thousands die, their slaughtered carcasses / Shall serve for walls and bulwarks to the rest' (III.iii.138–9). The uncanniness of Act V, in fact, is that it shows Bajazeth's vision of corpses as construction material eerily taking shape. Not only do playgoers hear that the virgins are on the walls of Damascus, but they subsequently learn from Zenocrate, who renarrates the virgins' murder and the desecration of their bodies, that 'Damascus' walls [are] dyed with Egyptians' blood' (V.ii.258) – that is, as the pun insists, death has literally been incorporated into the matter of the walls. Inviting us to contemplate the city's breached and bloody walls festooned with corpses, Part I crystallises its grim vision of necropower.

Making walls afresh

While Part I culminates with the transformation of Damascus into a death-world, Part II amplifies the terror, for many death-worlds come into view before the siege of Babylon and Tamburlaine's order to 'drown them all, man, woman, and child' (V.i.168). Most obviously, Tamburlaine creates a zone of living death when he carries out his promise to 'consume [Larissa] with fire / Because this place bereft [him] of [his] love' (II.iv.137–8): a zone where future visitors will see, amidst the scene of 'houses burnt' and land 'singe[d]', a monumental pillar inscribed in many languages, a 'mournful streamer', and a commemorative register of Zenocrate's virtues (II.iv.139; III.ii.11, 19). Several other scenes similarly highlight a 'creativity' that works hand in hand with killing. For example, when Tamburlaine's soldiers lay siege to Balsera, Marlowe details their construction projects, evoking the 'dimensions' of the trenches to be built and the need for a newly devised instrument, the 'Jacob's staff', to measure 'height' and 'distance' (III.iii.42, 50–1). Moreover, while scholars often read Tamburlaine's long discourse to his sons on warfare – the speech, following his elegy for Zenocrate, which paraphrases Ive's fortification treatise – as marking Tamburlaine's turn away from death, we might rather ask what fortification is, if it is not an attempt to establish an enclosure in close proximity to death? As this disquisition emphasises, to fortify is to be at risk of being 'assailed', to be vulnerable to 'assault', and to be preoccupied with 'sav[ing] the walls from breach' (66–7, 82). In fact, Tamburlaine conjures a stronghold in which

6,000 inhabitants, like the besieged captain at Balsera, are endangered from virtually every side (III.ii.74–5). Tamburlaine's prior conversation with his sons is instructive here: in it, he holds out a vision of his throne set in a battlefield 'whose superficies / Is covered with a liquid purple veil / And sprinkled with the brains of slaughtered men' (I.iv.79–81), and one son proposes to reach the throne by 'mak[ing] a bridge of murdered carcasses / Whose arches should be framed with bones of Turks' (I.iv.93–4). Through Tamburlaine's gory image, which evokes the technical term for a geometrical surface, and his son's reply, which clearly recalls Bajazeth's corpse architecture in Part I, Marlowe re-zones the battlefield and makes death an architectural feature of the landscape.

In Part II, city walls evoke death worlds even more hauntingly than in Part I, not least because the sequel uses the theatre's tiring-house wall as Part I seems not to have done.[16] As in Part I, the siege begins with the evocation of a terrified populace that remains off stage. Act V thus opens with several figures on the walls, including the Governor, who listens to a soldier lamenting the 'breach the enemy made' and to citizens urging surrender (V.i.2). Moments later, Tamburlaine and his troops scale the tiring-house wall in pursuit of the Governor. Lingering, far more than Part I, on the besieged city as a zone of living death, Marlowe ultimately depicts as arresting spectacle the shooting of the Governor, who hangs bound in chains on the walls begging for his life. Moreover, as is clear from the Governor's prior defiant language to Tamburlaine, 'Nor if my body could have stopped the breach / Shouldst thou have entered, cruel Tamburlaine', Marlowe represents the death by hanging and firing squad as literalising the Governor's wish to defend the city (V.i.101–2). Indeed, the equation between hanging corpse and city wall is rendered explicit as Tamburlaine notes that the Governor has 'as many bullets in his flesh / As there be breaches in her battered wall' (V.i.158–9).

While Part I stops with the similar equation of corpse and wall, Part II outdoes its progenitor in the death-centredness of its siege scenes by simultaneously suggesting the emergence of a death ecology: one focused on the lake encircling Babylon where Tamburlaine ultimately orders that the populace be drowned. As Act V opens, the Governor suggests the bituminous and presumably dark waters of this lake provide an endlessly renewable source of impregnable walls:

> Have we not hope, for all our battered walls,
> To live secure and keep his forces out,
> When this our famous lake of Limnasphaltis

>   Makes walls afresh with every thing that falls
>   Into the liquid substance of his stream,
>   More strong than are the gates of death or hell?
>   (V.i.15–20)

Significantly, the lake, which Marlowe seems to have named after the 'smouldering tar pits in the nearby basin of the Euphrates', is both a locale of busy manufacture – of 'mak[ing] walls afresh with everything' – and a landscape suggestive of 'death' and 'hell' not unlike that of Bajazeth's black Cocytus lake.[17] Part II emphasises this doubleness when Tamburlaine declares victoriously that Babylon's 'stately buildings' and 'lofty pillars' have been 'carried … by the cannon's force' and 'now fill the mouth of Limnasphaltis lake / And make a bridge unto the battered walls' (V.i.63, 64, 68–70). By bringing together the majestic towers and the walls marking Part II's zone of living death, Tamburlaine's words clearly equate the lake with a topography of absolute destruction. But the speech is also peculiarly attuned to the Governor's insistence on the lake's creative faculties insofar as Tamburlaine envisages the lake as a 'mouth' that does not so much consume the city as ingeniously transform it into something else: a bridge to the nowhere that is Babylon after it has been razed by the besieging army. When, moments later, Techelles reports to Tamburlaine on the massacre, Part II develops this notion, offering a striking image of the lake as a site of war's grotesque creations:

>   I have fulfilled your highness' will, my lord:
>   Thousands of men drowned in Asphaltis lake
>   Have made the water swell above the banks,
>   And fishes fed by human carcasses,
>   Amazed, swim up and down upon the waves,
>   As when they swallow asafoetida,
>   Which makes them fleet aloft and gasp for air.
>   (V.i.201–7)

Through Techelles' account of the tar-filled lake as a site where dead bodies serve for medicinal food, like the foul-smelling asafoetida, to dying fish, Marlowe offers his final vision of the oddly generative death-worlds created by Tamburlaine's warring soldiers. Just as the slaughter has upset the ecology of the lake, making for waters that cover the land and fish that, having been 'fed' by corpses, float above the water and to their death in the air, so too has the staging of siege disrupted the narrative of conquest otherwise inscribed in Part II, generating only a fecund realm of the dead.

It is hard to square this grotesque vision of a death-clogged atmosphere with the more usual accounts of *Tamburlaine* as drama of robust imperial and economic aspirations. If, for example, we were to restage Peter Hall's famous 1976 production, which began by projecting onto the stage floor a map showing all the places Tamburlaine claimed for himself, how would we represent the burnt landscape of Larissa or the macabre geography of lake Limnasphaltis post-siege?[18] As Hall's production underscores, interpretations of *Tamburlaine* as about overseas commercial enterprises often hinge on its cartographic imaginary and on Tamburlaine's dying request for a map so that he might 'see how much / Is left for [him] to conquer all the world, / That these [his] boys may finish all [his] wants' (V.iii.123–5). But to take seriously the play's staging of military violence is to notice the longing for deterritorialisation that is encrypted in Tamburlaine's mournful evocation of 'how much is left' and what must be 'finish[ed]', and, more importantly, is writ large in both parts of the play. Given Marlowe's repeated visions of ingenious siegecraft and indiscriminate slaughter – obsessions that Marlowe will revisit in a farcical key in the final act of *The Jew of Malta* – perhaps what *Tamburlaine* most ardently represents is not so much the longings that propelled Elizabethan mercantile and colonial pursuits as the beginnings of a global politics premised on perpetual warfare and disposable populations.

Notes

1. S. J. Ervine, *The Organized Theatre: A Plea in Civics* (London: Allen and Unwin, 1924), 186.
2. Stephen Greenblatt, *Renaissance Self-Fashioning: From More to Shakespeare* (University of Chicago Press, 1980), 194.
3. David R. Lawrence, *The Complete Soldier: Military Books and Military Culture in Early Stuart England, 1603–1645* (Leiden: Brill, 2009), 313–70.
4. Achille Mbembe, 'Necropolitics', *Public Culture* 15:1 (2003): 11–40.
5. *Ibid.*, 40; emphasis in original.
6. Christopher Marlowe, *Tamburlaine Parts One and Two*, ed. Anthony B. Dawson (London: A. & C. Black; New York: Norton, 1997) (IV.i. 190–2). Further references will be cited in the text.
7. Michael Neill, *Issues of Death: Mortality and Identity in English Renaissance Tragedy* (Oxford: Clarendon Press, 1997), 93.
8. See 'chariot, n.', at *OED Online*, www.oed.com, accessed 20 March 2012, which cites a 1581 definition as follows: 'a certeine Engine of warre, made with long and sharpe pikes of yron, set in the forefront'.
9. See 'smouldering, adj.' at *ibid.*
10. See the title page of *Certain Waies for the Orderyng of Souldiers in Battelray* (1562), which was reprinted in 1573 and 1588.

11 See, for example, accounts of battle array in R. Barret, *The Theorike and Practike of Modern Warres* (London, 1598).
12 For the 1587 anecdote, see E. K. Chambers, *The Elizabethan Stage*, 4 vols. (Oxford University Press, 1923), Vol. II, 135.
13 Jonathan Gil Harris, *Untimely Matter in the Time of Shakespeare* (Philadelphia: University of Pennsylvania Press, 2009), 119.
14 Paul Ive, *The Practise of Fortification* (1589).
15 Quoted in Charles Edelman, *Shakespeare's Military Language: A Dictionary* (New Brunswick, NJ: Athlone, 2000), 37.
16 On the play's staging, see Leslie Thomson, 'Marlowe's Staging of Meaning', *Medieval and Renaissance Drama in England* 18 (2005): 19–36.
17 David Riggs, *The World of Christopher Marlowe* (London: Faber and Faber, 2004), 218.
18 J. S. Cunningham and Roger Warren, '*Tamburlaine the Great* Re-Discovered', *Shakespeare Survey: An Annual Survey Of Shakespeare Studies and Production* 31 (1978): 155–62.

CHAPTER SIXTEEN

Education, the university, and Marlowe

Elizabeth Hanson

Christopher Marlowe's life and art were, to an unusual degree, determined by a single social development, the so-called 'educational revolution' in sixteenth-century England, which saw both the rise of a network of town grammar schools and a transformation of the universities from fundamentally clerical institutions to ones also engaged in the production of a more general educated elite. Marlowe owed his career to both the grammar school and the university, which together constituted a system linked by, among other mechanisms, merit scholarships of the kind that carried Marlowe, 'base of stock' like Doctor Faustus, from the King's School in Canterbury to Corpus Christi College, Cambridge in 1580.[1] Marlowe would stay at Cambridge for seven years, completing both the B.A. and the M.A. courses. Although his command of poetry and drama was shaped by both grammar school and university, this chapter will consider the grammar school primarily as a context for its main focus, the university. As Marlowe's biographer David Riggs notes, at the time of his death Marlowe 'was the greatest playwright that England had ever seen'.[2] He was also 'the first university graduate to forge a lasting professional bond with the adult players' whose commercial playing companies drove the flowering of the drama in early modern England.[3] These two 'firsts' are undoubtedly connected. To understand that connection, however, one must grasp the nature of the institution where Marlowe passed nearly one-quarter of his life and the more general transformation in the social place of learning that shaped the universities.

The social place of learning

That Marlowe, the son of a shoemaker, could become a Master of Arts does not indicate that either the schools or the universities in early modern England were 'accessible' in the modern sense of widely available to a significant segment of the population. Only a tiny minority of English males, and males only, could attend the institutions that trained boys, first at school in Latin grammar and rhetoric, and then at university in logic and the art of disputation and, in the case of more advanced students, mathematics, astronomy, cosmography, and, sometimes, divinity and civil law. However, it is a truism among historians of education that it would not be until the twentieth century that English educational institutions would again be as socially heterogeneous as they were in the sixteenth century. The reasons for this heterogeneity are complex and have as much to do with residual social attitudes as with progressive ones. These attitudes found expression in the town grammar schools as well as in the universities, and the social complexion of the schools inflected that of the universities.

The founding of grammar schools in English towns had begun apace in the latter part of the fifteenth century and had accelerated under the Tudors, with many schools being re-founded at the Reformation and new ones continuing to be established throughout Elizabeth's reign. This long wave of school foundations was driven, it is often argued, by the crown's effort to establish religious conformity through the regulated training of a cadre of Church ministers and bureaucrats. That explanation, however, does not fully account for the conviction expressed by town corporations and individual sponsors that the establishment of a grammar school would serve the honour of the town and the cause of virtue. The rise of the grammar school marked a shift in the value accorded learning from the specific equipment of clerics to a more widely desirable condition of cultivation.

However, what is also clear and remarkable in the founding documents of school after school is the assertion that schools are not to be limited to the well-born. The statutes of the Merchant Taylors' School, founded in 1561 in London, provide that of the 250 places in the school, 100 are for 'poore men's sonnes coming thether to be taught & being found meete and apt to learne'.[4] Those words come from the 1561 statutes of the school; the statutes of the King's School, which Marlowe attended, similarly make provision for 'fifty poor boys both destitute of the help of friends and endowed with minds apt for learning'.[5] That provision preceded by a few years a debate between Archbishop of Canterbury Thomas Cranmer, and some of the other commissioners visiting the school in the wake of the Chantries Act of 1547, about whether or not the school should be restricted to 'younger brethren and gentlemen's sons', with Cranmer successfully advocating for places for 'poor men's children' as they are 'commonly more given to apply their study'.[6]

Cranmer's stance in this debate, and the insistence on access for the poor in school statutes, sound progressive to our ears but are better understood as conservative positions, insofar as they reflect a long established conceptual link between education in letters and provision for the poor. This link depended on the fact that the primary use for Latin literacy was a career in the Church, a career that until the Reformation meant joining the one estate in which inheritance supposedly played no part. Endowing a poor boy with learning provided for him and the Church without, in theory, materially affecting the social order. After the Reformation and the end of clerical celibacy, the separateness of the clerical estate diminished, though the link between a degree of poverty and clerical training persisted. Meanwhile, the rise of the humanist curriculum, which stressed classical Latin literature and rhetorical skill, made the education the school offered more suitable to a general elite than to a specifically clerical estate. While the claim that education in letters was the prerogative of gentlemen's sons was seldom as explicitly made as it was at Canterbury, the increasing presence at grammar schools of such boys along with the sons of wealthy merchants and professional men meant that, on a practical level, the affinity between these groups and the schools was becoming increasingly robust at the same time that the link between the poor and schooling persisted.

Thus when Christopher Marlowe embarked on his studies at the King's School, he entered into a very complex social space. His poverty and aptness to learn made him a natural candidate both for a place in the school and for the scholarship, established by Archbishop of Canterbury Matthew Parker with the intention of supplying the Church with godly, literate ministers, which took Marlowe from the school to Cambridge. At the same time, however, he was acquiring attributes that sharply distinguished him from the vast majority of his countrymen and made him a member of a learned elite that now also consisted of gentlemen and some noblemen as well as men like himself. This is not to say, however, that Marlowe's education was a vehicle for social mobility in the sense of facilitating movement up a social ladder, or that that learned elite was internally meritocratic. Learning dislocated individuals and subjected them to new modes of distinction without having a material impact on the hierarchical social order they inhabited.

This tension between a rigidly hierarchical social order and the complicating effect of learning was arguably even more pronounced at Elizabethan Cambridge and Oxford than it was in the grammar schools. Though historians of early modern education dispute the degree, pace, timeline, and implications of the transformation, they are generally agreed that, over the course of the sixteenth century, the English universities saw both an overall increase in total student numbers and a change in culture wrought by the increased presence of well-born young men, many of whom were not pursuing degrees or Church careers. As historian Mark Curtis puts it, the result was that 'the academic haunts of the medieval clergy had become a normal resort for the sons and heirs of the English gentry and nobility'.[7] Over the course of the sixteenth century the claim that the purpose of the university is, as one commentator wrote in 1529, to 'nourish the children of poor men in letters' gives way to complaints such as the one voiced in 1573 that 'now the youth of nobility and gentlemen, taking up their scholarships and fellowships do disappoint the poor of their livings and advancements'.[8] This is not to say, however, that the well-born had *replaced* the more traditional types of students. The traditional students also continued to arrive at the university in increased numbers – an increase that was fuelled by the expanding network of grammar schools.

At Marlowe's Cambridge there were in fact four official categories of students, based on financial relation to the college. At the top were 'fellow-commoners', well-born young men who were often not studying for degrees but sojourning there before passing on to the more elite Inns of Court. They paid substantial fees for privileges such as eating at the high table with the college fellows. Next, if academic distinction is the criterion, came the scholarship holders such as Marlowe. These students were pursuing degrees and constituted a socially heterogeneous category insofar as their members comprised sons of gentlemen as well as low-born men such as Marlowe. Then came pensioners, who were wealthy enough to pay for their places and who, for a variety of reasons academic or social, had not procured a scholarship. Last came sizars, who supported themselves by serving in the dining hall, emptying chamber pots, and occasionally receiving small grants from benefactors back home. Often these were poor but promising students from grammar schools that had no scholarships linking them with Cambridge and Oxford colleges. The poet Edmund Spenser attended Cambridge in this capacity.

We can gain a sense of the social complexity produced by the jostling of men of different status from a 1597 letter from Brian Twyne, a student at Corpus Christi College, Oxford, to his father, a well-to-do physician. Begging his father to keep him in better style, Twyne observes:

> The time was and custom was in your being here that no scholar of our house might be suffered to have a poor scholar, but every scholar did his own affairs and business, but for me to have done it in these times (as you would have had me) and no man else, it had been worse than homely and

beggarly: should I have carried wood and dust, and emptied chamber pots and no man, no scholar so doing but myself? It had been intolerable, and too base for my mind; yea and I had disgraced many a mean man's son who were fellow scholars with me, myself being a gentleman.[9]

What initiates the well-born Twyne's exhortation to his father, it is worth noting, is a request for a 'yarde and a quarter of good taffeta' for his bachelor's gown, without which he will be 'less than every man'.[10] Doctor Faustus' dream of magic that will 'fill the public schools [university debating halls] with silk' (i.90) is usually read as evidence of the kind of status envy that a poor scholar such as Marlowe would have experienced at the university, but Twyne's anxiety suggests a much more complex situation. Like Marlowe, Twyne was the holder of a scholarship, and the letter shows his awareness that he shares the status of 'scholar' with 'meaner men' whose positions are enhanced because he is in that category with them. But his own status as a gentlemanly scholar is apparently fragile, requiring a servant to shore it up, though that servant is also a 'scholar'. Indeed, later in the letter Twyne claims that if he has to 'do his own affairs' as his father wishes him to, he himself will be taken to be a 'poor scholar'. The multiple, shifting meanings of 'scholar' in the letter and Twyne's claim that that meaning has changed over time suggest both that the social place of learning was unfixed and that the culture of the university did not merely reproduce the rigid hierarchical structure of Elizabethan society but challenged it, albeit in subtle ways.

Some historians, however, have disputed this possibility, arguing that multiple mechanisms enforced social distinction and limited cross-status interactions: gentlemen gravitated to particular colleges, special rooms were built to house them, and they lived with tutors who gathered groups of gentlemen into their chambers. This social segregation, the argument goes, also manifested academically so that there were essentially two tracks at the university: a rigorous academic one for men such as Marlowe who were taking degrees and (at least in theory) pursuing careers in the Church, and another for the well-born who would often spend only two years at the university before proceeding to the Inns of Court, where they would study enough law to allow them to manage their estates and participate in Parliament. One frequently adduced piece of evidence for this arrangement is a study handbook (drawn up in the 1620s but apparently reflecting longstanding practice) by Richard Holdsworth, later Master of Emmanuel College, Cambridge. This handbook offers daily study schedules that will permit students to master a challenging four-year course but also offers an alternative programme, *Studia leviora* ('lighter studies'), consisting mostly of modern literature for 'such as come to the University not with intention to make Scholarship their profession, but only to get such learning as may serve for delight and ornament and such as the want whereof would speak a defect in breeding'.[11]

Other historians have persuasively countered, however, that the idea of a two-track university is far too simple. For one thing, as we have seen, the scholarship-holders pursuing a degree could be well-born as well as poor, a fact that had become a matter of concern when Marlowe was at the university. For another, even where well-born students were not taking degrees there is evidence that some took their studies seriously. Sir Philip Sidney, who went up to Christ Church, Oxford twelve years before Marlowe arrived in Cambridge, is described by his family's friend Thomas Moffett as frequently employing himself at the 'public assembly hall', meaning that he often engaged in the oral disputations that were the academic performance demanded of students, even though he was not pursuing a degree.[12] The rise over the course of the sixteenth century of the colleges as communities where students not only lived but took instruction closely supervised by tutors enhanced the subjection of all men, no matter their status, to academic discipline. While well-born students may have brought to the university both the envy-provoking accoutrements of social distinction and anxiety about maintaining such distinction, once there they were shaped by a clerical culture epitomised by men like Marlowe, with the result that the powers cultivated by university training acquired more than a narrowly clerical value. As historian Victor Morgan observes, from the early years of Elizabeth's reign 'the Latinate, linguistically sophisticated, pedantically theological culture of the early modern universities, together with the premium that they placed on eloquence, largely set the style of th[e] wider culture'.[13]

Becoming learned

The humanist training that Marlowe received at the King's School in Canterbury had focused on grammar and rhetoric, two of the three branches of the medieval trivium of disciplines. The third branch, logic or dialectic, was the focus of the university arts course leading to the Bachelor's degree. Grammar meant primarily the study of Latin, which was pursued at the grammar school through a method of double translation, whereby a pupil would translate a text from Latin to English and then back into Latin. Grammar also included the analysis, memorisation, and use in verse composition of syllable 'quantities' – that is, the different duration of spoken syllables that was the metrical principle on which Latin poetry was based. Rhetoric taught students how to organise their thoughts and adorn them with figures of speech so as to persuade their listeners – an outcome that was dependent on also moving those listeners. Obviously the boundary between grammar and rhetoric was somewhat fluid, insofar as the skills of verse-making might be harnessed for the task of moving an audience. Both were studied with reference to Latin drama, which furnished an object of analysis and an occasion for speaking aloud, an important ingredient of eloquence. There was also overlap between the grammar-school subject of rhetoric and the university subject of logic, insofar as the analytical procedures of logic afforded the matter and strategies for the arguments a rhetorician could pursue. The Elizabethan statutes for Cambridge specify that Latin grammar be taught only to choristers; all others were to have already mastered this subject. These statutes thus position university studies in a sequential relation to the work of the grammar school. They also provide that the first year of study be devoted to rhetoric, the second and third years to dialectic or logic, and the fourth to 'philosophy', suggesting a sequence of disciplines. However, the complicated and somewhat contradictory evidence of how university study actually proceeded suggests that it is more accurate to understand this sequence in terms of mastery of the single art of dialectic, which was nourished by the oratorical skills cultivated by an ongoing study of grammar and rhetoric.

What did it mean, with respect to both content and method, to study dialectic? A plan of studies drawn up by Robert Norgate, Master of Corpus Christi College during Marlowe's time there, specifies that the week was to begin at six o'clock on Monday morning with a lecture (literally a reading aloud with commentary) of Seton's *Dialectic … with Annotations by Peter Carter,* the most commonly used textbook on the subject. Seton identifies dialectic as 'the skill of arguing credibly' and the art 'to reason probably, on both parts [sides] of all matters that be put forth, so far as the nature of the thing can bear'.[14] Regarding these definitions David Riggs comments that probability is a matter of persuasion rather than a claim about the real world. In other words, dialectical reasoning was in the service less of discovery of the truth than of achieving political effects. One very important implication of this tendency is that, despite the fact that the primary purpose of educating men like Marlowe was to furnish the Church with ministers who would cultivate religious conformity, training in dialectic, as Riggs puts it, 'provided Renaissance undergraduates with a prolonged education in scepticism'.[15] This effect was produced above all by that emphasis on reasoning 'on both parts' of a question, or *in utramque partem*, as Marlowe and his fellow students would have said. This intellectual discipline meant that no proposition, no matter how orthodox, could be imagined without the student also entertaining and developing a contrary argument. Riggs cites a list of theses to be disputed in 1580 that includes 'The will acts freely' and 'Nothing is done without prior consent and volition by God.'[16] In each case a young undergraduate would have had to develop convincing opposing arguments to prove what were, in effect, heretical positions.

The contestatory stance of the dialectician and the provisional quality of the truths he arrived at were evident in the chief mode of academic performance demanded of students: the oral disputation. A disputation required one student acting as 'respondent' to offer arguments in support of a proposition like the ones cited above. Next 'opponents' (usually more than one) would offer contrary propositions and discover the flaws in the respondent's arguments. Finally, a 'determiner' would summarise and criticise the arguments on both sides, evaluate the disputers' performances, and 'determine' the answer to the problem debated. The Elizabethan statutes at both universities required that students dispute twice at the end of the first year, once as opponent and once as respondent. Fulfilment of this requirement admitted the student to the position of 'general sophister', which he would occupy for the rest of the B.A. course, regularly attending disputations and serving as an opponent in them at least once a term and as a respondent in the special disputations of 'determining' or graduating bachelors. Before a bachelor could 'determine' himself, he was subject to an oral examination, followed by his final, public disputation. When the First Scholar says that Faustus was 'wont to make our schools ring with *sic probo* ['thus I prove'], he is referring to Faustus' brilliant performance in such disputations (ii.2).

There is evidence that the requirements of the university statutes were not always rigorously enforced, but this laxity was only because much work of this kind was conducted in colleges instead of in the 'schools' or public rooms serving the entire university. Norgate's schedule for Corpus Christi College, for instance, provided that the sophisters work on disputation on Mondays through Thursdays at four in the afternoon in the college. That this constant focus on public oral performance was both demanding and nerve-wracking is suggested by Holdsworth's study guide, which admonishes students to keep up their studies lest they 'be baffled in [their] disputes, disgraced and vilified in Public examinations, [and] laughed at in speeches and Declamations'.[17] It has been argued that the element of display in university work helped to assimilate academic and aristocratic cultures to one another. However, given the potential for public humiliation afforded by such exercises and the complex social composition of the student body, disputation might have carried considerable social risk for the well-born, affording occasions for the demonstration of superior intellectual powers by poor boys such as Marlowe. The records are remarkably silent about whether college authorities permitted such cross-status encounters or took steps to avoid them.

One thing that will be apparent from the foregoing is that the course leading to a bachelor's degree was focused on the mastery less of specific content than of a method of investigation with no end other than its own perfection. Faustus' question, 'Is, to dispute well logic's chiefest end?' (i.8), and the yearning for a 'greater subject' (i.11) it bespeaks, might have resonated with more than one determining bachelor. Nevertheless, the early modern undergraduate arts course was probably less frustrating than the medieval one had been, insofar as the early modern course had been enriched by the humanist focus on Latin and some Greek letters. Holdsworth's schedule has students spending every afternoon reading at a more advanced level many of the authors they would have first encountered at grammar school: Cicero, Virgil, Ovid, Seneca and Plautus, Livy, Statius, and Homer. This combination of the art of disputing with the study of literature permitted the bachelor's course to serve as an education for gentlemen scholars. But for a scholarship student such as Marlowe, in an older, more clerical mode, it was merely preparation for his studies in the M.A. course.

The M.A. course derived from the medieval quadrivium of arithmetic, geometry, astronomy, and music, though in the 1580s Marlowe would have actually studied mathematics, geometry, astronomy, and cosmography. Cosmography, an ancestor of geography, would have entailed acquaintance with classical authorities such as Strabo and Ptolemy but also with the work of the great Renaissance cartographer, Abraham Ortellius, whose atlas may be what Marlowe imagined when he has Tamburlaine request a map so that he can chart his conquests at the conclusion of *Tamburlaine the Great*, Part II. Similarly, astronomy was pursued through reading Ptolemy but such reading would have allowed students to grasp the implications of Copernicus' findings, which were being published in England throughout this period. If the names of Ortellius and Copernicus suggest that these studies would have been pulling students towards modern notions of science, however, we also need to grasp how proximate fields such as mathematics and astronomy remained to the occult. Both universities in this period nurtured astrologers and magicians. The best known were John Dee, famed mathematician and astrologer to the queen, who had commenced his studies at Cambridge in 1542, and Robert Fludd, who began his studies at Oxford fifty years later. But John Caius, a well-known physician and the founder of Gonville and Caius College, Cambridge, also studied magic, leaving a manuscript with conjurations in his own hand to mathematician John Fletcher, who in turn made a name for himself as an astrologer. The Puritan polemicist William Perkins, who was a student at Cambridge at the same time as Marlowe, studied magic avidly while a student, to the point where, according to seventeenth-century historian of Cambridge Thomas Fuller, he 'bordered on Hell it selfe' but later came to denounce his obsession.[18]

Doctor Faustus, learned but of low birth like Marlowe, is thus less an allegorical figure than a typical one in the sense of representing, with some imaginative enhancement, a possible way of being cultivated by the university. The educational path that Marlowe, and others like him, trod was a transforming one, with respect both to the intellectual powers it afforded individuals and to their imaginable purchase on the world. But while the university could flavour the culture of the larger society, it did little to change that society's structure. There was thus nowhere for a man like Marlowe to take his learning save into an increasingly scarce Church living or to the unstable and emergent market of the commercial theatre. The early modern university may have helped to reproduce the social order but it also jammed it, inviting the university's denizens to *imagine* a power for learning because the actual relation between learning and power was so fraught with contradiction.

Notes

1 Christopher Marlowe, *Dr Faustus*, ed. Roma Gill (London: A. & C. Black; New York: W. W. Norton, 1989), Prologue, 11. All quotations are from this edition. Spelling has been modernised for all quotations from sixteenth- and seventeenth-century texts regardless of how it appeared in the cited text.
2 David Riggs, *The World of Christopher Marlowe* (New York: Henry Holt, 2004), 1.
3 *Ibid.*, 184.
4 Statutes of the Merchant Taylors' School, printed in Frederick William Marsden Draper, *Four Centuries of the Merchant Taylors' School* (London: Oxford University Press, 1962), 243.
5 From the King's School Statutes, 1541, in Arthur F. Leach, *Educational Charters and Documents, 598 to 1909* (Cambridge University Press, 1911), 457.

6 The quotations are from a sixteenth-century account of the debate printed in John Gough Nichols, *Narratives of Days of the Reformation* (London: Camden Society, 1859), 273–4.
7 Mark H. Curtis, *Oxford and Cambridge in Transition* (Oxford: Clarendon Press, 1959), 56.
8 Thomas Starkey, *A Dialogue between Pole and Lupset*, ed. Thomas Frederick Mayer, Camden Fourth Series 37 (London: Offices of the Royal Historical Society, 1989), 124; Sir Humphrey Gilbert, *Queene Elizabethes Achademy* [British Library, Lansdowne MS 98], Early English Text Society, Extra Series 8–16 (London: Early English Text Society, 1872), 10.
9 Brian Twyne, to his father, 26 September 1597, Oxford, Bodleian Library MS Gr. Misc. d. 2, fo. 46, printed in *Bodleian Quarterly Record* 5 (1926–8): 216.
10 *Ibid.*
11 Richard Holdsworth, 'Directions for a Student in the Universitie', printed in Harris Francis Fletcher, *The Intellectual Development of John Milton*, 2 vols., Vol. II (Urbana: University of Illinois Press, 1961), 623–64 (647).
12 Thomas Moffett, *Nobilis; or, A View of the Life and Death of a Sidney*, ed. Virgil B. Heltzel and Hoyt H. Hudson (San Marino: The Huntington Library, 1940), 77.
13 Victor Morgan, *A History of the University of Cambridge*, 4 vols., Vol. II: *1546–1750* (Cambridge University Press, 2004), 134.
14 John Seton, *Dialectica Ioannis Setonis Cantabrigiensis, annotationibus Petri Carteri* (London: Excudebant Gerardus Dewes & Henricus Marsh ex assignatione Thomae Marsh, 1584), 154, sig. A1r. Translated and quoted in Riggs, *The World of Christopher Marlowe*, 80–1.
15 *Ibid.*, 83.
16 University Archives, Cambridge University Library Miscellaneous Collections 10, 1–15, translated and cited in Riggs, *The World of Christopher Marlowe*, 91.
17 Holdsworth, 'Directions', 637.
18 Thomas Fuller, *Abel redivivus* (1651), 432, quoted in Mordechai Feingold, 'The Occult Tradition in the English Universities of the Renaissance: A Reassessment', in *Occult and Scientific Mentalities of the Renaissance*, ed. Brian Vickers (Cambridge University Press, 1984), 73–94 (83).

CHAPTER SEVENTEEN

Marlowe and the question of will

Kathryn Schwarz

> Time present and time past
> Are both perhaps present in time future,
> And time future contained in time past.
> If all time is eternally present
> All time is unredeemable.
> What might have been is an abstraction
> Remaining a perpetual possibility
> Only in a world of speculation.
> What might have been and what has been
> Point to one end, which is always present.[1]

Christopher Marlowe's *Tamburlaine* plays execute a temporal sleight of hand. The individual will that motivates action coincides with the grammatical 'will' that anticipates the future, only to be displaced by the 'will have been' of prophecy and history. When Tamburlaine announces '*will* and *shall* best fitteth Tamburlaine', he implies his surrender to an overriding impulse that drives the teleology of conquest.[2] Resistless to a force within, he becomes irresistible to the world without, and exemplifies an anarchic supremacy that preoccupies early modern theorists of the psyche. Pierre de la Primaudaye, author of the philosophical compendium *The French Academie*, compares ascendant will to an insurgent sovereign: 'shee accounteth this Lordshippe which shee taketh to her selfe to bee a great good, and so maketh knowne her power and magnificence, as it were a tyrannicall prince'.[3] For the tyrant who capitulates to his own lawless desires, there is no meaningful difference between triumph and devastation; Johannes H. Birringer's account of 'Tamburlaine's creative and destructive will to power' sums up the indiscriminate effects of arbitrary volition.[4] In his treatise on the soul, the didactic poet John Davies offers advice – 'Then let *Reason* raine / Thy head-strong *Will*, and thy high thoughts restraine' – that links unrestrained will to an apocalyptic fall:

> For if thy thoughts flie higher then that pitch,
> And *Luciferian* pride thy *Minde* inflate,
> Thou mayst with him fall hedlong in the ditch,
> And runne into *Gods* unrevoked hate.⁵

Davies' warning closely echoes the King of Jerusalem's threat to Tamburlaine: 'Thy victories are grown so violent, / That shortly heaven, fill'd with the meteors / Of blood and fire thy tyrannies have made, / Will pour down blood and fire on thy head' (*2 Tamb.*, IV.i.142–5).

Tamburlaine explodes these clichés of internal disorder and ungoverned acts, arguing that the will that masters him is not his own: 'But, since I exercise a greater name, / The Scourge of God and terror of the world, / I must apply myself to fit those terms' (*2 Tamb.*, IV.i.155–7). His peculiar resolve — 'to fit those terms' — subordinates linear progress to an intricate fusion of what has been and what will be. The King of Jerusalem anticipates a causal sequence in which change is just a matter of time. But both time and change resist anticipation, for Tamburlaine enacts what has been done, presenting himself less as an agent who makes history than as the agent of a history already made. His comment on 'will' and 'shall' lays a false trail unless we follow the thought to its conclusion: 'For *will* and *shall* best fitteth Tamburlaine, / Whose smiling stars give him assured hope / Of martial triumph ere he meet his foes' (*1 Tamb.*, III.iii.41–3). The verb form that subtends this claim is 'will *have*', the form of the future anterior. If Tamburlaine equates words with deeds – 'I speak it, and my words are oracles' (*1 Tamb.*, III.iii.102) – and if he is, as Marjorie Garber writes, 'a master of speech-acts', it is because his future has become the past.⁶ History plays by definition present episodes that have occurred. The two parts of *Tamburlaine* make active use of this axiomatic structure; by uniting character and audience in explicit knowledge of what will have been, the plays set up a complex relationship between subjectivity and time. What does it mean to act in the future anterior, to be at once subject to its laws of foreclosure and a subject within its paradoxical space? What scope does agency have, what shape can selfhood take, under the shadow of remembered acts? What ethical choices are offered or withheld when the future becomes a Möbius strip?

'A subject always declares meaning in the future anterior', Alain Badiou writes, and defines this subject as a contingent yet crucial element in the validation of belief: 'A subject emptily names the universe to-come which is obtained by the supplementation of the situation with an indiscernible truth. At the same time, the subject is the finite real, the local stage, of this supplementation.'⁷ As the 'local stage' for a process that provisionally figures what is to come, Badiou's subject participates in realised truths, but neither adequately anticipates nor retrospectively knows its own effect. Such a subject hardly seems congruent with Tamburlaine, whose habitation of a finished history retrojects hypothesis into fact, and for whom declaration meets meaning in a consummated future that fills with substantiation even as it is named. But Badiou offers precise terms for the temporal anomaly of this process: 'A subject is a knowledge suspended by a truth whose finite moment it is.'[8] Tamburlaine is out of time, suspended by his own stipulated truth in a finite moment that masquerades as a progress narrative. 'And, till by vision or by speech I hear / Immortal Jove say "Cease, my Tamburlaine", / I will persist a terror to the world', he declares (*2 Tamb.*, IV.i.201–3). Pre-empted by 'until', the defiant 'I will' commits to a persistence that is legibly superfluous, not only for the 'we' who read or watch but for Tamburlaine himself: he will continue to do what he has done until he has done what he has been destined to do. The pattern built on this circular logic attracts frequent comment, from 'the almost plotless episodic structure, barren of dramatic conflict' to 'the *repetition compulsion* of Marlowe's heroes', from the 'compulsively repetitive structure of Tamburlaine's game of conqueror' to the description of that game as 'numbingly repetitious'.[9] Repetition without difference collapses a line to a point, the single point at which Tamburlaine's trajectory starts and ends.

As the votary of an ordained future, Tamburlaine believes what we know, a convergence that situates the plays at the intersection of prophecy and history. And his idiosyncratic prophecy works like history, in the sense that the prophecy erases even the illusion of alternative routes. Meander describes Tamburlaine as 'misled by dreaming prophecies' (*1 Tamb.*, I.i.41), citing a truism of oracular predictions: Tamburlaine may arrive at his fate, but only through a process that leads him astray. From *Oedipus* to the *Arcadia*, destiny follows from ill-conceived attempts to escape it; all action is errant, and understanding comes after the fact. Indeed, Mathew R. Martin argues that even Tamburlaine's emergence as 'a man whose being is anterior to his becoming' is an attempt to elude trauma.[10] Whether we focus on psyches or structures, prophecies interlock misreading with truth, an effect Slavoj Žižek associates with 'the way so-called historical necessity itself *is constituted through misrecognition*'.[11] Through a repetitive process mediated by a founding error, experience belatedly accrues the status of the inevitable; 'that is why we are all the time "rewriting history", retroactively giving the elements their symbolic weight by including them in new textures – it is this elaboration which decides retroactively what they "will have been"'.[12] But if we look at Tamburlaine from this angle, we encounter an obstacle because he encounters none. Whatever those 'dreaming prophecies' might say, they define his end as immanent in his beginning. His insistence that he will control destiny merges with his awareness that destiny has determined him; mortality and immortality, like intention and execution, become reciprocal affirmations. When he says 'I hold the Fates bound fast in iron chains, / And with my hand turn Fortune's wheel about; / And sooner shall the sun fall from his sphere / Than Tamburlaine be slain or overcome' (*1 Tamb.*, I.ii.174–7), he might as well say, as Jean-Luc Nancy says, 'In the span of its lifetime, the body is also a dead body, the body of a dead person, this dead person I am when alive. Dead or alive, neither dead nor alive, I *am* the opening, the tomb or the mouth, the one inside the other.'[13] Mouths and tombs, the bodies through which the living speak and the tablets on which the dead are spoken: what differentiates such artifacts for the subject of what must have been?

Tamburlaine, subject of the prophetic end he will have existed to fulfil, both bears and exacts the costs of certainty. His proleptic role disallows counter-factuals, those conditional statements that create a web of futurities. The fugitive 'what if' has been lost to a predicative 'if ... then', in which 'if' has the force of 'when' and 'then' folds the future into the past. 'If thou wilt stay with me' (*1 Tamb.*, I.ii.188); 'if I should desire the Persian crown' (II.v.76); 'if I prosper' (II.v.84): such propositions banish alternatives. As Tamburlaine's line of action contracts to a point, so too does the maze of thought experiments that might surround it. The plays manifest an extreme version of Jacques Derrida's tenet, 'for that which guides our future anterior, there is as yet no exergue'.[14] Etymologically, 'exergue' indicates 'something lying outside the work'; here what will have been occupies no space outside the work of Tamburlaine, the text of his prophecy, the foreshortened arc of his acts. There is something eerie about this compressed purpose, which destroys not only human enemies but imaginative possibilities. The future anterior mystifies agents as it fixes effects, and Nancy's subtle shifts 'Dead or alive, neither dead nor alive' – recall the example with which Freud begins his study of the uncanny: 'doubts whether an apparently animate being is really alive; or conversely, whether a lifeless object might not be in fact animate'.[15] History plays have a generic investment in reanimating the dead. *Tamburlaine*'s parade of uncanny bodies constructs a citational relationship to this practice, an intratextual meditation on what it means to pack life and death into one corporeal moment that is over before it begins.

That one moment is most obviously Tamburlaine's. Oracular, prophetic, divinely decreed, his habitation of a prefigured future conflates animate subject-effects with static object lessons. We see him in the present, know him from the past, register his claim on the future; in his reincarnate occurrence we engage the living to recall the dead. The signs of his enigmatic ontology are familiar points of plot. Innumerable battles leave him unscathed, and his self-mutilation highlights this unlikelihood; describing himself as 'void of scars and clear from any wound', he cuts himself 'to teach you all' (*2 Tamb.*, III.iii.112, 114). We might reasonably wonder what he teaches us.[16] When he says 'Now look I like a soldier' (III.iii.117), what links the presentist 'now' to the double-timed, historicist and futurist 'then'? His prophesied body anticipates his blazoned body, which anticipates his wounded body, which anticipates his dying body; yet at each moment Tamburlaine is inseparably deadly subject and deathly object (of intention, of desire, of violence, of death). The moments are coincident, as his states of being are coincident, imbricated in an always-now projected back from the already-has-been. 'Now', like 'if', is enclosed by 'then'. Judith Haber cogently describes 'repeated, paradoxical attempts to immortalize the flesh by wounding it'; such reiterative, episodic, ambiguous acts affirm an uncanny duality that remains constant to the end.[17] And at the end, Tamburlaine's notorious diagnosis again confuses life with death, as his desiccated blood, his extinguished substance, and his voided spirit define a body that is operational but not viable (*2 Tamb.*, V.iii.82–97). The alternatives of revival and dissolution become the same predestined choice – 'See, my physicians, now, how Jove hath sent / A present medicine to recure my pain!' (V.iii.106–7), he says of the final battle – and fate is the *pharmakon*, the prescription that conserves and kills. Michel de Certeau's insight resonates here: 'To be spoken without knowing it is to be caught dead unawares; it is to proclaim death, believing all the while it is conquered; it is to bear witness to the opposite of what one affirms.'[18] But it resonates oddly, for Tamburlaine knows he has been spoken, even as this knowledge means he must bear witness in oppositional terms. He fights his last battle as he has fought all battles, a lifeless object that is perversely animate, an animate being who is not plausibly alive, an agent, irreducibly double, which puts in question the evidentiary value of flesh.

Tamburlaine's abrupt, futile investment in lineage underscores his embodied paradox. The worries about legitimacy (*2 Tamb.*, I.iv.21–34), the murder of Calyphas, 'a form not meet to give that subject essence / Whose matter is the flesh of Tamburlaine' (*2 Tamb.*, IV.i.114–15), the stress on continuation, all fantasise a history that exceeds his own future presence. Lee

Edelman pinpoints the recursive drive of such fantasies: 'Futurism thus generates generational succession, temporality, and narrative sequence, not toward the end of enabling change, but, instead, of perpetuating sameness, of turning back time to assure repetition.'[19] Tamburlaine makes this drive explicit – 'My flesh, divided in your precious shapes, / Shall still retain my spirit, though I die, / And live in all your seeds immortally' (*2 Tamb.*, V.iii.173–5) – but sequential similitude is not an option for a figure whose own existence violates time.[20] Although Tamburlaine singles out Calyphas as 'my abortive son' (*2 Tamb.*, IV.iii.66), each son represents a line cut short, an awareness that circulates both in historical accounts and in the plays. Thomas Fortescue records that Tamburlaine '[left] behinde hym twoo soonnes, not such as was the father, as afterwarde appeared by many plaine, and evident signes'.[21] And when Amyras says 'Your soul gives essence to our wretched subjects, / Whose matter is incorporate in your flesh' (*2 Tamb.*, V.iii.165–6), he identifies himself not just as a flesh-puppet for the paternal spirit, but as one whose expiration date coincides with his father's own. The living death of patrilineal succession has been forestalled by the death-in-life of Tamburlaine.

I would suggest, however, that Tamburlaine is not the most salient sign of uncanniness in these plays. He surrounds himself with figures that are indifferently living and dead, as if, interred within his anachronistic futurity, he transmits imprisonment as a form of contagion. Allies and enemies meet in the category 'prisoner', which suspends bodies between personhood and matter; when the Turkish emperor Bajazeth appears as an enraged footstool, his role is as paradigmatic as it is strange. False contraries – persuasion versus coercion, maintenance versus slaughter – resolve into spectacles of mystified animation, so that the targets of two-fold aggression exhibit both outcomes. Bajazeth lives in a cage and brains himself against it; Zenocrate follows Tamburlaine in his train and in her coffin. These may be sequential spectacles, but they overlap in the depleted yet evocative subject–objects who blur the lines of mortality. Bajazeth's imprisonment outlives his body; invocations span the second play, from Orcanes' reference to 'the mighty Callapine, / Who lives in Egypt prisoner to that slave / Which kept his father in an iron cage' (*2 Tamb.*, I.i.3–5) to Tamburlaine's mention of 'Bithynia, where I took / The Turk and his great empress prisoners' (*2 Tamb.*, V.iii.129–30). Zenocrate is still more present: 'At every town and castle I besiege, / Thou shalt be set upon my royal tent' (*2 Tamb.*, III.ii.36–7), Tamburlaine vows of her portrait; dying, he demands, 'Now fetch the hearse of fair Zenocrate; / Let it be plac'd by this my fatal chair, / And serve as parcel of my funeral' (*2 Tamb.*, V.iii.211–13).

Rival or lover, alive or dead, each figure is perversely constant in function and effect, inviting us to ask what knowable difference attends the fact of dying. 'Bodies are evident – and that's why all justice and justness start and end with these', Nancy writes. 'Injustice is the mixing, breaking, crushing, and stifling of bodies, making them indistinct.'[22] This indistinction, which commingles not only flesh but the seductions and exterminations that collect it, is precisely what makes bodies evidence for Tamburlaine. Surrounded by Zenocrate's grief, Arabia's corpse, and the brained remains of Zabina and Bajazeth, he announces, 'And such are objects fit for Tamburlaine, / Wherein, as in a mirror, may be seen / His honour' (*1 Tamb.*, V.ii.414–16). It is easy to recognise error: he is the prince of the *de casibus* tradition, heedless of lessons and omens; he is the subject of the Lacanian mirror stage, drunk on orthopaedic totality. But there is truth here as well. Tamburlaine views this array of bodies, each caught on the cusp of what will have been, and sees his own uncanny image.

In 'The Uncanny', Freud defines the porous boundary between living and dead as an atavistic remainder: 'it is no matter for surprise that the primitive fear of the dead is still so strong within us and always ready to come to the surface on any provocation'.[23] *Tamburlaine* provokes through cumulation, the messy heaping-up of things into masses of things that refuses the comforts of discretion. The protagonist's equivocal state is enmeshed in the suspended bodies he imprisons, which are entangled with bodies we barely see but must conjure for ourselves: the soldiers who, in their unfathomable multitudes, proliferate the confusion of death and life. Karen Cunningham writes of Marlowe's elaborate deaths, 'discussions of aesthetics compound one another until our interest in the style of dying overcomes our response to the fact'.[24] For soldiers there is not even a style of dying; to be alive is to be dead, the shift from one side of the equation to the other leaving no mark on the zero-sum game. This logic amalgamates killers and corpses: 'Let thousands die: their slaughter'd carcasses / Shall serve for walls and bulwarks to the rest' (*1 Tamb.*, III.iii.138–9). The ruthlessness with which 'if' leads to 'then' is inescapable: 'Suppose they be in number infinite' (*1 Tamb.*, II.ii.43) becomes 'And numbers more than infinite of men' (*2 Tamb.*, II.ii.18); 'Let him bring millions infinite of men' (*1 Tamb.*, III.iii.33) becomes 'My sword hath sent millions of Turks to hell' (*2 Tamb.*, V.i.178); 'He brings a world of people to the field' (*2 Tamb.*, I.i.67) becomes 'For half the world shall perish in this fight' (*2 Tamb.*, I.vi.44). In the space of our complicit imagination, speculative soldiers slide into actual soldiers, and violent throngs slip into mass graves. Patricia A. Cahill describes *Tamburlaine*'s militarism in terms of 'uniform personhood and

Marlowe and the question of will 199

mathematically rationalized violence' but notes that rationalisation has its limit: 'Marlowe repeatedly hints at the way numerical thinking unexpectedly morphs into a spectacle of horror, in which, for example, human flesh can be imagined as undifferentiated multitude.'[25] It is difficult to imagine Tamburlaine's limit; an evacuated animation, he can only aspire to do it all again. 'Techelles, let us march, / And weary Death with bearing souls to hell' (2 *Tamb.*, v.iii.76–7).

Cahill's point, like Cunningham's, suggests that the more urgent issue may be *our* response. *Tamburlaine* is a ghost story on a grand scale. It revisits a familiar moment, but embeds this moment in corollary iterations that illuminate the costs. So how do we count those costs, and what principles inform our maths? We can turn to Judith Halberstam's point about accountability – 'to tell a ghost story means being willing to be haunted'[26] – and to Carla Freccero's explication: 'This willingness to be haunted is an ethical relation to the world, motivated by a concern not only for the past but also for the future, for those who live on in the borderlands without a home.'[27] But we might then find that *Tamburlaine* exposes a gap, between the pleasure of being haunted and the obligation of ethical response. Do we really care about those anonymous soldiers from the borderlands? Perhaps. Or perhaps to be haunted by the knowledge of history, and by the material reanimation of that knowledge, is simply to use bodies for our own ends. Cahill's 'spectacle of horror' is only horror if it matters. And to everything in us that insists it *must* matter, Nancy offers a sobering answer: 'The cadavers in a mass grave aren't the dead, they aren't our dead: they are wounds heaped up, stuck in, flowing into one another, the soil tossed right on top, no winding-cloth to define the spacing of one, and then another, death ... Through another concentration, bodies are only signs annulled.'[28] It remains a problem of time: the always-already of the soldiers, the will-have-been of their deaths, raises the question of whether they can ever call for justice. Do such mechanisms operate in the foreclosed space of the future anterior? Does will-have-been leave room for should-not-be? Trapped among immutable data, we might find refuge in the verdicts of evaluative historiography. Still, there is the curious fact that it has always been difficult to moralise Tamburlaine, the prince who never really falls. Those of us in the business of using people might be left to decide for ourselves: what responsibilities attend our pleasures, and what do we owe to those who, for us, will only ever have been dead? Freud concludes, 'Most likely our fear still implies the old belief that the dead man becomes the enemy of his survivor and seeks to carry him off to share his new life with him.'[29] It seems all too likely that we – the 'we' who can claim that pronoun of survivors – may enact an efficient if inadvertent annexation of our own.

Notes

1. T. S. Eliot, 'Burnt Norton', 1–10, in *Collected Poems, 1909–1962* (New York: Harcourt, Brace & World, 1963), 175.
2. Christopher Marlowe, *Tamburlaine the Great*, Part I, III.iii.41, in *The Complete Plays*, ed. J. B. Steane (New York: Penguin, 1986). Subsequent quotations of *Tamburlaine* follow this edition.
3. Pierre de la Primaudaye, *The Second Part of the French Academie* (London: G. B[ishop], R[alph] N[ewbery], and R. B[arker], 1594), 213. In citing early modern texts, I have modernised typography in several ways, revising consonantal *u* and *i* to *v* and *j*, vocalic *v* to *u*, and long *s* to *s*.
4. Johannes H. Birringer, 'Marlowe's Violent Stage: "Mirrors" of Honor in *Tamburlaine*', *ELH* 51:2 (1984): 219–39 (223).
5. John Davies, *Mirum in modum* (London: printed for William Aspley, 1602), sig. C2v.
6. Marjorie Garber, '"Here's Nothing Writ": Scribe, Script, and Circumscription in Marlowe's Plays', *Theatre Journal* 36:3 (1984): 301–20 (302). See also Birringer, 'Marlowe's Violent Stage', esp. 234–7.
7. Alain Badiou, *Being and Event*, trans. Oliver Feltham (London and New York: Continuum, 2007), 400, 399–400.
8. *Ibid.*, 406.
9. Irving Ribner, 'The Idea of History in Marlowe's *Tamburlaine*', *ELH* 20:4 (1953): 251–66 (265); Stephen Greenblatt, *Renaissance Self-Fashioning: From More to Shakespeare* (University of Chicago Press, 1980), 200, emphasis in original; Mathew R. Martin, '"This tragic glass": Tragedy and Trauma in *Tamburlaine Part One*', in *Staging Pain, 1580–1800: Violence and Trauma in British Theater*, ed. James Robert Allard and Mathew R. Martin (Farnham: Ashgate, 2009), 15–29 (21); Matthew Greenfield, 'Christopher Marlowe's Wound Knowledge', *PMLA* 119:2 (2004): 233–46 (239).
10. Martin, '"This tragic glass"', 22.
11. Slavoj Žižek, *The Sublime Object of Ideology* (London and New York: Verso, 1989), 61, emphasis in original. For his comments on prophecy, see 58.
12. *Ibid.*, 56.
13. Jean-Luc Nancy, *Corpus*, trans. Richard A. Rand (New York: Fordham University Press, 2008), 15; emphasis in original.
14. Jacques Derrida, *Of Grammatology*, trans. Gayatri Chakravorty Spivak (Baltimore and London: Johns Hopkins University Press, 1976), 5.
15. Sigmund Freud, 'The Uncanny' (1919), in *The Standard Edition of the Complete Psychological Works of Sigmund Freud*, ed. and trans. James Strachey, 24 vols. (London: Hogarth Press, 1955), Vol. XVII, 217–56 (226). Freud takes this example from Ernst Jentsch's 1906 essay 'On the Psychology of the Uncanny'.

16 Alan Shepard argues that self-wounding reveals a fear of inauthenticity; Greenfield identifies self-wounding with theatrical power: Alan Shepard, 'Endless Sacks: Soldiers' Desire in *Tamburlaine*', *Renaissance Quarterly* 46:4 (1993): 734–53, esp. 752; Greenfield, 'Christopher Marlowe's Wound Knowledge', esp. 238–40.
17 Judith Haber, *Desire and Dramatic Form in Early Modern England* (Cambridge University Press, 2009), 25.
18 Michel de Certeau, *Heterologies: Discourse on the Other*, trans. Brian Massumi (Minneapolis: University of Minnesota Press, 1986), 181.
19 Lee Edelman, *No Future: Queer Theory and the Death Drive* (Durham, NC and London: Duke University Press, 2004), 60.
20 See Mark Thornton Burnett's description of the sons as 'alien to Tamburlaine'; '*Tamburlaine* and the Body', *Criticism* 33:1 (1991): 31–47 (37).
21 Thomas Fortescue, *The Forrest; or, Collection of Histories* (London: Jhon Kyngston for Willyam Jones, 1571), 87; see also George Whetstone, *The English Myrror* (London: J. Windet for G. Seton, 1586), esp. 82.
22 Nancy, *Corpus*, 47.
23 Freud, 'The Uncanny', 242.
24 Karen Cunningham, 'Renaissance Execution and Marlovian Elocution: The Drama of Death', *PMLA* 105.2 (1990): 209–22 (215).
25 Patricia A. Cahill, *Unto the Breach: Martial Formations, Historical Trauma, and the Early Modern Stage* (Oxford University Press, 2008), 19, 69.
26 Judith Halberstam, *In a Queer Time and Place: Transgender Bodies, Subcultural Lives* (New York and London: New York University Press, 2005), 60.
27 Carla Freccero, *Queer/Early/Modern* (Durham, NC and London: Duke University Press, 2006), 75.
28 Nancy, *Corpus*, 77.
29 Freud, 'The Uncanny', 242.

CHAPTER EIGHTEEN

Marlowe and the self

Lars Engle

From the beginning of Renaissance studies to the present day, the emergence of a modern kind of selfhood has been one of the chief alleged features of Renaissance culture and one of the main claims for its importance. Jacob Burckhardt in 1860 writes: 'this period ... first gave the highest development to individuality, and then led the individual to the most zealous and thorough study of himself'; Stephen Greenblatt in 2011 writes: 'something happened in the Renaissance, something that surged up against the constraints that centuries had constructed around curiosity, desire, individuality, sustained attention to the material world, the claims of the body ... it became possible – never easy, but possible – in the poet Auden's phrase to find the mortal world enough'; Richard Strier in 2011, quoting Burckhardt, writes: 'Aside from believing that there was a major shift in European culture (or "civilization") beginning in Italy in the late thirteenth century, I accept the view that there were many persons in the period who "knew little of false [or any] modesty" ... and were committed to being recognized as – dare I say it? – "individuals".'[1] Christopher Marlowe is a natural exhibit in support of this claim about Renaissance selfhood. While not a pioneer of Renaissance consciousness, he is the breakthrough artist for English Renaissance public theatre, and one could hardly find a stronger announcement of the possibilities of enhanced selfhood through irreverent overthrow of inherited structures of deference and identity than *Tamburlaine the Great*. Indeed, Marlowe's own life arguably culminates in a secular martyrdom brought about by his proto-Nietzschean search for true selfhood: his insistence on recasting the world he found as a world he willed.[2]

In its presentation of a scholar-magician whose revolt against God seems not only doomed but also misguided and sometimes silly, *Doctor Faustus* offers an obstacle to this view of Marlowe and selfhood. The play can be read as Marlowe's equivalent to the Retraction at the end of *The Canterbury Tales*. In such a reading, Marlowe wants us to see through

Faustus' individualistic self-assertion and, more generally, to reinsert human subjects into a cosmos where the only sane path is to recognise divine authority and bow to it. This is what Milton makes of *Doctor Faustus* in *Paradise Lost*. My chapter combats the idea that *Doctor Faustus* presents an obstacle to an account of Marlowe as proto-Nietzschean, and thus seeks to preserve him as a strong piece of evidence for the sweeping but useful view of Renaissance selfhood as a precursor of the modern self. I will argue that, in *Faustus* as elsewhere, Marlowe anticipates a modern secular goal of emancipatory self-recreation.

A question I have often encountered in teaching *Doctor Faustus* deals with an aspect of the hero's selfhood and interior mental life. It is this: if Faustus is so smart, why does he often act so stupid? This question might be asked globally of Faustus' initial choice: why condemn yourself to eternal torture for temporal rewards, especially when it turns out that there is nothing very substantive that you want to accomplish in this world beyond impressing people? We have developed some fairly helpful answers to the global question – basically pointing out that almost everybody who lives a secular life at least risks eternal damnation by focusing on the temporal at the expense of the spiritual, and that Faustus thus counts as a super-Everyman, doing in a more egregious and self-conscious way what almost everyone else does without thinking it through.

The question can also be asked (and I think is usually first asked) about particular moments early in the play, moments where Faustus' fateful choices seem bumptious and arbitrary, where, as David Riggs puts it, most interpreters see him as 'a bookish dunce'.[3] Such moments include Faustus' response to Mephistopheles' magnificent evocation of hell (used later in its essentials by Milton's Satan, who combines aspects of Faustus with aspects of Mephistopheles):

> MEPHISTOPHELES: Hell hath no limits, nor is circumscribed
> In one self place, for where we are is hell,
> And where hell is must we ever be,
> And, to conclude, when all the world dissolves,
> And every creature shall be purified,
> All places shall be hell that is not heaven.
> FAUSTUS: Come, I think hell's a fable.[4]

Faustus' reply is not only intellectually perverse in denying an eye-witness report from someone who would surely deny hell's reality if he could; it is also graceless, breaking the rhythm of Marlowe's mighty line. What is Marlowe up to?

Similarly, in his opening soliloquy, Faustus is notoriously partial in his quotation from a Latin Bible that, as Riggs points out, turns out to be not Jerome's Vulgate, but Marlowe's or Faustus' translation back into Latin from English Bibles of the time.⁵ (The reverse translation might signal Marlowe's irreverent impatience, but it also suggests that the verses Faustus 'views' in 'Jerome' were inscribed in English in Marlowe's mind.)

> When all is done, divinity is best.
> Jerome's Bible, Faustus, view it well.
> [*He reads.*] '*Stipendium peccati mors est.*' Ha!
> '*Stipendium*', etc.
> 'The reward of sin is death.' That's hard.
> [*He reads.*] '*Si pecasse negamus, fallimur*
> *Et nulla est in nobis veritas.*'
> If we say that we have no sin,
> We deceive ourselves, and there's no truth in us.
> Why then belike we must sin,
> And so consequently die.
> Ay, we must die an everlasting death.
> What doctrine call you this? *Che serà, serà*,
> What will be, shall be? Divinity, adieu!
>
> (1.i.37–50)

Note that once again Faustus' discovery, 'Why then belike we must sin', breaks rhythm, with the 'belike' signalling awkward surprise. Generations of professors have pointed out that Faustus leaves off the redemptive half of each of his scriptural verses. David Bevington's Norton introduction is representative: 'Any good Christian in Marlowe's audience would presumably know, however, that Faustus is quoting selectively and unfairly, playing games with the profundities of Christian faith that concede the inevitable sinfulness of humankind only to insist that God's great mercies are open to those who truly repent. From the start, Faustus betrays himself as a fool.'⁶ As Riggs points out, however, Faustus' misleading combination of half a line from Romans with half a line from the first epistle of John distils the essence of Calvinist double-predestination from the point of view of a reprobate: the wage of reprobation is death; and if we deny our reprobation, there's no truth in us. Robert Hunter claims that 'if Calvin is right and if Faustus is right in assuming his "thoughts against Joves Deity" to be the unpardonable sin, then Faustus is right in deeming himself already damned … His very thinking so suggests that he has already been numbered among the reprobate.'⁷ Riggs comments,

> The so-called 'devil's syllogism' based on Romans 6:23 and 1 John 1:8 held a special fascination for Marlowe's contemporaries because it so closely resembled the Calvinist dogma adopted in England and Wurtemburg. Calvin too isolates the first half of Romans 6:23 and insists that 'all sin is mortal'. Article 15 of the Church of England ended with the first half of 1 John 1:8 followed by a full stop. The Thirty-Nine Articles that constituted the Elizabethan Church nowhere suggest that all who confess their sins will be forgiven; on the contrary, God reserves the gift of grace only for the elect, who 'feel in themselves the working of the Spirit of Christ ... So for curious and carnal persons, lacking the Spirit of Christ, to have continually before their eyes the sentence of God's Predestination is a most dangerous downfall.' Critics rightly point out that Faustus is hideously mistaken about the Bible; but the Church he is rejecting has taught him to make precisely these mistakes. Marlowe, who had already been taxed with atheism, unveils in *Dr Faustus* the ecclesiastical basis of his own unbelief.[8]

Riggs' final sentence suggests that the errors of Faustus may be part of an ironic strategy on Marlowe's part, and Riggs' way of resolving the problem they raise is to pose Faustus' own evident fictionality as the governing irony of the play: 'Marlowe ... used his poetic gift of irony, indirectness and erudite allusion to notify patient judges that Dr Faustus is a fictional being – a character in a book or an unwitting actor in the theatre of God's judgments.'[9] Riggs is surely right that the play creates a double audience for itself or a double impression in individual readers and viewers.

But it is possible to see Faustus as a more intelligible intellectual, a Renaissance self of a particular proto-modern kind, rather than as a metafiction. The key to seeing Faustus in this way is a particularly puzzling, initially ludicrous exchange between Faustus and Mephistopheles. Mephistopheles gives his greatest speech, and Faustus gives one of his bumptious and aesthetically unappreciative replies:

> MEPHISTOPHELES: Why, this is hell, nor am I out of it.
>   Think'st thou that I, who saw the face of God
>   And tasted the eternal joys of heaven,
>   Am not tormented with ten thousand hells
>   In being deprived of everlasting bliss?
>   O Faustus, leave these frivolous demands,
>   Which strike a terror to my fainting soul!
> FAUSTUS: What, is great Mephistopheles so passionate
>   For being deprivèd of the joys of heaven?
>   Learn thou of Faustus manly fortitude,
>   And scorn those joys thou never shalt possess.
>   Go bear these tidings to great Lucifer:

> Seeing Faustus hath incurred eternal death
> By desperate thoughts against Jove's deity,
> Say he surrenders up to him his soul.
> (1.iii.77–91)

'Learn thou of Faustus manly fortitude.' What does this imperative mean? Surely Faustus is not merely being self-aggrandising here. He's saying to Mephistopheles, stop revelling in despair and pay attention to the ways a resolute human being deals with the spiritual situation we share. Act like a Renaissance epicurean atheist and 'scorn those joys you never shall possess'.[10] Why never? Because exemplars of 'manly fortitude' know, as surely as do devils, that they are human reprobates who have 'incurred eternal death' by the very way they think about God. But unlike Mephistopheles, Faustus finds something better to do than to complain magnificently about what he has lost: humans like Faustus construct an alternative intellectual framework in which God's judgements do not matter.

Given this understanding of Faustus' attitude – an attitude Faustus here consciously strikes, at a moment where he must to some degree feel the overwhelming spiritual pathos of Mephistopheles' grief at being deprived of the divine presence – many of Faustus' odd remarks become understandable. Comments such as 'I think hell's a fable', spoken to a being who has just come from there, count as exemplifications for Mephistopheles of 'manly fortitude' vis-à-vis God and God's system. Remember that Richard Baines and Thomas Kyd – the first in a letter denouncing Marlowe to the Privy Council, the second in testimony under torture ordered by that Council – both accuse Marlowe of leading others to atheism or to the setting-aside of God that constituted 'atheism' in the English Renaissance.[11] In the Faustus–Mephistopheles relation we have a weird paradigm of intimate conversation between two men, both knowing themselves at odds with God, in which the bolder of the two tries to get the other to put a braver face on the deprivation they share.

Blaise Pascal, writing half a century after Marlowe's murder, famously proposed that, however improbable the existence of God may be, the rewards of believing in God are so great that they justify belief in an improbability: God is a bet worth taking. Faustus anticipates Pascal's wager but in reverse and, as Riggs has shown, in this calculation Faustus exhibits attitudes common among sixteenth-century atheists. Convinced that he is reprobate, Faustus balances the hideous near-certainty of eternal torment against the extremely difficult task of sustaining unbelief in a God-saturated world and finds the task worth the attempt even when success in it is improbable. If only he can *not* accept God's power, he may be able to lead a decent life while he has it. Faustus certifies that he is damned 'by desp'rate thoughts against Jove's deity' (I.iii.91), but, as Riggs helps us see, in sixteenth-century England one could easily pass *from* the conviction that one had been systematically damned since before the beginning of time *to* the hope that one could cast off the damning system by way of desperate thoughts against God's deity.[12] And Faustus appeals in a variety of ways to Mephistopheles to recognise in Faustus a superior accommodation to the exiled state. As Faustus declares to the newly summoned Mephistopheles, invoking his own performative self in the third person like a modern professional athlete: 'This word "damnation" terrifies not him, / For he confounds hell in Elysium. / His ghost be with the old philosophers!' (I.iii.59–61).

Moreover, Faustus' description of himself as damned by desperate thoughts presumably applies to his internal state before he takes up magic seriously at the play's opening. We can, in fact, see elements of partly suppressed anxiety about Faustus' relation to God's judgements and mercy in the apparently cavalier dismissals of non-magical fields of study in his opening soliloquy. Faustus dismisses medicine because it cannot 'make man to live eternally' (I.i.24). He dismisses law after quoting part of a phrase in Latin: '*Exhaereditare filium non potest pater nisi –*' (I.i.31); 'a father may not disinherit his son unless …'. Obviously, if Faustus is driven by a sense of being predestined to hell by God, he does not want to hear precisely how a father goes about disinheriting his sons. So he condemns law as 'servile and illiberal' (I.i.36) – that is, consigning one to slavishness and ungenerous in its basic terms – and turns to divinity. But, as we saw above, as soon as he thinks about theology he decides that he is disinherited: 'The reward of sin is death. That's hard' (I.i.41). Faustus finally turns to magic as an affirmation of human mental strength, a strength that allows mental life to be a god unto itself: 'his dominion that exceeds in this / Stretcheth as far as doth the mind of man. / A sound magician is a mighty god' (I.i.62–4). The opening soliloquy, then, illustrates how 'manly fortitude' consists in being a god for oneself.

But Doctor Faustus and *Doctor Faustus* differ crucially. What is one to make of the play's circumstantial refutation of the internalised and rejected Calvinism that drives Faustus himself?

While, as Hunter remarks, the 'necessary ingredient' in the play's 'terror' and 'mystery' for 'each variety of [sixteenth-century] believer' is 'the Calvinist conception of God', the play's basic plot is, after all, inconsistent with Calvinist double predestination.[13] If Faustus were eternally destined to be damned by a God, however inscrutable that God's judgements, why should demonic agents strive so energetically to seduce or daunt him? If Faustus has been predetermined to damnation since the beginning of time, all they have to do is wait for him. If he is of the elect, nothing they can do could damn him. Obviously *they*, knowing themselves damned without reprieve, do *not* know that there can be no reprieve for Faustus. Nor do the Good Angel and the Old Man. Is it simply that Marlowe, despite his atheism, reworks a deeply Christian morality plot that originates in Catholic moral thinking, though, as David Bevington demonstrates in *From 'Mankind' to Marlowe*, there is a long series of Protestant (and, at least in intention, Calvinist) moral plays between Marlowe and his Catholic precursors?[14] Or is Marlowe actually thinking creatively within the ferment of late-sixteenth-century Protestant doctrine about the issues of grace and predestination through this juxtaposition?

It is a telling coincidence that in 1586, roughly when Marlowe was coming down from Cambridge to London, Jacobus Arminius, a young Dutch theologian, returned from Geneva, where he had studied with Calvin's chief disciple Theodore Beza, to Leyden. In 1588, when Marlowe was, we think, beginning to write *Doctor Faustus*, Arminius undertook a defence of Calvin's doctrine of predestination against a Dutch theologian; that process led him to his own reinterpretation of Romans, rejection of double predestination, and development of Arminian doctrines of the availability of grace, even to the non-elect, within a covenant involving election that became a key element in the development of Protestant doctrine. Similar views developed independently in England in the 1580s. Samuel Harsnett, later an archbishop himself, was censured by the Archbishop of Canterbury when Harsnett 'attacked the harshness of the prevailing predestinarian doctrine in a famous sermon at Paul's Cross in 1584'.[15] That sermon aimed explicitly at the doctrine of double predestination, which Harsnett describes polemically as the belief that 'God should design many thousands of souls to Hell before they were, not in eye to their faults, but to his own absolute will and power, and to get him glory in their damnation. This opinion is grown huge and monstrous ... and men do shake and tremble at it; yet never a man reaches David's sling to cast it down.'[16] Marlowe could have heard similar argument at his university. Peter Baro and William Barrett preached and disputed against high Calvinism at Cambridge, and Baro at least did so during Marlowe's time there, though he was not officially censured by the Archbishop until 1595; he asserts the freedom of the will and God's interest in the contingency (as opposed to the necessity) of the sinner's sin and of the good person's virtue in a disputation published in 1588 and delivered before Marlowe went down to

London.[17] Harsnett ends his 1584 sermon by mapping what he sees as the quicksands of error surrounding the true path of the English Church:

> To conclude, let us take heed and beware, that we neither (with the Papists) rely upon our free will; nor (with the Pelagian) upon our nature: nor (with the Puritan), *Curse God and die*, laying the burden of our sins on his shoulders, and the guilt of them at the everlasting doors: but let us fall down on our faces, give God the glory, and say, Unto Thee O Lord belong mercy and forgiveness.[18]

Marlowe thought through these alternatives, and his Faustus exemplifies someone who is lost among them and who chooses, in effect, to make something creative and temporarily powerful out of the 'curse God and die' option.

The view that the Protestant way must include a less predetermined situation for sinners – a view that well describes everything in *Doctor Faustus* except Doctor Faustus' own attitudes – gets its most memorable summation in English poetry in the words of Milton's God in *Paradise Lost* (1667), describing a moral universe in which some are elect and some are not. Even those who are not elect should trust God to take an interest in their spiritual situation:

> Some have I chosen of peculiar grace
> Elect above the rest: so is my will.
> The rest shall hear me call, and oft be warned
> Their sinful state, and to appease betimes
> Th'incensed Deity, while offered grace
> Invites, for I will clear their senses dark
> What may suffice, and soften stony hearts
> To pray, repent, and bring obedience due.
> To prayer, repentance, and obedience due
> Though but endeavored with sincere intent
> Mine ear shall not be slow, mine eye not shut.[19]

The spiritual power of Marlowe's play, its exposition of a profound crisis in the inward life of Marlowe and his generation, derives from its portrayal of a Calvinist atheist attempting to be a resolute epicurean in an emerging Arminian dispensation. This description may not make the play sound proto-modern. Nonetheless, it is a way of describing *Doctor Faustus* that allows us to see the play as a support rather than as an obstacle to the view that Marlowe exemplifies Renaissance individualism and prefigures modern selfhood. The play shows the brilliant, moving, but ultimately fairly hollow attempt at epicurean fortitude and self-consolation by a man convinced that the alternative is a passive conformist acquiescence in his own predestined damnation. The play sets the character exemplifying this attempt, however, in a richly imagined spiritual universe that rejects predestined reprobation and damnation. Faustus may be a disappointing worldling who does not do much worthwhile with his hard-bought powers. But he is also a multivalent figure for those who, raised in the wrong set of beliefs, misunderstand the possibilities of the world in which they cast off those wrong beliefs and thus lose the chance for the most meaningful kind of life. This kind of tragic selfhood is not confined to those raised in Calvinist late-sixteenth-century England. People still map the developments in their inward lives according to their relations to the patterns of belief they have inherited. Many still try to get rid of aspects of inherited belief that they find stifling or unbelievable. When they attempt to do so, they still find that the alternatives they perceive as available are strongly conditioned by the belief-systems they used to hold. For this reason, Faustus speaks profoundly for his age – that is, for the difficulties of making the best use of the possibilities of Renaissance selfhood – and, by a set of analogies that will continue to hold as long as there are belief systems to cast off, for all time.

Notes

1 Jacob Burckhardt, *The Civilization of the Renaissance in Italy* (1860), trans. Samuel George Chetwynd Middlemore (New York: Modern Library, 2002), 212; Stephen Greenblatt, *The Swerve: How the World Became Modern* (New York: Norton, 2011), 9–11; Richard Strier, *The Unrepentant Renaissance: From Petrarch to Shakespeare to Milton* (University of Chicago Press, 2011), 4.
2 For accounts of Marlowe's death in rough consonance with this view, see David Riggs, *The World of Christopher Marlowe* (London: Faber and Faber, 2004), chapters 14 and 15; and Charles Nicholl, *The Reckoning: The Death of Christopher Marlowe* (University of Chicago Press, 1995), *passim*. On p. 55 Nicholl quotes Thomas Nashe's comment (probably about Marlowe) that 'His life he contemned in comparison of the liberty of speech.'
3 Riggs, *The World of Christopher Marlowe*, 238.
4 Christopher Marlowe, *Doctor Faustus* (A-version), II.i.121–7, in *Doctor Faustus and Other Plays*, ed. David Bevington and Eric Rasmussen (Oxford University Press, 1995), 154.
5 Riggs, *The World of Christopher Marlowe*, 239.
6 David Bevington, Lars Engle, Katherine E. Maus, and Eric Rasmussen, eds., *English Renaissance Drama: A Norton Anthology* (New York: Norton, 2002), 246.
7 Robert G. Hunter, *Shakespeare and the Mystery of God's Judgments* (Athens: University of Georgia Press, 1976), 51.

8 Riggs, *The World of Christopher Marlowe*, 241.
9 *Ibid.*, 247.
10 See *ibid.*, 29–31.
11 *Ibid.*, 328.
12 *Ibid.*, 29–31.
13 Hunter, *Shakespeare and the Mystery of God's Judgments*, 43.
14 David Bevington, *From 'Mankind' to Marlowe: Growth of Structure in the Popular Drama of Tudor England* (Cambridge, MA: Harvard University Press, 1962), 141–51, 245–62.
15 Austin Woolrych, *Britain in Revolution* (Oxford University Press, 2002), 36.
16 Harsnett quoted in Peter White, *Predestination, Policy, and Polemic: Conflict and Consensus in the English Church from the Reformation to the Civil War* (Cambridge University Press, 1992), 99.
17 See Peter Baro, *Two Theames or Questions*, in Andreas Hyperius, *A speciall treatise of Gods prouidence* (London: John Wolfe, 1588), 515–20.
18 In White, *Predestination*, 100. The italics are Harsnett's.
19 John Milton, *Paradise Lost*, ed. Alastair Fowler, 2nd edn (London: Longman, 1998), III.183–92.

CHAPTER NINETEEN

Race, nation, and Marlowe

Emily C. Bartels

What does it mean to look to Marlowe for representations of race? Race-based studies of Shakespeare have concentrated on a number of usual suspects: Shylock, the merchant/Jew of Venice; Aaron, the Moor of Rome; Othello, the Moor of Venice; and Caliban, the man/fish/monster/native of *The Tempest*'s 'brave new world'.[1] Marlowe's plays offer their own outstanding examples: the Scythian Tamburlaine and the opposing Turkish emperor, Bajazeth; Barabas, the Jew of Malta, and his Turkish slave, Ithamore; Dido, queen of Carthage. But to single them out as the racial representatives is not only to imply that race applies only to Others; it is to take race – which in early modern representations indicates species, lineage, family, disposition as well as identities coded by ethnicity, religion, and colour – as more of a stable, reliable, or extractable sign of difference than historically it was.[2]

Almost all of Marlowe's leading characters along with many of their peers, not to mention Marlowe himself, seem to stand out as Other in some way – socially, politically, sexually, as well as racially; and with good reason Stephen Greenblatt has argued that Marlowe's plays characteristically encourage 'subversive identification with the alien'.[3] Within this context in which difference is everything and everywhere, race competes with other features as the distinguishing mark of identity, preventing any easy correlation between race and difference. If we want to see how complicated, tentative, and undifferentiated early modern terms of racial identity are, Marlowe's plays offer an especially telling place to begin.

Take, for example, the idea of race as ethnicity, which hinges primarily on place. At the moment that Marlowe was writing, English entrepreneurs were exploring, in the hopes of exploiting, overseas markets, particularly in the Mediterranean and eventually in the New World. Within this context of extended cross-cultural contact, nationally based conceptions of race were appearing not only unusually pertinent but also unusually porous. To explain his purpose in publishing accounts of English ventures overseas, from the legendary times of King Arthur to the present, in his *Principal Navigations Voyages Traffiques and Discoveries of the English Nation* (1589) Richard Hakluyt sets England against Spain and 'all the nations and people of the earth' as unrivalled 'in searching the most opposite corners and quarters of the world'.[4] Yet beside such blatant and boastful nationalist claims surface fears, if not prospects, of cultural blending – of English entrepreneurs 'turning Turk' in the Mediterranean (as Robert Daborne stages in *A Christian Turn'd Turk*, in 1609–12) or 'going native' in the New World; of Moors, gatekeepers of the prized Barbary trades, entering into cross-cultural marriages or sexual liaisons, even producing offspring, with Europeans. Famously on Shakespeare's stage, the Moor Othello elopes with the Venetian Desdemona, and *Titus Andronicus* (1592–4) at once references a Moor, Muliteus, who fathers a 'fair' baby with his Roman wife, and features the Moor Aaron, who produces a 'black' son with the new Roman queen, a Goth.[5]

Perhaps no early modern play scrambles more than *Tamburlaine the Great* to explore the ethnic consequences of a global economy, with one man (a.k.a. Tamburlaine) gloriously on top. Introduced in the Prologue as a Scythian 'threatening the world with high astounding terms, / And scourging kingdoms with his conquering sword', Tamburlaine casts aside his Scythian heritage and parades around Persia, Africa, and Egypt in Part I with the not so small ambition of becoming 'monarch of the East' and 'win[ning] the world at last'.[6] His globally oriented quest unsettles the very tenets of national identity that it is simultaneously anchored on, however, creating an unresolved tension between the national and the global and leaving ethnicity and race suspended somewhere in between.

Part I starts and ends with a focus on the 'unhappy' kingdom of Persia, whose 'insufficient' king Mycetes is overthrown by his treasonous brother Cosroe, who is in turn overthrown by Tamburlaine (I.i.6, 2). Though Tamburlaine represents his conquest of Persia as merely a 'pretty jest' (II.v.90), he is obsessed with becoming the Persian king and, he likes to say, 'rid[ing] in triumph through Persepolis', a Persian city (II.v.50). While marketing himself as 'terror of the world' (III.iii.45), he repeatedly sets up Persia to be the ultimate standard of value. He assures the Egyptian Zenocrate (whom he kidnaps, rapes, and then marries) that her 'person is more worth to Tamburlaine / Than the possession of the Persian crown' (I.ii.90–1). He swears 'by this my sword that conquer'd Persia' (III.iii.82). In the final scene, he marks his triumph over territories extending 'from Barbary unto the Western India' (V.ii.457) by crowning Zenocrate 'Queen of Persia' as well as, secondarily and less specifically, of 'all the kingdoms and dominions' that he has 'subdued' (V.ii.446–8). Even at the end of Part II, which offers five more acts of global conquest, Tamburlaine sees nothing fitter than to 'depart to Persia, / To triumph after all [his] victories' (V.i.210–11).

Across *Tamburlaine*'s two parts, Persia stands out as the named seat of power and desire, even though on display with it is a spectacular conglomeration of cultures. Part I concludes in waves of glory, after all, with a promise of a mixed marriage between a Scythian and an Egyptian, staged in Africa, signifying Tamburlaine's hold over much of Asia, with Tamburlaine expecting tribute from 'Egyptians, Moors, and men of Asia' (V.ii.456). If this is how nationally based cultures take shape within a global economy, what then can it mean to speak of the Persian – or, for that matter, any – race? (Given the play's unrelenting emphasis on nation, we could also ask inversely, what does it mean to speak of a global economy?)

Within *Tamburlaine* this does seem to be how cultures take shape. Though Tamburlaine presents his campaign as extraordinary, his ambitions uniquely authorised by fates, gods, and oracles, the play suggests his actions and their multicultural consequences as the way of the world. In the very first scene we learn (from Cosroe) that Persia 'in a former age / Hast been the seat of mighty conquerors' who 'have triumph'd over Afric and the bounds / of Europe' (I.i.6–7, 9–10), and we have no guarantee that their origins, or the kingdom's, were ever purely Persian. In Part I as well, Tamburlaine is mirrored by a world-mongering precursor, the Turkish emperor Bajazeth, who declares himself

> Dread lord of Afric, Europe and Asia,
> Great king and conqueror of Graecia,
> The ocean, Terrene, and the Coal-black sea,
> The high and highest monarch of the world.
> (III.i.23–6)

Critics tend to treat the Turk – perhaps more than other non-European subjects – as fairly easy to classify, distinguishing, for example, a discrete set of Turk plays.[7] However apt the classification might be, we might well ask in the case of this 'monarch of the world': in what sense is he Turkish? (How) is he linked to a recognisably Turkish nation, people, race? In *The Jew of Malta*, place does provide an anchor: characters assert that the 'warlike' Turks who hover off the island's coast (and off the stage) for four acts, waiting for a monetary tribute from the Christian Governor, 'are come from Turkey' (I.i.149–50), though the Turks themselves chart their progress rather ominously across the other islands (Cyprus, Candy) that they control. But in *Tamburlaine*, the Turkish emperor is defined by an utter, if all-inclusive, placelessness. He appears first with the 'great kings of Barbary' and his own 'portly bassoes', engaged in a 'dreadful siege / Of the famous Grecian Constantinople' (*1 Tamb.*, III.i.1, 5–6). He then attempts to shore up his reputation as 'the greatest potentate of Africa' (III.iii.63) by fighting Tamburlaine over and in the terrains of Africa.

To be sure, race and rule are not the same. In the sixteenth and seventeenth centuries, the Turks maintained a vast, if changing, empire across North Africa and the Mediterranean by collecting monetary tribute from nations that were otherwise allowed their own autonomy, cultural practices, religions, and rule.[8] And yet, there is never a guarantee that the buck, as it were, stopped with tribute, conquest with culture. At the end of *The Jew of Malta*, the tables, in fact, turn on the Turks: they are bamboozled first by the 'busy' Jew, who invites them ashore only to trap them in 'a deep pit past recovery' (V.v.55, 38), and then by the Christian Governor, who exposes the plot only to insist that the Turks 'live in Malta prisoner' forever after (V.v.126). What then is the cultural future for the Turks or Malta? (How) will sexual intermixing change the nature of the Turkish or (such as it is) the Maltese race?

In *The Jew of Malta,* as in *Tamburlaine*, we've already seen global conquest complicating the designation of ethnicity. Critics almost automatically assume that Barabas' slave Ithamore is a Turk, taking their cues from Ithamore himself. When the conniving Pilia Borza introduces him to the also conniving Bellamira as 'the gentleman', Ithamore scoffs in an aside: 'what gentry can be in a poor Turk of tenpence?' (IV.ii.44, 45–6). Yet rather than being a reliable ethnic tag, 'poor Turk' serves also or instead as a figure of speech along with 'tenpence', emphasising class at least as much as race; accordingly, one modern editor glosses 'Turk of tenpence' as a 'common' – not Turk-specific – 'derogatory expression'.[9] In fact, Ithamore himself reports that he was born 'in Thrace' and 'brought up in Arabia' (II.iii.134). Even if he is technically a Turk, that label clearly accommodates a multicultural birth and rearing in places not necessarily Turkish. All this happens, of course, in a play where none of the characters of Malta – from the ruling Knights to the dispossessed Jew – seems to be originally 'of Malta' (hence the problem with defining a Maltese race).[10]

Tamburlaine brings the question of race explicitly to the level of blood. If Part I shows the terms and boundaries of nation – and nation or place as race – compromised by longstanding habits of conquest, Part II traces the racial legacy in terms of lineage and suggests the impact of intermixing on inherited identity. Tamburlaine first appears holding court in Egypt, dangling the 'crown of Persia' (still) in front of his three, not entirely promising sons while also urging them to 'wade up to the chin in blood' on the imperial battlefield (I.iv.74, 84). By the time we get to Part II, it's hard enough to imagine Tamburlaine as representative of any nation, despite editors who list Tamburlaine as 'King of Persia' in the dramatis personae, or characters who demean him as 'the sturdy Scythian thief' (*1 Tamb.*, I.i.36) or 'the Persian' (*1 Tamb.*, III.i.43).[11] It's harder still to assign an ethnicity to his sons. The scene emphasises the fact that these sons 'have their mother's looks', which, Tamburlaine fears, augur 'amorous' and not 'martial' demeanours (*2 Tamb.*, I.iv.35, 21–2). 'Be all a scourge and terror to the world', he warns them, 'Or else you are not sons of Tamburlaine' (*2 Tamb.*, I.iv.63–4). But as this display of tough love puts manly might above female blood as the crux of lineage, the gender bias clear, it nonetheless underscores the fact that Tamburlaine and Zenocrate carry visibly different bloodlines, not quite articulated but not quite erased by the imposition of a 'make war not love' imperative.

If these would-be kings of Persia are to be sons of their father, they must write this inheritance across the world, like Tamburlaine, undoing the particularity of the very places and bloodlines that they simultaneously stake their claims on. That undoing raises the question of when that particularity was ever 'done'. Given what we've seen or heard of the imperialist history of Persia, the world-mongering trajectory of the Turk, there is no reason to believe that Tamburlaine's attempt to leave his mark on the world, to absorb multiple peoples and nations into his own, all-encompassing realm, is a game-changer, at least as far as global conquests and their racial consequences are concerned. As the tension between the local and the global plays out on Marlowe's stage, we're invited to think backwards as well as forwards, to realise how racially and culturally mixed the local already is.

We could make a similar argument for inscriptions of race that are grounded on religion. In Part I of *Tamburlaine* Bajazeth and his wife Zabina profess their allegiance to Mahomet, and in Part II, religion distinguishes the King of Natolia (a Turkish province), Orcanes, who swears 'by sacred Mahomet', and 'the Christian' (I.i.11), Sigismund, King of Hungary, who swears by 'sweet Jesus Christ' (I.ii.58). Such racial distinctions lose some of their defining force in the world of conquest, however, as these leaders join in league with a *mélange* of others – for example 'Grecians, Albanese, / Sicilians, Jews, Arabians, Turks, and Moors, / Natolians, Sorians, black Egyptians, / Illyrians, Thracians, and Bithynians' – who are delineated but not otherwise differentiated (I.i.61–4, 67). Tamburlaine himself wields Christian, Muslim, and pagan vocabularies: he references 'angels', 'heavens', 'cherubins and holy seraphins', 'hellish' things, and the 'King of Kings' (*2 Tamb.*, II.iv.15, 26, 14, 27), and swears 'by Mahomet' (*2 Tamb.*, IV.i.123), while touting, and almost supplanting, the pagan god Jove as his champion. Crowns are what he worships, not religion, the 'childish toy' that the all-political Machevill dismisses in the prologue to *The Jew of Malta* (14). To be sure, at the end of Part II, Tamburlaine sets fire to 'the Turkish Alcoran', only to be immediately – and fatally – 'distemp'red' (V.i.171, 216). For the previously unstoppable conqueror, this is a tragic, if counterintuitive, moment of truth, proving him surprisingly, but undeniably, mortal (who knew?). Instead of serving as the capstone of a dedicated campaign against Islam, however, this climax comes out of a relentlessly secular and episodic blue: the burning of the Koran is merely one, albeit the last one, of Tamburlaine's many gestures of power, designed to show his incontestable might, not some religious right. If God is saying a word within the scene, it is not a word that can be translated readably into race, not in this world where religious terms and tempers arise variably to further the ends of conquest.

These kinds of complications do not stop at the borders of England, whose populace included more than a few 'strangers', despite discrete but not sustained efforts on the part of the English to push them out. In 1492, Richard I succeeded ostensibly in expelling all Jews from England, though by the seventeenth century efforts were underway to reverse the expulsion.[12] In the late sixteenth and early seventeenth centuries, Queen Elizabeth authorised the deportation from England of a select group of 'blackamoors'; yet one of her justifications for doing so – that her 'own liege people' 'perishe for want of service' (i.e. the jobs) that the blackamoors occupy and 'want [i.e. lack] the relief which those people consume' – suggests how embedded those strangers were in the English economy.[13] So similiarly in the case of the anonymous Dutch Church Libel, which calls for the English to attack the Dutch in their midst, who were competing with English citizens for jobs and resources.[14] Border-patrolling declarations such as these could only go so far in erasing what had become a fact of life, in the language, culture, race, since at least the Norman conquest of England in 1066: that England itself was never purely nor securely 'English'.

Marlowe's one 'English' history play, *Edward II*, takes on these matters as it exposes the inextricability of sexual and national politics.[15] The central conflict consists of a violent power-play, and eventually a civil war, between the English king and his rebellious peerage, all cathected around the outlandish figure of Gaveston, the king's favourite. Edward II spends the first half of the play insisting that it is his royal right and will to 'have' Gaveston (I.i.96), who has been exiled by the recently deceased Edward I; the peers in turn do everything they can first to resist the repeal of, and then to reinstate, that exile. Although the nobles use the charge of sodomy to incriminate the king and his 'base minion' (I.i.133) for abusing the body politic, the never fully articulated elephant-in-the room, which shadows and surpasses in scope these sexually and politically personalised animosities, is England's intimacy with France. 'Having' Gaveston means recalling him from – and so underscoring – his homeland, France. Accordingly, the peers bolster their authority over king and crown by incriminating Gaveston not only as a sodomite but also as 'that peevish' and 'sly inveigling' 'Frenchman' (I.ii.7, 57). Their attacks, however, draw attention at once to and away from the glaring but unspoken fact that Isabella, the queen of England, mother to the crown prince (who will be Edward III), and adulterous lover of the Younger Mortimer, the head of the noble faction, is sister to Lord Valois, the king of France.

No one on either side of the conflict makes a big issue of the fact that the English queen is French or that the adulterous activity of Mortimer, who is sexually and politically in bed with her, reproduces the king's. But the political consequences of these illicit intimacies with France are dire. In Act III, Isabella reports to Edward II that 'our brother, King of France, / Because your highness has been slack in homage, / Hath seized Normandy into his hands' (III.ii.64–6). Edward casts the news, and caution, to the winds and laments rather about his separation from Gaveston, sure (or wanting to be sure) that 'Valois and I will soon be friends again' (III.ii.69). Short-sightedly, Edward then sends Isabella and the prince to France to 'parley' on his behalf, directing them to 'go in peace' and 'leave us in wars at home' (III.iii.73, 87) – leaving out the very real possibility that what may be brewing is war with France. Indeed, it is there, with the backing of the nobleman Sir John of Hainault, that Isabella and the Younger Mortimer solidify their rebellion against Edward II, which results in the murder not only of the French Gaveston but also of the English king.

If we move beyond these literal and figurative character assassinations to consider England's political and cultural future, what may seem more ominous, because neither end-stopped nor predictable, is Prince Edward's rise to be England's king. While he is in France, the prince rejects both 'the king of England' and 'the court of France', professing his desire to stay rather by his 'gracious mother's side' (IV.ii.24–5). That side, of course, carries with it an indelible French connection, a mother who declares the English king 'unkind' – unsympathetic, with resonances also of 'not of kin/kind' (IV.ii.2). As king, Edward III insists on finding and punishing those, including possibly his mother, who 'spilt [his] father's blood' (V.vi.70). But this final emphasis on blood brings out the unspoken, perhaps unspeakable, racial consequences of Edward II's reign. If we are to take comfort in the undoing of either the wayward king or the rebellious queen and overreaching nobles, we have to rest easy with the recognition that the new king of England is tied to France – not, as before, by marriage, but now and hereafter by blood. In a play whose characters single out sodomy as a national ill, it is no small irony that what may prove most threatening to the English nation, to the illusion of its racial purity, is not the English king's sodomitical attachment to an eradicable French minion but his heterosexual marriage to a child-bearing French queen.

If this kind of intermixing has long been the way of the world, what are we to make then of the face and function, power and prominence, of racial designations? What can it mean to declare some Other a Scythian, Persian, Frenchman, Turk, blackamoor, or Jew? In staging worlds of difference, how do Marlowe's plays ask us to think about these race-defining, if not also race-defying, terms? Of course, in the background and foreground of early modern culture, stereotypes – of the Turk, for example, as a ruthless, oversized, frequently Christian-hating Muslim imperialist – swirl, creating the illusion that their abstract and, from iteration to iteration, inconsistent terms actually compose a definitive, simultaneously case-specific and inclusive, one-size-fits-all identity.[16] Spectators would likely have come to the theatre with certain if diverse assumptions, which Marlowe's plays might support (the Turkish Bajazeth is, after all, a ruthless imperialist) and/or challenge (but so, of course, is the Scythian/Persian Tamburlaine).

It is sometimes tempting, too tempting, to take these assumptions as the be-all and end-all of racial meaning and to presuppose race as cause (to assume that Bajazeth is a ruthless imperialist *because* he is a Turk or a Muslim, rather than that he is a Turk or a Muslim who happens also to be a ruthless imperialist). Yet plays are all about contingency, about the unpredictable set of circumstances, actions, and interactions that, in any given moment, come to together to produce (if the play is any good) an equally unpredictable outcome. Instead of taking meaning solely from some predetermined standards that exist before and outside the dramatic fiction, articulations of race are inextricably embedded in that fiction with all its twists and turns; they are the products, not just the prescripts, of an unfolding, ostensibly improvised exchange.

For any given play, then, we need to ask not simply what race *is* but what it *does*. Take, for example, the moment in *Tamburlaine*, Part I, when Bajazeth first confronts Tamburlaine and asks his audiences to 'note the presumption of this Scythian slave' who 'calls me Bajazeth, whom you call lord' (III.iii.67–8). Bajazeth's purpose here is not simply to point out Tamburlaine's Scythian heritage but to use that heritage to demean the 'slave' who won't call him lord. Etymologically, the Middle English word 'slave' takes root from the Latin *slavus*, also (as the *OED* records) the name for a Slavic people who were conquered in the ninth century. Right before our eyes and ears in *Tamburlaine*, a play preoccupied with 'working words' (*1 Tamb.*, II.iii.25), alliteration presses 'Scythian' and 'slave' together, creating an essentialising elision between a given ethnicity that is partly descriptively apt (Tamburlaine does come from Scythia) and a derogatory slur that isn't apt at all (Tamburlaine, who started his career as a shepherd, is not literally a slave). Similarly, when Tamburlaine replies 'And know thou, Turk, that those which lead my horse / Shall lead thee captive thorough Africa' (*1 Tamb.*, III.iii.72–3), he uses 'Turk' to derogate rather than to describe Bajazeth, who has just defined himself rather as 'the greatest potentate of Africa'. In these instances, and across the play and the period, racial terms emerge repeatedly as racist retorts, to the point that racism almost seems to precede race, scripting a single-minded, usually derogatory clarity around identities that, as we've seen, are provocatively complex.

To read race in Marlowe's plays, then, is to delve into the contingencies that are the heart and soul of any play. It is to understand that racial identities and inscriptions are invariably case-specific, settled and unsettled by changing actions, speech acts, times. In Marlowe, Scythians, Persians, Egyptians, Turks, Christians, and Jews are who they are. And if the plays prompt us to take these figures as representative of a given race, the plays simultaneously demand that we question in what terms, whose terms, and why.

Notes

1 William Shakespeare, *The Tempest*, ed. Stephen Orgel (Oxford University Press, 1987), V.i.183.
2 On early modern uses of race, see Ania Loomba, *Shakespeare, Race, and Colonialism* (Oxford University Press, 2002), 22–44; and Emily C. Bartels, *Speaking of the Moor: From Alcazar to Othello* (Philadelphia: University of Pennsylvania Press, 2008), 9–16.

3 Stephen Greenblatt, *Renaissance Self-Fashioning: From More to Shakespeare* (University of Chicago Press, 1980), 203.
4 Richard Hakluyt, *The Principal Navigations Voyages Traffiques & Discoveries of the English Nation: Made by Sea or Overland to the Remote & Farthest Distant Quarters of the Earth at any time within the compass of these 1600 Yeares*, ed. Ernest Rhys, intro. John Masefield, 10 vols., Vol. 1 (London: J. M. Dent & Sons, Ltd., 1910 [1907]), 3.
5 William Shakespeare, *Titus Andronicus*, ed. Eugene Waith (Oxford University Press, 1994), IV.ii.154, 66.
6 Christopher Marlowe, *The First Part of Tamburlaine the Great*, in *The Complete Plays*, ed. J. B. Steane (London: Penguin, 1969), Pro, 5–6, I.ii.185, III.iii.260. All references to Marlowe's plays are from this edition.
7 For example, see Daniel J. Vitkus, ed., *Three Turk Plays from Early Modern England* (New York: Columbia University Press, 2000).
8 For a good introduction to this history, see Daniel Vitkus, *Turning Turk: English Theater and the Multicultural Mediterranean, 1570–1630* (New York: Palgrave Macmillan, 2003), 16–19.
9 J. B. Steane, note to *JM*, IV.ii.46.
10 See my argument in *Spectacles of Strangeness: Imperialism, Alienation, and Marlowe* (Philadelphia: University of Pennsylvania Press, 1993), 82–108.
11 For example, the Penguin edition, which I'm using here.
12 A good resource is Donald S. Katz, *Philosemitism and the Readmission of Jews to England 1603–1655* (Oxford: Clarendon Press, 1982).
13 Quotations are from the letters of 1596 and 1601, cited in *Speaking of the Moor*, 113, 109; see my discussion, 100–17, which includes the full texts of the letters.
14 A full copy of the Dutch Church Libel is available at www2.prestel.co.uk/rey/texts.htm.
15 See Gregory W. Bredbeck, *Sodomy and Interpretation: Marlowe to Milton* (Ithaca, NY: Cornell University Press, 1991), 60–77, on the interplay of the sexual and political.
16 I am drawing on the rich theoretical analysis of stereotypes in Homi K. Bhabha, *The Location of Culture* (London: Routledge, 1994), 66–84.

CHAPTER TWENTY

Marlowe and religion

Gillian Woods

Religion was central to early modern experience. Far more than just a weekly visit to church, religion underpinned political, social, and domestic structures and influenced everything from education to architecture to land rights. Indeed, its significance was eternal: a matter not just of life and death, but of everlasting salvation or damnation. However, the title of this chapter is something of misnomer: early modern 'religion' was not single, but insistently and troublingly plural. In post-Reformation England, Christianity was fractured into different denominations; repeated shifts in state religion following Henry VIII's break with the Church in Rome in 1533 pushed England back and forth between Catholicism and Protestantism. Divisions within Christianity were further compounded by more frequent confrontations with non-Christian religions. New global trade routes increased contact with Islamic and Jewish merchants and brought encounters with aboriginal inhabitants of the New World whose behaviour seemed to recall the pagan practices of the ancient British past. Thus polemical insistence on 'one' theological truth was made against a plural backdrop that made such claims both urgent and difficult to maintain. Marlowe makes drama out of the tensions produced by this variegated religious situation. Where religion claims to answer questions, Marlowe's plays pose doubts. Indeed, Marlowe problematises the very relationship between religion and meaning: while religious affiliation often drives the action of his plots, it often dissolves rather than determines interpretation.

One of the many accusations the (not necessarily reliable) informant Richard Baines lodged against Marlowe was that 'almost into every company he cometh he persuades men to atheism'.[1] Rumours about an author's beliefs (or disbelief) do not define the meaning of the work. But perhaps the reason Marlowe's contemporary reputation as an atheist has remained so critically popular is that his plays have the subversive quality Baines tries to sensationalise. Nevertheless, the drama is much less didactic and much more interrogative than Baines' report of its writer might suggest. Marlowe's plays are bursting with a range of religious types and stereotypes: medieval English Catholics (*Edward II*); contemporary French Catholics and Huguenots (*The Massacre at Paris*); Moorish and Turkish Muslims, Spanish and Maltese Catholics, and an overdeterminedly Jewish Jew (*The Jew of Malta*); a Calvinist scholar and would-be atheist (*Doctor Faustus*); deceitful Christians, truthful Muslims, and a protagonist who variously identifies himself as Jove's scourge, the gods' enemy, Mahomet's follower and Mahomet's mocker (*Tamburlaine*); not to mention interfering pagan gods (*Dido, Queen of Carthage*). In making action out of such an assortment, Marlowe exposes the contested nature of religious meaning and the provisional moral standards these divisions produced.

Polemicists of all theological persuasions disputed the terms of early modern religion. Even writers of the same faith often disagreed about the extent to which other denominations and religions should be stigmatised, with attitudes varying further according to context. The ongoing English Reformation meant 'Catholicism' was no longer uncontroversially synonymous with Christianity. Some Protestant writers fought a losing battle to requisition the label Catholic (with its 'universal' significance), but the insults 'Romish' and 'papist' were more effective in linguistically narrowing the scope of the old Church. Militantly minded reformers redefined Catholicism as anti-Christian through a variety of rhetorical manoeuvres, including the association of 'papistry' with other religions. Protestant polemicists declared 'that Papisme is flat Paganisme' and collapsed Catholicism into other religious 'others'.[2] Luther saw Catholics as typologically linked to the Jews in their respective persecutions of Paul and reformers.[3] Elsewhere Catholics were bracketed with Muslims: for example, the radical reformer John Bale records a joking reference to Pope Urban II as 'Turban' in his *Pageant of Popes*, and in his dictionary of the Bible Thomas Wilson repeatedly matches Catholics and Muslims as interchangeable enemies of the true faith, so that 'Great City' is defined as 'Whatsoeuer Domination, Power, and Gouernment; either of Pope or Turke, or which any enemy of the Church doth enioy and exercise against Christ and his Church'.[4] Yet the comparative 'otherness' of a particular religion waned and intensified according to circumstance. One collection of character types mocked the 'Precisian' (or 'puritan') for his default 'opposition' to 'the *Papist*, though it bee sometimes accompanied with an absurditie'.[5] Even official positions on religious difference were fluid. Faced with the Islamic threat of the Ottoman Empire bearing down on Europe, in 1565 the English Church described the Catholic island of

Malta as 'part of Christendom' and issued a common prayer to be said for protection against 'Turks, infidels and sworn enemies of Christian religion'.[6] But just fourteen years later, Elizabeth opened relations with Sultan Murad III, spying an opportunity to capitalise on Protestant and Islamic opposition to a Catholic 'other' (Spain represented an economic and military threat to England and the Ottoman Empire).[7] Early modern religious sameness and difference were somewhat relative.

Marlowe not only reveals this relativity but also shows how it unfixes deeper ethical and linguistic meaning. His characters repeatedly cite religious difference as justification for unjust behaviour. For example, in *The Jew of Malta* the Islamic Ithamore and Jewish Barabas form a murderous compact based on (anti-)religious affiliation: 'Both circumcisèd, we hate Christians both' (II.iii.218). Unfortunately for Barbaras, Ithamore later finds it easy to adjust his religious antipathy: 'To undo a Jew is charity, and not sin' (IV.iv.88). While Ithamore and Barabas are self-professedly 'villains both' (II.iii.217), their theological pragmatism is shared by the play's Christians. Ferneze notoriously sets the action in motion by taxing the Jews not 'equally' but 'like infidels', claiming that Christian 'sufferance' of their 'hateful lives' provoked God's ire in the form of the Turkish demand for money (I.ii.62–7). One act later he reassesses God's plan: when Del Bosco suggests that Ferneze could keep his money and engage in a lucrative slave trade, the Maltese Governor discovers a differently pious need to defy 'these barbarous, misbelieving Turks' (II.ii.46). Although Ferneze and Del Bosco are Catholics, ripe for stereotyping on the post-Reformation stage, Barabas' insistent use of the label 'Christian' shrinks the audience's distance from what they see. Indeed, Barabas explicitly relates his own moral pragmatism to Christian example: 'It is no sin to deceive a Christian, / For they themselves hold it a principle, / Faith is not to be held with heretics' (II.iii.312–14). In this bizarrely farcical tragedy characters cross and double-cross one another without flinching, mouthing axioms that cancel one another out: it is acceptable to deceive Jews, Muslims, and Christians. The standard moral message – 'let due praise be given / Neither to fate nor fortune, but to heaven' (V.v.122–3) – actually undermines any final catharsis when the Jew is boiled alive, Muslim soldiers are massacred, and the Christians emerge supposedly triumphant.

Elsewhere in Marlowe's drama, nominal religion works to nullify some of the fundamentals of communication, as promises are cancelled for ostensibly theological reasons. In *Tamburlaine*, Part II Baldwin convinces Sigismond that oaths of peace made to 'infidels' may be broken since non-Christians have 'no faith nor true religion' (II.i.33–4), as if words only signify between men of one belief. The action of the plot seems to condemn this specious logic, as the Christians are subsequently defeated by the Muslims with whom they broke faith. Yet Marlowe complicates what could have been a relatively straightforward religious narrative. The Muslim Orcanes articulates the impiety of the Christian deceit, pointing out that the Christians clearly care 'little' (II.ii.35) for the Christ by whose name they swore the breached oath. Rather than see this dishonesty as proof of the turpitude of Christianity, Orcanes calls on Christ (a prophet in Islamic terms) to witness the wrong and support his retribution: 'If there be Christ, we shall have victory' (II.ii.64). At his subsequent success, Orcanes declares equivocally 'Christ or Mahomet hath been my friend' (II.iii.11). While the plot apparently punishes Christians for their infidelity, the dialogue puts a question mark over the religious meaning of the narrative. Rather than seizing an opportunity to assert Islamic righteousness, Orcanes speculates on what he thinks could be a sign of Christ's might, but Orcanes is nevertheless unconverted. Instead he proffers a pluralistic vision that undermines Christian certitude: 'in my thoughts shall Christ be honourèd, / Not doing Mahomet an injury, / Whose power had share in this our victory' (II.iii.33–5). The drama sets up a situation that calls for a single interpretation, but overlays different religious possibilities that obscure it.

Religion actively dissolves its own significance in *The Massacre at Paris* (an account of the St Bartholomew's Day Massacre of 1572 when Catholics killed thousands of Huguenots). Sectarianism drives the plot of the play but is denuded of theological substance. The play's Catholics are not only grotesquely homicidal but also aberrantly irreligious in their indifference to the faith for which they supposedly fight. In soliloquy the Guise (the Catholic duke who orchestrates the slaughter) confides in us that his 'policy hath framed religion' (ii.65), revealing that the theological dispute upon which the violence is predicated is empty of meaning. In the massacre itself, deaths are delivered with sectarian jokes. The Guise taunts the Protestant preacher Loreine with a reformed formula, '"Dearly beloved brother" – thus 'tis written' (vii.5), and immediately stabs him. In remaking a wordy reference to Scripture as a death wound, this joke (and others like it) see violence supplant the content of theological controversy. Oddly, religious difference (asserted through violence) removes religious meaning (expressed in words). At his own murder, the Guise refuses to pray to God ('I ne'er offended him' (xxi.76)) and instead swears revenge by a signifier that he has stripped of significance: '*Vive la messe!*' (xxi.85).

For much of its critical history this play has been read as rabidly anti-Catholic in its dramatisation of the bloody villainy of the St Bartholomew's Day Massacre. But more recent scholarship has challenged the play's ascription as jingoistic Protestant propaganda.[8] Indeed the early production history implies that the drama did not perform as straightforward polemic. Henslowe's *Diary* reveals that it continued to be performed after the real-life counterpart of the play's Protestant 'hero', Henri of Navarre, converted to Catholicism in 1593. For at least some of its early modern stage life, the play must have been tinged with a destabilising irony, since its Protestant figurehead was known to have switched sides: the war hero who fought the Catholic enemy had himself become a papist.[9] Had the theatrical Navarre's heroism been unequivocal, it seems unlikely that *Massacre* would have been revived in repertory after the historical Navarre's confessional shift. But while Marlowe's Navarre may call on God, he is one-dimensional and ineffectual (frequently seen fleeing danger). By the end of the play he adopts the language of brutality used by Catholic characters. The difference between the denominations collapses even as it continues to motivate the action. The drama's analogous structure (whereby Protestant deaths in the first half are replaced by Catholic deaths in the second) erases any ethical difference between the two factions that would give the play a clear-cut sectarian message.

Early modern readers and audiences were taught to make sense of earthly experience through a religious narrative. Christian (and, better still, Protestant) victories proved God's religious preferences, but so too did defeats. National triumphs such as the destruction of the Spanish Armada (perhaps more of a propaganda than a military victory) revealed God's special care of Protestant England; here was providential evidence of a reformed, Christian God. However, the routing of Christian forces was also taken as confirmation of God's Christian status, since such moments showed God scourging his people for their imperfect piety. Christian epistemology flexibly provided unanswerable readings of triumph and disaster, joy and suffering. The interpretive strain elasticity placed on the faithful is apparent in the prayerful addresses printed in news pamphlets that dutifully acknowledge the justice of God's scourging but anxiously plead for a clearer demonstration of his Christian credentials. For example, writing about *The Estate of Christians, Liuing vnder the Subiection of the Turke*, one anonymous writer begs God 'for thy honours sake' to overthrow the 'enemies of [Christ's] Gospell', to 'let them know that thou art the God of heauen and earth'.[10]

Marlowe's characters articulate the emotional difficulty of accepting this epistemological schema (albeit in a different theological paradigm). In the *Tamburlaine* plays characters repeatedly call for divine aid to make sense of the plot. Bajazeth calls on a 'sleepy Mahomet' who allows the royal body to be defiled (*1 Tamb.*, III.iii.269); Theridamas is uncertain whether 'Mahomet will suffer' the torture of Bajazeth and Zabina (*1 Tamb.*, IV.iv.53–4); and the starving Zabina is brought to question 'is there left no Mahomet, no God, / No fiend, no Fortune[?]' (*1 Tamb.*, V.i.239–40). Of course, early modern Christian audiences might not expect Islamic prayers to be answered, but Marlowe makes it hard to see such suffering as a definite punishment for wrongheaded religious belief. Instead he raises fundamental questions about God's (in)activity in human affairs. The dialogue never clarifies the meaning of the plot. In his spectacular brutality Tamburlaine seems to demand moral interpretation. His characterisation is saturated with symbolism: from his shepherd-to-warrior costume change, to his fatally colour-coded tents, to his appropriation of emperors as footstools and 'horses' for his chariots. Yet the signification is so excessive that it becomes difficult to pinpoint significance. This lack of clarity derives partly from the way Tamburlaine keeps changing his script: he is a scourge both of and to God (and/or the gods). It is unclear whether the plays invite us to accede to Tamburlaine's atrocities as a just divine punishment or to expect those atrocities to be divinely punished. The ambivalence makes a different kind of meaning whereby audiences are brought to wrestle with the ethical and logical difficulties of a providential narrative. Interestingly, the same rhetorical formula is used to question both God's failure to protect Tamburlaine's victims and his failure to keep Tamburlaine alive. Confronted with the sight of the slaughtered virgins of Damascus, Zenocrate rails: 'Blush, heaven, that gave them honour at their birth, / And let them die a death so barbarous!' (*1 Tamb.*, V.i.350–1); grieving for the dead Tamburlaine, Usumcasane cries: 'Blush, heaven, to lose the honour of thy name' (*2 Tamb.*, V.iii.28). The formulation is not striking enough for the memory of Part I to haunt Part II, but its repetition does reveal the way in which Marlowe puts pressure on providential epistemologies, which not only seem to be failing here, but which are also easily adapted to fit opposing viewpoints.

The broadly Muslim landscape of the *Tamburlaine* plays enables Marlowe to scrutinise religious belief at a safe distance. Tamburlaine openly – almost scientifically – tests the deity by burning a holy book and daring a divine response: 'if thou have any power, / Come down thyself and work a miracle' (*2 Tamb.*, V.i.186–7). Since the book in question is the Koran and the divinity Mahomet, Christian blasphemy is avoided. However, the anti-Islamic scene is not produced with a pro-Christian message. While burning a Koran is pointedly not the same thing as burning a Bible, the desecration of a holy text (as opposed to a more 'dissimilar' symbol of Islam) has risky connotations. Furthermore, Tamburlaine's reaction to Mahomet's failure to respond lacks the clarity that would explain Islamic impotence as evidence of Christian truth: 'Seek out another godhead to adore, / The God that sits in heaven, if any god, / For he is God alone, and none but he' (*2 Tamb.*, v.i.199–201). As Daniel Vitkus points out, the conditionality of 'if any god' and the curiously plural implications of 'another godhead' and 'none but he' hardly endorse Christian monotheism.[11] Marlowe seems uninterested in picking theological sides, but instead he interrogates the very concept of belief itself. His characters repeatedly ask where God is, while their plots keep divinity absent. Strikingly, the most eloquently faithful answer to this question is provided by Orcanes, who describes God as: 'He that sits on high and never sleeps, / Nor in one place is circumscriptible, / But everywhere fills every continent / With strange infusion of his sacred vigour' (*2 Tamb.*, II.ii.49–52). Omniscient and omnipresent, Orcanes' God sounds very much like the Christian deity, but the theological soundness of the depiction is undermined (in early modern Protestant England) by the Muslim status of the speaker. Marlowe plays with multiple theological paradigms to expose the difficulty (if not the impossibility) of knowing one truth.

If the representation of Mahomet's indifference is ideologically harmless, *Doctor Faustus* considerably raises the stakes when the protagonist's prayer for Christ's salvation is directly answered by Lucifer: 'Christ cannot save thy soul, for he is just' (vii.84). A number of critics have detected a theologically specific tension driving the tragedy.[12] In staging a protagonist who (falteringly) accepts Lucifer's line that human depravity renders redemption an unjust impossibility, Marlowe draws out some of the discomfiting implications of Calvinism (the dominant theology of the Elizabethan Church) and its controversial doctrine of predestination. Placing new emphasis on old teachings, Calvin posited that when God created the universe he decided who would be saved and who would be damned; human beings could not influence this unalterable decision. By having Faustus repeatedly voice concern that he might be doomed, Marlowe engages his audience with the anxieties produced by Calvinism. Is Faustus tragically damned because God has predetermined this fate, or because he *thinks* God has predetermined it? Either way, the tragedy is damningly bound up with Calvinist problems.

However, the play's exploration of the psychology of faith and doubt is not limited to one theological debate (important as it was). Faustus' doubts concern some of the organising principles of theistic belief: he struggles to distinguish between numinous, demonic, and earthly (specifically theatrical) conditions. Where Orcanes testified to God's immanence in all existence, in *Doctor Faustus* Mephistopheles twice warns Faustus that hell is everywhere: 'Why, this is hell, nor am I out of it' (iii.78); 'Within the bowels of these elements, / Where we are tortured and remain for ever. / Hell hath no limits, nor is circumscribed / In one self place, for where we are is hell, / And where hell is must we ever be' (v.121–5). Both physical and metaphysical, Mephistopheles' hell is empirical rather than topographical; eternally mobile, it functions in a horrifyingly endless present tense. Yet Faustus remains unmoved: 'Come, I think hell's a fable' (v.129); 'these are trifles and mere old wives' tales' (v.137). His damnation is the consequence not only of a lack of faith in God, but also of a failure of belief in the reality of hell. This obtuseness seems odd given that Faustus encounters, as Mephistopheles points out, 'an instance to prove the contrary' to the suggestion that hell is merely fictional (v.138). Except that Faustus' theatrical context makes his category confusion understandable, even inevitable. This thoroughly Renaissance character – a man (imperfectly) versed in humanist scholarship – is stranded in a medieval morality form. Older plays staged clear-cut (though not unsophisticated) allegorical stories of salvation in which 'Everyman' figures were beset by personified vices and finally saved by representative virtues. As David Bevington has shown, with the use of Good and Bad Angels and a full cast of devils, Marlowe rehabilitates the old form only to strip away its structural promise of redemption.[13] In declaring hell a fable, Faustus responds logically to a demonic figure who looks like a fictional character. Indeed, while Mephistopheles may accentuate our sense of Faustus' error by submitting himself as hellish evidence, elsewhere he and Lucifer distract Faustus with spectacles that are unreal in their conventional theatricality. Thus moments after the second disquisition on hell '*a* DEVIL *dressed like a woman, with fireworks*' enters the scene. A little earlier Mephistopheles had summoned dancing devils to divert Faustus from the somatic warnings against signing away his soul. Asked, in theatrically resonant language, 'What means this show?', Mephistopheles replies: 'Nothing, Faustus, but to delight thy mind withal' (v.83–4). The constant presence of devilish 'show' keeps Faustus thinking he is participating in an illusion, but leaves him unable to understand the actual significance it hides.

The audience is implicated in Faustus' inability to recognise the real meaning of the devils. From our perspective Faustus is right and wrong to think that he is in a fiction. As his tragic end draws near he tries to dissolve himself into literary myth, promising to be 'Paris' (xiii.97) for a demonic Helen of Troy; he remains distracted from the real soteriological business at hand. However, the audience necessarily shares Faustus' theatrical fascination. Three scenes earlier, the efficacy of demonic display was highlighted when Faustus conjured Alexander and his paramour for the German emperor. Faustus cautions that he cannot resurrect 'the true substantial bodies' (x.46) but only 'spirits' (x.50) that resemble them. Since these 'spirits' are represented by human actors, the illusion is very convincing. And the emperor duly exclaims: 'Sure these are no spirits, but the true substantial bodies of those two deceased princes' (x.69–70). The theatrical presence of the actors' bodies, within the fictional terms of the play, underwrites the quality of the demonic performance. But for the audience, these bodies are also our guarantee that we are watching only an illusion of devilry, not a devilish illusion. Yet the plot of the play dares the audience, like Faustus, not to take such display seriously and to play along with it as mere performance. This attitude does not work out so well for Faustus. The tragedy seems to refuse its representational limits, warning that the devilish illusions might be doing really devilish work. It is not surprising that this play proved so representationally unstable in its early modern performances: notoriously, on a number of occasions extra devils were reported as accompanying actors on stage, as if hell had somehow broken through the play's vexed boundary of illusion.[14]

Throughout the Marlowe canon various forms of category confusion threaten neat theological narratives of singular truth; the mixing of different religious paradigms is disorienting. But in *Doctor Faustus* a different interaction – between theatrical and devilish performance – proves damnably slippery. In *The Jew of Malta*, *The Massacre at Paris*, and *Tamburlaine*, scenes that conventionally puncture the authenticity of 'other' religions fail to complete the standard message and promote the orthodox reformed alternative. Marlowe dismantles the religious framework with which his audiences had been taught to make sense of existence. Yet in *Doctor Faustus* atheism is not the interpretive solution either. In this play the very mechanisms of dramatic representation trap the audience in the crux between faith and doubt. But the paradoxical 'moral' of this inverted morality play invites the audience to accept emphatically theatrical displays as a religious reality.

Notes

1 Reprinted in Christopher Marlowe, *The Complete Plays*, ed. Frank Romany and Robert Lindsey (Penguin: London, 2003), xxxv. All subsequent references to Marlowe are to this edition.
2 Oliver Ormerod, *The Picture of a Papist* (London, 1606).
3 James Shapiro, *Shakespeare and the Jews* (New York: Columbia University Press, 1996), 21.
4 John Bale, *The Pageant of Popes* ([London], 1574), sig. L6v; Thomas Wilson, *A Christian Dictionarie* (London, 1612), 62.
5 Thomas Overbury, *Sir Thomas Ouerburie his Wife* [...] *Whereunto are annexed, New Newes and Characters* (London, 1616), sig. [G8v].
6 *Liturgical Services: Liturgies and Occasional Forms of Prayer Set Forth in the Reign of Queen Elizabeth*, ed. William Keatinge Clay (Cambridge University Press, 1847), 519.
7 Jonathan Burton, 'Anglo-Ottoman Relations and the Image of the Turk in Tamburlaine', *Journal of Medieval and Early Modern Studies* 30:1 (2000): 125–56, 130–8.
8 See especially Julia Briggs, 'The Rites of Violence: Marlowe's *Massacre at Paris*', in *Christopher Marlowe*, ed. Richard Wilson (London and New York: Longman, 1999), 215–34.
9 Prior to 1593, Henri of Navarre had been a much vaunted Protestant hero in the English printing presses and Elizabethan soldiers fought his cause in France. See Paul Voss, *Elizabethan News Pamphlets* (Pittsburgh: Duquesne University Press, 2001).
10 *The Estate of Christians, Liuing vnder the Subiection of the Turke* (London, 1595), sig. [Av5].
11 Daniel Vitkus, *Turning Turk: English Theater and the Multicultural Mediterranean, 1570–1630* (New York: Palgrave Macmillan, 2003), 55.
12 See, for example, Jonathan Dollimore, *Radical Tragedy: Religion, Ideology and Power in the Drama of Shakespeare and His Contemporaries* (University of Chicago Press, 1984); Michael Hattaway, 'The Theology of Marlowe's *Doctor Faustus*', *Renaissance Drama* 3 (1970), 51–78; Alan Sinfield, *Faultlines: Cultural Materialism and the Politics of Dissident Reading* (Berkeley: University of California Press, 1992).
13 David Bevington, *From 'Mankind' to Marlowe: Growth of Structure in the Popular Drama of Tudor England* (Cambridge, MA: Harvard University Press, 1962).
14 E. K. Chambers, *The Elizabethan Stage*, 4 vols., Vol. III (Oxford: Clarendon Press, 1923), 423–4.

CHAPTER TWENTY ONE

Marlowe and queer theory
David Clark

Christopher Marlowe's *Edward II* (first published 1594) has become a relatively popular play in the last twenty or thirty years, at least partly because of the way it seems to intersect with turn-of-the-millennium anxieties about gay identity and social homophobia; and, more recently, Marlowe and his play have been prime exhibits in debates over early modern sexuality and selfhood. It is not difficult to see why, since Edward can easily be read as a tragic hero whose fatal error is that of loving Gaveston too much in a cruelly heterosexist society, and since Marlowe himself figures in some of the critical biographies as an intriguingly Wildean or Byronic character, an Elizabethan spy (or double agent) with a fatal fascination for the forbidden and the transgressive. Indeed, if, as the Baines note would have it, Marlowe's principal sins were atheism, sodomy, and tobacco-smoking, it is probably the last for which he would be most castigated today. Nonetheless, it is far from certain that Marlowe ever said or did the things attributed to him by his former friends and enemies. Clouds of uncertainty surround many aspects of his life and work: from scholarly doubts over the relative dating of the plays attributed to him to speculations that, on the one hand, his entire literary output may be assigned to Shakespeare, writing under an early *nom de guerre*, or, on the other, he may have faked his own death and in fact may have written most of the plays attributed to Shakespeare.

If Marlowe, therefore, is a slippery subject, queer theory is no less intangible, ever both questioning and self-questioning. It may embrace whatever is non-normative but is also invested in the reworking of what is normative. It holds out the promise of an overarching category of 'belonging' – leaving behind distinctions of gay, lesbian, bisexual, intersex, transvestite, transsexual – yet dismisses universality as illusory and privileges the individual, the various, the heterodox. As Judith Butler points out:

> If the term queer is to be a site of collective contestations, the point of departure for a set of historical reflections and futural imaginings, it will have to remain that which is, in the present, never fully owned, but always and only redeployed, twisted, queered from a prior usage and in the direction of urgent and expanding political purposes.[1]

Marlowe and queer theory are, therefore, perhaps suitable companions, and this chapter will explore a few of their many possible conversations: from notable queer characters and moments in Marlowe's plays, to the way those plays queer dramatic genres and key issues of power and identity. Finally, however, I will consider the ways in which Marlowe might critique (?queer) queer theory in the way he balances the ludic and subversive potential of his queer subjects with the finally irreducible pain and death with which their disruption of the norm is punished.

Queer(ing) Marlowe

Marlowe's protagonists are notoriously subversive; in many ways his plays bring the marginal and the alien to the centre and question that marginalisation and the demonisation of the Other. From Barabas the vengeful Jew to Edward the sodomitical king and Faustus the overweening seeker of knowledge and sensation, Marlowe's characters and others also indicate the perils of excessive desire. Most critical attention, however, has focused on Marlowe's homoerotics and their function and significance in the context of early modernists' debates about homosexuality, sodomy, friendship, and their intersections.

There are certainly several key homoerotic moments in the Marlovian canon, even leaving aside examples in *Edward II*. The unfinished poem *Hero and Leander* (1598), for instance, details Leander's beauty and desirability, emphasising that 'in his lookes were all that men desire',[2] and dwells on the sea-god Neptune's rebuffed attempts to woo him, as Neptune steals kisses, offers him toys, and caresses his limbs (665–75). Leander may reject Neptune's importunate advances, but there is no sense that the god's desire is absurd or wicked. It provides a counterpart and alternative to the male–female desire that motivates the poem's action. Neptune initially mistakes Leander for Ganymede, who also appears at the start of Marlowe's early play *Dido, Queen of Carthage*. The play opens with the boy sitting on Jupiter's knee, with the chief god of Olympus promising to punish his wife Juno if she threatens his paramour and to give Ganymede whatever jewels he desires 'if thou wilt be my love'.[3] 'Ganymede' was also a well-known contemporary term for a male prostitute, and there is plenty of evidence that male–male erotic relations were widely accepted in practice in the early modern period, as long as they did not conflict with the duty to sire an heir.

Homoeroticism is not necessarily queer in and of itself (although queer studies often homes in on homoerotic moments). Rather in the early modern period, it is sometimes accepted as normative, as long as it is not exclusive, excessive, or linked to other non-normative practices. The problem with the eponymous Edward II and with Henry III of France in *The Massacre at Paris* is not that they love their 'minions', but that such love causes them to neglect their kingly interests. This ambivalence towards homoeroticism raises intriguing questions as to whether a contemporary audience would read the love Doctor Faustus expresses for Mephistopheles as suitably affectionate or unsuitably sodomitical because of the diabolical nature of his companion, or whether the race of Mycetes, king of Persia in *Tamburlaine*, would colour an audience's perception of his love for Meander.

Perhaps the most productive focus for a queer investigation, however, is *Edward II*, which provokes (and refuses answers to) questions of sexuality and identity, personal motivation and performativity, in particularly complex and provocative ways.

Queer *Edward II*: homoeroticism and sodomy

Enter Gaveston, reading a letter from the King.
GAVESTON: 'My father is deceased. Come Gaveston,
　And share the kingdom with thy dearest friend.'
　Ah, words that make me surfeit with delight!
　What greater bliss can hap to Gaveston
　Than live and be the favourite of a King!
　Sweet prince, I come! These, these thy amorous lines
　Might have enforced me to have swum from France,
　And, like Leander, gasped upon the sand,
　So thou wouldst smile, and take me in thine arms.
　The sight of London to my exiled eyes
　Is as Elysium to a newcome soul:
　Not that I love the city or the men,
　But that it harbours him I hold so dear,
　The King, upon whose bosom let me die,
　And with the world be still at enmity.
　What need the arctic people love starlight,
　To whom the sun shines both by day and night?[4]

Thus begins *Edward II*, and Marlowe's choice to open the play with a soliloquy from Gaveston, rather than with speeches from the king or his grumbling barons and wife, is significant. The stage business with the letter enables Marlowe to present Gaveston as a key character and to force the audience to make judgements about him right from the start. The initial emphasis here falls on his love for Edward and their passionate friendship, invoking, for an Elizabethan audience, the dangerous political implications of the idea of sharing the throne (2).

Several critics have emphasised the apparently homosexual nature of Edward and Gaveston's relationship, and Marlowe does emphasise homo-erotic elements in Gaveston's soliloquy. In saying he would have swum from France to get to Edward, Gaveston compares himself to 'Leander' (8), the object of the sea-god Neptune's lustful attentions in *Hero and Leander*. There is also a sexual pun when Gaveston talks of the king 'upon whose bosom let me die' (14), death being regularly used as a metaphor for orgasm in Renaissance literature. Similarly, when Gaveston talks about the sun shining 'both by day and night' (17), he is drawing on the conventional iconographic representation of the monarch as the sun and suggesting he will be in Edward's presence by day *and* night. However, as Alan Bray emphasises, what we today might see as unambiguous signs of sexual or romantic love — 'the embraces and the protestations of love, the common bed and the physical closeness, the physical and emotional intimacy' — are part of the conventions of friendship in medieval and Renaissance discourse.[5]

The complicating factor is that, when an early modern writer wishes to discredit a rival or his ideas, these signs of friendship can also be produced as signs of sodomy. For example, when Mortimer, the lead noble objecting to Gaveston's insinuation into the English court, calls Gaveston a 'night-grown mushrump' (or 'mushroom', with a pun on 'rump'; I.iv.284), the phrase indicates Mortimer's disquiet about the king and his minion's night life and about the sexually enabled influence the low-born but now elevated Gaveston has over the king. As this example suggests, sodomy, in the early modern as in the medieval period, is not just a sexual sin; it has associations with political, theological, and social subversion as well as with both male–male *and* male–female sexual sins. In fact, Bray convincingly suggests that *Edward II* sets up an unresolved tension between the two interpretations of Edward and Gaveston's relationship, as one of friendship versus one of sodomy.

The ambivalence surrounding Edward and Gaveston's relationship is present in the main source upon which Marlowe draws, Raphael

Holinshed's *Chronicles of England*. Holinshed comments: 'A wonderfull matter that the king should be so inchanted with the said earle [Gaveston], and so addict himselfe, or rather fix his hart vpon a man of such a corrupt humor, against whome the heads of the noblest houses in the land were bent to deuise his ouerthrow'.[6] Holinshed is clearly not enamoured of Gaveston, but he maintains a balance between the negative tropes of addiction and enchantment and the idea that Edward has 'fix[ed] his hart' upon him – and in the full passage from which this extract is taken, Holinshed also repeats the word 'affection'. Is the whole relationship a tainted one, or is the problem that Edward has chosen the wrong object of affection? Holinshed raises the spectre of the sodomitical and implicitly criticises the king's association with this man of 'corrupt humor', but he is careful not to condone the barons' rebellion against the king: the barons are clearly seen to be wrong to oppose him.

Several historical figures contemporary to Marlowe have been called up as relevant to the story of Edward and Gaveston: from Henry II of France (reigned 1574–89), whom Marlowe dramatised in *The Massacre at Paris* and whose favouritism was openly criticised by contemporaries as sodomitical, to James VI of Scotland (reigned 1567–1625), not yet James I of England (reigned 1603–25), whose relationship with Esmé Stuart (whom he created Earl Lennox) was also the subject of public criticism and debate, some writers suggesting the relationship was sodomitical and immoderate, others treating it as a productive friendship. Accusations of sodomy could be applied to male–female relations, too, however. All sorts of anxieties surrounded Queen Elizabeth during her reign (1558–1603) because of her tendency towards political favouritism. The anonymous libel, *Leicester's Commonwealth* (1584), for example, questioned the interrelation of the monarch's public and private persona and the impact of her favour on questions of succession.[7] *Edward II* thus speaks to both a queer past and a queer present for its early modern audiences: it enshrines a queer monarch in England's constitutional history, deems him worthy of public attention in the theatre, and thereby provides a space for subversive comment on the behaviour and affiliations of contemporary monarchs.

Performance and performativity

The ambivalent dynamic of Gaveston's first soliloquy is more than matched by his second, in which he describes the *masques* or fantastic theatrical shows that he will put on for the king, where his pages will be cross-dressed as 'sylvan nymphs' (1.i.57) and his men will dance as satyrs:

> Sometime a lovely boy in Dian's shape,
> With hair that gilds the water as it glides,
> Crownets of pearl about his naked arms,
> And in his sportful hands an olive tree
> To hide those parts which men delight to see,
> Shall bathe him in a spring.
>
> (I.i.60–5)

Another actor in the role of Actaeon, 'peeping through the grove, / Shall by the angry goddess be transformed, / And, running in the likeness of an hart, / By yelping hounds pulled down, and seem to die' (I.i.66–9).

The homoeroticism of the lovely boy, playfully hiding 'those parts which men delight to see', sits uneasily next to the vicious death of doomed Actaeon, hunted by his own hounds – an image that recurs throughout the play and is proleptic of the fate of Edward, not a wounded kingly lion but a stricken deer, murdered by his own nobles. This is not simply a straightforward linkage of homoeroticism with morbidity, as some earlier critics have assumed, buying into homophobic tropes prevalent in the mid twentieth century. Rather it would seem to exemplify the dangers of desire in a context of performance and spectacle – the context both of the king at court, whose undisciplined favouritism threatens his country's exchequer and his barons' power, and of the early modern audience, watching an actor characterise a character, Gaveston, who is proposing to put on a homoerotic and transvestite performance while also performing a role ('play-acting') himself.

In Gaveston's opening speeches, there is an obvious attention to theatrical spectacle in his plan to divert the king with masques and shows. However, Gaveston is also performing himself in Judith Butler's sense of performativity as 'that reiterative power of discourse to produce the phenomena that it regulates and constrains'[8] – and not just in his intertextual likening of himself to Leander in the first soliloquy. It is a passage that, as a whole, reads like a rehearsal of what he is planning to say to Edward when they are reunited, whether one deems the signified emotion genuine or counterfeited.

Gaveston is also performing when, after his second soliloquy, he decides to give three poor men false hope that he will help them, saying 'it is no pain to speak men fair. / I'll flatter these and make them live in hope' (I.i.41–2) – an indication of the cruelty or expediency that is also one of his characteristics. After dismissing the indigents, he says

> These are not men for me;
> I must have wanton poets, pleasant wits,

> Musicians that, with touching of a string,
> May draw the pliant king which way I please.
>
> (I.i.49–52)

This speech and its context ask the audience to question how far Gaveston's advertised love for the king is founded on self-interest, and how far the 'bliss' in being 'the favourite of a king' (I.i.4–5) lies in the lavish lifestyle to which he can become accustomed. We are both presented with homoerotic desire and simultaneously denied its presence, as Gaveston's performance draws attention to the necessity of reading desire, motivation, and public identity and to the disquieting possibility of their ultimate unreadability.

Gaveston is clearly a good dissembler. Notwithstanding, he is not the only character in the play who is happy to 'speak men fair' (I.i.41). Edward recognises that, as far as the barons are concerned, 'it boots me not to threat; I must speak fair' (I.iv.63), and Gaveston urges him later to 'dissemble with [Isabella], speak her faire' (II.ii.28). Finally, Isabella likens herself to Juno, lamenting over Jove's attentions to Ganymede, but knows 'I must entreat him, I must speak him fair' (I.iv.183). That repeated phrase 'speak fair' links implicitly to the idea of 'acting false' and widens the possibilities of false acting from one homoerotically identified character to any given character in the play. As Claude Summers comments, 'The contrast between what individuals say and what they do reflects the identity crisis in which everyone ... participates, as they are torn between what is socially acceptable and what is self-fulfilling.'[9]

Space does not permit an exploration of the other performative constructions of self in the play – Edward's shifting self-presentation from defiant lover in Act I to tragic victim towards the end of Act V, for instance, or his assassin Lightborn's explicit invocation of the theatrical in the showmanship of his approach to the murder. The uncertainty as to characters' genuine motivations and private identities pervades the play, however, and reflects a deeper ambivalence surrounding the characters and even genre. One could read the play as the tragedy of the doomed love of Edward and Gaveston or as the tragedy of Edward's humiliated wife Isabella. Alternatively, one could characterise *Edward II* as a history play, where the patriotic barons recognise the danger to the realm from Edward's obsessive love and try to prevent the social disorder that might follow from the low-born Gaveston's rise to power. Such generic uncertainty is characteristic of early modern drama: there are similar debates over other plays, such as *King Lear* (a tragedy according to its categorisation in the 1623 Folio, but titled *The True Chronicle History of the Life and Death of King Lear and His Three Daughters* in the 1608 Quarto) and *Richard III* (categorised as a history, but titled *The Tragedy of Richard the Third* on its first page in the 1623 Folio). However, the balance of history and tragedy in *Edward II* may also represent a deliberate queering of genre: a resolve to make the audience choose how to take the drama set before them.

It was not just a matter of Marlowe queering the Renaissance stage, however: the theatre was already a very queer space in the way the normative was suspended, inverted, and parodied, as several contemporary commentators worried. Stephen Gosson, for instance, was anxious about the cross-dressing involved in an all-male acting company (of the kind that might put on Gaveston's 'masque' of Diana and Actaeon), fearing that theatres 'effeminate the minds, as pricks unto vice' and offer 'wanton spectacles'; others agreed that public theatres facilitated access to loose women and male prostitution.[10] Furthermore, Garrett Epp argues that acting itself is a sodomitical form in early modern terms, since actors – who were classed with rogues and vagabonds at the bottom of the social hierarchy, gendered male – destabilise 'hierarchical order', because performance allows the (unnormatively gendered) actor 'authority over the playtext equal to or greater than that of the legitimately masculine playwright'.[11]

Queer/early modern

Queer theatre, queer play, queer characters, queer themes: Marlowe, and certainly *Edward II*, seem very queer indeed. But what would Marlowe think of queer theory today? Queer theory has often been criticised for its perceived excesses, whether an overemphasis on the rhetorical, an undue obscurity of expression, or a lack of historical rigour. However, one of the most difficult charges to refute is that of social irresponsibility in an excessive commitment to social constructionism that neglects the real-world importance of identity politics. That is to say, a conviction that categories of identity are historically and culturally variable sometimes causes critics to treat them as irrelevant, when political groupings based on a community of identity are often crucial in resisting injustice and violence directed towards the non-normative.

For instance, as of the writing of this article in August 2012, same-sex activity is punishable by death in Iran, Mauritania, Saudi Arabia, Sudan, Yemen, Nigeria, Gambia, and Somalia and is criminalised in over seventy countries, including many in Africa, Asia, Latin America, the Caribbean, and Oceania. As well, homophobic murders have been documented so far this year in Belgium, Brazil, Chile, Iraq, South Africa, Tasmania, Turkey, and the United Kingdom, and in the US states of California, North Carolina, Texas; the list goes on. It is largely, though not exclusively, alliances of same-sex-oriented individuals who spearhead pressure groups aimed at increasing public awareness and legal and political sanctions against societal tolerance of and complicity in such acts.

Marlowe, in presenting his marginal and subversive characters and themes, also forces us to confront the pain and death that result from resisting the status quo or failing to conform, and nowhere more starkly than in the sadistic and overdetermined death of Edward II. This is not a reiteration of the trope of the queer as tragic victim. Marlowe not only draws attention to Edward's manipulation of the rhetoric of victimhood; he also makes it impossible to be sure whether Edward's murderer Lightborn in fact pierced the king's entrails with a poker or smothered him with a featherbed and, in creating this uncertainty, emphasises the punitive powers of normativity and the Other-oriented violence integral to its own self-definition and maintenance.[12] If Marlowe had anything to say to queer theorists today, perhaps it would be a reminder to balance the pleasures of discourse and performativity with the need to critique a world in which people are murdered for failing to conform to a perceived norm.

Notes

1 Judith Butler, *Bodies that Matter: On the Discursive Limits of 'Sex'* (New York: Routledge, 1993), 228.
2 Christopher Marlowe, *Hero and Leander*, in *The Complete Works of Christopher Marlowe*, 5 vols., Vol. I: *All Ovids elegies, Lucans first booke, Dido Queene of Carthage, Hero and Leander*, ed. Roma Gill (Oxford: Clarendon Press, 1986), line 84.
3 Christopher Marlowe, *Dido, Queen of Carthage*, I.i.49, in *ibid*.
4 All quotations from *Edward II* (here, I.i.1–17) are taken from Christopher Marlowe, *Edward the Second*, ed. Charles R. Forker (Manchester University Press, 1994).
5 Alan Bray, 'Homosexuality and the Signs of Male Friendship in Elizabethan England', repr. in *Queering the Renaissance*, ed. Jonathan Goldberg (Durham, NC: Duke University Press, 1994), 40–61 (46).
6 Holinshed's *Chronicles* (the 1587 edition of which is used here, VI.139) are most conveniently available online at www.english.ox.ac.uk/holinshed/ (designated as for the year 1309).
7 See further, Curtis Perry, 'The Politics of Access and Representations of the Sodomite King in Early Modern England', *Renaissance Quarterly* 53:4 (2000), 1054–83 (1058 and *passim*).
8 Butler, *Bodies that Matter*, 2.

9 Claude J. Summers, 'Sex, Politics, and Self-Realization in *Edward II*', in *'A Poet and a Filthy Play-Maker': New Essays on Christopher Marlowe*, ed. Kenneth Friedenreich, Roma Gill, and Constance Brown Kuriyama (New York: AMS Press, 1988), 221–40 (229).
10 Stephen Gosson, *The Schoole of Abuse* (1579), quoted in Jonathan Goldberg, *Sodometries: Renaissance Texts, Modern Sexualities* (Stanford University Press, 1992), 106.
11 Garrett P. J. Epp, 'To "Play the Sodomits": A Query in Five Actions', in *The Ashgate Research Companion to Queer Theory*, ed. Noreen Giffney and Michael O'Rourke (Farnham: Ashgate, 2009), 181–97 (187–8).
12 On the murder of Edward II, see Paul Menzer's excellent 'Marlowe Now', Chapter 33 in this collection (357–65).

CHAPTER TWENTY TWO

Marlowe and women

Alison Findlay

In what was probably Marlowe's first play, the tragic figure of Dido complains to Aeneas: 'Why look'st thou toward the sea? The time hath been / When Dido's beauty chain'd thine eyes to her. / Am I less fair than when you saw's me first?'[1] She realises, to her despair, that her speech has no more power than her looks: 'And wilt thou not be mov'd by Dido's words?' (V.i.155). Dido's feeling of neglect might be echoed by the other female characters in Marlowe's plays whose speeches receive relatively little attention. In Part II of *Tamburlaine*, Olympia pointedly draws attention to the destructive silencing of women in favour of male protagonists when she tricks Theridamas into stabbing her throat rather than become the victim of his rapacious desires (IV.ii.68–70). By considering image and speech, this chapter will consider what spaces exist for women in Marlowe's drama: first in relation to play worlds governed by homosocial networks of power, and then, with a special focus on *Dido* and *Tamburlaine*, in relation to the all-male environment of the theatre.

Simon Shepherd has argued that roles like Helen, the 'face that launch'd a thousand ships' (*DrF*, V.i.99) in *Doctor Faustus*, or Zenocrate in *Tamburlaine* make women into spectacular objects fetishised by men and the male gaze.[2] Tamburlaine's extravagant praise of his prisoner as 'brighter than is the silver Rhodope, / Fairer than whitest snow on Scythian hills' (I.ii.88–9), for example, emphasises Zenocrate's position as his object rather than as a self-determining subject. Abigail in *The Jew of Malta* exemplifies the difficulty female characters have in constructing their own stories. Abigail is cast in the traditional role of daughter-as-sacrifice, as LaGretta Lenker observes.[3] Barabas says he prizes her 'as Agamemnon did his Iphigen' (I.i.136), Iphigenia being the daughter offered as a sacrifice to the success of the Greek army. Iphigenia actively embraces her role as sacrifice in Lady Jane Lumley's translation of Euripides' *Iphigenia*, but the reference in Marlowe's play signals limits to Abigail's scope for action.[4] Barabas cannot even license her public protest against the Senate's confiscation of their property. When she determines to 'reprehend' the senators 'with fierce exclaims' (I.ii.236–7), he commands: 'Be silent, daughter, sufferance breeds ease' (I.ii.242). Abigail acts decisively but only briefly in Act III, Scene iii. In a mere eighty lines, she discovers that Barabas' plot has killed Don Mathias, confides to spectators 'I perceive there is no love on earth' (III.iii.52), asks to be admitted to the nunnery (III.iii.60), and vows not to betray her father (III.iii.78–80). Such brief expressions in the scripted text make it difficult to attribute subjective agency to Abigail. The role relies on the power of the actor to charge the sparse script with a sense of determination and emotion.[5]

Even where female speech is truncated, the characters' function as listeners or as marginalised speakers can disrupt the authority of male voices. Gina Bloom argues that early modern understandings of voice as reliant on the unstable phenomenon of breath, 'ephemeral, mobile, unpredictable, indeed invisible', cause particular anxiety for male speakers.[6] As critical listeners, female characters can subvert the authority of dominant male voices visually (as the captive Zenocrate deconstructs the romance of Tamburlaine's courtly love poetry) or by providing a point of focus for offstage female auditors whose experiences are also marginalised. In *Doctor Faustus*, for example, the two small roles of the Duchess of Vanholt and Helen of Troy act as a subversive point of identification between the women in the early modern audience and the protagonist. The female characters embody the forbidden desire, pleasure, and knowledge that Faustus seeks. The Duchess of Vanholt is tempted by 'the thing you most desire to have' (IV.iii.10), selecting grapes in an echo of Eve's desire for the forbidden fruit from the Tree of Knowledge. Helen's subsequent appearance, arguably, seals Faustus' fall and damnation, ravishing him with a kiss that 'suck[s] forth my soul, see where it flies' (V.ii.102). Intellectually curious female spectators who valued learning in spite of religious and moral warnings about its dangers may have identified sympathetically with Faustus' quest for forbidden knowledge, reading against the text's orthodox morality to construct a tragedy of failed self-realisation rather than one of damnation.[7]

Frustrated female ambition is vividly dramatised by Catherine de Medici's role in *The Massacre at Paris*. Marlowe reduces Catherine's part from the prime position she holds in his source text, Anne Dowriche's *The French Historie*, as Randall Martin has shown.[8] Dowriche recounts how 'the Mother Queen' appears 'first upon the Stage' and, 'like a divelish sorceresse', persuades the council to take up her 'bloodie plot'. Her advice of 'wisedome macht with pollicie' is straight out of Machiavelli, and Dowriche remarks in the margin: '*The queen mother was a good scholar of that divel of Florence, Machivel, of whom she learned manie bad lessons, as this.*'[9] To any reader aware of Catherine de Medici's reputation as a leading political plotter, her potent, truncated role in Marlowe's text would have effectively conveyed frustrated ambition. The character's desire for control bubbles through lines that identify her as the power behind the throne. The Duke of Guise reports that Catherine rifles 'the bowels of her treasury' to promote him 'and in my love entombs the hope of France' (I.ii.76–9), the corporeal imagery hinting at her uncanny maternal power to deal life and death. She directs the murders of Henry of Navarre and Charles: 'For Catherine must have her will in France' (xi.39). Her line 'For I'll rule France, but they shall wear the crown' (xi.44) betrays the same fascination with absolute power. With Henry III established in what Catherine assumes to be a figurehead role, she finally dares to reach for the crown herself: 'Tush, all shall die unless I have my will, / For while she lives Catherine will be queen' (xiv.66–7). This moment of female self-realisation is complemented in the following scene where Guise's wife undermines the status of the play's antihero by writing a letter to her lover. There is little the Guise can do except protest: 'O wicked sex, perjured and unjust' (xv.37–9). Queen Catherine's triumph is short lived. When Henry murders the Duke of Guise, she collapses emotionally and generically from political overreacher into the feminine genre of complaint: 'To whom shall I bewray my secrets now, / Or who will help to build religion?' (xxii.155–6).

Complaint can be a powerfully subversive form of speech for female characters, proving difficult to monitor or discipline once it is expressed into the air.[10] In Catherine's case the lament is a shocking anticlimax after her speeches of confident Machiavellian plotting. In *Edward II*, however, Queen Isabella traces an opposite trajectory, moving from complaint to politically astute rhetoric. Isabella's poignant wish to flee from court, 'to live in grief and baleful discontent' (I.ii.48), because Edward only has eyes for Gaveston, is prevented by the Younger Mortimer, who keeps her in the political arena as an ally and becomes her lover. Her subsequent soliloquy elaborates her emotional imprisonment in having to plead for Gaveston's repeal (I.iv.170–86), but her appeal is born of a keen political awareness that her sovereignty as a woman in a man's world depends upon her proximity to Edward (and later to their son). Joanna Gibbs notes how Isabella deftly manipulates Mortimer into supporting Gaveston's repeal in order to murder him (I.iv.225–7), a pragmatic strategy typical of Marlowe's 'politic women', who seek to 'subversively reinscribe themselves within patriarchy'.[11] Isabella and Mortimer's subsequent relationship as lovers mirrors her political complicity with male-dominated systems.

The question of why Marlowe's women are willing to enforce the terms of male dominance is, I will argue, linked to conditions of performance. A consideration of the boy actors who played the roles of Marlowe's female protagonists helps to illuminate the pattern of resistance to and complicity with homosocial networks of power observed by Emily Bartels.[12] To pursue this line of inquiry, I will focus on the different positions occupied by the lead boy actors in *Dido, Queen of Carthage* performed by 'Children of Her Majesties Chapel' and in *Tamburlaine* Parts I and II acted by the Admiral's Men.

In the boys' company, performances of adult males were, arguably, even more artificial than simulated performances of women, and Marlowe's rewriting of the *Aeneid* exploits the possibilities offered by these circumstances radically to deconstruct conventional hierarchies of gender and power. Robert Logan notes that 'the audience would have seen a boy acting unconventionally as an adult male (Aeneas) with an uncharacteristic lack of manliness and a second boy acting conventionally as a female (Dido) ... with uncharacteristic manliness'.[13] From the opening scene where Jove is enthralled by Ganymede, gender is simulated. Jove gives the boy the 'linked gems / My Juno ware upon her marriage day' (I.i.42–3), introducing a series of moments, strung through the play, that foreground props and costume as mobile markers, opening up space for a play of differences. Cupid's arrow is a mobile phallic signifier, while Dido takes the masculine part in actively wooing Aeneas, giving him the jewels, 'golden bracelets', and 'wedding ring / Wherewith my husband woo'd me' (III.iv.62–3).[14] In Marlowe's text Dido is placed centre-stage (following Ovid rather than Virgil's account of the myth of Aeneas). Indeed, the play advertises an alternative history to Virgil's: an emotionally driven herstory directed by women.[15] Dido's pursuit of desire – vocalised in powerfully passionate speeches – shapes the action even though she is controlled by Cupid's arrow. Other female characters emerge as powerful forces in the play. The role of Dido's sister, Anna, is expanded by Marlowe to create an outspoken, desiring subject. Venus chastises Jupiter, reminding him of his responsibilities to Aeneas and to the writing of epic history. Marlowe's focus on a heroine who rewrites conventional ideas of femininity (and history), along with Iarbus' reference to her as 'Eliza' (IV.ii.10), would have undoubtedly engaged the audience of a court performance, with Queen Elizabeth at its head.

The play's climax, in which Dido casts herself onto the funeral pyre, followed by Iarbus and Anna, has been interpreted in opposing ways by critics. Amongst readings that emphasise its comic absurdity, Frederick Tromly suggests that Marlowe as playwright sadistically tantalises Dido with fantasies of overarching romantic control only to satirise her 'obsessive self-delusion'.[16] On the other hand, Dido does have the mightiest lines in the play, and 'flashes of tragic sublimity' counterpoise the comedy to destabilise conventional modes of genre and tone as well as of gender.[17] The part certainly offered a serious challenge for the boy actor who took the lead. It is more demanding than other female roles from the 1580s and would have been a real test of his maturity as an actor. In the unique theatrical context of the boys' company, the actor playing Dido can literally take the lead and play unchallenged by the stage presence of a dominant male. Claire Kinney suggests that the theatrical context magnifies the plot's subversive mockery of adult agency and Marlowe's self-mockery as Jovian author who surrenders dramatic agency to 'those other Ganymedes, the children who will impersonate adult speaking subjects'.[18] The demands of the Dido part make me doubt that the actors playing the protagonists would have been indistinguishable in age and maturity, as Kinney suggests. Instead, I propose that Marlowe's text deliberately offers the lead boy actor an opportunity to star centre-stage as a woman and, from this unusual theatrical starting-point, generates alternative histories based on different configurations of gender, sexuality, and power.

By contrast, the first and second parts of *Tamburlaine*, played by the Admiral's Men, stage a reinscription of the female role and boy actor within a male gaze and mode of speaking. The spectacular masculinity displayed by Tamburlaine and his men is a seductive model for both female characters and mature boy actors. Zenocrate's part is as demanding as Dido's, and Zabina's also requires an experienced performer. In both cases, the boy actor's experience follows the same trajectory traced by the female characters: initial resistance to male dominance succeeded by willing complicity with it. The women in *Tamburlaine* learn that conventional forms of female speech may effectively critique masculine authority, but these are hopelessly ineffective in halting the ruthless trajectory of Tamburlaine's conquests. Tamburlaine ignores Zenocrate's feminine appeal for safe deliverance and ransom (*1 Tamb.*, I.ii.7–16), superimposing his own view of her as object of his desires, romantic and political (since marriage to a princess would legitimate his rise to power). In Act V, when the Virgins come to plead for mercy for the besieged city of Damascus, their powerful rhetoric falls on deaf ears. Initially, the humility and tears 'shed from the heads and hearts of all our sex' (V.i.26–8) cleverly veil an implicit critique of male obduracy and persuade the Governor to ask for peace, but the performance cuts no ice with Tamburlaine. Neither does the First Virgin's oratory, which deftly interweaves a conventional plea of 'Pity, O pity, sacred emperor' with appeals to Tamburlaine's ambition in the offer of the 'gilded wreath' that is 'the true Egyptian diadem' (V.i.99–105). The rhetoric is, of course, ineffectual: Tamburlaine summarily executes the virgins before launching into sadistic praise of Zenocrate's beauty in suffering (V.i.135–90) and then into an attack on Damascus.

Curses and complaints, other conventional forms of marginalised female speech, offer no more success for the women in *Tamburlaine*. Zabina's despair resonates passionately on stage at the futility of building 'nests / So high within the region of the air' (V.i.242–50) but cannot change her fate. Bajazeth presents her as an emblem of failed female power:

> You see my wife, my queen and emperess
> Brought up and propped by the hand of Fame
> Queen of fifteen contributory queens,
> Now thrown to rooms of black abjection.
> (V.i.263–6)

His death causes her rhetorical collapse from Marlovian verse into disordered prose. Once her husband is gone, Zabina's speech fragments into madness, looking forward to the idiolects of Ophelia and Lady Macbeth in its snatches of memorial reconstruction, changed perspective, and childlike sensory perception. Zabina notices Tamburlaine's streamers 'white, red, black, here, here, here!' and recalls the horror of her husband's starvation and, finally, her own role as queen: 'Make ready my coach, my chair, my jewels. I come, I come, I come!' (V.i.312–18). Zabina's lines appear to be a warning about the self-destructive nature of her reinscription into male power. She calls out: 'Go to, my child: away, away, away!' – words that, Pam Whitfield persuasively suggests, may be addressed to Zenocrate.[19]

Zenocrate takes up the lead provided by Zabina's mad prose but begins to speak with a male register. Her own vision of destruction – of 'Damascus' walls dy'd with Egyptian blood' – and her lament for Bajazeth and Zabina are tightly structured pieces of oratory. She appropriates the 'male narrative voice of truth' to offer the play's most powerful critique of 'fickle empery' and of Tamburlaine's ambitions 'for sceptres and for slippery crowns' (V.i.351–7).[20] Having exhausted the impossibilities of resistance, she then surrenders her divided duty as a female subject in a tragic swansong for her integrity (V.i.383–402). Her commitment to 'live and die with Tamburlaine' (III.ii.24) denies difference by subsuming herself into his ambitions.

Zenocrate's complicity with the ideology that aestheticises her and silences her difference comes from her role as a listener, which expands through the two parts of the play. Zenocrate is ravished by rhetoric of conquest. She finds that Tamburlaine's 'amorous discourse' of 'war and blood' (*1 Tamb.*, III.ii.44–5) is 'much sweeter than the Muses' song' (III.ii.50). The openness of her ears defies gender convention since, as Bloom points out, 'aural openness displays a heroic capacity for leadership' amongst male characters but, 'for the gentlewoman, aural generosity compromises honor'.[21] The relationship between listening and developing heroic leadership is evident in the exchanges between Tamburlaine and his followers. Those followers learn to value 'kingly joys in earth' (*1 Tamb.*, II.v.59) and win crowns by consuming Tamburlaine's verse and imitating his heroic style. Theridamas' rhetoric of victory over the Turks wins his leader's praise: 'Well said, Theridamas! Speak in that mood, / For *will* and *shall* best fitteth Tamburlaine' (III.iii.40–1). Rhetoric was imagined invading and colonising the ears of listeners. Henry Peacham, for example, regarded its figures as 'martial instruments both of defense and invasion' and thus advised men to 'hold these weapons always ready in our hands'.[22]

If the preservation of a chaste reputation excludes women from sharing aural openness to men's speech, then the virgin Zenocrate, who is also on stage during the preparations for battle, must listen differently, one might say androgynously, to the military counsel. Her political status as a prince (heir to the Soldan) offers one explanation for her androgynous listening. Corinne Abate describes Zenocrate as 'more than an emblematic beauty'; she is the political ally Tamburlaine needs in order to legitimate conquest by force of arms.[23] 'Prince' Zenocrate is attracted by the allure of imperial power. Her plea for Damascus is overridden by the prospect of worldwide domination: 'Calling the provinces, cities, and towns / After my name and thine, Zenocrate' (*1 Tamb.*, IV.iv.81–2). The early modern theatre adds another explanation for Zenocrate's marginalised androgyny in the apprentice boy actor learning to be a man, like Tamburlaine, who was played by his master. Manliness is, Simon Shepherd reminds us, 'an argument, a rhetorical construction, to be learnt. The "terms" precede the person and shape him.'[24] The role of Zenocrate, a character who is inaugurated into the male values and behaviour of Tamburlaine's court, is powerfully supplemented by the apprentice actor's journey to maturity as an adult male.

Zenocrate would surely have been played by the most experienced boy actor on the brink of manhood. Evidence from Henslowe's *Diary* indicates that the apprentices or servants bound to masters in the Admiral's Men played both female and young male roles and were likely in their late teens.[25] A strong candidate for the role of Zenocrate in the 1590s would be John Pig, an apprentice of Edward Alleyn, the definitive Tamburlaine. Pig was a member of Strange's Men in 1593 and the Admiral's Men from 1597 to 1599, playing the title role in a lost play, *Alice Pearce* (1597), as well as minor male roles. Articles of women's clothing for Pig as Alice and for men's jackets and suits appear in Henslowe's *Diary*. A joke letter to Mrs Alleyn, apparently from John Pig on tour but written in Alleyn's hand, suggests a playful trading of identities between Master and Boy. In a parodic echo of Tamburlaine, 'Pig' vows 'by the faith of a fustian kinge never to retorne' to London 'till fortune us bryng' back in triumph.[26] Perhaps Alleyn's Tamburlaine and the adult members of the all-male company who played the conquering heroes represented an idealised model of mastery for the apprentice boy actors playing the female leads, Zenocrate and Zabina.

In *1 Tamburlaine*, Act III, Scene iii, where Zenocrate sits opposite Zabina, both boy actors rehearse adult kingly power through their roles as queens. The male rulers pass on their thrones and crowns: Bajazeth directs Zabina to sit 'upon this royal chair of state / And on thy head wear my imperial crown', while Tamburlaine commands Zenocrate to 'take thou my crown, vaunt of my worth / And manage words with her, as we will arms' (III.iii.130–1). The process of kingmaking is enacted between the male hero and a woman character, and between a master actor and his boy. The subordinate figure (woman or apprentice) legitimises the mastery of the superior through deference, praise, and, in the case of Zenocrate, the symbolic crowning of Tamburlaine as Emperor of Africa (III.iii.218–20). In return, Tamburlaine warns Zenocrate: 'I will not crown thee yet, / Until with greater honours I be grac'd' (IV.iv.140–1). At the level of fiction, his sovereignty will be fully legitimated by granting hers. At the level of theatre, the boy's female role is not yet complete; he cannot yet pass to full possession of mastery which the crown symbolises.

The end of Part I celebrates how Zenocrate, who 'long hath ling'red for so high a seat', is finally rewarded for her loyalty by being enthroned as 'Queen of Persia'. She is literally the crowning glory of Tamburlaine's achievements (V.i.507–9). Pam Whitfield argues that this is a hollow victory for Zenocrate, who does not speak a word during the coronation: 'It is as a voiceless and defeated shell of a woman that she ascends the throne to take her venerated seat alongside the terror of the world.'[27] In Part II she serves Tamburlaine as an instrument giving immortality through the production of sons 'that shall be emperors' (I.iii.7). Tamburlaine's concern at their youthful femininity betrays a rejection of the female otherness embodied by Zenocrate, who pointedly remarks that they resemble their father in life and 'in death resemble me' (II.iv.72–3), a lesson Calyphas learns to his cost. Zenocrate's final speech is conventionally feminine, following the cultural tradition of using the deathbed as a stage to display a dying woman's virtue. Contrary to Zenocrate's wish to 'let me die' (II.iv.66), from henceforth she appears on stage as a talisman, the shell of a woman without a living body, in the effigy that Tamburlaine orders. The golden mummy-case symbolises how Zenocrate has been subsumed into Tamburlaine's identity as emperor, an identity of super-masculinity that she helped to create. As a theatrical story, the golden mummy is the female part that the boy actor has now outgrown. Having worshipped, followed, and effectively become the male hero, he abandons the 'gowne of calleco for the quene' as an empty shell, to adopt the 'red sewt of cloth for pyge'.[28] The boy actor's trajectory reiterates the narrative of abandonment in *Dido, Queen of Carthage* with which I began, where women are left behind in favour of expanding male horizons. Although the boy actor's progress seems to confirm the limited scope of most women's roles in Marlowe, female characters have significant opportunities to master the stage through powerful verse and offer tantalising possibilities of a world elsewhere where difference can thrive.

Notes

1 *Dido, Queen of Carthage*, V.i.113–15. For convenience, all references will be to texts in Christopher Marlowe, *Christopher Marlowe: Complete Plays and Poems*, ed. E. D. Pendry and J. C. Maxwell (London: Dent, 1976).
2 Simon Shepherd, 'Representing "Women" and Males: Gender Relations in Marlowe', in *Christopher Marlowe*, ed. Richard Wilson (London and New York: Longman, 1999), 62–82 (67).
3 LaGretta Tallent Lenker, 'The Hopeless Daughter of a Hapless Jew: Father and Daughter in Marlowe's *The Jew of Malta*', in *Placing the Plays of Christopher Marlowe: Fresh Cultural Contexts*, ed. Sara Munson Deats and Robert A. Logan (Aldershot: Ashgate, 2008), 63–73 (64).
4 Lady Jane Lumley, *Iphigenia at Aulis* (1555), in *Three Tragedies by Renaissance Women*, ed. Diane Purkiss (Harmondsworth: Penguin, 1998), 1–35
5 Lenker, 'The Hopeless Daughter', 72.
6 Gina Bloom, *Voice in Motion: Staging Gender, Shaping Sound in Early Modern England* (Philadelphia: University of Pennsylvania Press, 2007), 109.
7 Alison Findlay, *A Feminist Perspective on Renaissance Drama* (Oxford: Blackwell, 1998), 11–25.
8 Randall Martin, 'Anne Dowriche's *The French History*, Christopher Marlowe, and Machiavellian Agency', *SEL* 39:1 (1999): 69–87.

9. Anne Dowriche, *The French historie That is; a lamentable discourse of three of the chiefe, and most famous bloodie broiles that haue happened in France* (London, 1589), 23r–v.
10. Bloom, *Voice in Motion*, 109.
11. Joanna Gibbs, 'Marlowe's Politic Women', in *Constructing Christopher Marlowe*, ed. J. A. Downie and J. T. Parnell (Cambridge University Press, 2000), 164–76 (175).
12. Emily C. Bartels, *Spectacles of Strangeness: Imperialism, Alienation, and Marlowe* (Philadelphia: University of Pennsylvania Press, 1993), 25.
13. Robert A. Logan, *Shakespeare's Marlowe: The Influence of Christopher Marlowe on Shakespeare's Artistry* (Burlington, VT: Ashgate, 2007), 185.
14. See Sara Munson Deats, 'The Subversion of Gender Hierarchies in *Dido, Queene of Carthage*', in *Marlowe, History and Sexuality*, ed. Paul Whitfield White (New York: AMS Press, 1998), 163–78 (172).
15. Joyce Green MacDonald, 'Marlowe's Ganymede', in *Enacting Gender on the English Renaissance Stage*, ed. Viviana Comensoli and Anne Russell (Urbana: University of Illinois Press, 1999), 97–113 (105).
16. See, for example, Jackson Cope, 'Marlowe's *Dido* and the Titillating Children', *ELR* 4 (1974): 315–25. Frederick B. Tromly, *Playing with Desire: Christopher Marlowe and the Art of Tantalization* (University of Toronto Press, 1998), 63.
17. Sara Munson Deats, '*Dido, Queen of Carthage* and *The Massacre at Paris*', in *The Cambridge Companion to Christopher Marlowe*, ed. Patrick Cheney (Cambridge University Press, 2004), 193–206 (198, 204).
18. Claire R. Kinney, 'Epic Transgression and the Framing of Agency in *Dido, Queen of Carthage*', *SEL* 40:2 (2000): 261–76 (272).
19. Pam Whitfield, '"Divine Zenocrate", "Wretched Zenocrate": Female Speech and Disempowerment in *Tamburlaine I*', in *Renaissance Papers 2000*, ed. T. Howard-Hill and Philip Rollinson (Woodbridge: Boydell and Brewer, 2000): 87–97 (94).
20. Shepherd, 'Representing "Women"', 71.
21. Bloom, *Voice in Motion*, 132, 115.
22. Wayne A. Rebhorn, *Renaissance Debates on Rhetoric* (Ithaca, NY: Cornell University Press, 2000), 226.
23. Corinne S. Abate, 'Zenocrate: Not Just Another "Fair Face"', *English Language Notes* 41:1 (2003): 19–32 (23).
24. Shepherd, 'Representing "Women"', 81.
25. David Kathman, 'How Old Were Shakespeare's Boy Actors?', *Shakespeare Survey* 58 (2005): 220–46 (229). On the Admiral's Men see Andrew Gurr, *Shakespeare's Opposites: The Admiral's Company 1594–1625* (Cambridge University Press, 2009).
26. See Philip Henslowe, *Henslowe's Diary*, ed. R. A. Foakes, 2nd edn (Cambridge University Press, 2002), 73, 318, 321. The letter is on 282–3.
27. Whitfield, '"Divine Zenocrate"', 97.
28. Henslowe, *Diary*, 318.

CHAPTER TWENTY THREE

Marlowe and the new science

Mary Thomas Crane

We have the word of no less an expert than Marjorie Hope Nicolson that this chapter is a waste of time:

> The Elizabethan dramatist whose imagination would have responded most sensitively to the poetic implications of the 'new astronomy' died too early to know them. Had he lived longer, Christopher Marlowe might well today pre-empt the place accorded by literary students to John Donne, as the first English poet whose imagination was stirred by the new discoveries. And I venture to suggest – since one may comfortably surmise about the dead – that the 'new Philosophy' would not have called all in doubt to Marlowe. Optimism rather than pessimism, exultation rather than despondency might have been the early note of the 'new astronomy' in England.[1]

Nicolson cites Caroline Spurgeon's observation that Marlowe's imagery is predominantly centred on 'the dazzling heights and vast spaces of the universe' and on 'the movements of meteors and planets'.[2] However, Nicolson laments the fact that Marlowe's universe remains thoroughly Ptolemaic and Aristotelian.[3]

It is not the case that Marlowe 'died too early' to know about the 'new astronomy'. Robert Recorde alluded to Copernicus' heliocentric model in his popular English astronomy text, the *Castle of Knowledge*, published in 1556, and Thomas Digges published a translation of part of the *De revolutionibus* in his *A Perfit Description of the Caelestiall Orbes* in 1576. There is evidence that educated Londoners in the 1580s and 1590s, people like Gabriel Harvey and Thomas Hariot with whom Marlowe was acquainted, knew about the Copernican model of the universe.[4] Critics have noted Marlowe's use of cutting-edge cartography in *Tamburlaine*, his most 'scientific' play.[5] But scholars have been less clear on what is new in his meteorology and astronomy.[6]

It is true that descriptions of the universe in *Tamburlaine* and in Marlowe's other plays are resolutely Ptolemaic. But an ability to imagine the universe in Copernican terms is not, in fact, a reliable criterion for determining whether or not the 'new astronomy' influenced the person doing the imagining. For one thing, the ability to picture a heliocentric universe lagged behind its acceptance in theory: in sixteenth-century England, knowledge of and even belief in the correctness of Copernicus' mathematical account of the movement of the heavenly bodies did not necessarily mean acceptance of his theory as a physical model of the universe. Those sixteenth-century English mathematicians who were in a position to understand the superiority of Copernicus' calculations – John Dee, Robert Recorde, Thomas Digges, Thomas Hariot, and others – struggled to come to terms with the fact that the appearance of the heavens as observed from earth supported the Ptolemaic model.[7]

In sixteenth-century England, 'the new science' first emerged through a set of issues that a group of mathematically and technologically educated Londoners explored and discussed in the last half of the century as they embraced new technologies and struggled to reconcile the tenets of Aristotelian natural philosophy with new theories and observations that called them into question. We can identify three areas of innovation and speculation that provide a context for the moral universe of Marlowe's *Tamburlaine*. First, as several scholars have noted, advances in cartography and the publication of maps that allowed people to visualise an expanding world gave Marlowe a sense of imaginative control over vast geographical spaces, which provides a setting for Tamburlaine's imperial ambitions and the basis for Marlowe's verbal technology for projecting an illusion of vast space on the platform stage.[8]

Second, English Protestants invested Aristotelian meteorology with a newly intensified naturalism, arguing that because divine intervention in nature no longer occurred, meteorological events like comets and earthquakes were to be read not as signs of God's moral approbation or disapprobation, but simply as natural events caused by atmospheric conditions. Marlowe's meteorological images in *Tamburlaine* reflect this new sense of a world abandoned by God to human devices and ambitions.[9]

Finally, new technologies for determining the distance and location of astronomical phenomena meant that the supernova of 1572 could, for the first time, be definitely identified as a new event taking place above the moon, a realm that was supposed to be immune to change and that therefore guaranteed the stability of the universe as a whole. While Part I of *Tamburlaine* confines Tamburlaine's projected power to the area of the heavens located below the moon, Part II uses images that repeatedly imagine Tamburlaine's power projected above the moon and able to threaten the stability of the highest reaches of the heavens. The play mirrors the ambivalence with which educated Londoners greeted new ideas about the universe: Marlowe, like many of his contemporaries, seems to have experienced both exultation and pessimism in response to those ideas.

Critics have long been aware that Marlowe made use of Abraham Ortelius' recently published world atlas, the *Theatrum orbis terrarum* (1570), as a source for the geography of Tamburlaine's empire.[10] John Gillies has argued that Ortelius' atlas was 'new in the sense of adding unknown continents' and also in the sense that it represented space in a way that was newly 'indifferent to religious symbolism' (38). The atlas inspired Marlowe to express his 'hero's ambition and potency' in terms of 'an imagery of sheer geographic extent' (37). Henry Turner argues that Marlowe was also inspired by maps fundamentally to reimagine and expand the resources of the platform stage, using 'geometrical projection as a kind of poetic projection that is somehow necessary to stage performance'.[11]

If Ortelius' maps helped Marlowe give imaginative shape to Tamburlaine's imperial ambitions and also inspired a technology for realising his own ambitions for the Elizabethan stage, contemporary meteorological writing helped him create a three-dimensional space for Tamburlaine's ambition, making it possible to imagine an upward trajectory linked by the four Aristotelian elements and uninhibited by the kind of moral judgements previously thought to be expressed by God through the natural world.[12] In *1 Tamburlaine*, I.ii.48–51, Tamburlaine boasts to Zenocrate that his army will be 'so great an host, / As with their weight shall make the mountains quake, / Even as when windy exhalations, / Fighting for passage tilt within the earth'.[13] Aristotelian meteorology was based on the idea that many atmospheric phenomena were caused by dry 'exhalations' given off by earth, or moist 'vapours' given off by water that rose up (pulled by the heat of the sun) through the three regions of the air (a warm layer close to the earth, a cold layer in the middle, and a hot layer close to the sphere of fire).[14] If a cloud of water vapour was pulled up into the cold middle region, it was condensed into snow, hail, or rain. If dry exhalations were pulled up into the highest region and set on fire, they would fall back down towards earth as flaming comets. Dry exhalations trapped within the hollows of the earth caused earthquakes as they tried to escape.[15]

In classical antiquity, unusual meteorological events such as comets and earthquakes were believed to foretell disasters of various kinds. Christian writers adapted this idea to claim that comets and earthquakes represented a warning from God about impending events. In sixteenth-century England, however, Protestant belief that God's miraculous interventions in nature had ceased meant that writers increasingly cast doubt on the supernatural interpretation of 'meteors' (comets, rain, earthquakes, lightning were all called 'meteors'). Leonard Digges, writing in his *Prognostication Everlasting* (1556), repeats the belief that earthquakes foretell wars but casts some doubt by citing this belief in Latin: 'Plentie of winds, succed into holes, cones, or caves of the earth, which absent from above the earth causeth quietnesse: the violent brusting out of them (the earth closed againe) is the Earthquake: *signum est futurorum bellorum* [it is a sign of future wars].'[16] Gabriel Harvey in his letter about an earthquake felt in London in April of 1580 takes a middle view, explaining that the material cause of an earthquake is 'stoare of grosse and drye vapours' trapped in the earth, but the efficient cause is 'God himselfe'.[17] Therefore, the final cause could either be 'that the wynde shoulde recover his Naturall place' or else 'to testifie and denounce the secrete wrathe and indignation of God'.[18]

William Fulke, whose meteorological treatise *A Goodly Gallery* (London, 1563) has been called 'the only properly scientific discussion of the subject in English in the sixteenth century', presents a strongly Protestant guide to meteorological events.[19] His account of earthquakes is entirely naturalistic, listing a number of atmospheric conditions that are 'signes and tokens' that an earthquake is about to occur, but making no claims that earthquakes are signs of future wars.[20] His discussion of comets does take up their traditional 'significations', and he argues that the 'civile or politike effects' (fos. 15v–16r) result from natural causes: 'many whote and drie Exhalations; in the aire, which in drie men kindle heat, whereby they ar provoked to anger, of anger cometh brawling, of brawling fighting and war, of warre victory, and of victory chaunge of Commonwelths' (fo. 16r–v).

We can now see the audacity of Tamburlaine's claim that the weight of his vast army will cause earthquakes. Rather than supporting the older view that earthquakes are supernatural events representing a warning from God that wars or other disruptions are about to occur, Tamburlaine claims that his army itself is heavy enough to shake the earth. He eschews a supernatural interpretation: he, not God, has the power to shake the earth, and he is able to do so without employing the traditional mechanism of trapped exhalations.

Tamburlaine and the other characters in the play frequently use meteorological metaphors and analogies to measure and explain human ambition, and other characters refer to Tamburlaine himself in these terms as well. Tamburlaine's famous assertion that 'Nature that fram'd us of foure Elements, / Warring within our breasts for regiment, / Doth teach us all to have aspyring minds' (*1 Tamb.*, II.vii.18–20) is, as Gillies has argued, an unorthodox claim in terms of Galenic medicine, where a state of health demanded that the humours be in balance.[21] In meteorological terms, however, the four elements (which corresponded to the four humours) did vie with each other, and both air and fire did 'aspire' to rise above heavier earth and water. Theridamas constrasts Cosroe with Tamburlaine in elemental terms: 'For he [Cosroe] is grosse and like the massie earth, / That mooves not upwards, nor by princely deeds / Doth mean to soare above the highest sort' (II.vii.31–3). Tamburlaine's warring elements create a kind of internal earthquake, as his airy spirits attempt to break free from his grosser parts.

In an extended passage in *2 Tamburlaine*, Tamburlaine provides his own reworking of the premonitory power of meteors, replacing supernatural causation with his own agency. His burning of the town where Zenocrate has died will send flames 'to the highest regions of the aire, / And kindle heaps of exhalations, / That being fiery meteors, may presage, / Death and destruction to th' inhabitants!' (III.ii.2–5). He imagines the destruction of the town as the direct cause of meteors, which in turn stand as signs of the destruction that caused them. He also predicts that his triumph over the town will cause:

> a blazing star,
> That may endure till heaven be dissolv'd,
> Fed with the fresh supply of earthly dregs,
> Threatening a dearth and famine to this land,
> Flieng Dragons, lightning, fearfull thunderclaps,
> Sindge these fair plaines.
> (III.ii.6–11)

Here, the exhalations sent up by his destructive activities will create a range of meteorological effects that will themselves damage his enemies' lands. There are hints, unique to Part II, that these effects extend beyond the atmosphere, creating a 'blazing star' and predicting the eventual dissolution of the heavens.

In sixteenth-century England, the idea that the realm of the fixed stars could be subject to change was more shocking and destabilising than the new Copernican model of the universe had been. Previously, new stars that appeared were identified as comets, which, as we have seen, were thought to be atmospheric phenomena formed in the area below the moon, which was subject to change. In 1572, however, various observers, including the English mathematician Thomas Digges, were able to determine that the new star had no visible parallax and therefore must be located far above the moon.[22] The unchanging nature of the fixed stars had provided a limit to the change and mortality that plagued human existence. Robert Recorde, in his *Castle of Knowledge* (1556), emphasised that the fixed stars 'waxe not werye with labour, nother growe olde by continuance, but are as freshe in beutye and shape, as the firste daye of their creation' because they 'utterly stande cleere from all corruption of time'.[23] John Dee, writing in 1568 just before the appearance of the new star, affirmed the importance to the whole cosmos of a heavenly realm immune to change: 'That the mutual spaces among the fixed stars have never been altered in the whole eternity of time shows that the stars are very much superior even to those things in the elemental universe that strongly retain an unvarying condition in their situations.' He goes on to say that 'if this were not so [if the fixed stars were not immutable], no particle would be preserved naturally even for a single day'.[24]

Contemporaries reacted in different ways to the news that the new star rocked the foundations of the universe. Thomas Digges believed that it was a miracle, analogous to the star created by God to herald the birth of Christ. Others, like Francis Shakelton, writing in *A blazing Starre* (1580), after acknowledging the natural causes of most comets and meteors, cited Digges to argue that the star had been sent by God to 'stirre up all the sorte of us (beeyng moste wretched and miserable sinners) to be mindfull of the Judgment daie', a final miracle heralding the end of the world.[25] In Part 1, however, Tamburlaine's aspirations are bounded by the limits of the Aristotelian cosmos: they do not ascend by natural means above the lunar sphere. He describes aspiration to Theridamas in entirely orthodox terms: they will be united 'untill our bodies turn to Elements: / And both our soules aspire celestiall thrones' (I.ii.236–7). In this same scene Tamburlaine suggests that the heavenly spheres are stable and unchanging : 'Sooner shall the Sun fall from his Sphere, / Than *Tamburlaine* be slaine or overcome' (I.ii.176–7).

Only once in Part 1 does Tamburlaine seem to claim that he can project his transformative ambitions into the realm of the fixed stars, but his claim turns out to be based on an optical illusion: 'And with our Sun-bright armour as we march, / Weel chase the Stars from heaven, and dim their eies / That stand and muse at our admyred armes' (II.iii.22–4). Although it will appear as if the stars have been dislodged, this illusion is caused by the dazzling brilliance of sunlight reflected in the armour of his forces. Tamburlaine here hints at a cosmological crisis that occurred in 1572, when a new star suddenly appeared in the constellation Cassiopeia and slowly faded from view, shattering the belief that change could not occur above the moon and, as a result, threatening the stability of the universe.

For Marlowe, the removal of the lunar limit to change and mortality provides a setting for Tamburlaine's more extreme claims in Part II. In Part I, as we have seen, Tamburlaine aligns his extended power with geographical expansion across the surface of the earth and up into the atmosphere below the moon. In Part II, however, after the death of Zenocrate, he transgresses the lunar boundary, repeatedly imagining himself as able to change, or destroy, the realm of the fixed stars. These imaginings signal the excessive and destructive nature of Tamburlaine's aspirations, and it is this imagery, perhaps more than his burning of the Koran, that suggests he may have gone too far. Immediately after Zenocrate dies, Tamburlaine claims that in his grief he will:

> Raise Cavelieros higher than the cloudes,
> And with the cannon breake the frame of heaven,
> Batter the shining pallace of the Sun,
> And shiver all the starry firmament:
> For amorous *Jove* hath snatcht my love from hence.
>   (II.iv.103–7)

There is blasphemy here, of course, in his attack on Jove. But Tamburlaine spends three lines describing his assault on the 'frame of heaven', 'palace of the sun', and 'starry firmament', all of which were newly vulnerable after 1572.

Part II contains many such imagined transgressions of the heavens: Tamburlaine will 'with the flames that beat against the clowdes / Incense the heavens, and make the starres to melt' (IV.i.195). He has the power to extend meteorological phenomena up into the heavens, making 'meteors, that like armed men / Are seene to march upon the towers of heaven, / Run tilting round about the firmament, / And breake their burning Lances in the aire' (IV.i.203–6). As he dies, using a map to lament the geographic areas that he will never conquer, Tamburlaine leaves his sons with a warning that echoes the ambivalence of his imagined transgressions of the highest heavens. He urges them to 'be warned' by the example of Phaethon, whose attempt to drive the chariot of the sun was ended by Jupiter. His warning is not that they avoid a similar transgression but rather that they take care to guide the chariot as strongly and as competently as their father.

In subsequent plays Marlowe observes the lunar boundary, turning his attention to other forms of transgression. Faustus' dragon chariot allows him to see but not to visit the highest reaches of the heavens. Faustus questions Mephistopheles about the upper reaches of the heavens but receives only conventional Ptolemaic cosmology in response, knowledge that Faustus deems inadequate: 'Tush! These slender trifles Wagner can decide.'[26] In *Tamburlaine*, however, Marlowe's imagination was clearly imbued with the cosmological controversies of his day, and they contribute to his exhilarating but uneasy exploration of a universe that was newly devoid of traditional judgements and limits. In the two *Tamburlaine* plays, Marlowe represents transgression in spatial terms, linking his own newly ambitious projection of vastness onto the space of the platform stage with his protagonist's dangerous projection of power above the moon.

Notes

1 Marjorie Hope Nicolson, *Science and Imagination* (Ithaca, NY: Cornell University Press, 1962 [1956]), 41–2. Nicolson 'pioneered new scholarly approaches to the study of literature and science' and was the first woman to become a full professor at an Ivy League university when she was hired at Columbia in 1941. See http://250.columbia.edu/c250_celebrates_remarkable_ columbian/marjorie_hope_nicolson.html.
2 Caroline Spurgeon, *Shakespeare's Imagery and What It Tells Us* (Cambridge University Press, 1935), 13.
3 The Ptolemaic cosmology inherited from classical antiquity was based on the idea that the earth was located unmoving at the centre of the universe surrounded by rotating concentric spheres, to which the sun, moon, and planets were attached. A final fixed sphere contained the stars. Aristotle established the basic form of this system, which was elaborated by Claudius Ptolemaeus in the second century CE.
4 Gabriel Harvey mentions Copernicus several times in his marginalia, for which see Virginia F. Stern, *Gabriel Harvey: His Life, Marginalia, and Library* (Oxford: Clarendon, 1979), 166–7. The evidence for Hariot's Copernicanism comes chiefly from a reference to it in a letter to Hariot from his friend Sir William Lowrer; see Matthias Schemmel, *The English Galileo: Thomas Harriot's Work on Motion as an Example of Preclassical Mechanics*, 2 vols. (London: Springer, 2008), Vol. I, 20–1.
5 John Gillies, 'Tamburlaine and Renaissance Geography', in *Early Modern English Drama: A Critical Companion*, ed. Garrett Sullivan, Patrick Cheney, and Andrew Hadfield (New York: Oxford University Press, 2006).
6 *Ibid.*, 39–41, argues that 'subversive force is wrung from the old cosmology by a relentless focus on its creaking joins', noting the 'restless' spheres but not the new naturalistic meteorology or supralunar change. David Riggs, *The World of Christopher Marlowe* (New York: Henry Holt, 2004), 166–9 argues that 'Copernican astronomy had raised the Ptolemaic system to new heights'

by suggesting that man was capable of mathematically comprehending the universe. Riggs is mistaken, however, in arguing that Marlowe derived an Epicurean physics from his reading of Ovid's *Metamorphoses* (88–9).
7 See Francis Johnson, *Astronomical Thought in Renaissance England* (New York: Octagon Books, 1968 [1937]), 94–6.
8 See Gillies, 'Tamburlaine and Renaissance Geography'; and also Henry S. Turner, *The English Renaissance Stage: Geometry, Poetics, and the Practical Spatial Arts, 1580–1630* (Oxford University Press, 2006), 6.
9 Craig Martin, *Renaissance Meteorology: Pomponazzi to Descartes* (Baltimore: Johns Hopkins University Press, 2011), argues that early modern meteorological works represented a branch of Aristotelian natural philosophy that was in some ways compatible with the new science because meteorologies were 'open inquiries, which attempted to construct theories that corresponded to sensible evidence, observations, ancient texts, religious doctrines, and experiments' (154).
10 This connection was first made by Ethel Seaton, 'Marlowe's Map', *Essays and Studies by Members of the English Association* 10 (1924): 13–35. For an exploration of these maps for Marlowe's implication in imperialism, see Gillies, 'Tamburlaine and Renaissance Geography'.
11 Turner, *The English Renaissance Stage*, 6. Turner is talking primarily about Dekker but mentions Marlowe in this context.
12 Gillies notes that Tamburlaine's ambition 'unfolds in two dimensions – a geographic dimension and a cosmic dimension' ('Tamburlaine and Renaissance Geography', 37) but misses the role of the new meteorology and the supernova of 1572 in creating new possibilities for cosmic expansion.
13 Christopher Marlowe, *Tamburlaine the Great*, in *The Complete Works of Christopher Marlowe*, 5 vols., ed. Roma Gill, David Fuller, and Edward J. Esche, Vol. v (Oxford: Clarendon Press, 1998). All quotations from *Tamburlaine* are taken from this edition.
14 S. K. Heninger, *A Handbook of Renaissance Meteorology* (Durham, NC: Duke University Press, 1960), 45–61.
15 *Ibid.*, 128–34.
16 Leonard Digges, *Prognostication Everlasting* (London, 1556), fo. 13v.
17 Gabriel Harvey, *The Works of Gabriel Harvey*, 3 vols., ed. Alexander Grosart, Vol. I (New York: AMS, 1969 [1884]), 52.
18 *Ibid.*, 53.
19 On Fulke, see Heninger, *Handbook*, 20–2; and also Richard Bauckham, 'Science and Religion in the Writings of Dr William Fulke', *The British Journal for the History of Science* 8 (1975): 17–31 (28).
20 William Fulke, *A Goodly Gallerye ... to behold the natural causes of all kynde of Meteors ...* (London, 1563), fos. 22–3.
21 Gillies, 'Tamburlaine and Renaissance Geography', 40, who notes that warring elements would suggest 'illness' rather than 'an aspiring mind'.
22 Johnson, *Astronomical Thought*, 154–6. 'Parallax' is the apparent difference in location of an object when it is viewed from two different locations, and it is

measured by the angle of inclination between the two lines of sight. Closer objects have a larger parallax than more distant ones. In 1572 parallax could be measured for the moon, but not for stars. Digges determined that the new star had no visible parallax and therefore could not be located below the moon.
23 Robert Recorde, *Castle of Knowledge* (London, 1556), sigs. A4r, A5r.
24 John Dee, *Propaedeumata aphoristica*, ed. and trans. J. L. Heilbron and Wayne Shumaker (Berkeley: University of California Press, 1978), 162–3. 'Nullum, ne uno quidem die (naturaliter) praeservaretur Individuum.'
25 Francis Shakelton, *A blazing Starre* (London, 1580), sig. Biv.
26 Christopher Marlowe, *Doctor Faustus*, II.iii.676 (A-text), in *Doctor Faustus with the English Faust Book*, ed. David Wootton (Indianapolis: Hackett, 2005).

CHAPTER TWENTY FOUR

The professional theatre and Marlowe

Tom Rutter

In a pamphlet of 1590 called *Francesco's Fortunes*, Robert Greene has his narrator digress into a discussion 'of Playes, Playmakers and Players' in which he explains how the high esteem accorded actors in ancient Rome led them to become both covetous and proud. He writes that the actor Roscius was once arrogant enough to compare himself with Cicero when the two met at a dinner, 'which insolencie made the learned Orator to growe into these termes; why *Roscius*, art thou proud with *Esops* Crow, being pranct with the glorie of others feathers? of thy selfe thou canst say nothing, and if the Cobler hath taught thee to say, *Aue Cesar*, disdain not thy tutor, because thou pratest in a Kings chamber'.[1] Roscius is firmly put in his place: whatever acclaim he may have received, he is the human equivalent of a talking bird who can only repeat the lines others have given him.

This anecdote can be read as expressing some of the frustrations inherent in Greene's own position as a Cambridge graduate with literary ambitions, writing plays for actors who seem to reap the greater rewards – a situation discussed more explicitly in *Greene's Groatsworth of Wit, Bought with a Million of Repentance* (a pamphlet of uncertain authorship that claimed to be Greene's deathbed confession).[2] In his survey of the later Elizabethan drama, G. K. Hunter aligns Greene with other university-educated playwrights like Thomas Lodge, Christopher Marlowe, Thomas Nashe, and George Peele, explaining that 'mastery of Latin, the language of learning, had given these graduates the sense of having joined a European élite of power and privilege.' However, 'in the real world of power in Elizabethan England there was no social scope for such assumptions', and, instead of being able to turn their literary talents to public service or the more prestigious poetic genres, they were obliged to make money through writing plays and pamphlets.[3] For Hunter, Greene's expressions of resentment stem from the experience of escaping one's hereditary social class through education only to find oneself financially dependent on one's social and educational inferiors: players and their public.

Like Greene, Marlowe was a tradesman's son whose time at Cambridge may have inculcated values and expectations at odds with the realities of the literary marketplace; did he share the attitude towards the professional theatre suggested by Greene's comments? If so, it could explain the 'ambivalence toward ... drama' that Sara Munson Deats, for example, finds in *Doctor Faustus*, a play whose awareness of the power of spectacle to seduce and to distract is exemplified by the 'show' of devils 'giving crowns and rich apparel to Faustus' in order 'to delight his mind' and by the pageant of the Seven Deadly Sins that Lucifer offers Faustus as a 'pastime' after his short-lived attempt at repentance.[4] Unlike Greene or Nashe, however, Marlowe left no explicit comments on the professional drama of his time, and to read his plays in search of evidence one way or the other would be to risk circularity of reasoning. The current chapter will approach the question of Marlowe's relationship with the Elizabethan stage in a different way: by setting out some of its institutional practices and by discussing how successfully he worked within them.

Relationships with acting companies

The title page of *Tamburlaine the Great* (1590) – see Figure 6 – advertises that the play's two parts 'were sundrie times shewed vpon Stages in the Citie of London ... By the right honorable the Lord Admyrall, his seruantes',[5] and the records of the theatre owner and manager Philip Henslowe indicate that after the playwright's death the Admiral's Men would also regularly perform *The Jew of Malta*, *The Massacre at Paris*, and *Doctor Faustus*. The impression these facts might give, however, of an exclusive working relationship between Marlowe and a single company is somewhat misleading. Marlowe wrote at least two plays for other acting companies: the title pages of *Dido, Queen of Carthage* and *Edward II* ascribe them to the Children of the Queen's Chapel and to the Earl of Pembroke's Men respectively. Furthermore, the early performance history of *Doctor Faustus* is uncertain, while Henslowe refers to performances of *The Jew of Malta* by Lord Strange's Men, the Earl of Sussex's Men, and 'the Quenes men & my lord of Susexe to geather' before even mentioning the Admiral's Men.[6] Whoever Marlowe wrote the latter play for, its fortunes between 1591 and 1594 seem to have been bound up with a specific theatre – Henslowe's Rose – rather than with a particular company; or perhaps with the actor Edward Alleyn, who was an Admiral's Man in the late 1580s

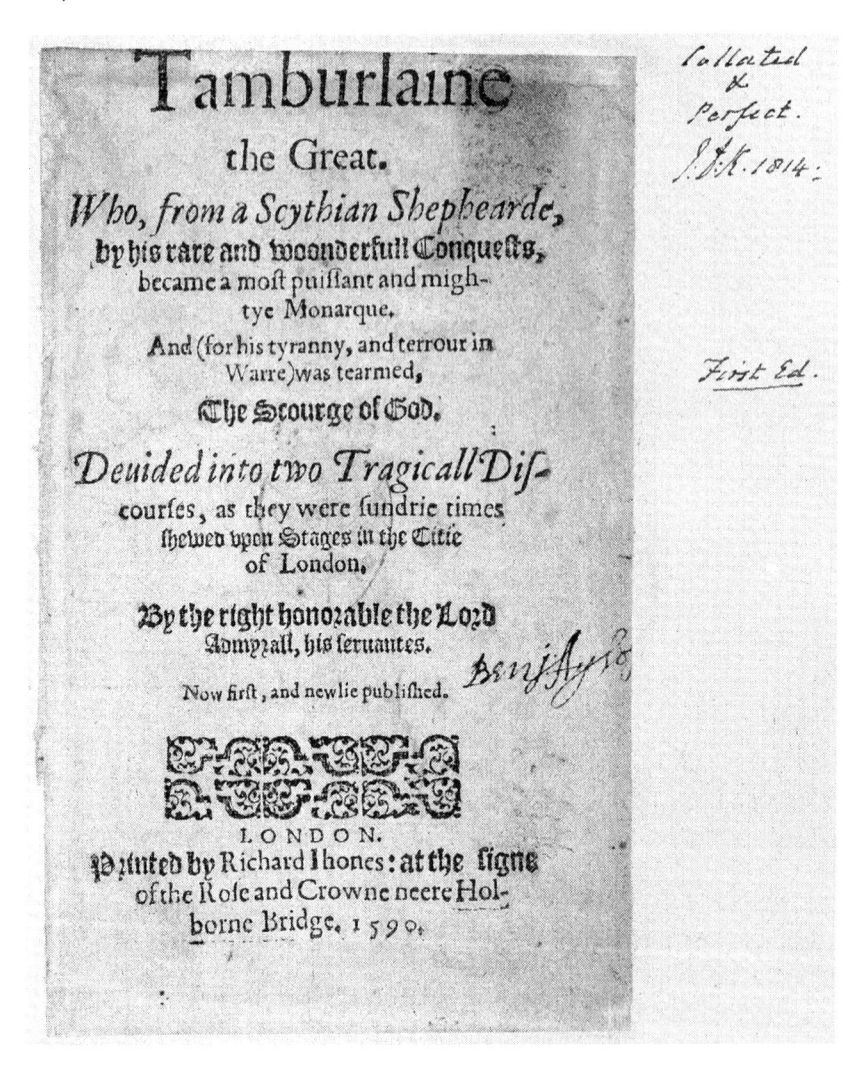

Figure 6   Marlowe's *Tamburlaine* (1590), title page

before working with Lord Strange's Men only to rejoin the Admiral's in 1594.

Marlowe's relationship with the actors who performed his plays was thus very different from the one that Shakespeare would go on to enjoy with the Lord Chamberlain's Men from 1594 onwards. As an actor and a sharer in the company, Shakespeare presumably had the opportunity to influence the manner in which a play he had written might be cast, revised, and performed. As a mere playwright, Marlowe had no control over any of these things. It may be worth noting that for all his plays' interest in dramatic spectacle, the concern with practices like rehearsal and touring that we see in *A Midsummer Night's Dream* or *The Taming of the Shrew* is entirely absent from them. Shakespeare uses the word 'cue', whether literally in a dramatic context or figuratively, in *Richard III*, *A Midsummer Night's Dream*, *Much Ado about Nothing*, *The Merry Wives of Windsor*, *Henry V*, *Hamlet*, *King Lear*, *Othello*, and *The Two Noble Kinsmen*. That the word appears in none of Marlowe's plays, however, suggests a lesser degree of interest in the actual work involved in performance.

We do not know exactly what financial arrangements existed between Marlowe and the companies for which he wrote. A letter from the playwright Thomas Kyd to Lord Keeper Sir John Puckering, following Kyd's imprisonment, suggests that (as seems to have been the case with other dramatists) Marlowe's professional relationship was with the players themselves, not with their aristocratic patron: Kyd says that Marlowe had claimed to be in the service of the same Lord, presumably Lord Strange, as himself, but that 'his L[ordshi]p never knewe his service, but in writing for his plaiers, ffor never cold my L[ord] endure his name or sight, when he had heard of his conditions'.[7] As to the terms of that relationship, we have to draw upon records of dealings between the Admiral's Men and other playwrights half a decade after Marlowe's death. It seems that by the late 1590s, a playwright might expect to be paid between £5 and £6 for a single play: Anthony Munday was paid £5 for the first part of *Robin Hood* on 15 February 1597–8, for example.[8] As G. E. Bentley notes, this compares favourably with the £10 per annum that a university graduate might earn as a schoolmaster or a curate.[9]

Matters were rarely that simple, however. For one thing, as I will discuss in more detail later, it was extremely common for dramatists to collaborate on a play: although Henslowe again paid a total of £5 (on the Admiral's Men's behalf) for the second part of *Robin Hood*, part of this money went to Munday and part to his co-writer Henry Chettle. If the going rate was similar in Marlowe's lifetime, then Marlowe would presumably have received less than £5 for any plays of which he was not sole author. A second complication has to do with the timing of payment. Dramatists did sometimes sell a finished product to the players: in a letter of 8 November 1599, the Admiral's Man Robert Shaa wrote to Henslowe of unnamed dramatists, 'Mr Henshlowe we haue heard their booke and lyke yt their pryce is eight pound[es].' However, they were more frequently lent money on the basis of work in progress, as Munday was lent 5s on 28 February 1597–8 'in p̱te of paymente of th*e* second p̱te of Roben Hoode'. On 3 December 1597, Ben Jonson was lent 20s 'vpon a boocke wch he showed the plotte vnto th*e* company', that is, on the basis of a play outline that the company approved. There was thus scope for the eventual form of a play to reflect the input of the actors for whom it was being written.[10]

Even leaving aside the gap of up to a decade between these records and Marlowe's writing career, however, it is difficult to be sure how far they reflect his own dealings with playing companies. Bentley, in *The Profession of Dramatist in Shakespeare's Time*, seems unsure how to place Marlowe: Marlowe is obviously not one of the 'amateurs' like Lodowick Carlell or Fulke Greville, occasional dramatists who did not write for profit, but nor is he included among the '22 writers who wrote or collaborated in a dozen or more plays for the commercial theatres in the period 1590–1642, who were clearly being paid for their literary efforts, who in a general sense may be considered more or less professional'.[11] Marlowe is presumably excluded on the grounds that death curtailed his productivity, but even so, on the basis of his surviving plays, which average one a year for the period 1587–93, it is a stretch to describe him as a 'professional dramatist'. Even if he worked on plays that have since been lost or misattributed, he seems to have sought income through other channels, including literary patronage, as is implied by his dedication of Thomas Watson's *Amintae gaudia* to the Countess of Pembroke, not to mention whatever he was up to when he was arrested for coining in Flushing in early 1592. It is possible, then, that (for example) Marlowe offered the first part of *Tamburlaine* to the Admiral's Men as a finished play that they might or might not choose to purchase, rather than Marlowe approaching them with a proposal. The sequel, however, seems to have been commissioned in response to the success of the first play: the Prologue asserts that 'the generall welcomes Tamburlain receiu'd, / When he arriued last vpon our stage, / Hath made our Poet pen his second part'.[12] In doing so Marlowe either set a trend or followed an existing one: 'By 1592 multi-part plays were an established feature of the Elizabethan repertory', as Roslyn Knutson shows.[13]

Acting companies and dramatic form

The available evidence suggests that Marlowe had neither the long-term attachment to a single company that Shakespeare would experience nor the sustained productivity of an Anthony Munday (who would be named by Henslowe in conjunction with fourteen plays in the space of five years).[14] Examination of Marlowe's plays, however, should banish any sense of their author as out of touch with the realities of dramatic production. As well as being epic in its chronological and topographical sweep, the first part of *Tamburlaine* has a cast of well over two dozen; yet, as David Bevington pointed out decades ago, the play accommodates itself to the limited personnel of the Admiral's Men through a dramatic structure that maximises the potential for doubling. While important roles such as those of Tamburlaine, his generals, and Zenocrate persist through the play, its episodic nature, whereby Tamburlaine encounters a series of antagonists (Mycetes, Cosroe, Bajazeth), means that actors playing the parts of defeated adversaries and their followers can reappear later in other roles. The first part of *Tamburlaine* can therefore be performed with, say, eleven men and four boy actors and would have readily suited the size of the Admiral's Men, which (on the basis of other theatrical documents) Bevington estimates at 'eight or ten regular players, some hired assistants and extras, and perhaps four boys'.[15]

This 'progressive suppression of character', whereby 'with each new incident in the life of his hero Marlowe suppresses one group of supporting roles in order to introduce another', informs the overall shape of each of *Tamburlaine*'s two parts.[16] However, Marlowe can be seen to use similar techniques at the level of individual scenes. For example, the long second scene of *The Jew of Malta* includes at least nineteen roles, but its structure allows some of these to be doubled. The first part of the scene is an encounter between Fernese, Governor of Malta, and Calymath, son of the Turkish emperor, along with their entourages. The Turks then leave, to be replaced by Barabas and three Jews. After Barabas has been deprived of his estate, the Maltese authorities leave, and Barabas bemoans his situation to his fellow Jews before being left alone. This gradual emptying of the stage enables some of the other actors to change and reappear in new roles for the latter part of the scene, which features Abigail, the friars, the nuns, Mathias, and Lodowick. The nineteen roles can thus easily be played by twelve actors.

Despite Marlowe's coming to the theatre from the university rather than being, like Shakespeare, an actor-turned-dramatist, his approach to role-distribution, entrances, and exits in *The Jew of Malta*, as in *Tamburlaine*, shows him to be (to use David Bradley's phrase) a 'prescient author' attuned to the needs of professional actors, rather than a naïve postgraduate whose scripts would have needed revision to make them stageable.[17]

Collaboration

In his introduction to *The Cambridge Companion to Christopher Marlowe*, Patrick Cheney stresses the 'absolute inaugural power' that, even in the early seventeenth century, other writers attributed to Marlowe, 'the best of Poets in that age', as Heywood would call him in his 'Prologue to the Stage' to *The Jew of Malta*.[18] Cheney is surely right both to emphasise the sublime qualities of the authorial genius evoked by, for example, Michael Drayton, who wrote that Marlowe 'had in him those brave translunary things, / That the first Poets had, his raptures were, / All Ayre, and fire' and, more recently, to protest at Marlowe's relegation from 'the received narrative of modern English "authorship"'. It needs to be emphasised, however, that this genius repeatedly expressed itself in collaboration – not just in the sense Cheney mentions, whereby early modern drama in general was 'the product of a complex cultural collaboration between authors, scribes, printers, actors, businessmen, and other social agents', but in the more basic sense that Marlowe was not the sole author of some of his plays.[19]

The most obvious instance is *Dido, Queen of Carthage*, whose title page attributes it to Marlowe and Thomas Nashe. While, as Martin Wiggins shows in an article on the play, various critics and editors have tried to minimise Nashe's contribution, the basis for doing so is flimsy: 'on the available evidence, the question editors should now be posing is not whether, but what, Nashe contributed to *Dido*'.[20] Both texts of *Doctor Faustus*, too, are generally held to be of multiple authorship. Eric Rasmussen finds evidence in the inconsistencies between some of the scenes, such as the discrepancy between the third scene of the A-text (where Mephistopheles insists that he came to Faustus of his own accord, not because of Faustus' conjuring) and the ninth (where the same character complains at being compelled to come from Constantinople at Robin's words). Rasmussen also argues that function-word tests divide authorship between Marlowe and a collaborator who was responsible for, broadly speaking, the comic scenes (those in the A-text featuring Wagner, Robin, Rafe, the pope, the emperor, the horse-courser, and the Duke and Duchess of Vanholt).[21]

Finally, in his epistle at the start of *Tamburlaine*, the printer Richard Jones writes that he has '(purposely) omitted and left out some fond and friuolous Iestures, digressing (and in my poore opinion) far vnmeet for the matter'.[22] It is conceivable that these omitted sections were written by Marlowe, but that attribution raises the question of why Jones would open a printed text by disparaging the author. It seems likelier that these lost parts of the play were written by another hand – either a fellow dramatist, as with *Faustus*, or one of the actors (as with the play *A Knack to Know a Knave*, whose title page advertised the inclusion of the clown Will Kemp's 'applauded Merrimentes of the men of Goteham').[23]

Marlowe was not unusual in writing at least some of his plays collaboratively: nearly two-thirds of the plays referred to in Henslowe's *Diary* were the work of more than one dramatist.[24] Furthermore, he can be deemed to have used the practice of collaboration to good effect in both commercial and aesthetic terms. It evidently resulted in plays that were popular with audiences: Jones' preface to *Tamburlaine*, as well as boasting that the two plays were 'delightfull for many of you to see, when the same were shewed in London vpon stages', acknowledges that the omitted material was by 'some vaine conceited fondlings greatly gaped at'.[25] As for the artistic success of Marlowe's collaborations, while the comic scenes of *Doctor Faustus* have tended to be less appreciated by critics than Faustus' tragic speeches and exchanges with Mephistopheles, the two dimensions of the play can be said to interact in a way that produces a satisfying whole. Rather than being mere light relief, Robin's conjuring can make us reassess the motives and meaning of Faustus' own use of magic, while (as Alan Dessen points out) the point of the horse-courser scene 'lies in a fairly obvious analogy: both the horse-courser and Faustus have made a bargain ... that seemed like a good idea at the time but has a catch ... that leads to an unfortunate conclusion'.[26]

While Marlowe cannot have envisaged it, the relationship between tragic and comic scenes in *Doctor Faustus* may also have facilitated the 'adicyones' to the play for which William Bird and Samuel Rowley were paid £4 in 1602, and which are usually taken to be reflected – albeit not straightforwardly – in the previously unpublished sections that appear in the 1616 B-text of the play.[27] The sequence of comic episodes that separate Faustus' pact with the devil from its terrible culmination can readily be added to without destroying the overall shape of the play, and the result is probably what we see in the B-text, with its extra Rome scenes, expanded Benvolio plot, and so on. The play's episodic structure both reflects its collaborative origins and leaves it open to revision, a widespread practice: as Bentley points out, available evidence suggests that 'if a play had sufficient theatrical appeal to be kept in the repertory ... it was normal for the text to be revised for at least one of its revivals'.[28]

Conclusion

In an essay of 2010, Holger Schott Syme asks 'what it might have meant for a play, a playing company, or even a stationer to be successful in 1594', and he goes on to challenge the assumption that Marlowe's plays enjoyed 'dominance or lasting central importance' in the repertory of the Admiral's Men. His plays may have 'generally performed well' and made a satisfying amount of money, but not to an extraordinary degree: after being staged frequently and lucratively in the company's first season at the Rose (1594), they declined both in their prominence in the repertory and in the returns they produced.[29]

One response to Syme might be to emphasise the longevity of Marlowe's plays on the Elizabethan stage: the success of *1 Tamburlaine* in 1594 is all the more remarkable when one remembers that it was seven years old by this time. For the current chapter, though, his insight that Marlowe's plays 'were entirely ordinary and played more or less the same role as other tried and tested items in the repertory' is surely apposite.[30] Irrespective of their artistic or historical significance, they were commercially successful precisely because they fitted so well within the structures of Elizabethan professional drama. Marlowe's career shows him to have been willing to repeat a commercially successful formula (with the sequel to *Tamburlaine*), to engage in collaboration with others, and to write in a way that recognised the practical limitations that faced acting companies. His plays were staged following commercial transactions that made them the property of the acting company, open to subsequent revision and augmentation. In *Greene's Groatsworth of Wit*, it is precisely for their willingness to be 'subiect to the pleasure of such rude groomes' – the actors – that 'Greene' takes Marlowe and other playwrights to task. Lacking any statement from Marlowe to the contrary, it seems legitimate to view him in the terms that are applied to him in that pamphlet: not as resentful or disdainful of actors, but as a 'famous gracer of Tragedians'.[31]

Notes

1 Robert Greene, *Francescos Fortunes; or, The Second Part of Greenes Neuer Too Late* (London, 1590), sigs. B4v–C1r.
2 Robert Greene [?], *Greenes, Groats-vvorth of Witte, Bought with a Million of Repentance* (London, 1592), sigs. D4v–E1r.
3 G. K. Hunter, *English Drama 1586–1642: The Age of Shakespeare*, Oxford History of English Literature (Oxford: Clarendon Press, 1997), 25.

4 Sara Munson Deats, '"Mark this show": Magic and Theater in Marlowe's *Doctor Faustus*', in *Placing the Plays of Christopher Marlowe: Fresh Cultural Contexts*, ed. Sara Munson Deats and Robert A. Logan (Aldershot: Ashgate, 2008), 13–24 (13); Christopher Marlowe, *Doctor Faustus: A- and B-Texts (1604, 1616)*, ed. David Bevington and Eric Rasmussen (Manchester University Press, 1993), A-text, II.i.82–3, II.iii.100.
5 Christopher Marlowe, *Tamburlaine the Great* (London, 1590), A1r.
6 Philip Henslowe, *Henslowe's Diary*, ed. R. A. Foakes, 2nd edn (Cambridge University Press, 2002), 16–21.
7 Thomas Kyd, *The Works of Thomas Kyd*, ed. F. S. Boas, 2nd edn (Oxford: Clarendon Press, 1955), cix.
8 Henslowe, *Diary*, 86.
9 G. E. Bentley, *The Profession of Dramatist in Shakespeare's Time 1590–1642* (Princeton University Press, 1971), 96.
10 Henslowe, *Diary*, 85–7, 288.
11 Bentley, *The Profession of Dramatist*, 17–26.
12 Marlowe, *Tamburlaine*, F3r.
13 Roslyn Lander Knutson, *The Repertory of Shakespeare's Company 1594–1613* (Fayetteville: University of Arkansas Press, 1991), 50.
14 Henslowe, *Diary*, 74–206.
15 David M. Bevington, *From 'Mankind' to Marlowe: Growth of Structure in the Popular Drama of Tudor England* (Cambridge, MA: Harvard University Press, 1968), 205, 202.
16 *Ibid.*, 131, 203.
17 David Bradley, *From Text to Performance in the Elizabethan Theatre: Preparing the Play for the Stage* (Cambridge University Press, 1991), 38.
18 Patrick Cheney, 'Introduction: Marlowe in the Twenty-First Century', in *The Cambridge Companion to Christopher Marlowe*, ed. Patrick Cheney (Cambridge University Press, 2004), 1–23 (7). Millar MacLure, ed. *Marlowe: The Critical Heritage 1588–1896* (London: Routledge and Kegan Paul, 1979), 49.
19 MacLure, ed., *Marlowe: The Critical Heritage*, 47; Patrick Cheney, *Marlowe's Republican Authorship: Lucan, Liberty, and the Sublime* (Basingstoke: Palgrave Macmillan, 2009), 1–2.
20 Martin Wiggins, 'When Did Marlowe Write *Dido, Queen of Carthage*?', *Review of English Studies* 59 (2008), 521–41 (526).
21 Eric Rasmussen, *A Textual Companion to Doctor Faustus* (Manchester University Press, 1993), 30, 66.
22 Marlowe, *Tamburlaine*, sig. A2r.
23 Anon., *A Most Pleasant and Merie Nevv Comedie, Intituled, A Knacke to Knowe a Knaue* (London, 1594), sig. A1r.
24 Bentley, *The Profession of Dramatist*, 199.
25 Marlowe, *Tamburlaine*, sig. A2r.
26 Alan Dessen, 'Robert Greene and the Theatrical Vocabulary of the Early 1590s', in *Writing Robert Greene: Essays on England's First Notorious Professional*

Writer, ed. Kirk Melnikoff and Edward Gieskes (Aldershot: Ashgate, 2008), 25–37 (37).
27 Henslowe, *Diary*, 206; Rasmussen, *A Textual Companion*, 42.
28 Bentley, *The Profession of Dramatist*, 262.
29 Holger Schott Syme, 'The Meaning of Success: Stories of 1594 and Its Aftermath', *Shakespeare Quarterly* 61 (2010): 490–525 (490, 499–505).
30 *Ibid.*, 505.
31 Greene, *Groats-vvorth of Witte*, sigs. F2r, E4v.

PART III

Reception

CHAPTER TWENTY FIVE

Marlowe in his moment

Holger Schott Syme

What exactly was Christopher Marlowe's 'moment'? Was it the late 1580s, when both parts of *Tamburlaine* were first staged? Was it 1590, the year the publication of those plays ushered drama originally written for the professional theatre into the world of literature? Was it the following years, up to his death in 1593, when most of his dramatic works were performed in front of capacity crowds at London's theatres, even as their author continued to live a life of notoriety? Or was Marlowe's moment a posthumous event, with the influence of his plays growing well into the 1590s and beyond, bolstered, in the realm of literature, by the publication of *Hero and Leander* in 1598?

There is a dominant version of literary and theatre history that would suggest all of the above are true: Marlowe burst onto the theatrical scene with *Tamburlaine*, a play that almost singlehandedly revolutionised English dramatic literature; the same play then ushered in the phenomenon of drama as a marketable print commodity; and Marlowe's works remained commercially successful enough to form the core of one of early modern England's leading acting companies, the Lord Admiral's Men, for decades. However, this account, as influential as it has been, has little evidence on its side and in some of its particulars contradicts what little concrete information we have about the Elizabethan theatre.

Marlowe's influence

How revolutionary was *Tamburlaine*? According to the conventional narrative, very. Even the most nuanced theatre-historical analyses cling to the idea that the play kicked off a 'cultural contest' between old and new in which Marlowe eventually 'prevailed'.[1] However, we now remain aware of only one side of this 'conflict', since almost all drama written for adult professional actors before *Tamburlaine* is lost. As Lukas Erne notes, 'what "the popular theatre of the day" was like when Marlowe arrived in

London is something we know next to nothing about'.[2] If Marlowe was a revolutionary, then, it is unclear what exactly he was rebelling against. That the two parts of *Tamburlaine*, first performed by the Lord Admiral's Men in 1587 or 1588, were a great success is beyond question; but given our near-total ignorance about the theatrical and dramatic contexts of his works, how can we claim that Marlowe's success was the result of his radical difference?

Even if *Tamburlaine* really broke with tradition as spectacularly as literary historians assert, however, was the play actually as influential as the conventional narrative suggests? It is true that the early 1590s saw a small flourishing of plays about conqueror figures – Robert Greene's *Alphonsus, King of Aragon*; *Selimus* (possibly also by Greene); George Peele's *The Battle of Alcazar*; and a few others. It is certainly possible that those works responded to or imitated *Tamburlaine*. Some of them, critics have argued, explicitly allude to Marlowe's text, at times almost recycling his images and ideas. But these plays make up a very small fraction of the theatrical repertory of the 1590s.

Revealingly, the acting company about which we have the most detailed information from the early 1590s, Lord Strange's Men, show no sign of having succumbed to the *Tamburlaine* fever. Among the twenty-seven plays we know they performed between February 1592 and February 1593 – the period when all their shows at the Rose Theatre were recorded in Philip Henslowe's business diary – only two or three seem to fit the mould: a two-part 'Tamer Cham' play and a play about 'Mully Mollocco' (which some scholars interpret as Henslowe's title for *The Battle of Alcazar*). Other offerings range from romances and biblical moralities to English chronicle history plays but also include two of Marlowe's own works: *The Jew of Malta* and *The Massacre at Paris*. What the Strange's Men's records suggest (to the extent that we can make sense of them at all, given that only nine or ten of the texts survive) is that Marlovian drama happily co-existed with works that sound to us like more old-fashioned fare – that companies who staged his plays did not instantly transform their entire repertories to fit what may have been a new paradigm but instead learnt to orchestrate and cycle through an increasingly wide range of dramatic styles and modes.

What makes Strange's Men a particularly pertinent case study is the fact that they may well have been the first company to think of London as their permanent home. As Sally-Beth MacLean has argued, unlike other troupes, they avoided touring between 1589 and 1592, possibly performing at the Rose for all those years.[3] A more typical company of actors would have travelled around Britain for most of the year. Such a company would not have been likely to feel the need to respond quickly to revolutionary new plays — partly because their audiences were diverse enough that there would have been little incentive to invest in radically new material, and partly because their absence from London and its professional writers kept those troupes out of the loop to some extent. It is therefore unclear why the Queen's Men, say, or Leicester's Men — to name just two of the many groups performing throughout Britain in those years — should have cared, or even known, that the Admiral's Men's *Tamburlaine* was stunning audiences elsewhere in the country. Strange's Men, on the other hand, with their settled London existence, would presumably have felt the impact of a new voice or a new style of drama much more acutely — to them, a competitor in or around the City (perhaps at one of the Shoreditch playhouses, the Theatre or the Curtain) would have posed a challenge, while a prominent travelling company such as the Queen's Men could easily have ignored a competitor passing through a town months before they performed there. Consequently, the relative absence of a clear Marlovian influence on the Strange's Men's repertory is especially telling: if the Marlowe 'revolution' did not utterly change their practices, why would it have had much of an impact on other troupes?

This is a point worth dwelling on. The conventional narrative conceives of acting troupes as participants in a cultural market and of Marlowe as near-unmatchable competition in that market, pitting him (and the Admiral's Men) against everybody else, forces of the new against defenders of the old. But such a binary model necessarily misrepresents the nature of the theatrical marketplace, in London as well as in the country at large. Consider this anonymous letter, written to Sir Francis Walsingham in January 1587:

> For every day in the week the players' bills are set up in sundry places of the City, some in the name of her Majesty's Men, some the Earl of Leicester's, some the Earl of Oxford's, the Lord Admiral's, and divers others; so that when the bells toll to the lecturer, the trumpets sound to the stages, whereat the wicked faction of Rome laugheth for joy, while the godly weep for sorrow ... It is a woeful sight to see two hundred proud players jet in their silks, where five hundred poor people starve in the streets.[4]

The figure of 200 actors strutting around in their fine costumes is likely inflated, and the picture of a City bustling with acting companies probably only represents what things were like in the winter, when troupes tended to avoid touring. But even if few, or no, groups of actors had made London their permanent home yet, it is undeniable that there were a large number of performance spaces in and around the City — spaces that needed to be filled somehow. By 1587, four large outdoor playhouses had opened their doors: the Theatre and the Curtain north of the City, the Rose south of the Thames, and the theatre in Newington Butts, a mile south of the City. And beyond these purpose-built houses, four inns served as theatres at least until the mid 1590s: the Bel Savage, the Bull, the Cross Keys, and the Bell. While none of these spaces may have been associated with particular acting companies, some of them at least had already developed a reputation for specific styles of performance or a distinctive type of drama by the early 1590s. The Bull, for instance, had become recognisable as a place where 'actors speak fustian', staging plays with titles like 'a fig for a Spaniard', and full of 'invent[ed] words running on the letter to content over curious fancies'.[5]

We thus know that London had eight professional performance venues, all of which were used for theatrical productions throughout the year. And despite a presumed high turnover of occupants, some of those venues managed to develop well-defined house styles. Walsingham's anonymous correspondent names four acting companies, and we can probably add at least another two or three that occasionally took up residence in one of the London theatres. This great diversity, however, poses a major challenge to the conviction that Marlowe's arrival on the scene in 1587 had a singular and revolutionary impact. Even if we grant that *Tamburlaine* was universally acknowledged as unlike anything anyone had ever seen before, and even if we were to imagine it as performed by the Admiral's Men during a long, uninterrupted stint in London, it would still have been only one theatrical event among many; even if it sold out every time, attracting spectators in unprecedented numbers, the playhouse where it was staged still only held a few thousand people – in an entertainment marketplace that could accommodate well over 10,000 spectators every day. There is thus no reason to assume that all the other companies would have felt compelled to offer similar plays, or that they would have anticipated that the theatregoers who were crowded out of performances of Marlowe's work would not go elsewhere for their daily entertainment. There was simply too much theatre on offer, in London and throughout the kingdom, for one playwright's or one company's innovative work to have the immediate transformative influence the conventional narrative of literary history implies.

Measuring any kind of influence is of course an inherently problematic undertaking. In Marlowe's case, we simply know too little of the other dramatic works produced in the 1580s to say with certainty whether his plays were in fact more transformative than other, lost ones; and although we have a somewhat larger number of plays from the following decade, we still cannot clearly demonstrate exactly how widespread the influence of Marlowe's works was – we would need a better sense of how representative the surviving sample of texts is. However, one might argue that it is less important to know that a given text or author influenced *a specific number* of others than to assess the *quality* of influence a particular author had on others. Marlowe's works evidently affected the way some of his contemporaries wrote plays: at least a number of authors whose texts reached print attempted to mimic or counter some of his writerly habits and attitudes. But such a perspective necessarily privileges the minority of plays that have survived to this day, implicitly suggesting that those works are representative of larger trends in the development of early modern theatre and tacitly equating the market for playbooks and that for live performances. Worse, in Marlowe's case, scholars have almost inevitably, if understandably, focused on Shakespeare's response.[6]

But that strategy comes with its own disadvantages: we do not know, after all, how similar Shakespeare's plays were to the bulk of drama written and performed in the 1590s and early 1600s. What is clear is that *literary history* has long traced the development of Elizabethan drama from humble beginnings to unparalleled artistic excellence through Marlowe to Shakespeare – a narrative that necessarily, and troublingly, ignores the hundreds of lost and dozens of surviving plays that fail to support a vision of ever greater aesthetic accomplishment and instead speak to the continued popularity and importance of old models, with their seemingly crusty poetics and hackneyed plotlines.

One striking instance of this persistent presence of a kind of drama that literary history wants to relegate to the dark pre-Marlovian past is the anonymous *Clyomon and Clamydes*. This romance, first printed in 1599 and performed by the Queen's Men – the leading acting company in England throughout Marlowe's career – could not be less like *Tamburlaine*. In place of Marlowe's overreaching characters fuelled by awe inspiring ambition, we get silly tales of knights in not especially shining armour, and damsels in highly contrived distress, instead of mighty blank-verse lines, we get rhymed hexameters and heptameters. And yet, this apparently anachronistic play, sometimes dated to the 1570s precisely because it seems so out of step with the Marlovian paradigm, was not only staged by a successful, if deliberately conservative, company but was considered a worthwhile investment for a publisher at the end of the sixteenth century – competing not just with Marlowe's playbooks, but also with Shakespeare's.

Clyomon and Clamydes thus offers one important corrective to the conventional narratives of theatre and literary history. It shows that plays of dubious poetic merit continued to appeal to audiences in the 1580s and 1590s. And perhaps even more importantly, it shows that such plays may have found a readership as well, although it is true that *Clyomon* was never reprinted and therefore probably sold poorly (but the same is true of Marlowe's *Massacre at Paris* – and of Shakespeare's *Much Ado about Nothing*, which saw its only single-volume edition the year after *Clyomon and Clamydes* was published). Stationers frequently invested in plays now considered inferior: in 1599 alone, they published Greene's *Alphonsus*; the anonymous *A Warning for Fair Women* (another 'old-fashioned' play, featuring a number of allegorical dumb shows); and the anonymous *George a Green, the Pinner of Wakefield*, yet another play that shows no trace of Marlowe's or Shakespeare's influence and thus feels 'old' – although it may in fact testify to the continued theatrical *and* literary currency of other dramatic models. Such seemingly outdated material was not simply considered marketable by stationers but also outsold many playbooks of a more 'post-revolutionary' bent. We may never know what contemporary readers saw in *Mucedorus* (the best-selling play of the age) or *A Looking Glass for London and England*, but the fact that these works and others like them continued to be read suggests that the market for printed plays at least partly reflected the heterogeneity of the theatrical world.

Marlowe's success

Much of my argument so far has been concerned with what we do not know – the wealth of theatrical activities and writing now lost to us but of crucial importance as context for Marlowe's drama. Let me now turn to something we *do* know: just how well plays such as *Tamburlaine*, *The Jew of Malta*, and *Doctor Faustus* did on stage. Henslowe's *Diary* is a unique source of information in this regard, at least for the years it covers in sufficient detail: 1592–7.

Any analysis of the daily takings Henslowe lists for Strange's Men must conclude that *The Jew of Malta*, for instance, was a true blockbuster. It was staged thirteen times and averaged just over 45 shillings a performance. Only two plays earned Henslowe more from 1592 to 1593: *The Spanish Tragedy* and a play about Henry VI that may or may not have been one of Shakespeare's. And *The Jew of Malta* remained a relatively steady money-maker for other companies at his Rose Theatre (the play probably belonged to Henslowe). It was staged ten times by the Admiral's Men in 1594 and revived by them for another eight shows in 1596. After that, Marlowe's play seems to have been retired along with Edward Alleyn, the actor long associated with the star parts of Barabas and Tamburlaine, but it returned to the Admiral's Men's repertory in 1601, when Alleyn rejoined them for a while after they had moved to a new theatre, the Fortune. The play made its next recorded appearance in the 1630s, when Queen Henrietta's Men staged it at court and at the Cockpit Theatre, complete with a prologue by Thomas Heywood apologising for the old-fashioned material. *The Jew of Malta* thus looks like a work of enduring popularity – one of the plays built to last through the decades leading up to the closure of theatres in 1642. Similar accounts can be constructed for *Doctor Faustus* and, with less confidence, for *Tamburlaine*.

However, what is less clear is just how exceptional Marlowe's plays were in either their immediate success or their longevity. The most remarkable thing about *The Jew of Malta* is not that it was an unparalleled success (other plays were more profitable), but that we know so much about its commercial fortunes. As a consequence, we are liable to overestimate just how unusual those fortunes were, simply because we have so little data for comparison. The surviving records in fact suggest that many similar success stories lie just beyond our archival reach. Take another profitable Strange's Men play, 'Titus and Vespasian'. This anonymous, and lost, work more or less matched *The Jew of Malta* in receipts, running for ten shows with average takings of just under 45 shillings. However, unlike Marlowe's play, it did not make it into the Admiral's Men's repertory – most likely because it went with the rest of Strange's Men to either the Lord Chamberlain's Men (Shakespeare's company) or elsewhere and drops out of recorded theatre history. 'Titus and Vespasian' thus looks insignificant: a flash in the pan, it only lasted on stage for a year and then vanished from sight, wasn't interesting enough to merit print publication, and didn't leave a record attesting to lasting theatrical popularity. This impression, however, is almost entirely an effect of the fragmentary evidence we rely on in constructing the history of early modern drama. 'Titus and Vespasian' may well have gone on to be the Chamberlain's Men's most enduringly popular play – but without any records about the company's commercial fortunes, we have no way of knowing.

In other words, just as what we *do not know* about Marlowe has distorted our conventional accounts of his influence, what we *think we know* about his plays' exceptional commercial success has distorted our understanding of their relative popularity. Worse, the traditional narrative tends to ignore what data we do have in its desire to sustain claims for Marlowe's unparalleled and perennial appeal. Contrary to what some theatre historians have asserted, none of his plays is in fact among the most profitable Admiral's Men productions recorded in Henslowe's *Diary*; in each of the years for which we have records (1594–7), Marlowe's works brought in fewer spectators than the average play; and by the troupe's third season at the Rose, none of his works played a significant role in their repertory any more – only *Doctor Faustus* was still being staged in the 1596–7 season, but just 4 times compared to 187 performances of other plays, earning Henslowe a total of 58 shillings, or just over 14 shillings per show. Marlowe's five plays (the two parts of *Tamburlaine*, *The Jew of Malta*, *Doctor Faustus*, and *The Massacre at Paris*) make up only 7 per cent of the works staged in those three years, and just over 2 per cent of the more than 230 plays known to have been performed by the Admiral's Men in total.[7] However one crunches those figures, the popular claim that the Marlovian oeuvre was 'the beating heart of the company's repertory' is impossible to sustain.[8]

Occasionally, however, the fog of our ignorance about what the English theatrical scene was really like in Marlowe's and Shakespeare's time lifts for a moment – and in those moments we get glimpses of a very unfamiliar landscape. Decades ago, a puzzling list of plays was found on the back of a manuscript in the hand of Sir George Buc, Master of the Revels from 1610 to 1622 and an antiquarian with a keen interest in the recent history of the stage. E. K. Chambers reasoned that the list must either refer to texts Buc had licensed for performance or to plays that he had considered for court entertainments. Strikingly, 'a very unexpected entry' refers to 'Titus, and Vespatian' – quite likely that old play we last encountered in Henslowe's *Diary* in 1593 and therefore possibly a work not just rivalling *The Jew of Malta* in popularity when first staged, but also matching Marlowe's play's longevity, considered fit for a revival at court over twenty-five years after its original performance.[9] How many other examples like 'Titus and Vespasian' may there have been? And how could we ever know how influential, how successful, and, most distressingly, how aesthetically impressive they were?

Marlowe out of date

From both the perspective of influence and that of commercial success, the notion that Marlowe really had a 'moment' may have lost some of its lustre by now. But even if we grant that such a moment in fact existed, just how long did it last? It would be difficult to dispute the continued influence of his poetry – *Hero and Leander* seems to have remained a shining reference point for later poets. But in the theatre and in the realm of dramatic writing, his star may have faded rather more quickly. I would suggest that by the time Ben Jonson called Marlowe's lines 'mighty' in 1623, that tag had become something of a poisoned compliment. Critics frequently accused dramatists of indulging in verbal noise and excess, and both features were increasingly associated with popular, unsophisticated plays in post-Elizabethan England. Take Edmund Gayton, admittedly writing with a lot of hindsight in the mid seventeenth century: 'I have heard, that the Poets of the Fortune and the Red Bull, had always a mouth-measure for their Actors (who were terrible tear throats) and made their lines proportionable to their compass, which were *sesquipedales*, a foot and a half.'[10] Earlier sources, such as Sir Thomas Overbury's *Characters*, also refer to 'wide-mouth'd *Poet*[s]' who speak 'nothing but bladders and bombast'.[11] And that word, 'bombast' (i.e. stuffing), takes us back to Marlowe's own lifetime and to Robert Greene's *Groatsworth of Wit*. Greene famously accused Shakespeare of thinking he could 'bombast out a blank verse as the best of you' – and the same Robert Greene also attacked Marlowe for 'filling the mouth' of his actors with his 'every word' 'like the faburden of Bo-Bell'.[12] This sense of excessive loudness, of words that take up too much space, attaches itself to Marlowe's plays from the beginning; fellow writers, from Greene to Joseph Hall to Ben Jonson, were particularly apt to criticise him for his lack of restraint.[13] Their critique has to qualify in important ways our understanding of Marlowe's revolutionary impact. When his plays were first performed, they were attacked, partly, for their excessive noise; and a generation later, that same noise already (or still) seemed uncouth to a courtly writer such as Overbury. Retrospectively, actors with over-stuffed mouths came to be associated with supposedly vulgar, overly popular, aggressively old-fashioned theatres of which the Red Bull was the archetype. So when exactly, and where, did Marlovian 'megaphonics' (to use Harry Berger's phrase) become mainstream?[14] And how long did that moment last? If within a generation the blank-verse insurgency wound up institutionalised as fustian populism at the Red Bull – the playhouse where plays no one reads any more go to die – Marlowe looks less like the author who ushered in a new way of writing plays, less like a perpetual influence and aesthetic reference point, and more like a writer devoured, within a few short years, by his own revolution.

Notes

1 Scott McMillin and Sally-Beth MacLean, *The Queen's Men and Their Plays* (Cambridge University Press, 1998), 155.
2 Lukas Erne, 'Biography, Mythography, and Criticism: The Life and Works of Christopher Marlowe', *Modern Philology* 103 (2005): 28–50 (39).
3 Sally-Beth MacLean, 'Adult Playing Companies, 1583–1593', in *The Oxford Handbook of Early Modern Theatre*, ed. Richard Dutton (Oxford University Press, 2009), 39–55 (46).
4 Excerpted in E. K. Chambers, *The Elizabethan Stage*, 4 vols. Vol. IV (Oxford: Clarendon Press, 1923), 303–4 (modernised).
5 Quoted in Glynne Wickham, Herbert Berry, and William Ingram, eds., *English Professional Theatre, 1530–1660* (Cambridge University Press, 2000), 303.
6 See Paul Menzer, '*c.f.* Marlowe', in *Richard II: New Critical Essays*, ed. Jeremy Lopez (Abingdon: Routledge, 2012), 117–35, for a perceptive critique of this scholarly tendency.
7 See my 'The Meaning of Success: Stories of 1594 and Its Aftermath', *Shakespeare Quarterly* 61 (2010): 490–525, for a more detailed account.
8 Andrew Gurr, *Shakespeare's Opposites: The Admiral's Company, 1594–1625* (Cambridge University Press, 2009), 171.
9 E. K. Chambers, review of *The King's Office of the Revels, 1610–1622: Fragments of Documents in the Department of Manuscripts, British Museum, transcribed by FRANK MARCHAM*', *Review of English Studies*, Original Series 1 (1925): 479–84 (483).
10 Edmund Gayton, *Pleasant notes upon Don Quixot* (London: William Hunt, 1654), sig. D4v (modernised).
11 Sir Thomas Overbury, *Characters*, ed. Donald Beecher (Ottawa: Dovehouse, 2003), 241 (modernised).
12 Robert Greene, *Groats-vvorth of witte, bought with a million of repentance* (London: J. Wolfe and J. Danter for William Wright, 1592), sig. F1v; *Perimedes the blacke-smith* (London: John Wolfe for Edward White, 1588), sig. A3r.
13 Joseph Hall, *Virgidemiarum sixe books* (London: Richard Bradock, for Robert Dexter, 1598), sigs. B4r–B5v; Ben Jonson, *Ben Jonson*, ed. C. H. Herford, Percy Simpson, and Evelyn Simpson, 11 vols. (Oxford: Clarendon Press, 1925–52), Vol. VIII, 587; Vol. XI, 145.
14 Harry Berger, Jr, *Imaginary Auditions: Shakespeare on Stage and Page* (Berkeley: University of California Press, 1989), 65.

CHAPTER TWENTY SIX

Marlowe and Shakespeare revisited

Thomas Cartelli

Approached, as it often is, as an analogue of Christopher Marlowe's *Edward II* (1592–3), Shakespeare's *Richard II* (1595–6) is usually interpreted along similar lines, as dramatising a weak king's inevitable loss of his crown through successive acts of misgovernance, in this instance to a stronger successor, Henry Bolingbroke, who better deserves to wear it. But however fertile the correspondences between the two plays are, *Richard II* is also representative of a more comprehensive (and complicated) reckoning with other works of Marlowe's that Shakespeare undertook in the immediate aftermath of Marlowe's death, particularly *Tamburlaine the Great* (c. 1588–90) and *Doctor Faustus* (1592–3). We may find therefore that conventional lines of interpretation need to be altered to accommodate a *Richard II* that both displays and interrogates the neo-Tamburlainean presumption Bolingbroke brings to bear against the established order of royal succession, while it forges formative dramatic ties between Marlowe's Faustus and Shakespeare's 'plume-plucked' king, especially as they embark on the downward incline of their fortunes.

Richard II's commerce with *Tamburlaine the Great* commences in the third scene of the play as Richard is about to bid farewell to his powerful antagonist, Henry Bolingbroke, when his sudden decision to abbreviate Bolingbroke's exile from ten to six years evokes the following response from the exiled duke: 'How long a time lies in one little word! / Four lagging winters and four wanton springs / End in a word; such is the breath of kings.'[1] Although this passage has elicited little commentary from scholars and directors, it not only helps confirm Richard's suspicion that 'the eagle-winged pride / Of sky-aspiring and ambitious thoughts' (I.iii.129–30) has motivated Bolingbroke to enter the lists against Richard's loyal supporter, Thomas Mowbray, but marks the emergence of the boundless presumption that will soon prompt Bolingbroke to abridge the already abbreviated term of his exile and mount an unanswerable challenge against Richard's royal pre-eminence.

Bolingbroke's reaction to Richard's reduction of his sentence operates as a kind of revelation or epiphany, designed not to be heard or noted by anyone apart from the audience. The awed fascination with power that Bolingbroke displays here retrospectively helps explain – not only to his audience but quite possibly to himself – what he was about in attempting, in Richard's words, 'to wake our peace' (I.iii.132) by accusing Mowbray of a crime that was just as much Richard's. To put it as plainly as possible, when Richard, prompted by seeing 'in the glasses of [John of Gaunt's] eyes' his 'grieved heart' (I.iii.208–9), summarily dissolves four years of Bolingbroke's sentence, what Bolingbroke witnesses is the power of kings to alter time itself, indeed, to swallow it up with a 'breath'. So 'rapt' is he that Bolingbroke is not party to the ensuing dialogue that takes shape around him between Richard and his father, Gaunt, who has a very different take on what kings can and cannot do about the passage of time.

In describing Bolingbroke as 'rapt', I allude, of course, to Macbeth's entrancement at being newly designated Thane of Cawdor, as he distractedly dwells on the apparent fulfilment of the witches' prophecy – instead of attending to the conversation of his comrades – in the third scene of *Macbeth*.[2] But a closer analogue to Bolingbroke's revery/revelation is that defining moment in the first part of Marlowe's *Tamburlaine the Great* when Tamburlaine eloquently elaborates on Cosroe's resolve to 'ride in triumph through Persepolis' (II.v.49):

> TAMBURLAINE: And ride in triumph through Persepolis?
> Is it not brave to be a king, Techelles?
> Usumcasane and Theridamas,
> Is it not passing brave to be a king,
> And ride in triumph through Persepolis?
> TECHELLES: O, my lord, 'tis sweet and full of pomp.
> USUMCASANE: To be a king is half to be a god.
> THERIDAMAS: A god is not so glorious as a king.
> (II.v.50–7)[3]

Tamburlaine's question – 'Is it not passing brave to be a king, / And ride in triumph through Persepolis?' – is both more and less rhetorical. Although directly addressed to his three associates, it emerges as a clarification of what had possibly been his unrefined motive in helping Cosroe achieve the Persian crown. And it becomes one of the most memorable lines uttered in the annals of Elizabethan drama, so perfectly does it rhapsodise on what is arguably the central fantasy-content of the age, transforming worldly ambition into both an ethic and an aesthetic of heroic aspiration.

In the economy of *Richard II*'s first three scenes, Bolingbroke's 'discovery' of what the breath of kings can do clarifies his formerly inchoate motivations in just the way the earlier passage serves Tamburlaine. Both characters set out to do something bold and daring. Both have 'aspiring minds'. But in the first flush of action (on Bolingbroke's part) and achievement (on Tamburlaine's), neither is quite ready to identify the destination that he has been moving towards.[4] That destination only becomes evident as it is named or proclaimed by the current possessor of the power each craves. 'Persepolis' is the metonymic embodiment of that destination (the Persian empery) for Tamburlaine; 'the breath of kings', the touchstone of the place to which Bolingbroke aspires, namely, Richard's throne. When Richard peremptorily abridges time itself in reducing Bolingbroke's sentence, he sets the course for his destruction just as surely as Cosroe does when he announces that he is setting off for Persepolis. At that point, both characters have their objectives, and destinies, clarified for them, becoming fully aware, as if for the first time, of what likely motivated them in the first place.

Tamburlaine the Great, of course, is not the first play of Marlowe's one thinks of when considering the intertextual correspondences of *Richard II*. Other Marlowe plays that *Richard II* mines more deeply include, as noted above, *Edward II*, but also *Doctor Faustus*, especially in terms of the rich textual echoes of *Faustus* found in *Richard II*'s parliament (or deposition) scene.[5] From *Edward II* Shakespeare drew on established precedents of plot and characterisation to model his own representation of a 'misgoverned' king's response to the aggressive challenges of ambitious aristocrats. But it may well have been the daring of the antagonists as much as the weakness of the protagonists that attracted Marlowe and Shakespeare to these chronicle accounts to begin with, especially given the established notoriety of Marlowe's 'proud Mortimer' and the historic challenge to political orthodoxy mounted by Henry Bolingbroke.[6] In *Edward II*, the sporadically Machiavellian Mortimer will defeat Edward and his minions but fail to reckon with the decisive response of the boy-king Edward III, the father's tragedy ceding to the son's triumph. In *Richard II*, the more Tamburlainean Bolingbroke – who notably returns to England at the head of an army *before* he can possibly know that he has been dispossessed of his inheritance – both unmakes Richard's royal authority and makes himself king and the father of a dynasty, becoming in the process as much the object of the play's dramatic scrutiny as Richard is.

Bolingbroke is, admittedly, Tamburlainean more on the level of presumption than in the one area where the overlap is greater between

Richard and Tamburlaine – that is, with respect to their shared belief in the working power of words. Indeed, where Tamburlaine is as much a talking machine as he is a 'desiring machine that produces violence and death',[7] Bolingbroke is more consistently the 'silent king', the still, stolid point around which his ambitions take concrete shape. Yet Bolingbroke demonstrates a decidedly Tamburlainean assurance in the power of his name alone to conjure the force necessary to execute his designs that is far from the wishful, merely 'poetic' nature of Richard's bouts of magical thinking. While Richard commands the 'breath' to mitigate Bolingbroke's exile, having already 'breathe[d] against' Mowbray the 'hopeless word of "never to return" … upon pain of life' (I.iii.152–3), Richard's word is far less efficacious than is Bolingbroke's when the latter issues the following command to his ally and henchman, the Duke of Northumberland:

> Noble lord,
> Go to the rude ribs of that ancient castle;
> Through brazen trumpet send the breath of parley
> Into his ruined ears, and thus deliver:
> Henry Bolingbroke
> On both his knees doth kiss King Richard's hand
> And send allegiance and true faith of heart
> To his most royal person, hither come
> Even at his feet to lay my arms and power
> Provided that my banishment repealed
> And lands restored again be freely granted.
> If not, I'll use the advantage of my power
> And lay the summer's dust with showers of blood
> Rained from the wounds of slaughtered Englishmen –
> The which how far off from the mind of Bolingbroke
> It is such crimson tempest should bedrench
> The fresh green lap of fair King Richard's land
> My stooping duty tenderly shall show.
> (III.iii.31–48)

It could be argued that Bolingbroke is not speaking of himself in the bombastic third person here so much as dictating in the first a message that he wants Northumberland to deliver. But his intermixing of first and third persons with overweening pride ('the mind of Bolingbroke') and false humility ('on both his knees'), combined with a preference for degrading and threatening formulations ('ruined ears', 'showered blood'), plainly indicate the boundless presumption of a character whose belief in himself has all the assurance of Tamburlaine's 'will and shall'.

This is not to suggest that *Richard II* is 'a *Tamburlaine* play' in the manner of such earlier exercises in emulation as Robert Greene's *Alphonsus of Aragon* (1590), George Peele's *Battle of Alcazar* (1591), and the anonymous *Selimus* (1592). Whereas Tamburlaine operates on a stage freed from the constraints of likelihood and history alike (however much Marlowe may have mapped his drama on historical accounts), Shakespeare contextualises Bolingbroke's will to power in a thicket of political realism, if not of faithfully recorded fact. As Richard notes, Bolingbroke is as much a figure of the modern politician, reserving the thunder of his boasts for his royal opponent while doffing 'his bonnet to an oyster-wench' (I.iv.31) to gain favour with commoners. Although Bolingbroke's Tamburlainean aspirations will inexorably drive the character forwards to the goal he desires – the 'fruition of an earthly crown' – that fruition will never taste as sweet to Bolingbroke as it does to Tamburlaine, so qualified will his gain of the crown be by Richard's embodiment of its cost and loss, so long will the taint of the crown's acquisition remain the prevailing theme of his reign.[8] It is, moreover, far from an incidental irony that the words that inspire Bolingbroke's ascent to the crown are contrastingly echoed by those Richard utters on 'the death of kings' as he begins orchestrating his precipitous descent. Nor does it seem merely incidental that as he acts out that descent, Richard will adopt a similarly self-reflective position in relation to another Marlovian overreacher, namely, Doctor Faustus.

Given the didactic import of so much that Richard has to say about the limits and lies of kingship, it hardly seems rash to claim that *Richard II* – like *Doctor Faustus* – is as much a cautionary text on the corrosive effects that ambition visits on those who harbour 'sky-aspiring and ambitious thoughts' as it is a play about the delusions and misdeeds of a king too self-indulgent and reckless to sustain what he takes to be his royal mandate. In light of *Richard II*'s critical reception as a play focused on a king too weak even to rise above pathos to the level of tragedy, such a conclusion may seem counterintuitive. Ostensibly emblematic moments like the famous garden scene presumably confirm John of Gaunt's early identification of Richard as 'landlord of England', and Richard himself, the quondam lord of time, later testifies movingly to his own failure to use time wisely. But – as noted above – the play from first to last also concentrates its anatomising gaze on a character sufficiently presumptuous to use his name as a line of blank verse – 'Henry Bolingbroke' (III.iii.35) – and sufficiently hypocritical to 'protest my soul is full of woe / That blood should sprinkle me to make me grow' (V.vi.45–6) as he walks behind a funeral bier of his own most persistent making at play's end.

The critical gaze that fastens on Bolingbroke from the moment he makes his premature return to England closely resembles the scepticism with which the transparently self-serving actions and motives of Mortimer Junior are presented in *Edward II*.[9] Bolingbroke's subjection to the play's critical gaze is particularly pronounced in *Richard II*'s parliament scene, which is orchestrated (if not controlled) by Richard, though not for his benefit alone.[10] The most powerful effect of Richard's performance comes towards the end of the scene after he has already dispossessed himself of his crown and sceptre. Richard asks for a mirror, looks into it, moralises on what he sees, and then breaks it into 'an hundred shivers':

> Give me that glass, and therein will I read.
> *[He takes the mirror.]*
> No deeper wrinkles yet? Hath sorrow struck
> So many blows upon this face of mine,
> And made no deeper wounds? O flattering glass,
> Like to my followers in prosperity,
> Thou dost beguile me! Was this the face
> That every day under his household roof
> Did keep ten thousand men? Was this the face
> That, like the sun, did make beholders wink?
> Is this the face which outfaced so many follies,
> That was at last outfaced by Bolingbroke?
> A brittle glory shineth in the face –
> As brittle as the glory is the face,
> *[He throws down the mirror.]*
> For there it is, cracked in an hundred shivers.
> Mark, silent king, the moral of this sport:
> How soon my sorrow hath destroyed my face.
> (IV.i.277–92)

In this theatrical tour de force, Richard evokes two memorable lines from Marlowe that dramatise both an inspiring and a deluded vision of human transcendence – *Doctor Faustus*' 'Was this the face that launched a thousand ships / And burnt the topless towers of Ilium?' (V.i.99–100) – and redeploys them to mock both his own inflated sense of self-importance and the importance credited to him by his 'beholders', in the process bringing the whole notion of transcendence crashing down. Unlike Faustus, who desperately clings to a vision of Helen as the quintessence of mortal beauty and human desire before coming to a final reckoning with his vainglory and arrogance, Richard is unbeguiled by the fair face he continues to see reflected in the mirror, which he mocks with clinical detachment. Seemingly cured of the delusions of grandeur that made him, like Faustus, think he could soar above the orbit of ordinary men, Richard offers this vision of the 'brittleness' of glory as a moral exemplum to the silent king, Bolingbroke, who remains so taken with (and taken in by) the ostensibly time-altering power of 'the breath of the kings' that his impatience seems tasked by what Richard has to show and tell. Like other ambitious men who have climbed to the top of the ladder of Fortune (*Edward II*'s proud Mortimer among them), the 'mounting Bolingbroke' does not appear to be listening, or, if he is listening, does not see how the moral spun by the 'light-headed' Richard applies to him. What, after all, can a self-styled 'mockery king of snow', spinning out self-pitying scenarios as the clock winds down, have to say to a confident heavyweight who has never lost a fight?

In one of the best essays ever written on Marlowe, Edward A. Snow contends that 'it might help to clarify Marlowe's perspective [on Faustus] if we were to think of [him] as the dialectical, ironical counterpart of Tamburlaine (rather than as a developmental, autobiographical recantation of him), and the two of them together as complementary considerations of a single human problematic'.[11] One may, I believe, see a corresponding dialectic played out on the stage of *Richard II* in the seemingly uneven competition between Bolingbroke and Richard, which critics have persisted in assessing in terms of the former's developmental, if not autobiographical, recantation of the latter. In *Imaginary Audition*, however, Harry Berger makes the commerce between Shakespeare and Marlowe seem considerably more resonant than the reshading of a succession of characters, though his insight into how 'the self-slandering undertone of Richard's rhetoric has no parallel in *Doctor Faustus*' seems crucial to the argument he develops.[12] Berger contends that 'if both Faustus's spiritual melodrama and the megaphonics of Marlovian theater are heard in the echo chamber of *Richard II*, they are present as a model to be corrected or repudiated, and the similarities between the heroes serve to draw attention to their differences'.[13] He expands on this point in the following passage:

> Shakespeare's citational use of *Doctor Faustus* is more than a revision. It is a parodistic representation both of Faustus's spiritual melodrama as conceived by Marlowe and of Marlowe's own rhetorical theatricality. The two are compacted into a single effect and displaced to Richard. That is, insofar as Faustus's morality play and Marlowe's, Faustus's bombastic grandeur and Marlowe's, are glimpsed in *Richard II*, they are present as an identity, a single citational system which is localized in Richard rather than in the play as a whole.[14]

Berger first sees Shakespeare conflating 'Faustus's spiritual melodrama' with the 'rhetorical theatricality' that conceives it. This conflation makes Faustus appear to embody and express Marlowe's own aesthetic agenda, thereby disallowing Marlowe a critical detachment from his surrogate's subject position. Berger then has Shakespeare 'displace' this conflated 'single effect' to Richard only to have Richard, in turn, retain the same critical distance from Faustus that allows Shakespeare to sustain a 'parodistic representation' of Faustus' plight, Marlowe's manner of presenting it, and, presumably, the 'single effect' that is 'localized' in Richard. The net result of these transactions is a Marlowe with no critical detachment from his own dramatic idiom, a Richard who both is and is not able to escape his defining medium, and a Shakespeare seeking to 'repudiate and correct' both models of authorship and character.

As suggestive as Berger's reading of this intertextual transaction is, he evinces a better feel for what Marlowe is about when he reads Faustus' singing of Helen's praises, recitation of outlandish claims, and anticipation of erotic delights as a last desperate and overcharged attempt to distract himself from his accelerating fate rather than as evidence of complete self-abandon.[15] Indeed, if Snow is right in claiming that 'the words that for Tamburlaine are the cornerstones of the will to power … betray, when Faustus utters them, the deeply conditional nature of the self and its compromises with circumstance, situation, other wills, and its own inner tensions',[16] Marlowe could hardly want, much less expect, the parade of seductive conceits generated by 'Is this the face that launched a thousand ships' to arouse the answering fervour of 'Is it not passing brave to be a king[?]'. However compelling these lines may sound and seem, Faustus has already entered, by this point, a domain certainly as desperate as and considerably more ominous than the scene of impending doom and self-pity Richard experiences and elaborates on in the fourth act of Shakespeare's play. When Shakespeare has Richard call for a mirror and enact his 'parodistic' representation of Faustus and his already famous lines, he is, as Berger notes, clearly performing a likeness with a difference, but that difference is not entirely, and hence need not be construed as, a repudiation or correction of Faustus, much less of Marlowe, both of whom are always already ahead of him in packing alms for oblivion. Richard is rather summoning the ghost of Faustus here as a kindred spirit of desperation and delusion while at the same time culling out for mockery his own mistakes in (and of the extreme ego-gratifying) kind. As Faustus is to Tamburlaine, in Snow's formulation, Richard is to Faustus in mine, that is, 'his dialectical, ironical counterpart': a character made capable by defeat of recognising what Faustus may embody and gesture towards but cannot yet fully acknowledge, namely, the 'brittleness' of earthly glory.

Like Shakespeare, Richard has the advantage of belatedness, of occupying the Marlowe aftermath and using what he finds there to drive his difference-in-sameness forwards, as Shakespeare has Richard demonstrate in his earlier response to Northumberland's relentless ministrations, 'Fiend, thou torments me ere I come to hell!' (4.1.270) (which Berger aptly terms his 'Faustian bellow').[17] Here Shakespeare has Richard evoke and inhabit a Marlovian context and idiom in order to fashion his defeat by Bolingbroke in terms of an overmatched Faustus being gratuitously tortured by a sadistic Mephistopheles, agent and henchman of a silently approving king (who more than once likens himself to Jehovah). The shared affective condition of intense self-regard and self-pity – which Richard is dwelling in, dwelling on, and seeking to liberate himself from through aggressive self-assertion in the mirror scene – activates an exchange of reflections, one play, one character, reflecting, mirroring, even colliding with the other, with the differences between them enriching, rather than inhibiting, their interplay.[18]

If the allusion to Mephistopheles carries, as I think it does, more than the strain of Richard's offended vanity and desperation, and conveys the impression of inexorable force pressing against an already defeated subject, then we may also be witnessing here something Marlowe seldom allows us to witness in his *Tamburlaine* plays, namely, the human consequences of Tamburlaine's will to power. Indeed, except for the light, virtually comic scenes in *Richard II*'s closing movement – which Shakespeare seems to have designed to set the scene for *1 Henry IV* – Bolingbroke is positioned here and elsewhere as carrier of a contagion of Tamburlainean ruthlessness that promises to poison the well of 'this new world' (IV.i.79) he has brought into being at the beginning of the play's fourth act. By contrast, as we witness Richard's fifth-act conversion into an introspective philosopher-sage and compare that figure with the all too morally mobile self-crowned 'King Henry' (IV.i.221) who, in the end, 'hate[s] the murderer, love[s] him murdered' (V.vi.40), we may find that it is the neo-Tamburlainean Bolingbroke – not Marlowe, Faustus, or Richard II, his neo-Faustian counterpart – that stands corrected, if not repudiated, by Shakespeare.

Notes

1 William Shakespeare, *Richard II*, I.iii 213–15. All quotations from Shakespeare are drawn from *The Complete Works of Shakespeare*, ed. David Bevington, 6th edn (New York: Longman, 2008).

2 Wilbur Sanders is, to my knowledge, the only other critic to note the resemblance between the unspecified motives of Bolingbroke and 'the somnambulist power-lust of a Macbeth', in *The Dramatist and the Received Idea* (Cambridge University Press, 1968), 165.
3 All quotations from Marlowe are drawn from Christopher Marlowe, *The Complete Plays of Christopher Marlowe*, ed. Irving Ribner (Indianapolis: Bobbs–Merrill, 1963).
4 As he explores Bolingbroke's possible motives, Sanders claims that 'Shakespeare can have seldom thrown so little light on a key motivation as he does on the process by which Bolingbroke moves towards his goal'; Sanders, *The Dramatist and the Received Idea*, 164.
5 The play's most sustained intertextual commerce with *Doctor Faustus* occurs in this scene (IV.i.155–318), which was omitted from the first three quarto editions of the play (Q1–3) published in 1597 and 1598, possibly for reasons of formal censorship or anticipation of the same, and appeared for the first time in the quarto edition of 1608.
6 Marlowe's contemporary Michael Drayton would move Mortimer to the forefront of literary concern, first, in *Mortimeriados* (1596) and later, in revised form, in *The Barons' War* (1603).
7 Stephen Greenblatt, 'Marlowe and Renaissance Self-Fashioning', in *Two Renaissance Mythmakers: Christopher Marlowe and Ben Jonson*, ed. Alvin Kernan (Baltimore: Johns Hopkins University Press, 1977), 47.
8 As the dying Henry IV will say to Prince Hal in *2 Henry IV*, 'For all my reign hath been but as a scene / Acting that argument' (IV.v.197–8).
9 For a fuller account of the critical remarks made here about Marlowe's *Edward II*, see the chapter on the play, entitled 'King Edward's Body', in my book, *Marlowe, Shakespeare, and the Economy of Theatrical Experience* (Philadelphia: University of Pennsylvania Press, 1991); or its reprinting in Richard Wilson, ed., *Christopher Marlowe* (London and New York: Longman, 1999), 174–90.
10 In an incisive essay that problematises everything from the name normally given to this scene to whether or not its absence from the Elizabethan quartos can properly be called an omission, Emma Smith contends that its inclusion in Q4 fairly radically alters the terms of engagement in Richard's favour insofar as the scene 'endorses Richard's kingly authority even at the moment when that authority is most under threat', in '*Richard II*'s Yorkist Editors', *Shakespeare Survey* 63 (2010): 37–48 (40).
11 Edward A. Snow, 'Marlowe's *Doctor Faustus* and the Ends of Desire', in Kernan, *Two Renaissance Mythmakers*, 70–110 (98).
12 Harry Berger, Jr, *Imaginary Audition: Shakespeare on Stage and Page* (Berkeley and Los Angeles: University of California Press, 1989), 66.
13 *Ibid.*, 65.
14 *Ibid.*, 66.
15 *Ibid.*, 69.
16 Snow, 'Marlowe's *Doctor Faustus*', 99.
17 Berger, *Imaginary Audition*, 67.

18 In light of the array of possibilities generated by this collision, I find it curious that Shakespeare's sustained engagement with Marlowe's most provocative play should have been consigned to textual oblivion for over ten years after *Richard II*'s initial publication, and I wonder what – if anything – Faustus' linkage to the deposition material might have had to do with the scene's censorship or omission.

CHAPTER TWENTY SEVEN

Marlowe in Caroline theatre

Lucy Munro

One of the best-known examples of the ongoing life of Marlowe's work in the period between the accession of Charles I in 1625 and the outbreak of the Civil War in 1642 is the 1633 publication of *The Jew of Malta*. Although the play had been performed as early as 1589, this was its first appearance in print. The edition unites a set of issues with which recent scholars have engaged: the publication of plays and, in particular, old plays; the evidence for their theatrical revival and ongoing prestige; and the emergence of playwrights as 'authors' in print. These interconnected concerns are suggested by the text of the 1633 title page:

> *The Famous*
> TRAGEDY
> OF
> THE RICH IEVV
> OF *MALTA*.
> AS IT WAS PLAYD
> BEFORE THE KING AND
> QVEENE, IN HIS MAJESTIES
> Theatre at *White-Hall*, by her Majesties
> Servants at the *Cock-pit*.
>
> *Written by* CHRISTOPHER MARLO.
>
> Printed by *I. B.* for *Nicholas Vavasour*, and are to be sold
> at his shop in the Inner-Temple, neere the
> Church. 1633.

The title page credits not only the author of the play, but also its theatrical owners in the 1630s, Queen Henrietta Maria's Men, and the owner of its rights in print, the publisher Nicholas Vavasour. It also foregrounds not one but two performance contexts: performance at court, before the king and queen; and performance at the Cockpit, a small indoor playhouse on Drury Lane, which was the usual home of Queen Henrietta Maria's Men.

Taking the 1633 edition of *The Jew of Malta* as its starting point, this chapter explores the afterlife of Marlowe's plays and poems in the Caroline playhouse from three angles. First, it examines the representation of Marlowe in theatrical contexts, highlighting the contested and ambivalent ways in which he was represented in print and on the stage. Second, it explores the evidence for revivals of Marlowe's plays between 1625 and 1642, tracing the different theatrical repertories with which they were associated. Third, it looks at a significant example of Marlowe's ongoing theatrical life: explicit allusions to the plays and poems within Caroline works, suggesting that even before his biographical legend was fully established his works could be exploited as symbols of erotic transgression.

Author

Marlowe is not the only 'author' to figure in Vavasour's edition of *The Jew of Malta*. As Zachary Lesser has shown us, the edition should be viewed in the context of Vavasour's activities as a whole and of his Laudian religious politics.[1] My interest here, however, lies specifically in the interactions between writers and actors. The play itself is preceded by a series of introductory texts written by the dramatist Thomas Heywood: a dedication to 'MY VVORTHY FRIEND', Thomas Hammon (A3r–v); a prologue and epilogue 'spoken at Court' (A4r); and a prologue and epilogue 'to the Stage, at the Cocke-pit' (A4v). Heywood was a regular writer for Queen Henrietta Maria's Men, and he appears to have been employed to write new prologues and epilogues for the revived play – a common practice at this time. However, these texts and the dedicatory note are intriguing in the ways in which they situate both the play and Marlowe himself.

Heywood begins his dedication with Marlowe, noting that *The Jew of Malta* was 'composed by so worthy an Authour as Mr. *Marlo*'; he also emphasises the contribution of Edward Alleyn, the first actor to play Barabas: 'the part of the Jew presented by so vnimitable an Actor as Mr. *Allin*' (A3r). However, the printed play is not presented here primarily as a tribute to Marlowe's genius, or even Alleyn's, but as part of a system of patronage. Heywood had already dedicated two plays to Hammon, the second part of *The Fair Maid of the West* (1631) and the first part of *The Iron Age* (1632); *The Jew of Malta* thus continues an established tradition. This fact is emphasised in the dedication, which concludes with the words: 'I had no better a New-yeares gift to present you with; receiue it therefore as a continuance of that inuiolable obliegement, by which, he rests stil ingaged; who as he euer hath, shall always remaine, *Tuissmus* [your very own]: THO HEYVVOOD' (A3v). The New Year's gift was an important part of the patronage system, and *The Jew of Malta* is thus transformed from a relic of the popular stage, or of an individual dramatist, to a means of sealing the affective and financial bond between poet and patron.

Elsewhere in the 1633 edition, Marlowe's contribution is again qualified by, or juxtaposed with, that of others. The epilogue for the court performance concludes with the lines '*And if ought here offend your eare or sight, / We onely Act, and Speake, what others write*' (A4r). The author – here unnamed – is made to bear responsibility for the play instead of the actors, who merely speak the lines given to them; the epilogue elides the fact that, in the absence of the dead author, responsibility for the choice of *The Jew of Malta* can only lie with the actors or, possibly, with Heywood, the playwright answerable for the lines that the epilogue is at that moment speaking.

The issue of authority is again raised in the court prologue, which focuses on the play's age and on its title character, and concludes by handing judgement on both the actor and the author over to the king: '*He that hath past / So many Censures, is now come at last / To haue your princely Eares, grace you him; then / You crown the Action, and renowne the pen.*' Despite the age of the play and its record of theatrical success, it is only Charles' approval that can secure the reputation of its (again unnamed) author. The Cockpit prologue alludes to Marlowe more explicitly, but again the figures of the author and actor are intertwined:

                 We know not how our Play may passe this Stage,
Marlo.   But by the best of Poets in that age
                 The Malta Jew *had being, and was made;*
*Allin.   *And He, then by the best of** *Actors play'd:*
                 In Hero *and* Leander, *one did gaine*
                 A lasting memorie: in Tamberlaine,
                 This Jew, *with others many: th'other man*
                 The Attribute of peerelesse, being a man
                 Whom we may ranke with (doing no one wrong)
                 Proteus *for shapes, and* Roscius *for a tongue,*
                 So could he speake, so vary[.]

Although Marlowe and Alleyn are not named within the prologue itself, Heywood takes advantage of the print medium to add marginal notes specifying the playwright and actor that he has in mind.

It is striking that Marlowe's fame is said to derive primarily from his authorship of a non-dramatic work, *Hero and Leander*. Although

Heywood's reference to this text is in part designed so that he can balance the two genres and praise Alleyn for his portrayals of Tamburlaine and Barabas, the importance of the non-dramatic works in Marlowe's Caroline afterlife is demonstrated in the two new editions of *Hero and Leander* (1629 and 1637) and *All Ovid's Elegies* (1630 and 1640), the former credited as 'Begun by CHRISTOPHER MARLOE, and finished by GEORGE CHAPMAN' and the latter as '*By C. M.*' The period also saw repeated reprints for an anonymous broadside ballad version of 'Come Live with Me and Be My Love', later described as 'that smooth Song which was made by *Kit Marlow*, now at least fifty years ago' in Izaac Walton's *The Compleat Angler*.[2] In contrast, *Doctor Faustus* was the only one of Marlowe's plays to be reprinted between 1625 and 1642, appearing in 1631, although a 1657 edition of *Lust's Dominion* was to claim the authorship of '*Christofer Marloe*, Gent.'.[3] Marlowe in the Caroline period was thus as much a non-dramatic as a dramatic poet, and he is as prone to having others' works attributed to him as to be denied the authorship of works now often considered to be his.

The Caroline Marlowe is, it appears, a shifting and evasive figure. Something of this ambivalence can be seen in John Suckling's *The Goblins* (King's Men, *c.* 1638–41), in which a group of thieves disguised as devils capture a somewhat brain-addled poet who, thinking he is in hell, requests to meet poets such as Shakespeare and Fletcher. But there are, apparently, limits as to which writers might be in this fictional hell. When the poet asks to consult the author of *Querer por solo Querer* and 'he that made the fairie Queene', the first thief replies that they are 'by themselves in some other place'; he offers instead 'he that writ *Tamerlane*'.[4] While Antonio Hurtado de Mendoza, author of *Querer por solo Querer*, and Edmund Spenser are apparently in heaven, Marlowe is available in hell, along with 'the Author of the *bold Beauchams*, / And *Englands Joy*'. The first allusion is to a play, *The Bold Beauchamps*, now lost, which appears to have been considered old-fashioned by 1607–8, when it was mentioned in Francis Beaumont's *The Knight of the Burning Pestle*; the second is to a notorious summary or 'argument' of an unperformed play, *The Plot of the Play, called England's Joy*, by Richard Vennar, published in 1602.[5] *The Goblins* thus playfully suggests that Marlowe's works – and, perhaps, *Tamburlaine* in particular – are to be grouped with old-fashioned and popular, even exploitative, entertainment rather than with literary texts such as *Querer por solo Querer* and *The Faerie Queene*. It also appears to nod at Marlowe's reputation for transgressive behaviour and his authorship of the devil-invoking *Doctor Faustus*.

Theatre

As described above, the 1633 edition of *The Jew of Malta* does not only draw attention to Marlowe as the author of the play; it also focuses on Alleyn's performance of Barabas and on the part that this role played in establishing his reputation. It is noticeable that Heywood devotes more of his prologue to Alleyn than to Marlowe, but it is not entirely surprising, given that he devotes the remainder of the prologue to establishing the claim of a new actor, Richard Perkins, to the title role:

>   *nor is't hate:*
> *Perkins   *To merit: in* him who doth personate*
>   *Our* Jew *this day, nor is it his ambition*
>   *To exceed, or equall, being of condition*
>   *More modest; this is all that he intends,*
>   *(And that too, at the urgence of some friends)*
>   *To proue his best, and if none here gaine-say it,*
>   *The part he hath studied, and intends to play it.*
>   (A4v)

Heywood again omits the actor's name from the script of the prologue, supplying it in the printed text. Spectators must have been aware that Perkins – the leading actor in Queen Henrietta Maria's Men – was due to play the role, but his anonymity is appropriate given the emphasis that is laid in the prologue on his unassuming modesty. The tactic is maintained in the epilogue for the Cockpit, which claims that '*our Actor* [...] *onely aym'd to goe, but not out-goe*'. Perkins' role is to negotiate with memories of Alleyn's performance, not to seek to outdo it.

While the 1633 edition of *The Jew of Malta* provides the strongest surviving evidence for the revival of Marlowe's works in the Caroline period, the play's performance at court and at the Cockpit is at odds with prevailing trends. In Abraham Cowley's *The Guardian*, performed at Trinity College, Cambridge, in March 1642, a character is said to 'roar like *Tamerlin* at the Bull'.[6] Cowley refers to the Red Bull, an amphitheatre, to the north of the City of London, which attracted a more mixed and (possibly) rowdier audience than did indoor theatres like the Cockpit.[7] Similarly, Edward Gayton looks back to Caroline performances at the amphitheatres in his *Pleasant Notes upon Don Quixot* (1654), recalling that on Shrovetide, a time of holiday and festive release for apprentices,

> the Players have been appointed, notwithstanding their bils to the contrary, to act what the major part of the company had a mind to; sometimes *Tamerlane*, sometimes Iugurth, sometimes the Jew of *Malta*, and sometimes

parts of all these, and at last, none of the three taking, they were forc'd to undresse and put off their Tragick habits, and conclude the day with the merry milk-maides.[8]

Gayton appears to remember occasions on which spectators exercised their power over the players, calling repeatedly for old favourites and even refusing to allow the company to settle into any one play. *The Two Merry Milkmaids* had been first performed at the Red Bull around 1620, while the Elizabethan play *Jugurth* was relicensed for the Fortune, another amphitheatre, in 1624.[9] Cowley's and Gayton's accounts therefore suggest the ongoing popular life of Marlowe's plays.

Doctor Faustus was also associated by tradition with the amphitheatres. *Knavery in All Trades* (1664), probably written by John Tatham – who had been active as a dramatist before the Civil War – includes a sequence in which old playgoers discuss their memories of the Caroline stage. One describes a performance by Richard Fowler, the leading actor at the Fortune, to which another responds: 'I but what d'ye call him was the man; he plaid the devil in Doctor *Faustus*, and a fellow in the Gallery throwing a Tobacco-Pipe at him; I hope to see thee (quoth He) e're long as bad as I am, what's that quoth the fellow? the Son of a Whore quoth He.'[10] Like many old plays, Marlowe's had begun to gather theatrical anecdotes around them, but in comparison with allusions to Shakespeare or Jonson these anecdotes seem especially likely to focus on performance.

These accounts and allusions, and others like them, suggest both the ongoing theatrical vitality of at least some of Marlowe's plays, and the extent to which they were associated with popular theatre. However, the court and Cockpit performances of *The Jew of Malta* complicate this picture, reminding us not to stereotype amphitheatre repertories in the way that Gayton appears to or to assume that there were no overlaps between the repertories of the amphitheatres and of the indoor theatres. Moreover, the apparent failure of playing companies to revive *Dido, Queen of Carthage* or *Edward II* suggests the incomplete, fragmented nature of Marlowe's Caroline canon. It is, however, dangerous to assume that absence of evidence is evidence of absence. *Dido, Queen of Carthage* is strongly associated with an Elizabethan children's company aesthetic but would not have been too out of place alongside Thomas Randolph's *Amyntas* in the repertory of the short-lived Caroline children's company, the Children of the Revels, active around 1629–32.[11] Similarly, *Edward II* would sit easily in a repertory alongside Caroline history plays such as John Ford's *Perkin Warbeck* or Robert Davenport's *King John and Matilda*, both performed by Queen Henrietta Maria's Men around the time when the company revived *The Jew of Malta*.

Allusion

The 1633 court prologue to *The Jew of Malta* painstakingly portrays the play as old; not only was it '*writ many yeares agone*', but it is cautiously presented '*'Mongst other Playes that now in fashion are*' (A4r). However, Marlowe's works were also part of a living theatrical tradition: through revival itself; through their influence on playwrights such as Ford, Thomas Rawlins, and Nathanael Richards; and through allusions within the texts of plays.[12] These allusions follow the patterns of publication and revival described above. There are many references to *Hero and Leander*, *Doctor Faustus*, *Tamburlaine*, and, to a lesser extent, *The Jew of Malta*, but few or none to *Dido* or *Edward II*. Allusions appear within plays written by a number of different dramatists, for a variety of playhouses and companies, and they provide an intriguing picture of what attracted Marlowe's successors to his work.

In Suckling's *The Goblins*, mentioned above, when the Poet is offered 'h[e] that writ *Tamerlane*' he replies,

> I beseech you bring me to him,
> There's something in his Scene
> Betwixt the Empresses a little high and clowdie,
> I would resolve my selfe.[13]

Although it is not immediately clear what the Poet finds obscure about the altercation between Zenocrate and Zabina in Act III of *Tamburlaine*, the allusion may suggest one way in which Marlowe's works were open to Caroline reinterpretation. Sophie Tomlinson has recently argued that the increased visibility of female theatricality at court had important effects on the transvestite commercial stage; she suggests that the work of dramatists such as Ford, James Shirley, and William Cartwright – writing for the Blackfriars, Cockpit, and Court stages – 'testifies to a newly awakened perception of women's abilities as actors and artists in the Caroline period, and to a fresh valuation of their intellectual and moral qualities'.[14] On the other hand, the Poet might simply display a prurient interest in a scene in which two high-status women exchange insults.

Elsewhere, *Hero and Leander* is presented within plays as a kind of textual aphrodisiac, wielded by men in an attempt to woo women that is often unsuccessful or unresolved. A typical example can be found in

Thomas Nabbes' comedy *Covent Garden* (Queen Henrietta Maria's Men, 1632–3), in which Artlove is advised on wooing techniques by his cynical associate Jerker:

> Sure thou hast not boldnes enough to speake to her. Thou wouldst blush, and fall into some patheticall booke discourse, or tell her the story of *Hero and Leander*, to make her tendernesse whine. Tis not the way. Get accesse to her; and after one mannerly salute, double and treble thy kisses; tumble her a little, and if opportunity serve, offer the rest: Magick hath not a Philter like it.[15]

Hero and Leander is stigmatised as an inadequate erotic tool, one that must be rejected in favour of more direct tactics. Given that the two young men are standing under the balcony on which Dorothy, Artlove's target, is positioned, the rejection of 'pathetical booke discourse' and the recommendation of force take on a greater force.

Marlowe's plays are also often invoked in the context of transgressive desire. In Randolph's *Amyntas* (Children of the Revels, 1630), Amaryllis is required to write the name of the shepherd who should marry Laurinda: Alexis or her own beloved, Damon. Damon, who suspects a trick to deny him Laurinda, wounds Amaryllis, whereupon she attempts to write Damon's name in her own blood:

> This paper is too course;
> O that I had my heart, to write it there!
> But so it is already. Would I had
> A Parchment made of my own skin, in that
> To write the truth of my affection,
> A wonder to posterity! – Hand make hast
> As my bloud does, or I shall faint I feare
> Ere I have done my story. –

Fainting, she declares, 'My blood congeales / Within my quill, and I can write no more.'[16] The allusion to Faustus' pact with the devil underlines both the violence of Amaryllis' masochistic action and the unnaturalness of her attempt to sign away, to another woman, the man that she is in love with; it suggests the tragic potential of the emotionally excessive Caroline pastoral tragicomedy and also, perhaps, the comedic edge of Marlovian tragedy.

A quotation from *Tamburlaine* is treated in a similarly ambivalent fashion in William Cavendish and James Shirley's comedy *The Variety* (King's Men, 1641). Simpleton and James plot to abduct Lucy, the reluctant object of Simpleton's affections. James comments, 'The Coachman is a lusty fellow too, and will help to clap her abroad; the curtaines being close she cannot be heard, and the horses will runne, as the devill were in the poope, for he drives like a Tamberlaine', to which Simpleton cries, 'Holla ye pamperd Jades'.[17] Simpleton is described in the dramatis personae and within the text as a 'chiaus'; the term had been adapted from the Turkish *chāush* in the late sixteenth century to refer to a Turkish messenger or sergeant.[18] The allusion to *Tamburlaine* thus restates Simpleton's association with outlandish mores or appetites, rendering him ambivalent in terms of his sexual desires, his class-status, and his nationality.

Conclusion

In many ways, the picture that we gain of Marlowe's afterlife in the Caroline theatre is in accord with that offered by other periods and contexts. His authorship is often contested or ambivalent; select plays are familiar enough for dramatists to build complex associations around allusions to them; and a faint aura of transgression surrounds many of the references to his works. In other respects, however, the Caroline period provides a less familiar view. Here, we find a Marlowe whose works are somewhat old-fashioned, sometimes in tune with new theatrical aesthetics but as often at odds with them, dependent upon the actors that perform them, and defiantly popular despite attempts to make them appeal to the elite.

Notes

1 Zachary Lesser, *Renaissance Drama and the Politics of Publication: Readings in the English Book Trade* (Cambridge University Press, 2004), 81–114. For an alternative account of the topicality of *The Jew of Malta* in the 1630s see John Parker, 'Barabas and Charles I', in *Placing the Plays of Christopher Marlowe: Fresh Cultural Contexts*, ed. Sara Munson Deats and Robert A. Logan (Aldershot: Ashgate, 2008), 167–81.
2 Izaac Walton, *The Compleat Angler; or, The Contemplative Man's Recreation* (London, 1653), 63–4.
3 *Lust's Dominion* is more commonly associated with Dekker, Day, Houghton, and, possibly, Marston. See Charles Cathcart, '*Lust's Dominion; or, The Lascivious Queen*: Authorship, Date, and Revision', *Review of English Studies*, New Series 52 (2001): 360–71.
4 John Suckling, *The Goblins: A Comedy*, in *Fragmenta aurea: A Collection of all the Incomparable Peeces, Written by Sir John Suckling* (London, 1646), 45 (*The Goblins* has separate pagination).

5 The Citizen's Wife claims that her husband 'hath promised me any time this twelvemonth to carry me to *The Bold Beauchamps*' (Francis Beaumont, *The Knight of the Burning Pestle*, ed. Michael Hattaway (London: Ernest Benn, 1969), Induction, 52–3). On *England's Joy* see Tiffany Stern, *Documents of Performance in Early Modern England* (Cambridge University Press, 2009), 70–2. Vennar advertised a one-off performance at the Swan but only uttered a few words of the prologue before running off with the profits.
6 Abraham Cowley, *The Guardian* (London, 1650), C3v.
7 For reappraisals of the Red Bull see Lucy Munro, Anne Lancashire, John H. Astington, and Marta Straznicky, 'Issues in Review: Popular Theatre and the Red Bull', *Early Theatre* 9 (2006): 99–156.
8 Edmund Gayton, *Pleasant Notes upon Don Quixot* (London, 1654), 271.
9 On *Jugurth*, see N. W. Bawcutt, ed., *The Control and Censorship of Caroline Drama: The Records of Sir Henry Herbert, Master of the Revels 1623–73* (Oxford: Clarendon Press, 1996), 151.
10 John Tatham[?], *Knavery in All Trades; or, The Coffee-House: A Comedy* (London, 1664), E1r.
11 The best overview is G. E. Bentley, 'The Theatres and the Actors', in *The Revels History of Drama in English*, 8 vols., Vol. iv, ed. Philip Edwards, Gerald Eades Bentley, Kathleen McLuskie, and Lois Potter (London and New York: Routledge, 1981), 69–124 (105–8).
12 For more complete lists of allusions, see John Edwin Bakeless, *The Tragicall History of Christopher Marlowe*, 2 vols. (Cambridge, MA: Harvard University Press, 1942); C. F. Tucker Brooke, *The Reputation of Christopher Marlowe*, Transactions of the Connecticut Academy of Arts and Sciences 25 (New Haven: Connecticut Academy of Arts and Sciences, 1922), 347–408.
13 Suckling, *The Goblins*, 45.
14 Sophie Tomlinson, *Women on Stage in Stuart Drama* (Cambridge University Press, 2005), 81.
15 Thomas Nabbes, *Covent Garden: A Pleasant Comedie* (London, 1638), 12.
16 Thomas Randolph, *Poems with the Muses Looking-Glass: And Amyntas* (Oxford, 1638), 79–80.
17 William Cavendish and James Shirley, *The Variety*, In *The Country Captaine and the Variety, Two Comedies Written by a Person of Honor* (London, 1649), 72 (the plays have separate pagination).
18 See *ibid.*, A2r, 45; *OED*, s.v. 'chiaus, *n.*'.

CHAPTER TWENTY EIGHT

Marlowe's literary influence
Lisa Hopkins

Although Marlowe has never achieved the iconic status of his exact contemporary Shakespeare, his seven extraordinary plays, great unfinished epyllion *Hero and Leander*, and exquisite lyric 'The Passionate Shepherd to His Love' have all in their own ways exerted a substantial, if not always durable, literary influence. (His translation of the first book of Lucan's *Pharsalia* has always been a more minority taste, though by no means entirely neglected.) Marlowe's literary influence can be crudely divided into two sorts: response (usually in the form of imitation or parody) to his style and response to the content of his works (principally his plays), chiefly but not necessarily exclusively in the form of engagement with the sceptical, questioning ethos of his oeuvre. Notably, these two separate strands of Marlowe's influence have largely tended to focus on different plays, with *Tambulaine* being the preferred model for echoes of Marlowe's language and *Doctor Faustus* more likely to be invoked in any exploration or appropriation of Marlowe's reputation for dissidence, and these two different kinds of response each have their own historical moments, imitation of Marlowe's style being a phenomenon mainly of the century after his death and interest in his radical potential only coming later.

Some years ago, an overly zealous copy-editor picked me up on the fact that I had referred to 'Marlowe's mighty line', as it was famously termed by Ben Jonson, without giving an act, line, and scene reference for it. Giving my inner pedant full rein, I attempted to explain what was meant by the phrase, but actually I could have saved myself the trouble by giving a reference to more or less any line from either part of *Tamburlaine*, because when writers in the late sixteenth and early seventeenth centuries echoed Marlowe what they almost always tried to do was make a noise like Tamburlaine. This was, after all, the man who made his followers kings and exhorted them to 'march against the powers of heaven / And set black streamers in the firmament / To signify the slaughter of the gods'.[1] Particularly memorable was the moment when Tamburlaine, having harnessed four conquered kings to his chariot, whips them on in a speech beginning 'Holla, ye pampered jades of Asia!' (2 *Tamb.*, IV.ii.1); as late as 1629 this was apparently still being shouted at Bridewell inmates being made to clean the streets of London.

The desire to reproduce the blood-and-thunder rhythms and exotic, rolling polysyllables of *Tamburlaine* could be illustrated from any one of a large number of plays. In the anonymous 1590s university play *Caesar's Revenge*, for instance, Caesar says to Cleopatra,

> Not onely Aegipt but all Africa,
> Will I subject to Cleopatras name.
> Thy rule shall stretch from unknowne Zanziber,
> Unto those Sandes where high erected poastes []
> Of great Alcides, do up hold his name,
> The sunne burnt Indians, from the east shall bring:
> Their pretious store of pure refined gould,
> The laboring worme shall weave the Africke twiste,
> And to exceed the pompe of Persian Queene,
> The Sea shall pay the tribute of his pearles,
> For to adorne thy goulden yellow lockes,
> Which in their curled knots, my thoughts do hold,
> Thoughtes captivd to thy beauties conquering power.[2]

The idea of Persia is geographically quite alien in this reference to Africa; it, along with the grand polysyllables, is clearly an import from *Tamburlaine the Great*, Part I. Coupled with the extravagant promises to Cleopatra that are so obviously reminiscent of those Tamburlaine makes to Zenocrate, this effects not only a temporal but also by implication a cultural dislocation, prising open the grave in which the classical past was entombed and setting the story free to evoke more urgent and contemporary resonances. Although Tamburlaine himself lived in the fourteenth century, Marlowe anachronistically inserts an episode from a later period of history in the shape of events linked to the 1444 Battle of Varna; a story of invasion and military might inevitably looked all too urgently contemporary in the build-up to and immediate aftermath of the Armada.

Paradoxically, though topicality was always latent in Roman plays because of the supposed colonisation of Britain by the great-grandson of Aeneas and of the consequent blood-link to Rome and Troy, it did require activation. In the case of *Caesar's Revenge*, the story of Tamburlaine, maker and breaker of kingdoms, might well help audiences notice that *Caesar's Revenge* itself was not uninterested in the question of who might be a king, specifically with reference to the fact that there was no clear successor to

Elizabeth's throne. Brutus' comment on Pompey that 'the rising sun, not setting, doth men please' (II.iv.36) echoes Elizabeth's own remark to the Scottish ambassador, William Maitland of Lethington: 'I know the inconstancy of the people of England, how they ever mislike the present government and has [*sic*] their eyes fixed upon that person that is next to succeed; and naturally men be so disposed: *Plures adorant solem orientem quam occidentem* [More people adore the rising sun than the setting one].'³ Moreover, the survival of two separate titles for the play, *Caesar's Revenge* and *Caesar and Pompey*, suggests a lack of clarity about the generic template within which audiences are expected to respond. *Tamburlaine* helps by evoking the easily familiar narrative of the exceptional man for whom death is fundamentally contingent rather than implicit in, and a summation of, the meaning of his life.

In another Roman play that may well derive originally from much the same times as *Caesar's Revenge*, the anonymous *Claudius Tiberius Nero* (c. 1607), Drusus too uses clearly Tamburlainian language when he declares,

> The orient does shine in warlike steel,
> And bloody streamers, wavèd in the air,
> By their reflections dye the plains in red,
> As ominous unto destructive wars,
> As are the blazing comets in the East.
> (II.iii.127–31)⁴

Here the primary allusion is to the mad Zabina's 'streamers white, red, black, here, here, here'(*1 Tamb.*, V.i.315). But once again the evocation is of *Tamburlaine* as a whole, pulling the play forwards in time and allowing the audience to see that its story of a corrupt court and ambitious favourites might map quite neatly onto the home life of their own dear king. Above all, the figure of Tamburlaine evoked war, and questions of military prowess and preparedness were to the fore in both of these Roman plays themselves and the contexts in which they were produced, with first Elizabeth's wars in Ireland and then the potential consequences of her successor's pacifism looming particularly large. The extent to which stylistic imitation of Tamburlaine lent itself to discourses of war is perhaps most pithily encapsulated when Shakespeare's Pistol demands, in *Henry IV, Part Two*:

> Shall pack-horses,
> And hollow pampered jades of Asia,
> Which cannot go but thirty mile a day,
> Compare with Caesars and with Cannibals,
> And Troyant Greeks?⁵

As Bertie Wooster says of Shakespeare himself, it sounds well enough, but it doesn't actually mean anything; what it does do, however, is precisely nail both the extent to which Pistol is nothing more than a purveyor of empty bombast and the extent to which the play itself fails to register completely unqualified enthusiasm for war and its effects.

The vogue for *Tamburlaine* did not last, though. In 1681, a play called *Tamerlane the Great*, by Charles Saunders, was acted in London. When it was censured as 'only an Old Play transcrib'd' – that is, an unacknowledged rehashing of Christopher Marlowe's *Tamburlaine the Great* – Saunders claimed never to have heard of Marlowe's play or to have found anyone else who had, while in 1675 Milton's nephew Edward Phillips in his *Theatrum poetarum* had ascribed *Tamburlaine* to Thomas Newton, author of *A Notable Historie of the Saracens*.[6] Milton himself, however, appears to have had a more informed interest in Marlowe. Milton's newly fallen Satan is tormented by the 'thought ... of lost happiness', the theological concept of *poena damni*, the pain of loss experienced by the damned. And Satan's statement in Book IV, 'Which way I fly is hell; myself am hell',[7] recalls Mephistopheles'

> Why this is hell, nor am I out of it.
> Think'st thou that I, who saw the face of God,
> And tasted the eternal joys of heaven,
> Am not tormented with ten thousand hells,
> In being deprived of eternal bliss?[8]

The fear of an almost incomprehensible suffering that can never end is found in Faustus' closing soliloquy – 'Let Faustus live in hell a thousand years, / A hundred thousand, and at last be saved' (V.ii.101–2) – and Marlowe's play too offers us a strong sense of hell but can imagine heaven only as what it is not. Finally, the idea of a 'doom' that had been 'reserved' for Satan and the fact that a place had already been 'prepared' for him even before his revolt (I.54–5, 71) raise the same issues of predestination and choice as the opening Chorus' reference to how Faustus' 'waxen wings did mount above his reach, / And melting heavens conspired his overthrow' (Pro., 21–2)

When interest in Marlowe finally did begin to return, it was no longer on *Tamburlaine* that it centred. In 1744 Dodsley included *Edward II* in his *Old Plays*, and in 1818 Oxberry brought out a further edition of that and also of *The Jew of Malta* and *Doctor Faustus* (as well as *Lust's Dominion*, which he erroneously identified as by Marlowe). In the same year Kean's revival brought further attention to *The Jew of Malta*, with Kean's own

Barabas singled out for special praise: 'He illumined and rendered tolerable a dark and gloomy portrait ... He seized upon every passage that could diffuse an air of truth and probability around the character with instinctive discrimination.'[9] Not until 1820 did Oxberry add the two parts of *Tamburlaine* to his suite of editions. Attention also began to turn to the rest of the canon, with *Dido, Queen of Carthage* appearing in Hurst and Robinson's *Old English Drama* in 1825 and with John Payne Collier announcing in the same year that he had 'discovered' a missing leaf from *The Massacre at Paris* (although the subsequent revelation of Collier's predilection for forgery has raised a question mark over this claim). Marlowe's poetry had also received renewed attention from Byron, whose interest in the Faust story seems to have been channelled through Goethe rather than through Marlowe, but whose 1810 poem 'Written after Swimming from Sestos to Abydos' begins,

> If, in the month of dark December,
> Leander, who was nightly wont
> (What maid will not the tale remember?)
> To cross thy stream, broad Hellespont!
> (1–4)[10]

The poem goes on to remind us that Leander did this 'according to the doubtful story, / To woo – and Lord knows what beside' (14–15), clearly recalling the comic inexperience of Leander and the delicious vagueness of the poem's oft-repeated 'it': 'She, with a kind of granting, put him by it, / And ever as he thought himself most nigh it' (557–8).[11] Byron's own aesthetic sensibility and delicate versification here sustain a sympathetic dialogue that annihilates the years to present him and the Marlowe of *Hero and Leander* as twinned spirits.

Thus throughout the 1820s interest shifted and floated without gravitating to any specific centre, until in 1829 the relative estimation of the canon took a decisive step towards its current state, with Goethe singling out *Faustus* for praise that proved highly influential. The time was obviously ripe for such a shift in preference: as the careers of Byron and his friend Shelley abundantly demonstrate, iconoclasm and challenge to established authority had both found their moment. I have already suggested, though, that when Milton echoes Faustus what he remembers may be echoes of ideas and situations rather than of specific terms and phrases. This choice results of course partly because Milton has such a strongly developed style of his own, but in general, when *Doctor Faustus* is remembered, it is for its ideas rather than for its actual language. The survival of two distinct texts leaves room for uncertainty about what Marlowe actually wrote, but even lines found in both have less of an afterlife than might have been expected. Astonishingly, *Early English Books Online* finds only one other instance of a question beginning 'Was this the face that', in *The Tragedy of Julia Agrippina* by Thomas May (whose interest in Lucan clearly attests to the direct influence of Marlowe). To be Tamburlainian is to sound like Tamburlaine, but to be Faustian is not, it seems, to sound like Faustus.

It was in the nineteenth century that this pattern of adaptation without quotation became definitively established, perhaps partly as a result of Goethe's famous preference for the shape of the play rather than for its detail ('How greatly is it all planned!'). *Faustus* clearly informed the 1818 first version of Mary Shelley's *Frankenstein*, which was revised and republished in 1831 – not least when the monster, like Faustus, asks for a wife; (*Edward II* is also an important presence in another Shelley novel, *Valperga*, which is set partly in the court of the historical Edward II and includes Gaveston as a character). *Faustus* can also be seen as an influence on the creation of another celebrated literary monster, since recent work on Bram Stoker has pointed out that his creation of Dracula was influenced by the portrayal of Goethe's Faust by Henry Irving, whose theatre Stoker managed.[12] The story of the Faustian pact also underlines *The Picture of Dorian Gray*, whose author Oscar Wilde had been a childhood friend of Stoker in Dublin and remained close to him in London. Dorian Gray says that he 'would give my soul' not to grow old; the woman in the opium den calls him 'the devil's bargain'; Dorian's attempts to repent are unavailing; and although Shakespeare would appear to be the dominant influence, the narrative does at one point mention Edward II and Gaveston, suggesting that Marlowe too is being remembered.[13]

Marie Corelli's *The Sorrows of Satan*, which was published in the same year as *Dracula* and mentions Irving as a particular friend of its Mephistopheles figure, offers a novel version of the traditional legend in which the devil can be restored to heaven if enough human souls resist him, although he is doomed to tempt them to the utmost of his power.[14] Corelli, whose Stratford home coincidentally now houses the Shakespeare Institute, mentions Shakespeare repeatedly but Marlowe never. Nevertheless, the novel is haunted and shaped by *Doctor Faustus* at every turn. At the outset, the impoverished narrator Geoffrey Tempest finds himself at 'a moment when if ever good and evil angels play a game of chance for a man's soul, they were surely throwing the dice on the last wager for mine' (8). To him enters the charismatic and mysterious foreign prince Lucio Rimânez (a name that we later learn derives from

Ahrimanes, a Persian name for the spirit of darkness), who, in an echo of Mephistopheles' costuming as a Franciscan friar, is announced as 'particularly fond of the society of the clergy' (10). To Tempest he is a 'Maecenas' (15), a name that may recall Faustus' desire to see the tomb of Virgil, to whom Maecenas was a patron, and Rimânez has 'wonderful eyes … suggestive of both tears and fire' (22). Tempest at once inherits a fortune from an uncle who claimed to have sold his soul to the devil (41), meets 'the paralysed Helen of a modern Troy' (131), marries a woman who claims her soul has been corrupted by the knowledge offered by books (162), wins the Derby with a mysterious horse named Phosphor whom no one but its jockey may touch (200), is shown tableaux of some modern varieties of wickedness and misery as a form of entertainment (220), and is granted a vision of the long-dead king of Alexandria and his paramour (335). There is also an echo of *Frankenstein* when the devil tells how he once saved a literary critic on the Mer de Glace (84). Here too heaven can be described only as what it is not (122). Only once, however, do we catch even the faintest echo of the actual language of Marlowe – when the devil sings of aspiring and of 'the noise of a myriad wheels that run / Ever round and round the sun' (283). Here it is of course the music of *Tamburlaine* rather than of *Faustus* that is being heard.

In her extremely long suicide note (part of which is apparently written after she is dead, as a demonstration of the existence of an afterlife), Tempest's beautiful but damned wife, who like the heroine of *The Picture of Dorian Gray* is called Sibyl, blames the poetry of Swinburne for corrupting her (325). Swinburne too was interested in Marlowe, and a rare exception to the general nineteenth-century preference for *Faustus* is found in his sonnet on the playwright, which directly quotes 'If all the pens that ever poets held' from *Tamburlaine*. However, even this is an exception proving the rule that when *Tamburlaine* is remembered, it is remembered for specific verbal details. Swinburne himself turned to *Faustus* as the inspiration for his poem 'Faustine', in which 'the devil threw dice with God' for the soul of the eponymous heroine.

A more subtle and far less obviously moralising version of the Faustus story than Corelli's can be detected a few years later in Conrad's *Heart of Darkness*, where a reflection on those who had sailed from Deptford prefaces the introduction of a narrator named Marlow, who muses that 'this also … has been one of the dark places of the earth' like Mephistopheles observing that he is even now in hell.[15] Conrad's suggestively named Marlow, who like his near-namesake has a passion for maps, goes out to Africa, and sails up a river along whose banks weird cries of grief echo at the sight of a ship (59–61) like the wailings of devils excluded from heaven. Marlow meets Mr Kurtz, who like Faustus excels at every art and who may or may not have 'made a bargain for his soul with the devil' (70) but has certainly participated in 'midnight dances ending with unspeakable rites' (71); around Kurtz cluster a Helen-like 'wild and gorgeous apparition of a woman' (87) and a figure with horns on its head (94) resembling those of Marlowe's Benvolio. Once again, there are no direct verbal echoes of the play, but in *Doctor Faustus* Conrad has clearly found a vision of hell with the subtlety and sophistication needed to interweave appropriately with his own oblique and nuanced narration.

In our own century, Bart Simpson and his father Homer both at different times sell their souls to the devil, and the motif is also found in the film *Bedazzled* and the musical *Damn Yankees*.[16] Faustus is a recurrent figure in the crime fiction both of Margery Allingham and of Reginald Hill, as in *Child's Play*, where 'the bar was pretty crowded and rustic drinkers were clearly as sensitive to the approach of last orders as Faustus was to his last mid night'.[17] He is also found in Philip K. Dick's *Galactic Pot-Healer*, where the Glimmung is compared to Marlowe's version of the Faust legend, but again what is being recalled in both cases is the shape of the narrative rather than any specific lines from the play.[18] Ursula LeGuin's popular children's book *A Wizard of Earthsea*, in which the hero Ged endangers his soul by a quest for knowledge and conjures the phantom of a long-dead beauty, can also be seen as a version of the Faust story, not least since its hero takes to the air and does magic,[19] while in *The Farthest Shore*, the final book of the trilogy, the dead hero Erreth-Akbe is summoned – like the spirit Alexander in *Faustus* – in a form of magical peep-show. In the twenties, Michael Butor and Henri Pousseur collaborated on *Votre Faust, fantasie variable, genre opéra*, which, although influenced primarily by Goethe, also glances at Marlowe,[20] as does Aymanan Krishna Kaimal's 1976 Kathakali dance *Faust*.[21] Even the popular TV series *Yes, Minister* has been described by Gerald Kaufman as 'The Rt Hon. Faust MP, constantly beset by the wiles of Sir Mephistopheles'.[22] While it was the mighty line of Tamburlaine that caught the imagination of Marlowe's contemporaries, it is the urgent, agonised scepticism of Faustus, shoring up fragments amidst the ruins of certainty and of monolithic knowledge and belief systems, that sings more loudly now.

Notes

1 Christopher Marlowe, *Tamburlaine the Great*, ed. Mark Thornton Burnett (London: J. M. Dent, 1999), Part II, V.ii.48–50. All references to *Tamburlaine* are to this edition.

2 Anon., *The tragedie of Caesar and Pompey or Caesars reuenge* (London, 1607), I.vi.29–41. The original text had an erroneous full stop after 'poastes' (32).
3 Queen Elizabeth I, *Elizabeth I: Collected Works*, ed. Leah S. Marcus, Janel Mueller, and Mary Beth Rose (University of Chicago Press, 2000), 66.
4 I quote from the version of *Claudius Tiberius Nero* edited by my student Sharon McDonnell as part of the 'Editing a Renaissance Play' module on the M.A. in English Studies (Renaissance Literature) at Sheffield Hallam University: http://extra.shu.ac.uk/emls/iemls/resources.html.
5 William Shakespeare, *Henry IV, Part Two*, ed. P. H. Davison (Harmondsworth: Penguin, 1977), II.iv.158–62.
6 F. S. Boas, *Christopher Marlowe: A Biographical and Critical Study* (Oxford: Clarendon Press, 1940), 300.
7 John Milton, *Paradise Lost*, in *The Portable Milton*, ed. Douglas Bush (Harmondsworth: Penguin, 1976 [1949]), Book IV.75.
8 Christopher Marlowe, *Doctor Faustus*, in *The Complete Plays*, ed. Mark Thornton Burnett (London: J. M. Dent, 1999), 1604 text, I.ii.78–82. All quotations are taken from this edition.
9 Frederick William Hawkins, *The Life of Edmund Kean*, 2 vols. (London: Tinsley Brothers, 1869), Vol. II, 42.
10 George Gordon, Lord Byron, 'Written after Swimming from Sestos to Abydos', in *Byron: Poetical Works*, ed. Frederick Page (Oxford University Press, 1970), 59. On Byron's interest in Goethe, see Fred Parker, '"Much in the mode of Goethe's Mephistopheles": *Faust* and Byron', in *International Faust Studies: Adaptation, Reception, Translation*, ed. Lorna Fitzsimmons (London: Continuum, 2008), 107–23 (107).
11 Christopher Marlowe, *Hero and Leander*, in *The Collected Poems of Christopher Marlowe*, ed. Patrick Cheney and Brian J. Striar (Oxford University Press, 2006).
12 See for instance David J. Skal, '"His Hour upon the Stage": Theatrical Adaptations of *Dracula*', in Bram Stoker, *Dracula*, ed. Nina Auerbach and David J. Skal (London: W. W. Norton, 1997), 371–81 (372–3).
13 Oscar Wilde, *The Picture of Dorian Gray* (Harmondsworth: Penguin, 1984), 34, 217, 254–5, 158.
14 Marie Corelli, *The Sorrows of Satan* (Oxford University Press, 1996), 29. All further quotations from the novel will be taken from this edition, and reference will be given in the text.
15 Joseph Conrad, *Heart of Darkness* (Harmondsworth: Penguin, 1973), 7. Further references will be cited in the text.
16 With thanks to my colleague Tom Rutter.
17 Reginald Hill, *Child's Play* (London: HarperCollins, 2003 [1987]), 300.
18 Philip K. Dick, *Galactic Pot-Healer* (London: Gollancz, 2005 [1969]), 151.
19 Ursula LeGuin, *A Wizard of Earthsea* (Berkeley, CA: Parnassus Press, 1968).
20 Steven R. Cerf, 'The Faust Theme in Twentieth-Century Opera', in *Lives of Faust: The Faust Theme in Literature and Music*, ed. Lorna Fitzsimmons, rev. edn (Berlin: Walter de Gruyter, 2008), 461–72 (469).

21 David G. John, 'Goethe's *Faust* in India: The Kathakali Adaptation', in *International Faust Studies: Adaptation, Reception, Translation*, ed. Lorna Fitzsimmons (London: Continuum, 2008), 161–76 (165).
22 Gerald Kaufman, in *The Guinness Book of Classic TV*, ed. Paul Cornell, Martin Day, and Keith Topping (Enfield: Guinness, 1993), 113–18 (117).

CHAPTER TWENTY NINE

Marlowe in the movies

Pascale Aebischer

Since *Shakespeare in Love* (1999) enshrined Marlowe's status as the principal precursor Shakespeare had to get out of the way in order to achieve genius, Marlowe has developed a recognisable 'brand' identity as radical, dangerous, and queer, and he has become an ever more marketable commodity. As a result, the core corpus of Marlowe films – Richard Burton and Nevill Coghill's *Doctor Faustus* (1967), Jan Švankmajer's post-Communist *Faust* (1994), and Derek Jarman's *Edward II* (1991) – has expanded. It now includes new films, like the Stage on Screen DVD of a production of *Doctor Faustus* at the Greenwich Theatre (2009) and Douglas Morse's low-budget *The Jew of Malta* (2012). Adaptation studies' more flexible definition of what constitutes an adaptation adds to the corpus F. W. Murnau's silent *Faust* (1926), which like Švankmajer's film relied on a number of Faust texts including Marlowe's, and Sidney Lumet's *A Deadly Affair* (1966). Finally, the BBC's DVD release in 2009 of Toby Robertson's 1969–70 Prospect Theatre production of *Edward II*, with Ian McKellen as the king, has enabled one of the most important twentieth-century productions of a Marlowe play to re-enter the corpus thirty-nine years after its first airing and subsequent disappearance from circulation in Britain.[1]

It is the recent release of the BBC DVD of Ian McKellen's performance of *Edward II* that prompts the questions that preoccupy me here, not just because this promises to be a popular film that has not yet been subjected to critical analysis, but because its relationship with the most influential and widely known Marlowe film to date, Derek Jarman's provocatively queer *Edward II*, defies linear chronology. How may we read the relationship between these films, bearing in mind that there is no evidence that might support the assumption that Jarman saw, or was even aware of, McKellen's performance? To what extent is the film shot in 1970 changed upon its DVD release in 2009 by the fact that Jarman filmed the same play in 1991? To what extent may the 2009 release of the McKellen film affect our reading of Jarman's *Edward II*?

A typical reception-studies approach to the two films might, in Barbara Klinger's terms, be synchronic (each film analysed in its own historical context) and diachronic (the McKellen performance considered at two points thirty-nine years apart); it would, thus, acknowledge 'the radical flux of meaning' for McKellen's performance 'brought on by changing social and historical horizons over time'.[2] A combination of synchronic and diachronic analyses as suggested by Klinger, however, is rendered insufficient in this case by the hostile entanglement of McKellen's biography with Jarman's. Since Jarman's death, the publication of his life-writing and McKellen's political activism have resulted in constant changes to their 'biographical legends' that have affected the relationship between their films of *Edward II*.[3] The films therefore demand a response that is not only synchronic and diachronic but also *anachronic*; that is, an approach that recognises the inchoate intersections of mutual influences that render it difficult, after the release of the McKellen DVD in 2009, to read this film solely as a precursor rather than also as a successor to Jarman's film. Anachronic viewing of this kind allows what follows after to change the meaning of what comes before and creates dialogues between films that defy the laws of chronology.

A synchronic history of Toby Robertson and Richard Marquand's film of McKellen's performance in 1970 would see that film as the culmination of a series of fringe and amateur performances on the one hand and as a successor to Sidney Lumet's *A Deadly Affair* (1966) on the other. Director Toby Robertson had himself played King Edward for the Cambridge ADC in 1951 and had then gone on to direct a production for the Marlowe Society in 1958. This production had emphasised 'the relationship between power and suffering' and had discreetly treated the play's articulation of same-sex desire 'as love in the classical sense'.[4] Same-sex desire is even more obviously suppressed in the scenes from *Edward II* directed by Peter Hall that are woven into the climactic moments of Lumet's *A Deadly Affair*. The performance of Marlowe's play by the RSC within this cold war spy thriller emphasises the slow build-up to the horrible murder rather than the sexual politics of the play. David Warner's Edward does not share the stage with Gaveston in the scenes selected, and the camera pays as much attention to the interactions of secret agents and policemen dotted among the audience as it does to the play. The onstage sodomitical murder is arguably even 'straightened', for want of a better word, by the parallel murder, in the stalls, of Simone Signoret's East German spy by her handler (Maximilian Schell); his hand slipping under her shawl to kill her without being detected while they exchange significant glances is synchronised with Lightborn's 'secret' insertion of the poker, replaying the sodomitical murder in a heterosexual key.[5]

The casting of Timothy West, the Matrevis of *A Deadly Affair*, as Mortimer Junior in the 1969–70 Prospect Theatre production makes it the more significant that young McKellen took a course that was radically different from that of his predecessors. Toby Robertson recalls McKellen 'almost sort of parading … his homosexuality', even though the actor had not come out as homosexual at this point.[6] His extravagant performance of same-sex desire was part of a larger strategy aimed at distinguishing Marlowe's king as much as possible from Shakespeare's Richard II, whom McKellen was playing in repertory with *Edward II*. While surviving footage of *Richard II* shows a consistent attempt at 'accurate' period costume, the costumes for *Edward II* are self-consciously eclectic and use modern touches, like tight leggings with modern patterns, topped by prominent 'medieval' codpieces, to distinguish Edward's homoerotic entourage from the more conservative period outfits of the barons.[7] Where McKellen's Richard is self-possessed and haughty in the deposition scene, his Edward is highly emotional, even petulant and camp. Against the background of the Stonewall riots in New York in June 1969 and, in the UK, the decriminalisation of homosexual acts between consenting adults in 1967 and the abolition of theatre censorship in 1968, it was possible for McKellen to welcome James Laurenson's Gaveston with a kiss on the mouth.[8]

That kiss, in the performance of *Edward II* that Richard Marquand filmed for the BBC towards the end of the run in London's Piccadilly Theatre,[9] became 'the first kiss between two men on British television'.[10] In the film, McKellen portrays Marlowe's king as moving from self-indulgent, exuberant youth to bearded manhood and, eventually, to the abjection of a tortured death in the sewers. In language that betrays the attitudes the production was up against, Benedict Nightingale's review described 'the creature that Lightborn finally dispatches' as 'a raddled, defeated, pathetic old queer, weakly grappling with his executioner, a parody of his former self'.[11] Lightborn's tights, worn in the same fashion as those of Edward, Gaveston, and Spencer, cue the viewer to consider him a member of the homosexual faction in Edward's court. The murder, as a result, carries a strong sado-erotic charge, with Robert Eddison's sadistic Lightborn comforting and stroking the wretched king, even kissing Edward on the mouth before proceeding with his grim preparation for the murder. The camera focuses on Edward's screaming face, but not before allowing a glimpse of the chilling precision with which Lightborn aims the red-hot poker towards Edward's bottom. With Lightborn stroking dead Edward's legs, Matrevis stabs him in the back, so that the executioner collapses over Edward's body in a final sexualised embrace. If the kiss between Edward and Gaveston at the beginning of the production speaks of the onset of an era in which homosexual desire can be expressed and valued, the murder with which it concludes suggests an affinity between homoeroticism and sadistic violence that disturbs a reading of the production as a progressive portrayal of same-sex desire.

Moving diachronically to the release of the BBC DVD in 2009, it is striking that the production is nevertheless marketed for its North American viewer as a progressive milestone in its portrayal of a homosexual king. The DVD's title, *Ian McKellen in* Edward II, privileges the actor above either the playwright or the director, selling itself as a classic performance by a performer whose star status relies on a series of high-profile heterosexual roles set against the backdrop of belated gay advocacy. The image shows Gaveston and Edward holding one another at arm's length and is matched, on the reverse, by a citation from the *Time Magazine* review of 19 September 1969 stating that 'McKellen and Director Toby Robertson have confronted with stark candor the fact that Edward II is a play by a homosexual about a king who was homosexual.' This emphasis is reinforced by the blurb's reminder that '[t]he BBC broadcast of this critically lauded production caused a sensation with its uncompromised portrayal of Edward's sexuality'.[12] With its additional provision of a special feature of a 1985 BBC programme in which actors improvise a reconstruction of 'The Marlowe Inquest', the DVD emphasises the production's age and origin as a television broadcast and frames it in relation to Marlowe's scandalous life, alleged homosexuality, and violent death.[13] This is classic theatre with a star actor and an extra sensationalist twist that allows the viewer to smile at the prudishness of a former generation with a flattering feeling of superiority.

While the connection between Marlowe and the production's flagging-up of his play's concern with same-sex desire is made explicit by the DVD, it stays silent about the connection between the performance and the biography of Ian McKellen. It is McKellen's star status, which cannot be disentangled from his sexual politics, that keys an anachronic reading of the DVD in relation to Derek Jarman's *Edward II* and to the two men's differing attitudes towards gay rights and the Conservative government in the UK in the late 1980s and early 1990s. Jarman, who had been openly gay since the 1970s, was one of the first artists to have gone public about carrying HIV in 1987. A supporter of the radical activist group OutRage!, which 'outed' prominent figures and performed carnivalesque publicity stunts that drew attention to the homophobia of the Thatcher government, Jarman was openly resentful of other public figures who had remained in the closet during the 1980s. McKellen, by contrast, had only come out about his homosexuality on BBC Radio 3 in 1987 in the context of a debate about Section 28 of the Local Government Act, the homophobic legislation that prompted Derek Jarman's work on *Edward II* between 1986 and 1991. McKellen went on to lobby the government on behalf of Stonewall, a moderate gay rights organisation that sought dialogue with all political parties.[14] Jarman's smouldering resentment of McKellen's position came to a head on 4 January 1991, when, in response to McKellen's acceptance of a knighthood from the same government that had passed Section 28, Jarman denounced his former friend in an open letter to the *Guardian* in which he asserted his 'dismay [at McKellen's] acceptance of this honour from a government which has stigmatised homosexuality'.[15]

The public row between the two men and their supporters continued throughout the early months of 1991, during which Jarman filmed *Edward II* and incorporated OutRage! activists in his anachronistic vision of a medieval king persecuted for his homosexuality by vindictive spitting churchmen and the Conservative government of 1991. When McKellen, in an interview, accused Jarman of jealousy and of not 'living in the real world', Jarman noted in his diary: 'Peripheral is the way the straight world sees us. It's a sorry day when "England's leading gay man" sees the rest of us this way. Maybe Ian has just a gay façade and has a heart as straight as a die.'[16] Significantly, Jarman reworked McKellen's opposition between straight Richard II and gay Edward II, and his own opposition to McKellen's politics, as an opposition between what he saw as Shakespeare's assimilationist politics and craving for popularity and Marlowe's sexual and political dissidence. Writes Jarman: 'I suspect if Elizabeth I was dishing out knighthoods, Shakespeare would have been at the front door with a begging bowl, Marlowe would have run a mile.'[17]

Seen anachronically in the context of a conflict whose extent and implications have only become obvious in the past decade (with the posthumous publication of Jarman's final diary in 2000 and with Michael D. Friedman's analysis, in 2009, of McKellen's performance of Richard III in the Loncraine film of 1995 as 'a monstrous version of "the queer activist", whose refusal to curb his sexual promiscuity despite his AIDS status threatens the health of society'),[18] each of the 1970 and 1991 *Edward II*s remembers and responds to the other's vision of how Marlowe's play enables an exploration of the sexual politics of the present. The very 'classic' presentation of the McKellen DVD, and the verse-speaking that betrays

McKellen's Cambridge training by George Rylands and John Barton, enshrine his position as someone who 'owns' classical theatre and is at ease within the conservative Establishment. The DVD lends authority to McKellen's desire, evident from his school visits in 2008, to act as a role model for the modern homosexual that is acceptable to parents, the mainstream press, and middle-ground politicians. His portrayal of Edward as camp, self-obsessed, and in thrall to his more dominant lover caters to a homophobic stereotype that is clearly differentiated from his personal star image; like his portrayal in *Richard III* of 'the queer activist', his Edward II is projecting an image of Nightingale's 'pathetic old queer' over whose tortured body McKellen can rise to promote an image of the modern homosexual celebrity as a benign wizard. Key is the sympathetic portrayal, in the film, of Laurenson's 'virile' Gaveston, who acts as a positive foil to McKellen's unattractive king, and of Diane Fletcher's Queen Isabella, whose emotional turmoil becomes a convenient point of identification for a straight-identified audience.

Seen as an anachronic response to the McKellen DVD, Jarman's choice of working-class actors Stephen Waddington and Andrew Tiernan as Edward and Gaveston contributes to his depiction of the modern homosexual as an everyman figure who is oppressed by the game-hunting Establishment, whose figurehead is Tilda Swinton's icy Queen Isabella. Whereas the king and his lover speak Marlowe's verse as prose but enjoy performances of classical music, dance, and readings from Dante, Swinton's verse-speaking is as crisp as are her glamorous outfits: Edward's queer court can be without pretensions in its appreciation of the arts, while verse-speaking of the kind associated with McKellen and Swinton's Isabella is combined with a lack of artistic appreciation and, in Swinton's performance, even of soul. Considered side-by-side with Diane Fletcher's sympathetic, warm, and distraught queen, Swinton's performance forbids the viewer to identify with Isabella's predicament. Even as Andrew Tiernan's thuggish Gaveston, when he brutalises a bishop or toys with Isabella, is not set up as a gay role model, the film presents the lovers as anything but '*the limp-wristed lisping fags so beloved of the tabloids*'.[19] Jarman thus quite explicitly avoids the effeminate, submissive stereotype McKellen's performance buys into, presenting instead a relationship based on love and the presumption of equality. Jarman's film portrays a political struggle that associates the king with the OutRage! activists in their provocative drag without making them a point of mockery. McKellen's incongruous combination of leggings and codpiece is, in Jarman's film, transferred onto Nigel Terry's Mortimer, who appears bare-legged in a leopard-skin coat to berate the lovers. In Jarman's final image of Mortimer and Isabella covered in dust and locked in a cage, the heterosexual couple are, to adapt Nightingale's phrase, the ones portrayed as raddled, defeated, pathetic, weak parodies of their former selves, while a very queer boy Edward III, wearing his mother's accessories, peers down at them with dispassionate curiosity. With its drag queens, nude rugby scrum, and camp vampirism, Jarman's *Edward II* resists commodification as 'fit … for wholesome family entertainment', as Swinton acknowledged in 2002, and is unlikely to be screened in schools even today, when Section 28 has been dropped from the Local Government Act and Jarman has achieved canonical status.[20]

The McKellen DVD, true to the actor's mission as an ambassador for gay rights in schools, anachronically answers the queer image of the cross-dressed boy king on top of the caged queen and her lover with a final scene in which Edward III, played as a dignified young man by Myles Reithermann, regretfully but sternly banishes his tearful mother before being ceremonially robed in a royal cloak. He then impales young Mortimer's head on a sword with his own hands and, having performed this manly business, bends over his father's cleaned-up body to kiss him on the mouth. The kiss as a signifier of same-sex desire is transformed in this gesture into a sign of filial piety; only the young man's tights suggest that he, too, may be read as 'gay', though in a discreet manner that makes him blend in with the barons. As Jarman's *Edward II* queers McKellen's performance, the McKellen DVD counters Jarman's film with a version of the play more suitable for use in educational contexts, where Edward III may operate as an intradiegetic representative of the extradiegetic politics of its star actor. Read anachronically, neither film thus holds chronological precedence, while each impacts on how the other may be understood by a present-day viewer.

Although the space available here will not permit me to follow through the implications of such an anachronic approach for the remainder of the corpus of Marlowe films, it is tempting to suggest, as a parting shot, that Murnau's 1926 *Faust* and the 2009 Stage on Screen *Doctor Faustus* permit a similar anachronic reconsideration of Burton and Coghill's 1967 *Doctor Faustus* and Švankmajer's 1994 *Faust*. The Stage on Screen *Faustus*, with its filmed theatre format, anachronically stresses the association of the Burton/Coghill film with the Oxford University Dramatic Society stage production from which it originated. Meanwhile, the re-release of the restored German print of F. W. Murnau's *Faust* in 2006 as a 'Masters of Cinema' DVD that draws attention to Murnau's indebtedness to Marlowe's 'tone' enables a fuller appreciation of Švankmajer's surrealist animation's debt

Marlowe in the movies 323

to expressionist cinema, just as Švankmajer's film anachronically imprints Murnau's *Faust* with the politics of a reunited Europe that had not yet been divided in 1926. Douglas Morse's *Jew of Malta*, too, participates in this anachronic revisioning of the Marlowe corpus, in that its medley of rented costumes and uneven acting, combined with an ambitious vision, prompts a reconsideration of the missionary zeal and the connections to amateur performance shared by the majority of film adaptations of Marlowe's plays, including Jarman's polished film, with its amateur performers, and McKellen's *Edward II*, with its origins in student theatre. An anachronic view of these films thus highlights the gap that continues to separate 'small-time' Marlowe on screen from the glitzy big-budget professionalism of 'big-time Shakespeare'.

Notes

1 The film, as references to it in Sara Munson Deats, *Sex, Gender, and Desire in the Plays of Christopher Marlowe* (Newark: University of Delaware Press; London: Associated University Presses, 1997) suggest, was available for US-based scholars during the period in which it had dropped from circulation in the UK.
2 Barbara Klinger, 'Film History Terminable and Interminable: Recovering the Past in Reception Studies', *Screen* 38:2 (1997): 107–28 (111).
3 *Ibid.*, 126.
4 Toby Robertson and John Russell Brown, 'Directing *Edward II*', *Tulane Drama Review* 8:4 (Summer 1964): 174–83 (176, 177); George Geckle, *Tamburlaine and Edward II: Text and Performance* (London: Macmillan, 1988), 83.
5 On the homoeroticism of *Edward II* and the cold war plot of *A Deadly Affair*, see Deborah Willis, 'Marlowe Our Contemporary: *Edward II* on Stage and Screen', *Criticism* 40 (1998): 599–622. It is true that there are homoerotic elements in the film; yet the scenes from *Edward II* on their own cannot be read as stressing this aspect of the play.
6 Toby Robertson interviewed by George L. Geckle in Geckle, *Tamburlaine and* Edward II, 96.
7 'Richard II's Deposition Scene (Ian McKellen and Fiona Shaw)', at www.youtube.com/watch?v=q7-i1MVjnYM, accessed 1 December 2011.
8 David Fuller, 'Love or Politics: The Man or the King? *Edward II* in Modern Performance', *Shakespeare Bulletin* 27:1 (Spring 2009): 81–115 (91).
9 The film was aired on the BBC on 6 August 1970, with further screening 'over various PBS stations in 1975 and 1977'. Charles R. Forker, 'Introduction', in Christopher Marlowe, *Edward the Second*, ed. Charles R. Forker (Manchester University Press, 1994), 108.
10 DVD cover, *Ian McKellen in* Edward II, BBC Worldwide Ltd, 2009.

11 Benedict Nightingale, Review of *Edward II*, *New Statesman* 5 (Sept. 1969); cited in Geckle, *Tamburlaine and* Edward II, 85.
12 *Ibid.*
13 DVD special feature, 'The Marlowe Inquest', dir. Anthony Garner, with Michael Pennington, Matthew Marsh, and John Woodvine, BBC, 1985.
14 Mark Barratt, *Ian McKellen: An Unofficial Biography* (London: Virgin, 2005), 139.
15 *Ibid.*, 49.
16 Derek Jarman, *Smiling in Slow Motion*, ed. Keith Collins (London: Century, 2000), 163.
17 *Ibid.*, 162. See also Roland Wymer, *Derek Jarman* (Manchester University Press, 2005), 143; and Kate Chedgzoy, *Shakespeare's Queer Children: Sexual Politics and Contemporary Culture* (Manchester University Press, 1995), 214.
18 Michael D. Friedman, 'Horror, Homosexuality, and Homiciphilia in McKellen's *Richard III* and Jarman's *Edward II*', *Shakespeare Bulletin* 27:4 (2009): 567–88 (575).
19 Derek Jarman, *Queer Edward II* (London: BFI, 1991), 30; emphasis Jarman's.
20 Tilda Swinton, 'No Known Address … or … Don't Look Down …', in *Derek Jarman: Brutal Beauty*, ed. Isaac Julien (London: Koenig Books and Serpentine Gallery, 2008), 11–16 (11).

CHAPTER THIRTY

Editing Marlowe's texts

Andrew Duxfield

When a student, teacher, actor, or academic reads Marlowe, the likelihood is that he or she will be holding a modern edition whose tidy appearance belies the complexity of its textual origins. Depending on the publisher and the intended audience, there may be, below the main text, a strip of what looks to the general reader like an arcane cipher, a mysterious code that provides the initiated with a record of decisions taken by the editor. Those decisions are manifold; in producing an edition, an editor will introduce orthographical and grammatical regularity, emend oddities, select preferable readings where multiple options are available, and determine which aspects of the text require further explication in accompanying notes or appendices. These decisions will be influenced by a number of factors, including the editor's interpretation of the text and his or her aesthetic sensibility, as well as the intended audience of the edition. The Marlowe that one might read in a modern edition has undergone a complex process of mediation in order to exist in its presentable format; a modern edition doesn't give us unalloyed access to 'what Marlowe wrote' but rather a (re)construction informed by its editor's interpretive and aesthetic preference and by the cultural and political climate in which it was produced.

It is tempting to think that more might be revealed to us, both about Christopher Marlowe and about the plays and poems attributed to him, by looking beyond the modern edition to the 'original' printed texts; perhaps bypassing these intervening layers of editorial and cultural interference will allow us access to a genuine sense of 'what Marlowe wrote'. A quick look at the early history of Marlowe in print reveals some serious problems with this notion, however. The first Marlovian works to see publication were the two parts of *Tamburlaine the Great*, in a combined quarto edition printed in 1590 by the experienced artisan Richard Jones. The title page, which does not mention Marlowe, provides an eye-catching synopsis of Tamburlaine's achievements in a dizzying range of typefaces, and states that the action is 'Devided into two Tragicall Discourses, as they were sundrie times shewed upon Stages in the Citie of London'.[1] This statement is complicated on the following page, on which Richard Jones addresses 'the Gentlemen Readers: and others that take pleasure in reading Histories'.[2] Jones declares:

> I have here published in print for your sakes, the two tragical Discourses of the Scythian Shepheard, Tamburlaine ... I have (purposely) omitted and left out some fond and frivolous jestures, digressing (and in my poore opinion) far unmeet for the matter, which I thought, might seeme more tedious unto the wise, than any way els to be regarded, though (happily) they have bene of some vaine conceited fondlings greatly gaped at, what times they were shewed upon the stage in their graced deformities: nevertheless now, to be mixtured in print with such matter of worth, it wuld proove a great disgrace to so honorable & stately a historie: Great folly were it in me, to commend unto your wisdomes, either the eloquence of the author that writ them, or the worthinesse of the matter it selfe.[3]

Jones implicitly equates tragedy with history here (as the title of the 1604 publication *The Tragical History of Doctor Faustus* also does), identifying them as forms dignified by a gravitas befitting an erudite reading public. In contrast to this gravity are the 'fond and frivolous' gestures that Jones has apparently cut from the play, gestures which, given the assertion that 'fondlings' have 'gaped' at them, would seem to be more fit for theatrical entertainment than for serious reading. For many nineteenth- and early-twentieth-century editors of *Tamburlaine*, this all meant quite simply that some extra-authorial material (perhaps extemporised by a comic actor and inserted into a theatrical script) was helpfully excised by a judicious and tasteful editor, a decision of which Marlowe would have approved and in which he might have been involved.[4] As Laurie Maguire has pointed out, the eccentric numbering of scenes in the text (across both plays at least eight scene numbers are skipped) lends some credence to Jones' statement, as does the fact that he initially registered the plays with the Stationers' Register as 'Two comical discourses of Tamburlaine'.[5] It seems safe to say that the content of the 1590 text of *Tamburlaine* is somewhat different from the content of the copy-text Jones worked from, whatever kind of document that may have been. What exactly has been 'omitted and left out', however, it is impossible to discern, and the 'author' whose eloquence Jones thinks it would be folly to commend might as easily be Marlowe as any actor or collaborator. Rather than offering a glimpse of the dramatist's work unmediated by editorial practice, Marlowe's earliest printed work is, to all intents and purposes, an edition itself.

Virtually all of the early printed texts of Marlowe's works are distanced from their author by chronology; it is quite probably the case that *Tamburlaine* was the only of Marlowe's works to be printed during his lifetime. Indeed, it seems that the dramatist's untimely demise may have provided the impetus for publication of his work to begin in earnest. *Dido, Queen of Carthage* and *Edward II* both appeared in 1594 as printers doubtless capitalised on the sensation surrounding Marlowe's inglorious death (*The Jew of Malta* was registered with the Stationers in this year also, although no sixteenth-century text of the play survives). *The Massacre at Paris* was printed in 1596 (not, as Roger Carter Hailey has recently shown, the previously favoured date of 1594).[6] The year 1598 saw the printing of *Hero and Leander*, by some distance the most successful early Marlowe publication, as nine reprints testify (from 1600 onwards these reprints included Marlowe's translation of the first book of Lucan's *Pharsalia*). Around 1599 Marlowe's translation of Ovid's *Elegies* appeared together with the *Epigrams* of John Davies in a book sufficiently provocative to be the subject of a bishop's order for public burning. *Doctor Faustus* was published first in 1604 and then again in a different guise in 1616, and *The Jew of Malta* saw print in 1633, some forty or so years after the play was first performed on the London stage. Like the 1590 *Tamburlaine* quarto, the 1633 *Jew of Malta* contains a preface written by an extra-authorial figure, in this case the playwright Thomas Heywood. While Heywood does not suggest any alterations have been made to the text, critics and editors have often been ready to suggest that additions made by him or another jobbing playwright of the early 1630s account for the play's perceived disunity of tone.[7]

No play of Marlowe's has attracted more attention from editors and textual scholars than *Doctor Faustus*, however, and few Renaissance works better encapsulate in their editorial history the major points of disagreement in modern textual theory. There are two main candidates for the date of the play's composition, some scholars favouring a date towards the beginning of Marlowe's professional writing career in 1588–9, with others positing it as the culmination of his dramatic development, written in 1592–3. Both of the early printed versions are Jacobean, however, with the 'A-text' published in 1604 and the 'B-text' following in 1616. The two texts are significantly different, with the longer B-text offering a fuller account of Faustus' travels in the middle of the play and generally demonstrating a greater leaning towards theatrical spectacle than its earlier counterpart. Even in the first and final acts, where the two texts largely correspond, there are numerous localised variations. To complicate matters further, an entry in the *Diary* of Philip Henslowe, owner of the Rose Theatre, records a payment of £4 to playwrights William Bird and Samuel Rowley for additions to *Doctor Faustus* made in 1602, before the appearance of either printed text. Once again the spectre of extra-authorial revision looms. Even the very earliest Marlovian texts, then, cannot be said to give us direct access to the work of the author; there are no 'originals' to which we can return.

Since the editing of early modern texts began to be comprehensively theorised in the early twentieth century, textual debate has focused on how an editor should approach a text in the absence of an original. Given that we don't have unmediated, uncorrupted access to what the author originally wrote, what exactly is it that a modern edition should aim to reproduce? For the majority of the century, predominance in textual scholarship belonged to an approach known as 'New Bibliography', the most illustrious practitioners of which were W. W. Greg and Fredson Bowers, both of whom produced editions of *Doctor Faustus*. The premise of the New Bibliography was that the role of the editor was to act as a kind of textual archaeologist. That is, the editor takes the artifacts available to him or her, namely the available early texts, complete with their imperfections and corruptions, and uses them to reconstruct a hypothetical authorial original. Through painstaking examination of textual evidence and a keen aesthetic sensibility, a good editor should be able to differentiate the work of the true artist from the error of a compositor or the addition of a hack and to make editorial decisions accordingly. As such, the object of inquiry was not so much the printed text or texts in and of themselves, but rather what they concealed; Bowers wrote in 1950 that 'one of the chief functions of textual bibliography is to pierce this veil of the printing process and to restore, however imperfectly, the authority of the manuscript, which we know only through its printed and thus secondary form'.[8] Given the extreme rarity of extant manuscript sources for printed texts (a fragment of a leaf of manuscript with a passage from *The Massacre at Paris*, intriguingly more complete than the corresponding passage in the printed version, is all that remains of any such documents pertaining to Marlowe's work),[9] their reconstruction was necessarily an imaginative process, but one that was nonetheless deemed essential if editors were to liberate themselves from what Greg called 'the tyranny of the copy-text'.[10]

The result of this editorial philosophy is that, for many years, *Doctor Faustus* was predominantly presented to modern readers as a coherent, unified entity; since the editorial goal was to reproduce the work in its pre-print state, the edition need not be concerned with replicating the divergence of its early print history. Generally speaking, the first task of the *Faustus* editor was to establish which of the two texts was more likely to be derived from a properly authorial source and to use that as the copy-text, blending and substituting elements from the other text when they seem more 'Marlovian'. The tendency in early editions of the play was to use the A-text as copy, until W. W. Greg's landmark edition of 1950, which broke from tradition by including both texts and which devoted its considerable introduction to demonstrating the primacy of the B-text. Greg's overall argument – that the A-text was a memorial reconstruction put together for the purposes of provincial touring and that the B-text was copied from Marlowe's foul papers and supplemented by material from the 1611 reprint of the A-text – formed the basis of a number of subsequent major editions of the play, including those of John Jump (1962), Leo Kirschbaum (1962), and Roma Gill (1965) as well as Fredson Bowers' complete works of 1973, all of which use the B-text as copy.

The technical terminology and painstaking detail of the New Bibliographical editorial approach lends it an air of scientific method; yet Greg's logic is animated throughout his work on *Faustus* by a necessarily subjective sense of aesthetic, and sometimes moral, value. His hypothesis regarding the provenance of the A-text is a case in point:

> The text we have in A appears to be a version prepared for the less critical and exigent audiences of provincial towns, and prepared ... by memorial reconstruction from the London performance ... This report or reconstruction served as a new prompt-book for provincial performance, and in the course of its use as such it suffered further degeneration, partly by the insertion of bits of gag, sometimes of a topical sometimes of an unseemly character, that had proved attractive to a vulgar audience.[11]

For all the textual deciphering that fills his very long introduction, the basis of Greg's hypothesis regarding the relative authority of the two texts is that he finds some of the A-text's content to be 'unseemly', 'vulgar', and artistically inferior. A number of critics who from the 1970s onwards began to argue for the authority of the A-text disagreed with Greg's preference without departing from his approach. Constance Kuriyama states in 1975, for example, that 'acceptance of the B text as "original" or authoritative leaves us with a work that is, to put it plainly, an aesthetic monstrosity and a critical nightmare'.[12] One of the problems of an editorial practice that seeks to filter the author's artistic vision from the textual dross into which it has been subsumed is that this practice inevitably involves the construction of the author in the editor's own image. Implicit in Greg's thinking is that, like himself, Marlowe was a serious literary man who would have had little time for larking about, and as a result we end up with a textual hypothesis that distances Marlowe from comic or lowbrow elements of the play. For Greg, as for earlier editors like Dyce and perhaps even Richard Jones, Marlowe cannot be 'held responsible for the scenes of clownage'.[13]

More recently, textual critics have highlighted the tendency of author-centric editing to obscure significant possibilities of meaning that subtle variants between texts, or quirks that would ordinarily be dismissed as 'accidentals', can produce. Leah Marcus, who advocates a process named 'un-editing', convincingly demonstrates how a variance in setting between the two texts is one such case. The A-text locates the action in 'Wertenberg', while the B-text has 'Wittenberg' as its base. Editions of the play, including those that use the A-text as copy, have almost universally adopted the B-text reading; Wittenberg, as the home of Faustus in the play's prose source *The English Faust-Book* and as the base of that other controversial early-sixteenth-century doctor of divinity, Martin Luther, seems like the logical setting, and 'Wertenberg' can quite easily be explained as an error on the part of the compiler of the manuscript source or the compositor at the print-house. Marcus notes, however, that 'Wertenberg' is a common Anglicisation of 'Würtemburg' and that, by locating the action there, the A-text 'draws on an alternative tradition associating Faustus with a German duchy that was a hotbed of left wing Protestantism rather than a place which had become, by the late sixteenth century at least, the centre of a more conservative Lutheran orthodoxy'.[14] Rather than a slip, Marcus argues, the A-text's relocation of Faustus to Würtemburg represents a conscious attempt to reinvigorate an ageing play with freshly radical associations, reproducing what she calls the 'Marlowe effect', and is consistent with several other unique aspects of the 1604 version that accord with a hotter brand of Protestantism. The text thus coherently registers the cultural and artistic circumstances in which it was produced in a way that is obscured by editorial standardisation.

Marcus' argument reflects a broader shift in textual theory that gathered pace in the wake of the decentring of the author by post-structuralist thought. As theorists such as Barthes and Foucault characterised texts as cultural products that generate meaning in their reception rather than in their conception, textual critics began to question the value of the standard editorial project of recovering the work as it was envisaged by the author. For scholars such as Marcus, Jerome McGann, Stephen Orgel, Randall McLeod, Paul Werstine, and David Scott Kastan, the material and 'social' aspects of the text – the very aspects that editing has traditionally sought to expunge – are precisely what the edition, if we should have editions at all, should strive to incorporate; the input of 'extra-authorial' agents like collaborators, revisers, actors, compositors, theatre owners, and censors is not to be subordinated to the reconstruction of an authorial vision, but rather is to be acknowledged as central to the ontology of the text. And it is the text, not a Platonic ideal lying somewhere beyond it, that should be the object of inquiry.

In the light of these developments, the modern standard in the editing of *Doctor Faustus* is to present it in the bifurcated state of its early print history. David Bevington and Eric Rasmussen's benchmark Revels edition of the play, and their Oxford World's Classics collection, both present the A- and B-texts as related but nonetheless distinct entities, each available for consideration on its own terms as well as in relation to its counterpart.[15] The question of retaining textual indeterminacy in the modern edition goes beyond the acknowledgement of variant texts, however. Whether or not the editors base their decisions on the perceived intentions of the author, they must still make those decisions, and the practical limitations of print mean that where multiple readings are possible one must always be favoured. Bevington and Rasmussen, for example, reproduce both texts of the play but not all of their unique quirks, and this edition follows others in standardising the A-text's setting to Wittenberg. Indeed, if the theoretical impetus towards the restoration of textual diversity is pursued to its logical conclusion, then editing, which is by definition a standardising process, begins to seem unnecessary and indeed counterintuitive. Yet, despite calls by Randall McLeod for the abandonment of the edition in favour of the study of facsimiles of early texts, the modern edition remains essential if early modern literature is to remain accessible to students, actors, and general readers.[16] R. A. Foakes, in a spirited defence of traditional editing values, has pointed out the gulf between theory and practice, noting that 'one of the curious aspects of the explosion of writing about textual criticism and about editing in recent years is that many of those publishing advice or admonitions to editors have never edited a work themselves'.[17]

Whether editing can perform its function whilst meeting the challenges of textual theory remains to be seen, but undoubtedly the most promising development in this respect is the electronic hypertext edition. Online editions that allow instant navigation between variant texts and sources – an example being Hilary Binda's edition of *Faustus* currently hosted by the Perseus Project[18] – provide a potential solution to the problem of incorporating the fluidity of the Renaissance text in a modern edition. This technology is not new, but the impracticality and discomfort of reading from a computer screen has for the most part kept its impact in relative check. The rapid developments currently being made in e-readers and tablet computing technology, however, represent a genuine opportunity for the meaningful incorporation of textual diversity and material aspects of textual production into the edition; there is no reason why a perfectly readable and portable electronic edition may not now accommodate flexible navigation among an edited text (with the option to rotate between local variants), transcriptions and facsimiles of early printed versions, variant texts in cases such as that of *Doctor Faustus*, and even audiovisual material such as videos of scenes in performance.

However successful such a reimagining of the edition might prove to be in registering extra-authorial input and reincorporating textual indeterminacy, its capacity to provide us an unalloyed text is still limited. The likelihood is that its effect will not be to remove the tyranny of editorial decision-making, but rather to position the reader in the role of editor. However we read Marlowe in the future, one certainty is that what we read will not be what Marlowe wrote.

Notes

1. Christopher Marlowe, *Tamburlaine the Great* (London, 1590), STC (2nd edn) 17425, sig. A.
2. *Ibid.*, sig. A2.
3. *Ibid.*, sig. A2r–v.
4. Alexander Dyce describes in his 1850 edition the fond and frivolous gestures as the 'buffooneries' of a clown and suggests that 'probably we have no cause to lament the curtailments which it suffered from the publisher of the first edition'; in Christopher Marlowe, *The Works of Christopher Marlowe*, 3 vols., ed. Alexander Dyce (London: William Pickering, 1850), Vol. I, ix–x. Editors who concur include A. H. Bullen, *The Works of Christopher Marlowe* (London: John C. Nimmo, 1885); and Una Ellis-Fermor, *Tamburlaine the Great: In Two Parts* (London: Methuen, 1930).
5. Laurie E. Maguire, 'Marlovian Texts and Authorship', in *The Cambridge Companion to Christopher Marlowe*, ed. Patrick Cheney (Cambridge University Press, 2004), 41–54 (42–3).
6. See Roger Carter Hailey, 'The Publication Date of Marlowe's *Massacre at Paris*, with a Note on the Collier Leaf', *Marlowe Studies: An Annual* 1 (2011): 25–40.
7. E. K. Chambers characterises the play as 'one of the comparatively rare cases, in which a play has only come down to us in a form rehandled to suit an audience of an inferior mentality to that aimed at by the original author'; 'Review of *The Jew of Malta and The Massacre at Paris*, ed. H. S. Bennett', *The Modern Language Review* 27:1 (1932): 77–9 (78).

8 Fredson Bowers, 'Some Relations of Bibliography to Editorial Problems', *Studies in Bibliography* 3 (1950), 37–62 (61–2).
9 See J. Q. Adams, 'The *Massacre at Paris* Leaf', *The Library* 14 (1934): 447–69.
10 W. W. Greg, 'The Rationale of Copy-Text', *Studies in Bibliography* 3 (1950): 19–36 (26).
11 Christopher Marlowe, *Doctor Faustus: 1604–1616*, ed. W. W. Greg (Oxford University Press, 1950), 60.
12 Constance Brown Kuriyama, 'Dr Greg and Doctor Faustus: The Supposed Originality of the 1616 Text', *English Literary Renaissance* 5 (1975): 171–97 (177).
13 Marlowe, *Doctor Faustus*, ed. Greg, 19.
14 Leah Marcus, 'Textual Indeterminacy and Ideological Difference: The Case of *Doctor Faustus*', *Renaissance Drama* 20 (1989): 1–29 (24).
15 See Christopher Marlowe, *Doctor Faustus: A- and B-Texts* (1604, 1616), ed. David Bevington and Eric Rasmussen (Manchester University Press, 1993); and *Doctor Faustus and Other Plays*, ed. David Bevington and Eric Rasmussen (Oxford University Press, 1995).
16 Randall McLeod, 'Un "Editing" Shakespeare', *SubStance* 33–4 (1981–2): 26–55.
17 R. A. Foakes, 'Shakespeare Editing and Textual Theory: A Rough Guide', *Huntington Library Quarterly* 60:1 (1997): 425–42 (425).
18 See Christopher Marlowe, *The Works of Christopher Marlowe*, ed. M. Eccles, A. F. Stocker, and Hilary Binda, in *The Perseus Collection*, at www.perseus.tufts.edu/hopper/collection?collection=Perseus%3Acollection%3AMarlowe, accessed 27 January 2012.

CHAPTER THIRTY ONE

Marlowe's biography

Thomas Healy

In truth, we know little about Christopher Marlowe's life, even whether we should rightly call him Marlowe. He is variously referred to as Marley, Marle, Marlo, Marlin, or Merling in official records.[1] In the only signature of his we confidently possess, he signs himself as Marley, and this is what his father is often called in documents. So it is as probable that he introduced himself as 'Marly' rather than as 'Marlow'. While we know the exact date of his death (30 May 1593), we are not precisely certain of his birthday. He was baptised in Canterbury on 26 February 1564, a date that suggests he was born earlier in this month.

Given the paucity of information about Marlowe, his biographers inevitably rely heavily on contextualising his life within the late Elizabethan world or drawing inferences about Marlowe from his plays and poems. While such biographical methodologies may help make Marlowe's life more comprehensible to modern readers, it should be recognised that – even with the most careful sifting of inferences from the evidence – there loom other plausible explanations that account for the events he was caught up in and, thus, that prompt alternative ideas about his character and motivations, even around the incidents we know in some detail. In particular, what the majority of Marlowe's biographers understandably succumb to is a tendency to allow Marlowe's life to attain a significance that few of his contemporaries likely felt it possessed. While unquestionably celebrated by some as a playwright and a poet of the first order – for example in 1627 Drayton praises him for possessing 'brave translunary things / That the first poets had' and places him in exalted company with Chaucer, Spenser, and Sidney – Marlowe's life was too unsettled and too short to allow him to attain the reputation of his longer-lived exact contemporary Shakespeare.[2] Yet given the exotic nature of many of Marlowe's dramatic characters and his writing's fascination with the shocking and spectacular, there is a tendency to inflate Marlowe, endowing him with a stature his life almost certainly did not possess.

A prime illustration is the ostensible portrait of him discovered in his old Cambridge College, Corpus Christi, in 1953. The portrait is of a richly dressed, attractive young man who is unidentified but who a Latin inscription, which dates the portrait as 1585, proposes is twenty-one years old. There is also a Latin motto – *Quod me nutrit me destruit* ('That which nourishes me destroys me'). This heavily restored portrait has now become so thoroughly identified with Marlowe that it can be difficult to accept that doubtlessly it has nothing to do with him.[3] Nothing indicates that this portrait was continuously hidden at Corpus for 360 years until its twentieth-century discovery, and so its contemporary associations with Cambridge are not clear. Marlowe had graduated with his B.A. the previous year as a poor and a fairly undistinguished student. He stayed on to do his M.A., though, like many students undertaking this degree, he did not stay continuously in Cambridge and certainly was back with his family in Canterbury for at least part of 1585. He is also likely to have begun being used as an intelligencer by Sir Francis Walsingham, Elizabeth's Principal Secretary, and to have been abroad for a time. Only if we imagine Marlowe to have been singled out at Cambridge as a high-flyer in a secret service that resembles more Ian Fleming's world of James Bond than the actuality of the piecemeal, mostly socially misfit group employed irregularly by Walsingham in his drive to protect the queen's security, does it become possible to imagine that Marlowe might have amassed the wealth or patronage to afford the clothing or the commission for this portrait at any point in his career, let alone when he was a new graduate in 1585.[4] Nothing of his later movements suggests that he moved familiarly as an equal in the social circles of the young man portrayed in the portrait. Further, the pertinence of the motto is only realised if we are inclined to see its commissioner or painter possessing a foresight about Marlowe's modern reputation as a doomed overachiever, a thesis particularly advanced by Harry Levin's influential 1954 study.[5]

There are four sources of information about Marlowe's life. First, the official records that record his presence in certain places at certain times and his involvement with institutions. These include entries in registers at his Canterbury school, his Cambridge college, and in legal documents. They also include court and state records that outline at greater length charges made against Marlowe, that speak on his behalf, or that examine his violent death. These provide us with at least some information about the circles he moved in, if not usually his actual role in them, let alone what he thought about others in them. These documents provide the only hard information we possess about Marlowe's life and, as with most similar documents of the early modern period, they are usually tantalising in their brevity, enticing biographers to draw considerably augmented surmises about Marlowe from them.

Second, there are the contemporary or near contemporary comments made about Marlowe by friends and by those who harboured grudges against him, whether genuinely or expediently so. The reliability of most, if not all, of these remarks must be questioned – particularly since the notorious attributions to Marlowe of atheism or homosexuality stem from sources that are highly partisan and recorded in contexts that actively sought to discredit him. Most notorious of these is Richard Baines' 'A note containing the opinion of one Christopher Marley concerning his damnable judgment of religion and scorn of Gods word', which was presented to the Privy Council in 1593. This document, and a similar statement made by the dramatist Thomas Kyd about Marlowe's 'monstruous opinions', have provided fertile material for those seeking to portray a heretical, socially unorthodox character.[6] Kyd's document, however, dates from after Marlowe's death, and possibly Baines' too, and both were almost certainly coerced from their authors by the authorities.

Third, there are Marlowe's own writings, his poetry and plays. While what Marlowe chose to write about and translate indicates his imaginative and cultural inclinations as well as something of his educational training and his place in his immediate literary environment, literary biography needs to tread cautiously in interpreting fictional creations as mirrors of their creators. Further, when seeking to apply Marlowe's art to his life, it needs to be recalled that little of his writing appeared during his lifetime, and that which does – probably only the two parts of *Tamburlaine* – was almost certainly printed without his involvement. The uncertain provenance surrounding Marlowe's writings makes it highly speculative to claim particular poems or plays as tied to episodes or even periods of his life. In plays such as *Doctor Faustus*, which exists in two versions dating from eleven and twenty-three years after his death, or the popular *Jew of Malta*, which has come down to us only in a printed version from 1633, forty years after his death, it is virtually inconceivable that what we possess is precisely what emerged from Marlowe's pen. Confusing and indistinct artistic progeny makes problematic many basic assumptions about what Marlowe wrote and when.

Fourth, we have modern scholarship, which, especially since the mid twentieth century, has attempted to contextualise Marlowe's life in relation to the scant evidence we have of it. While often acknowledging that it is difficult to be precise about Marlowe specifically, such investigations have enabled us to gain a more distinct idea of his environment, for example how and what he was taught at school and university. There have been a number of meticulous attempts at reconstructing his life through reliance on context – notably John Bakeless, William Urry, Charles Nicholl, and David Riggs – while less scrupulous or informed commentators have used the opportunities provided by slight evidence to engage in flights of historical fantasy.[7] Paradoxically, however, the more we understand about the Elizabethan era, the less familiar it becomes. Recent work in the archives has revealed a nuanced, intricate social, political, and cultural maze, making general or uniform assertions about the period less credible than previously. As a result commentators' assessment of Marlowe's life tries to draw plausible scenarios about him from reconstructions that are based on the social operations of an era that we increasingly realise we only partially comprehend. An illustration is provided by the longstanding perception that Marlowe was employed as a spy working for the Elizabethan secret service. While the evidence does suggest that Marlowe acted as an 'intelligencer', working for a number of influential court figures or their lieutenants, this is not a role that easily equates with a modern image of a spy. An intelligencer gathered information (or disseminated misinformation), and the term covered roles extending from conveying social gossip to engaging in serious espionage. For Marlowe (as for most) it was a casual occupation rather than a career. Further, the conduct of espionage during the period was not undertaken by a coordinated agency. Powerful peers at court, with their own ambitions and rivalries, paid a variety of people for information about plots, machinations, or sometimes mere tittle-tattle concerning one another as much as they sought intelligence to counter the external threats to England. It was widely acknowledged that most intelligencers worked for their own advantage rather than through loyalty to the sovereign or even to their employer. Yet labelling Marlowe a spy accords him glamour, creating a sense of him as an exceptional figure who might have occupied important roles within the Elizabethan state, sharing similarities with his dramatic creations, who can move from humble origins to conquer the world, entertain emperors, or become intimate with monarchs.

At the risk of being witnessed as a stolid pedant who is dull to the raptures of Marlowe's 'ayre and fire',[8] I would like to consider Marlowe's life as less glamorous than most of his recent commentators have tended to make it. This doesn't diminish his importance as a writer; but it allows that in reality Marlowe was unlikely to be the figure that his subsequent reputation has made him. Marlowe paints his literary canvas with bold, embellished sumptuousness; what we know of his life makes him a more ordinary figure.

Christopher Marlowe was born and grew up in Canterbury.[9] His father, John, had moved a few miles to the city from north Kent and became a shoemaker. Marlowe's mother, Katherine, had come from Dover, and both were considered as immigrants in Canterbury. John Marlowe appears to have been a competent, if sometimes quarrelsome, tradesman who nevertheless held a number of minor civic offices. In one respect his social origins place Marlowe among the group of Elizabethan writers such as Shakespeare or Spenser who came from modest backgrounds. In comparison with Shakespeare, however, Marlowe's background was considerably less affluent. Shakespeare's family owned property in and around Stratford, and Shakespeare's father acquired more. Crucial besides wealth were connections. Shakespeare's family, and likely Spenser's, were better allied socially than Marlowe's. Christopher's father had apprenticed himself to another Canterbury outsider, the impoverished Gerard Richardson, and the Marlowes lived in one of the poorest districts of the city. John Marlowe's advancement to join the Guild of Shoemakers and to become a freeman of the city in 1564 appears principally due to an outbreak of plague in Canterbury that decimated the artisans in the city – including Richardson – creating a labour shortage. Opportunity in the Elizabethan world was heavily dependent on family connections and patronage, even for gaining relatively modest employment among grand households, with mercantile companies, or in the Church. Christopher had no obvious substantial prospects from his family connections.

Where Marlowe's opportunity did come from was through education. We do not know where he first went to school, but he clearly showed himself an apt pupil as he gained a scholarship to Canterbury's King's School worth £4 a year. This was a substantial amount and certainly would have helped family finances. Christopher gained his scholarship in 1578, making him about fourteen, which was late for starting at the school. It may be that he was enrolled previously, but if so he would have needed financial support, which his family would not have been easily able to provide.

Marlowe obviously thrived in the King's School since he won a scholarship to Cambridge. Endowed by Matthew Parker, a former archbishop of Canterbury and previously a master of Corpus Christi College, Cambridge, this scholarship was granted on merit to a student with high proficiency in grammar and 'if it may be such as can make a verse'.[10] The recipient was intended ultimately to follow a career in the English Church.

At both the King's School and Cambridge, Marlowe's generation was among the first in England to be immersed in a humanist curriculum.[11]

Above all this sought to develop *eloquentia*, an effective understanding and employment of language. Focusing on the perceived greatest exponents of Latinity – Virgil, Ovid, Cicero, Horace, Livy – but drawing on a wide range of Latin and Greek authors (mostly read in Latin translation) as well as modern masters such as Erasmus and Valla, boys at school or university were instructed in grammar, oratory, and rhetoric celebrating *copia* – stylistic abundance and variety – as eloquent language's proper element. This instruction rested on the humanist view that to speak or write well was in effect to speak or write ethically, correctly, and truthfully. Renaissance education centred on rhetoric as a positive art of persuasion – a means to negotiate truth through language. Thus, when Parker favoured giving his scholarship to a boy who 'can make a verse' – that is, verses in Latin, the language of Elizabeth education – his presumption was that this ability to use language elegantly would demonstrate the fundamental moral soundness of the recipient, not the boy's talent as a budding poet.

The terms of the scholarship also point to what appears a contradiction in Elizabethan education. In promoting an eloquence manifested by the classics, there was a ready awareness that these texts often wrote about humanity in ways that did not accord with Protestant ideals. With virtually a universal belief in sixteenth-century Europe that the human will was 'infected' and that a satanic reality actively lured humanity to destruction, even humanism's proponents acknowledged that it was almost impossible to distinguish confidently between truth and falsehood in language with the completeness that was sought. This doubleness of perspective around language was unintentionally reinforced by the main teaching vehicle of Marlowe's university curriculum, the disputation. Students demonstrated their *eloquentia* through taking part in debates where they were arbitrarily asked to defend or attack a position. While tutors largely steered away from serious controversies to dispute upon, students were expected to be able to draw upon collections of precepts gathered from eminent authors and to forge these into convincing rhetorical and oratorical displays that would demonstrate the inadequacy of their opponent's position. Marlowe was raised in an academic environment that was formally highly orthodox in upholding the social, intellectual, and especially religious status quo, but that then gave him access to materials that challenged these positions and trained him to think how it might be possible to promote what the established Church and state dictated should not be encouraged.

The impact of this educational model is observed in all of Marlowe's writing: Faustus disputing with the devil, Tamburlaine extolling virtue that leads to an earthly – not heavenly – crown, Leander persuading Hero about the appropriateness of their having sex, the Guise or Machiavel declaring their contempt of the religious/moral world that *eloquentia* was supposed to uphold. Pre-eminent among late Elizabethan writers who challenge conventions, part of Marlowe's dramatic genius rests with his ability to engage a public who relished such heterodoxies, at least as performed in the theatre. Marlowe's plays provoke through unleashing ambiguous characters and actions within a dramatic environment of circus-like sensationalism. His educational training may have provided some of the tools to deliver his defiant perspectives, but Marlowe's grasp of showmanship seems something innate in him.

Marlowe graduated B.A. from Cambridge in 1584. There are no documents that reveal anything of his activities there beyond the fact that he followed the course of study. His scholarship permitted him to remain at Cambridge for another three years to work towards his M.A. if he intended to become a priest in the English Church, and Marlowe duly registered. However, he clearly had little obvious intention of becoming a cleric (though no doubt he needed the scholarship income), and he began to be increasingly absent from Cambridge for extended periods. Marlowe's decision not to pursue a career in the Church probably had little to do with religious conviction. A reasonable appointment in the English Church required patronage that Marlowe did not possess, and had he taken orders he would likely have ended up as a £10-a-year curate, supplemented by a little tutoring to youngsters, in a rural parish. As a university graduate Marlowe technically became a gentleman, but without the resources to sustain this rank. One option was to seek secretarial employment within an aristocratic household, as Spenser did. But here, too, connections were important. In many respects, Marlowe belongs to the university graduates of this period who have been labelled alienated intellectuals.[12]

Marlowe became an intelligencer. In 1587 as he approached taking his M.A., the minutes from the Queen's Privy Council record a warranty sent to Cambridge to attest Marlowe's loyalty. The minutes suggest that suspicions had been raised that Marlowe was about to go to the English College at Douai in France and convert to Catholicism: a course taken by a number of alienated graduates of the period and much feared by the authorities. The Privy Council minutes record that Marlowe had 'done her Majestie good service' and should be allowed to graduate M.A., which he duly did.[13]

What acts Marlowe performed as an intelligencer are largely uncertain, and indeed he largely disappears from the record between 1589 and early 1592. He is associated with figures such as Richard Baines or Thomas

Walsingham, cousin to Sir Francis and ultimately a literary patron of Marlowe, who were associated with intelligence work in France in the 1580s. He can also be persuasively placed working for Lord Burghley, Elizabeth's chief minister, during the early 1590s. Marlowe himself claimed to be linked with Ferdinando Stanley, Lord Strange, and Henry Percy, ninth Earl of Northumberland – a noted intellectual, friend of Sir Walter Ralegh, and patron of many of the poets, mathematicians, and scientists who also gathered in Ralegh's Durham House in London.[14] The dramatist Thomas Kyd, with whom Marlowe lodged from at least 1591, later claimed, however, that Marlowe was only known to Strange as a writer of plays for his theatre company – which produced *The Jew of Malta* in 1592 and probably *The Massacre at Paris* in 1593 – and that Strange could not bear Marlowe's 'name or sight'.[15]

In 1592, Marlowe was arrested at Flushing (Vlissingen) in the Netherlands for counterfeiting coins and was sent back to England for trial. That he was quickly freed suggests his presence in the Netherlands – if not the actual counterfeiting – had official backing. The man who denounced Marlowe to the authorities was Richard Baines, with whom Marlowe shared rooms in Flushing and with whom he had previously lodged in the late 1580s. Baines plays a significant role in the posthumous reputation of Marlowe, as the author of a 1593 account to the Privy Council about Marlowe's ostensibly heretical opinions, cited above. It is hard to determine whether his denunciation of Marlowe on this occasion stems from a falling out between them or whether Baines panicked and turned Marlowe in to protect himself.

The other occupation Marlowe sought was as a poet and dramatist. His choice of the stage was opportune, since the commercial theatres were expanding during this period following the establishment of James Burbage's Theatre in Shoreditch in 1576. It is possible that Marlowe's *Dido, Queen of Carthage* was performed as early as 1584 (the title page of the first printed edition in 1594 claims that it was 'Played by the Children of Her Maiesties Chappell', and this group effectively ceased to perform after 1584, though there is some evidence of them operating in East Anglia and in Kent during the late 1580s and early 1590s).[16] The first play to win Marlowe serious attention, though, was the first part of *Tamburlaine*, mostly likely performed in the summer of 1587 by the Admiral's Men. Its success prompted the immediate writing of the second part, which seems to have been hastily put into performance by November of that year. In writing for the theatre, Marlowe would be expecting payment for his play script and possibly some of the proceeds of the first production's box office. But writing plays was hardly lucrative, and, likely as significant, would be the hoped-for attention of peers, such as Charles Howard, Earl of Nottingham and Lord High Admiral, or Lord Strange, who sponsored theatre companies. Unlike Shakespeare, though, who was an actor, director, and ultimately part-owner of a theatre company, Marlowe does not appear to have been professionally involved with the theatre outside writing for it. Nor did Marlowe try to emulate Robert Greene or Thomas Nashe and write pamphlets and popular romances as well as plays.

The success of *Tamburlaine* led to the part of Marlowe's life we know more about than any, its ending. On the evening of 5 May 1593, doggerel verses advocating violence against immigrant traders in London were posted on the Dutch Church in Broad Street. They were signed 'Tamberlaine' and written by someone who knew Marlowe's work, since there is reference to the recent production of *The Massacre at Paris*.[17] The Privy Council took this incident seriously as part of a wave of anti-immigrant protest that could potentially destabilise the city, and ordered a round-up of suspects. Though Marlowe was then residing at Thomas Walsingham's house in Kent, the rooms he shared in London with Thomas Kyd were searched, and Kyd was questioned.

Suspicion of Marlowe in the Dutch Church libel was convenient for many in London and at court. By the 1580s some strident elements within the Church of England orchestrated a series of pamphlet attacks on the London theatres as sinful places that directly conflicted with the efforts of the godly to win souls to religion. Within the Corporation of London some equated the city's ostensible moral health with its physical and commercial health, arguing that the playhouses operating just beyond the Corporation's jurisdiction offended God, who might punish London. The Privy Council, too, had closed the theatres in June 1592 for a period, fearing that public disorder might stem from them.[18] Depositions, pamphlets, and other denunciations made against Marlowe both during his life and after it indicate that a case against him as the most sensational of the English dramatists had been developing for some time, with the authorities seeking to denounce Marlowe as a dangerous atheist as part of a wider plan to discredit Sir Walter Ralegh through similar accusations.[19] The authorities searching Kyd's lodging claimed to find a tract owned by Marlowe full of 'vile hereticall Conceiptes denying the deity of Jhesus Christ'. This is a huge exaggeration: what was found was a transcript of a treatise that was not particularly seditious, which Marlowe had probably read while at school.[20] A writ against Marlowe was issued on 18 May, ordering him to report to the authorities daily. Marlowe returned from Kent to do so and was left at liberty on bail.

On 30 May, at a house in Deptford and on the invitation of Ingram Frizer, Marlowe gathered with a small group connected with Burghley and Thomas Walsingham in various nefarious aspects of espionage. According to the inquest into Marlowe's death, they passed the day together walking in the garden and dining. However, a quarrel broke out when it came to settling the bill. Daggers were employed, and Frizer killed Marlowe, who seems to have died instantly.

The inquest accepted Frizer's plea of self-defence. There are anomalies in the evidence, and it is difficult to draw conclusions from it. Many would like to see this as Marlowe murdered on the order of the Privy Council, or of a powerful peer, to prevent him from incriminating some at court, or because he was a dangerous, popular intellectual, who threatened the state's security.[21] It is just as possible that this was a fight that got out of hand and that Frizer called in favours from Thomas Walsingham or the Cecils to avoid a murder charge, just as Marlowe himself may have sought support when he was caught counterfeiting in the Netherlands. There is nothing directly that links this dinner with Marlowe's troubles over the verses posted on the Dutch Church.

Once Marlowe was dead, however, his reputation could be forged to suit a variety of ends. Most problematic of these character assassinations is Richard Baines' 'A note containing the opinion of one Christopher Marley', prepared for the Privy Council, which accuses Marlowe of various heretical utterances. It is not clear when this was written. The document states that it was delivered to the Council on 27 May, three days before Marlowe died, while elsewhere it is claimed that it was delivered on 'Whitsun Eve', which was 2 June, three days after he died.[22] Attempts to silence Marlowe, however, failed. His plays became more frequently performed after his demise and a number remained produced up to the closing of the theatres in 1640, while his poetic and dramatic reputation also gained stature through the posthumous publication of his work.

Marlowe's short adult life after leaving Cambridge appears volatile. In his plays he often depicts characters who gain celebrity despite inconspicuous social origins. In doing so, Marlowe captures something of the social desires of his theatregoing public, for whom wealth and prominence were largely improbable dreams. Marlowe depicts these implausible aspirations adeptly as they engage his own situation. He died too young during the advance of the English theatre to have envisaged a serious accounting of his work such as that accorded Jonson or Shakespeare during the early seventeenth century, let alone the salaried position in the City of London eventually gained by Thomas Middleton. At his death in 1593, the literary stature accorded him by Drayton in 1627 would likely have seemed an impossible distinction.

Notes

1 Charles Nicholl, 'Marlowe, Christopher (bap. 1564, d. 1693)', in *Oxford Dictionary of National Biography*, at www.oxforddnb.com, accessed 3 January 2013; hereafter *ODNB*.
2 Michael Drayton, 'To my most dearely-loued friend Henery Reynolds, Esquire, of Poets & Poesie', in *The Minor Poems of Michael Drayton*, ed. Cyril Brett (Oxford: Clarendon Press, 1907), 108–13.
3 In 2012, twelve editions of Marlowe's plays or poems, biographies of him, or critical studies devoted to him on sale in the UK (omitting fictional work about Marlowe) feature this portrait on their covers. Generations of students will recognise it from the cover of J. B. Steane's edition of Christopher Marlowe, *The Complete Plays* (Harmondsworth: Penguin Books, 1969), much reprinted until 2003.
4 See John Cooper, *The Queen's Agent: Francis Walsingham at the Court of Elizabeth I* (London: Faber and Faber, 2011), esp. 157–89. Marlowe's role as intelligencer is most comprehensively considered by Charles Nicholl, *The Reckoning: The Murder of Christopher Marlowe*, rev. edn (London: Vintage, 2002), esp. 122–37.
5 Harry Levin, *The Overreacher: A Study of Christopher Marlowe* (London: Faber and Faber, 1954).
6 Richard Baines, British Library, Harley MS 6848, fols. 185–6; Thomas Kyd, in *ibid.*, fo. 154. See Nicholl, 'Marlowe'.
7 John E. Bakeless, *The Tragicall History of Christopher Marlowe*, 2 vols. (Cambridge, MA: Harvard University Press, 1942); William Urry and Andrew Butcher, *Christopher Marlowe and Canterbury* (London: Faber and Faber, 1988); Nicholl, *Reckoning*; David Riggs, *The World of Christopher Marlowe* (London: Faber and Faber, 2004). A striking recent example of a flight of fantasy is Ros Barber's various attempts to suggest Marlowe's death was faked, a thesis also proposed by the Marlowe Society (www.marlowe-society.org/). Although Barber develops this hypothesis at greatest length in her fiction, *The Marlowe Papers* (London: Sceptre, 2012), she has published various academic investigations trying to support this supposition.
8 Drayton, 'Of Poets & Posie'.
9 Our knowledge of Marlowe's life in Canterbury principally stems from the meticulous shifting of documents by William Urry, the Cathedral and City Archivist of Canterbury for many years; see Urry and Butcher, *Marlowe and Canterbury*.
10 Cited in A. D. Wright and Virginia F. Stern, *In Search of Christopher Marlowe: A Pictorial Biography* (London: MacDonald, 1965), 63.

11 See Lisa Jardine, 'Lorenzo Valla: Academic Skepticism and the New Humanist Dialectic', in *The Skeptical Tradition*, ed. Myles Burnyeat (Berkeley: University of California Press, 1983), 253–86. At Cambridge, a new curriculum was introduced by statute in 1570; Riggs, *The World of Christopher Marlowe*, 77–9.
12 Mark H. Curtis, 'The Alienated Intellectuals of Early Stuart England', *Past and Present* 23:1 (1962): 25–43.
13 Nicholl, 'Marlowe'.
14 *Ibid.*; Mark Nicholls, 'Percy, Henry, Ninth Earl of Northumberland (1564–1632)', in *ODNB*; and Mark Nicholls and Penry Williams, 'Ralegh, Sir Walter (1554–1618)', in *ODNB*. There is no evidence that these figures formed a distinct grouping, let alone a 'School of Night' or 'School of Atheism' as some of their detractors proposed. See Susanne S. Webb, 'Raleigh, Hariot, and Atheism in Elizabethan and Early Stuart England', *Albion: A Quarterly Journal Concerned with British Studies* 1 (1969): 10–18.
15 Cited in Riggs, *The World of Christopher Marlowe*, 261.
16 See *Records of Early English Drama*, online edition, at http://link.library.utoronto.ca/reed/troupe.cfm?TroupeListID=1196, accessed 17 May 2012.
17 'A Libell, fixte vpon the French Church Wall, in London. Ann° 1593°', Oxford, Bodleian Library MS Don. d. 152, fol. 4v. See Arthur Freeman, 'Marlowe, Kyd, and the Dutch Church Libel', *English Literary Renaissance* 3 (1973), 50–1 for a transcribed version.
18 The fullest study of the relation between stage and Church is Peter Lake with Michael Questier, *The Antichrist's Lewd Hat: Protestants, Papists and Players in Post-Reformation England* (New Haven and London: Yale University Press, 2002).
19 Robert Parsons, *An Advertisement Written to a Secretary of my Lord Treasurers of England, by an English Intelligencer as he Passed through Germany towards Italy* (1592), 18: 'Of Sir VValter Rauleys schoole of Atheisme by the waye, and of the Coniurer that is M. thereof, and of the dilige-ce vsed to get young gentleme- to this schoole, where in both Moyses, and our Sauior; the olde, and new Testamente are iested at, and the schollers taught amonge other things, to spell God backwarde'. It should be noted that Parsons' tract is an attempt to show how Elizabeth's Protestant faction unjustly persecutes Catholics, and this section is part of a long denunciation of Leicester, Walsingham, the Cecils, and Bacon among others.
20 Nicholl, 'Marlowe'.
21 Nicholl, *Reckoning*, in the 1992 first edition, tried to link Marlowe's death with the Earl of Essex; Nicholl retracts this claim in the 2002 second edition; Park Honan, *Christopher Marlowe: Poet and Spy* (Oxford University Press, 2005), tries to link it to Thomas Walsingham; Riggs claims that the evidence 'leads back to the Palace'; *The World of Christopher Marlowe*, 334.
22 Nicholl, 'Marlowe'.

CHAPTER THIRTY TWO

Marlowe and the critics

Adam Hansen

This chapter uses the critical heritage to identify key questions defining (and perhaps limiting) the study of Marlowe. This is not a history of that critical heritage. Instead, the chapter highlights criticism addressing questions responsive to the contexts in which Marlowe worked and the contexts in which Marlowe is reworked. 'Criticism' means and involves lots of things. Critics ask diverse questions about Marlowe, as this collection proves. How can we begin to evaluate these questions? By recognising that the first critic writing on or about Marlowe was Marlowe. His works raise questions about his writing and the writing of others, and about the conditions affecting both. These questions inform later interpretations, including this one.

Marlowe the critic

Tamburlaine Part I's prologue surveys the literary scene, promising to lead us from one aesthetic experience ('jigging veins of rhyming mother wits ... such conceits as clownage') to another ('high astounding terms').[1] Understandably, then, critics have asked: what was Marlowe's relationship with his precursors, his contemporaries, or pre-existing, popular forms of drama? Such questions generate stimulating answers, but perhaps at some cost: 'Marlowe-who-isn't-Shakespeare obscures discussion of Marlowe-who-is-Marlowe (or of Shakespeare-who-isn't-Marlowe).'[2] Marlowe's attempts to distinguish his work from others' paralleled his desire to overreach his own efforts. The 1592 Latin dedicatory epistle to Mary, Countess of Pembroke, attributed to 'C. M.', is conventionally humble about the author's 'yet rude quill'. Yet that 'yet' intimates that he expects greater things of himself: 'I believe that I can achieve more than my unripe natural talents are accustomed to bring forth.'[3] Critical self-consciousness paid dividends: Marlowe exceeded the assumptions of consumers, 'vain-conceited fondlings' and 'courteous readers' alike.[4]

Accordingly, critics have asked: what did Marlowe make of his audiences' expectations, and what did those audiences make of Marlowe? Some answers to such questions might be limiting: 'the search for a predominant audience' can involve 'the quest' for a 'single, predominating response', perhaps 'incompatible' with the 'dynamic (and divided) nature of Elizabethan society', especially when those audiences exhibited 'unrestraint, impiety, and occasional sedition'.[5] Marlowe prospered with that crowd, yet knew that less local contexts also mattered: his work responds to 'an increasingly dominant cultural obsession with foreign worlds and peoples', which developed 'with England's nascent imperialism'.[6]

Marlowe also understood that different contexts make words mean differently, as Mortimer's ambiguous instructions in *Edward II* suggest:

> The king must die, or Mortimer goes down ...
> This letter ...
> Contains his death yet bids them save his life ...
> '*Edwardum occidere nolite timere, bonum est*';
> Fear not to kill the king, 'tis good he die.
> But read it thus, and that's another sense:
> '*Edwardum occidere nolite, timere bonum est*';
> Kill not the king, 'tis good to fear the worst.
> (V.iv.1–12)

The possible (and eventual) responses to Mortimer's 'unpointed' (that is, unpunctuated) letter betray not simply that the language, indeed all language, is unstable, but, more concretely, that when, how, and what we read or perceive is a matter of life and death (V.iv.13). This reality is unavoidable for the powerful and the disempowered alike. To Mortimer, 'lascivious shows' dissipate the resources both of the rulers and of the 'murmuring commons' (II.ii.156–9). What power of 'moving' people through words (or πρᾶξις (praxis), in Sir Philip Sidney's and Aristotle's terms) did Marlowe, or should we, attribute to his 'lascivious shows' on page and stage, in his period and since?[7] Mimicking Sidney's *A Defence of Poetry*, Marlowe's translations of Ovid's *Elegies* claim that 'poets' large power is boundless and immense', because their words do not require 'true history's pretence' (III.xi.41–2).

But since the very poems professing these ideals were burnt under religious authority in 1599, how 'boundless' will repression, and history, let texts be? Marlowe's texts ask this of themselves. One of the *Elegies* terms verse 'soft' because it is written in an age of 'great barbarism', where the 'liberal arts' mean nothing (III.vii.1–4). Comparably, in *1 Tamburlaine*, Mycetes says ''tis a pretty toy to be a poet' (II.ii.54). But because he is an idiot, are we to believe the opposite: poetry is ugly work, and deadly serious play? Another elegy avers: "'Tis doubtful whether verse avail or harm' (III.xi.13). But as intensified, concentrated language, it does *something*: 'Outrageous death profanes all holy things, / And on all creatures obscure darkness brings ... / Verses alone are with continuance crown'd' (III.viii.19–20, 28). Translating Ovid's words makes them live on: 'Verse is immortal' (I.xv.32). In turn, the translation affirms that *Marlowe's* subversive words will survive, surpassing any power, 'holy' or 'crown'd'. Yet these lines also suggest that while poetry lasts, 'creatures', including poets, do not; 'life' and 'work' are not identical. Did Marlowe anticipate the idea that texts and authors are different, with different potentials?

Critics have responded to Marlowe's ambivalence about writers' or writing's powers in several ways. One is to ask: how can we claim any agency for cleft or corrupt works like *The Massacre at Paris* or *Doctor Faustus*? Establishing their textual integrity might exemplify nineteenth-century criticism (and biblical hermeneutics), intent on consolidating a canon. But as Leah S. Marcus proves, moving beyond such approaches facilitates accounts concerned less with texts' holy holism than with their bedevilling diversity: 'The different versions [of *Doctor Faustus*] carry different ideological freight – the A text could be described as more nationalist and more Calvinist, Puritan, or ultra-Protestant, the B text as more internationalist, imperial, and Anglican, or Anglo-Catholic.' These 'differences' appear in different critical decisions about which texts to prioritise or assimilate. But these decisions are also often based on assumptions about who Marlowe was or what he believed. These assumptions create what Marcus terms a '*Marlowe* effect', in which textual fluidity, ambiguity, and inconsistency compel audiences, editors, and scholars to make Marlowe himself mean things: alternative versions construct alternative Marlowes, none definitive.[8]

And so another critical response to Marlowe's sense of the differences between writer and text has been to debate the extent to which we can (or should) separate Marlowe's seemingly unorthodox life from his partially canonical works. The infamous 1593 note attributed to Richard Baines, accusing Marlowe of various deviant beliefs and practices, is literary *and* personal critique daring us to indulge biographical fallacy. Baines' claim that Marlowe claimed that 'the New Testament is filthily written' combines Marlowe's perceived superciliousness with his aesthetic irreverence: Marlowe rewrites theology as much as he rewrites theatre.[9] In the sixteenth and seventeenth centuries, Marlowe's unorthodoxy seemed self-evident: he or his characters tried 'daring God out of heauen' with 'monstrous opinions' or by 'suffering ... lust to haue the full raines'; Marlowe's death, like his characters', manifested 'the iustice of God'.[10] Here criticism serves in its 'truest', etymological sense, to discriminate good from bad. Latterly, such concerns have been superseded, as David Riggs' comments about Marlowe's supposed atheism suggest: 'The right question is not "Was he or wasn't he?" but rather "Why Marlowe?" Why was he chosen by history to fill this role? The answers to this question cannot lie in his conscious choices, about which there is nothing to know; they lie in the history of the role itself as it evolved over time.'[11] The (unanswerable) question of 'Was he or wasn't he' an atheist has wider significance, because of slippages in early modern taxonomies of deviance and between those taxonomies and later periods' moralities: 'was he or wasn't he' orthodox in his texts, beliefs, and actions; a sodomite; political subversive; counterfeiter? So what significance has criticism invested in Marlowe in order to ask the questions it has asked?

Critical interventions

To paraphrase Terry Eagleton, discussing the functions of criticism in a 'nuclear age' (for which substitute 'age of austerity', or 'age of terror'), the world needs 'yet another study' of an early modern author such as 'Robert Herrick' like a hole in the head.[12] Such studies still happen, but not as frequently as those on Marlowe. Why? This question animates critics who like to question:

> To engage seriously with Marlowe, theatrically or critically, is (and was) not only to question Marlowe; it is (and was) also to question the ostensibly unquestionable mainstays of Western 'civilization' – Christian doctrines, imperialism, capitalism, heteronormality, and the like – to step outside the status quo and its illusion of truth and see how or whether that 'truth' or Marlowe's version of it measures up, and to invite controversy, challenge and change. It is (and was), in effect, to get political.

This is 'the interventionist edge of interpretation'.[13] Marlowe's poetic praxis informs critical theory and practice, understood in the post-Second World War sense of working on or against coercive ideologies. Yet Marlowe has long been implicated in such interventions as readers conjectured: is he our contemporary and/or a critical contrast *to* the contemporary?

An 1818 review of Edmund Kean's revival of *The Jew of Malta* asked of Ithamore's conduct: 'Who shall limit the effects of slavery on the human mind?'[14] Pitched between the Abolition of the Slave Trade Act (1807) and the Slavery Abolition Act (1833), this review used Marlowe to weigh into arguments during a period of transition. Comparably, nineteenth-century researches into Marlowe's life asserted that he had been bad-mouthed by the 'rancorous malignity' of 'vindictive' Puritans; the 'spirit' of such aesthetophobes still exists 'in our times', when 'the pulpit' designates a 'conflagration' at a theatre 'a national blessing'.[15] Marlowe intervenes here in the 'competition' between theatre and Church as 'forums for public assembly'.[16]

The conditions of the mid twentieth century generated other contexts in which Marlowe was made to participate. Harry Levin's *The Overreacher* appeared in 1954, one year after the first performances of Arthur Miller's *The Crucible* in New York. Levin was based at Harvard; Miller's play was set in Massachusetts' past. Like Miller, Levin sought to read history in terms of local concerns. So Levin opens by recounting an invocation of Marlowe 'before a Congressional hearing', when someone asked: 'Is he a Communist?' Levin goes on to suggest that we understand Marlowe's depiction of Machiavellianism because, in a post-war context, '*Realpolitik*' has become 'the virtual law of nations'.[17] We understand Marlowe's skill at 'dramatizing geopolitics' because 'the problem of defence was not less vital than it has latterly become'.[18] And so we understand Marlowe because we understand what paranoia makes people do, and what the costs of freedom, 'domination and subjection' are:

> It is a sobering comment on our age, *if not on Marlowe's tragedy*, that, after having all but dropped out of the repertory for more than three hundred years, [*Tamburlaine*'s] recent revival has been greeted as peculiarly meaningful and appropriate. The massing of armies, the breaking of treaties, the cult of despots, the regimentation of satellites, the clashing of extremes of East and West – hyperbole seems powerless to exaggerate the commonplaces of our daily news.[19]

Some have questioned Levin's contextual consciousness.[20] Yet Levin was painfully aware of 'the … agonies of the old world'.[21] In *The Overreacher*, these feature with significant understatement: 'thousands of lurid effigies swing behind Barabas; and Abigail's sacrifice is one of millions'.[22]

Levin proved hugely influential: Stephen Greenblatt and others have stated that his work 'is "what we know"'.[23] Like Levin, Greenblatt has been accused of obscuring the 'submerged politics of his own reading'.[24] On the contrary, like Levin, Greenblatt has explicated how his work has been 'decisively shaped' by both the cultural 'uproar' and the political conservatism of the moments in which he worked.[25] For, like Levin, Greenblatt knew that when we 'speak with the dead', we attend to 'the voices of the living'.[26] Reading about previous subversion is not 'inherently liberating', but neither is discussing it without an eye (or ear) to the now: 'Writing that was not engaged, that withheld judgments, that failed to connect the present with the past seemed worthless.' Yet Greenblatt's experiences, work, and subjects (like Marlowe) suggested that though 'historical processes' are not 'unalterable', 'alteration' is not 'easy'.[27] The more 'subversive' an intervention, the more it is contained, by those in authority and, perhaps, counterintuitively, by those seeking to subvert: 'Marlowe's protagonists rebel against orthodoxy, but they do not do so just as they please; their acts of negation not only conjure up the order they would destroy but seem at times to be themselves conjured up by that very order.'[28] Marlowe therefore assumed a new status in the period of the Eastern Bloc and Berlin Wall, enemies within and double agents, when game theory managed mutually assured destruction and marginal analysis shaped defence budgets. Scholars concerned by how the past informed their present fixated on an author whose '*omnimpotent*' characters were obsessed with transgressing material, moral, and linguistic 'enclosures and barriers' but were enclosed by them; whose deviance was in direct proportion to their orthodoxy; whose yearning for transgressive power disempowered them; and who inhabited dramas exhibiting 'dark playfulness' as they made social 'aliens' symbolic centres.[29]

Jonathan Dollimore's *Radical Tragedy* acknowledged the pervasiveness of 'cold-war rhetoric'; yet with each republication Dollimore's work on Marlowe there intervened in other political contexts.[30] The 2004 edition was mindful of the attacks on the United States on 11 September 2001. Dollimore refers to these events to ask: 'what has all this got to do with … Renaissance drama?'[31] His answer echoes Levin and Greenblatt: 'Faustus is situated at the centre of a violently divided universe.'[32] In an age of ongoing global conflicts, so are we. Dollimore suggests that Faustus' search for 'a more complete knowledge' is 'a search for security'.[33] This twinned desire for knowledge and security is readily comprehensible when defences of, and attacks on, 'homelands' depend on information spun in dossiers. But, unlike Greenblatt, Dollimore emphasises how the end of *Doctor Faustus* reveals that the 'punitive intervention which validates divine power also compromises it': 'Faustus has to be destroyed since in a very real sense the credibility of that heavenly power depends upon it.'[34] In 1984, with international hostilities showing no sign of thaw, and with Thatcherite policies or Reaganomics egregiously concentrating financial capital while depleting cultural and social capital, readers may have focused on the *power* aspect of 'heavenly power'. Yet, by 2004, the resonance of Dollimore's work on tragedy shifted, as powers mobilised in the name of the 'heavenly' assumed greater significance.

Marlowe always finds a home in interesting times. Ethel Seaton, writing just after the end of the First World War, compared Marlowe to someone who conducts 'a great game of chess, with kings and conquerors for pieces ... such as many recently have played with the aid of flags on pins'.[35] But in the past twenty or so years of globalised (if also localised) war, many more scholars have sought to understand how Marlowe's characters exhibit, suffer, or query 'imperial resolve'.[36] Influenced in large part by Emily C. Bartels' work in this area, these understandings realise that modern conceptions of conflict between selves and alien others 'had their beginnings', if not a 'local habitation', in early modern ideas and practices, like Marlowe's, as Bartels' use of the present tense suggests: 'what is out there and what is here are not so different after all, despite the plethora of contemporary representations invested in proving the contrary'.[37]

Building on Dollimore and Greenblatt, Sara Munson Deats identified other vital points of conflict and intervention by studying how Marlowe's plays 'foreground ... crucial differences' between 'sex, gender and desire'. Deats concatenated elements in Marlowe criticism, attending to recent scholarship engaging with the politics of sexuality: 'in the England of the 1590s sodomy functioned as a symbolic synecdoche for all kinds of subversive behavior, even as ... in the America of the 1950s communism became a code word for any kind of behavior deemed deviant'.[38] While looking back to the contexts encompassing Levin and Greenblatt, Deats acknowledged a new phase of interventionist Marlowe commentary. New, or *revived*: as editor, biographer, and psychologist, Havelock Ellis was 'the first' to identify Marlowe with 'all of the characteristics of a "sexual invert"', in 1897: 'Marlowe ... became part of Ellis's effort to attack the Victorian sexual conventions that repressed what he found to be the essential passions of the artistic temperament.'[39] Ellis' interventions have underscored critics using Marlowe to generate 'unease' in readers 'about their ability to know what the word *homosexual* means' in early modern texts, to make them 'wonder whether ... we know what it means today'.[40] Such critics are mindful of the problems of being 'attentive to the alterity of the past' but do not want their work to be seen as 'antiquarianism'.[41] Jonathan Goldberg therefore connects Renaissance literature with 'current political realities': 'an escalation of homophobia ... assaults on political correctness ... the recent war [the USA in Kuwait in 1991] ... writing about AIDS in the media'.[42] Given such contexts, Goldberg rewrites his own ambivalence about the hope that 'menaced and vulnerable' identities could survive being 'crushed', in the societies of Marlowe's plays and after.[43] Instead, Marlowe serves as 'a site of political resistance', offering works where 'Modern heterosexist presumptions are not in place.'[44]

Conclusion

Some commentators try to contain interventions generated by Marlowe and his critics. A 2002 collection of essays notes that 'recent studies' of Marlowe view his texts 'feelingly': does 'feelingly' exclude *historically*?[45] The introduction to that collection suggests Marlowe was 'an iconoclast who challenges the conventional wisdom of his day'.[46] Does this exclude *our* day? Or should we be more sceptical about how we make Marlowe intervene, and the questions we ask about him? Perhaps we see what we want to see, and err to think otherwise, if our thinking relies on erroneous assumptions:

> Marlowe's cultural and, in particular, academic capital results to no slight degree from a mythographic creation with which it is in our best interest to be complicit. Marlowe was an atheist, and people who think subversively and differently matter. Marlowe was a homosexual, and sexual difference matters. So Marlowe matters. Which academic would like to start a seminar or lecture on Marlowe by candidly admitting that we know next to nothing about the playwright?[47]

But if we want to consider Marlowe's distinction from and relation to his contexts, contemporaries, and ourselves, we might focus on what is distinct and knowable about *how*, not just *what* or *why*, he wrote. How, in other words, did and do his works' 'high astounding terms' astound the 'eye (or ear)' at linguistic, rhetorical, cognitive, and, ultimately, *ideological* levels?[48] Answering that question requires close textual analysis, but not for its own sake: such analysis occurs in the classroom and beyond, as much as with the lone critic 'sitting at his [or her] book', as *The Massacre at Paris* puts it (ix.2). Reworking Marlowe in these various contexts involves, needs, and generates critical interventions keeping him 'new' and 'exciting', in his time and in ours.[49]

Notes

1 Christopher Marlowe, *Tamburlaine the Great: Part 1* (1590), in *Complete Plays and Poems*, ed. E. D. Pendry (London: Everyman, 1995), Prologue, 1–8. All subsequent references to Marlowe are to this edition and are inserted parenthetically in the text.

2 Simon Shepherd, *Marlowe and the Politics of Elizabethan Theatre* (Brighton: Harvester, 1986), xiii.
3 Marlowe, *Complete Plays and Poems*, 397.
4 R[ichard] J[ones], 'To the Gentlemen Readers' (1590), in *ibid.*, 5.
5 Thomas Cartelli, *Marlowe, Shakespeare, and the Economy of Theatrical Experience* (Philadelphia: University of Pennsylvania Press, 1991), 44–56.
6 Emily C. Bartels, *Spectacles of Strangeness: Imperialism, Alienation, and Marlowe* (Philadelphia: University of Pennsylvania Press, 1993), 3.
7 Sir Philip Sidney, *A Defence of Poetry* (1595), ed. J. A. Van Dorsten (Oxford University Press, 1996), 38–9.
8 Leah S. Marcus, 'Textual Indeterminacy and Ideological Difference: The Case of *Doctor Faustus*', *Renaissance Drama* 20 (1989): 1–29; reprinted in *Critical Essays on Christopher Marlowe*, ed. Emily C. Bartels (London: Prentice Hall, 1997), 15–38 (18).
9 Reprinted in *Marlowe: The Critical Heritage, 1588–1596*, ed. Millar MacLure (London: Routledge and Kegan Paul, 1979), 36–8.
10 Robert Greene, *Perimedes the Blacksmith* (1588), in MacLure, *Marlowe: The Critical Heritage*, 29–30 (29); Thomas Kyd (1593), in *ibid.*, 32–6 (35); Thomas Beard, 'The Theatre of Gods Iudgements' (1597), in *ibid.*, 41–2.
11 David Riggs, 'Marlowe's Quarrel with God', in Bartels, *Critical Essays*, 39–58 (43).
12 Terry Eagleton, *The Function of Criticism: From the Spectator to Post-Structuralism* (London: Verso, 1987), 108.
13 Bartels, 'Introduction', in *Critical Essays*, 1–11 (1–2, 7).
14 *Blackwood's Magazine* (May 1818), in MacLure, *Marlowe: The Critical Heritage*, 70–3 (71).
15 James Broughton, 'Life and Writings of Christopher Marlowe', *Gentleman's Magazine* (January–June 1830), in MacLure, *Marlowe: The Critical Heritage*, 84–9 (85).
16 Thomas Dabbs, *Reforming Marlowe: The Nineteenth-Century Canonization of a Renaissance Dramatist* (Lewisburg: Bucknell University Press; London and Toronto: Associated University Presses, 1991), 55.
17 Harry Levin, *The Overreacher: A Study of Christopher Marlowe* (London: Faber and Faber, 1954), 18–19.
18 *Ibid.*, 54–5.
19 *Ibid.*, 69, 73–4; emphasis mine.
20 Susanne Klingenstein, *Enlarging America: The Cultural Work of Jewish Literary Scholars, 1930–1990* (New York: Syracuse University Press, 1998), 65–9.
21 Harry Levin, *Contexts of Criticism* (Cambridge, MA: Harvard University Press, 1957), 6.
22 Levin, *Overreacher*, 91.
23 Cited in Klingenstein, *Enlarging America*, 67.
24 Howard Felperin, *The Uses of the Canon: Elizabethan Literature and Contemporary Theory* (Oxford: Clarendon Press, 1990), 113.

Marlowe and the critics

25 Stephen Greenblatt, *Learning to Curse: Essays in Early Modern Culture* (London and New York: Routledge, 2007 [1990]), 224, 5.
26 Stephen Greenblatt, *Shakespearean Negotiations: The Circulation of Social Energy in Renaissance England* (Oxford: Clarendon Press, 1988), 1.
27 Greenblatt, *Learning*, 221–4.
28 Stephen Greenblatt, *Renaissance Self-Fashioning: From More to Shakespeare* (University of Chicago Press, 1980), 210.
29 Constance Brown Kuriyama, *Hammer or Anvil: Psychological Patterns in Christopher Marlowe's Plays* (New Brunswick, NJ: Rutgers University Press, 1980), 110; Marjorie Garber, '"Infinite Riches in a Little Room": Closure and Enclosure in Marlowe', in *Two Renaissance Mythmakers: Christopher Marlowe and Ben Jonson. Selected Papers from the English Institute, 1975–76*, ed. Alvin Kernan (Baltimore and London: Johns Hopkins University Press, 1977), 3–21 (8); Greenblatt, *Renaissance Self-Fashioning*, 220, 194.
30 Jonathan Dollimore, *Radical Tragedy: Religion, Ideology and Power in the Drama of Shakespeare and His Contemporaries*, 3rd edn (Durham, NC: Duke University Press, 2004 [1984]), lxxix.
31 *Ibid.*, xvii.
32 *Ibid.*, 110.
33 *Ibid.*, 113.
34 *Ibid.*, 118.
35 Ethel Seaton, 'Marlowe's Map', *Essays and Studies by Members of the English Association* 10 (1924): 13–35.
36 Thomas Cartelli, 'Marlowe and the New World', in *Christopher Marlowe and English Renaissance Culture*, ed. Darryll Grantley and Peter Roberts (Aldershot: Ashgate, 1999 [1996]), 110–18 (116).
37 Bartels, *Spectacles of Strangeness*, 9, 24.
38 Sara Munson Deats, *Sex, Gender, and Desire in the Plays of Christopher Marlowe* (Newark: University of Delaware Press; London, Associated University Presses, 1997), 14–15, 194.
39 Dabbs, *Reforming*, 128.
40 Gregory W. Bredbeck, *Sodomy and Interpretation: Marlowe to Milton* (Ithaca, NY and London: Cornell University Press, 1991), xii.
41 Jonathan Goldberg, *Sodometries: Renaissance Texts, Modern Sexualities* (Stanford University Press, 1992), 18.
42 *Ibid.*, 20, 25.
43 Jonathan Goldberg, 'Sodomy and Society: The Case of Christopher Marlowe', *Southwest Review* 69 (1984): 371–8, reprinted in *Christopher Marlowe*, ed. Richard Wilson (London and New York: Longman, 1999), 54–61 (61).
44 Goldberg, *Sodometries*, 141, 125.
45 Robert A. Logan, 'Introduction: Marlowe's Empery', in *Marlowe's Empery: Expanding His Critical Contexts*, ed. Sara Munson Deats and Robert A. Logan (London: Associated University Presses, 2002), 13–21 (15).
46 *Ibid.*, 20.

47 Lukas Erne, 'Biography, Mythography, and Criticism: The Life and Works of Christopher Marlowe', *Modern Philology* 103 (2005): 28–50 (30).
48 Russ McDonald, 'Marlowe and Style', in *The Cambridge Companion to Christopher Marlowe*, ed. Patrick Cheney (Cambridge University Press, 2009 [2004]), 55–69 (56).
49 Lisa Hopkins, 'Marlowe', in *Teaching Shakespeare and Early Modern Dramatists*, ed. Andrew Hiscock and Lisa Hopkins (Houndmills: Palgrave, 2007), 42–53 (46).

CHAPTER THIRTY THREE

Marlowe now

Paul Menzer

A faint fug of glamour hangs over Marlowe – a compound of sulphur, tobacco, and unease. Consider the following list, titles or subtitles from the last decade of scholarly work on Christopher Marlowe:

- 'What Shakespeare did to Marlowe in Private'
- 'Arms and the Boy'
- 'Sodomy Revisited in Marlowe's *Edward II*'
- 'To Sodomize a Nation'
- 'Tobacco and Boys: How Queer Was Marlowe?'
- 'Breeching the Boy in Marlowe's *Edward II*'
- 'The Rebel and the Red-Hot Spit'
- 'Marlowe's *Edward II*: Penetrating Language in Shakespeare's *Richard II*'.[1]

This sort of thing happens less often in Shakespeare studies. Or this:

- 'Who Killed Christopher Marlowe?'
- 'The Murder of Christopher Marlowe'
- 'On Her Majesty's Secret Service'
- 'Journeys through the Elizabethan Underground'
- 'To Catch a Spy'
- 'Marlowe's Murderer Revealed!'
- 'Scribblers and Assassins'
- 'The Killing of Christopher Marlowe'.[2]

It is enough to raise the suspicion that the real 'Cambridge Companion to Christopher Marlowe' was Sir Francis Walsingham. Taken together, these titles epitomise the anality and espionage schools of Marlowe criticism. Whether it is skulduggery or boy-buggery, these acts of critical engagement produce a deviant Marlowe, whose racy pronouncements and shadowy demise position him on the outskirts of Elizabethan respectability, a fugitive from the past and a harbinger of our contemporary preoccupations.

Above all, they provide a biographical filter through which to read his work, be it through a hermeneutics of sodomy or as a double agent, a counterfeiter whose forgeries extended to the literary.

Marlowe had a flair for spectacular endings, both in his life and in his letters. The plays all drive towards violent conclusions, their heroes – like their author – defined by their demise. Dido flames out; Faustus goes to hell; Henry dies of a poisoned knife; Barabas boils; Edward suffocates; and while Tamburlaine escapes his first play unscathed, even he finally grows sick of all the drama. Moreover, Marlowe favoured finales in which the protagonists either produce the dramaturgy of their own demise or – like Barabas – unwittingly succumb to it. In either case, the ends of these plays eerily prefigure the death of their writer. Furthermore, the plays all appeared in print after Marlowe's death; he left his poetry scattered across a motley of manuscripts and miscellanies; and he left an extended poetic project – *Hero and Leander* – unfinished. The plays underwrite the biography of an author whose greatest drama was to suffer an ending that matched those of his protagonists. 'Cut is the branch that might have grown full straight', as the epilogue to *Faustus* puts it. Marlowe died in 1593, and we've been writing his epilogue ever since.

The death of the author dominates treatments of Marlowe today – on the stage, in the study, and in the classroom. Not, however, the 'death of the author' in the sense that Roland Barthes intended, in which authorial agency spreads so wide it evaporates. To the contrary, with Marlowe the preoccupation with the author's death is a literal business, which, far from effecting a post-modern erasure of biography, produces a neoconservative critical practice that reads the plays and poems backwards, a preposterous poetics that starts with the author's end.

Our challenge today might therefore be to read Marlowe without Marlowe, or, at any rate, to read Marlowe without the death drive. For while his biography offers tantalising details (and maddening elisions), the enchantments of his life end up producing oddly allegorical readings of his poems and plays. To make over Marlowe as the pin-up boy of transgressive poetics, we have to root our readings in biographical 'fact', however dubious the evidence. The paradox, therefore, is that to produce a radical Marlowe, the critic employs a reading practice that views the work as allegorical, the proleptic autobiography of an untimely end. The paradox is plain. It takes a conservative reading practice to make Marlowe modern.

Consider the parallel case of Shakespeare, who died quietly at home having written a respectable valediction to the stage. Shakespeare's biography provides an unremarkable though legible frame in which to read his work: after some fitful early efforts the fledgling writer ripens towards the full maturation of his creative powers, which yield to an inevitable dark period before resolving themselves in autumnal twilight. After a decent interval of seven years come the 'complete works'. Corpse and *corpus* coalesce with a fitting fullness, as life and art cohere to round out the whole journey. While this reading turns Shakespeare's life into its own allegory, its genre is romance, not tragedy. His allegory is of wholeness, and reading Shakespeare backwards would see the arc of his career as bending towards romance. Marlowe, by contrast, had the tragic taste to die before thirty, just escaping the '27 Club', a modern meme for the early deaths of musicians like Robert Johnson, Janis Joplin, Jimi Hendrix, Kurt Cobain, and Amy Winehouse, all pictures of health who, as a recent review put it, pursued 'precipitous lifestyles that made them candidates for early self-destruction'.[3] The comparison is facile, but it speaks to the tenacious allegorical allure of a young artist and an untimely end. In fact, the brevity of Marlowe's life produces oddities like studies of his 'Late Years', meaning the early 1590s, when the swan of Avon was yet unfledged.[4] Marlowe was done before Shakespeare really got started, and the sense of incompleteness, of a life and art left unfinished, dominates the Marlowe we produce today. Underwritten by death, defined largely by their endings, they are all 'late' plays.

To diagnose the place of Marlowe on the stage, in the classroom, and in the study today is to understand the way(s) he is appropriated by and for modernity and the allegories of authorship we produce. Julia Reinhard Lupton, for one, has argued that Marlowe proves less assimilable than Shakespeare to 'educational instrumentalization' because 'his plays are too much in love with tyranny, whether political, erotic, or cerebral, to lend support to the national programs of the modern state'.[5] Indeed, it is hard to imagine Marlowe substituting for Shakespeare in the various 'Shakespeare in the Schools' initiatives sponsored by the Folger Shakespeare Library or Shakespeare's Globe or the American Shakespeare Center (try it for yourself: 'Marlowe for Kids', 'Marlowe Made Easy', 'Marlowe Set Free', 'Marlowe Camp'). It is, furthermore, impossible to see Marlowe mustering the cultural capital to underwrite the sort of institutions that support such programming: 'The Marlowe Institute', 'The American Marlowe Center', 'Marlowe's Rose'. It is not that Marlowe's *plays* or *poetry* do not carry capital by themselves: Marlowe's poetic and dramatic range could, after all, make him *the* exemplary figure of English Renaissance letters (as, indeed, Patrick Cheney has argued).[6] But the jagged edges of Marlowe's life make him an odd fit for such initiatives. Marlowe's capital lies elsewhere.

That 'elsewhere' is on the stage and in film, since Marlowe allures industries with radical pretences, offering the irresistible shimmer of artistic pedigree, dissident politics, and a glamorous bio. (The art of Caravaggio provides a near analogue in the graphic arts.)[7] Deborah Willis, in the tellingly titled 'Marlowe Our Contemporary', claims that Derek Jarman and Bertolt Brecht harnessed Marlowe's erotic and political charge to power, respectively, film and theatre adaptations of *Edward II*, which served up a brew of '"heroic" sexual politics' and a 'critique of state power and class privilege'.[8] Yet here, as elsewhere, Marlowe's biography overshadows all. A production of *Faustus* in the chapel of Jesus College, Cambridge in 1980 began with a reading of the Baines note, which prompted Lois Potter's perceptive critique that 'many recent productions of the major works could be described as dramatizations of "the Baines note"'.[9] Similarly, in the films *Shakespeare in Love* (1998) and *Anonymous* (2011), 'Marlowe' shadows Shakespeare. In the first, Shakespeare believes that he's responsible for Marlowe's death; the second unavoidably concludes that he is. Both films summon Marlowe only to kill him off, and, in both, Marlowe's death is literally vital to Shakespeare's success. If the stage dramatises Richard Baines' note, films dramatise Jonathan Bate's observation that 'metaphorically ... Shakespeare was the rival who killed Marlowe'.[10] The teaching, critiquing, and performing of Marlowe today are all versions of inverted biography that start with death and work backwards.

Lupton and Willis summarise Marlowe's position in the now: too heterodox for evangelical pedagogy, he is limited by his heterodoxy to vague citations of his radical promise, a radical promise leveraged on his death. He thus resists widespread dissemination in the educational arena and achieves his greatest impact in the boutique industries of the stage and art house. It is unsurprising that these seemingly incompatible positions arrive at the same place – marginalisation – since they arise from the same assumption. Both positions are products of new historicist or cultural materialist readings that grant unilateral authority to the centralised state. Such a reading model sees literature – and drama in particular – as having only two real options: assent to or dissent from centralised authority (which, of course, amount to the same thing). Marlowe is pressed into service as a radical foot soldier for modernist preoccupations, but these ideological readings turn into allegories of subject–state relations. And we all know how such stories end.

The modern desire to read Marlowe's work as thinly veiled autobiography has precedent, since Marlowe's death seemed allegorically apt to his contemporaries as well. They greeted his death by trying to square his astonishing literary achievements with his turbulent existence and horrifying end. His death was viewed, as now, in largely allegorical terms, either providential or prophetic. His admirers, like Peele, Chapman, Nashe, and Drayton, placed him at the Elysian table reserved for writers, apotheosising Marlowe by seating him in the celestial company of what Drayton called the 'first Poets'. His detractors, by contrast, saw his untimely end as a fit punishment for his blasphemy, reading in his death an allegory of excess punished. Robert Greene presciently predicted that Marlowe would be struck down for his blasphemies, and divines saw his end as just desserts. 'See what a hook the Lord put in the nostrils of this barking dog', Thomas Beard vividly concluded in *The Theatre of God's Judgment*, since Marlowe had 'denied God and his son Christ'. Beard for one sees the aptness of Marlowe's end:

> It so fell out that in London streets as he purposed to stab one whom he owed a grudge unto with his dagger, the other party perceiving so avoided the stroke, that withal catching hold of his wrist, he stabbed his own dagger into his own head … But herein did the justice of God most notably appear, in that he compelled his own hand which had written those blasphemies to be the instrument to punish him, and that in his brain, which had devised the same.[11]

Beard posthumously rewrites Marlowe's career, seeing his death as poetic justice with a vengeance. Now, as then, attention to Marlowe produces an allegory that reads the plays as deathly retrospect.

Killed by the self-hand with which he wrote his blasphemies, Marlowe drafted the argument of his own demise by scripting Faustus' fortunes, Barabas' pot-boiler, and, in particular, Edward's gruesome murder in *Edward II*. Edward's murder is arguably the most scandalous moment in Marlowe's dramatic canon and an exemplar of the way Marlowe's biographical allure quite literally rewrites his work. Though the play has been called the most 'modern' play by early modern England's 'most modern playwright', the play's ending has generated both editorial emendation and critical readings that rely on conservative reading practices to rewrite Edward's death as Marlowe's murder.[12] On the modern stage and in contemporary criticism, *Edward II* ends with a bed trick, with Edward swapped out for Marlowe.

Critics have harried Edward's end to produce readings the text only flirts with. To review, in the 1594 octavo of *Edward II*, Lightborn calls for various accessories to Edward's murder, including a 'spit', a 'table', and a 'featherbed'.[13] Marlowe borrowed these props from Holinshed's *Chronicles*, with which he was clearly conversant. There, Edward's murder is described in ways that leave little to the imagination. Yet, in Marlowe's play, at the moment of Edward's murder, Lightborn calls only for 'the table', and for Matrevis and Gurney to 'lay the table down, and stamp on it, / But not too hard, lest that you bruise his body' (xxv.113–14). As Stephen Orgel sensibly asserts, 'Edward is pressed to death'.[14] Nevertheless, editors frequently insert a stage direction calling for the spit and implying its application ('*As* EDWARD *is trapped under a table*, LIGHTBORN *pushes the spit up his anus*. EDWARD *screams and dies*'; 'MATREVIS *and* GURNEY *bring in a table and a red-hot spit*'.).[15] Oddly, readers who caution that the play is at least unclear about the part the poker plays can be accused of 'editorial squeamishness'.[16] Even Orgel's sensible reading is a remnant of the 'fastidious past'.[17] The oddity speaks for itself. To avoid being tarred as squeamish or fastidious (than which nothing could be worse under the terms of the 'modern'), editors aggressively emend the text to make it comply with their desires: 'we want the murder to be precisely what Marlowe refuses to make it', Orgel writes, 'the mirror of Edward's unspeakable vice'.[18] If the poker is missing from the scene of the crime, critics seem intent upon planting it there.[19]

Modern productions of *Edward II* find this ending irresistible as well (with the possible exception of the Jarman film, where it plays out as a dream sequence but does not result in Edward's death), and *Edward II* has become nearly as popular on the contemporary stage as *Doctor Faustus*.[20] There, as with Chekhov's famously loaded rifle, once the spit is introduced, it has to go off, or in. It is easy enough, on one hand, to arraign critics and producers of homophobia in their reading of this scene, as Orgel and others imply.[21] The more curious phenomenon is the critical desire to rewrite Edward's ending at all. The desire to finish off Edward/*Edward* in terms that satiate a critical need may be in part generated by a language that cannot help itself. It is, in short, impossible for critics to talk about the end of *Edward II* without talking about the end of Edward II. Criticism that reads anal rape as the fitting point of the play rescript Marlowe to form a gruesome pun, much like the death of an author by his own hand.

Indeed, editions or productions that insist on the spit take their cue from Thomas Beard, who wrested the evidence of Marlowe's murder to conform to the dramaturgy of death that operates within a theatre of God's judgement. In sum, readings of Edward's end/*Edward*'s end read the play's closing as Marlowe's premonitory rendering of his own reckoning. After all, Marlowe also got it in the socket with the sharp end of a stick. The irony abounds, since to produce an ending to *Edward II* that adheres to a 'modern' hermeneutics of sodomy, critics end up straitjacketing the play in a Dantean hairshirt. Such readings of Marlowe – that map the death of the author back onto his plays – end up conforming to what Beth Lynch calls the early modern 'genre of judgement literature' like that of Thomas Beard.[22] Perhaps, finally, *Edward II* does not quite produce the ending we demand since it is among this late medieval writer's most medieval plays.

The attempts of modernity to rationalise Marlowe to its terms have produced a strange spectacle: the friction between the canonising imperatives of modern criticism and the unwieldy mess of Marlowe's written work have produced allegory where we might expect interpretation. Rather than read Marlowe's literary legacy as an extended chronicle of a death foretold, we could instead see in Marlowe the sheer stubborn strangeness of the past, the inaccessible agents and intensities of creative expression in a time radically unlike our own. We might, that is, resist the urge to allegorise Marlowe and turn instead to a criticism less in love with death. For all of Marlowe's plays are early plays: from the lyric delights of *Dido* to the martial tattoo of the *Tamburlaine*s, from the brimstone of *Faustus* to the chronicle history of *Edward II*. And what to do with *The Massacre at Paris*, which reads like it was written on the back of a cocktail napkin, or *The Jew of Malta*, a pilot for a sitcom that was never picked up? If Marlowe must represent something about the English Renaissance, it is wild profusion, exuberant energy, the amateur anarchy of a literary temperament working within imperfectly understood inherited schemes with an eye towards a vernacular audience.

As for the poems, they are all juvenilia – smutty Ovidian translations, a witty though unfinished epyllion, a counter-imperial Lucanian epic, and pastoral fantasies about horny shepherds. It is difficult to detect a 'programme' here, since Marlowe's poetry seems far more opportunistic than programmatic. For all its astonishments, it feels amateur in intention – though certainly not in effect – conveying the effortless charms of a Leonardo sketch or a Beatles outtake. The output is above all varied, the work of a writer exercising his imagination across prescribed poetic forms, though all, it seems, for a lark.

Marlowe's death *was* a tragedy, robbing us of more than can be measured. It is not so much that his branch might have grown full straight, but that it would have grown and produced unknown pleasures. Imagine a Marlowe at the height of his powers, his work in its full maturity, a subsequent dark period, and a late autumn harvest. Imagine Marlowe at forty or fifty. But that is to revise Marlowe's ending as well, to project the

Marlowe I want onto the Marlowe we have. There is no end to the pleasures of what survives of Marlowe. And that is enough.

Notes

1 Meredith Skura, 'What Shakespeare Did to Marlowe in Private: *Dido, Faustus,* and Bottom', in *Christopher Marlowe the Craftsman: Lives, Stage, and Page*, ed. Sarah K. Scott and M. L. Stapleton (Farnham: Ashgate, 2010), 79–90; Timothy D. Crowley, 'Arms and the Boy: Marlowe's Aeneas and the Parody of Imitation in *Dido, Queen of Carthage*', *English Literary Renaissance* 38 (2008): 408–38; Jonathan Crewe, 'Disorderly Love: Sodomy Revisited in Marlowe's *Edward II*', *Criticism* 51 (2009): 385–99; Marcie Bianco, 'To Sodomize a Nation: *Edward II*, Ireland, and the Threat of Penetration', *Early Modern Literary Studies*, special issue 16 (2007): 11.1–21; Stephen Orgel, 'Tobacco and Boys: How Queer Was Marlowe?', *GLQ: A Journal of Lesbian and Gay Studies* 6 (2000): 555–7; Marie Rutkoski, 'Breeching the Boy in Marlowe's *Edward II*', *SEL* 46 (2006): 281–304; Jon Surgal, 'The Rebel and the Red-Hot Spit: Marlowe's *Edward II* as Anal-Sadistic Prototype', *American Imago* 61 (2004): 165–200; Meredith Skura, 'Marlowe's *Edward II*: Penetrating Language in Shakespeare's *Richard II*', *Shakespeare Survey* 50 (1997): 41–55.
2 Stephen Greenblatt, 'Who Killed Christopher Marlowe?', *New York Review of Books* 53:6 (6 April 2006): 42–6; Manabu Tsuruta, 'The Murder of Christopher Marlowe', *Eigo Seinen/Rising Generation* 152:7 (October 2006): 414; Himmet Umunç, 'On Her Majesty's Secret Service: Marlowe and Turkey', *Belleten* 70:259 (December 2006): 903–18; Roy Christopher Kendall, *Marlowe and Richard Baines: Journeys through the Elizabethan Underground* (Madison, NJ: Fairleigh Dickinson University Press, 2003); Frank Ardolino, 'To Catch a Spy: John le Carré and Sidney Lumet's Use of Marlowe's *Edward II* in Performance', *Journal of Evolutionary Psychology* 22:1–2 (2002): 40–6; Charles Marowitz, 'Marlowe's Murderer Revealed!', *Shakespeare Bulletin* 20:4 (2002): 31–2; Charles Nicholl, 'Scribblers and Assassins: Charles Nicholl Reopens the File on Thomas Drury and the Prosecution of Christopher Marlowe', *London Review of Books* 24:21 (31 October 2002): 30–3; David Riggs, 'The Killing of Christopher Marlowe', *Stanford Humanities Review* 8 (2000): 239–51.
3 David Weiss, 'Amy Winehouse and the 27 Club', at *Life Goes Strong*, http://play.lifegoesstrong.com/article/amy-winehouse-27-club, accessed 30 January 2012.
4 David Bevington, 'Christopher Marlowe: The Late Years', in *Placing the Plays of Christopher Marlowe: Fresh Cultural Contexts*, ed. Sara Munson Deats and Robert A. Logan (Aldershot: Ashgate, 2008), 209–22.
5 Julia Reinhard Lupton, 'Shakespace on Marloan', in *Shakespeare without Class: Misappropriations of Cultural Capital*, ed. Donald Hedrick and Bryan Reynolds (New York: Palgrave, 2000), 277–85 (281).
6 Patrick Cheney calls Marlowe 'Renaissance England's first great poet-playwright', in Christopher Marlowe, *The Collected Poems of Christopher Marlowe*, ed. Patrick Cheney and Brian Striar (Oxford University Press, 2005), xi.

7 See Graham Hammill, *Sexuality and Form: Caravaggio, Marlowe, and Bacon* (University of Chicago Press, 2000).
8 Deborah Willis, 'Marlowe Our Contemporary: *Edward II* on Stage and Screen', *Criticism* 40 (1998): 599–622.
9 Lois Potter, 'What Happened to the Mighty Line? Recent Marlowe Productions', *Shakespeare Bulletin* 27:1 (2009): 63–9 (64).
10 Jonathan Bate, *The Genius of Shakespeare* (London: Picador, 1997), 105.
11 Thomas Beard, *The Theatre of Gods Judgement* (London, 1597).
12 Thomas Cartelli, '*Edward II*', in *The Cambridge Companion to Christopher Marlowe*, ed. Patrick Cheney (Cambridge University Press, 2004), 158–73 (158).
13 Christopher Marlowe, *Edward II*, ed. Peter J. Smith (London: Nick Hern, 1998), xxv.30, 33). All quotations are taken from this edition unless otherwise noted.
14 Stephen Orgel, *Impersonations: The Performance of Gender in Shakespeare's England* (Cambridge University Press, 1996), 47.
15 The latter stage direction appears in both *The Complete Plays*, ed. Frank Romany and Robert Lindsey (Penguin: London, 2003); and in *Doctor Faustus and Other Plays*, ed. David Bevington and Eric Rasmussen (Oxford University Press, 1995).
16 Marlowe, *Edward II*, ed. Smith, xix.
17 *Ibid.*
18 Orgel, *Impersonations*, 42, 49.
19 For a thorough summary of the 'evidence' for Edward's sodomy and the anal-rape narrative, see Ian Mortimer, 'Sermons of Sodomy: A Reconsideration of Edward II's Sodomitical Reputation', in *The Reign of Edward II: New Perspectives*, ed. Gwilym Dodd and Anthony Musson (Woodbridge: Boydell and Brewer, 2006), 48–60.
20 See Potter, 'What Happened to the Mighty Line?'.
21 Kate Chedgzoy characterises and censures such moves, noting that 'as the action unfolds, it moves away from the spit, so punitively homophobic interpretations of Edward's death that suggest that its manner is a punishment fitting his supposedly sodomitical crime can only do so by subjecting the text to a certain amount of ideological strain'; Kate Chedgzoy, 'Marlowe's Men and Women: Gender and Sexuality', in Cheney, *The Cambridge Companion to Christopher Marlowe*, 245–61 (258).
22 Beth Lynch, *John Bunyan and the Language of Conviction* (Woodbridge: Boydell and Brewer, 2004), 104.

Further reading

PART I   MARLOWE'S WORKS

1   Marlowe's chronology and canon

Rasmussen, Eric. *A Textual Companion to Doctor Faustus.* Manchester University Press, 1993.

Thomas, Vivien and William Tydeman, eds. *Christopher Marlowe: The Plays and Their Sources.* London and New York: Routledge, 1994.

Wiggins, Martin. 'When Did Marlowe Write *Dido, Queen of Carthage?*' *Review of English Studies* 59 (2008): 521–41.

Wiggins, Martin, in association with Catherine Richardson. *British Drama, 1533–1642: A Catalogue.* Oxford University Press, 2012– .

2   Marlowe's magic books: the material text

Brown, Georgia E. 'The Other Black Arts: *Doctor Faustus* and the Inky Worlds of Printing and Writing'. In *Doctor Faustus: A Critical Guide.* Ed. Sara Munson Deats. London and New York: Continuum, 2010. 140–58.

Byville, Eric. 'How to Do Witchcraft Tragedy with Speech Acts'. *Comparative Drama* 45 (2011): 1–33.

Chambers, E. K. *The Elizabethan Stage.* 4 vols. Vol. III. Oxford: Clarendon Press, 1923.

Maguire, Laurie E. 'Marlovian Texts and Authorship'. In *The Cambridge Companion to Christopher Marlowe.* Ed. Patrick Cheney. Cambridge University Press, 2004. 41–54.

Marcus, Leah S. 'Marlowe *in tempore belli*'. In *War and Words: Horror and Heroism in the Literature of Warfare.* Ed. Sara Munson Deats, LaGretta Tallent Lenker, and Merry G. Perry. Lanham and New York: Lexington Books, 2004. 295–316.

Unediting the Renaissance: Shakespeare, Marlowe, Milton. London and New York: Routledge, 1996.

Rebhorn, Wayne A. *The Emperor of Men's Minds: Literature and the Renaissance Discourse of Rhetoric.* Ithaca, NY: Cornell University Press, 1995.

3 Marlowe and the limits of rhetoric

Carver, Gordon. 'The Elizabethan Erotic Narrative: Sex(y) Reading'. *Explorations in Renaissance Culture* 31 (2005): 107–34.
Cheney, Patrick. *Marlowe's Counterfeit Profession: Ovid, Spenser, Counter-Nationhood*. University of Toronto Press, 1997.
Logan, Robert A. *Shakespeare's Marlowe: The Influence of Christopher Marlowe on Shakespeare's Artistry*. Burlington, VT: Ashgate, 2007.
Orgel, Stephen. 'Musaeus in English'. *George Herbert Journal* 29:1–2 (2005–6): 67–75.
Rhodes, Neil. *The Power of Eloquence and English Renaissance Literature*. New York: St Martin's Press, 1992.
Weaver, William P. 'Marlowe's Fable: *Hero and Leander* and the Rudiments of Eloquence'. *Studies in Philology* 105:3 (2008): 388–408.

4 Marlowe and character

Anthony Burgess. *A Dead Man in Deptford*. London: Hutchinson, 1993.
Ruth Lunney. *Marlowe and the Popular Tradition: Innovation in the English Drama before 1595*. Manchester University Press, 2002.
Peter Whelan. *The School of Night*. New York: Josef Weinberger Plays, 1992.

5 Marlowe's dramatic form

Dollimore, Jonathan. *Radical Tragedy: Religion, Ideology and Power in the Drama of Shakespeare and His Contemporaries*. 3rd edn. Durham, NC: Duke University Press, 2004.
Kelly, Henry Ansgar. *Ideas and Forms of Tragedy from Aristotle to the Middle Ages*. Cambridge University Press, 1993.
Neill, Michael. *Issues of Death: Mortality and Identity in English Renaissance Tragedy*. Oxford: Clarendon Press, 1997.
Norland, Howard B. *Drama in Early Tudor Britain, 1485–1558*. Lincoln: University of Nebraska Press, 1995.
Silk, M. S. *Tragedy and the Tragic*. Oxford: Clarendon Press, 1996.
Stern, Tiffany. *Documents of Performance in Early Modern England*. Cambridge University Press, 2009.

6 Marlowe's poetic form

Boutcher, Warren. '"Who taught thee Rhetoricke to deceive a maid?": Christopher Marlowe's *Hero and Leander*, Juan Boscán's *Leandro*, and Renaissance Vernacular Humanism'. *Comparative Literature* 52:1 (2000): 11–52.
Braden, Gordon. *The Classics and English Renaissance Poetry: Three Case Studies*. New Haven: Yale University Press, 1978.

Brown, Georgia E. 'Breaking the Canon: Marlowe's Challenge to the Literary Status Quo in *Hero and Leander*'. In *Marlowe, History, and Sexuality: New Critical Essays on Christopher Marlowe*. Ed. Paul Whitfield White. New York: AMS Press, 1998. 59–75.
Haber, Judith. '"True-loves blood": Narrative and Desire in *Hero and Leander*'. *English Literary Renaissance* 28 (1998): 372–86.
Hardie, Philip, ed. *The Cambridge Companion to Ovid*. Cambridge University Press, 2002.
Hulse, Clark. *Metamorphic Verse: The Elizabethan Minor Epic*. Princeton University Press, 1981.

7 Marlowe and the Elizabethan theatre audience

Cook, Ann Jennalie. *The Privileged Playgoers of Shakespeare's London*. Princeton University Press, 1981.
Dessen, Alan. *Elizabethan Stage Conventions and Modern Interpreters*. Cambridge University Press, 1984.
Gurr, Andrew. *Playgoing in Shakespeare's London*. 3rd edn. Cambridge University Press, 2004.
Harbage, Alfred. *Shakespeare's Audience*. New York: Columbia University Press, 1941.
Low, Jennifer A. and Nova Myhill, eds. *Imagining the Audience in Early Modern Drama, 1558–1642*. New York: Palgrave, 2011.
Whitney, Charles. *Early Responses to Renaissance Drama*. Cambridge University Press, 2006.

8 Marlowe and classical literature

Bartels, Emily C. 'Reproducing Africa: *Dido, Queene of Carthage* and Colonialist Discourse'. In *Spectacles of Strangeness: Imperialism, Alienation, and Marlowe*. Philadelphia: University of Pennsylvania Press, 1993. 29–52.
Blissett, William. 'Lucan's Caesar and the Elizabethan Villain'. *Studies in Philology* 53 (1956): 553–75.
Gill, Roma. 'Marlowe and the Art of Translation'. In *'A Poet and a Filthy Play-Maker': New Essays on Christopher Marlowe*. Ed. Kenneth Friedenreich, Roma Gill, and Constance Brown Kuriyama. New York: AMS Press, 1988. 327–42.
Hooley, Dan. 'Raising the Dead: Marlowe's Lucan'. In *Translation and the Classic: Identity as Change in the History of Culture*. Ed. Alexandra Lianeri and Vander Zajko. Oxford University Press, 2008. 243–60.
Summers, Claude J. '*Hero and Leander*: The Arbitrariness of Desire'. In *Constructing Christopher Marlowe*. Ed. J. A. Downie and J. T. Parnell. Cambridge University Press, 2000. 133–47.

9 Marlowe's medievalism

Beckwith, Sarah. *Signifying God: Social Relation and Symbolic Act in the York Corpus Christi Cycle*. University of Chicago Press, 2001.
Bevington, David. *From 'Mankind' to Marlowe: Growth of Structure in the Popular Drama of Tudor England*. Cambridge, MA: Harvard University Press, 1962.
Lunney, Ruth. *Marlowe and the Popular Tradition: Innovation in the English Drama before 1595*. Manchester University Press, 2002.
Muir, Lynette R. *Love and Conflict in Medieval Drama: The Plays and Their Legacy*. Cambridge University Press, 2007.
Parker, John. *The Aesthetics of Antichrist: From Christian Drama to Christopher Marlowe*. Ithaca, NY and London: Cornell University Press, 2007.
Sponsler, Claire. *Drama and Resistance: Bodies, Goods, and Theatricality in Late Medieval England*. Medieval Cultures 10. Minneapolis and London: University of Minnesota Press, 1997.

10 Marlowe's libraries: a history of reading

Eamon, William. *Science and the Secrets of Nature: Books of Secrets in Medieval and Early Modern Culture*. Princeton University Press, 1994.
Eisenstein, Elizabeth L. *Divine Art, Infernal Machine: The Reception of Printing in the West from First Impressions to the Sense of an Ending*. Philadelphia: University of Pennsylvania Press, 2011.
Johns, Adrian. 'The Physiology of Reading: Print and the Passions'. In *The Nature of the Book: Print and Knowledge in the Making*. University of Chicago Press, 1998. 380–443.
Manguel, Alberto. *A History of Reading*. New York: Penguin, 1997.
Summit, Jennifer. 'Reading Reformation: The Libraries of Matthew Parker and Edmund Spenser'. In *Memory's Library: Medieval Books in Early Modern England*. University of Chicago Press, 2008. 101–36.
Wall-Randell, Sarah. '*Doctor Faustus* and the Printer's Devil'. *SEL* 48:2 (2008): 259–81.

11 Marlowe's translations

Cheney, Patrick. *Marlowe's Counterfeit Profession: Ovid, Spenser, Counter-Nationhood*. University of Toronto Press, 1997.
James, Heather. 'The Poet's Toys: Christopher Marlowe and the Liberties of Erotic Elegy'. *Modern Language Quarterly* 67:1 (March 2006): 103–27.
Lyne, Raphael. 'Lyrical Wax in Ovid, Marlowe, and Donne'. In *Ovid and the Renaissance Body*. Ed. Goran V. Stanivukovic. University of Toronto Press, 2001.
Moulton, Ian Frederick. '"Printed Abroad and Uncastrated": Marlowe's *Elegies* with Davies' *Epigrams*'. In *Marlowe, History, and Sexuality: New Critical Essays on Christopher Marlowe*. Ed. Paul Whitfield White. New York: AMS Press, 1998.

Stapleton, M. L. *Harmful Eloquence: Ovid's* Amores *from Antiquity to Shakespeare*. Ann Arbor: University of Michigan Press, 1996.

'Marlowe's First Ovid: "Certaine of Ovids Elegies"'. In *Christopher Marlowe the Craftsman: Lives, Stage, and Page*. Ed. Sarah K. Scott and M. L. Stapleton. Farnham: Ashgate, 2010. 137–48.

PART II MARLOWE'S WORLD

12 Geography and Marlowe

Gillies, John. *Shakespeare and the Geography of Difference*. Cambridge University Press, 1994.

Jones, Emrys. '"A World of Ground": Terrestrial Space in Marlowe's *Tamburlaine* Plays'. *The Yearbook of English Studies* 38:1–2, Tudor Literature (2008): 168–82.

Klein, Bernhard. *Maps and the Writing of Space in Early Modern England and Ireland*. Basingstoke: Palgrave, 2001.

Sullivan, Garrett. 'Geography and Identity in Marlowe'. In *The Cambridge Companion to Christopher Marlowe*. Ed. Patrick Cheney. Cambridge University Press, 2004. 231–44.

Turner, Henry S. *The English Renaissance Stage: Geometry, Poetics, and the Practical Spatial Arts, 1580–1630*. Oxford University Press, 2006.

West, Russell. *Spatial Representations and the Jacobean Stage: From Shakespeare to Webster*. Basingstoke and New York: Palgrave, 2002.

13 Marlowe, history, and politics

Adams, Simon L. *Leicester and the Court: Essays on Elizabethan Politics*. Manchester University Press, 2002.

Briggs, Julia. 'Marlowe's *Massacre at Paris*: A Reconsideration'. *RES* 34 (1983): 257–78.

Dillon, Anne. *The Construction of Martyrdom in the English Catholic Community, 1535–1603*. Aldershot: Ashgate, 2011.

Kewes, Paulina. 'History Plays and the Royal Succession'. In *The Oxford Handbook of Holinshed's* Chronicles. Ed. Paulina Kewes, Ian W. Archer, and Felicity Heal. Oxford University Press, 2013. 497–513.

Perry, Curtis. *Literature and Favouritism in Early Modern England*. Cambridge University Press, 2006.

Shagan, Ethan H., ed. *Catholics and the 'Protestant Nation': Religious Politics and Identity in Early Modern England*. Manchester University Press, 2005.

14 Marlowe and social distinction

Cheney, Patrick. 'Biographical Representations: Marlowe's Life of the Author'. In *Shakespeare, Marlowe, Jonson: New Directions in Biography*. Ed. Takashi Kozuka and J. R. Mulryne. Aldershot: Ashgate, 2006. 183–203.

Hardin, Richard F. 'Irony and Privilege in Marlowe'. *Centennial Review* 33 (1989): 207–27.
Riggs, David. 'The Poet in the Play: Life and Art in *Tamburlaine* and *The Jew of Malta*'. In *Shakespeare, Marlowe, Jonson: New Directions in Biography*. Ed. Takashi Kozuka and J. R. Mulryne. Aldershot: Ashgate, 2006. 205–23.
The World of Christopher Marlowe. New York: Henry Holt, 2004.
Scott, Sarah K. and M. L. Stapleton, eds. *Christopher Marlowe the Craftsman: Lives, Stage, and Page*. Farnham: Ashgate, 2010.
Wilson, Richard. 'Tragedy, Patronage, and Power'. In *The Cambridge Companion to Christopher Marlowe*. Ed. Patrick Cheney. Cambridge University Press, 2004. 207–30.

15 Marlowe, death-worlds, and warfare

Cahill, Patricia A. *Unto the Breach: Martial Formations, Historical Trauma, and the Early Modern Stage*. Oxford University Press, 2008.
DeSomogyi, Nick. *Shakespeare's Theatre of War*. Aldershot: Ashgate, 1998.
Logan, Robert A. 'Violence, Terrorism, and War in Marlowe's *Tamburlaine* Plays'. In *War and Words: Horror and Heroism in the Literature of Warfare*. Ed. Sara Munson Deats, LaGretta Tallent Lenker, and Merry G. Perry. Lanham and New York: Lexington Books, 2004. 65–81.
Shepard, Alan. *Marlowe's Soldiers: Rhetorics of Masculinity in the Age of the Armada*. Aldershot: Ashgate, 2002.
Taunton, Nina. *1590s Drama and Militarism: Portrayals of War in Marlowe, Chapman and Shakespeare's Henry V*. Aldershot: Ashgate, 2001.
Wilson, Richard. 'Visible Bullets: Tamburlaine the Great and Ivan the Terrible'. *ELH* 62:1 (Spring 1995): 47–68.

16 Education, the university, and Marlowe

Curtis, Mark H. *Oxford and Cambridge in Transition, 1558–1642*. Oxford: Clarendon Press, 1959.
Feingold, Mordechai. 'The Occult Tradition in the English Universities of the Renaissance: A Reassessment'. In *Occult and Scientific Mentalities of the Renaissance*. Ed. Brian Vickers. Cambridge University Press, 1984. 73–94.
Jardine, Lisa. 'Humanism and the Sixteenth Century Cambridge Arts Course'. *History of Education* 4 (1975): 16–31.
   'The Place of Dialectic Teaching in Sixteenth-Century Cambridge'. *Studies in the Renaissance* 21 (1974): 31–62.
Morgan, Victor. *A History of the University of Cambridge*. 4 vols. Vol. II: *1546–1750*. Cambridge University Press, 2004.
Riggs, David. *The World of Christopher Marlowe*. New York: Henry Holt, 2004.

372 *Further reading*

17 Marlowe and the question of will

Bartels, Emily C. 'The Double Vision of the East: Imperialist Self-Construction in Marlowe's *Tamburlaine Part One*'. *Renaissance Drama* 23 (1992): 3–24.

Burnett, Mark Thornton. *Constructing 'Monsters' in Shakespearean Drama and Early Modern Culture*. New York: Palgrave Macmillan, 2002.

Cahill, Patricia. 'Killing by Computation: Military Mathematics, the Elizabethan Social Body, and Marlowe's *Tamburlaine*'. In *Arts of Calculation: Quantifying Thought in Early Modern Europe*. Ed. David Glimp and Michelle R. Warren, New York: Palgrave Macmillan, 2004. 165–86.

Moore, Roger E. 'The Spirit and the Letter: Marlowe's *Tamburlaine* and Elizabethan Religious Radicalism'. *Studies in Philology* 99:2 (2002): 123–51.

Thomson, Leslie. 'Marlowe's Staging of Meaning'. *Medieval and Renaissance Drama in England* 18 (2005): 19–36.

Whitfield, Pam. '"Divine Zenocrate", "Wretched Zenocrate": Female Speech and Disempowerment in *Tamburlaine i*'. In *Renaissance Papers 2000*, ed. T. Howard-Hill and Philip Rollinson (Woodbridge: Boydell and Brewer, 2000). 87–97.

18 Marlowe and the self

Greenblatt, Stephen. *The Swerve: How the World Became Modern*. New York: Norton, 2011.

Hunter, Robert G. *Shakespeare and the Mystery of God's Judgments*. Athens: University of Georgia Press, 1976.

Nicholl, Charles. *The Reckoning: The Death of Christopher Marlowe*. University of Chicago Press, 1995.

Riggs, David. *The World of Christopher Marlowe*. New York: Henry Holt, 2004.

Strier, Richard. *The Unrepentant Renaissance: From Petrarch to Shakespeare to Milton*. University of Chicago Press, 2011.

19 Race, nation, and Marlowe

Bartels, Emily C. *Spectacles of Strangeness: Imperialism, Alienation, and Marlowe*. Philadelphia: University of Pennsylvania Press, 1993.

Floyd-Wilson, Mary. *English Ethnicity and Race in Early Modern Drama*. Cambridge University Press, 2003.

Hendricks, Margo and Patricia Parker, eds. *Women, 'Race', and Writing in the Early Modern Period*. London: Routledge, 1994.

Iyengar, Sujata. *Shades of Difference: Mythologies of Skin Color in Early Modern England*. Philadelphia: University of Pennsylvania Press, 2005.

Loomba, Ania. *Shakespeare, Race, and Colonialism*. Oxford University Press, 2002.

Spiller, Elizabeth. *Reading and the History of Race in the Renaissance*. Cambridge University Press, 2011.

20 Marlowe and religion

Lake, Peter. 'Religious Identities in Shakespeare's England'. In *A Companion to Shakespeare*. Ed. David Scott Kastan. Oxford: Blackwell, 1999. 57–84.

Patrides, C. A. '"The Bloody and Cruell Turke": The Background of a Renaissance Commonplace'. *Studies in the Renaissance* 10 (1963): 126–35.

Poole, Kristen. 'The Devil's in the Archive: *Doctor Faustus* and Ovidian Physics'. *Renaissance Drama* 35 (2006): 191–219.

Riggs, David. 'Marlowe's Quarrel with God'. In *Critical Essays on Christopher Marlowe*. Ed. Emily C. Bartels. New York: G. K. Hall, 1997. 39–60.

Daniel Vitkus. *Turning Turk: English Theater and the Multicultural Mediterranean, 1570–1630*. New York: Palgrave Macmillan, 2003.

21 Marlowe and queer theory

Chedzgoy, Kate. 'Marlowe's Men and Women: Gender and Sexuality'. In *The Cambridge Companion to Christopher Marlowe*. Ed. Patrick Cheney. Cambridge University Press, 2004. 245–61.

DiGangi, Mario. 'Marlowe, Queer Studies, and Renaissance Homoeroticism'. In *Marlowe, History, and Sexuality: New Critical Essays on Christopher Marlowe*. Ed. Paul Whitfield White. New York: AMS Press, 1998. 195–212.

Green, Adam. 'Gay but not Queer: Toward a Post-Queer Study of Sexuality'. *Theory and Society* 31:4 (2002): 521–45.

Greenblatt, Stephen. *Renaissance Self-Fashioning: From More to Shakespeare*. University of Chicago Press, 1980.

Morland, Iain and Annabelle Willox, eds. *Queer Theory*. New York: Palgrave, 2005.

22 Marlowe and women

Bartels, Emily C. *Spectacles of Strangeness: Imperialism, Alienation, and Marlowe*. Philadelphia: University of Pennsylvania Press, 1993.

Bloom, Gina. *Voice in Motion: Staging Gender, Shaping Sound in Early Modern England*. Philadelphia: University of Pennsylvania Press, 2007.

Findlay, Alison. *A Feminist Perspective on Renaissance Drama*. Oxford: Blackwell, 1998.

Gibbs, Joanna. 'Marlowe's Politic Women'. In *Constructing Christopher Marlowe*. Ed. J. A. Downie and J. T. Parnell. Cambridge University Press, 2000. 164–76.

Shepherd, Simon. 'Representing "Women" and Males: Gender Relations in Marlowe'. In *Christopher Marlowe*. Ed. Richard Wilson. London and New York: Longman, 1999. 62–82.

Tromly, Frederick B. *Playing with Desire: Christopher Marlowe and the Art of Tantalization*. University of Toronto Press, 1998.

23 Marlowe and the new science

Gillies, John. 'Tamburlaine and Renaissance Geography'. In *Early Modern English Drama: A Critical Companion*. Ed. Garrett Sullivan, Patrick Cheney, and Andrew Hadfield. New York: Oxford University Press, 2006.

24 The professional theatre and Marlowe

Bentley, G. E. *The Profession of Dramatist in Shakespeare's Time 1590–1642*. Princeton University Press, 1971.
Bradley, David. *From Text to Performance in the Elizabethan Theatre: Preparing the Play for the Stage*. Cambridge University Press, 1991.
Hirschfeld, Heather A. *Joint Enterprises: Collaborative Drama and the Institutionalization of the English Renaissance Theater*. Amherst: University of Massachusetts Press, 2004.
Hunter, G. K. *English Drama 1586–1642: The Age of Shakespeare*. Oxford History of English Literature. Oxford: Clarendon Press, 1997.
Knutson, Roslyn Lander. *The Repertory of Shakespeare's Company 1594–1613*. Fayetteville: University of Arkansas Press, 1991.
Masten, Jeffrey. *Textual Intercourse: Collaboration, Authorship, and Sexualities in Renaissance Drama*. Cambridge University Press, 1997.

PART III RECEPTION

25 Marlowe in his moment

Downie, J. A. 'Marlowe: Facts and Fiction'. In *Constructing Christopher Marlowe*. Ed. J. A. Downie and J. T. Parnell. Cambridge University Press, 2000. 13–29.
Erne, Lukas. 'Biography, Mythography, and Criticism: The Life and Works of Christopher Marlowe'. *Modern Philology* 103 (2005): 28–50.
Knutson, Roslyn Lander. *Playing Companies and Commerce in Shakespeare's Time*. Cambridge University Press, 2001.
Syme, Holger Schott. 'The Meaning of Success: Stories of 1594 and Its Aftermath'. *Shakespeare Quarterly* 61 (2010): 490–525.
Whitney, Charles. *Early Responses to Renaissance Drama*. Cambridge University Press, 2006.

26 Marlowe and Shakespeare revisited

Cartelli, Thomas. *Marlowe, Shakespeare, and the Economy of Theatrical Experience*. Philadelphia: University of Pennsylvania Press, 1991.

27 Marlowe in Caroline theatre

Astington, John. 'Playing the Man: Acting at the Red Bull and the Fortune'. *Early Theatre* 9 (2006): 130–43.

Brooke, C. F. Tucker. *The Reputation of Christopher Marlowe*. Transactions of the Connecticut Academy of Arts and Sciences 25. New Haven: Connecticut Academy of Arts and Sciences, 1922.
Lesser, Zachary. *Renaissance Drama and the Politics of Publication: Readings in the English Book Trade*. Cambridge University Press, 2004.
Munro, Lucy. 'Marlowe on the Caroline Stage'. *Shakespeare Bulletin* 27 (2009): 39–50.
Parker, John. 'Barabas and Charles I'. In *Placing the Plays of Christopher Marlowe: Fresh Cultural Contexts*. Ed. Sara Munson Deats and Robert A. Logan. Aldershot: Ashgate, 2008. 167–81.
Shawcross, John T. 'Signs of the Times: Christopher Marlowe's Decline in the Seventeenth Century'. In *'A Poet and a Filthy Play-Maker': New Essays on Christopher Marlowe*. Ed. Kenneth Friedenreich, Roma Gill, and Constance Brown Kuriyama. New York: AMS Press, 1988. 63–71.

28 Marlowe's literary influence

Dabbs, Thomas. *Reforming Marlowe: The Nineteenth-Century Canonization of a Renaissance Dramatist*. Lewisburg: Bucknell University Press; London and Toronto: Associated University Presses, 1991.
Hopkins, Lisa. 'Marlowe's Reception and Influence'. In *The Cambridge Companion to Marlowe*. Ed. Patrick Cheney. Cambridge University Press, 2004. 282–96.

29 Marlowe in the movies

Aebischer, Pascale. 'Renaissance Tragedy on Film: Defying Mainstream Shakespeare'. In *The Cambridge Companion to English Renaissance Tragedy*. Ed. Emma Smith and Garrett Sullivan. Cambridge University Press, 2010. 116–31.
Barker, Roberta. *Early Modern Tragedy, Gender and Performance, 1984–2000*. Houndmills: Palgrave Macmillan, 2007.
Chedgzoy, Kate. *Shakespeare's Queer Children: Sexual Politics and Contemporary Culture*. Manchester University Press, 1995.
Fuller, David. 'Love or Politics: The Man or the King? *Edward II* in Modern Performance'. *Shakespeare Bulletin* 27:1 (Spring 2009): 81–115.
Potter, Lois. 'Marlowe in Theatre and Film'. *The Cambridge Companion to Christopher Marlowe*. Ed. Patrick Cheney. Cambridge University Press, 2004. 262–81.
Willis, Deborah. 'Marlowe Our Contemporary: *Edward II* on Stage and Screen'. *Criticism* 40 (1998): 599–622.

30 Editing Marlowe's texts

Duxfield, Andrew. 'Modern Problems of Editing: The Two Texts of Marlowe's *Doctor Faustus*'. *Literature Compass* 2 (2005): n.p.

Maguire, Laurie E. 'Marlovian Texts and Authorship'. In *The Cambridge Companion to Christopher Marlowe*. Ed. Patrick Cheney. Cambridge University Press, 2004. 41–54.

Marcus, Leah S. *Unediting the Renaissance: Shakespeare, Marlowe, Milton*. London and New York: Routledge, 1996.

Murphy, Andrew, ed. *The Renaissance Text: Theory, Editing, Textuality*. Manchester University Press, 2000.

Orgel, Stephen. 'What Is an Editor?' *Shakespeare Studies* 24 (1996): 23–46.

Werstine, Paul. 'Editing after the End of Editing'. *Shakespeare Studies* 24 (1996): 47–54.

31 Marlowe's biography

Bakeless, John E. *The Tragicall History of Christopher Marlowe*. 2 vols. Cambridge, MA: Harvard University Press, 1942.

Nicholl, Charles. *The Reckoning: The Murder of Christopher Marlowe*. Rev. edn. London: Vintage, 2002.

Riggs, David. *The World of Christopher Marlowe*. New York: Henry Holt, 2004.

32 Marlowe and the critics

Burnett, Mark Thornton. 'Marlowe and the Critics'. In *Christopher Marlowe: The Complete Plays*. Ed. Mark Thornton Burnett. London: Everyman, 1999. 615–31.

DiGangi, Mario. 'Marlowe, Queer Studies, and Renaissance Homoeroticism'. In *Marlowe, History, and Sexuality: New Critical Essays on Christopher Marlowe*. Ed. Paul Whitfield White. New York: AMS Press, 1998. 195–212.

Logan, Robert A. 'Marlowe Scholarship and Criticism: The Current Scene'. In *Christopher Marlowe the Craftsman: Lives, Stage, and Page*. Ed. Sarah K. Scott and M. L. Stapleton. Farnham: Ashgate, 2010. 5–22.

Ribner, Irving. 'Marlowe and the Critics'. *Tulane Drama Review* 8:4 (1964): 211–24.

Tydeman, William and Vivien Thomas. *Christopher Marlowe: A Guide through the Critical Maze*. Bristol Press, 1989.

Wilson, Richard. '"Writ in blood": Marlowe and the New Historicists'. In *Constructing Christopher Marlowe*. Ed. J. A. Downie and J. T. Parnell. Cambridge University Press, 2000. 116–32.

33 Marlowe now

Hammill, Graham. *Sexuality and Form: Caravaggio, Marlowe, and Bacon*. University of Chicago Press, 2000.

Lopez, Jeremy. 'Alleyn Resurrected'. *Marlowe Studies: An Annual* 1 (2011): 167–80.

Lupton, Julia Reinhard. 'Shakespace on Marloan'. In *Shakespeare without Class: Misappropriations of Cultural Capital*. Ed. Donald Hedrick and Bryan Reynolds. New York: Palgrave, 2000. 277–85.

Orgel, Stephen. 'Tobacco and Boys: How Queer Was Marlowe?' *GLQ: A Journal of Lesbian and Gay Studies* 6 (2000): 555–7.
Potter, Lois. 'What Happened to the Mighty Line? Recent Marlowe Productions'. *Shakespeare Bulletin* 27:1 (2009): 63–9.
Shepherd, Simon. 'A Bit of Ruff: Criticism, Fantasy, Marlowe'. *Constructing Christopher Marlowe*. Ed. J. A. Downie and J. T. Parnell. Cambridge University Press, 2000. 102–15.

Index

Admiral's Men 8, 11, 245, 246, 249, 263, 265, 266, 267, 270, 275, 276, 277, 278, 280, 281, 282, 341
All Ovid's Elegies see Ovid's Elegies
Alleyn, Edward 68, 249, 263, 281, 297, 298, 299, 300
antitheatricalism 239
Ascham, Roger 104
astronomy 182, 189, 252, 253, 259
audiences i, 8, 15, 16, 29, 40, 41, 44, 49, 52, 62, 70–77, 91–9, 132, 135, 144, 145, 152, 193, 204, 205, 228, 230, 235, 237, 239, 243, 245, 278, 286, 300, 321, 329, 347, 363

Badiou, Alain 193, 194
Baines, Richard 340, 341
   'Baines note' 206, 222, 232, 336, 341, 343, 348, 360
Bale, John 223
Bartels, Emily C. 48, 245, 352
Barthes, Roland 330, 358
Bate, Jonathan 120, 360
Beard, Thomas 354, 361, 362, 363
Berger, Harry 283, 291, 292, 293
Bevington, David 90, 136, 204, 208, 229, 267
Bird, William 269, 328
Bishops' Ban 80, 82, 110, 119, 327, 347
blackletter type 18, 21
blank verse 50, 51, 58, 111, 283, 289
Bloom, Harold 27
Blunt, Edward 35, 38
Book of Secrets 107
Bowers, Fredson 328, 329
boy acting companies 8, 85, 245, 246, 301, 303
Bradley, A. C. 110, 111
Bray, Alan 235
Brecht, Bertolt 360
Briggs, Julia 74, 147, 148
Brown, Georgia 23, 31, 65, 113
Burbage, James 9, 341
Burton, Richard 316

Butler, Judith 232, 237
Byron, Lord 2, 310, 314

Callaghan, Dympna 112
Calvinism 49, 55, 77, 159, 204, 205, 207, 208, 209, 210, 223, 228, 348
Caravaggio 2, 360
cartography 47, 125–36, 189, 252, 253, 254, 260, 312
Catholicism 73, 74, 75, 88, 90, 91, 92, 98, 138–48, 149, 150, 151, 208, 222–6, 340, 348
Caxton, William 15
Cecil, William, Lord Burghley 139, 140, 148, 149, 150, 341, 343
Chapman, George 38, 66, 299, 361
Chaucer, Geoffrey 202, 334
Cheney, Patrick 58, 268, 359, 374
Children of the Chapel Royal 8, 245, 263
classical drama 53, 54, 55, 82, 242
Clyomon and Clamydes 279
Collier, John Payne 310
comedy 38, 47, 49, 50, 72, 83, 246, 303
commonplacing 104
Conrad, Joseph 312, 313
Copernicus 189, 252, 253, 256, 259
Corelli, Marie 311, 312
Corpus Christi College, Cambridge 103, 181, 184, 187, 188, 335, 338
   Parker Library 103, 106

Davies, John 67, 82, 119, 192, 193, 327
de Certeau, Michel 196
Deats, Sara Munson 25, 26, 48, 74, 263, 352
Dee, John 108, 129, 131, 136, 190, 253, 257
Dekker, Thomas 13, 80
Deloney, Thomas 151, 156
Derrida, Jacques 195
Devereux, Robert, second Earl of Essex 141, 147, 345
dialectic 186, 187

Dido, Queen of Carthage 8, 11, 27, 28, 81, 138, 160, 212, 223, 233, 242, 245, 250, 263, 268, 301, 310, 327, 341
Digges, Leonard 255
Digges, Thomas 252, 253, 256, 257, 261
Doctor Faustus 1, 10, 11, 12, 15, 16, 22, 23, 27, 29, 39–45, 47, 49–55, 73, 75, 76, 77, 90, 91, 97, 99, 118, 136, 138, 159–63, 181, 185, 188, 189, 202–10, 223, 228, 229, 230, 233, 234, 242, 243, 258, 259, 263, 268–71, 280, 281, 282, 285, 287, 289, 290–3, 299–303, 306, 309–313, 316, 322, 326–32, 336, 339, 348, 351, 358, 360, 361, 362, 363
  attitude to learning 108, 190
  Chorus 39, 49, 52, 54, 101, 309, 358
  ending 76, 118
  Helen of Troy 11, 43, 163, 230, 242, 243, 290, 292, 312
  hell 27, 45, 49, 54, 102, 163, 198, 203, 206, 207, 229, 230, 293, 299, 309, 312, 313, 358
  in print 102, 332
  Lucifer 42, 102, 106, 228, 229, 263
  textual differences 21, 23, 41, 44, 51, 53, 269, 327, 329, 332, 348
  woodcut 21, 23
Dollimore, Jonathan 56, 231, 351, 352
Drayton, Michael 268, 294, 334, 337, 344, 361
Dutch Church Libel 39, 151, 217, 221, 342

Earl of Pembroke's Men 9, 263
editing 325–33
editions 2, 7, 15, 18, 19, 145, 299, 310, 325, 328, 329, 331, 344, 362
Edward II 1, 9–14, 29, 45, 75, 98, 135–43, 147–53, 156, 160, 165, 166, 217, 218, 219, 223, 232–40, 244, 263, 285, 287, 290, 291, 301, 302, 309, 311, 316–23, 327, 347, 360–3
  ending 319, 362
  sexuality 240, 323
  topicality 140, 144, 147
Eisenstein, Elizabeth L. 102
elegy 58, 80, 82, 84, 110–16, 157, 158, 348
Eliot, T. S. 28, 47, 192
Elizabeth I, queen of England 10, 75, 81, 139, 141–9, 173, 182, 217, 224, 236, 245, 308, 320, 335, 339, 341
Erasmus, Desiderius 27, 29, 31, 32, 34, 61, 339
Euripides 242

film studies 317
Ford, John 39, 301, 302
Foucault, Michel 330
Foxe, John 145, 146, 150
Freud, Sigmund 198, 199
  uncanny 195, 198

Frizer, Ingram 343
Fust, Johann 16, 23, 102

Galen 101, 103, 105
Garber, Marjorie 193
Gillies, John 131, 136, 254, 256, 259
Goethe, Johann von 310, 311, 313
Goldberg, Jonathan 240, 241, 352
Gorboduc 50, 53, 54
Gorges, Arthur 87, 88
grammar schools 112, 181–90
Grandage, Michael 45
Greenblatt, Stephen 28, 169, 202, 212, 350
Greene, Robert 9, 11, 39, 143, 262, 263, 270, 276, 280, 283, 289, 342, 361
Greg, W. W. 328, 329, 330
Gresshop, John (headmaster of the King's School, Canterbury) 103

Haber, Judith 33, 196
Hakluyt, Richard 213
Hall, Peter 179, 317
Hariot, Thomas 252, 253, 259
Harsnett, Samuel 208, 209
Harvey, Gabriel 161, 162, 165, 166, 252, 255, 259
Henri III, king of France 75, 139, 141, 142, 143, 146, 147, 148, 149, 152, 236
Henri IV, king of France 148, 149, 151, 152
Henslowe, Philip 9, 12, 13, 14, 226, 248, 249, 263, 265, 267, 269, 276, 280, 282, 328
Hero and Leander 8, 30, 33, 35, 57–65, 83, 155, 156, 163, 233, 235, 275, 283, 298, 302, 303, 306, 310, 327
  ending 83, 358
  Neptune 33, 61, 83, 233, 235
  rhetoric 36
  vocabulary 59
Heywood, Thomas 50, 268, 281, 297, 298, 299, 300, 327
Holinshed, Raphael 103, 138, 140, 141, 143, 144, 145, 236, 361
homosexuality 61, 65, 85, 141, 232–40, 317, 318, 319, 320, 321, 322, 323, 336, 352, 353
humanism 28, 30, 32, 57, 61, 97, 104, 105, 107, 117, 161, 164, 183, 186, 189, 229
hypertext 331

interiority 41
Islam 11, 17, 72, 216, 217, 219, 222–8
  Koran 217, 228, 258

James VI, king of Scotland 139, 142, 143, 144, 236
Jarman, Derek 316, 317, 319, 320, 321, 322, 323, 360, 362
Jew of Malta, The 7, 12, 14, 39–47, 68, 71, 98, 132, 133, 134, 138, 156, 157, 163, 165, 179, 212, 214,

215, 217, 223, 224, 230, 242, 263, 267, 268, 276, 280, 281, 282, 296–302, 309, 316, 323, 327, 336, 341, 349, 363
genre 224
Jewishness 40, 41, 46, 216, 217, 220, 222, 223, 224
prologue 12, 39, 45, 297, 302
Jones, Richard 18, 268, 269, 325, 326, 330
Jonson, Ben i, 39, 56, 80, 81, 86, 115, 266, 283, 301, 306, 343
Poetaster, The 80

Kean, Edmund 309, 314, 349
Kyd, Thomas 13, 166, 206, 265, 336, 341, 342
Spanish Tragedy, The 53, 54, 280

Latin 8, 30, 35, 40, 57, 60, 66, 82, 87, 112–17, 182, 183, 186, 189, 204, 207, 220, 255, 262, 339
drama 187
Levin, Harry 27, 111, 335, 350
Lodge, Thomas 11, 262
Logan, Robert 245
Lopez, Jeremy 69, 70
Lord Chamberlain's Men 264, 281
Lord Strange's Men 9, 13, 249, 263, 264, 276, 277, 280, 281
Lucan 13, 57, 81, 86, 87, 88, 110, 311
Lucan's First Book 88, 111, 119, 167, 306, 327
Lupton, Julia Reinhard 359
Luther, Martin 104, 120, 223, 330

Maguire, Laurie 326
Manutius, Aldus 18, 30
Marcus, Leah S. 330, 348
Marlowe, Christopher
 allusions to 301–4, 309, 313
 biographical readings 1, 202, 222, 232, 319, 336, 358, 360
 characterisation 39–48, 73, 86, 91, 200, 293
 collaboration 12, 265, 268, 269
 death 2, 327, 334, 343, 358, 361, 363
 depictions of race 42, 212–20
 depictions of religion 74, 144, 145, 151, 210, 212, 216, 217, 222–31, 244, 330
 doubtful attributions 13, 299, 309
 early modern performance 245, 246, 250, 267, 282, 301, 304
 early responses 36, 39, 162, 166, 276, 283, 304, 306, 307
 education 103, 104, 112, 156, 158, 182–92, 259, 262, 335, 338
 female characters 242–51
 film 323, 360

genre 8, 38, 47, 49–56, 58, 65, 82, 83, 84, 195, 238, 239, 244, 246, 326
geography 94, 125–38, 179, 189, 214
history 138–54
in print 332
lost plays 13, 266
'mighty line' 86, 115, 203, 283, 306, 313
modern performance 47, 179, 316, 362
names 1, 334
performance 310
popularity 15, 51, 71, 78, 86, 119, 150, 270, 276, 279, 280, 281, 283, 299, 301, 320
printing 332
soliloquies 41, 132, 134, 137, 162, 163, 168, 204, 207, 225, 235, 236, 237, 244, 309
sources 10, 11, 33, 57, 59, 66, 84, 85, 91, 101, 103, 107, 108, 138, 140, 142, 145, 243, 328, 330, 331, 336
stage spectacle 15, 16, 17, 53, 68, 91, 92, 93, 94, 96, 97, 170, 172, 177, 199, 229, 237, 263, 265, 327
television 318, 319
topicality 12, 75, 88, 138–54, 235, 236, 308, 351
translation 80, 82, 88, 89, 110–23, 157, 204
vocabulary 155
Marprelate Controversy 149
Marston, John 80
Mary, Queen of Scots 144
masculinity 61, 110, 111, 112, 113, 116, 117, 216, 245, 246, 248, 250, 322
Massacre at Paris, The 9, 10, 11, 12, 13, 28, 39, 44, 73, 74, 75, 98, 138–43, 147–52, 155, 223, 225, 226, 230, 234, 236, 243, 263, 276, 280, 282, 310, 327, 328, 341, 342, 348, 353, 363
 Duke of Guise 9, 28, 39, 44, 73–5, 86, 90, 98, 142, 148, 155, 225, 244, 340
 Henri of Navarre 142, 147, 148, 149, 151, 226, 231, 244
 politics 151
Master of the Revels 282
May, Thomas 311
Mbembe, Achille 169
McDonald, Russ 58
McKellen, Ian 316–23
medieval cycle drama 90, 91, 95, 99
Middleton, Thomas 48, 344
Milton, John 203, 209, 309, 310
Montaigne, Michel de 116, 121
morality plays 40, 91, 208, 229, 276
More, Sir Thomas 104
Morse, Douglas 316, 323
Mucedorus 280
Munday, Anthony 39, 265, 266
Murnau, F. W. 316, 322, 323

N-Town plays 92, 95, 96
Nashe, Thomas 12, 157, 161, 162, 166, 262, 263, 268, 342, 361
Neill, Michael 170
New World exploration 212, 213, 222

Ong, Walter 112
Orgel, Stephen 37, 66, 81, 330, 362, 376
Ortelius, Abraham 103, 125, 189, 254
Ovid 7, 30, 34, 60, 65, 80–4, 110–18, 157, 158, 165, 189, 245, 260, 339, 347, 348
Ovid's Elegies 57, 58, 80, 85, 110, 111, 117, 118, 155, 299, 327

'Passionate Shepherd to His Love, The' 1, 57, 58, 72, 85, 299, 306
pastoral 73, 303, 363
patronage 7, 81, 151, 266, 297, 335, 338, 340
Peacham, Henry 27, 248
Peele, George 10, 140, 141, 143, 146, 262, 276, 289, 361
Petrarchism 57, 59, 65, 66, 81
plague 9, 338
playhouses 9, 68, 277, 278, 281, 283, 300
Potter, Lois 305, 360
predestination 55, 204, 207, 208, 228, 309
Preston, Thomas 50
Puritanism 16
Puritans 74, 149, 150, 209, 223, 348, 350
Puttenham, George 27, 30, 34

Queen Henrietta's Men 281, 296, 297, 300–3
Queen's Men 263, 277, 279
queer theory 232–41

Ralegh, Sir Walter 139, 141, 341, 342
Ramus, Peter 28, 103
reading 101, 104, 108, 161
Red Bull theatre 283, 300, 301, 305
rhetoric 17, 27, 28, 31, 36, 41, 66, 101, 103, 131, 132, 146, 182, 186, 244, 248, 291, 339, 351
  blazon 33, 61, 65, 92
  copia 29, 32, 34, 35, 57, 339
  ekphrasis 57, 64, 83
Rhodes, Neil 28
Riggs, David 181, 187, 188, 203, 204, 205, 206, 207, 260, 337, 345, 349
Rose Theatre 9, 11, 12, 172, 263, 270, 276, 278, 280, 282, 328, 359
Rowley, Samuel 269, 328
Rowley, William 77
Royal Shakespeare Company 317

selfhood 133, 193, 202, 203, 209, 210, 232
Seneca 53, 54, 116, 189
sexuality 60, 113, 232, 240, 317, 318
Shakespeare in Love 2, 316, 360
Shakespeare, William 1, 9, 10, 12, 18, 47, 53, 54, 69, 90, 131, 170, 232, 264–7, 279–85, 287, 289, 291, 292, 293, 299, 301, 306, 309, 311, 316, 318, 320, 323, 334, 338, 342, 343, 346, 357, 358, 359, 360, 374
  Antony and Cleopatra 85
  Hamlet 54, 247, 265
  Henry IV, Part II 308
  Henry V 53, 265
  King Lear 47, 238, 265
  Macbeth 46, 247, 286
  Merchant of Venice, The 132, 212
  Much Ado about Nothing 265, 280
  Othello 212, 213, 265
  Richard II 147, 285, 287, 289, 290, 291, 293, 318, 320, 357
  Richard III 239, 265, 320, 321
  Romeo and Juliet 52, 53
  Sonnets 38, 64
  Tempest, The 212
  Titus Andronicus 212, 213
  Venus and Adonis 64, 72
  Winter's Tale, The 53
Shelley, Mary 311
Shepherd, Simon 242, 248
Shirley, James 302, 303
Sidney, Sir Philip 10, 51, 64, 104, 109, 163, 164, 165, 167, 186, 334, 347
social status 70, 166, 182, 184, 186, 189, 190, 248, 263
Spanish Armada 141, 143, 226, 307
Spenser, Edmund 64, 184, 299, 334, 338, 340
Stoker, Bram 311
subversion 2, 30, 40, 51, 155, 212, 222, 233, 236, 240, 243, 244, 246, 259, 348, 349, 351, 352
Švankmajer, Jan 316, 322, 323
Swinburne, Algernon 312

Tamburlaine, Part I 15, 17, 18, 27, 29, 39, 40, 42, 43, 47, 51, 52, 70, 86, 94, 98, 126, 136, 138, 156, 158–65, 195, 200, 220, 227, 242, 247, 254, 255, 257, 267, 270, 285, 286, 302, 347
  ending 162, 176
  in print 325
  prologue 39, 44, 51, 93, 213, 266, 346
  Triumph of Death motif 171
  warfare 169–79
Zenocrate 11, 18, 20, 29, 94, 163, 172, 176, 197, 213, 216, 227, 242, 243, 246, 247, 248, 249, 250, 254, 258, 267, 302, 307

Tamburlaine, Part II 8, 9, 11, 15, 17, 47, 52, 138, 189, 193, 196, 215, 224, 227, 228, 256, 306
  ending 52
  staging 177
  warfare 169–79
tragedy 38, 40, 49–55, 72, 83, 84, 86, 98, 113, 139, 142, 228, 238, 243, 289, 303, 326, 350, 352
Turner, Henry 254

Vennar, Richard 299
Verstegan, Richard 139, 140, 149, 150
Vice character 40, 46

Virgil xxii, 11, 30, 81, 84, 85, 86, 114, 189, 245, 312, 339
Vitkus, Daniel 228

Walsingham, Sir Francis 143, 277, 335, 357
Walsingham, Thomas 341, 342, 343, 345
Watson, Thomas 157, 266
Weaver, William 34
Whitgift, John 149, 150
Whitney, Charles 70, 73
Wiggins, Martin 50, 55, 268
Wilde, Oscar 232, 311
Wilson, Thomas 27, 32, 223

Žižek, Slavoj 194

Printed in Great Britain
by Amazon